Zabbix 4 Network
Third Edition

Monitor the performance of your network devices and applications using the all-new Zabbix 4.0

Patrik Uytterhoeven
Rihards Olups

BIRMINGHAM - MUMBAI

Zabbix 4 Network Monitoring
Third Edition

Copyright © 2019 Packt Publishing

All rights reserved. No part of this book may be reproduced, stored in a retrieval system, or transmitted in any form or by any means, without the prior written permission of the publisher, except in the case of brief quotations embedded in critical articles or reviews.

Every effort has been made in the preparation of this book to ensure the accuracy of the information presented. However, the information contained in this book is sold without warranty, either express or implied. Neither the authors, nor Packt Publishing or its dealers and distributors, will be held liable for any damages caused or alleged to have been caused directly or indirectly by this book.

Packt Publishing has endeavored to provide trademark information about all of the companies and products mentioned in this book by the appropriate use of capitals. However, Packt Publishing cannot guarantee the accuracy of this information.

Commissioning Editor: Pavan Ramchandani
Acquisition Editor: Rahul Nair
Content Development Editor: Ronn Kurien
Technical Editor: Swathy Mohan
Copy Editor: Safis Editing
Project Coordinator: Jagdish Prabhu
Proofreader: Safis Editing
Indexer: Priyanka Dhadke
Graphics: Tom Scaria
Production Coordinator: Jyoti Chauhan

First published: March 2010
Second edition: August 2016
Third edition: January 2019

Production reference: 1160119

Published by Packt Publishing Ltd.
Livery Place
35 Livery Street
Birmingham
B3 2PB, UK.

ISBN 978-1-78934-026-6

www.packtpub.com

`mapt.io`

Mapt is an online digital library that gives you full access to over 5,000 books and videos, as well as industry leading tools to help you plan your personal development and advance your career. For more information, please visit our website.

Why subscribe?

- Spend less time learning and more time coding with practical eBooks and Videos from over 4,000 industry professionals

- Improve your learning with Skill Plans built especially for you

- Get a free eBook or video every month

- Mapt is fully searchable

- Copy and paste, print, and bookmark content

Packt.com

Did you know that Packt offers eBook versions of every book published, with PDF and ePub files available? You can upgrade to the eBook version at `www.packt.com` and as a print book customer, you are entitled to a discount on the eBook copy. Get in touch with us at `customercare@packtpub.com` for more details.

At `www.packt.com`, you can also read a collection of free technical articles, sign up for a range of free newsletters, and receive exclusive discounts and offers on Packt books and eBooks.

Contributors

About the authors

Patrik Uytterhoeven has over 16 years of experience in IT, mostly with HP UNIX and Red Hat Linux. In late 2012, he joined Open-Future, a leading open source integrator and the first Zabbix reseller and training partner in Belgium. When Patrik joined Open-Future, he also became a Zabbix certified trainer. Since then, he has provided training and public demonstrations around the world, from Belgium to America and Asia. His next step was to author a book, so the first *Zabbix Cookbook* was born. Because Patrik also has a deep interest in configuration management, he wrote some Ansible roles. Patrik was also a technical reviewer of *Learning Ansible* and *Ansible Configuration Management*, both published by *Packt Publishing*.

Rihards Olups has over 20 years of experience in IT, most of it with open source solutions. He started using Zabbix in 2001, and joined Zabbix company later. Rihards spent 6 years at Zabbix, helping users and customers get the most value out of the monitoring tool. He briefly gets his mind off of Zabbix by improving OpenStreetMap.

About the reviewers

Werner Dijkerman is a lead infrastructure engineer from the Netherlands. He has more than 10 years of experience in IT operations departments in different organizations. He started working with the leading online retailer in the Netherlands and moved on to one of the leading software companies for general practitioners. He now works for iWelcome, the only established IDaaS provider in Europe.
He started the Puppet module for Zabbix, which is now available from the people behind Vox Pupuli. He has also created several Ansible roles for Zabbix, to automatically install and configure Zabbix components on your infrastructure for various operating systems.

Andrea Dalle Vacche is a known name in the Zabbix world, between his products we must at least mention Orabbix and DBforBIX. Andrea, during his career, has covered many critical roles, his involvement has always been very wide reaching and deals with critical aspects of the platforms. He is considered a subject matter expert of Site Reliability Engineering. Indeed he is now covering a key technical role in a leading global financial company where he is responsible for the stability/availability of large-scale mission critical server farm.

> *First, I would like to thank my wife, Anna, for her support and encouragement. She is always a pleasant presence in my life. Then, a special thanks goes to the whole Packt team, as it is always a pleasure working with them.*

Packt is searching for authors like you

If you're interested in becoming an author for Packt, please visit authors.packtpub.com and apply today. We have worked with thousands of developers and tech professionals, just like you, to help them share their insight with the global tech community. You can make a general application, apply for a specific hot topic that we are recruiting an author for, or submit your own idea.

Table of Contents

Preface

This book is a perfect starting point for monitoring with Zabbix. Even if you've never used a monitoring solution before, this book will get you up and running quickly, before guiding you into more sophisticated operations with ease. You'll soon feel in complete control of your network, ready to meet any challenges you might face.

Starting with the installation, you will discover the new features in Zabbix 4.0. You will then get to grips with native Zabbix agents and SNMP devices. You will also explore Zabbix's integrated functionality for monitoring Java application servers and VMware.

The book also covers notifications, permission management, system maintenance, and troubleshooting, so you can be confident that every potential challenge and task is under your control. If you're working with larger environments, you'll also be able to find out more about distributed data collection using Zabbix proxies.

Once you're confident and ready to put these concepts into practice, you will find out how to optimize and improve performance. Troubleshooting network issues is vital for anyone working with Zabbix, so the book is also on hand to help you work through any technical snags and glitches you might face. By the end of this book, you will have learned many more advanced techniques to fine-tune your system and make sure it is in a healthy state.

Who this book is for

If you're new to Zabbix, look no further than this book. This book is for system and network administrators who are looking to put their knowledge to work with Zabbix 4.0.

What this book covers

Chapter 1, *Getting Started with Zabbix*, gives an overview of Zabbix features and architecture, and guides you through installing a Zabbix server, frontend, and agent on the same system. We will set up a Zabbix database as well. The information in this chapter will give you an idea of what the product is capable of and help you understand the main components, as well as getting you started with a real, working installation.

Chapter 2, *Getting Your First Notification,* teaches you how to navigate around the Zabbix UI. This will be continued with setting up a monitored host, an item, and a trigger. The collected data will be viewed in a visual way, and then the system will be configured to send an email when a threshold is exceeded. This setup will be tested.

Chapter 3, *Monitoring with Zabbix Agents and Basic Protocols,* explores the differences between passive and active agents/items. The benefits and drawbacks of each will be discussed to aid you in deciding which one to use. Several types of agentless checks will be covered, including ICMP ping checks.

Chapter 4, *Monitoring SNMP Devices,* covers a very popular monitoring method, especially for network devices—SNMP. Industry-standard tools for SNMP will be briefly introduced. Adding MIB files so that Zabbix can use them will be explained. Both SNMP polling and trapping with Zabbix will be shown in a practical way. SNMP bulkget support will be covered, including potential pitfalls.

Chapter 5, *Managing Hosts, Users, and Permissions,* looks at the management of hosts, host groups (including nested group functionality), users, and user groups.

Chapter 6, *Detecting Problems with Triggers,* expands on the ways to define problem conditions. To help you understand the concept of separate problem conditions, the way triggers are not directly attached to hosts will be covered.

Chapter 7, *Acting upon Monitored Conditions,* uses the new knowledge on data collection and problem definitions (items and triggers) to demonstrate the possible ways to send out alerts. Ways to configure email and integration with issue-tracking systems will be covered. Repeated alerts and escalations to other users and user groups will be explained.

Chapter 8, *Simplifying Complex Configurations with Templates,* introduces templates and advocates for their use. The benefits of templates will be clearly explained, and the template management process will be demonstrated.

Chapter 9, *Visualizing Data with Screens and Slideshows,* ties in closely with the previous chapter, introducing additional visualization elements—dashboards, screens, and slide shows. It also expands on the sharing of these elements, which also applies to network maps.

Chapter 10, *Advanced Item Monitoring*, deep-dives into many of the remaining data collection and transformation options. You will learn how to monitor log files and use calculated and aggregate items that reuse previously collected values. The most popular way to extend Zabbix agent with new items, user parameters, will be demonstrated in detail, along with a similar way to collect data on the server side, external checks.

Chapter 11, *Automating Configuration*, introduces and provides lots of detail on the ways to automate both host entity creation and the creation of hosts themselves in Zabbix. The built-in LLD features, including the Zabbix agent (filesystems, network interfaces, CPUs, and more) and SNMP, will be explored in detail, and ways to completely customize it by scripting will be demonstrated, too.

Chapter 12, *Monitoring Web Pages*, delves into monitoring web pages in two main ways—using web scenarios and web page-related Zabbix agent items. With web scenarios, data storage details will be shared and alerting approaches will be discussed. Both simple and more complicated monitoring (involving logging in) will be covered.

Chapter 13, *High-Level Business Service Monitoring*, uses the data collection, alerting, and visualization knowledge that you will have gained as a springboard to gain a high-level overview of the services that can calculate SLA. In this chapter, you will learn how best to design, configure, and test the service tree with a generated dataset and view the results in the built-in reports.

Chapter 14, *Monitoring IPMI Devices*, covers most of the things needed to monitor IPMI, a protocol supported by nearly all server class systems nowadays. You will learn how to create IPMI items in Zabbix, and look at the more complex discrete sensor monitoring. For sensors that return bit-mapped values, a special Zabbix trigger function, bitwise(), will be explained in detail.

Chapter 15, *Monitoring Java Applications*, looks into the built-in support for JMX monitoring and Zabbix Java gateway. We'll start by installing and configuring it to work with Zabbix server and proceed with basic JMX value gathering.

Chapter 16, *Monitoring VMware*, demonstrates using the built-in VMware monitoring by applying the default templates. After an easy start, you will get familiar with the way these templates and VMware monitoring and discovery works, and you'll be exposed to host prototypes.

Chapter 17, *Using Proxies to Monitor Remote Locations*, teaches you about Zabbix proxies—remote data collectors. Both active and passive Zabbix proxies will be configured, and the benefits of using one or the other will be explained.

Chapter 18, *Encrypting Zabbix Traffic*, looks at the encryption between Zabbix components (the server, proxy, and agent) and trying it out in a practical manner. An overview of the supported backend libraries will be provided.

Chapter 19, *Working Closely with Data*, looks at some low-level things, including database structure and some content, in detail. You will find out where collected data is stored and learn how to perform some modifications, such as restoring access after forgetting your Zabbix password.

Chapter 20, *Zabbix Maintenance*, focuses on keeping Zabbix itself running. An important topic covered will be internal monitoring, which shows cache usage, process busy rates, unsupported item count, value collection count, and other statistics. You will also learn about the best practice for backing up and restoring a Zabbix database.

Chapter 21, *Visualizing Data with Graphs and Maps*, starts a more detailed section on visualization options, beyond the previously discussed simple graphs. Simple, custom, and ad hoc graphs will be covered in detail, especially the configuration possibilities of custom graphs. To read this chapter, go to the link: `https://www.packtpub.com/sites/default/files/downloads/Visualizing_Data_with_Graphs_and_Maps.pdf`.

Chapter 22, *Monitoring Windows*, concerns Windows, providing coverage of most of the available functionality, starting with the native agent installation and configuration. Two of the most popular metric-gathering methods will be demonstrated–performance counters and WMI. Ways to find out the desired performance counters will be shown. Windows service state, including service discovery, will be explained, along with Windows Eventlog monitoring and filtering by severity, facility, and other parameters. To read this chapter, go to the link: `https://www.packtpub.com/sites/default/files/downloads/Monitoring_Windows.pdf`.

Appendix A, *Troubleshooting*, describes problems that users frequently encounter with data collection and general Zabbix operations. The best ways to detect them and fix them will be detailed. To prepare you for less common and new problems, detailed information will be provided on the log file format, ways to modify the behavior of a running daemon, finding out what daemon processes are doing, and other tasks.

Appendix B, *Being Part of the Community*, leaves you prepared to find more information on the things not covered in this book. Suggestions concerning the Zabbix IRC channel, forums, wiki, issue tracker, and possible in-person meetups will be provided. To be more informed about upcoming changes or to obtain some changes before full release, a code management system will be described. For users who require commercial support, brief references will be included.

To get the most out of this book

You will need at least one Linux system, which could be a virtual machine as well.

Depending on the specific features discussed, you might also benefit from the following:

- Access to an SMTP (email) server
- More Linux systems
- A device with SNMP support
- A Windows system
- A device with IPMI support
- A Java virtual machine
- A VMware instance

Some of these can be replicated on the same Linux box—for example, running SNMPD or a Java virtual machine will allow you to try out all the monitoring solutions without a separate system.

Download the example code files

You can download the example code files for this book from your account at www.packt.com. If you purchased this book elsewhere, you can visit www.packt.com/support and register to have the files emailed directly to you.

You can download the code files by following these steps:

1. Log in or register at www.packt.com.
2. Select the **SUPPORT** tab.
3. Click on **Code Downloads & Errata**.
4. Enter the name of the book in the **Search** box and follow the onscreen instructions.

Once the file is downloaded, please make sure that you unzip or extract the folder using the latest version of:

- WinRAR/7-Zip for Windows
- Zipeg/iZip/UnRarX for Mac
- 7-Zip/PeaZip for Linux

The code bundle for the book is also hosted on GitHub at `https://github.com/PacktPublishing/Zabbix-4-Network-Monitoring-Third-Edition`. In case there's an update to the code, it will be updated on the existing GitHub repository.

We also have other code bundles from our rich catalog of books and videos available at `https://github.com/PacktPublishing/`. Check them out!

Download the color images

We also provide a PDF file that has color images of the screenshots/diagrams used in this book. You can download it here: `https://www.packtpub.com/sites/default/files/downloads/9781789340266_ColorImages.pdf`.

Conventions used

There are a number of text conventions used throughout this book.

`CodeInText`: Indicates code words in text, database table names, folder names, filenames, file extensions, pathnames, dummy URLs, user input, and Twitter handles. Here is an example: "This allows the `zabbix` user to use `sudo` and restart the Apache web server."

A block of code is set as follows:

```
PROBLEM: SNMP trap has arrived on snmptraps on snmptraps
```

When we wish to draw your attention to a particular part of a code block, the relevant lines or items are set in bold:

```
BB +5.0V         | 4.97 Volts      | ok
Baseboard Temp   | 23 degrees C    | ok
System Fan 2     | 3267 RPM        | ok
Power Unit Stat  | 0x00            | ok
```

Any command-line input or output is written as follows:

```
$ snmptrap -Ci -v 2c -c public <Zabbix server> "" "NET-SNMP-
MIB::netSnmpExperimental" NET-SNMP-MIB::netSnmpExperimental s
"Critical Error"
```

Bold: Indicates a new term, an important word, or words that you see onscreen. For example, words in menus or dialog boxes appear in the text like this. Here is an example: "Go to **Configuration** | **Actions** and click on **SNMP action** in the **Name** column."

Warnings or important notes appear like this.

Tips and tricks appear like this.

Get in touch

Feedback from our readers is always welcome.

General feedback: If you have questions about any aspect of this book, mention the book title in the subject of your message and email us at customercare@packtpub.com.

Errata: Although we have taken every care to ensure the accuracy of our content, mistakes do happen. If you have found a mistake in this book, we would be grateful if you would report this to us. Please visit www.packt.com/submit-errata, selecting your book, clicking on the Errata Submission Form link, and entering the details.

Piracy: If you come across any illegal copies of our works in any form on the Internet, we would be grateful if you would provide us with the location address or website name. Please contact us at copyright@packt.com with a link to the material.

If you are interested in becoming an author: If there is a topic that you have expertise in and you are interested in either writing or contributing to a book, please visit authors.packtpub.com.

Reviews

Please leave a review. Once you have read and used this book, why not leave a review on the site that you purchased it from? Potential readers can then see and use your unbiased opinion to make purchase decisions, we at Packt can understand what you think about our products, and our authors can see your feedback on their book. Thank you!

For more information about Packt, please visit `packt.com`.

Getting Started with Zabbix 1

It's Friday night and you are at a party outside the city with old friends. After a few beers, it looks as if this is going to be a great party, when suddenly your phone rings. A customer can't access some critical server that absolutely has to be available as soon as possible. You try to connect to the server using SSH, only to discover that the customer is right—it can't be accessed.

As driving after those few beers would quite likely lead to an inoperable server for quite some time, you get a taxi—expensive because of the distance (while many modern systems have out-of-band management cards installed that might have helped a bit in such a situation, our hypothetical administrator does not have one available). After arriving at the server room, you find out that some log files have been growing more than usual over the past few weeks and have filled up the hard drive.

While the preceding scenario is very simplistic, something similar has probably happened to most IT workers at one point or another in their careers. Most will have implemented a simple system monitoring and reporting solution soon after that.

We will learn how to set up and configure one such monitoring system—Zabbix. In this very first chapter, we will cover the following topics:

- First steps in monitoring
- Zabbix architecture and choosing the version and repository
- Setting up Zabbix from packages
- Setting up Zabbix from the source
- Configuring the Zabbix frontend

Technical requirements

You will need a server or virtual machine with the option to install CentOS/Red Hat or Debian/Ubuntu.

The first steps in monitoring

Situations similar to the one just described are actually more common than desired. A system fault that had no visible symptoms before is relatively rare. A subsection of UNIX administration horror stories (`http://www-uxsup.csx.cam.ac.uk/misc/horror.txt`) only containing stories about faults that weren't noticed in time could probably be compiled easily.

As experience shows, problems tend to happen when we are least equipped to solve them. To work with them on our terms, we turn to a class of software commonly referred to as **network monitoring software**. Such software usually allows us to constantly monitor things happening in a computer network using one or more methods and notify the persons responsible if a metric passes a defined threshold.

One of the first monitoring solutions most administrators implement is a simple shell script invoked from `crontab`, which checks some basic parameters, such as disk usage, or some service state, such as an Apache server. As the server and monitored parameter count grows, a neat and clean script system starts to grow into a performance-hogging script hairball that costs more time in upkeep than it saves. While the do-it-yourself crowd claims that nobody needs dedicated software for most tasks (monitoring included), most administrators will disagree as soon as they have to add switches, UPSes, routers, IP cameras, and a myriad of other devices to the swarm of monitored objects.

So, *what basic functionality can expect from a monitoring solution?* Let's take a look:

- **Data gathering**: This is where everything starts. Usually, data is gathered using various methods, including **Simple Network Management Protocol (SNMP)**, **Zabbix agents**, **Intelligent Platform Management Interface (IPMI)**, and **Java Management Extensions (JMX)**.

- **Data storage**: Once we have gathered the data, it doesn't make sense to throw it away, so we will often want to store it for later analysis.
- **Alerting**: Gathered data can be compared to thresholds and alerts sent out when required using different channels, such as email or SMS.
- **Visualization**: Humans are better at distinguishing visualized data than raw numbers, especially when there's a lot of data. As we have data already gathered and stored, it is easy to generate simple graphs from it.

Sounds simple? That's because it is. But then we start to want more features, such as easy and efficient configuration, escalations, and permission delegation. If we sit down and start listing the things we want to keep an eye out for, it may turn out that that area of interest extends beyond the network, for example, a hard drive that has **Self-Monitoring, Analysis, and Reporting Technology (S.M.A.R.T)** errors logged, an application that has too many threads, or a UPS that has one phase overloaded. It is much easier to manage the monitoring of all of these different problem categories from a single configuration point.

In the quest for a manageable monitoring system, wondrous adventurers stumbled upon collections of scripts much like the way they themselves implemented obscure and not-so-obscure workstation-level software and heavy, expensive monitoring systems from big vendors.

Many went with a different category—free software. We will look at a free software monitoring solution, Zabbix.

Zabbix features and architecture

Zabbix provides many ways of monitoring different aspects of your IT infrastructure and, indeed, almost anything you might want to hook up to it. It can be characterized as a semi-distributed monitoring system with centralized management. While many installations have a single central system, it is possible to use distributed monitoring with proxies, and most installations will use Zabbix agents.

What features does Zabbix provide? Let's have a look:

- A centralized, easy to use web interface
- A server that runs on most UNIX-like operating systems, including Linux, AIX, FreeBSD, OpenBSD, and Solaris
- Native agents for most UNIX-like operating systems and Microsoft Windows versions
- The ability to directly monitor SNMP (SNMPv1, SNMPv2c, and SNMPv3) and IPMI devices
- The ability to directly monitor Java applications using JMX
- The ability to directly monitor vCenter or vSphere instances using the VMware API
- Built-in graphing and other visualization capabilities
- Notifications that allow easy integration with other systems
- Flexible configuration, including templating
- **Low-Level Discovery** (**LLD**) and the ability to generate items, graphs, and triggers (among others) in an automated way
- A lot of other features that allow you to implement a sophisticated monitoring solution

If we look at a simplified network from the Zabbix perspective, placing the Zabbix server at the center, the communication of the various monitoring aspects matters. The following diagram depicts a relatively simple Zabbix setup with several of the monitoring capabilities used and different device categories connected:

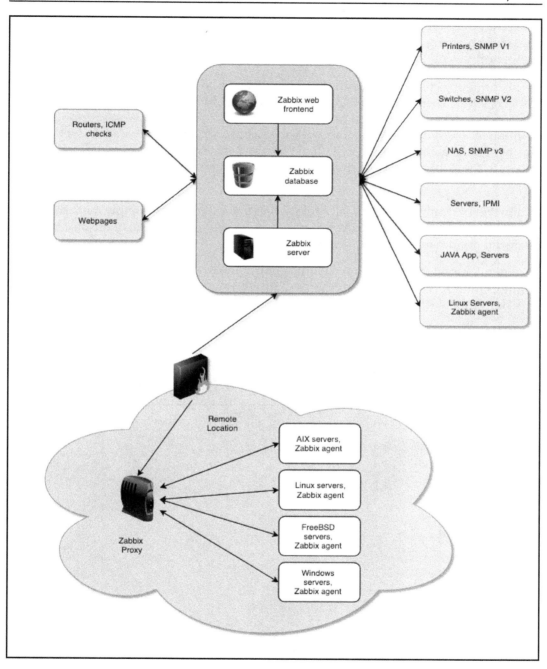

The Zabbix Server directly monitors multiple devices, but a remote location is separated by a firewall, so it is easier to gather data through a Zabbix proxy. The Zabbix proxy and Zabbix agents, just like the server, are written in the C language.

Our central object is the Zabbix database, which supports several backends. The Zabbix server, written in the C language, and the Zabbix web frontend, written in PHP, can both reside on the same machine or on another server. When running each component on a separate machine, both the Zabbix server and the Zabbix web frontend need access to the Zabbix database, and the Zabbix web frontend needs access to the Zabbix server to display the server status and for some additional functionality.

While it is perfectly fine to run all three server components on a single machine, there might be good reasons to separate them, such as taking advantage of an existing high-performance database or web server.

In general, monitored devices have little control over what is monitored—most of the configuration is centralized. Such an approach seriously reduces the ability of a single misconfigured system to bring down the whole monitoring setup.

In the following diagram, we have an overview of the basic Zabbix setup with our Zabbix server, web server and relational database. In our setup, we will install the three components on one machine. It is possible, however, to split up components over three different machines, something we will see later in this book:

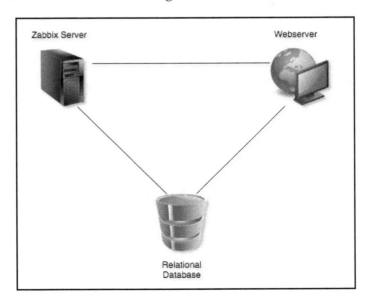

Installation

Alright, enough with the dry talk—*what use is that?* Let's look at the dashboard screen of the Zabbix web frontend, showing only a very basic standard configuration:

The Zabbix dashboard shows you a high-level overview of the overall status of the monitored system, the status of Zabbix, some of the most recent problems, and a few more things. This particular dashboard shows a very tiny Zabbix setup. Eventually, your Zabbix installation will grow and monitor different devices, including servers of various operating systems, different services and the hardware state on those servers, network devices, UPSes, web pages, other components of IT, and other infrastructure.

The frontend will provide various options for visualizing data, starting from lists of problems and simple graphs and ending with network maps and reports, while the backend will work hard to provide the information that this visualization is based on and send out alerts. All of this will require some configuration that we will learn to perform along the course of this book.

Before we can configure Zabbix, we need to install it. Usually, you'll have two choices—installing from packages or setting it up from the source code. Zabbix packages are available in quite a lot of Linux distribution repositories, and it is usually a safe choice to use those. Additionally, a Zabbix-specific repository is provided by SIA Zabbix (the company developing the product) for some distributions.

 It is a good idea to check the latest installation instructions at `https://www.zabbix.com/documentation/4.0/manual/installation`.

Choosing the version and repository

At first, we will set up the Zabbix server, database, and frontend, all running on the same machine and using a MySQL database.

Should you use the packages or install from the source? In most cases, installing from the packages will be easier. Here are a few considerations that might help you select the method:

- There are certain benefits of using distribution packages. These include the following:
  - Automated installation and updating
  - The dependencies are usually sorted out
  - Easy and proper cleanup when uninstalling
  - No installation of compilers needed on your systems
- Compiling from source also has its share of benefits. They are as follows:
  - You can get newer versions with more features and improvements.
  - You have more fine-grained control over compiled-in functionality.

But *which version to choose?* You might see several versions available in repositories, and those versions might not be equal. Since Zabbix 2.2, the concept of a **Long-Term Support** (**LTS**) release has been introduced. This determines how long support in the form of bug fixes will be available for. An LTS release is supported for five years (three years full support and two years limited support), while a normal release is supported until a month after the release date of the next version. Zabbix 2.2 and 3.0 are LTS releases, while 2.4, 3.2, and 3.4 are normal releases. Choose an LTS release for an installation that you don't plan to upgrade for a setup where you want vendor (Zabbix SIA) support. A normal release can be used for a setup you intend to keep up-to-date. In this book, we will use the latest LTS release Zabbix version 4.0.

This policy might change. Verify the details on the Zabbix website:
`http://www.zabbix.com/life_cycle_and_release_policy.php`.

The most widely used Zabbix architecture is a server that queries agents. This is what we will learn to set up initially so that we can monitor our test system.

As with most software, there are some prerequisites that we will need in order to run Zabbix components. These include requirements of hardware and other software that the Zabbix server and agent depend on. For the purpose of our installation, we will settle for running Zabbix on Linux, using a MySQL database. The specific Linux distribution does not matter much—it's best to choose the one you are most familiar with.

Hardware requirements

Hardware requirements vary wildly depending on the configuration. It is impossible to provide definite requirements, so any production installation should evaluate them individually. For our test environment, though, even as little RAM as 128 MB should be enough. CPU power in general won't play a huge role; Pentium II-class hardware should be perfectly capable of dealing with it, although generating graphs with many elements or other complex views could require more powerful hardware to operate at an acceptable speed. You can take these as a starting point as well when installing on a virtual machine.

Of course, the more resources you give to Zabbix, the snappier and happier it will be.

Installing from the packages

If you have decided to install Zabbix from the packages, package availability and the procedure will differ based on the distribution. A few distributions will be covered here—read the distribution-specific instructions for others. For the installation, we need root rights.

Red Hat Enterprise Linux (RHEL)/CentOS

RHEL or CentOS users have two repositories to choose from: the well-known **Extra Packages for Enterprise Linux** (**EPEL**) and the Zabbix repository. EPEL might be a safer choice, but it might not always have the latest version. (In fact, at the time of writing, the latest version in EPEL was still 3.0.22, so it's possible that 4.0 will not be available in EPEL). In production, most of the time you will encounter setups with **Security-Enhanced Linux** (**SELinux**) enabled. However, SELinux is rather complex on its own, so it's out of the scope of this book; please disable SELinux before you start with the installation of Zabbix. If you have no clue how to do so, this can be done by editing the /etc/selinux/config file and putting disable or permissive instead of enabled. Don't forget to reboot afterwards so that changes are applied to the system. You can verify the status with the getenforce command.

EPEL

If EPEL is not set up already, it must be added. For RHEL/CentOS 7, the command is similar to this:

```
# rpm -Uvh
http://ftp.colocall.net/pub/epel/7/x86_64/e/epel-release-7-5.noarch.rp
m
```

For CentOS7 only, run the following command:

```
# yum install epel-release
```

 Check the latest available version at https://fedoraproject.org/wiki/EPEL.

If you would like to check the available Zabbix versions in EPEL, it is possible with the next command:

```
# yum --disablerepo="*" --enablerepo="epel" search zabbix
```

Once the repository has been set up, you may install the packages (except the following is for 3.0 not for 4.0 as it was not available when this book was written):

```
# yum install zabbix30-agent zabbix30-dbfiles-mysql zabbix30-server-mysql zabbix30-web-mysql
```

The Zabbix repository

First, the package that will define that the Zabbix repository should be installed:

```
# rpm -ivh
http://repo.zabbix.com/zabbix/4.0/rhel/7/x86_64/zabbix-release-4.0-1.e
l7.noarch.rpm
```

Once the repository has been set up, you may install the packages:

```
# yum install zabbix-server-mysql zabbix-web-mysql zabbix-agent
```

Ubuntu/Debian

Zabbix has repositories available for Debian and Ubuntu just as it does for CentOS/Red Hat, so both are equally supported. Just be aware that Zabbix SIA has a slight preference lately for CentOS/Red Hat, and that this is the preferred OS for their training as well, but both are equally supported and tested:

```
# For Ubuntu 18.04
# wget
https://repo.zabbix.com/zabbix/4.0/ubuntu/pool/main/z/zabbix-release/z
abbix-release_4.0-1+bionic_all.deb

# For Debian 9
# wget
https://repo.zabbix.com/zabbix/4.0/debian/pool/main/z/zabbix-release/z
abbix-release_4.0-1+stretch_all.deb
# dpkg -i zabbix-release_4.0-1+bionic_all.deb
```

Once the repository has been set up, you may want to update the cache and install the packages, as follows:

```
# apt update
# add-apt-repository universe # (This is needed
                              # for package
                              # like fping ...)
# apt install zabbix-server-mysql zabbix-agent zabbix-frontend-php
```

Installing from source

If you have decided to install Zabbix from the source, you will need to obtain the source, configure it, and compile it. After the daemons are put in place, the frontend will have to be set up manually as well.

The server and agent

At first, we will only set up the Zabbix server and agent, both running on the same system. We will set up additional components later during the course of this book.

Software requirements

Now, we should get to compiling the various components of Zabbix, so make sure to install the minimum required packages to get Zabbix working with MySQL. Here they are:

- GCC
- Automake
- MariaDB (or any compatible MySQL DB)

Depending on your distribution and the desired functionality, you might also need some or all of the following packages:

- zlib-devel
- mariadb-devel (for MySQL support)
- glibc-devel
- curl-devel (for web monitoring)
- libidn-devel (curl-devel might depend on it)

- `openssl-devel` (`curl-devel` might depend on it)
- `net-snmp-devel` (for SNMP support)
- `popt-devel` (`net-snmp-devel` might depend on it)
- `rpm-devel` (`net-snmp-devel` might depend on it)
- `OpenIPMI-devel` (for IPMI support)
- `libssh2-devel` (for direct SSH checks)
- `libxm2-devel` (for VMware monitoring)
- `unixODBC-devel` (for database monitoring)
- Java SDK (for Java gateway/JMX checks)

Downloading the source

There are several ways of downloading the source code of Zabbix. You can get it from a **Subversion** (**SVN**) repository, which will be discussed in `Appendix B`, *Being part of the Community*; however, for this installation procedure, I suggest you download version 4.0.0 from the Zabbix home page, `https://www.zabbix.com/`. While it should be possible to use the latest stable version, using 4.0.0 will allow you to follow instructions more closely. Go to the **Download** section and grab the compressed source package. Usually, only the latest stable version is available on the download page, so you might have to browse the source archives, but do not take a development or beta version, which might be available.

To make further references easy, I suggested you choose a directory to work in, for example, `~/zabbix` (~ being your `home` directory). Download the archive into this directory.

Compilation

Once the archive has finished downloading, open a Terminal and extract it:

```
$ cd ~/zabbix; tar -zxvf zabbix-4.0.0.tar.gz
```

I suggest you install the prerequisites and compile Zabbix with external functionality right away so that you don't have to recompile as we progress.

For the purpose of this book, we will compile Zabbix with server, agent, MySQL, CURL, SNMP, SSH, ODBC, XML (VMware), and IPMI support.

To continue, enter the following in the Terminal:

```
$ cd zabbix-4.0.0
$ ./configure --enable-server --with-mysql --with-net-snmp --with-
libcurl --with-openipmi --enable-agent --with-libxml2 --with-unixodbc
--with-ssh2 --with-openssl
```

In the end, a summary of the compiled components will be printed. Verify that you have the following enabled:

```
Enable server:          yes
Server details:
With database:          MySQL
WEB Monitoring:         CURL
SNMP:                   yes
IPMI:                   yes
SSH:                    yes
TLS:                    OpenSSL
ODBC:                   yes
Enable agent:           yes
```

If the configuration completes successfully, it's all good. If it fails, check the error messages printed in the console and verify that all prerequisites have been installed. A file named config.log might provide more detail about the errors. If you can't find out what's wrong, check Appendix A, *Troubleshooting*, which lists some common compilation problems.

To actually compile Zabbix, issue the following command:

```
$ make
```

You can grab a cup of tea, but don't expect to have much time—Zabbix compilation doesn't take too long; even an old 350-MHz Pentium II compiles it in approximately five minutes. On a modern machine, give it less than a minute. After the make process has finished, check the last lines for any error messages. If there are none, congratulations—you have successfully compiled Zabbix!

Now, we should install it. I suggest you create proper packages, but that will require some effort and will be distribution dependent. Another option is to run make install. This will place the files in the filesystem but will not register Zabbix as an installed package—removing and upgrading such software is harder.

If you have experience with creating distribution packages, do so—it is a better approach. If this is just a test installation, run the following:

```
# make install
```

Here and later in this book, a $ prompt will mean a normal user, while a # prompt will mean the root user. To run commands as root, su or sudo are commonly used.

But remember that test installations have a tendency of becoming production installations later—it might be a good idea to do things properly from the very beginning.

Dash or underscore

Depending on the method of installation, you might get Zabbix binaries and configuration files using either a dash (minus) or an underscore, as in the following:

- zabbix_server versus zabbix-server
- zabbix_agentd versus zabbix-agentd
- zabbix_server.conf versus zabbix-server.conf

While Zabbix itself uses an underscore, many distributions will replace it with a dash to follow their own guidelines. There is no functional difference; you just have to keep in mind the character that your installation uses. In this book, we will reference binaries and files using an underscore.

Initial configuration

After compilation or installation from the package, we have to configure some basic parameters for the server and agent. Default configuration files are provided with Zabbix. The location of these files will depend on the installation method you chose:

- Source installation: /usr/local/etc
- RHEL/CentOS/Debian/Ubuntu package installation: /etc

On other distributions, the files might be located in a different directory. In this book, we will reference binaries and configuration files using relative names, except in situations where the absolute path is recommended or required.

To configure the Zabbix agent, we don't have to do anything. The default configuration will do just fine for now. That was easy, *right?*

For the server, we will need to make some changes. Open the `zabbix_server.conf` file in your favorite editor (you will need to edit it as the `root` user) and find the following entries in the file:

- `DBName`
- `DBUser`
- `DBPassword`

`DBName` should be `zabbix` by default; we can leave it as is. `DBUser` is set to `root`, and we don't like that, so let's change it to `zabbix`. For `DBPassword`, choose any password. You won't have to remember it, so be creative.

In UNIX-like solutions, a hash character or # at the beginning of a line usually means that the line is commented out. Make sure not to start lines you want to have an effect with a hash.

Creating and populating the database

For the Zabbix server to store the data, we need a database. As we have installed our Zabbix server with MySQL support, we need to install the MySQL server first. You will see that we install MariaDB instead of MySQL. This is because now most distributions prefer to deliver MariaDB instead of MySQL as MySQL was acquired by Oracle and people were afraid Oracle would change the license. Zabbix also has support for other databases, such as Oracle, IBM DB2, and PostgreSQL. The reason we use MySQL is because it's the most widely known and also the preferred database by Zabbix SIA. This does not mean other solutions are worse or less tested. It's just because the best knowledge in Zabbix SIA is with MySQL and not PostgreSQL or any other supported database:

```
CentOS/Red Hat 7
# yum install mariadb-server

Ubuntu/Debian
# apt install mysql-server
```

We also have to create a database. Start a MySQL client to connect to the MySQL Server:

```
CentOS/Red Hat 7  Start the database first and set a DB root password
# systemctl start mariadb; systemctl enable mariadb
# mysql_secure_installation
# mysql -u root -p
```

```
Ubuntu/Debian Start the database first and set a DB root password
# mysql_secure_installation
# mysql -u root -p
```

Using `mysql_secure_installation` is easy to set a root password for your database. It also allows you to configure MySQL/MariaDB easy in a more secure way.

Enter the `root` user's password for MySQL (you will have set this during the installation of MariaDB or the password could be something that is the default for your distribution). If you do not know the password, you can try omitting `-p`. This switch will tell the client to attempt to connect without a password (or with an empty password).

If you are using MySQL Community Edition from the packages and the version is 5.7.6 or higher, it generates a random password that is stored in `logfiles`. Check out the MySQL documentation at `http://dev.mysql.com/doc/refman/5.7/en/linux-installation-rpm.html` for more details.

Now, let's create the database. Add the user through which Zabbix will connect to the database and grant the necessary permissions to this user:

```
mysql> create database zabbix character set utf8 collate utf8_bin;
Query OK, 1 row affected (0.01 sec)
mysql> grant all privileges on zabbix.* to 'zabbix'@'localhost'
identified by 'mycreativepassword';
Query OK, 0 rows affected (0.12 sec)
```

Use the password you set in the `zabbix_server.conf` file instead of `mycreativepassword`.

Quit the MySQL client by entering the following command:

```
mysql> quit
```

Let's populate the newly created database with a Zabbix schema and initial data. The following commands refer to the files as they appear in the Zabbix source. When installing from packages, this file could be located in a directory such as `/usr/share/doc/zabbix-server-mysql-4.0.0/` or `/usr/share/zabbix-server-mysql`:

```
# zcat /usr/share/doc/zabbix-server-mysql*/create.sql.gz | mysql -
uzabbix -p zabbix
```

This processes should complete without any messages. If there are any errors, review the messages, fix the issue, and retry the failed operation. If the import is interrupted in the middle of the process, you might have to clear the database—the easiest way to do this is to delete the database by typing this:

```
mysql> drop database zabbix;
Query OK, 0 rows affected (0.00 sec)
```

> Be careful not to delete a database with important information! After deleting the Zabbix database, recreate it as we did before.

By now, we should have the Zabbix server and agent installed and ready to start.

Starting up

You should never start the Zabbix server or agent as `root`, which is common sense for most daemon processes. If you installed Zabbix from distribution packages, system users should have been created already—if not, let's create a new user to run these processes. You can use tools provided by your distribution or use the most widely available command, `useradd`, which we need to execute as `root`:

```
# useradd -m -s /bin/bash zabbix
```

For production systems, consider using different user accounts for the Zabbix server and agent. Otherwise, users with configuration rights will be able to discover Zabbix database credentials by instructing the agent to read the server configuration file. Some distribution packages, such as the EPEL and OpenSUSE ones, already use a separate user account called `zabbixsrv` or `zabbixs` by default.

This will create a user named `zabbix` with a `home` directory in the default location, `/home/zabbix` usually, and a shell at `/bin/bash`.

> While using `bash` on a test system will make it easier to debug issues, consider using `/bin/nologin` or `/bin/false` on production systems.

If you installed from source, let's try the direct approach—running the binaries. The location of the binaries will depend on the chosen method of installation. Installing from the source without any extra parameters will place the agent and server binaries in /usr/local/sbin; distribution packages are likely to place them in /usr/sbin. Assuming they are in your path, you can determine where the binaries are by running this:

```
# which zabbix_server
```

Keep in mind the potential use of a dash or minus instead of an underscore.

This will show something similar to the following:

```
/usr/sbin/zabbix_server
```

Alternatively, the whereis command can also list configuration and other related files:

```
# whereis zabbix_server
```

This would likely list the binary, configuration file, and main page:

```
zabbix_server: /usr/sbin/zabbix_server
/usr/local/etc/zabbix_server.conf /usr/share/man/man3/zabbix_server
```

Once you know the exact location of the binaries, execute the following as the root user:

```
# <path>/zabbix_agentd
```

We are using zabbix_agentd, which runs as a daemon. Older versions also had the zabbix_agent executable, which provided an option to be run within **internet service daemon** (**inetd**); it did not support active items and, in most cases, had worse performance than the agent daemon.

This will start the Zabbix agent daemon, which should start up silently and daemonize. If the command produces errors, resolve them before proceeding. If it succeeds, continue by starting the Zabbix server:

```
# <path>/zabbix_server
```

Check the Zabbix server log file, configurable in `zabbix_server.conf`. If there are database-related errors, fix them and restart the Zabbix server.

If you installed from the packages, execute this:

```
# systemctl start zabbix-agent
# systemctl start zabbix-server
```

With `systemd` no output should be printed on the screen if the service was started without issues.

Feel free to experiment with other parameters, such as `stop` and `restart`—it should be obvious what these two do.

You can verify whether services are running with the `status` parameter. For a service that is not running, you would get the following:

```
# systemctl status zabbix-server
```

A running service would yield the following:

```
zabbix-server.service - Zabbix Server
Loaded: loaded (/usr/lib/systemd/system/zabbix-server.service;
disabled; vendor preset: disabled)
Active: active (running) since Sun 2018-08-05 12:57:13 CEST; 1min 39s
ago
Process: 1972 ExecStart=/usr/sbin/zabbix_server -c $CONFFILE
(code=exited, status=0/SUCCESS)
Main PID: 1974 (zabbix_server)
CGroup: /system.slice/zabbix-server.service
├─1974 /usr/sbin/zabbix_server -c /etc/zabbix/zabbix_server.conf
├─1979 /usr/sbin/zabbix_server: configuration syncer [synced
configuration in 0.008373 sec, idle 60 sec]
....
```

While it's nice to have Zabbix processes running, it's hardly a process one expects to do manually upon each system boot, so the server and agent should be added to your system's startup sequence. This is fairly distribution specific, so all possible variations can't be discussed here. With RHEL or CentOS, a command such as this should help:

```
# systemctl enable zabbix-agent
# systemctl enable zabbix-server
```

This will add both services to be started at boot time.

A nice summary of Systemd can be found at `https://fedoraproject.org/wiki/SysVinit_to_Systemd_Cheatsheet`.

Verifying the service's state

While the `systemd` method is a nice way to check a service's state for some distributions, it's not available everywhere and isn't always enough. Sometimes, you might want to use these other methods to check whether the Zabbix server or agent is running:

- **Checking running processes**: The most common method to check whether a particular process is running is by looking at the running processes. You can verify whether the Zabbix agent daemon processes are actually running using this command:

  ```
  $ ps -C zabbix_agentd
  ```

- **Output from the** `ss` **command**: Sometimes, an agent daemon might start up but fail to bind to the port or the port might be used by some other process. You can verify whether some other process is listening on the Zabbix port or whether the Zabbix agent daemon is listening on the correct port by issuing this command:

  ```
  # ss -tlnp
  ```

Process names won't be printed for other users' processes unless you are the `root` user. In the output, look for a line similar to this:

 `ss` is a replacement for `netstat` on CentOS/Red Hat; if you would still like to use `netstat`, that is possible by installing the `net-tools` package—just remember that `netstat` is deprecated.

```
State   Recv-Q Send-Q Local Address:Port Peer Address:Port
LISTEN  0      128     *:10050            *:*
users:(("zabbix_agentd",pid=1965,fd=4),("zabbix_agentd",pi
d=1964,fd=4),("zabbix_agentd",pid=1963,fd=4),
...
LISTEN  0      128     *:10051            *:*
users:(("zabbix_server",pid=2011,fd=5),("zabbix_server",pi
d=2010,fd=5),("zabbix_server",pid=2009,fd=5),
...
LISTEN  0      50      *:3306             *:*
users:(("mysqld",pid=1832,fd=14))
LISTEN 0 128 *:22 *:* users:(("sshd",pid=1033,fd=3))
LISTEN  0      100     127.0.0.1:25       *:*
users:(("master",pid=1278,fd=13))
LISTEN 0 128 :::10050 :::*
users:(("zabbix_agentd",pid=1965,fd=5),
...
LISTEN  0      128     :::10051           :::*
users:(("zabbix_server",pid=2011,fd=6),("zabbix_server",pi
d=2010,fd=6),("zabbix_server",pid=2009,fd=6),
...
LISTEN  0      128     :::22              :::*
users:(("sshd",pid=1033,fd=4))
LISTEN 0 100 ::1:25 :::* users:(("master",pid=1278,fd=14))
```

This indicates that the `zabbix_agentd` process is running and listening on all addresses on port `10050`—just what we need.

- **Telnetting to the port**: Even when a service starts up and successfully binds to a port, there might be some connectivity issues, perhaps due to a local firewall. To quickly check connectivity on the desired port, you can try this:

  ```
  $ telnet localhost 10050
  ```

This command should open a connection to the Zabbix agent daemon, and the daemon should not close the connection immediately. All of this applies to the Zabbix server as well, except that it uses a different port by default: `10051`.

On CentOS, it is possible that `telnet` will not work—that's because we have to install it first. This can be done by running the following:

```
# yum install telnet
```

The web frontend

Now that we have the Zabbix server and agent either compiled and installed or installed from the distribution packages, and both daemons are running, you probably have a feeling that something's missing. We have only configured some low-level behavior, so *where's the meat?*

That's what the frontend is for. While, in theory, Zabbix can have multiple frontends, the only one with full functionality so far is the Zabbix web frontend, which is written in PHP. We have to set it up to configure Zabbix and get to those nice graphs everybody likes.

Prerequisites and setting up the environment

Of course, being a Zabbix web frontend, it will require a platform to run on—a web server with a PHP environment. We will need the following installed:

- A web server that is supported by PHP; Apache is the most common choice
- PHP version 5.4.0 or higher

 The following instructions apply when installing from source. Installing from packages usually installs the Zabbix frontend as well. On CentOS make sure you have Apache enabled and started.

In the next code block, we will show you how to install the webserver on CentOS and Debian:

```
On CentOS
# yum install httpd php php-ldap php-mysql
# systemctl enable httpd
# systemct start httpd
```

```
On Debian/Ubuntu
# apt install apache2 php php7.2-cli php7.2-mysql php7.2-common
php7.2-curl php7.2-json php7.2-cgi libapache2-mod-php7.2 php7.2
php7.2-ldap
```

It is easiest to install these from the distribution packages as it will take care of all of the dependencies we need. Just make sure you install the correct PHP connector for your database—in our case, this is php-mysql. If you would like to make a connection to your AD/LDAP, you also need to make sure that php-ldap is installed.

> Some distributions split out the core PHP modules. These might include ctype, net-socket, libxml, and others.

Once you have all of these installed, it's time to set up the frontend. Again, there's a choice of using packages or installing from source. If you decided to go with the packages, you should have the frontend installed already and should be able to proceed with the configuration wizard section explained next. If you went with the source installation, it's just a simple copying of some files.

First, you have to decide where the frontend code has to go. Most distributions that package web servers use /srv/www/htdocs or /var/www. If you compiled the Apache web server from the source, it would be /usr/local/apache2/htdocs (unless you manually changed the prefix or installed an older Apache version). We will place the frontend in a simple subdirectory, zabbix.

Assuming you have Apache distribution packages installed with the web root directory at /srv/www/htdocs, placing the frontend where it is needed is as simple as executing the following as the root user:

```
# cp -r frontends/php /srv/www/htdocs/zabbix
```

The last thing we need to do is open our firewall so that our browser can connect on the web server port of our server:

```
CentOS/Red Hat
# firewall-cmd --add-service=http --permanent
# firewall-cmd --reload

Debian / Ubuntu
(standard there is no firewall installed you could use iptables or ufw
or similar solution)
 # apt install firewalld
```

Zabbix provides out of the box a configuration for HTTP. This is not really best practice and it's advised in production to configure Zabbix properly with HTTPS.

Using the web frontend configuration wizard

The web frontend has a wizard that helps you to configure its basics. Let's go through the simple steps it offers.

It's time to fire up a browser and navigate to Zabbix's address: `http://<server_ip_or_name>/zabbix`. It should work just fine in the latest versions of most browsers, including Firefox, Chrome, Safari, Opera, Konqueror, and Internet Explorer.

Step 1 – welcome

If everything has been configured properly, you should be greeted by the installation wizard:

If you are not, there are several things that could have gone wrong. If the connection fails completely, make sure Apache is started up and there is no firewall blocking access. If you see a blank page or some PHP code, make sure that PHP is properly installed and configured to parse files ending with the `.php` extension through the `AddType application/x-httpd-php` directive. If you see a file and directory listing instead of the installation wizard, make sure you have added `index.php` to the `DirectoryIndex` directive. If these hints do not help, check the PHP documentation at `https://secure.php.net/manual/en/`.

This screen doesn't offer us much to configure, so just click on **Next step**.

Step 2 – PHP prerequisites

In this step, the installation wizard checks PHP-related prerequisites. If you are lucky, all will have been satisfied, and you will be greeted with all green entries:

ZABBIX	Check of pre-requisites			
		Current value	Required	
Welcome	PHP version	5.4.16	5.4.0	OK
Check of pre-requisites	PHP option "memory_limit"	128M	128M	OK
Configure DB connection	PHP option "post_max_size"	16M	16M	OK
Zabbix server details	PHP option "upload_max_filesize"	2M	2M	OK
Pre-installation summary	PHP option "max_execution_time"	300	300	OK
Install	PHP option "max_input_time"	300	300	OK
	PHP option "date.timezone"	Europe/Riga		OK
	PHP databases support	MySQL		OK
	PHP bcmath	on		OK
	PHP mbstring	on		OK
Cancel			Back	Next step

If so, just click on the **Next step** button to continue to *Step 3 – database access*.

However, more often than not, one or more entries will have a red **Fail** warning listed next to them. This is where things get more interesting. Problems at this point fall into two categories—**PHP installation** or **configuration**.

Entries such as **PHP version, PHP databases support, PHP bcmath, PHP mbstring, PHP gd, PHP gd PNG/JPEG/FreeType support**, and others that are not listed as an **option** are PHP installation problems. To solve these, either install the appropriate distribution packages (sometimes called **php5-bcmath, php5-gd, php5-mysql**, and so on), or recompile PHP with the corresponding options.

PHP option "memory_limit", PHP option "post_max_size", PHP option "upload_max_filesize", PHP option "max_execution_time", PHP option "max_input_time", and PHP time zone are configuration issues that are all set in the php.ini configuration file. This file is usually located at /etc/php5 or similar for distribution packages and /usr/local/lib for PHP source installations. Set the following options:

```
max_execution_time 300
memory_limit 128M
post_max_size 16M
upload_max_filesize 2M
max_input_time 300
always_populate_raw_post_data -1
date.timezone Europe/Riga
```

For the time zone, set the date.timezone option to a time zone that best matches your environment. The default for Zabbix is Europe/Riga, and you can see valid options at http://www.php.net/manual/en/timezones.php.

Make sure you restart Apache after changing the PHP configuration file. If you can't find php.ini, or you make changes but the installation wizard does not pick them up, create a file named test.php in the htdocs directory with only this content:

```
<?php phpinfo() ?>
```

Navigate to this file using your browser and check the value for a **Configuration File (php.ini) Path** entry—this is where you should look for php.ini.

Once everything is fixed, click on the **Next step** button to continue.

If you install from packages then you only have to edit the `zabbix` config file in your web server's `config` folder and after applying the correct changes restart your web server:

```
CentOS/Red Hat
# /etc/httpd/conf.d/zabbix.conf
Debian/Ubuntu
#/etc/apache2/conf-enabled/zabbix.conf
```

Step 3 – database access

Remember the database we created earlier? That's the information we'll supply here:

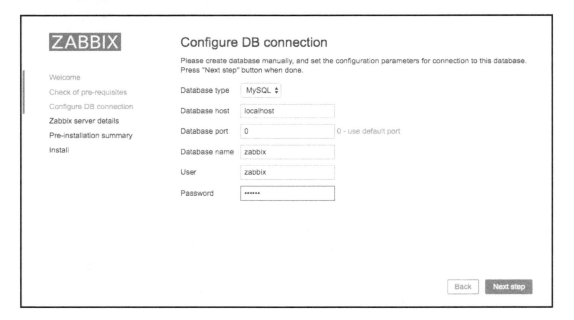

We already configured database credentials for the Zabbix server, but the Zabbix frontend uses a different configuration file. The default **Database type**, **Database host**, and **Database port** values should work for us. Set both **Database name** and **User** to `zabbix`. If you have forgotten the password, just look it up or copy it from `zabbix_server.conf`. After entering the data, click on the **Next step** button. If all of the information is correct, the wizard should proceed to the next step.

Step 4 – Zabbix server details

The next screen lets you specify the Zabbix server's location:

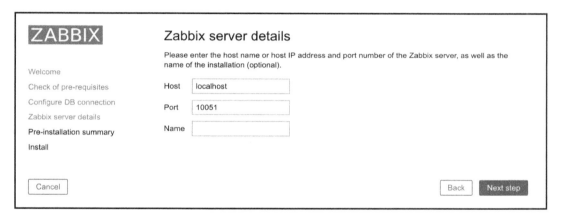

The defaults for the host and port are suitable for us, but we could benefit from filling in the **Name** field. The contents of this field will be used for page titles and a label in the upper-right corner of the Zabbix interface—this could be really handy if we had multiple Zabbix installations. Feel free to enter any name here, but for this book, we'll call the server **Zabbix One**. When you're done, it's over to the **Next step** again. The next screen is a summary of the choices made in the previous screens.

Step 5 – summary

If you left the defaults where appropriate and your database connection test was successful, it should be safe to continue by clicking on **Next step**:

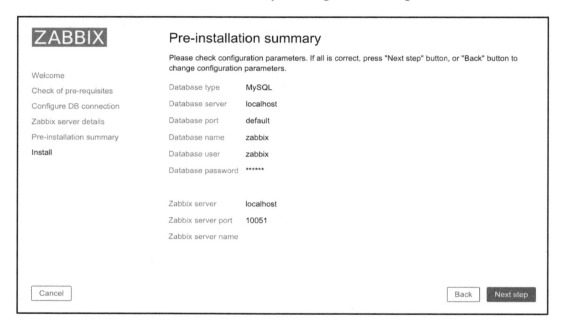

Step 6 – writing the configuration file

It is quite likely that in the next screen, you will be greeted with failure:

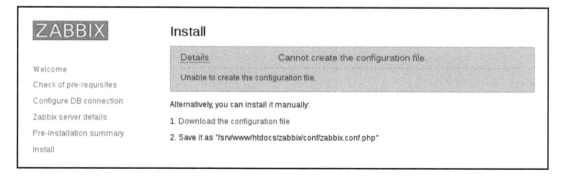

The installation wizard attempted to save the configuration file, but with the access rights that it has, it should not be possible. Previous versions of Zabbix explained two alternatives for proceeding. Unfortunately, Zabbix 4.0 has lost the explanation for one of those. The two possible solutions are as follows:

1. Click on **Download the configuration file** and manually place this file in the `htdocs/zabbix/conf` directory.
2. Make the `htdocs/zabbix/conf` directory writable by the web server user (execute as `root`). Use these commands:

```
# chown <username> /path/to/htdocs/zabbix/conf
# chmod 700 /path/to/htdocs/zabbix/conf
```

Obviously, we need to insert the correct username and directory in these commands. Remember, common locations are `/var/www/html` and `/usr/local/apache2/htdocs`—use the one you copied the Zabbix frontend code to. Common users are `wwwrun`, `www-data`, `nobody`, and `daemon`—you can find out which one the correct user is for your system by running this:

```
$ ps aux | grep http
```

You could also run this:

```
$ ps aux | grep apache
```

The username that most `httpd` processes are running under will be the correct one. Once the permissions have been changed, click on **Finish**. That should successfully save the configuration file.

 You can also skip the configuration wizard by copying `zabbix.conf.php.example` in the `conf` directory to `zabbix.conf.php` and editing it directly. In this case, you should manually verify that the PHP installation and configuration requirements have been met.

It is suggested that you restrict the permissions on this file afterwards to be readable only by the web server user, by issuing these commands as `root`:

```
# chmod 440 /path/to/htdocs/zabbix/conf/zabbix.conf.php
# chown root /path/to/htdocs/zabbix/conf/
```

The file contains the database password, which is best kept secret.

Step 7 – finishing the wizard

Congratulations, this is the last wizard screen, which only wants you to be friendly to it and press **Finish**:

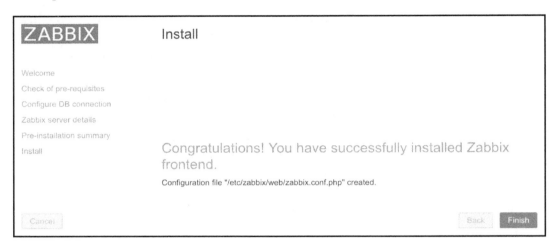

Step 8 – logging in

Immediately after clicking on **Finish**, you should see a login form:

The Zabbix database data that we inserted previously also supplied the default username and password. The default credentials are as follows:

- **Username**: Admin
- **Password**: zabbix

That should get you to the initial frontend screen, which drops you into a quite empty dashboard:

Congratulations! The web frontend is now set up and we have logged in.

 It is possible to easily change the Zabbix frontend configuration later. The `zabbix.conf.php` configuration file can be edited to change database access details, the Zabbix server host and port, and the server name that we entered in the fourth step as well. Most of the parameters in that file should be self-explanatory; for example, `$ZBX_SERVER_NAME` will change the server name.

If you take a closer look at the upper-right corner, you'll spot something familiar: it's the server name we entered earlier in the configuration wizard. This makes it easier to distinguish this installation from other Zabbix instances; for example, if you had a testing and a production instance. Additionally, this name is also used in the page title, and hence in the tab title in most modern browsers. When multiple tabs are open, you should be able to see the instance name right there in the tab. There's no need to click on each tab individually and check the URL or upper-right corner of the Zabbix frontend:

The dashboard isn't too exciting right now, except maybe for that table labeled **System information**. The same view is also available somewhere else, though—click on **Reports** and then click on **System information**, the very first report:

System information		
Parameter	Value	Details
Zabbix server is running	Yes	localhost:10051
Number of hosts (enabled/disabled/templates)	91	7 / 0 / 84
Number of items (enabled/disabled/not supported)	76	76 / 0 / 0
Number of triggers (enabled/disabled [problem/ok])	24	24 / 0 [8 / 16]
Number of users (online)	4	2
Required server performance, new values per second	5.04	

Now we can concentrate on this widget. The frontend successfully sees that the Zabbix server is running and displays the host and port to which it is trying to connect. It also knows some basic things about Zabbix's configuration—there are 76 hosts configured in total. Wait, *what's that?* We have only set it up and have not configured anything; *how can there be 76 hosts already?* Let's take a closer look at the **DETAILS** column. These values correspond to the descriptions in parentheses located in the **PARAMETER** column. So, there are 0 monitored hosts, 1 that is not monitored, and 75 templates. Now that makes more sense—75 of those 76 are templates, not actual hosts. Still, there's one host that isn't monitored, *what's up with that?*

Click on **Configuration** and choose **Hosts**. You should see the following screenshot:

 The first thing to do here is click on that **Filter** button at the right side of the page. In the older versions of Zabbix, it was a huge button. As you can see, all filters are open by default; we will discuss and use filters later. For now, whenever you see a filter preceding the information we came for, just close it.

So, there it is. It turns out that the default Zabbix database already has one server configured—the local Zabbix server. It is disabled by default, as indicated in the **System information** screen and here by the **Disabled** string in the **Status** column.

 There's a lot of technical details in the Zabbix online manual at `https://www.zabbix.com/documentation/4.0/`.

Summary

In this chapter, we set up a fresh Zabbix installation consisting of a database, a server, and an agent daemon, all running on the same machine. We also installed and configured the Zabbix web frontend, based on PHP, to access the database.

We will use the results of this work in all of our future chapters. To see how we can get from a monitored metric to an alert email, we'll go through a simple scenario in the next chapter: think of it as a sort of quick start guide.

Questions

1. What are the three main components that we need to set up a Zabbix server ?
2. In what language is the Zabbix server written ?
3. In what language is the Zabbix frontend written ?
4. What databases other than MySQL are supported ?

Further reading

The next list contains a list of URLs that should help you find some extra information concerning what we have seen in this chapter.

- **Requirements**: https://www.zabbix.com/documentation/4.0/manual/installation/requirements
- **Installation from sources**: https://www.zabbix.com/documentation/4.0/manual/installation/install
- **Why MariaDB Scores Over MySQL**: https://opensourceforu.com/2018/04/why-mariadb-scores-over-mysql/
- **mysql_secure_installation**: https://mariadb.com/kb/en/library/mysql_secure_installation/

Getting Your First Notification

2

We have now installed Zabbix, but it's not doing much—this is what we'd expect. Software that starts doing something on its own would probably be a bit undesirable, at least for now. The promise of Zabbix is to inform you about problems as soon as possible, preferably before your users and management notice them. But how do we get data, where do we place it, and *how do we define what a problem is?* We will try to quickly get Zabbix working and alerting us on a single monitored item, which is the most common scenario. Before we can tell Zabbix who to send notifications to, we will have to explore and use some basic Zabbix concepts. They are as follows:

- Exploring the frontend
- Monitoring quickstart
- Information flow in Zabbix
- Let's create some load
- Basic item configuration
- Using global search

Exploring the frontend

Although we have already looked at some data that was provided by the frontend, we should get a bit more familiar with it before attempting some more configuration tasks.

The configuration steps will be followed by verifying the results in the *Monitoring quickstart* section. We will then explain some generic **item** terms that are used in Zabbix and their uses. Items, being the basis of information gathering, have a fair amount of configuration possibilities.

In your browser, go to the URL that contains the IP of your Zabbix setup, as mentioned in the following steps. Zabbix should be properly configured now and manageable from the UI:

1. Open Zabbix's root URL (`http://<server_ip_or_name>/zabbix`) and log in again if you have been logged out. You should now see a pretty empty dashboard with a little information.
2. Click on the entries in the top menu bar and observe how the lower menu bar shows subentries of your chosen category.
3. Click on **Configuration**, and then click on **Host groups** in the second-level menu—here, all configured host groups are shown.

You will be using these menus a lot so, in the future, we'll refer to the action we just performed as **Configuration | Host groups**. (Whenever you see such a notation, the first is the main category, and the second is the entry under it.)

As you can see in the following screenshot, there are five main categories, and they are as follows :

The tabs in the preceding screenshot are explained as follows:

- **Monitoring**: This category contains most of the monitoring-related pages. You will be able to view data, problems, and graphs here.
- **Inventory**: Here, inventory data for monitored systems can be viewed.
- **Reports**: This section contains some simple reports.
- **Configuration**: Setting up everything related to the monitoring of systems, parameters, notification sending, and so on happens here.
- **Administration**: This section allows you to set up more of the Zabbix internals, including authentication methods, users, permissions, and global Zabbix configuration.

The user profile

Before we venture deeper into these categories, it might be worth visiting the profile section (see the person-like icon in the upper-right corner):

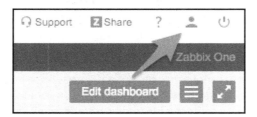

Clicking on it should open your profile:

Here, you can set some options concerning your user account, for example, you can change your password, the frontend language, or the frontend theme. As we will be using an **English (en_GB)** frontend, I suggest you leave that as the default. Zabbix 3.0 versions shipped two different themes, but that has been changed in Zabbix 4.0. Now, we have the *Blue* and *Dark* themes, like we used to have in 3.0, but also a *high-contrast-light* and a *high-contrast-dark* theme. We'll stick with the default theme, but both of the themes shipped with Zabbix 4.0 seem to be visually appealing.

Notice that you can find out the user account you are currently connected to by moving the mouse cursor over the profile icon in the upper-right corner. A tooltip will show your username, as well as your name and surname, as configured in the user profile. When you are not logged in, no profile icon is shown.

There are two options related to logging in: **Auto-login**, which will automatically log the user in using a cookie saved by their browser, and **Auto-logout**. By default, **Auto-login** should be enabled, and we will not change these options.

 Be aware that, sometimes, the auto logout function will not work as you would expect it to work. This is due to some pages extending the session lifetime. You can find more information in the documentation or in the ticket system of Zabbix at `https://support.zabbix.com/browse/ZBX-8051`.

We won't change the **URL** option at present, but we'll discuss the benefits of setting a custom default URL for a particular user later. The **Refresh** option sets the period in seconds, after which some pages in the frontend will refresh automatically to display new data. It might be beneficial to increase this parameter for huge screens, which we do not yet have.

The **Rows per page** option will limit the amount of entities displayed at a time. In larger installations, it might be useful to increase it, but making it too large can negatively affect the performance of the frontend.

Let's make another change here—switch over to the **Messaging** tab:

This allows you to configure frontend messages. For now, just mark the **Frontend messaging** option to enable them and change **Message timeout** to 180. We will discuss what the various options do later in this chapter, when the messages start to appear.

 Verify that all the checkboxes in the **Trigger severity** section are marked; if you saved the user profile before, they might have a different default state.

After you have changed the theme and enabled frontend messages, click on the **Update** button:

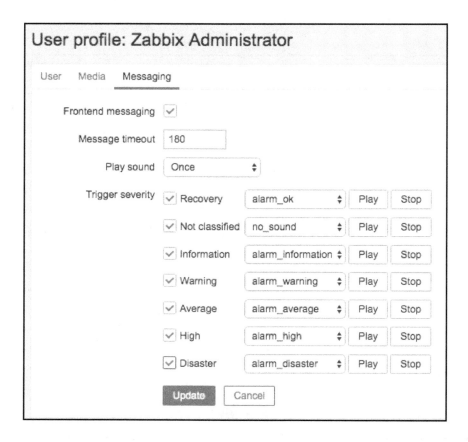

Monitoring quickstart

Now that we have a basic understanding of the frontend navigation, it's time to look at the basics of data gathering in Zabbix **Items**. In general, anything you want to gather data about will eventually go into an *item*.

 An item in Zabbix is a configuration entity that holds information on gathered metrics. It is the very basis of information flowing into Zabbix, and without items, nothing can be retrieved. An item does not hold any information on thresholds—that functionality is covered by triggers.

If items are so important in Zabbix, we should create some. After all, if no data retrieval is possible without items, we can't monitor anything without them. To get started with item configuration, open **Configuration | Hosts**. If it's not selected by default, choose **All** in the **Group** drop-down menu (in the top-right corner). This is a location we will visit quite a lot, as it provides easy access to other entity configurations, including **Items** and **Triggers**. Let's figure out what's what in this area. The most interesting functionality is the host list:

Primarily, it provides access to host details in the very first column, but that's not all. The usefulness of this screen comes from the other columns, which not only provide access to elements that are associated with hosts, but also list the count of those elements. Further down the host entry, we can see a quick overview of the most important host configuration parameters, as well as status information, which we will explore in more detail later:

We came here looking for items, so click on **Items** next to the Zabbix server. You should see a list similar to the one in the following screenshot:

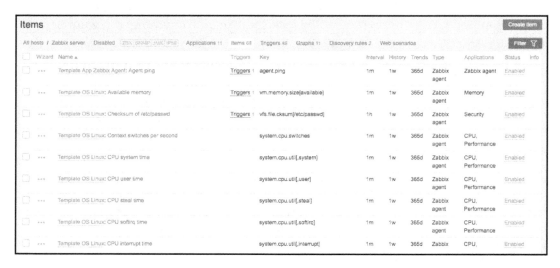

Note the method we used to reach the items list for a particular host—we used convenience links for host elements, which is a fairly easy way to get there and the reason why we will use **Configuration | Hosts** often.

Back to what we were after, we can see a fairly long list of pre-existing items. But wait, *didn't the Zabbix status screen that we saw in the first screenshot claim there's a single host and no supported items?* That's clearly wrong! Return to **Reports | System Information** (or **Monitoring | Dashboard**, which shows the same data). It indeed shows zero supported items. Now, move the mouse cursor over the text that reads **Number of items (enabled/disabled/not supported)**, and take a look at the tooltip:

System information

Parameter	Value	Details
Zabbix server is running	Yes	localhost:10051
Number of hosts (enabled/disabled/templates)	91	7 / 0 / 84
Number of items (enabled/disabled/not supported)	76	76 / 0 / 0
Number of triggers (ena Only items assigned to enabled hosts are counted		3 / 16]
Number of users (online)	4	1
Required server performance, new values per second	5.04	

Aha! So it counts only those items that are assigned to enabled hosts. As this example host, Zabbix server, is disabled, it's now clear why the Zabbix status report shows zero items. This is handy to remember later, once you try to evaluate a more complex configuration.

Creating a host

Instead of using this predefined host configuration, we want to understand how items work. But items can't exist in an empty space—each item has to be attached to a host.

In Zabbix, a host is a logical entity that groups items. The definition of what a host is can be freely adapted to specific environments and situations. Zabbix in no way limits this choice; thus, a host can be a network switch, a physical server, a virtual machine, or a website; it can even be a host that we make up.

If a host is required to attach items to, then we must create one. Head over to **Configuration** | **Hosts** and click on the **Create host** button, located in the top-right corner. You will be presented with a host creation screen. This time, we won't concern ourselves with the details, so let's input only the relevant information:

- **Host Name**: Enter A test host.
- **Groups**: Select the **Linux servers** group. This can be done by typing **Linux Servers** in the empty box. As you will see, Zabbix will show you a list of existing groups that match what you typed. Another option is to click the **Select** button and choose the correct group from the list of groups that will show up. Note that it is also possible to select multiple groups at the same time.

 Why did we have to select a group for this host? All permissions are assigned to host groups, not individual hosts. A host must belong to at least one group. We will cover permissions in more detail in Chapter 5, *Managing Hosts, Users, and Permissions*.

The fields that we changed for our host should look as follows:

When you are ready, click on **Add** at the bottom.

 Pay attention to **Host name**—it's important that this name is exactly the same as in our example! We will see later why this is so important.

Creating an item

So, we have created our first very own host. But, given that items are the basis of all the data, it's probably of little use right now. To give it more substance, we should create items. So, still on the **Configuration | Hosts** page, select **Linux servers** from the **Groups** drop-down, and then click on **Items** next to the host we just created, A test host. This host has no items to list—click on the **Create item** button in the upper-right corner.

There's a form, vaguely resembling the one for host creation, so let's fill in some values:

- **Name**: Enter CPU Load into this field. This is how the item will be named—basically, the name that you will use to refer to the item in most places.
- **Key**: The value in this field will be system.cpu.load. This is the *technical name* of the item, which identifies what information it gathers.
- **Type of information**: Choose Numeric (float). This defines which formatting and type the incoming data will have.

After filling in all the required information, you will be presented with the following screenshot:

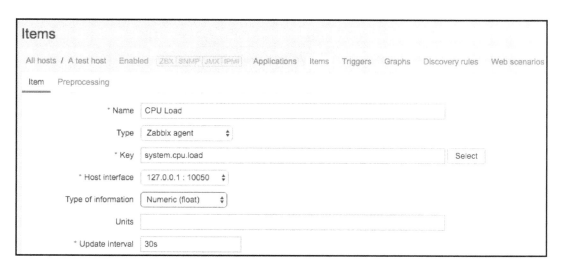

We will look at the other defaults in more detail later, so click on **Add** at the bottom.

More information on item keys is provided in `Chapter 3`, *Monitoring with Zabbix Agents and Basic Protocols*.

You should now see your new item in the list. But we are interested in the associated data, so navigate to **Monitoring | Latest data**. Notice the filter that takes up half the page? This time, we will want to use it right away.

Starting with Zabbix 2.4, the **Latest data** page does not show any data by default for performance reasons; thus, we have to set the filter first.

In **Filter**, type `test` in the **Hosts** field. Our new host should appear. Click on it, then click on **Apply** below the filter. You might have to wait for up to a minute to pass after saving the item, and then you should see that this newly created item has already gathered some data:

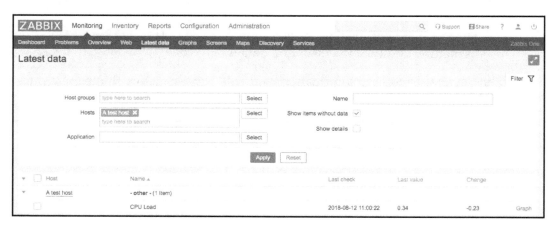

It is possible that there will be no CPU load and that your value will stay at 0. If this is the case for you, then you could run something like `md5sum /dev/zero` from your command line. This will calculate an MD5 check from `/dev/zero` and you will see your CPU load go up.

What should you do if you don't see any entries at all? This usually means that data has not been gathered, which can happen for a variety of reasons. If this is the case, check for these common causes:

- *Did you enter item configuration exactly as in the screenshot?* Check the item key and type of information.
- *Are both the agent and the server running?* You can check this by executing the following as `root`:

  # ss -lpn | grep zabbix

- The output should list both the server and agent daemons running on the correct ports:

  ```
  tcp LISTEN 0 128 *:10050 *:*
  users:(("zabbix_agentd",pid=1001,fd=4),("zabbix_agentd",pi
  d=1000,fd=4)
   tcp LISTEN 0 128 :::10051 :::*
  users:(("zabbix_server",pid=1509,fd=6),("zabbix_server",pi
  d=1508,fd=6)
  ```

- *Can the server connect to the agent?* You can verify this by executing the following from the Zabbix server:

  # telnet localhost 10050

  ```
  Trying ::1...
  Connected to localhost.
  Escape character is '^]'.
  Connection closed by foreign host.
  ```

- If the connection fails, it could mean that either the agent is not running or some restrictive firewall setting is preventing the connection. In some cases, SELinux might prevent that connection, too.
- If the connection succeeds but is immediately closed, then the IP address that the agent receives the connection from does not match the one specified in the `zabbix_agentd.conf` configuration file for the `Server` directive. On some distributions, this can be caused by IPv6 being used by default, so you should try to add another comma-delimited value to the same line for the IPv6 localhost representation to this directive, `::1`.

The Zabbix server reads into the cache all the information on items to monitor every minute by default. This means that configuration changes such as adding a new item might show an effect in the data that's collected after one minute. This interval can be tweaked in `zabbix_server.conf` by changing the `CacheUpdateFrequency` parameter.

Once data starts arriving, you might see no value in the **Change** column. This means that you moved to this display quickly, and the item managed to gather only a single value, thus, there's no change yet. If that is the case, waiting a bit should result in the page automatically refreshing (look at the page title—remember the 30-second refresh we left untouched in the user profile?), and the **Change** column will be populated. So, we are now monitoring a single value: the UNIX system load. Data is automatically retrieved and stored in the database. If you are not familiar with this concept, it might be a good idea to read the overview at `https://www.tecmint.com/understand-linux-load-averages-and-monitor-performance/`.

Introducing simple graphs

If you went away to read about system load, several minutes should have passed. Now is a good time to look at another feature in Zabbix—**Graphs**. Graphs are freely available for any monitored numeric item, without any additional configuration.

You should still be on the **Latest data** screen with the **CPU Load** item visible, so click on the link named **Graph**. You'll get something like this:

While you will probably get less data, unless reading about system load took you more than an hour, your screen should look very similar overall. Let's explore some basic graph controls.

If you don't see any data even after several minutes have passed, try to click on the filter at the top-right of the screen:

When you click on the filter, it will flap open and show you a more advanced version, where you will be able to make more fine-grained selections in your time-frame:

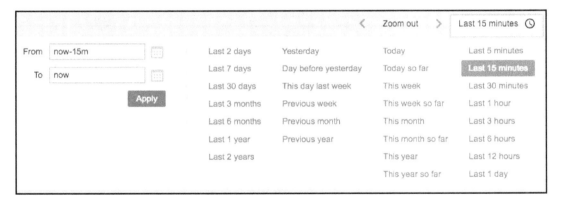

In previous versions, Zabbix relied on a time bar that was not always easy to use. Now, in Zabbix 4, it has received a mayor overhaul and, as you can see, it's much, much more user-friendly.

Let's say we have only 15 minutes of data. We could click on the last 15 minutes selection, as in the preceding screenshot, and the graph would show us the last 15 minutes of data. We can now do this from 5 minutes up to the last 2 years. With the zoom out buttons < >, we are able to move back and forward in jumps based on the time-frame we have selected. For example, if we had selected the last 5 minutes, then we would be able to jump back and forward in jumps of 5 minutes.

If we are not happy with the predefined set of time-frames that Zabbix SIA has put in the menu, then it is possible to select our own time-frame. Imagine you would like to investigate a time slot of 2 minutes at a specific point in time. This can be done by selecting the exact start date and end time from the box on the left-hand side of the filter and pressing the **Apply** button. This is a huge improvement on the previous versions!

Depending on the time at which you are looking at the graphs, (probably 2 days or more) some areas of the graph might have a gray background. This is the time outside of working hours, as defined in the Zabbix configuration. We will explore this in more detail later.

Clicking and dragging over the graph area will zoom in on the selected period once the mouse button is released. This is handy for a quick drill-down to a problematic or interesting period:

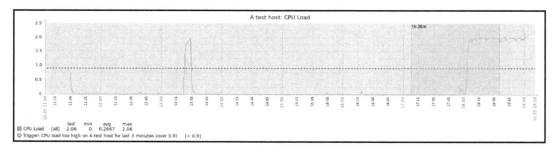

The yellow area denotes the time period we selected by clicking, holding down the mouse button, and dragging over the graph area. When we release the mouse button, the graph is zoomed to the selected period.

Another nice feature is that, if we like to see the raw values instead of the graph, we can do this by clicking in the upper-right corner on **View As | Graph.** This will open a drop-down selection menu, where we can select to see the raw values or the latest 500 raw values:

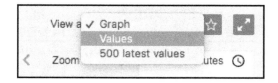

The graph period can't be shorter than one minute in Zabbix. Attempting to set it to a smaller value will do nothing. Before version 3.0, the shortest possible time period was one hour.

Creating triggers

Now that we have an item successfully gathering data, we can look at it and verify whether it is reporting as expected (in our case, that the system is not overloaded). Sitting and staring at a single parameter would make for a very boring job. Doing that with thousands of parameters doesn't sound too entertaining, so we are going to create a trigger. In Zabbix, a trigger is an entry containing an expression to automatically recognize problems with monitored items.

An item alone does nothing more than collect data. To define thresholds and things that are considered a problem, we have to use triggers.

Navigate to **Configuration** | **Hosts**, click on **Triggers** (next to **A test host**), and click on **Create trigger**.

Here, only two fields need to be filled in:

- **Name**: Enter `CPU load too high on A test host for last 3 minutes`
- **Expression**: Enter `{A test host:system.cpu.load.avg(180)}>1`

It is important to get the expression correct, down to the last symbol. Once done, click on **Add** at the bottom. Don't worry about understanding the exact trigger syntax yet; we will get to that later.

Another way to create the expression is to click **Add**, create the correct condition by selecting the item and function, and filling in the **Last of (T)** and **N** fields, as in the following screenshot:

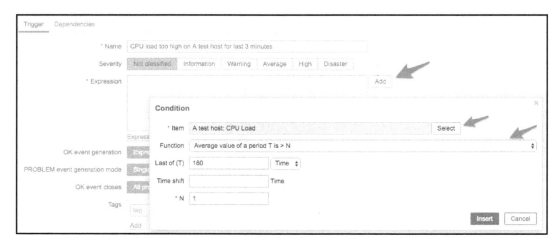

Notice how our trigger expressions refer to the item key, not the name. Whenever you have to reference an item inside Zabbix, it will be done by the item key.

The trigger list should now be displayed with a single trigger—the one we just created. Let's take a look at what we just added: open **Monitoring | Overview** and open the filter if it is closed, and then press the **Any** button. You should see our freshly added trigger, hopefully already updated, with a green color, as in the following screenshot:

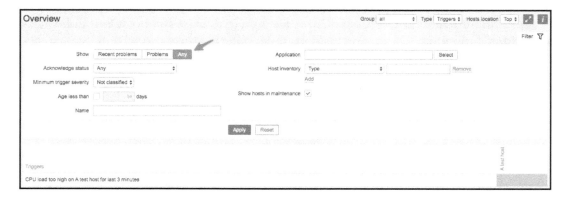

With Zabbix 4.0, we now have the possibility to filter for **Recent Problems**, **Problems**, and **Any** in the filter. With older versions, we had to look to the trigger page, where we would have a mix of filters in an OK and a problem state. Click on **Filter** to close the filter. We will explore this filter in more detail later.

Configuring email parameters

The most common notification method is email. Whenever something interesting happens in Zabbix, an action can be taken. We will set it up so that an email is sent to us. Before we decide when and what should be sent, we have to tell Zabbix how to send it.

To configure the parameters for sending emails, do the following:

1. Open **Administration** | **Media types**
2. Click on **Email** in the **Name** column

You'll get a simple form that you can fill in with the appropriate values for your environment:

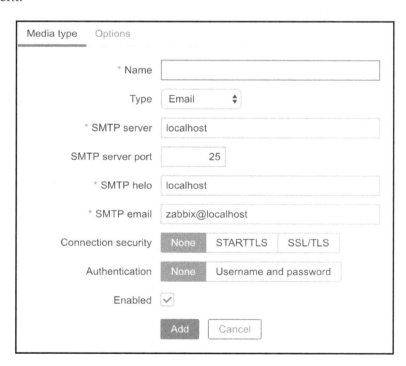

Change the **SMTP server**, **SMTP helo**, and **SMTP email** fields to use a valid email server. The **SMTP email** address will be used as the **From address**, so make sure it's set to something your server will accept. If needed, configure the SMTP authentication, and then click on the **Update** button.

Additionally, you can also make use of the **Connection security** and the **Authentication** options if you need to authenticate when connecting to your mail-server.

New in Zabbix 4.0 is the **Options** tab. The **Options** tab contains the alert processing settings. Concurrent sessions allow you to select one. This setting will only allow one process to send emails. This is fine for small setups. **Unlimited** will allow Zabbix to spin up an unlimited list of processes to send out emails. This can be needed in larger setups to get out the amount of messages needed to ensure everybody is informed on time. **Custom** will allow you to specify a custom number of processes.

The other option, **Attempts**, allows us to specify how many attempts Zabbix will make to get those emails out when it fails to deliver the message to the mail-server. The **Standard** option is 3 times and the maximum number of attempts is 10. The **Retry interval** option will specify how much time Zabbix waits between every attempt to send that message again. Times between 0 and 60 (seconds) are supported, but also time suffixes such as 1 m and 5 s.

Now that we have configured the server to send emails and set what the **From address** should be, it still doesn't know the email addresses that our defined users have, which is required to send alerts to them.

To assign an email address to a user, take the following steps:

1. Open **Administration | Users**. You should see only two users: **Admin** and **Guest**.
2. Click on **Admin** in the **Alias** column and switch to the **Media** tab, as follows:

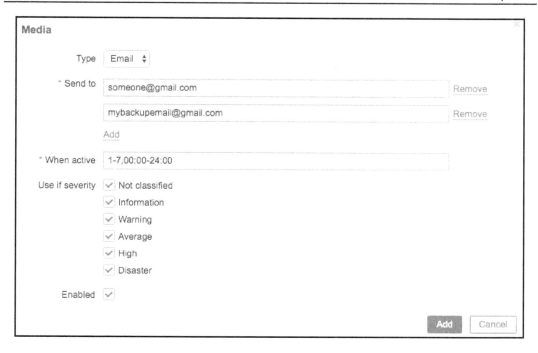

3. Click on the **Add** button. The only thing you have to enter here is a valid email address in the **Send to** textbox, preferably yours.

4. Once you are done, click on **Add** and then **Update** in the **User properties** screen.

In Zabbix 4, it is now possible to add multiple **Send to** email addresses. If this is the case, then Zabbix will send one email to all the specified recipients.

> You can specify more than one time period using a semicolon (;) separator: d-d, hh:mm-hh:mm; d-d, hh:mm-hh:mm...

The **When active** option is used in Zabbix to let it know that it can only send emails during these times. See the documentation for more details on how to define those times: https://www.zabbix.com/documentation/4.0/manual/appendix/time_period.

By marking the boxes **Use if severity**, we tell Zabbix to only send emails if the trigger has a certain severity level.

That finishes the very basic configuration required to send out notifications to users via email.

Creating an action

Now, it's time to tie all this together and tell Zabbix that we want to receive email notifications when our test box is experiencing a heavy load.

Things that tell the Zabbix server to do something upon certain conditions are called **actions**. An action has three main components:

- **Main configuration**: This allows us to set up general options, such as the email subject and the message.
- **Action operations**: These specify what exactly has to be done, including who to send the message to and what message to send.
- **Action conditions**: These allow us to specify when this action is used and when operations are performed. Zabbix allows us to set many detailed conditions, including hosts, host groups, times, specific problems (triggers) and their severity, among others.

To configure actions, take the following steps:

1. Open **Configuration** | **Actions**.
2. Click on **Create action**. (Make sure that the drop-down box **Event source** in the top-right corner has **Triggers** selected.)

A form is presented that lets you configure preconditions and the action to take:

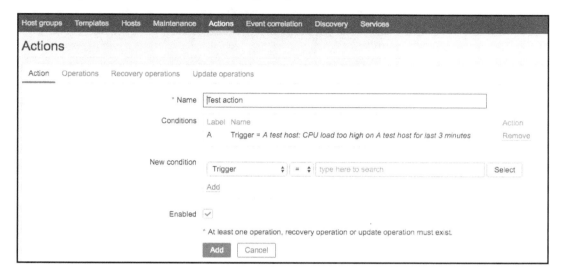

3. First, enter a name for your new action, such as `Test action`, and add a new condition by selecting **Trigger** and **=**.

4. Next, use the **Select** button to select the trigger that you made on your test host.

5. Click **Add**, then select the **Recovery operations** checkbox, and select **Send message** for **Operation type**.

6. Next, select **Admin** as the user to send the recovery message under **Send to Users**, and click **Add**:

7. Next, we should define the operation to perform, so switch to the **Operations** tab.

8. In the **Operations** tab, insert `1h` in **Default operation step duration**, as shown in the following screenshot:

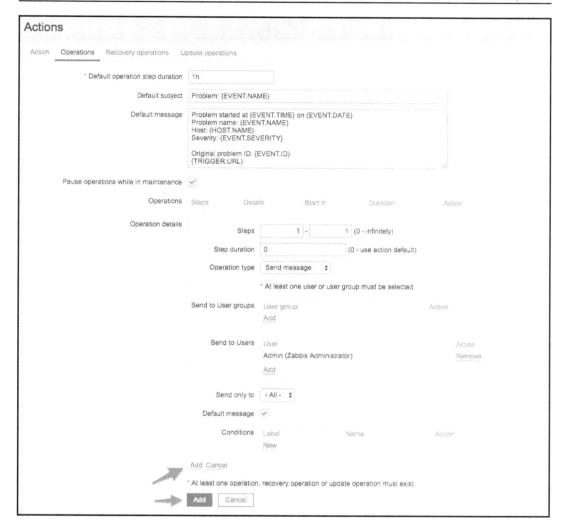

9. In here, click on **New** in the **Operations** block. This will open the
   Operation details block.
10. In the **Send to Users** section, click on the **Add** button. In the resulting
    popup, click on the **Admin** user.
11. Now, locate the **Add** control for the **Operation details** block. This is the
    first arrow in the screenshot.
12. Next, click on **Add** (the second arrow) in the preceding screenshot.

Congratulations! You have just configured the simplest possible action.

Information flow in Zabbix

We have now configured various things in the Zabbix frontend, including data gathering (**Item**), threshold definition (**Trigger**), and instructions on what to do if a threshold is exceeded (**Action**). But *how does it all work together?* The flow of information between Zabbix entities can be non-obvious at first glance. Let's look at a schematic showing how the pieces go together:

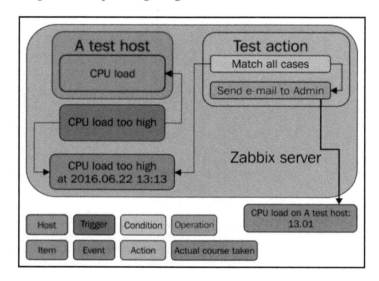

In our Zabbix server installation, we created a host (A test host), which contains an item (CPU load). A trigger references this item. Whenever the trigger expression matches the current item value, the trigger switches to the **PROBLEM** state. When it ceases to match, it switches back to the **OK** state. Each time the trigger changes its state, an event is generated. The event contains details of the trigger state change: when it happened and what the new state is. When configuring an action, we can add various conditions so that only some events are acted upon. In our case, we did not add any, so all events will be matched. Each action also contains operations, which define exactly what has to be done. In the end, some operation is actually carried out, which usually happens outside of the Zabbix server, such as sending an email.

A trigger can also be in the **UNKNOWN** state. This happens if there is not enough data to determine the current state. As an example, computing the average value for the past 5 minutes when there's no data for the past 10 minutes will make the trigger go into the **UNKNOWN** state. Events that cause a change to or from the **UNKNOWN** state do not match normal action conditions.

Let's create some load

Right, so we configured sending email. But it's not very interesting until we actually receive some notifications. Let's increase the load on our test system. In the console, launch the following:

```
$ cat /dev/urandom | md5sum
```

This grabs a pseudo random, never-ending character stream and calculates its MD5 checksum, so system load should increase as a result. You can observe the outcome as a graph—navigate to **Monitoring** | **Latest data** and click on **Graph** for our single item again.

Notice how the system load has climbed. If your test system can cope with such a process really well, it might not be enough—in such a case, you can try running multiple such MD5 checksum calculation processes simultaneously.

Allow **3 minutes** to pass and there should be a popup in the upper-right corner, accompanied by a sound alert:

There is one of the frontend messages we enabled earlier in our user profile. Let's look at what's shown in the message window:

- The small grey rectangle represents trigger severity. For recovery messages, it is green. We will discuss triggers in `Chapter 6`, *Detecting Problems with Triggers*.
- The first link leads to the **Monitoring** | **Problems** page, displaying the current problems for the host that are causing the message.
- The second link leads to the **Monitoring** | **Problems** page, displaying the problem history for the trigger in question.

The third link leads to the event details, displaying more information about this particular occurrence.

The window itself can be repositioned vertically, but not horizontally—just drag it by the title bar. At the top of the window, there are three buttons.

These buttons also have tooltips to remind us what they do, as follows:

- The snooze button silences the alarm sound that is currently being played.
- The mute/unmute button allows you to disable/enable all sounds.
- The clear button clears the currently visible messages. A problem that is cleared this way will not show up later unless it is resolved and then happens again.

Frontend messaging is useful as it provides the following:

- Notifications of new and resolved problems when you aren't explicitly looking at a list of current issues
- Sound alarms
- Quick access to problem details

Now is a good time to revisit the configuration options of these frontend messages. Open the profile again by clicking on the link in the upper-right corner, and switch to the **Messaging** tab:

Here is what these parameters mean:

- **Frontend messaging**: This enables/disables messaging for the current user.
- **Message timeout**: This is used to specify how long a message should be shown. It affects the message itself, although it may affect the sound alarm as well.
- **Play sound**: This drop-down has the options **Once**, **10 seconds**, and **Message timeout**. The first one will play the whole sound once. The second one will play the sound for 10 seconds, looping if necessary. The third will loop the sound for as long as the message is shown.
- **Trigger severity**: This lets you limit messages based on trigger severity (see Chapter 6, *Detecting Problems with Triggers*, for more information on triggers). Unmarking a checkbox will not notify you about that specific severity at all. If you want to get a message but not a sound alert, choose no_sound from the drop-down.

Adding new sounds is possible by copying `.wav` files to the audio sub-directory in the frontend directory.

Previously, when configuring frontend messaging, we set the message timeout to `180` seconds. The only reason was to give us enough time to explore the popup when it first appeared; it is not a requirement for using this feature.

Now, let's open **Monitoring** | **Problems** and select **Recent Problems** for show, and **A test hosts** for Hosts. We should see the `CPU load too high on A test host for last 3 minutes` trigger visible with red, flashing **PROBLEM** text in the **Status** column.

The flashing indicates that a trigger has recently changed state, which we just made it do with that increased system load.

However, if you have a new email notification, you should already be aware of this state change before opening **Monitoring** | **Triggers**. If all went as expected, you should have received an email informing you about the problem, so check your email client if you haven't yet. There should be a message with the subject **PROBLEM: CPU load too high on A test host for last 3 minutes**.

Did the email fail to arrive? This is most often caused by some misconfiguration in the mail delivery chain preventing the message from passing. If possible, check your email server's log files as well as network connectivity and spam filters. Going to **Reports** | **Action log** might reveal a helpful error message.

You can stop all MD5 checksum calculation processes now with a simple *Ctrl + C*. The trigger should then change status to **OK**, though you should allow at least the configured item interval of `30` seconds to pass.

Again, check your email: there should be another message, this time informing you that it's alright now, having the subject **OK: CPU load too high on A test host for last 3 minutes**.

Another place where we can see our trigger is on the dashboard in the **Problems** widget. We see that stat status is **RESOLVED**, and at the end, we will be able to see an arrow in red under **Actions** if something has failed. When we move our mouse over the arrow, we will see three actions: the first one was the email that was sent; the second icon is the calendar with the V in it, when the problem was resolved; and the third is the calendar with the exclamation mark inside, when the problem happened. After the envelope, you will see the reason why the email was not sent:

If all went fine, then congratulations! You have set up all the required configuration to receive alerts whenever something goes wrong, as well as when things go back to normal. Let's recall what we did and learned:

- We created a host. Hosts are monitored device representations in Zabbix that can have items attached to them.
- We also created an item, which is a basic way of obtaining information about a Zabbix system. Remember: the unique item identifier is key, which is also the string specifying what data will actually be gathered. A host was required to attach this item to.
- We explored a simple graph for the item that was immediately available without any configuration. The easy-to-use time-period selection controls allowed us to view any period and quickly zoom in for drill-down analysis.
- Having data already is an achievement in itself, but defining what a problem is frees us from manually trying to understand a huge number of values. That's where triggers come in. They contain expressions that define thresholds.
- Having a list of problems instead of raw data is a step forward, but it would still require someone looking at the list. We'd prefer being notified instead—that's what actions are for. We were able to specify who should be notified and when.

Basic item configuration

We rushed through the configuration of our simple item, so you might have gotten curious about the parameters we didn't change or talk about. Let's take a quick look at what can be monitored and what we can configure for each item.

Zabbix can monitor quite a wide range of system characteristics. Functionally, we can split them into categories, while technically, each method used corresponds to an item type.

Monitoring categories

Let's take a look at the generic categories that we can keep an eye on. Of course, this is not an exhaustive list of things to monitor—consider this as an example subset of interesting parameters. You'll soon discover many more areas to add in your Zabbix configuration.

Availability

While the simplified example we started with (the unlucky administrator at a party—remember him?) might not frighten many, there are more nightmare scenarios available than we'd want to think about. Various services can die without a sign until it's too late, and a single memory leak can bring the system down easily.

We'll try to explore the available options for making sure such situations are detected as early as possible in order to, say, help our administrator deal with disk space problems during the working day and not find out that an important service has died because of a database hiccup just as they go through the door.

Performance

Performance is one of several holy grails in computing. Systems are never fast enough to accommodate all needs, so we have to balance desired operations with available resources. Zabbix can help you both with evaluating the performance of a particular action and monitoring the current load.

You can start with simple things, such as network performance, indicated by a ping round-trip, or the time it takes for a website to return content, and move forward with more complex scenarios, such as the average performance of a service in a cluster coupled with the disk array throughput.

Security

Another holy grail in computing is security, a never-ending process where you are expected to use many tools, one of which can be Zabbix.

Zabbix can, independently of other verification systems, check simple things such as open ports, software versions, and file check sums. While these would be laughable as the only security measures, they can turn out to be quite valuable additions to existing processes.

Management

System management involves doing many things, and that means following a certain set of rules in all of those steps. Good system administrators never fail at that, except when they do.

There are many simple and advanced checks you can use to inform you about tasks to perform or problems that arise when configuring systems: cross-platform notifications about available upgrades, checking whether the DNS serial number has been updated correctly, and a myriad of other system management pitfalls.

Efficiency

While generally considered a subset of availability or performance, some aspects of efficiency do not quite fit in there. Efficiency could be considered the first step to improved availability and performance, which increases the importance of knowing how efficient your systems are.

Efficiency parameters will be more service-specific than others, but some generic examples might include Squid hit ratios and MySQL query cache efficiency. Other applications, including custom in-house ones, might provide other efficiency-measuring methods.

Item types

As explored previously, Zabbix gathers all its data within items. But surely, we'll want to get information in more ways than just through the Zabbix agent. What are our options? Let's have a look:

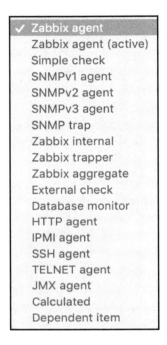

This is the item type configuration drop-down that opens when editing an item. We pretty much skipped this selection when creating our item, because the default value suited us. Let's take a quick look at the types available now:

- **Zabbix agent**: This is the default type. The server connects to the agent and gathers data.
- **Zabbix agent (active)**: This can be considered the opposite of the previous type. The Zabbix agent gathers data and connects to the server as required.
- **Simple check**: As the name implies, this type groups simple checks that are performed by the server. This includes checking for open TCP ports, ICMP ping, VMware, and so on. We will discuss both Zabbix agent types and simple checks in Chapter 3, *Monitoring with Zabbix Agents and Basic Protocols*.

- **SNMP agents**: These three types deal with gathering SNMP data. Versions, obviously, denote the protocol version to use when connecting to the monitored host.

- **SNMP trap**: While still relying on Net-SNMP's `snmptrapd` to obtain traps from the network, Zabbix offers the functionality of receiving SNMP traps easily. This item type allows you to do that, including automatic sorting per host. We will cover SNMP polling and trapping in Chapter 4, *Monitoring SNMP Devices*.

- **Zabbix internal**: This groups items that gather information about the internal state of Zabbix. We will discuss internal monitoring in Chapter 3, *Monitoring with Zabbix Agents and Basic Protocols*.

- **Zabbix trapper**: This item type accepts incoming data instead of querying for it. It is useful for any data you might want to feed into Zabbix that is obtained using other tools, customs scripts, or any other method.

- **Zabbix aggregate**: These items aggregate values across a host group. This is mostly useful for clusters or server farms where the overall state is more important than the state of individual machines.

- **External check**: External checks allow the Zabbix server to execute external commands and store the returned values in the item. This allows it to pass along any information that isn't accessible using any of the other item types. We will use Zabbix trapper items, aggregate items, and external checks in Chapter 10, *Advanced Item Monitoring*.

- **Database monitor**: This type includes checks by using the unixODBC drivers from the OS for querying various database parameters.

- **HTTP Agent**: This type of item allows us to poll data from a web page by making use of the HTTP/HTTPS protocol. Imagine Zabbix being able to connect to a website, read data from that website, and place it in an item. It sounds basic but we can do much more advanced things, such as converting headers to JSON or reading data in XML or JSON.

- **IPMI agent**: The **Intelligent Platform Management Interface** (**IPMI**) is a specification for managing and monitoring (which we're mostly after) systems, especially for out-of-band solutions. The IPMI item type allows direct access to this data. We will cover IPMI monitoring in Chapter 14, *Monitoring IPMI Devices*.

- **SSH agent**: It is possible to directly query a host with SSH and retrieve shell-command output. This check supports both password and key-based authentication.

- **TELNET agent**: For some systems where SSH is unavailable, a Telnet check can be used. While insecure, it might be the only way to access some devices, including older generation switches or UPSes. We will discuss SSH and Telnet -items in `Chapter 10`, *Advanced Item Monitoring*.

- **JMX agent**: Zabbix provides a component called the Zabbix Java gateway. It allows you to monitor JMX-capable applications directly. JMX monitoring will be discussed in `Chapter 15`, *Monitoring Java Applications*.

- **Calculated**: These are advanced items that allow you to create new values from other, pre-existing Zabbix items without duplicating data retrieval. We will use these items in `Chapter 10`, *Advanced Item Monitoring*.

- **Dependent Item**: Sometimes, it makes sense to gather data in bulk, and at other times there is no other way then to retrieve data in bulk. The dependent item can be used to retrieve necessary data out of the master item that contains the bulk data.

While all of these types might look a bit confusing at this point, an important thing to remember is that they are available for your use, but you don't have to use them. You can have a host with a single ICMP ping item, but if you want to monitor more, the advanced functionality will always be there.

As you might have noticed, the item type is set per individual item, not per host. This allows for great flexibility when setting up monitored hosts. For example, you can use ICMP to check general availability, a Zabbix agent to check the status of some services and simple TCP checks for others, a trapper to receive custom data, and IPMI to monitor parameters through the management adapter-all on the same host. The choice of item type will depend on network connectivity, the feature set of the monitored host, and the ease of implementation. Zabbix will allow you to choose the best fit for each item.

How items can be monitored

While that covered categories and item types, we skipped some other parameters when creating the item, so it might be helpful to learn about the basic values that will have to be set for most item types. Let's take a quick look at the fields in the item creation/editing window:

- **Name**: A user-level item name. This is what you will see in most places where data is shown to users.

- **Type**: This is the main property, affecting other fields and the way item data is gathered, as discussed previously.

- **Key**: This is the property that explicitly specifies what data has to be gathered for this item. It is sort of a technical name for the item. The key value must be unique per host. For certain other item types, the field that is actually identifying collected data might be **Simple Network Management Protocol Object Identifiers** (**SNMP OID**) or IPMI sensor, and the key will be only used to reference the item.

- **Type of information**: This allows you to choose the data type that will be gathered with the item. You'll have to set it according to the values provided: integers, decimals, and so on.

- **Data type**: This property provides a way to query data in hexadecimal or octal format and convert it to decimal values automatically. Some SNMP-capable devices (mostly printers) send information in these formats. There's also the Boolean data type that converts several inputs to 1 or 0.

- **Units**: This property allows you to choose the unit to be displayed besides data, and for some units, Zabbix will calculate corresponding conversions as required (called **human-readable** in many tools, so you get 32.5 GB instead of the same value in bytes).

- **Use custom multiplier**: This property multiplies incoming data with the value specified here and stores the result. This is useful if data arrives in one unit but you want to store it as another (for example, if the incoming data is in bytes but you want it in bits, you'd use a multiplier of 8).

- **Update interval**: This sets the interval between data retrieval attempts.

- **Custom intervals**: This setting allows you to modify the update interval during specific times or use cron-like item scheduling—either because you have no need for a particular item during the night or because you know a particular service will be down, for example, during a backup window. You can choose Flexible or Scheduling when creating a custom interval.

- **History storage period**: This sets the time period for which actual retrieved values are stored in the database.

- **Trend storage period**: This does the same as the **History storage period** option, but for trends. Trends are data that's been calculated from history and averaged for every hour to reduce long-term storage requirements.

- **Store value**: This property is for numeric data only and allows the Zabbix server to perform some basic calculations on the data before inserting it into the database, such as calculating the difference between two checks for counter items.

- **Show value**: In this drop-down, a value map may be selected. It allows you to show human-readable values for numeric codes, for example, as returned by the SNMP interface status. Refer to `Chapter 3`, *Monitoring with Zabbix Agents and Basic Protocols*, for more information on value mapping.

- **Applications**: This property makes it possible to perform logical grouping of items, for example, on the **Monitoring** | **Latest data** screen.

- **Populates host inventory field**: Allows you to place collected item values in an inventory field (explored in `Chapter 5`, *Managing Hosts, Users and Permissions*).

- **Description**: This field, available for several entities in Zabbix 3.0, allows you to describe an item. You may explain the way data is collected, manipulated, or what it means.

- **Enabled**: This allows you to enable or disable the item.

- **Preprocessing**: At the top, just on the right-hand side of item, there is a tab called **Preprocessing**. Preprocessing allows us to manipulate data that we retrieve from our items before we save it in our Zabbix database, like using regular expressions to cut a certain part out of our data or trim the left or right number from our received data, and so on:

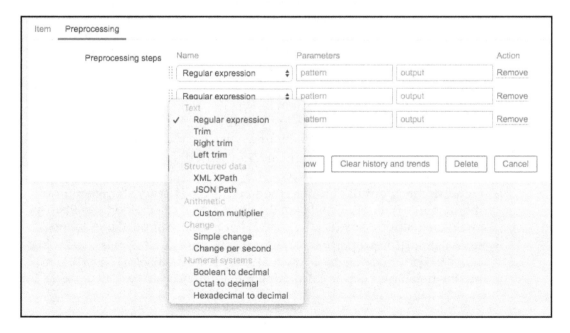

Don't worry if these short descriptions didn't answer all of your questions about each option. We'll dig deeper into each of these later. There are more options available for other item types as well.

Using global search

So far, we have navigated to a host or its items and other entities by going to specific pages in the frontend and then looking up the group and host. This is a convenient enough method in smaller installations, and it's also what we will mostly use in this book. In a larger installation, navigating like this could be very time-consuming, thus, a feature called **global search** becomes very useful. Actually, many users almost completely skip the classic navigation method and use search exclusively.

The global search field is available in the upper right corner of the Zabbix frontend. In there, type a single letter, a. Anything entered here is matched against the beginnings of host-names, and the results are shown in a drop-down. In our case, **A test host** matches:

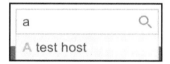

You can choose one of the drop-down entries with your keyboard or mouse, or search using your original string. Let's choose the single entry in the drop-down by either clicking on it with the mouse or highlighting it with the keyboard and hitting *Enter*. In the search results, we can see three blocks that correspond to the three types of entities that can be searched in Zabbix:

- Hosts
- Templates
- Host groups

This is how the entry looks:

Hosts									
Host	IP	DNS	Latest data	Problems	Graphs	Screens	Web	Applications	Items
A test host	192.168.1.29		Latest data	Problems	Graphs	Screens	Web	Applications 1	Items 36

Search: A test host

Host groups				
Host group	Latest data	Problems	Graphs	Web
		No data found.		

Templates					
Template	Applications	Items	Triggers	Graphs	Screens
			No data found.		

For all of them, searching by name is possible. Additionally, for hosts, a search can be performed by **IP** address and **DNS**.

In the search results, clicking on the hostname will open the host's properties. There are also additional links for each host, but the column headers can be confusing: **Triggers**, **Graphs**, and **Web** are duplicated. While it's not very intuitive, the difference is the use of a number next to the links: if there's a number, this is a link to the configuration section. If there's no number, it is a link to the monitoring section, or maybe there are no entities of that type configured. In that case, you sort of have to remember that the rightmost column with the same name is for configuration. The number for the configuration links, if present, is the count of the entities.

Summary

This was the chapter where we finally got some real action: monitoring an item, creating a trigger, and getting a notification on that trigger. We also explored the Zabbix frontend a bit and looked at basic item parameters. Let's review what basic steps were required to get our first alert:

- We started by creating a host. In Zabbix, everything to be monitored is attached to a logical entity called a **host**.
- Next, we created an item. Being the basis of information gathering, items define parameters about monitored metrics, including what data to gather, how often to gather it, how to store the retrieved values, and other things.
- After the item, we created a trigger. Each trigger contains an expression that is used to define thresholds. For each trigger, a severity can be configured as well. To let Zabbix know how to reach us, we configured our email settings. This included specifying an email server for the media type and adding media to our user profile.
- As the final configuration step, we created an action. Actions are configuration entities that define actual operations to perform and can have conditions to create flexible rules for what to do about various events.
- We actually did one more thing to make sure it all works—we *created a problem*. It is useful to test your configuration, especially when just starting with Zabbix. Our configuration was correct, so we were promptly notified about the problem.

While this knowledge is already enough to configure a very basic monitoring system, we'll have to explore other areas before it can be considered a functional one. In the next chapter, we will figure out what the differences between passive and active items are and what the important things to keep in mind are when setting up each of them. We'll also cover basic ICMP items and other item properties, such as positional parameters, value mapping, units, and custom intervals.

Questions

1. Name the 5 severity levels in Zabbix.
2. Can Zabbix send messages to different users or groups, and where do we configure this?
3. Does Zabbix allow items to be pre-processed before it saves them into the database?

Further reading

Read the following articles for more information:

- **Setting time periods**: https://www.zabbix.com/documentation/4.0/manual/appendix/time_period
- **Items**: https://www.zabbix.com/documentation/4.0/manual/config/items
- **VMware monitoring item keys**: https://www.zabbix.com/documentation/4.0/manual/config/items/itemtypes/simple_checks/vmware_keys

Monitoring with Zabbix Agents and Basic Protocols

Now that we have explored the basics of gathering and acting upon information in Zabbix, let's take a closer look at two simple and widely used methods for obtaining data—the already-mentioned Zabbix agents and so-called **simple checks**, which include **TCP connectivity** and **ICMP checks**.

In this chapter, we will cover the following topics:

- Using the Zabbix agent
- Item scheduling
- Creating a simple check
- Binding it all together
- Value mapping
- Units

Using the Zabbix agent

Previously, we installed the Zabbix agent on the same host and monitored a single item for it. It's now time to expand and look at how inter-host connectivity works.

To continue, install the Zabbix agent on another host. The easiest way might be installing from the distribution packages—or you may choose to compile it from the source. If installing from the packages on **Red Hat Enterprise Linux** (**RHEL**)/Debian-based systems, refer to Chapter 1, *Getting Started with Zabbix*, for repository instructions. A potential agent package name could be `zabbix-agent`.

Compiling the agent only from the source is done in a similar way to how all components were included for compilation in Chapter 1, *Getting Started with Zabbix*. Instead of the full `configure` line, we will use a single flag this time:

```
$ ./configure --enable-agent
```

Configuration should complete successfully, and the following summary lines are important:

```
Enable server:          no
Enable proxy:           no
Enable agent:           yes
```

If the output you see matches the preceding output, continue by issuing the following command:

```
$ make install
```

Compilation should complete without any errors, and it should do so relatively quickly. However, be aware that we compile the agent without support for encryption. I have added the URL to the documentation at the end of this chapter, which explains what options are needed to add encryption.

If you install distribution packages on a distribution different from where the server is installed, don't worry when the agent daemon has an older version than the server. This is supported and should work well. However, if the agent is older then 1.4 it will not work on Zabbix 4.0 as changes have been made in how the agent communicates with the Zabbix server. A newer agent with a newer server might not work and is not supported. You should avoid using an older server with newer agents as this has not been tested so there is no guarantee it will work as intended.

Staying with an older agent can be more convenient as you already have one installed and working well. When setting up new ones, it is suggested you go with the latest one, as it might have bugs fixed, improved performance, more supported items for a particular platform, and other benefits.

With the agent installed, now is the time to start it up. How this is done exactly depends on the installation method—and if you installed from the packages, it depends on the distribution as well. For examples on how to start up the agent, refer to Chapter 1, *Getting Started with Zabbix*. As a quick reminder, if you installed from packages on an RHEL/Debian-based system, the agent daemon can likely be started up like this:

```
# systemctl start zabbix-agentd
```

If you installed from the source, directly execute the binary:

```
# <path>/zabbix_agentd
```

Once the agent has been started, we also have to add this new host to the configuration:

1. Go to **Configuration** | **Hosts**
2. Make sure that the **Group** drop-down menu in the upper-right corner says **Linux servers**
3. Click on the **Create host** button and fill in this form:

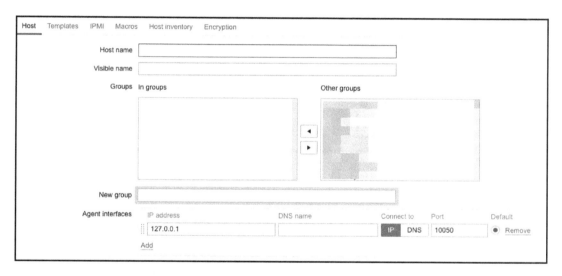

Here are some tips on filling out the form:

- **Host name**: Feel free to choose a descriptive name, or simply enter **Another host**
- **Agent interfaces**: Fill in either the **IP address** or **DNS name**, depending on which connection method you want to use
- **Connect to**: If you decide to go with **DNS name**, switch to **DNS**

When you're done, click on the **Add** button at the bottom.

Passive items

The item we created before was a so-called passive item, which means that the Zabbix server initiates a connection to the agent every time a value has to be collected. In most locations, they are simply referred to as being of the Zabbix agent type.

An easy way to remember what's passive or active in Zabbix is to think from the agent's perspective. If the agent connects to the server, it's active. If not, it's passive:

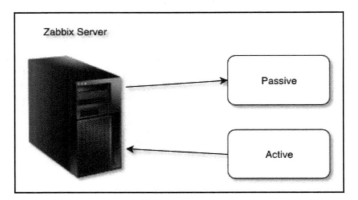

Let's create another passive item to check for the remote host:

1. Go to **Configuration | Hosts**.
2. Click on **Items** next to the host you just created.
3. Click on the **Create item** button, and fill in the following values. This will create our passive item, so make sure you copy it exact as it is written here. In this item, we will try to monitor our web server status as it runs for the frontend already on port 80:
   - **Name**: Enter Web server status
   - **Key**: Enter net.tcp.service[http,,80] (that's two subsequent commas preceding 80)
   - **Update interval**: Change to 60 from the default (30)—once a minute should be more than enough for our needs
   - **History storage period**: Change to 7 from the default (90)—that's still a whole week of exact per-minute service status records kept

The end result should be as shown in the following screenshot:

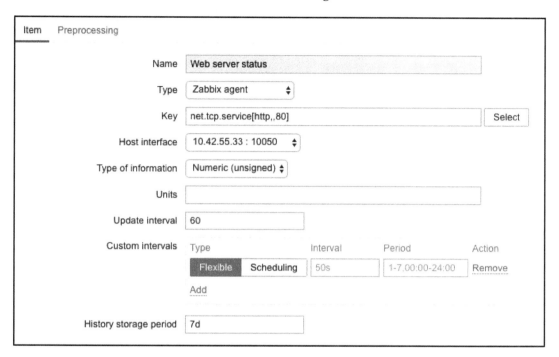

But *what's up with that* , , 80 *added to the service name?* Click on the **Select** button next to the **Key** field. This opens a window with a nice list of keys to choose from, along with a short description of each:

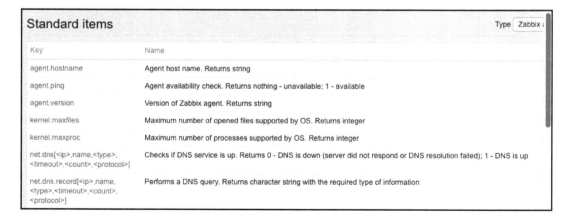

The **Type** drop-down menu in the upper-right corner will allow you to switch between several item types—we'll discuss the other types later. For now, find `net.tcp.service` in the list and look at the description. There are two things to learn here:

- Firstly, we didn't actually have to add that `80`—it's a port, and given that the default is already `80`, adding it was redundant. However, it is useful if you have a service running on a nonstandard port.
- Secondly, there's a key list just one click away to give you a quick hint in case you have forgotten a particular key or what its parameters should be like.

This key, `net.tcp.service`, is a bit special: it tries to verify that the corresponding service actually does respond in a standard manner, which means the service must be explicitly supported. As of the time of writing, Zabbix supports the following services for the `net.tcp.service` key:

- FTP
- HTTP
- HTTPS
- IMAP
- LDAP
- NNTP
- POP
- SMTP
- SSH
- TCP
- Telnet
- NTP

The TCP service is a bit special in its own way. While others perform service-specific checks, TCP is not really a service; it just checks the TCP connection. It's closer to a key you can see a couple of rows above in the item list, `net.tcp.port`. As the description says, this one just tries to open a TCP connection to any arbitrary port without performing any service-specific checks on the returned value. If you try to use an arbitrary service string that is not supported, you would simply get an error message saying that such an item key is not supported.

There's also a `net.udp.service` key that currently supports only one service—**Network Time Protocol** (**NTP**).

Feel free to look at the other available keys—we will use a couple of them later as well—then close this popup and click on the **Add** button at the bottom. You have probably already noticed the green strip at the top of the screen when some operation successfully completes. In older versions there was a control called Details available. Since Zabbix 4.0 this has changed and we will not see any details, only that the item was added:

Now, we could go over to **Monitoring** | **Latest data** and wait for the values appearing there, but that would be useless. Instead, after a couple of minutes, you should visit **Configuration** | **Hosts**. Depending on your network configuration, you might see a red **ZBX** marker next to this host. This icon represents errors that have occurred when attempting to gather data from a passive Zabbix agent.

To see the actual error message, move your mouse cursor over the icon, and a tooltip will open. Clicking on the error icon will make the tooltip permanent and allow you to copy the error message:

The three additional entries represent the SNMP, JMX, and IPMI data-gathering statuses. We will monitor SNMP devices in `Chapter 4`, *Monitoring SNMP Devices*, IPMI devices in `Chapter 14`, *Monitoring IPMI Devices*, and JMX applications in `Chapter 15`, *Monitoring Java Applications*.

If you see an error message similar to **Get value from agent failed: cannot connect to [[192.168.1.100]:10050]: [111] Connection refused** (most likely with a different IP address), it means that the Zabbix server was unable to connect to the agent daemon port. This can happen because of a variety of reasons, the most common being a firewall—either a network one between the Zabbix server and the remote host or a local one on the remote host. Make sure to allow connections from the Zabbix server to the monitored machine on port 10050. If you see something like what was displayed in the previous screenshot with *no route to host* then you probably made a configuration mistake and the Zabbix server cannot connect to the host with the Zabbix agent.

If you did this correctly (or if you did not have a firewall blocking the connection), you could again go to **Monitoring | Latest data**—only that would be pointless, again. To see why, refresh the host list. Soon, you should see the Zabbix agent status icon turn red again, and moving your mouse cursor over it will reveal another error message, **Received empty response from Zabbix Agent at [192.168.1.100]**, assuming that the agent dropped the connection because of access permissions. Now that's different. *What access permissions is it talking about*, and *why did they work for our first host?*

From the Zabbix server, execute this (replace the IP address with the correct one from your host):

```
$ telnet 192.168.1.100 10050
```

 You should always verify network connectivity and access permissions from the Zabbix server. Doing it from another machine can have wildly differing and useless results.

Replace the IP address with your remote host's address. You should see the following output, and the connection should immediately be closed:

```
Trying 192.168.1.100...
Connected to 192.168.1.100.
Escape character is '^]'.
Connection closed by foreign host.
```

Now, try the same with localhost:

```
$ telnet localhost 10050
Trying 127.0.0.1...
Connected to localhost.
Escape character is '^]'.
```

Notice how, this time, the connection is not closed immediately, so there's a difference in the configuration. The connection will most likely be closed a bit later—three seconds later, to be more specific. If this does not happen for some reason, press *Ctrl +]*, as instructed, then enter quit—this should close the connection:

```
^]
telnet> quit
Connection closed.
```

It turns out that configuring the Zabbix agent daemon on another machine is going to be a tiny bit harder than before.

As opposed to the installation on the Zabbix server, we have to edit the agent daemon configuration file on the remote machine. Open zabbix_agentd.conf as root in your favorite editor and take a look at the **Server** parameter. It is currently set to 127.0.0.1, which is the reason we didn't have to touch it on the Zabbix server. As the comment states, this parameter should contain the Zabbix server IP address, so replace 127.0.0.1 with the correct server address here.

 If you have older Zabbix agent instances in your environment, make sure to use and edit zabbix_agentd.conf, with d in the name. The other file, zabbix_agent.conf, was used by the limited-functionality zabbix_agent module, which has been removed.

Save the file and restart the agent daemon. How exactly this is done depends on the installation method, again. If you installed from the distribution packages, the following will most likely work:

```
# systemctl restart zabbix-agentd
```

If you installed from the source and did not create or adapt some init scripts, you will have to manually stop and start the agent process:

```
# killall -15 zabbix_agentd; sleep 3; zabbix_agentd
```

The preceding command will stop all processes called zabbix_agentd on the system. This should not be used if multiple agents are running on the system. Additionally, the delay of 3 seconds should be more than enough in most cases, but if the agent does not start up after this, check its log file for potential reasons. It is also possible that you have to specify the location of the zabbix_agentd binary if this file is not in a location that is in your path, for example, /usr/bin/zabbix_agentd.

Never use `kill -9` with Zabbix daemons. Just don't. Even if you think you could, do not do it. Signal 15 is SIGTERM—it tells the daemon to terminate, which means writing any outstanding data to the database, writing out and closing the log files, and potentially doing other things to shut down properly. Signal 9 is SIGKILL—the process is brutally killed without allowing it to say goodbye to the loved database and files. Unless you really know what you are doing, you do not want to do that—seriously, don't.

To verify the change, try Telnetting to the remote machine again:

```
$ telnet 192.168.1.100 10050
```

This time, the outcome should be the same as we had with the localhost—the connection should be opened and then closed approximately three seconds later.

While some host interface must be specified for all hosts, even for those only using active items, it is only used for passive Zabbix agent checks. If such items are not configured, this interface is simply ignored.

Finally, it should be worth opening **Monitoring | Latest data**. We will only see our previously created item, though; the reason is the same filter we changed earlier. We explicitly filtered for one host; hence, the second host we created does not show up at all.

In the filter, which should still be expanded, clear the host field and select **Linux servers** in the **Host groups** field, and then click on **Apply.**

In many filter fields in Zabbix, we can either start typing and get a list of matching entries or click on the **Select** button to see a list of all available entities. Typing in is a very convenient way when we know at least part of the name. Being able to see the list is helpful when working in an environment we are less familiar with.

We should see two monitored hosts now, each having a single item:

Notice how we can click the triangle icon next to each entry or in the header to collapse and expand either an individual entry or all of the entries.

Cloning items

Let's try to monitor another service now, for example, the one running on port 22, SSH:

1. To keep things simple for us, we won't create an item from scratch this time; instead, go back to **Configuration** | **Hosts**.
2. Click on **Items** next to **Another host**.
3. Click on **Web server status** in the **Name** column. This will open the item editing screen, showing all of the values we entered before.

This time, there are different buttons available at the bottom. Among other changes, instead of the **Add** button, there's an **Update** one.

Notice how one of the previously seen buttons is different. What was labeled **Add** previously is **Update** now. This change identifies the operation that we are going to perform: either adding a new entity or updating an existing one. We might open a configuration form intending to clone the entity, scan the fields, change some values, but forget to click on the **Clone** button. In the end, the existing item will be changed. The difference in the labels of the **Add** and **Update** buttons might help spot such mistakes before they are made.

There's also **Delete**, which, obviously, deletes the currently open item. We don't want to do that now. Instead, click on **Clone.**

Notice how the opened form proposes to create a new item, but this time, all values are set to those that the original item we cloned had. The **Update** button is changed to **Add** as well. Click on the **Add** button—it should fail. Remember, we talked about the key being unique per host; that's what the error message says as well:

Details   Cannot add item   ✕

Item with key "net.tcp.service[http,,80]" already exists on "Another host".

The item editing form is still open, so we can correct our mistake. Make the following modifications:

- **Name**: Change it to SSH server status
- **Key**: Change http,,80 to ssh so that it looks like this: net.tcp.service[ssh]

That's all we have to do for now, so click on the **Add** button at the bottom again. This time, the item should be added successfully. Now navigate to **Monitoring | Latest data**, where **Another host** should have two items listed—**SSH server status** and **Web server status**. Their status will depend on which services are running on the remote host. As it's remote, SSH most likely is running (and hence has a value of 1), but whether or not the web server is running will be specific to your situation. Be aware that it can take a few minutes before you get the first value in the latest data for our new item:

▼	A test host	**- other -** (2 Items)			
☐		SSH server status	2018-12-12 18:26:45	1	Graph
☐		Web server status	2018-12-12 18:26:22	Up (1)	Graph

> The monitoring of a port is often done to make sure the service on it is available, but that is not a strict requirement. If some system is not supposed to have SSH available through the internet, we could use such a check to verify that it has not been accidentally exposed either by the inadvertent starting of the SSH daemon or an unfortunate change in the firewall.

Manually querying items

Adding items to the frontend and waiting for them to update is one way of seeing whether you got the item key right. It is not a very quick method, though—you have to wait for the server to get to checking the item. If you are not sure about the parameters or would like to test different combinations, the easiest way to do this is with a utility called `zabbix_get`. When installing from source, it is installed together with the Zabbix agent. When installing from the packages, it could be installed together with the Zabbix agent or it could also be in a separate package. Using it is very simple: if we want to query the agent on the Zabbix server, we will run this on our Zabbix server, a **test host.**

On Debian/Ubuntu, run the following command:

```
# apt install zabbix-get
```

On Red Hat/Centos run the following command:

```
# yum install zabbix-get
```

This is the command to run from the shell of our Zabbix server:

```
$ zabbix_get -s 127.0.0.1 -k system.cpu.load
```

This will obtain the value in the exact same way as the server would do it. If you would like to get values like this from another host, you could run `zabbix_get` on the Zabbix server. Attempting to run it from the same host on which the agent runs will fail as we changed the `Server` parameter to accept connections from the Zabbix server only. If you would like to query the agent from the localhost for debugging purposes, `127.0.0.1` can be added to the `Server` parameter through a comma—this is sometimes done on all systems when deploying the agent. The `-s` option is to specify the IP/hostname of the host and `-k` is to specify the item key as we defined in Zabbix for our item. Run `zabbix_get --help` to check out all of the options you can specify.

This covers the basics of normal, or passive, Zabbix items, where the server queries agents. Let's move on to other item types.

Active items

Passive Zabbix items are fine if you can connect to all of the monitored hosts from the Zabbix server, but *what if you can't allow incoming connections to the monitored hosts because of security or network topology reasons?*

This is where active items come into play. As opposed to passive items, for active items, it's the agent that connects to the server; the server never connects to the agent. When connecting, the agent downloads a list of items to check and then reports the new data to the server periodically. Let's create an active item, but this time, we'll try to use some help when selecting the item key:

1. Go to **Configuration | Hosts**
2. Click on **Items** next to **Another host**
3. Click on **Create item**

For now, use these values:

- **Name:** `Incoming traffic on interface $1`
- **Type: Zabbix agent (active)**
- **Update interval:** `60s`
- **History storage period:** `7d`

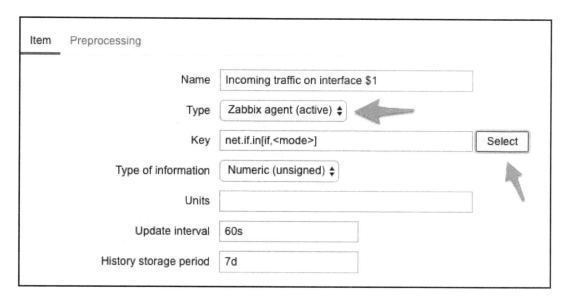

We'll do something different with the **Key** field this time.

Click on the **Select** button and, in the upcoming dialog that we saw before, click on `net.if.in[if,<mode>]`. This will fill in the chosen string, as follows:

net.if.in[if,<mode>]	Incoming traffic statistics on network interface. Returns integer

Replace the content in the square brackets with the name of your network card, so that the field contents read `net.if.in[enp0s3]`. When you're done, click on the **Add** button at the bottom. Never leave placeholders such as `<mode>`—they will be interpreted as literal values and the item will not work as intended.

If your system has a different network interface name, use that here instead of `eth0`. You can find out the interface names with the `ifconfig` or `ip addr show` commands. In many modern distributions, the standard `ethX` naming scheme has been changed to one that will result in various different interface names such as `enp0s3` and `em1`. Further, replace any occurrences of `eth0` with the correct interface name:

```
1: lo: <LOOPBACK,UP,LOWER_UP> mtu 65536 qdisc noqueue state UNKNOWN group default qlen 1000
    link/loopback 00:00:00:00:00:00 brd 00:00:00:00:00:00
    inet 127.0.0.1/8 scope host lo
       valid_lft forever preferred_lft forever
    inet6 ::1/128 scope host
       valid_lft forever preferred_lft forever
2: enp0s3: <BROADCAST,MULTICAST,UP,LOWER_UP> mtu 1500 qdisc fq_codel state UP group default qlen 1000
    link/ether 08:00:27:ca:63:71 brd ff:ff:ff:ff:ff:ff
    inet 192.168.1.14/24 brd 192.168.1.255 scope global dynamic enp0s3
       valid_lft 3133sec preferred_lft 3133sec
    inet6 fe80::a00:27ff:feca:6371/64 scope link
       valid_lft forever preferred_lft forever
```

Go to **Monitoring** | **Latest data** and check whether new values have arrived.

Well, it doesn't look like they have. You could wait a bit to be completely sure, but most likely, no data will appear for this new active item, which means we're in for another troubleshooting session.

First, we should test basic network connectivity. Remember, active agents connect to the server, so we have to know which port they use (by default, it's port `10051`). So, let's start by testing whether the remotely monitored machine can connect to the Zabbix server:

```
$ telnet <Zabbix server IP or DNS name> 10051
```

This should produce output similar to the following:

```
Trying <Zabbix server IP>...
Connected to <Zabbix server IP or DNS name>.
Escape character is '^]'.
```

Press *Ctrl +]* and enter quit in the resulting prompt:

```
telnet> quit
Connection closed.
```

Such a sequence indicates that the network connection is working properly. If it isn't, verify possible network configuration issues, including network firewalls and the local firewall on the Zabbix server. Make sure to allow incoming connections on port 10051:

```
# To check you local firewall rules run
# For iptables
iptables -S

# For firewalld
$ firewall-cmd --list-all
```

 Both agent and server ports for Zabbix are registered with the **Internet Assigned Numbers Authority (IANA)**.

So, there might be something wrong with the agent; let's take a closer look. We could try to look at the agent daemon's log file, so find the LogFile configuration parameter. If you're using the default configuration files from the source archive, it should be set to log to /tmp/zabbix_agentd.log. If you installed from packages, it is likely to be in /var/log/zabbix or similar. Open this log file and look for any interesting messages regarding active checks. Each line will be prefixed with PID and timestamp in the syntax, PID:YYYYMMDD:HHMMSS. You'll probably see lines similar to these:

```
15794:20141230:153731.992 active check configuration update from
[127.0.0.1:10051] started to fail (cannot connect to
[[127.0.0.1]:10051]: [111] Connection refused)
```

The agent is trying to request the active check list, but the connection fails. The attempt seems to be wrong—our Zabbix server should be on a different system than the localhost. Let's see how we can fix this. On the remote machine, open the zabbix_agentd.conf configuration file and check the ServerActive parameter. (This file can probably be located under /etc/zabbix/) The default configuration file will have a line like this:

```
ServerActive=127.0.0.1
```

This parameter tells the agent where it should connect to for active items. In our case, the localhost will not work as the Zabbix server is on a remote machine, so we should modify this. Replace 127.0.0.1 with the IP address or DNS name of the Zabbix server, and then restart the agent either using a systemd script or the manual method: killall.

While you have the configuration file open, take a look at another parameter there—StartAgents. This parameter controls how many processes are handling incoming connections for passive items. If set to 0, it will prevent the agent from listening on incoming connections from the server. This enables you to customize agents to support either or both of the methods. Disabling passive items can be better from a security perspective, but they are very handy for testing and debugging various problems. Also, some items will only work as passive items. Active items can be disabled by not specifying (commenting out) ServerActive. Disabling both active and passive items won't work; the agent daemon will complain and refuse to start up and it's correct—starting with both disabled would be a pointless thing to do. Take a look:

```
zabbix-agentd [16208]: ERROR: either active or passive checks must be
enabled
```

We could wait for values to appear on the frontend again, but again, they would not. Let's return to the agent daemon log file and see whether there is any hint about what's wrong:

```
15938:20141230:154544.559 no active checks on server
[192.168.1.3:10051]: host [Zabbix server] not monitored
```

If we carefully read the entry, we will notice that the agent is reporting its hostname as Zabbix server, but that is the hostname of the default host, which we decided not to use and left disabled. The log message agrees: it says that the host is not monitored.

If we look at the startup messages, there's even another line mentioning this:

```
15931:20141230:154544.552 Starting Zabbix Agent [Zabbix server].
Zabbix 4.0.0 (revision 85308)
```

You might or might not see the SVN revision in this message depending on how the agent was compiled. If it's missing, don't worry about it as it does not affect the ability of the agent to operate.

As that is not the hostname we want to use, let's check the agent daemon configuration file again. There's a parameter named `Hostname`, which currently reads `Zabbix server`. Given that the comment for this parameter says **Required for active checks and must match hostname as configured on the server**, it has to be what we're after. Change the agent configuration parameter to **Another host**, save and close the configuration file, and then restart the Zabbix agent daemon. Check for new entries in the `zabbix_agentd.log` file; there should be no more errors.

While we're at it, let's update the agent configuration on **A test host** as well. Modify `zabbix_agentd.conf` and set the `Hostname=A` test host and restart the agent daemon.

If there still are errors about the host not being found on the server, double-check that the hostname in the Zabbix frontend host properties and agent daemon configuration file (the one we just changed) match.

This hostname is case sensitive.

It's now time to return to the frontend and see whether data has started flowing in at the **Monitoring | Latest data** section:

		Host	Name ▲	Last check	Last value	Change	
▼	☐						
▼		Another host	- **other** - (1 Item)				
	☐		Incoming traffic on enp0s3	2018-12-12 18:31:40	239	+8	Graph

Notice how the system in this screenshot actually has an interface named `enp0s3`, not `eth0`. We will find out how to allow Zabbix to worry about interface names and discover them automatically in `Chapter 11`, *Automating Configuration*.

If you see no data and the item shows up unsupported in the configuration section, check the network interface name.

Great, data is indeed flowing, but the values look really weird. If you wait for a while, you'll see how the number in the **Last Value** column just keeps on increasing. So, *what is it?* Well, network traffic keys gather data from interface counters, that is, the network interface adds up all traffic, and this total data is fed into the Zabbix database. This has one great advantage—even when data is polled at large intervals, traffic spikes will not go unnoticed as the counter data is present, but it also makes data pretty much unreadable for us, and graphs would also look like an ever-growing line (if you feel like it, click on the **Graph** link for this item). We could even call them *hill graphs*:

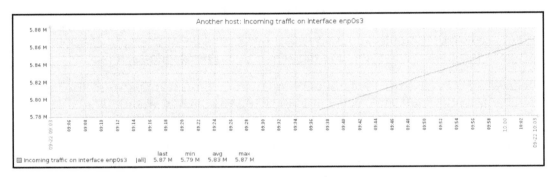

Luckily, Zabbix provides a built-in capability to deal with data counters like this:

1. Go to **Configuration | Hosts**
2. Click on **Items** next to **Another host**
3. Click on **Incoming traffic on interface eth0** in the **Name** column
4. Go to the **Preprocessing** tab and change the **Preprocessing steps** to **Changes per second**
5. Click on **Update**:

We will have to wait a bit for the changes to take effect, so now is a good moment to discuss our choice for the **Type of information** option for this item. We set it to **Numeric (unsigned)**, which accepts integers. The values that this item originally receives are indeed integers—they are counter values denoting how many bytes have been received on this interface. The **Preprocessing steps** option we changed to **Changes per second** (in previous versions, **Delta speed per second**), though, will almost always result in some decimal part being there; it is dividing the traffic between two values according to the number of seconds passed between them. In cases where Zabbix has a decimal number and has to store it in an integer field, the behavior will differ depending on how it got that decimal value, as follows:

- If the decimal value arrived from a Zabbix agent source such as a `system.cpu.load` item, the item will turn up unsupported
- If Zabbix received an integer but further calculations resulted in a decimal number appearing, like with our network item, the decimal part will be discarded

This behavior is depicted in the following diagram:

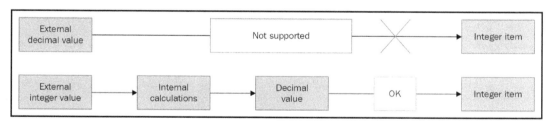

Why is there a difference like this, and why did we leave this item as an integer if doing so results in a loss of precision? Decimal values in the Zabbix database schema have a smaller number of significant digits available before the decimal point than integer values. On a loaded high-speed interface, we might overflow that limit, and it would result in values being lost completely. It is usually better to lose a tiny bit of precision—the decimal part—than the whole value. Note that precision is lost on the smallest unit: a byte or bit. Even if Zabbix shows 5 Gbps in the frontend, the decimal part will be truncated from this value in bits; hence, this loss of precision should be really, really insignificant. It is suggested to use integers for items that have a risk like this, at least until database schema limits are increased.

Check out **Monitoring** | **Latest data** again, you will see that the number under change is negative as we are now calculating a change per second instead of an ever-increasing value. So, our received value will probably be lower then the previous one.

Keep in mind that, in the worst case scenario, configuration changes might take up to three minutes to propagate to the Zabbix agent—one minute to get into the server configuration cache and two minutes until the agent refreshes its own item list. On top of this delay, this item is different from the others we created—it needs to gather two values to compute per second, one of which we are interested in; hence, we will also have to wait for whatever the item interval is before the first value appears in the frontend.

That's better; Zabbix now automatically calculates the change between every two checks (that's what the delta is for) and stores it, but the values still don't seem to be too user friendly. Maybe they're better in the graph—let's click on the **Graph** link to find out:

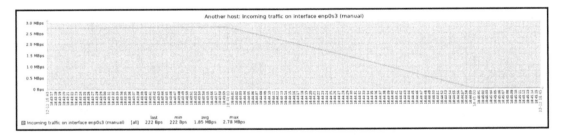

Ouch. While we can clearly see the effect our change had, it has also left us with very ugly historical data. The Y-axis of that graph represents the total counter value (hence showing the total since the monitored system was started up), but the X-axis represents the correct (delta) data. You can also take a look at the values numerically, go to the drop-down menu in the upper-right portion, which currently reads **Graph**. Choose **500 latest values** from there. You'll get the following screenshot:

Timestamp	Value
2018-12-12 18:46:30	249
2018-12-12 18:46:00	216
2018-12-12 18:45:30	254
2018-12-12 18:45:00	222
2018-12-12 18:44:00	2917670
2018-12-12 18:43:30	2910581
2018-12-12 18:43:00	2902951
2018-12-12 18:42:30	2896697
2018-12-12 18:42:00	2889398

In this list, we can nicely see the change in data representation as well as the exact time when the change was performed. But those huge values have come from the counter data, and they pollute our nice, clean graph by being so much out of scale—we have to get rid of them:

1. Go to **Configuration** | **Hosts**.
2. Click on **Items** next to **Another host**.
3. Mark the checkbox next to the **Incoming traffic on interface enp0s3** (or whatever interface you have) item, and look at the buttons positioned at the bottom of the item list:

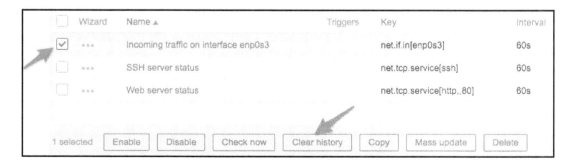

The fourth button from the left, named **Clear history**, probably does what we want. Notice the **1 selected** text to the left of the activity buttons—it shows the amount of entries selected, so we always know how many elements we are operating on. Click on the **Clear history** button. You should get a JavaScript popup asking for confirmation to continue. While history cleaning can take a long time with large datasets, in our case, it should be nearly instant, so click on the **OK** button to continue. This should get rid of all history values for this item, including the huge ones.

Still, looking at the *Y* axis in that graph, we see the incoming values being represented as a number without any explanation of what it is, and larger values get *K*, *M*, and other multiplier identifiers applied. It would be so much better if Zabbix knew how to calculate it in bytes or a similar unit:

1. Navigate to **Configuration** | **Hosts**.
2. Click on **Items** next to **Another host**.
3. Click on the **Incoming traffic on the enp0s3** (or whatever your interface is) interface in the **Name** column. Edit the **Units** field and enter Bps
4. Click on **Update.**

Let's check whether there's any improvement in the **Monitoring** | **Latest data**:

Wonderful; data is still arriving. Even better, notice how Zabbix now automatically calculates KB, MB, and so on where appropriate. Well, it would in our example host if there were more traffic. Let's look at the network traffic; click on **Graph**:

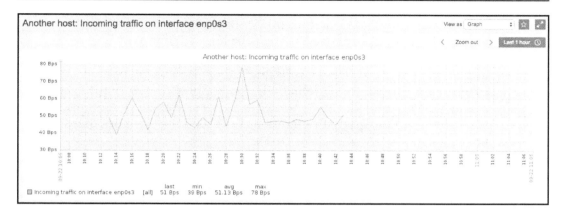

Take a look at the *Y*-axis—if you have more traffic, units will be calculated there as well to make the graph readable, and unit calculations are retroactively applied to the previously gathered values.

Units do not affect stored data like the **Store value** option did, so we do not have to clear the previous values this time.

One parameter that we set, the update interval, could have been smaller, hence resulting in a better-looking graph. But it is important to remember that the smaller the intervals you have on your items, the more data Zabbix has to retrieve and, each second, more data has to be inserted into the database and more calculations have to be performed when displaying this data. While it would have made no notable difference on our test system; you should try to keep intervals as large as possible.

So far, we have created items that gathered numeric data—either integers or decimal values. Let's create another one, a bit different this time:

1. As usual, go to **Configuration | Hosts**.
2. Click on **Items** next to **Another host**. Before continuing with item creation, let's look at what helpful things are available in the configuration section, particularly for items. If we look above the item list, we can see the navigation and information bar.

This area provides quick and useful information about the currently selected host—the hostname, whether the host is monitored, and its availability. Even more importantly, on the right-hand side, it provides quick shortcuts back to the host list and other elements associated with the current host—applications, items, triggers, graphs, discovery rules, and web scenarios. This is a handy way to switch between element categories for a single host without going through the host list all the time. But that's not all yet.

3. Click on the **Filter** button to open the filter we got thrown in our face before. The sophisticated filter appears again:

Using this filter, we can make complex rules about what items to display. Looking at the top-left corner of the filter, we can see that we are not limited to viewing items from a single host; we can also choose a **Host group**. When we need to, we can make filter choices and click on the **Filter** link underneath. Currently, it has only one condition—the **Host** field contains **Another host**, so the **Items** link from the host list we used was the one that set this filter:

1. Clear out the **Host** field
2. Choose **Linux servers** from the **Host group** field
3. Click on the **Apply** button below the filter

Host information and the quick link bar is only available when items are filtered for a single host.

Now, look right below the main item filter—that is a **Subfilter**, which, as its header informs, only affects data already filtered by the main filter.

The entries in the subfilter work like toggles—if we switch one on, it works as a filter on the data in addition to all other toggled subfilter controls. Let's click on **Zabbix agent (active)** now. Notice how the item list now contains only one item; this is what the number 1 represented next to this **Subfilter** toggle. But the subfilter itself now also looks different:

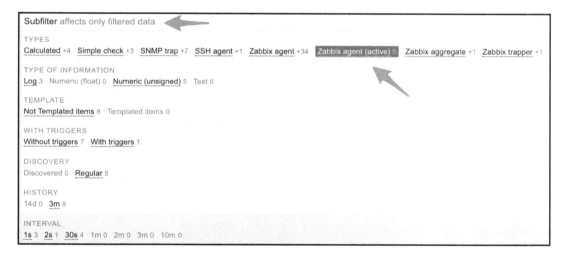

The option we enabled, **Zabbix agent (active)**, has been highlighted. **Numeric (float)**, on the other hand, is grayed out and disabled, as activating this toggle in addition to already active ones results in no items being displayed at all. While the **Numeric (unsigned)** toggle still has **1** listed next to it, which shows that enabling it will result in those many items being displayed, the **Zabbix agent** toggle instead has **+3** next to it. This form represents the fact that activating this toggle will display three more items than are currently being displayed, and it is used for toggles in the same category. Currently, the subfilter has five entries, as it only shows existing values. Once we have additional and different items configured, this subfilter will expand. We have finished exploring these filters, so choose **Another host** from the **Host** field, click on the **Filter** button under the filter, and click on **Create item**.

When you have many different hosts monitored by Zabbix, it's quite easy to forget which version of the Zabbix agent daemon each host has, and even if you have automated software deploying in place, it is nice to be able to see which version each host is at, all in one place.

Use the following values:

- **Name**: Enter `Zabbix agent version`
- **Type**: Select **Zabbix agent (active)** (we're still creating active items)
- **Key**: Click on **Select** and then choose the third entry from the list—**agent.version**
- **Type of information**: Choose **Character**
- **Update interval**: Enter `86400s`

When done! Click on the **Add** button. There are two notable things we did. Firstly, we set the information type to **Character**, which reloaded the form, slightly changing available options. Most notably, fields that are relevant for numeric information were hidden, such as units, multiplier, and trends.

Secondly, we entered a very large update interval, `86400`, which is equivalent to 24 hours. While this might seem excessive, remember what we will be monitoring here, the Zabbix agent version, so it probably (hopefully) won't be changing several times per day. Depending on your needs, you might set it to even larger values, such as a week.

To check out the results of our work, go to **Monitoring | Latest data**.

If you don't see the data, wait a while; it should appear eventually. When it does, you should see the version of the Zabbix agent installed on the listed remote machine, and it might be a higher number than displayed here, as newer versions of Zabbix have been released. Notice one minor difference—while all the items we added previously have links named **Graph** on the right-hand side, the last one has one called **History**. The reason is simple—for textual items, graphs can't be drawn, so Zabbix does not even attempt to do that.

Now, about that waiting—*why did we have to wait for the data to appear?* Well, remember *how active items work?* The agent queries the server for the item list it should report on and then sends in data periodically, but this checking of the item list is also done periodically. To find out how often, open the `zabbix_agentd.conf` configuration file on the remote machine and look for the `RefreshActiveChecks` parameter. The default is two minutes, which is configured in seconds, hence listing 120 seconds.

So, in the worst case, you might have had to wait for nearly three minutes to see any data as opposed to normal or passive items, where the server would have queried the agent as soon as the configuration change was available in its cache. In a production environment with many agents using active items, it might be a good idea to increase this value. Usually, item parameters aren't changed that often.

An active agent with multiple servers

The way we configured `ServerActive` in the agent daemon configuration file, it connects to a single Zabbix server and sends data on items to the server. An agent can also work with multiple servers at the same time; we only have to specify additional addresses here as a comma-separated list. In that case, the agent will internally spawn individual processes to work with each server individually. This means that one server won't know what the other server is monitoring—values will be sent to each of them independently. On the other hand, even if several servers request data on individual items, this data will be collected several times, once for each server.

 Always check comments in the configuration files; they can be very useful. In the case of `ServerActive`, the comment shows that an agent may also connect to non-default ports on each server by using syntax like this: `server1:port` and `server2:port`.

Working with multiple servers in active mode can be useful when migrating from one Zabbix instance to another. For a while, an agent could report to both the old and new servers. Yet another case where this is useful is a customer environment where the customer might have a local Zabbix server performing full-fledged monitoring, while an external company might want to monitor some aspects related to an application they are delivering.

For passive items, allowing incoming connections from multiple Zabbix servers is done the same way—by adding multiple IP addresses to the `Server` parameter.

Supported items

We created some items that use the Zabbix agent in both directions and gather data. But those are hardly the only ones available. You could check out the list while creating an item again (go to **Configuration** | **Hosts**, click on **Items** for any host, and click on the **Create item** button, followed by the **Select** button next to the **Key** field) in order to see which items are built in for Zabbix agents, along with a short description for most of them.

Not all Zabbix agent items are available as both passive and active items. For example, `log` and `event log` items (for gathering log file and Windows event log information, respectively) are only available as active items. Log monitoring is covered in Chapter 10, *Advanced Item Monitoring*, and Windows-specific items in Chapter 22, *Monitoring Windows*.

Looking at the list, we can find out which categories of items Zabbix agents support natively—system configuration, network traffic, network services, system load and memory usage, filesystem monitoring, and others. But that does not mean everything you see there will work on any system that the Zabbix agent daemon runs on. As every platform has a different way of exposing this information and some parameters might even be platform-specific, it isn't guaranteed that every key will work on every host.

For example, when the disk drive statistics report changes to `userspace`, the Zabbix agent has to specifically implement support for the new method; hence, older agent versions will support fewer parameters on recent Linux systems. If you are curious about whether a specific parameter works on a specific version of a specific operating system, the best way to find out is to check the Zabbix manual and then test it. Some of the most common agent item keys are as follows:

- `agent.ping`: This returns 1 when the agent is available and nothing at all when the agent is not available
- `net.if.in/out/total`: This provides incoming/outgoing or total traffic information
- `net.tcp.service`: This tries to make a simplistic connection to a TCP service
- `proc.num`: This counts the number of processes and can filter by various parameters
- `vfs.fs.size`: This provides filesystem usage information
- `vm.memory.size`: This provides memory usage information
- `system.cpu.load`: This provides CPU load information in a standard decimal representation
- `system.cpu.util`: This provides CPU utilization information, for example, `iowait`

For most of these, various parameters an be specified to filter the result or choose a particular piece of information. For example, `proc.num[,zabbix]` will count all processes that the Zabbix user is running.

Choosing between active and passive items

Even though we discussed Zabbix agents being active or passive, an agent really is neither one nor the other—the direction of the connections is determined by the item level. An agent can (and, by default, does) work in both modes at the same time. Nevertheless, we will have to choose which item type—active or passive—to use. The short version—active items are recommended.

To understand why, let's compare how the connections are made. With a passive agent, it is very simple:

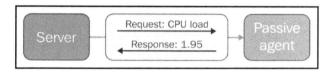

 The arrow direction denotes how connections are made.

One value means one connection. An active agent is a bit more complicated. Remember—in the active mode, the agent connects to the server; hence, the agent first connects to the Zabbix server and asks for a list of items to be monitored. The server then responds with items, their intervals, and any other relevant information:

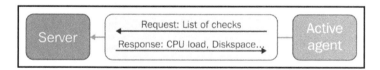

At this point, the connection is closed and the agent starts collecting the information. Once it has some values collected, it sends them to the server:

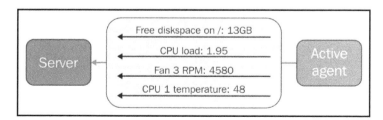

Note that an active agent can send multiple values in one connection. As a result, active agents will usually result in a lower load on the Zabbix server and a smaller amount of network connections.

The availability icon in the host list represents passive items only; active items do not affect it at all. If a host has active items only, this icon will stay gray. In previous Zabbix versions, if you added passive items that failed and then converted them all into active items, this icon would still stay red. Zabbix 3.0.0 is the first version in which the icon is automatically reset back to gray.

Of course, there are some drawbacks to active items and benefits to passive items too. Let's try to summarize what each item type offers and in which situation they might be better.

The benefits of active items are as follows:

- They have a smaller number of network connections
- They cause lower load on the Zabbix server
- They will work if the network topology or firewalls do not allow connecting from the server to the agent (for example, if the monitored hosts are behind an NAT)
- Items such as log or Windows event log monitoring are supported

Here are the benefits of passive items:

- They are easier to set up for beginners
- Custom intervals are supported (they are not supported by active items)
- Polling a virtual IP address on a cluster allows you to always query the active cluster node
- The default templates use passive items; hence, no modification or other configuration is required to use them

We will discuss using and modifying templates in Chapter 8, *Simplifying Complex Configurations with Templates*.

Item scheduling

Earlier, we discussed what introduces delay before a new item is checked—the Zabbix server configuration cache was mentioned. For passive items, there is another factor involved as well, and it is the way Zabbix schedules items to be polled. Each item is scheduled to be polled at a certain time, and the time between two polls is always constant. Even more, a specific item is always scheduled the same way, no matter when the Zabbix server was started. For example, if an item has a 60-second interval, it could be configured to be polled at second 13 of every minute. If the Zabbix server is restarted, this item will still be polled at second 13 of every minute. This scheduling is based on an **internal item ID**; hence, a specific item will not get this timing changed during its lifetime unless it is deleted and recreated or the item interval is changed.

 This logic is similar for all polled item types and will be relevant when we configure SNMP and other item types.

Active items get their polling started upon agent startup; hence, the specific time when values arrive will change based on when the agent was started. Additionally, active items are processed in a serial fashion; hence, one slow item can delay the values for other items from the same agent.

To summarize, after we add a new passive item, it is saved in the database, the Zabbix server does not know about it yet. This item is then loaded into the configuration cache. The configuration cache is refreshed every 60 seconds by default. After the server finds out about the new item, it schedules the item to be polled for the first time at some point between that moment and the item interval.

This means that, with the default interval of 30 seconds, it may take from 30 to 90 seconds before the first value arrives for the item. If the item has a very long interval, such as a serial number or agent version configured earlier, it may take a very long time until the first value appears automatically. There is no way to speed up item polling except by adding it with a short interval at first and then increasing the interval when the item has been verified to work as expected.

After a new active item is added, it is saved in the database again and the Zabbix server does not know about it yet. The active Zabbix agent periodically connects to the server to gather information about items it is supposed to monitor but, as it is not in the configuration cache yet, the server does not tell the agent about the item. This item is then loaded into the configuration cache. The configuration cache is refreshed every 60 seconds by default. After the server finds out about the new item, the item is available to the agent, but the agent connects to the server every two minutes by default. Once the agent finds out about the new item, it immediately attempts to collect the first value for it.

Refer to `Chapter 20`, *Zabbix Maintenance*, for details on how to tune these intervals.

In both cases, if an item is set to delta, we have to obtain two values before we can compute the final value that will be stored in the database and displayed in the frontend, we can't compute the difference from just one value.

However, with Zabbix 4.0 a feature was introduced that was the most voted feature for years that allows us to speed up things but only for passive checks at the moment. Also, we still have to wait till the configuration cache has picked up the changes before we can use this feature. By going to a passive item, we have at the bottom of the page a **Check now** button that allows us to retrieve the latest value of this item. Hopefully, this feature will be improved in the future so that it will work for active and passive items:

To be able to use the **Check now** button, the item config must be present in configuration cache in order to get executed. So it is not possible to check for a new value for an item/rule that has been created just now. Unless we wait till the configuration cache has picked up the information. We can however do a force reload of the configuration cache. Something that we will see in our `Chapter 17`, *Using Proxies to Monitor Remote Locations*.

Simple checks

The previously created items all required the Zabbix agent daemon to be installed, running, and able to make a connection in either direction. But *what if you can't or don't want to install the agent on a remote host and only need to monitor simple things?* This is where simple checks can help you. These checks do not require any specialized agent running on the remote end and only rely on basic network protocols such as **Internet Control Message Protocol** (**ICMP**) and TCP to query monitored hosts.

> Host-availability icons only cover the Zabbix agent, SNMP, JMX, and IPMI status, that is, things where we expect the response to arrive. Our expectations for simple checks could go both ways—an open port could be good or bad. There is no status icon for simple checks.

Let's create a very basic check now:

1. Go to **Configuration** | **Hosts**
2. Click on **Items** next to **Another host**
3. Click on **Create item**

Use the following values:

- **Name**: Enter SMTP server status
- **Type**: Select **Simple check**
- **Key**: Click on the **Select** button

The **Type** drop-down menu at the upper-right corner should already say **Simple check**. If it doesn't, change it to that. In the **Key** list, click on the net.tcp.service[service,<ip>,<port>] key and then edit it. Replace service with smtp and remove everything after it in the square brackets so that it becomes net.tcp.service[smtp], like so:

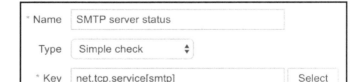

When configuring simple checks in Zabbix, beware of *paranoid* network security configurations that might trigger an alert if you check too many services too often.

When done, click on the **Add** button at the bottom. To check the result, go to **Monitoring** | **Latest data**—our new check should be there and, depending on whether you have the SMTP server running and accessible for the Zabbix server, should list either **1** (if running and accessible) or **0**.

Setting up ICMP checks

What if we care only about the basic reachability of a host, such as a router or switch that is out of our control? ICMP ping (echo request and reply) would be an appropriate method for monitoring in that case, and Zabbix supports such simple checks. Usually, these won't work right away; to use them, we'll have to set up a separate utility, `fping`, which Zabbix uses for ICMP checks. It should be available for most distributions, so just install it using your distribution's package-management tools. If not, you'll have to download and compile `fping` manually; it's available at `http://fping.sourceforge.net/`.

`fping` should come with your distribution if not make sure it is installed on your system. If you make use of SELinux, then it might be that SELinux prevents Zabbix from using `fping` as `fping` needs to be run as `root`. In that case, the solution is to create a proper SELinux rule for this.

Once `fping` is properly installed, the Zabbix server must know where to find it and be able to execute it. On the Zabbix server, open `zabbix_server.conf` and look for the `FpingLocation` parameter. It is commented out by default, and it defaults to `/usr/sbin/fping`. You can quickly find the `fping` binary location with this command:

```
$ which fping
```

If one of the results is `/usr/sbin/fping`, you don't have to change this parameter. If not, modify the parameter to point to the correct `fping` location and restart the Zabbix server so that it knows about the configuration change. That's not it yet. Zabbix also needs to be able to run `fping` with administrative privileges, so execute the following as `root`:

```
# chgrp zabbix /usr/sbin/fping
# chmod 4710 /usr/sbin/fping
```

 Permissions are usually already correct in Fedora/RHEL-based distributions. If you're using distribution packages, don't execute the previous commands; they might even disallow access for the Zabbix server, as it might be running under a different group.

As the `fping` binary should have been owned by `root` before, this should be enough to allow its use by the Zabbix group as required; let's verify that.

As usual, navigate to **Configuration** | **Hosts**, click on **Items** next to **Another host**, and click on **Create item**. Set the following details:

- **Name**: `ICMP ping performance`
- **Type**: **Simple check**
- **Key**: Click on the **Select** button; in the list, click on the **icmppingsec** key, and then remove everything inside the square bracket and the brackets themselves
- **Type of information**: `Numeric (float)`
- **Units**: `ms`
- **Custom multiplier** (from the **Preprocessing** tab): Select the checkbox and enter `1000`

The options in **Preprocessing** tab are as follows:

When all fields have been correctly set, click on the **Add** button at the bottom. Perform the usual round trip to **Monitoring | Latest data**—ICMP ping should be recording data already. If you wait for a few minutes, you can also take a look at a relatively interesting graph to notice any changes in the network performance.

Here, we set up ICMP ping measuring network latency in seconds. If you wanted to simply test host connectivity, you would have chosen the `icmpping` key, which would only record whether the ping was successful or not. That's a simple way to test connectivity on a large scale, as it puts a small load on the network (unless you use ridiculously small intervals). Of course, there are things to be aware of, such as doing something different to test Internet connectivity—it wouldn't be enough to test the connection to your router, firewall, or even your provider's routers. The best way would be to choose several remote targets to monitor that are known to have a very good connection and availability.

For ICMP ping items, several parameters can be specified. For example, the full `icmpping` key syntax is as follows:

```
icmpping[<target>,<packets>,<interval>,<size>,<timeout>]
```

By default, `target` is taken from the host this item is assigned to, but that can be overridden. The `packets` parameter enables you to specify how many packets each invocation should issue—usually, the `fping` default is 3. The `interval` parameter enables you to configure the interval between these packets—usually, the `fping` default is one second against the same target, specified in milliseconds. As for `size`, here, the default of a single packet could differ based on the `fping` version, architecture, and maybe other parameters. And the last one—`timeout`—sets individual target timeouts, with a common default being 500 milliseconds.

These defaults are not Zabbix defaults, if not specified, `fping` defaults are used.

Note that we should not set ICMP ping items with very large timeouts or packet counts; it can lead to weird results. For example, setting the packet count to 60 and using a 60-second interval on an item will likely result in that item missing every second value.

If you set up several ICMP ping items against the same host, Zabbix invokes the `fping` utility only once. If multiple hosts have ICMP ping items, Zabbix will invoke `fping` once for all hosts that have to be pinged at the same time with the same parameters (such as `packet,` `size,` and `timeout`).

> `fping` needs the SUID bit set to work properly. This is because `fping` needs root permissions to work but we run our Zabbix setup as a regular Zabbix user. In most cases, this will be set out of the box by your distribution but, just in case, check it if you run into issues. The proper settings can be verified like this:

```
[root@localhost ~]# ls -al /usr/sbin/fping
-rwsr-xr-x. 1 root root 32960 Oct 26  2014 /usr/sbin/fping
```

> If you don't use IPV4 but IPV6, then you need to configure `fping` for IPV6 in the Zabbix server configuration; that also means that you need to install `fping6` next to `fping`. The usual location is `/usr/sbin/fping6`.

Connecting all of the pieces

So, we found out that a normal or passive agent waits for the server to connect, while an active agent connects to the server, grabs a list of items to check, and then reconnects to the server periodically to send in the data. This means that using one or the other kind of Zabbix agent item can impact performance. In general, active agents reduce the load on the Zabbix server because the server doesn't have to keep a list of what and when to check. Instead, the agent picks up that task and reports back to the server. But you should evaluate each case separately: if you only have a few items per host that you monitor very rarely (the update interval is set to a large value), converting all agents into active ones that retrieve the item list more often than the items were previously checked won't improve Zabbix server performance.

It is important to remember that you can use a mixture of various items against a single host. As we just saw, a single host can have passive Zabbix agent items, active Zabbix agent items, and simple checks assigned. This allows you to choose the best fit for monitoring every characteristic to ensure the best connectivity and performance and the least impact on the network and the monitored host. And that's not all yet—we'll explore several additional item types, which again can be mixed with the ones we already know for a single configured host.

Key parameter quoting

Zabbix key parameters are comma-delimited and enclosed in square brackets. This means that any other character can be used in the parameters as is. If your parameters include commas or square brackets, they will have to be in quote marks. Here are a few examples:

- `key[param1,param2]`: This key has two parameters, `param1` and `param2`
- `key["param1,param2"]`: This key has one parameter, `param1` and `param2`
- `key[param1[param2]`: This is an invalid key
- `key['param1,param2']`: This key has two parameters, `'param1` and `param2'`

What's up with the last one? Well, Zabbix item keys are not shell-interpreted. Zabbix specifically supports double quotes for key parameter quoting. Single quotes are treated like any other character.

Positional parameters for item names

While we're working with items, let's explore some more tricks:

1. Go to **Configuration** | **Hosts**
2. Click on **Items** next to **Another host**
3. Click on **Incoming traffic on interface enp0s8** (or whatever interface you have) in the **Name** column

4. In the item-editing form, click on the **Clone** button at the bottom
5. In the new form, modify the **Key** field so that it reads `net.if.in[lo]`
6. Click on the **Add** button at the bottom

You might notice it right away, or go to **Monitoring | Latest data** and look at the list. Despite the fact that we only modified the key, the item name was updated accordingly as well:

That's what the `$1` part in the item **Name** field is doing. It's working like a common positional parameter, taking the first parameter of the item key. If we had more parameters, we could access those for inclusion in the name with `$2`, `$3`, and so on. This is mostly useful in cases where you want to create several items that monitor different entities so that when cloning the items, you have to change only a single instance of the identifier. It's easier than it seems to miss some change when there are multiple locations, hence creating items with mismatched configuration.

Now that we have some more items configured, it's worth looking at another monitoring view. While we spent most of our time in **Monitoring | Latest data**, this time, navigate to **Monitoring | Overview**. The **Type** drop-down menu in the upper-right corner currently lists **Triggers**, which does not provide a very exciting view for us: we only have a single trigger created. But we did create several items, so switch this drop-down menu to **Data**:

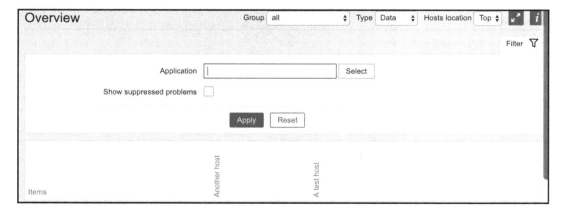

This time, the overview page is a bit more interesting: we can see which hosts have which items and item values.

 The usage of `$1` to `$9` in item names is deprecated so it's advised to not use this anymore as, in later versions, this might not work anymore. This is already true in 4.2 and it can also be that it is in 5.0; there is no plan yet when it will be removed completely (`https://support.zabbix.com/browse/ZBXNEXT-4591`).

Using mass update

Now this looks quite good—we can see all of the monitored data in a compact form. Those 1 results that denote the status for various servers—*what do they mean?* Was 1 for a running state, or was it an error, like with exit codes? They surely aren't intuitive enough, so let's try to remedy that. Go to **Configuration | Hosts,** and click on **Items** for **Another host**. Select all three server status items (**SMTP, SSH**, and **Web**), and then look at the buttons at the bottom of the item list.

This time, we will want to make a single change for all of the selected items, so the second button from the right looks like what we need—it says **Mass update**. Click on it:

Now that's an interesting screen—it allows us to change some parameters for multiple items at once. While doing that, only changes that are marked and specified are performed, so we can change some common values for otherwise wildly differing items. It allows us to set things such as the **Update interval** or any other parameter together for the selected items:

Type ☐	Original
Host interface ☐	Original
JMX endpoint ☐	Original
URL ☐	Original
Request body type ☐	Original
Request body ☐	Original
Headers ☐	Original
SNMP community ☐	Original
Context name ☐	Original
Security name ☐	Original
Security level ☐	Original
Authentication protocol ☐	Original
Authentication passphrase ☐	Original
Privacy protocol ☐	Original
Privacy passphrase ☐	Original
Port ☐	Original
Type of information ☐	Original
Units ☐	Original

Value mapping

This time, we are interested in only one value, the one that decides how the value is displayed to us. Mark the checkbox next to the **Show value entry** to see the available options.

It looks like somebody has already defined entries here, but let's find out what it actually means before making a decision. Click on the **Show value mappings** link to the right on the same line:

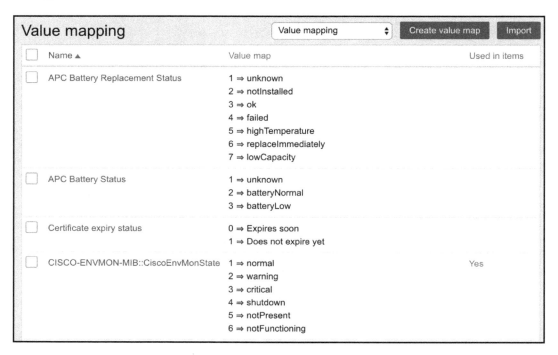

Looking at the list, we can see various names, each of them having a list of mapped references. Look at the **Name** column, where the predefined entries have hints about what they are good for. You can see UPS-related mappings, generic status/state, SNMP, and Windows service-related mappings. The **Value map** column shows the exact mappings that are assigned to each entry. But *what exactly are they?* Looking at the entries, you can see things such as **0 => Down** or **1 => Up**. Data arriving for an item that has a value mapping assigned will expose the descriptive mappings. You are free to create any mapping you desire. To create a new category of mapped data, you need to use the button in the upper-right corner called **Create value map**. We won't do that now, because one of the available mappings covers our needs quite well. Look at the entries—*remember the items we were curious about?* They were monitoring a service and they used 1 to denote a service that is running and 0 to denote a service that is down. Looking at the list, we can see an entry, **Service state**, which defines 0 as **Down** and 1 as **Up**—exactly what we need. Well, that means we don't have to create or modify any entries, so simply close this window.

You can access the value map configuration screen at any time by navigating to **Administration** | **General** and choosing **show value mappings** from the drop-down menu in the upper-right corner.

Back in the mass-update screen, recall the mapping entries we just saw and remember which entry fit our requirements the best. Choose **Service state** from the drop-down menu for the only entry whose checkbox we marked, **Show value.**

When you are done, click on the **Update** button. This operation should complete successfully. You can click on the **Details** control in the upper-left corner to verify that all three items we intended were updated.

Let's see how our change affected information display. Configured and assigned value mappings are used in most Zabbix frontend locations where it makes sense. For example, let's visit that old friend of ours, **Monitoring** | **Latest data**. Take a close look at the various server status entries—Zabbix still shows numeric values for the reference, but each has conveniently listed an appropriate *friendly name* mapped value:

| Web server status | 2018-12-12 19:44:22 | Up (1) |

We have currently stopped the SMTP server to verify whether both **1 => Up** and **0 => Down** mappings work—as we can see, they do. Value mapping will be useful for returned data that works like code values—service states, hardware states (such as batteries), and other similar monitored data. We saw some predefined examples in the value-mapping configuration screen before, and you are free to modify or create new mappings according to your needs.

Value mapping can be used for integers, decimal values (floats), and strings. One use case for strings could be the mapping of different backup levels that a backup software might return:

- `I => Incremental`
- `D => Differential`
- `F => Full`

Navigate back to **Monitoring** | **Overview** and again, look at the various server status entries for **ANOTHER HOST**:

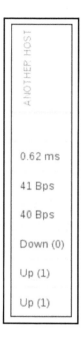

While value mapping doesn't seem too useful when you have to remember a single monitored characteristic with only two possible states, it becomes very useful when there are many different possible states and many possible mappings so that in most locations, you will have a quick hint about what each numeric value means and you are always free to invent your own mappings for custom-developed solutions.

Units

We previously configured units for some items, using values such as B or ms. While the effect was visible in the monitoring section quite easily, there are some subtle differences in the handling of different units.

Units is a free-form field. You can type anything in there, but some units will change their behavior when data is displayed:

- **B/Bps**: By default, when applying **K**, **M**, **G**, **T** and other unit prefixes, Zabbix will use a multiplier of 1,000. If the unit is set to **B** or **Bps**, the multiplier used will be changed to 1,024.
- **s**: An incoming value in seconds will be translated to a human-readable format.
- **uptime**: An incoming value in seconds will be translated to a human-readable format.
- **unixtime**: An incoming Unix timestamp will be translated to a human-readable format.

Interestingly, for our ICMP ping item, we did not use any of these; we used ms instead. The reason is that in certain cases of a very small roundtrip, a value in seconds might be too small to properly store in the Zabbix database schema. By applying the multiplier of 1,000 in the item configuration, we converted the incoming value in seconds into milliseconds, which should never exceed the limits of the database schema. One downside would be that, if a ping takes a long time, the value will not be displayed in seconds—we will have to figure it out from the millisecond value.

Units do not affect the stored values, only what gets displayed. We may safely change them back and forth until we get them right. With older versions of Zabbix, there was a fixed blacklist for certain units, such as rpm and % so that we would not get anything crazy such as 5KRPM or 1K%. With Zabbix 4, this blacklist has been removed and replaced with a new feature that allows us to blacklist any unit we like just by adding an ! in front of the unit: https://www.zabbix.com/documentation/4.0/manual/config/items/item#unit_blacklisting.

Custom intervals

Another item property that we just briefly discussed was custom intervals. Most item types have their intervals configurable, which determines how often the item values should be collected. But *what if we would like to change this interval based on the day of the week or the time of day?* That is exactly what custom intervals enable us to do. There are two modes for custom intervals:

- Flexible intervals
- Custom scheduling

Flexible intervals

Flexible intervals override the normal interval for the specified time. For example, an item could collect values every 60 seconds, but that item might not be important during the weekend. In that case, a flexible interval could be added with an interval of 3600 and time specification of 6-7,00:00-24:00. During Saturdays and Sundays, this item would only be checked once an hour:

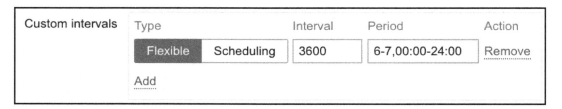

Custom intervals	Type			Interval	Period	Action
	Flexible	Scheduling		3600	6-7,00:00-24:00	Remove
	Add					

Up to seven flexible intervals may be added for a single item.

Days are represented with the numbers 1-7 and a 24-hour clock notation of HH:MM-HH:MM is used.

In case you were wondering, the week starts with a Monday here.

It is also possible to set the normal interval to 0 and configure flexible intervals. In this case, the item will only be checked at the times specified in the flexible intervals. This functionality can be used to check some item on a specific weekday only or even to simulate a crude scheduler. If an item is added with a normal interval of 0, a flexible interval of 60 seconds, and a time specification of 1,09:00-09:01, this item will be checked on Monday morning at 9 o'clock.

Overlapping flexible intervals: If two flexible intervals with different values overlap, during the overlap period, the smallest value is used. For example, if flexible intervals with periods 1-5,00-24:00 and 5-6,12:00-24:00 are added to the same item, during Friday, from 12:00 to 24:00, the one that has the smallest interval will be used.

Custom scheduling

The example of having a flexible interval of one minute works, but it's not very precise. For more exact timing, the other custom interval type can be used—**scheduling**. This enables you to obtain item values at an exact time. It also has one major difference from flexible intervals. Flexible intervals change how an item is polled, but custom scheduling does not change the existing polling. Scheduled checks are executed in addition to the normal or flexible intervals.

It may sound a lot like `crontab`, but Zabbix custom scheduling uses its own syntax. The time prefix is followed by a filter entry. Multiple time prefix and filter values are concatenated, going from the biggest to the smallest. The supported time prefixes are as follows:

- `md`: month days
- `wd`: weekdays
- `h`: hours
- `m`: minutes
- `s`: seconds

For example, an entry of `m13` will schedule this item to be polled every hour at the beginning of minute 13. If it is combined with a weekday specification such as `wd3m13`, it will be polled every hour at the beginning of minute 13 on Wednesdays only. Changing the weekday reference to the month day—or date—reference as `md13m13` would make this item be polled every hour at the beginning of minute 13 on the thirteenth day only.

The example of polling the item on Monday morning at 09:00 that we looked at before would be `wd1h9`:

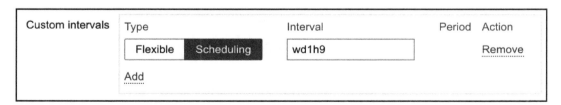

The filter can also be a range. For example, polling an item at 09:00 on Monday, Tuesday, and Wednesday would be done as `wd1-3h9`.

At the end of the filter, we can also add a step through a slash. For example, `wd1-5h6-10/2` would poll the item from Monday to Friday, starting at 06:00 every other hour until 10:00. The item would get polled at 06:00, 08:00, and 10:00. To make an item be polled every other hour all day long on all days, the syntax of `h/2` can be used.

Multiple custom intervals may also be specified by separating them with a semicolon; `wd1-5/2` and `wd1;wd3;wd5` would both poll an item at the beginning of Monday, Wednesday, and Friday.

Copying items

Looking at the same overview screen, the data seems easier to understand with textual hints provided for previously cryptic numeric values, but there's still a bit of not-so-perfect displaying. Notice the dashes displayed for the **CPU load** item for **Another host** and all other values for **A test host**. We didn't create corresponding items on both hosts, and item data is displayed here, which means missing items should be created for each host to gather the data. But recreating all items would be very boring. Luckily, there's a simple and straightforward solution to this problem.

Go to **Configuration** | **Hosts** and click on **Items** next to **A test host**. We had only a single item configured for this host, so mark the checkbox next to this item. Let's look at the available buttons at the bottom of the list again:

This time, we don't want to update selected items, but copy them to another host:

1. Click on the **Copy** button.
2. We want to copy these items to a specific host, so choose **Hosts** in the **Target type** drop-down menu.
3. Select **Linux servers** in the **Group** drop-down menu, which should leave us with a short list of hosts. We are copying from **A test host** to **Another host**; mark the checkbox next to the **Another host** entry.

4. Click on the **Copy** button:

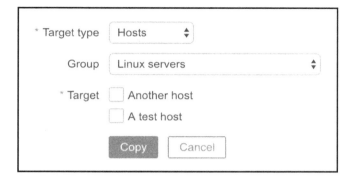

When the operation has completed, change the **Host filter** field (expand the filter if it is closed) to **Another host**, and then click on **Filter** below the filter itself. Notice how the **CPU load** item has appeared in the list. This time, mark all the items except **CPU load**, because that's the only item **A test host** has. You can use the standard range selection functionality here-mark the checkbox next to the ICMP ping performance item (the first item in the range we want to select), hold down *Shift* on the keyboard, and click on the checkbox next to the Zabbix agent version (the last item in the range we want to select). This should select all the items between the two checkboxes we clicked on.

Using the *Shift* key and clicking works to both select and deselect arbitrary entry ranges, including items, hosts, triggers, and other entries in the Zabbix frontend. It works both upward and downward. The result of the action depends on the first checkbox marked—if you select it, the whole range will be selected, and vice versa.

With those items selected, do the following:

1. Click on **Copy** below the item list.
2. Choose **Hosts** in the **Target type** drop-down menu.
3. Choose **Linux servers** in the **Group** drop-down menu.
4. Mark only the checkbox next to **A test host**, and click on **Copy**.

5. After that, click on the **Details** link in the upper-right corner. Notice how all of the copied items are listed here. Let's take another look at **Monitoring | Overview**:

ITEMS	ANOTHER HOST	A TEST HOST
CPU load	0	0.19
ICMP ping performance	0.76 ms	0.07 ms
Incoming traffic on interface enp0s8	53 Bps	859 Bps
Incoming traffic on interface lo	41 Bps	194 Bps
SMTP server status	Down (0)	Up (1)
SSH server status	Up (1)	Up (1)
Web server status	Up (1)	Up (1)

Great, that's much better! We can see all the data for the two hosts, with the numeric status nicely explained. Basically, we just cross-copied items that did not exist on one host from the other one.

But it only gets better—with a mouseover of the displayed values, you can notice how the chosen row is highlighted. Let's click on one of the **CPU load** values:

HISTORY
Last hour graph
Last week graph
Last month graph
Latest values

As you can see, the overview screen not only shows you data in a tabular form, it also allows quick access to common timescale graphs and the **Latest values** for the item. Feel free to try that out.

When you have looked at the data, click on one of the Zabbix agent version values:

Notice how this time there are no entries for graphs. Remember: graphs were only available for numeric data, so **Monitoring | Latest data** and these overview screen pop-up menus offer the value history only.

Summary

This time, we created a new host and added several normal or passive agent items and active agent items.

We learned that it is good practice to disable active items if they are not used by commenting out the `ServerActive` parameter. If passive items are not used, they can be disabled by setting `StartAgents` to `0`, although leaving them enabled can help with testing and debugging.

We set up simple checks on two different hosts and explored many tricks and mechanisms to ease managing in the frontend, such as item cloning, copying, and value mapping.

It might be worth remembering how connections are made for active and passive Zabbix agent item types, that's important when you have to decide on monitoring mechanisms based on existing network topology and configuration. Let's look at the following diagram, summarizing those connections. The arrow direction denotes how connections are made:

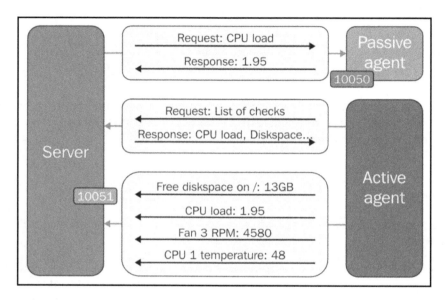

Discussing benefits and drawbacks, we found that active items are recommended over passive items in most cases.

Listed here are the default ports that can be changed if necessary:

- **Normal or passive items**: The Zabbix server connects to a Zabbix agent, which in turn gathers the data (port 10050)
- **Active items**: The Zabbix agent connects to a Zabbix server, retrieves a list of things to monitor, gathers the data, and then periodically reports back to the server (port 10051)
- **Simple checks**: The Zabbix server directly queries the exposed network interfaces of the monitored host; no agent is required

The simple checks were different: they never used the Zabbix agent and were performed directly from the Zabbix server. Simple checks included TCP port checking.

This covers the two basic, most commonly used check types—a Zabbix agent with bidirectional connection support and simple checks that are performed directly from the server.

In the next chapter, we will look at SNMP monitoring. We will start with a quick introduction to the Net-SNMP tools and basic **Management Information Base** (**MIB**) management, and we will set up SNMP polling with fixed and dynamic OIDs. We will also receive SNMP traps and map them to hosts and items both using the built-in method and a very custom approach.

Questions

1. When we talk about active or passive communication between Zabbix server and agent, is this from the agent or the server perspective ?
2. When I configure an item, can I click the **Check now** button and expect Zabbix to give me the information right away?
3. When I need to know the total throughput of my network interface, do I have to calculate in and out traffic together ?

Further reading

Read the following articles for more information:

- **Zabbix Documentation 4.0**: `https://www.zabbix.com/documentation/4.0/manual/installation/install`
- **Encryption**: `https://www.zabbix.com/documentation/4.0/manual/encryption#compiling_zabbix_with_encryption_support`
- **10 Implementation details of net.tcp.service and net.udp.service checks**: `https://www.zabbix.com/documentation/4.0/manual/appendix/items/service_check_details`

Monitoring SNMP Devices

4

Now that we are familiar with monitoring using Zabbix agents and the agentless method, let's explore an additional method that does not require Zabbix agent installation, even though it needs an agent of some kind anyway. **Simple Network Management Protocol** (**SNMP**) is a well-established and popular network-monitoring solution. We'll learn to configure and use SNMP with Zabbix, including SNMP polling and trap receiving.

Being more than two-decades old, SNMP has had the time to become widespread across a whole range of networked devices. Although the name implies management functionality, it's mostly used for monitoring. As the first versions had security drawbacks, the ability to modify configuration over SNMP did not become as popular as its read-only counterpart.

SNMP as the primary monitoring solution is especially popular in embedded devices, where running a complete operating system and installing separate monitoring agents would be overkill. Two of the most popular device categories implementing SNMP out of the box are printers and various network devices, such as switches, routers, and firewalls. SNMP allows the easy monitoring of these otherwise quite closed devices. Other devices with SNMP agents provided include UPSes, **Network-Attached Storage** (**NAS**) devices, and computer rack temperature/humidity sensors. Of course, SNMP is in no way restricted to devices with limited processing power—it's perfectly fine to run a generic SNMP agent instead of a specialized monitoring agent on standard servers. Reasons to use SNMP agents instead of Zabbix agents might include already installed and set up SNMP agents, no access to monitored hosts to install Zabbix agents, or a desire to keep systems relatively free from dependencies on monitoring software.

Given the prevalence of SNMP, it's no wonder Zabbix supports it out-of-the-box. SNMP support in Zabbix builds upon another quality open source product—**Net-SNMP** (http://net-snmp.sourceforge.net/).

In this chapter, we will do the following:

- Look at basic Net-SNMP tools
- Learn how to add **Management Information Base** (**MIB**) files so that Zabbix recognizes them
- Poll SNMP items in Zabbix
- Receive SNMP traps

Using Net-SNMP

If you installed Zabbix from the distribution packages, SNMP support should be already included. If you compiled Zabbix from the source, it should still have SNMP support, as we included that in the configure flags. All that's left to do is set up SNMP monitoring configuration. Before we do that, we'll need a device that has an SNMP agent installed. This is where you can choose between various options; you can use any networked device that you have access to, such as a manageable switch, network printer, or a UPS with an SNMP interface. As SNMP agents usually listen on port 161, you will need the ability to connect to such a device on this port over **User Datagram Protocol** (**UDP**). Although TCP is also supported, UDP is much more widely used.

If you don't have access to such a device, you could also start up an SNMP daemon on a computer. For example, you could easily use **Another host** as a test bed for SNMP querying. Many distributions ship with the SNMP daemon from the Net-SNMP package, and often it is enough to simply start the snmpd service. If that's not the case for your chosen distribution, you'll either have to find one of those networked devices with an SNMP agent already available or configure snmpd manually.

For testing, it may be enough to have a line like the following in /etc/snmp/snmpd.conf:

```
rocommunity public
```

This allows full read access to anybody who uses the public community string.

Do not use such a configuration in production.

Whichever way you choose, you will have to find out what data the device actually provides and how to get it. This is where Net-SNMP comes in, providing many useful tools to work with SNMP-enabled devices. We will use several of these tools to discover information that is required to configure SNMP items in Zabbix.

Let's start by verifying whether our SNMP device is reachable and responds to our queries.

While SNMPv3 has been the current version of SNMP since 2004, it is still not as widespread as SNMPv1 and SNMPv2. There are a whole lot of old devices in use that only support older protocol versions, and many vendors do not hurry with SNMPv3 implementations.

To complicate things further, SNMPv2 also isn't widely used. Instead, a variation of it, the community-based SNMPv2, or SNMPv2c, is used. While devices can support both v1 and v2c, some only support one of these. Both use so-called **community authentication**, where user authentication is performed based on a single community string. Therefore, to query a device, you would have to know which protocol version it supports and the community string to use. It's not as hard as it sounds. By default, many devices use a common string for access, `public`, as does the Net-SNMP daemon. Unless you explicitly change this string, you can just assume that's what is needed to query any host.

In some distributions, the Net-SNMP daemon and tools can be split out in separate packages. In such cases, install the tool package as well.

If you have installed and started Net-SNMP daemon on **Another host**, you can perform a simple query to verify SNMP connectivity:

```
$ snmpstatus -v 2c -c public <IP address>
```

If the daemon has been started correctly and network connectivity is fine, you should get some output, depending on the system you have:

```
[UDP: [<IP address>]:161->[0.0.0.0]:51887]=>[Linux another 3.11.10-29-
default #1 SMP Thu Mar 5 16:24:00 UTC 2015 (338c513) x86_64] Up:
10:10:46.20
Interfaces: 3, Recv/Trans packets: 300/281 | IP: 286/245
```

We can see here that it worked, and by default, communication was done over UDP to port `161`. We can see the target system's operating system, hostname, kernel version, when was it compiled and what hardware architecture it was compiled for, and the current uptime. There's also some network statistics information tacked on.

If you are trying to query a network device, it might have restrictions on who is allowed to use the SNMP agent. Some devices allow free access to SNMP data, while some restrict it by default and every connecting host has to be allowed explicitly. If a device does not respond, check its configuration—you might have to add the IP address of the querying machine to the SNMP permission list.

Looking at the `snmpstatus` command itself, we passed two parameters to it—the SNMP version (2c in this case) and community (which is, as discussed before, `public`).

If you have other SNMP-enabled hosts, you can try the same command on them. Let's look at various devices:

```
$ snmpstatus -v 2c -c public <IP address>
[UDP: [<IP address>]:161]=>[IBM Infoprint 1532 version NS.NP.N118
kernel 2.6.6 All-N-1] Up: 5 days, 0:29:53.22
Interfaces: 0, Recv/Trans packets: 63/63 | IP: 1080193/103316
```

As we can see, this has to be an IBM printer. And hey, it seems to be using a Linux kernel.

While many systems will respond to version 2c queries, sometimes you might see the following:

```
$ snmpstatus -v 2c -c public <IP address>
Timeout: No Response from <IP address>
```

This could of course mean network problems, but sometimes SNMP agents ignore requests coming in with a protocol version they do not support or an incorrect community string. If the community string is incorrect, you would have to find out what it has been set to; this is usually easily available in the device or SNMP daemon configuration (for example, Net-SNMP usually has it set in the `/etc/snmp/snmp.conf` configuration file). If you believe a device might not support a particular protocol version, you can try another command:

```
$ snmpstatus -v 1 -c public <IP address>
[UDP: [<IP address>]:161]=>[HP ETHERNET MULTI-
ENVIRONMENT,SN:CNBW71B06G,FN:JK227AB,SVCID:00000,PID:HP LaserJet P2015
Series] Up: 3:33:44.22
Interfaces: 2, Recv/Trans packets: 135108/70066 | IP: 78239/70054
```

So, this HP LaserJet printer did not support SNMPv2c, only v1. Still, when queried using SNMPv1, it divulged information such as the serial number and series name.

Let's look at another SNMPv1-only device:

```
$ snmpstatus -v 1 -c public <IP address>
[UDP: [<IP address>]:161]=>[APC Web/SNMP Management Card (MB:v3.6.8
PF:v2.6.4 PN:apc_hw02_aos_264.bin AF1:v2.6.1 AN1:apc_hw02_sumx_261.bin
MN:AP9617 HR:A10 SN: ZA0542025896 MD:10/17/2005) (Embedded PowerNet
SNMP Agent SW v2.2 compatible)] Up: 157 days, 20:42:55.19
Interfaces: 1, Recv/Trans packets: 2770626/2972781 | IP:
2300062/2388450
```

This seems to be an APC UPS, and it's providing a lot of information stuffed in this output, including serial number and even firmware versions. It also has considerably longer uptime than the previous systems: over 157 days.

But surely, there must be more information obtainable through SNMP,; also, this looks a bit messy. Let's try another command from the Net-SNMP arsenal, snmpwalk. This command tries to return all of the values available from a particular SNMP agent, so the output could be very large—we'd better restrict it to a few lines at first:

```
$ snmpwalk -v 2c -c public 10.1.1.100 | head -n 6
SNMPv2-MIB::sysDescr.0 = STRING: Linux zab 2.6.16.60-0.21-default #1
Tue May 6 12:41:02 UTC 2008 i686
SNMPv2-MIB::sysObjectID.0 = OID: NET-SNMP-MIB::netSnmpAgentOIDs.10
DISMAN-EVENT-MIB::sysUpTimeInstance = Timeticks: (8411956) 23:21:59.56
SNMPv2-MIB::sysContact.0 = STRING: Sysadmin (root@localhost)
SNMPv2-MIB::sysName.0 = STRING: zab
SNMPv2-MIB::sysLocation.0 = STRING: Server Room
```

 This syntax did not specify OID, and snmpwalk defaulted to SNMPv2-SMI::mib-2. Some devices will have useful information in other parts of the tree. To query the full tree, specify a single dot as the OID value, like this:
snmpwalk -v 2c -c public 10.1.1.100

As we can see, this command outputs various values, with a name or identifier displayed on the left and the value itself on the right. Indeed, the identifier is called the **Object Identifier (OID)**, and it is a unique string, identifying a single value.

Calling everything on the left-hand side an OID is a simplification. It actually consists of an **MIB**, **OID**, and **UID**, as shown here:

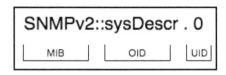

Nevertheless, it is commonly referred to as just the OID, and we will use the same shorthand in this book. Exceptions will be cases when we will actually refer to the MIB or UID part.

Looking at the output, we can also identify some of the data we saw in the output of snmpstatus-SNMPv2-MIB::sysDescr.0 and DISMAN-EVENT-MIB::sysUpTimeInstance. Two other values, SNMPv2-MIB::sysContact.0 and SNMPv2-MIB::sysLocation.0, haven't been changed from the defaults, and hence aren't too useful right now. While we are at it, let's compare this output to the one from the APC UPS:

```
$ snmpwalk -v 1 -c <IP address> | head -n 6
SNMPv2-MIB::sysDescr.0 = STRING: APC Web/SNMP Management Card
(MB:v3.6.8 PF:v2.6.4 PN:apc_hw02_aos_264.bin AF1:v2.6.1
AN1:apc_hw02_sumx_261.bin MN:AP9617 HR:A10 SN: ZA0542025896
MD:10/17/2005) (Embedded PowerNet SNMP Agent SW v2.2 compatible)
SNMPv2-MIB::sysObjectID.0 = OID: PowerNet-MIB::smartUPS450
DISMAN-EVENT-MIB::sysUpTimeInstance = Timeticks: (1364829916) 157
days, 23:11:39.16
SNMPv2-MIB::sysContact.0 = STRING: Unknown
SNMPv2-MIB::sysName.0 = STRING: Unknown
SNMPv2-MIB::sysLocation.0 = STRING: Unknown
```

The output is quite similar, containing the same OIDs, and the system contact and location values aren't set as well. But to monitor some things, we have to retrieve a single value per item, and we can verify that it works with another command, snmpget:

```
$ snmpget -v 2c -c public 10.1.1.100 DISMAN-EVENT-
MIB::sysUpTimeInstance
DISMAN-EVENT-MIB::sysUpTimeInstance = Timeticks: (8913849) 1 day,
0:45:38.49
```

We can add any valid OID, such as `DISMAN-EVENT-MIB::sysUpTimeInstance` in the previous example, after the host to get whatever value it holds. The OID itself currently consists of two parts, separated by two colons. As discussed earlier, the first part is the name of a **Management Information Base** (**MIB**). MIBs are collections of item descriptions, mapping numeric forms to textual ones. The second part is the OID itself. There is no UID in this case. We can look at the full identifier by adding a `-Of` flag to modify the output:

```
$ snmpget -v 2c -c public -Of 10.1.1.100 DISMAN-EVENT-
MIB::sysUpTimeInstance
.iso.org.dod.internet.mgmt.mib-2.system.sysUpTime.sysUpTimeInstance =
Timeticks: (8972788) 1 day, 0:55:27.88
```

To translate from the numeric to the textual form, an MIB is needed. In some cases, the standard MIBs are enough, but many devices have useful information in vendor-specific extensions. Some vendors provide quality MIBs for their equipment; some are less helpful. Contact your vendor to obtain any required MIBs. We will discuss basic MIB management later in this chapter.

That's a considerably long name, showing the tree-like structure. It starts with a no-name `root` object and goes further, with all the values attached at some location to this tree. Well, we mentioned numeric form, and we can make `snmpget` output numeric names as well with the `-On` flag:

```
$ snmpget -v 2c -c public -On 10.1.1.100 DISMAN-EVENT-
MIB::sysUpTimeInstance
.1.3.6.1.2.1.1.3.0 = Timeticks: (9048942) 1 day, 1:08:09.42
```

So, each OID can be referred to in one of three notations—short, long, or numeric. In this case, `DISMAN-EVENT-MIB::sysUpTimeInstance`, `.iso.org.dod.internet.mgmt.mib-2.system.sysUpTime.sysUpTimeInstance`, and `.1.3.6.1.2.1.1.3.0` all refer to the same value.

Take a look at the `snmpcmd` man page for other supported output-formatting options.

But how does this fit into Zabbix SNMP items? Well, to create an SNMP item in Zabbix, you have to enter an OID. *How do you know what OID to use?* Often, you might have the following choices:

- You just know it
- Ask somebody
- Find out yourself

More often than not, the first two options don't work, so finding it out yourself will be the only way. As we have learned, Net-SNMP tools are fairly good at supporting such a discovery process.

Using SNMPv3 with Net-SNMP

The latest version of SNMP, version 3, is still not that common yet, and it is somewhat more complex than the previous versions. Device implementations can also vary in quality, so it might be useful to test your configuration of Zabbix against a known solution—Net-SNMP daemon. Let's add an SNMPv3 user to it and get a value. Make sure Net-SNMP is installed and that snmpd starts up successfully.

To configure SNMPv3, first stop snmpd, and then, as root, run this:

```
# net-snmp-create-v3-user -ro zabbix
```

This utility will prompt for a password. Enter a password of at least eight characters—although shorter passwords will be accepted here, it will fail the default length requirement later. Start snmpd again, and test the retrieval of values using v 3:

```
$ snmpget -u zabbix -A zabbixzabbix -v 3 -l authNoPriv localhost
SNMPv2-MIB::sysDescr.0
```

This should return data successfully, as follows:

```
SNMPv2-MIB::sysDescr.0 = STRING: Linux another 3.11.10-29-default #1
SMP Thu Mar 5 16:24:00 UTC 2015 (338c513) x86_64
```

We don't need to configure versions 1 or 2c separately, so now we have a general SNMP agent, providing all common versions for testing or exploring.

The engine ID

There is a very common misconfiguration done when attempting to use SNMPv3. According to RFC 3414 (`https://tools.ietf.org/html/rfc3414`), each device must have a unique identifier. Each SNMP engine maintains a value, `snmpEngineID`, which uniquely identifies the SNMP engine.

Sometimes, users tend to set this ID to the same value for several devices. As a result, Zabbix is unable to successfully monitor those devices. To make things worse, each device responds nicely to commands such as `snmpget` or `snmpwalk`. These commands only talk to a single device at a time; hence, they do not care about `snmpEngineID` much.

In Zabbix, this could manifest as one device working properly but stopping when another one is added to monitoring.

If there are mysterious problems with SNMPv3 device monitoring with Zabbix that do not manifest when using command-line tools, `snmpEngineID` should be checked very carefully.

Authentication, encryption, and context

With SNMPv3, several additional features are available. Most notably, one may choose strong authentication and encryption of communication. For authentication, Zabbix currently supports the following methods:

- **Message-Digest 5 (MD5) algorithm**
- **Secure Hash Algorithm (SHA)**

For encryption, Zabbix supports these:

- **Data Encryption Standard (DES)**
- **Advanced Encryption Standard (AES)**

While it seems that one might always want to use the strongest possible encryption, keep in mind that this can be quite resource intensive. Querying a lot of values over SNMP can overload the target device quite easily. To have reasonable security, you may choose the `authNoPriv` option in the **Security level** drop-down menu. This will use encryption for the authentication process but not for data transfer.

Another SNMPv3 feature is context. In some cases, one SNMP endpoint is responsible for providing information about multiple devices—for example, about multiple UPS devices. A single OID will get a different value, depending on the context specified. Zabbix allows you to specify the context for each individual SNMPv3 item.

Adding new MIBs

One way to discover usable OIDs is to redirect the full SNMP tree output to a file, find out what interesting and useful information the device exposes, and determine what the OIDs are from that. It's all good as long as the MIB files shipped with Net-SNMP provide the required descriptors, but SNMP MIBs are extensible—anybody can add new information, and many vendors do. In such a case, your file might be filled with lines like this:

```
SNMPv2-SMI::enterprises.318.1.1.1.1.2.3.0 = STRING: "QS0547120198"
```

That's quite cryptic. While the output is in the short, textual form, part of it is numeric. This means that there is no MIB definition for this part of the SNMP tree. Enterprise number `318` is assigned to APC and, luckily, APC offers an MIB for download from their site, so it can be added to Net-SNMP configured MIBs. *But how?*

Getting SNMP MIBs isn't always easy. A certain large printer manufacturer representative claimed that they do not provide SNMP MIBs, and everybody should use their proprietary printer-management application. Most manufacturers do provide MIBs, though, and in some cases, freely accessible MIB collection sites can help better than official vendor sites.

After downloading a new MIB, you have to place it in a location where Net-SNMP will search for MIB files and configure them as well. Net-SNMP searches for MIBs in two locations: `.snmp/mibs` in the user's home directory and `/usr/share/snmp/mibs`; which one you use is your decision. If you want something for the current user only, or don't have access to the `/usr` directory, you can use `.snmp/mibs`; otherwise, use `/usr/share/snmp/mibs`. Whichever you choose, that's not enough—you also have to instruct tools to include this MIB.

While Zabbix server uses the same directory to look for MIBs, specifying MIBs to be used is only required for the Net-SNMP tools—Zabbix server loads all MIBs found.

The first method is to pass MIB names directly to the called command. But hey, we don't know the MIB name yet. To find out what a particular name in some file is, open the file in a text editor and look for MIB DEFINITIONS ::= BEGIN near the beginning of the file. The string before this text will be the MIB name we are looking for. Here's an example:

```
PowerNet-MIB DEFINITIONS ::= BEGIN
```

So, APC has chosen to name its MIB PowerNet-MIB. Armed with this knowledge, we can instruct any command to include this file:

```
$ snmpget -m +PowerNet-MIB -v 1 -c public <IP address> SNMPv2-
SMI::enterprises.318.1.1.1.1.2.3.0
PowerNet-MIB::upsAdvIdentSerialNumber.0 = STRING: "QS0547120198"
```

Excellent; snmpget included the correct MIB and obtained the full textual string, which confirms our suspicion that this might be a serial number. You can now use the same flag for snmpwalk and obtain a file with much better value names. Quite often, you will be able to search such a file for interesting strings such as serial number and find the correct OID.

> The + sign instructs us to include the specified MIBs in addition to otherwise configured ones. If you omit +, the MIB list will be replaced with the one you specified.

Feel free to look at the MIB files in the /usr/share/snmp/mibs directory. As you can see, most files here have their filename the same as their MIB name without the extension, which is not required. Actually, the filename has nothing to do with the MIB name; hence, sometimes, you might have to resort to tools such as grep to find out which file contains which MIB.

While passing individual MIB names on the command line is nice for a quick one-time query, it gets very tedious once you have to perform these actions more often and the MIB list grows. There's another method, somewhat more durable—the MIB's environment variable. In this case, the variable could be set like this:

```
$ export MIBS=+PowerNet-MIB
```

In the current shell, individual commands do not need the MIB names passed to them anymore. All of the MIBs specified in the variable will be included upon every invocation.

Of course, that's also not that permanent. While you can specify this variable in profile scripts, it can get tedious to manage for all the users on a machine. This is where a third method comes in: configuration files.

Again, you can use per-user configuration files, located in `.snmp/snmp.conf` in their home directories, or you can use the global `/etc/snmp/snmp.conf` file.

The location of the global configuration file and MIB directory can be different if you have compiled Net-SNMP from source. They might reside in `/usr/local`.

The syntax to add MIBs is similar to the one used in the environment variable—you only have to prefix each line with `mibs`, like so:

```
mibs +PowerNet-MIB
```

If you want to specify multiple MIB names in any of these locations, you have to separate them with a colon. Let's say you also need a generic UPS MIB; in that case, the MIB name string would be as follows:

```
+PowerNet-MIB:UPS-MIB
```

In some Net-SNMP versions, lines in configuration files might be silently cut at 1,024 characters, including newline characters. You can specify multiple `mibs` lines to get around this limitation.

And if you feel lazy, you can make Net-SNMP include all of the MIB files located in those directories by setting `mibs` to `ALL`—this works in all three locations. Beware that this might impact performance and lead to some problems if some parts are declared in multiple locations, including warnings from Net-SNMP tools and incorrect definitions being used.

Zabbix server always loads all available MIBs. When a new MIB is added, the Zabbix server must be restarted to pick it up.

Polling SNMP items in Zabbix

Armed with this knowledge about SNMP OIDs, let's get to the real deal—getting SNMP data into Zabbix. To make the following steps easier, you should choose an entry that returns string data. We could use a UPS serial number, such as the one discovered previously to be `PowerNet-MIB::upsAdvIdentSerialNumber.0`. Do the same for some network printer or manageable switch; if you don't have access to such a device, you can choose a simple entry from the Net-SNMP enabled host, such as the already mentioned system description, `SNMPv2-MIB::sysDescr.0`.

Now is the time to return to the Zabbix interface:

1. Go to **Configuration** | **Hosts**, and click on **Create host**. Then, fill in the following values:

   - **Host name**: Enter `SNMP device`.
   - **Groups**: In the **Groups** list-box, if there's a group, select it and click on the button.
   - **New group**: Enter `SNMP devices`.
   - **SNMP interfaces**: Click on **Add**.
   - **DNS name** or **IP address**: Enter the correct DNS name or IP address next to the SNMP interfaces we just added. If you have chosen to use an SNMP-enabled device, input its IP or DNS here. If you don't have access to such a device, use the **Another host** IP address or DNS name. If your SNMP device supports the retrieval of items in bulk then also mark bulk requests as, performance-wise, it's better to retrieve items in bulk than item by item:

   - **Connect to**: Choose **DNS** or **IP**, according to the field you populated.

If no agent items will be created for this host, the agent interface will be ignored. You may keep it or remove it.

2. When you are done, click on the **Add** button at the bottom. It's likely that you won't see the newly created host in the host list. The reason is the **Group** drop-down menu in the upper-right corner, which probably says **Linux servers**. You can change the selection to **All** to see all configured hosts or to **SNMP devices** to only see our new device. Now is the time to create an item, so click on **Items** next to **SNMP devices** and click on the **Create item** button. Fill in the following values:

   - **Name**: Enter something sensible, such as `Serial number`, if you are using an OID from an SNMP agent, or `System description` if you are using the Net-SNMP daemon.
   - **Type**: Change to the appropriate version of your SNMP agent. In the displayed example, `SNMPv1 agent` is chosen because that's the only version our device supports.
   - **Key**: This is not restricted or too important for SNMP items, but required for references from triggers and other locations. You can choose to enter the last part of the textual OID, such as `upsAdvIdentSerialNumber.0` or `sysDescr.0`.
   - **SNMP OID**: This is where our knowledge comes in. Paste the SNMP OID you have found and chosen here. In the example, `PowerNet-MIB::upsAdvIdentSerialNumber.0` is entered. If you are using the Net-SNMP daemon, enter `SNMPv2-MIB::sysDescr.0`.
   - **SNMP community**: Unless you have changed it, keep the default `public` value.
   - **Type of information**: Select **Character**.
   - **Update interval**: This information doesn't really change that often, so use some large value, such as `86400`.

If you left the agent interface in place, notice how it cannot be chosen for this item—only the SNMP interface can. While some item types can be assigned to any interface type, SNMP items must be assigned to SNMP interfaces.

3. When you are done, click on the **Add** button at the bottom.

Now, the outcome will depend on several factors. If you are lucky, you will already see the incoming data in **Monitoring | Latest data**. If you have chosen some vendor-specific OID, like in our example, it is possible that you will have to go back to **Configuration | Hosts**, click on **Items** next to **SNMP device**, and observe the status of this item:

TYPE	APPLICATIONS	STATUS	INFO
			✕

snmp_parse_oid(): cannot parse OID "PowerNet-MIB::upsAdvIdentSerialNumber.0".

Now, what's that? How could it be? We saw in our tests with Net-SNMP command-line tools that there actually is such an OID. Well, one possible situation when this error message appears is when the specified MIB is not available, which could happen if you tried SNMP queries previously from a different host.

Zabbix server works as if `ALL` is set for MIB contents; hence, you don't have to do anything besides copy the MIB to the correct directory (usually `/usr/share/snmp/mibs`) on the Zabbix server and restart the server daemon. If you did not copy the OID, deciding instead to retype it, you might have made a mistake. Verify that the entered OID is correct.

Even though Zabbix has done a great job to improve the readability of the error messages in the frontend, it might be misleading in some cases as it does not show the full log information. Check the server log to be sure.

After fixing any problems, wait until the Zabbix server refreshes the item configuration and rechecks the item. With the item configured, let's see what data we can get in Zabbix from it. Navigate to **Monitoring | Latest data**, expand the filter, clear the **Host groups** field, and start typing SNMP in the **Host** field—**SNMP device** should appear, so choose it and click on **Filter**. Expand the other category if needed, and look for the serial number. You should see something like this:

Serial number	2016-03-16 22:27:40	XA123PO

The serial number has been successfully retrieved and is visible in the item listing. This allows us to automatically retrieve data that, while not directly tied to actual availability or performance monitoring, is still quite useful. For example, if a remote device dies and has to be replaced, you can easily find the serial number to supply in a servicing request, even if you neglected to write it down beforehand.

Translating SNMP OIDs

If you can't or don't want to copy vendor-specific MIB files to the Zabbix server, you can always use numeric OIDs, like we did before. While not being as descriptive, they are guaranteed to work even if the copied MIBs are not available for some reason or are removed during a system upgrade.

But *how do we derive the corresponding numeric OID from a textual one?* While we could use snmpget to retrieve the particular value and output it in numeric form, that requires the availability of the device and network round trip. Fortunately, there's an easier way—the snmptranslate command. To find out the numeric form of the OID, we can use PowerNet-MIB::upsAdvIdentSerialNumber.0:

```
$ snmptranslate -On PowerNet-MIB::upsAdvIdentSerialNumber.0
.1.3.6.1.4.1.318.1.1.1.1.2.3.0
```

 You must have MIBs placed correctly and pass their names to Net-SNMP tools for the translation to work.

The default output format for Net-SNMP tools is the short textual one, which only outputs the MIB name and object name. If you would like to find out the corresponding textual name, use the following:

```
$ snmptranslate .1.3.6.1.2.1.1.1.0
SNMPv2-MIB::sysDescr.0
```

You can also use the -Of flag to output an OID in full notation:

```
$ snmptranslate -Of PowerNet-MIB::upsAdvIdentSerialNumber.0
.iso.org.dod.internet.private.enterprises.apc.products.hardware.ups.up
sIdent.upsAdvIdent.upsAdvIdentSerialNumber.0
```

Dynamic indexes

Previously, we monitored incoming traffic on the eth0 device using an active Zabbix agent daemon item. If we have snmpd set up and running, we can also try retrieving outgoing traffic but, this time, let's try to use SNMP for that.

Monitoring network traffic using the Zabbix agent daemon is usually easier, but SNMP monitoring is the only way to obtain this information for many network devices, such as switches and routers. If you have such a device available, you can try monitoring it instead, though the network interface name will most likely differ.

One way to find the item we are interested in would be to redirect the output of snmpwalk to a file and then examine that file. Looking at the output, there are lines such as these:

```
IF-MIB::ifDescr.1 = STRING: lo
IF-MIB::ifDescr.2 = STRING: eth0
```

Great, so the desired interface, eth0 in this case, has an index of 2. Nearby, we can find actual information we are interested in-traffic values:

```
IF-MIB::ifOutOctets.1 = Counter32: 1825596052
IF-MIB::ifOutOctets.2 = Counter32: 1533857263
```

So, theoretically, we could add an item with the IF-MIB::ifOutOctets.2 OID and name it appropriately. Unfortunately, there are devices that change interface index now and then. Also, the index for a particular interface is likely to differ between devices, hence potentially creating a configuration nightmare. This is where dynamic index support in Zabbix comes into use.

Let's look at what a dynamic index item OID would look like in this case:

Database OID	Literal string "index"	Index-based OID	Index string
IF-MIB::ifOutOctets[	"index",	"ifDescr",	"eth0"]

Let's have a quick overview what this all means to us:

- **Database OID**: This is the base part of the OID that holds the data we are interested in, that is, without the actual index. In this case, it's the OID leading to ifOutOctets, in any notation.
- **Literal string "index"**: This is the same for all dynamic index items.

- **Index-based OID**: This is the base part of the OID that holds the index we are interested in. In this case, it's the OID leading to `ifDescr`, in any notation.
- **Index string**: This is the string that the index part of the tree is searched for. This is an exact, case-sensitive match of all OIDs from the previous base OID. Here, the name of the interface we are interested in, `eth0`, will be searched for. No substring or other matching is allowed here.

The index that this search will return will be added to the database OID, and the following queries will gather values from the resulting OID.

You can easily view the index to determine the correct string to search for with Net-SNMP tools:

```
$ snmpwalk -v 2c -c public localhost
.iso.org.dod.internet.mgmt.mib-2.interfaces.ifTable.ifEntry.ifDescr
IF-MIB::ifDescr.1 = STRING: lo
IF-MIB::ifDescr.2 = STRING: eth0
IF-MIB::ifDescr.3 = STRING: sit0
```

As can be seen, this machine has three interfaces—**loopback**, **Ethernet**, and a **tunnel**. The picture will be very different for some other devices. For example, an HP ProCurve Switch would return (with the output shortened) the following:

```
$ snmpwalk -v 2c -c public 10.196.2.233
.iso.org.dod.internet.mgmt.mib-2.interfaces.ifTable.ifEntry.ifDescr
IF-MIB::ifDescr.1 = STRING: 1
IF-MIB::ifDescr.2 = STRING: 2
...
IF-MIB::ifDescr.49 = STRING: 49
IF-MIB::ifDescr.50 = STRING: 50
IF-MIB::ifDescr.63 = STRING: DEFAULT_VLAN
IF-MIB::ifDescr.4158 = STRING: HP ProCurve Switch software loopback
interface
```

Now that we know the OID to use for dynamic index items, let's create one such item in Zabbix:

1. Navigate to **Configuration | Hosts**, click on **Items** next to the correct host you want to create the item for, and click on **Create item**. Fill in the following values:

    - **Name**: Outgoing traffic on interface $1
    - **Type: SNMPv2 agent**
    - **Key**: ifOutOctets[eth0]

- **SNMP OID**: `IF-MIB::ifOutOctets["index","ifDescr","eth0"]`
- **Units**: `Bps`
- **Store value**: **Delta (speed per second)**

Same as before, replace `eth0` with an interface name that exists on the target system.

2. When you are done, click on the **Add** button at the bottom.

Make sure that the compound OID is entered correctly, paying close attention to quotes and spelling. We discussed the reason to use the **Numeric (unsigned)** type of information in `Chapter 3`, *Monitoring with Zabbix Agents and Basic Protocols*.

The newly added item should start gathering data, so let's look at **Monitoring | Latest data**. If you don't see this item or the data for it, navigate back to **Configuration | Hosts** and click on **Items** next to the corresponding host—there should be an error message displayed that should help with fixing the issue. If you have correctly added the item, you'll see the traffic data, as follows:

2018-11-25 17:02:30	163 Bps	+31 Bps	Graph

Remember that if the index matches the exact string, a substring match will not work here.

Dynamic index items are quite common. Many network devices have fixed port names but varying indexes. Host-based SNMP agents place things such as disk usage and memory statistics in dynamic indexes; thus, if you have such devices to monitor, Zabbix support for them will be handy.

Using dynamic index items can slightly increase overall load, as two SNMP values are required to obtain the final data. Zabbix caches retrieved index information, so the load increase should not be noticeable.

A dynamic SNMP index enables us to easily monitor a specific interface or other entity by name, but it would not be a very efficient method for monitoring a larger number of interfaces. We will discuss an automated solution, low-level discovery, in `Chapter 10`, *Advanced Item Monitoring*.

SNMP bulk requests

You might have spotted the checkbox next to the **SNMP interfaces** section, **Use bulk requests**:

When requesting values from SNMP hosts, Zabbix may request one value at a time or multiple values in one go. Getting multiple values in one go is more efficient, so this is what Zabbix will try to do by default—it will ask for more and more values in one connection against a device until all SNMP items can be queried in one go or the device fails to respond. This approach enables us to find the number of values that a device is configured to return, or is technically capable of returning, in one go. No more than 128 values will be requested in one attempt, however.

Only items with identical parameters on the same interface will be queried at the same time—for example, if the community or the port is different, Zabbix will not try to get such values in one attempt.

There are quite a lot of devices that do not work properly when multiple values are requested; hence, it is possible to disable this functionality per interface.

Receiving SNMP traps

While querying SNMP-capable devices is a nice method that requires little or no configuration of each device in itself, in some situations, information flow in the reverse direction is desired. For SNMP, these are called **traps**. Usually, traps are sent upon some condition change, and the agent connects to the server or management station on port 162 (as opposed to port 161 on the agent side, which is used for queries). You can think of SNMP traps as being similar to Zabbix active items; as with those, all connections are made from monitored machines to the monitoring server.

The direction of the connections isn't the only difference, SNMP traps have some other pros and cons when compared to queries. For example, SNMP traps are usually more capable of detecting short-lived problems that might have been missed by queries. Let's say you are monitoring incoming voltages on a UPS. You have decided on a reasonable item interval that would give you useful data and wouldn't overload the network and Zabbix server—let's say some 120 seconds, or two minutes. If the input voltage suddenly peaks or drops for a minute, your checks might easily miss this event, hence making it impossible to correlate it with problems with other devices that are not connected to the UPS. Another benefit that traps provide is reduced network and Zabbix server load as the information is only sent when an event occurs and there is no constant querying by the server. One drawback is partial decentralization of the configuration. SNMP trap-sending conditions and parameters have to be set for each device or device group individually. Another drawback is a lack of the guaranteed sending of the traps. Almost all SNMP implementations will use UDP, and trap information might get lost without any trace.

As such, SNMP traps aren't used to replace SNMP queries. Instead, they supplement them by leaving statistical information-gathering to the queries and providing notifications of various events happening in the devices, usually notifying us of emergencies.

In Zabbix, SNMP traps are received by `snmptrapd`, a daemon again from the Net-SNMP suite. These traps then have to be passed to the Zabbix daemon with some method. There are several ways of doing it, and we will explore two different approaches:

- Using the built-in ability of Zabbix to receive traps from the Net-SNMP trap daemon
- Using a custom script to push SNMP values to Zabbix

The first method, especially when using the embedded Perl code approach, is the most simple one and will offer the best performance. A custom script will provide the most flexibility but will also require more effort.

Using embedded Perl code

Using embedded Perl code in `snmptrapd` is the easiest method to set up. Unless you need extra functionality, it is suggested to stick with this method.

We'll start by configuring `snmptrapd` to pass information to Zabbix. There is an example script in the Zabbix sources called `misc/snmptrap/zabbix_trap_receiver.pl`. Place this file in some reasonable location—perhaps a `bin` subdirectory in the Zabbix `home` directory. If the directory does not exist, create it, as follows:

```
# mkdir -p /home/zabbix/bin; chown zabbix /home/zabbix
```

 If using distribution packages, you might have to use a different username. Check your distribution packages for details.

Place the `zabbix_trap_receiver.pl` file in this directory:

```
# cp misc/snmptrap/zabbix_trap_receiver.pl /home/zabbix/bin
```

 On some distributions, Net-SNMP Perl support could be split out into a separate package, such as `net-snmp-perl`.

Now, on to instructing `snmptrapd` to use that script. We only need to tell the trap daemon to process all of the received traps with this script. To do this, you'll have to find the location where your distribution places the Net-SNMP configuration files—usually, `/etc/snmp/`. In this directory, look for a file named `snmptrapd.conf`. If it's there, edit it (create a backup copy before you do anything); if it's missing, create it. Edit it as `root` and make it look as follows:

```
authCommunity execute public
perl do "/home/zabbix/bin/zabbix_trap_receiver.pl";
```

This will accept all traps that have the community set to `public` and pass them to the Perl receiver script.

 If you expect to receive traps with various community strings that are not known in advance, you could disable the authorization or checking of the community string with the `disableAuthorization yes` option in `snmptrapd.conf`.

Start or restart the trap daemon. It might be worth taking a quick look at the `zabbix_trap_receiver.pl` file. Notice the line that specifies the path:

```
$SNMPTrapperFile = '/tmp/zabbix_traps.tmp';
```

Behind the scenes, traps are passed to the Zabbix server through a temporary file. We'll discuss this in a bit more detail later in this chapter.

Filtering values by received data

Now, let's move on to the items on the Zabbix side. To test the most simple thing first, we will try to send values from the Zabbix server. Navigate to **Configuration** | **Hosts**, click on **A test host** in the **Name** column, and click on **Add** in the **SNMP interfaces** section. Click on the **Update** button at the bottom, and then click on **Items** next to **A test host**. Click on **Create item** and enter these values:

- **Name**: SNMP trap tests
- **Type**: **SNMP trap**
- **Key**: snmptrap[test]
- **Type of information**: **Character**

When you're done, it should look like this:

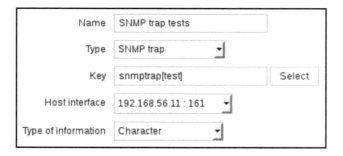

This item will collect all traps that this host gets, if the traps contain the test string. We have the trap daemon configured to place traps in a file, and we have the item to place these traps in. What's left is telling the Zabbix server where to get the traps. Open zabbix_server.conf and modify the StartSNMPTrapper parameter:

```
StartSNMPTrapper=1
```

There is a special process in Zabbix that reads traps from a temporary file. This process is not started by default, so we changed that part of the configuration. Take a look at the parameter just preceding this one:

```
SNMPTrapperFile=/tmp/zabbix_traps.tmp
```

Notice how it matches the file in the Perl script. A change in the script should be matched by a change in this configuration file and vice versa. At this time, we will not change the location of this temporary file.

After these changes have been made, restart the Zabbix server daemon. Now, we are ready to test this item. Let's send a trap by executing the following from the Zabbix server:

```
$ snmptrap -Ci -v 2c -c public localhost "" "NET-SNMP-
MIB::netSnmpExperimental" NET-SNMP-MIB::netSnmpExperimental s "test"
```

This slightly non-optimal Net-SNMP syntax will attempt to send an SNMP trap to localhost using the public community and some nonsense OID. It will also wait for a response to verify that snmptrapd has received the trap successfully—this is achieved by the -Ci flag. It uses the default port, 162, so make sure the port is open in your firewall configuration on the Zabbix server to receive traps.

 Waiting for confirmation also makes snmptrap retransmit the trap. If the receiving host is slow to respond, the trap might be received multiple times before the sender receives confirmation.

If the command is successful, it will finish without any output. If it fails with the snmpinform: Timeout error message, then several things could have gone wrong. As well as double-checking that UDP port 162 is open for incoming data, verify that the community in the /etc/snmp/snmptrapd.conf file matches the one used in the snmptrap command and that the snmptrapd daemon is actually running.

If everything goes well, we should be able to see this item with a value on the latest data page:

| SNMP trap tests | 2016-03-18 23:17:48 | 23:17:46 2016/03/18 PDU INF... |

Now, let's send a different trap. Still on the Zabbix server, run this:

```
$ snmptrap -Ci -v 2c -c public localhost "" "NET-SNMP-
MIB::netSnmpExperimental" NET-SNMP-MIB::netSnmpExperimental s "some
other trap"
```

This trap will not appear in the item we created. *What happened to it?* As the value that we sent did not contain the `test` string, this value did not match the one in the item. By default, such traps are logged in the server log file. If we check the log file, it should have something similar to the following:

```
9872:20160318:232004.319 unmatched trap received from "127.0.0.1":
23:20:02 2016/03/18 PDU INFO:
  requestid                     253195749
  messageid                     0
  transactionid                 5
  version                       1
  notificationtype              INFORM
  community                     public
  receivedfrom                  UDP: [127.0.0.1]:54031→[127.0.0.1]:162
  errorindex                    0
  errorstatus                   0
VARBINDS:
  DISMAN-EVENT-MIB::sysUpTimeInstance type=67 value=Timeticks:
(2725311) 7:34:13.11
  SNMPv2-MIB::snmpTrapOID.0      type=6  value=OID: NET-SNMP-
MIB::netSnmpExperimental
  NET-SNMP-MIB::netSnmpExperimental type=4  value=STRING: "some other
trap"
```

This is not so easy to trigger on, or even see in, the frontend at all. We will improve the situation and tell Zabbix to handle such unmatched traps for this host by placing them in a special item:

1. Navigate to **Configuration** | **Hosts**, click on **Items** next to **A test host**, click on **Create item**, and then fill in these values:

   - **Name**: SNMP trap fallback
   - **Type**: **SNMP trap**
   - **Key**: snmptrap.fallback
   - **Type of information**: **Character**

2. When you're done, click on the **Add** button at the bottom

The key we used here, `snmptrap.fallback`, is a special one. Any trap that does not match any of the `snmptrap[]` items will be placed here. Retry sending our previously unmatched trap:

```
$ snmptrap -Ci -v 2c -c public localhost "" "NET-SNMP-
MIB::netSnmpExperimental" NET-SNMP-MIB::netSnmpExperimental s "some
other trap"
```

Let's check the latest data page again:

| SNMP trap fallback | 2016-03-18 23:33:04 | 23:33:03 2016/03/18 PDU INF... |
| SNMP trap tests | 2016-03-18 23:17:48 | 23:17:46 2016/03/18 PDU INF... |

The fallback item got the value this time. To see what the value looks like, let's click on the **History** link next to one of these items:

TIMESTAMP	VALUE
2016-03-18 23:33:04	23:33:03 2016/03/18 PDU INFO: community public receivedfrom UDP: [127.0.0.1]:54642->[127.0.0.1]:162 errorindex 0 errorstatus 0 requestid 108168159

It contains quite a lot of information, but it also looks a bit strange, almost as if the value was cut. It turns out that, with this method, the trap information that is recorded in the database is quite verbose and the character information type does not offer enough space for it—this type is limited to 255 characters. We cannot even see the string we sent in the trap that matched or failed to match the filter. Let's try to fix this with the mass update functionality again:

1. Go to **Configuration** | **Hosts**
2. Click on **Items** next to **A test host**
3. Mark the checkboxes next to both SNMP trap items and click on the **Mass update** button
4. In the resulting form, mark the checkbox next to **Type of information** and choose **Text**
5. Click on the **Update** button

This should have fixed it, but we don't know that for sure yet. Let's verify—send both of these traps again:

```
$ snmptrap -Ci -v 2c -c public localhost "" "NET-SNMP-
MIB::netSnmpExperimental" NET-SNMP-MIB::netSnmpExperimental s "test"
$ snmptrap -Ci -v 2c -c public localhost "" "NET-SNMP-
MIB::netSnmpExperimental" NET-SNMP-MIB::netSnmpExperimental s "some
other trap"
```

If we look at the history of one of these items now, we will see that this change has indeed helped, and much more information is displayed—including the custom string we used for distributing these values across items:

```
TIMESTAMP              VALUE

                       00:14:55 2016/03/19 PDU INFO:
                           messageid                0
                           transactionid            11
                           requestid                973564866
                           notificationtype         INFORM
                           version                  1
2016-03-19 00:14:56        receivedfrom             UDP: [127.0.0.1]:40852->[127.0.0.1]:162
                           community                public
                           errorstatus              0
                           errorindex               0
                       VARBINDS:
                           DISMAN-EVENT-MIB::sysUpTimeInstance type=67 value=Timeticks: (3054527) 8:29:05.27
                           SNMPv2-MIB::snmpTrapOID.0      type=6  value=OID: NET-SNMP-MIB::netSnmpExperimental
                           NET-SNMP-MIB::netSnmpExperimental type=4  value=STRING: "some other trap"
```

> If the value is still cut, you might have to wait a bit more for the configuration cache to be updated and resend the trap.

The first item we created, with the `snmptrap[test]` key, can actually have a regular expression as the item parameter. This allows us to perform more advanced filtering, such as getting a link up and down traps in a single item. If a trap matches expressions from multiple items, it would get copied to all of those items.

Filtering values by originating host

We figured out how to get values in specific items, but *how did Zabbix know that it should place these values in* **A test host**? This happens because the address of the host that the trap came from matches the address in the SNMP interface for these items. To test this, let's copy the trap items to **Another host**:

1. Navigate to **Configuration** | **Hosts** and click on **Items** next to **A test host**
2. Mark the checkboxes next to both SNMP trap items and click on the **Copy** button
3. Choose **Hosts** from the **Target type** drop-down menu and mark the checkbox next to **Another host**

4. Click on **Copy**

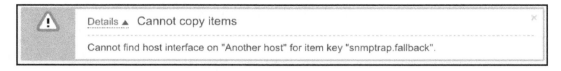

If you added an SNMP interface to **Another host** earlier, this operation might succeed.

It looks like that failed, and Zabbix complains that it can not find an interface. **Another host** did not have an SNMP interface; hence, these items can not be attached to any interface at all:

1. Go to **Configuration** | **Hosts** and click on **Another host**
2. Add a new SNMP interface with the address that this host has and click on **Update**
3. Try to copy the SNMP trap items from A test host to **Another host** the same way as done previously, and it should succeed now

With the items in place, let's test them. Send two test traps from **Another host**, the same way we sent them from the Zabbix server before:

```
$ snmptrap -Ci -v 2c -c public <Zabbix server> "" "NET-SNMP-
MIB::netSnmpExperimental" NET-SNMP-MIB::netSnmpExperimental s "test"
$ snmptrap -Ci -v 2c -c public <Zabbix server> "" "NET-SNMP-
MIB::netSnmpExperimental" NET-SNMP-MIB::netSnmpExperimental s "some
other trap"
```

Replace <Zabbix server> with the IP or DNS name of the Zabbix server. These commands should complete without any error messages.

The traps should be placed properly in the items on **Another host**.

Debugging

If traps do not arrive at all or do not fall into the correct items, there are a few things to check. If the traps do not appear when sent from a remote host, but work properly when sent from the Zabbix server, check the local firewall on the Zabbix server and make sure incoming UDP packets on port 162 are allowed.

Also make sure that the IP address the Zabbix server sees in the incoming traps matches the address in the SNMP interface for that host.

Sometimes, you might see that traps arrive at the SNMP trap daemon but do not seem to be passed on. It might be useful to debug snmptrapd in this case—luckily, it allows a quite detailed debug output. Exact values to use for various file locations will differ, but the following might work to manually start the daemon while enabling all debug output:

```
# /usr/sbin/snmptrapd -A -Lf /var/log/net-snmpd.log -p
/var/run/snmptrapd.pid -DALL
```

Here, -Lf specifies the file to log to and -DALL tells it to enable full debug.

If the received trap is in a numeric format and not very readable, you might have to add specific MIBs to the /etc/snmp/snmp.conf file so that they are found by snmptrapd.

What happens if Zabbix decides that a trap does not belong to any item on any host? This could happen because there are no trap items at all, the fallback item is missing, or the address in the incoming trap is not matched with any of the SNMP interfaces. By default, the Zabbix server logs such traps in the log file. An example record from the log file is as follows:

```
2271:20150120:124156.818 unmatched trap received from
[192.168.168.192]: 12:41:55 2015/01/20 PDU INFO:
  errorindex                 0
  transactionid              1
  requestid                  1752369294
  messageid                  0
  receivedfrom               UDP:
[192.168.168.192]:45375->[192.168.1.13]:162
  errorstatus                0
  version                    1
  notificationtype           INFORM
  community                  public
VARBINDS:
  DISMAN-EVENT-MIB::sysUpTimeInstance type=67 value=Timeticks:
(77578087) 8 days, 23:29:40.87
  SNMPv2-MIB::snmpTrapOID.0      type=6  value=OID: NET-SNMP-
MIB::netSnmpExperimental
  NET-SNMP-MIB::netSnmpExperimental type=4  value=STRING: "non-
matching trap"
```

The logging of non-matching traps can be controlled. If we go to **Administration |
General** and choose **Other** from the drop-down menu in the upper-right corner; the
last checkbox there is **Log unmatched SNMP traps**. Unmarking it will stop logging
such traps:

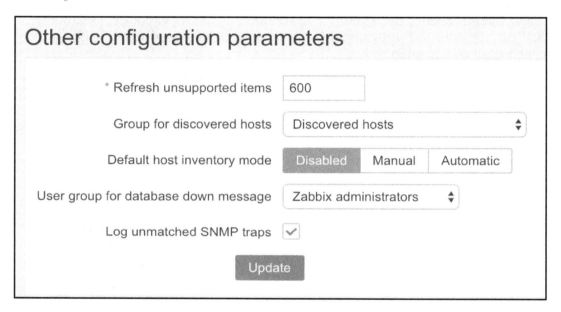

And *what if you would like to try out Zabbix's SNMP trap handling without setting up an
SNMP trap daemon, perhaps on some development server?* That should be very easy as
you can simply append trap information to the temporary file. It's a plain-text file,
and Zabbix does not know who added content, the trap daemon, user, or somebody
else. Just make sure to add all of the data for a single trap in one go.

Handling the temporary file

The temporary file to pass traps from the trap daemon to Zabbix is placed in /tmp by
default. This is not the best practice for a production setup, so I suggest you change it
once you are satisfied with the initial testing.

Note that the temporary file can grow indefinitely—Zabbix only reads data from it,
and never rotates or removes the file. Rotation should be set up separately, probably
with the logrotate daemon.

SNMP Trap Translator (SNMPTT)

Zabbix may also receive traps that are parsed by SNMPTT: http://www.snmptt.org/. This method uses the same temporary file and internal process approach as the embedded Perl trap receiver solution. SNMPTT can be useful for making received data human-readable.

Remember that it changes passed data so, depending on how things are set up, adding SNMPTT might require changes to item mapping, triggers, or other configuration.

Using a custom script

The method covered earlier, the embedded Perl receiver, is easy to set up and performs well. If it is not possible to use it for some reason or some advanced filtering is required, a custom script could push trap values to items. This subsection will use an example script shipped with Zabbix to demonstrate such a solution.

We'll place the example SNMP trap-parsing script in the Zabbix user's home directory:

```
# cp misc/snmptrap/snmptrap.sh /home/zabbix/bin
```

Let's take a look at that script now. Open the file we just copied to /home/zabbix/bin/snmptrap.sh. As you can see, this is a very simplistic script, which gets passed trap information and then sends it to the Zabbix server, using both host snmptrap and key snmptrap instances. If you are reading carefully enough, you've probably already noticed one problem—we didn't install any software as ~zabbix/bin/zabbix_sender, so that's probably wrong.

First, let's find out where zabbix_sender is actually located:

```
$ whereis zabbix_sender
zabbix_sender: /usr/local/bin/zabbix_sender
```

On this system, it's /usr/local/bin/zabbix_sender. It might be a good idea to look at its syntax by running this:

```
$ zabbix_sender --help
```

This allows you to send a value to the Zabbix server, specifying the server with the `-z` flag, port with `-p`, and so on. Now let's return to the script. With our new knowledge, let's look at the last line—the one that invokes `zabbix_sender`. The script seems to pass values retrieved from the SNMP trap as parameters to `zabbix_sender`; hence, we can't make any decisions and information transformation between `snmptrapd` and Zabbix. Now, let's fix the problem we noticed:

- Change `ZABBIX_SENDER` to read `/usr/local/bin/zabbix_sender` (or another path if that's different for you)
- Additionally, change the last line to read `$ZABBIX_SENDER -z $ZABBIX_SERVER -p $ZABBIX_PORT -s "$HOST" -k "$KEY" -o "$str"`—this way, we are also quoting host and key names, just in case they might include spaces or other characters that might break command execution

Save the file. Let's prepare the Zabbix side now for trap receiving. On the frontend, do the following:

1. Navigate to **Configuration** | **Hosts** and click on **Create host**. Fill in the following values:

     - **Name**: `snmptraps`
     - **Groups**: Click on **SNMP devices** in the **Other groups** box, then click on the button; if there are any other groups in the **Groups** listbox, remove them

2. Click on the **Add** button at the bottom.

Notice that the hostname used here, `snmptraps`, must be the same as the one we configured in the `snmptrap.sh` script; otherwise, the traps won't be received in Zabbix.

Now, click on **Items** next to the **snmptraps** host, and then click on **Create item**. Enter these values:

- **Name**: `Received SNMP traps`
- **Type: Zabbix trapper**
- **Key**: `snmptraps`
- **Type of information: Character**

We used the **Character** type of information here as our script is expected to pass less information to the item. If large amounts of information would have had to be passed, we would have set this parameter to **Text** again.

When you are done, click on the **Add** button at the bottom. Again, notice how we used the exact same key spelling as in the `snmptrap.sh` script.

We're done with configuring Zabbix for SNMP trap receiving, but *how will the traps get to the script we edited and, in turn, to Zabbix?* The same as before, this is where `snmptrapd` steps in.

Let's create a simplistic configuration that will pass all the received traps to our script. To do this, we will edit `snmptrapd.conf`. If you created it earlier, edit it (you may comment out the lines we added previously); if it's missing, create the file. Edit it as `root` and make it look as follows:

```
authCommunity execute public
#perl do "/home/zabbix/bin/zabbix_trap_receiver.pl";
traphandle default /bin/bash /home/zabbix/bin/snmptrap.sh
```

We commented out the Perl receiver line and added a line to call our new script. The default keyword will make sure that all received traps go to this script (that is, unless we have other `traphandle` statements with OIDs specified, in which case only those received traps will get to this script that don't match any other `traphandle` statement). Save this file, and then start or restart the `snmptrapd` daemon as appropriate for your distribution.

Now, we should be able to receive SNMP traps through all the chain links. Let's test that by sending a trap same the way as before from the Zabbix server:

```
$ snmptrap -Ci -v 2c -c public localhost "" "NET-SNMP-
MIB::netSnmpExperimental" NET-SNMP-MIB::netSnmpExperimental s "test"
```

Once the command completes successfully, check the frontend for the results. Go to **Monitoring** | **Latest data** and select **SNMP devices** in the filter:

Received SNMP traps	2016-03-19 00:41:52	localhost "test" NET-SNMP-MI...

Great, data from our test trap has been received here. It's trimmed in the table view, though, so click on **History** to view all of it:

TIMESTAMP	VALUE	
2016-03-19 00:41:52	localhost "test"	NET-SNMP-MIB::netSnmpExperimental

Excellent, we can see our trap in its entirety. Notice how with this custom script we decided to parse out only the specific string, instead of pushing all the details about the trap to Zabbix. Let's check what it looks like with several traps received one after another. From the console again, execute the following:

```
$ snmptrap -Ci -v 2c -c public localhost "" "NET-SNMP-
MIB::netSnmpExperimental" NET-SNMP-MIB::netSnmpExperimental s "another
test"
```

Refresh the **History** screen we had open in the browser and check whether the result is satisfactory:

TIMESTAMP	VALUE	
2016-03-19 00:44:31	localhost "another	NET-SNMP-MIB::netSnmpExperimental
2016-03-19 00:41:52	localhost "test"	NET-SNMP-MIB::netSnmpExperimental

Our latest trap is nicely listed, with entries being ordered in descending order.

If the trap did not arrive, refer to the *Debugging* section earlier in this chapter.

But wait, everything after the first space is missing from the informative text. That's not desirable, so let's try to fix this problem. As root, open the /home/zabbix/bin/snmptrap.sh file and look for the line that strips out addresses from received information:

```
oid=`echo $oid|cut -f2 -d' '`
address=`echo $address|cut -f2 -d' '`
community=`echo $community|cut -f2 -d' '`
enterprise=`echo $enterprise|cut -f2 -d' '`
```

As seen here, when using a space as the separator, only the second field is grabbed. We want the full details captured instead as, otherwise, a very important failure would simply show up as A for us. Let's add a dash to the field parameter so that all trailing fields are captured as well:

```
address=`echo $address|cut -f2- -d' '`
```

This should solve the problem, so let's test it again:

```
$ snmptrap -Ci -v 2c -c public localhost "" "NET-SNMP-
MIB::netSnmpExperimental" NET-SNMP-MIB::netSnmpExperimental s "A Very
Important Failure"
```

Return to the frontend and refresh the history listing:

TIMESTAMP	VALUE
2016-03-19 00:47:09	localhost "A Very Important Failure" NET-SNMP-MIB::netSnmpExperimental
2016-03-19 00:44:31	localhost "another NET-SNMP-MIB::netSnmpExperimental
2016-03-19 00:41:52	localhost "test" NET-SNMP-MIB::netSnmpExperimental

Finally! The data from our important traps will no longer be lost.

Filtering the traps

While that is great for receiving all traps in a single location, it also makes traps harder to correlate to particular hosts, and especially hard to observe if you have lots and lots of trap-sending hosts. In such a case, it becomes very desirable to split incoming traps in some sort of logical structure, similar to the way we did with the Perl receiver solution earlier. At the very least, a split based on existing hosts can be performed. In this case, all received traps would be placed in a single item for that host. If there are particular traps or trap groups that are received very often or are very important, these can be further split into individual items.

For example, if a network switch is sending various traps, including link up and down ones, we'll probably want to place these in a single item so they do not obscure other traps that much. If the switch has many workstations connected that are constantly switched on and off, we might even want to drop these traps before they reach Zabbix. On the other hand, if this switch has very important connections that should never go down, we might even go as far as creating an individual item for notifications coming from each port.

All the methods work by either replacing, improving, or hooking into the handler script, `snmptraps.sh`.

Custom mapping

One way to approach trap distribution is to create custom mappings that choose an appropriate destination for the trap depending on any parameters, including source host, OID, and trap details. Such mapping, while being relatively cumbersome to set up, is also the most flexible, as you can perform all kinds of specific case handling. It also requires double configuration—most changes have to be made both to the Zabbix configuration and to these mappings.

Custom mapping can use file-based lookup, a separate database, or any other kind of information storage.

Database lookups

Another method is to tap into existing knowledge, through the Zabbix database. As the database already holds information on host/IP address relationships, we can simply look up the corresponding hostname. Let's modify `snmptraps.sh` so that all traps coming from hosts defined in Zabbix end up in an `snmptraps` item for that specific host, but other traps are collected in the generic `snmptraps` host instead.

Start by modifying `/home/zabbix/bin/snmptraps.sh` and adding two lines:

```
oid=`echo $oid|cut -f11 -d'.'`
community=`echo $community|cut -f2 -d'"'`
zabbixhost=$(HOME=/root mysql -N -e "select host from zabbix.hosts
left join zabbix.interface on
zabbix.hosts.hostid=zabbix.interface.hostid where ip='$hostname' order
by 'hostid' limit 1;" 2>/dev/null)
[[ $zabbixhost ]] && HOST=$zabbixhost
str="$hostname $address $community $enterprise $oid"
$ZABBIX_SENDER $ZABBIX_SERVER $ZABBIX_PORT -s "$HOST" -k "$KEY" -o
"$str"
```

So *what do these do?*:

- The first line queries the MySQL database and checks whether a host is defined with the same IP as the trap source. If it is, the Zabbix host variable gets the hostname, as defined in Zabbix, assigned. Returned results are sorted by host ID and only the first match is taken. Hence, if there are multiple hosts with the same IP address (which is perfectly fine in Zabbix), only the oldest entry is selected. Any error output is discarded (redirected to /dev/null), so in case of a database misconfiguration, traps are not lost but end up in the generic trap-handling host.
- The second line simply sets the host used for sending data to Zabbix to the entry returned from the database, if it exists.
- But *what's that* HOME *variable in the first line?* The mysql command used there does not specify user, password, or any other connection information, so for the command to succeed, it would have to get this information from somewhere. For MySQL, this information can be placed in the .my.cnf file located in the user's HOME directory. Given that snmptrapd runs as root, but services often do not get all the environment variables normal logins do, we are directing further commands to look in /root for that file.

This means we're not done yet; we have to create the /root/.my.cnf file and fill it with the required information. As root, create /root/.my.cnf and place the following content in it:

```
[client]
user=zabbix
password=mycreativepassword
```

For the password, use the same one you used for the Zabbix server and frontend (if you don't remember this password, you can look it up in zabbix_server.conf).

Now, we should prepare for trap receiving on the Zabbix side.

Open **Configuration | Hosts**, click on **Items** next to **Another host**, and then click on the **Create item** button. Enter these values:

- **Name**: snmptraps
- **Type: Zabbix trapper**
- **Key**: snmptraps
- **Type of information: Character**

When you are done, click on the **Add** button at the bottom.

Before we send a test trap, let's do one more thing: make sure that snmptrapd does not perform reverse lookups on received traps. While that might slightly decrease the prettiness of the data, we want to keep this script simple for now and this will also improve performance a bit. To do this, add the -n flag for snmptrapd to the startup scripts and restart it. This procedure is distribution specific.

Finally, we are ready to test our tricky setup. From **Another host**, execute this:

```
$ snmptrap -Ci -v 2c -c public <Zabbix server> "" "NET-SNMP-
MIB::netSnmpExperimental" NET-SNMP-MIB::netSnmpExperimental s "test"
```

Replace <Zabbix server> with the IP or DNS name of the Zabbix server. This command should complete without any error messages.

> This won't work with A test host—the oldest host with the IP address of 127.0.0.1 would be the Zabbix server example host.

Back in the frontend, navigate to **Monitoring** | **Latest data**:

Another host	- **other** - (1 Item)		
	snmptraps	2016-03-19 11:35:34	192.168.56.11 "test" NET-SNM...

Great, snmptrap instances are now successfully sorted by host, if present.

If this trap was not sorted properly and still went into the snmptraps host, it could be caused by different output in some Net-SNMP versions. Instead of passing the IP address or hostname of the incoming connection as the first value, they pass a string like this:

```
UDP: [192.168.56.11]:56417->[192.168.56.10]:162
```

In that case, try adding another line before the zabbixhost assignment:

```
oid=`echo $oid|cut -f11 -d'.'`
community=`echo $community|cut -f2 -d'"'`
hostname=$(echo "$hostname" | awk -F'[][]' '{print $2}')
```

It will extract the first string enclosed in square brackets from the `hostname` variable. After making this change to the script, send the trap again.

That took us some time to set up, but now it's very simple. If we want traps from some host to be handled by a specific host, we create that host and an `snmptraps` item for it. All other traps go to the generic `snmptraps` host and `snmptraps` item.

But *what about item lookup?* The database holds information on item keys as well, so perhaps we could try using that.

We need to retrieve the item key from any database field based on the information received in the trap. As traps include SNMP OIDs, they are the best candidates to map traps against items. Now, the OID can be in numeric or textual form. In the Zabbix configuration, we have two fields that could be used:

- **Name**: While pretty much a free-form field, it is a *friendly name*, so we'd better keep it human-readable.
- **Key**: This field has more strict rules on the characters it accepts, but OIDs should be fine. While not used by humans much, this field is still referred to in the trigger expressions.

That means we will use the **Key** field. To keep it both short enough and somewhat human-readable, we'll set it to the last part of the received textual-form OID. As the trap will be received by `snmptraps.sh`, it will try to match the received OID to the item key and based on that decide where to send the data.

Remember that specific MIBs might have to be added to `/etc/snmp/snmp.conf` so that they are found by `snmptrapd`.

Again, as `root,` edit the `/home/zabbix/bin/snmptraps.sh` script. Replace the two lines we just added, so that it looks like this:

```
community=`echo $community|cut -f2 -d' '`
enterprise=`echo $enterprise|cut -f2 -d' '`
oid=`echo $oid|cut -f11 -d'.'`
community=`echo $community|cut -f2 -d'"'`
hostname=$(echo "$hostname" | awk -F'[][]' '{print $2}')
zabbixhostid=$(HOME=/root mysql -N -e "select hosts.hostid,host from
zabbix.hosts left join zabbix.interface on
zabbix.hosts.hostid=zabbix.interface.hostid where ip='$hostname' order
by 'hostid' limit 1;" 2>/dev/null)
zabbixhost=$(echo $zabbixhostid | cut -d" " -f2-)
[[ "$zabbixhost" ]] && {
    zabbixid=$(echo $zabbixhostid | cut -d" " -f1)
```

```
        trapoid=$(echo $oid | cut -d: -f3)
        if [ "$trapoid" ]; then
            zabbixitem=$(HOME=/root mysql -N -e "select key_ from
zabbix.items where key_='$trapoid' and hostid='$zabbixid';" 2>
/dev/null)
            if [ "$zabbixitem" ]; then
                HOST=$zabbixhost
                KEY=$zabbixitem
            fi
        fi
}
[[ $KEY = snmptraps ]] && {
    if [ "$(HOME=/root mysql -N -e "select key_ from zabbix.items
where
key_='snmptraps' and hostid='$zabbixid';" 2> /dev/null)" ]; then
        HOST=$zabbixhost
    fi
}
str="$hostname $address $community $enterprise $oid"
```

Save the file. In functional terms, as regards our current configuration, it will work exactly the same as the previous version, with one minor improvement: if you look at the previous version carefully, you'll see it only checks for host availability, so if you created a host but forgot to create an item with the snmptraps key for it, the sent trap would be lost. This version will check whether an item with such a key exists for that host. If not, the generic host, snmptraps, will receive the trap.

Note that this is one benefit of the custom-script solution over the embedded Perl trap receiver we configured earlier. It is easier to have triggers for traps landing in this fallback host than checking for them in the Zabbix server log file.

Additionally, it will now check whether the host also has an item with a key, matching the last part of the OID received. A simple decision flow representation is shown in the following diagram:

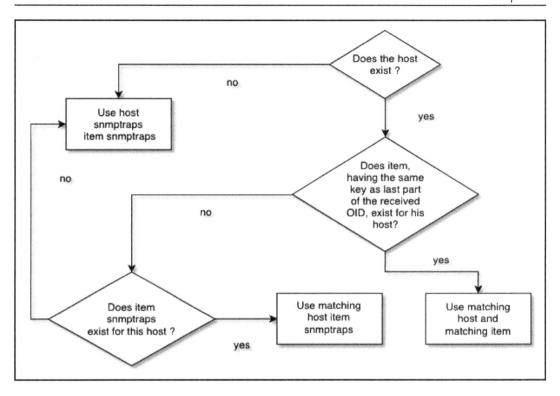

To test this, send an SNMP trap from **Another host** (there is no need to restart snmptrapd):

```
$ snmptrap -Ci -v 2c -c public <Zabbix server> "" "NET-SNMP-
MIB::netSnmpExperimental" NET-SNMP-MIB::netSnmpExperimental s "test"
```

Replace <Zabbix server> with the Zabbix server's IP or DNS name. If you now check **Monitoring** | **Latest data** for **Another host**, the trap should be correctly placed in the snmptraps item for this host. A trap sent from any other host, including the Zabbix server, should be placed in the snmptraps host and snmptraps item—feel free to try this out. Previously, a trap sent from the Zabbix server would be lost, because the script did not check for the snmptraps item's existence—it would find the host and then try to push the data to this nonexistent item.

Let's try out our item mapping now:

1. Go to the Zabbix interface, **Configuration** | **Hosts**, click on **Items** next to **Another host**, and click on the **Create item** button. Fill in the following values:

    - **Name**: Experimental SNMP trap
    - **Type**: **Zabbix trapper**
    - **Key**: netSnmpExperimental
    - **Type of information**: **Character**

2. When you're done, click on the **Add** button at the bottom.

Again, send a trap from **Another host**:

```
$ snmptrap -Ci -v 2c -c public <Zabbix server> "" "NET-SNMP-
MIB::netSnmpExperimental" NET-SNMP-MIB::netSnmpExperimental s "test"
```

In the frontend, look at **Monitoring** | **Latest data**. If all went right, this time the trap data should have been placed in yet another item—the one we just created:

Experimental SNMP trap	2016-03-20 03:12:07	192.168.56.11 "test" NET-SNM...

Now, whenever we have a host that will be sending us traps, we will have to decide where we want its traps to go. Depending on that, we'll decide whether it needs its own host with an snmptraps item, or perhaps even individual items for each trap type.

Summary

Having explored basic monitoring with a Zabbix agent before, we looked at a major agentless monitoring solution in this chapter—SNMP. Given the wide array of devices supporting SNMP, this knowledge should help us with retrieving information from devices such as printers, switches, UPSes, and others, while also listening and managing incoming SNMP traps from those.

Beware of starting to monitor a large number of network devices, especially if they have many interfaces. For example, adding 10 switches with 48 ports, even if you monitor a single item per switch once a minute only, will make Zabbix poll eight new values per second (480 ports once a minute results in *480/60=8* new values per second). Usually, more values per port are monitored, so such an increase can bring a Zabbix server down and severely impact network performance even when SNMP bulk get is used.

While we have created several hosts by now, we only paid attention to the host properties that were immediately useful. In the next chapter, we will look some more into what we can control on hosts, including host and host group maintenance. We'll also discover how we can provide access for other users to what we have been configuring so far, using user and permission management.

Questions

1. Is it possible to retrieve snmp items in groups instead of item by item?
2. What is the advantage of dynamic indexes?
3. What options do we have when configuring snmptraps in Zabbix?

Further reading

The following is a list of URLs with some more information about SNMP traps in Zabbix that should help you to get started:

- **SNMP agent**: https://www.zabbix.com/documentation/4.0/manual/config/items/itemtypes/snmp?s[]=bulks[]=requests#internal_workings_of_bulk_processing
- **Start with SNMP traps in Zabbix**: http://zabbix.org/wiki/Start_with_SNMP_traps_in_Zabbix

Managing Hosts, Users, and Permissions

5

We created some hosts and host groups earlier, thus exploring the way items can be grouped and attached to hosts. Now is the time to take a closer look at these concepts and see what benefits they provide. In this chapter, we will cover the following topics:

- Hosts and host groups
- Host maintenance
- Users, user groups, and permissions

Hosts and host groups

A host can be considered a basic grouping unit in Zabbix configuration. As you might remember, hosts are used to group items, which in turn are basic data-acquiring structures. Each host can have any number of items assigned, spanning all item types—Zabbix agents, simple checks, **Simple Network Management Protocol (SNMP)**, **Intelligent Platform Management Interface** (**IPMI**), and so on. An item can't exist on its own, so hosts are mandatory.

Zabbix does not allow a host to be *left alone*, that is, to not belong to any group. Let's look at what host groups we currently have defined—from the frontend, open **Configuration** | **Host groups**, as shown in the following screenshot:

The first thing that should catch your eye is that the **Templates** group seems to have a large number of templates already. These are provided as examples so that you can quickly refer to them later for some hints on items. We'll ignore these for now. We can also see an empty **Discovered hosts** group and the Zabbix servers group, which contains a single example host. The interesting part is in the first half of the table—we can see both groups we used along the way, with all the corresponding members. This table is fairly simple, with just a group name, a count of the number of group members (individually denoting hosts and templates contained in the group), and individual members being listed.

As you will see, individual members are color-coded, and use the following convention:

- **Green**: Normal, enabled host
- **Red**: Normal, disabled host
- **Gray**: Template

As you will see, some of the groups have / in their name, such as, for example, **Templates/Applications**. This is the new way of allowing the creation of subgroups in Zabbix. So, when you would like to create a host in a sub-group, it is possible to do so by just adding a / in the name.

Let's create another host group and assign some hosts to it:

1. Click on the **Create host group** button.
2. Enter **Linux servers/Test group**. This will allow you to create a host group nested in the **Linux servers** group with the name **Test group**. Let's also create a **Linux servers/SNMP** group. As you can see, there is a box that allows you to apply permissions and tags to all subgroups. This box can be helpful if you would like sub-groups to inherit the permissions from the host group.
3. Now, we will add our another host and our test host to the group **Linux servers/Test group** and our snmptrap host to the group **Linux servers/SNMP group** by going to **Configuration | Hosts** followed by <our host>.

4. In the **Groups** box, we can now type the name of our new group, or we can select it with the **Select** button.

5. Next, we click **Update**. For the `snmptrap` host, we remove the **Linux servers** group by clicking on the **x** just after the name of the group, so that it only belongs to **Linux servers/SNMP group**:

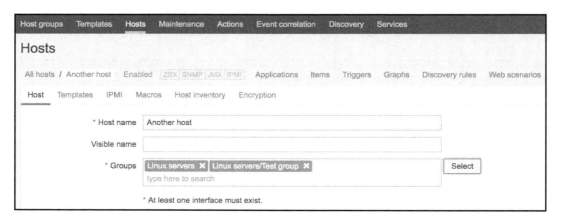

You have probably guessed by now that a host can belong to any number of groups or subgroups. This allows you to choose groupings based on any arbitrary decision, such as having a single host in groups called **Linux servers**, **Europe servers**, and **DB servers**.

Now, we are back in the host list, so return to the host group list by navigating to **Configuration** | **Host groups**. The group **Linux servers/Test group** contains two hosts, as it should, and **Linux servers/SNMP group** only contains our host, `snmptrap`. Let's say you want to disable a whole group of hosts, or even several host groups. Perhaps you have a group of hosts that are retired but that you don't want to delete just yet, or maybe you want to disable hosts that were created for testing when creating an actual production configuration on the Zabbix server. The group listing provides an easy way to do that—mark the checkboxes next to **Linux servers/SNMP group**, click on the **Disable hosts** button at the bottom of the list, and confirm the popup.

After this operation, all green hosts should be gone—they should be red now, indicating that they are in a disabled state:

☐ Linux servers	Hosts 2	Templates	Another host, A test host
☐ Linux servers/SNMP group	Hosts 1	Templates	snmptrap

After doing this, you should remember that `snmptrap` is a generic SNMP trap-receiving host, which probably should be left enabled. Click on it to open the host details editing page.

While you have the host details page open, you can take a quick look at the **Interface** section. As you can see, there are four different interface types available. For each of them, a single IP and DNS field is available, along with connect to controls, which are used for checks that are initiated from the server side. We've already used agent and SNMP interfaces. We will also use IPMI and JMX interfaces when configuring monitoring using those protocols.

Mark the **Enabled** checkbox and click on **Update**.

You should now see a host list with a status that shows in green, **Enabled**, per host. By clicking on the **Enabled** status, we can disable/enable each host individually.

 Finally, we are back to having all the hosts enabled again. Zabbix has four methods to change the state of a host. Let's have a look at them:

- Changing the state for the whole group in the **Configuration** | **Host groups** area
- Changing the state for a single host using the **Enabled** checkbox in that host's properties page
- Changing the state for a single host using controls for each host in the **Status** column in the host configuration list
- Changing the state for a single host or multiple hosts by marking the relevant checkboxes in the host configuration list and using the enable and disable buttons at the bottom of the list

We created the previous host group by going through the group configuration screen. As you might remember, another way to do this is to use the **New group** field when creating or editing a host—this creates the group and simultaneously adds the host to that group.

The host list on the configuration screen is also useful in another way. It provides a nice, quick way of seeing which hosts are down. While the monitoring section gives us quite extensive information on the state of specific services and the conditions of each device, sometimes you will want a quick peek at the device status, for example, to determine the availability of all the devices in a particular group, such as printers, routers, or switches. The configuration provides this information in a list that contains almost no other information to distract you. If we were to now select **all** from the **Group** drop-down, we would see all the hosts this installation has:

This time, we are interested in two columns—**Status** and **Availability**. The **Availability** column shows the internal state, as determined by Zabbix, for each host and polled item type. If Zabbix tries to get data from a host but fails, the availability of that host for this specific type of information is determined to be absent. Both the availability status and error message are preserved for the following four separate types of items, which are polled by the Zabbix server:

- Zabbix agent (passive)
- SNMP
- JMX
- IPMI

Error messages are preserved for each interface and are calculated by the Zabbix server internally. Error messages are shown when you move your mouse over the red icon. Here, we have an overview of all the different possible statuses in Zabbix:

- Green—available
- Red—not available (error shown when the mouse is moved over the red icon)
- Gray—unknown or not configured:

Remember that the availability icon in the host list represents passive Zabbix agent items only—active items do not affect it at all. If a host has active items only, this icon will remain gray. If you add passive items that fail and then convert them all to active items, the icon should revert to gray. This is an improvement in Zabbix that has been around since version 3.0. In previous versions, the icon would remain red throughout and you had to reset it in the database manually.

The Zabbix server will set the icon to grey in the following situations:

- There are no enabled items on the interface
- The host is set to be monitored by a proxy, a different proxy, or by a server (until Zabbix is updated and the host is checked again for availability, the icon will remain grey)
- The host is monitored by a proxy that is offline
- When our host is disabled

Availability information is aimed more at Zabbix administrators—it shows problems related to gathering data from a host, not information such as resource usage, process status, or performance metrics.

That just about wraps it up for host and host group management in Zabbix. The usefulness of host groups extends a bit past frontend management, though we'll see how exactly later in this chapter when we talk about permissions.

 With older versions of Zabbix, it was possible to add hosts to the host group when creating it. In Zabbix 4.0, this option has been removed, as selection boxes were removed in 4.0. Let's hope that this functionality comes back in another way.

Host inventory

We looked at managing hosts, but there's one area of host properties that warrants a slightly longer section.

Editing inventory data manually

Let's have a look how we can use Zabbix to manage our inventory:

1. Go to **Configuration** | **Hosts**, and make sure **Linux servers** has been selected in the **Group** drop-down. Then, click on **A test host**, and switch to the **Host inventory** tab. By default, the inventory is set to **Disabled**, as shown in the following screenshot:

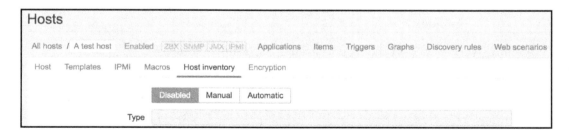

2. Click on **Manual** to enable the inventory fields. Notice how there are a lot of fields, starting with simple things such as type, name, operating system, and hardware, and ending with hardware maintenance dates, location data, and point-of-contact information. In the **Type** field, enter `test`, and then click on **Update.**

3. Now, click on **Another host**, switch to the **Host inventory** tab, and click on **Manual**. Then, enter the same `test` string in the **Type** field again. Click on **Update**. Now, let's mark the checkboxes next to both SNMP hosts and click on **Mass update** at the bottom of the list. In the **Mass update** form, switch to the **Inventory** tab and mark the checkbox next to **Inventory mode**. Switch to **Manual**, mark the checkbox next to **Type**, and enter `snmp` in that field:

4. Click on **Update**. With some inventory data populated, let's go to **Inventory** | **Overview**. Choose **all** from the **Group** drop-down and **Type** from the **Grouping by** drop-down. Notice how we can see all the available values for this field and how many hosts we have for each of them:

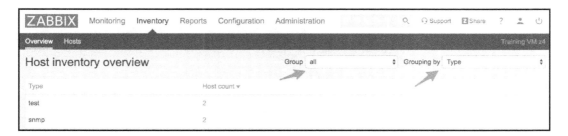

5. Click on the number **2** in the **Host count** column next to `snmp`. Here, we can see individual hosts and some of the inventory fields, including the field that we used, **Type.** This list was filtered to show only those hosts that have the exact `snmp` string in the **Type** field. You can verify that by looking at the filter:

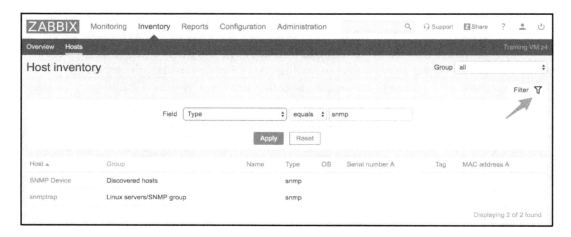

6. Collapse the filter and click on **SNMP Device** in the **Hosts** column. This will open the host overview page, displaying some basic configuration information. Notably, host interfaces are displayed here. While users without configuration permissions on hosts are not able to open host properties in the configuration section, they may see this host overview page and see the host interfaces this way:

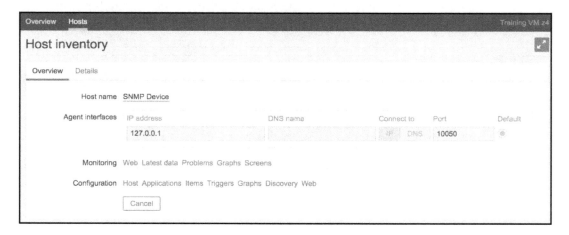

7. There are also two lines of links at the bottom of this form—**Monitoring** and **Configuration**. As you might expect, they provide quick access to various monitoring and configuration sections for this host, similar to the global search we discussed in `Chapter 2`, *Getting Your First Notification*. Clicking on hostname **SNMP Device** will provide access to global scripts. We will explore and configure those in `Chapter 7`, *Acting upon Monitored Conditions*.

8. Let's return to **Configuration** | **Hosts** and click on **SNMP Device**. Switch to the **Host inventory** tab, and in the **OS** column, enter `Linux` (`http://www.kernel.org`) and click on **Update**. Let's go directly to **Inventory** | **Hosts** this time—notice how this was the page we ended up at when we clicked on the host count from the inventory overview. Looking at the **OS** column, we can see that Zabbix recognized the URL and made it clickable:

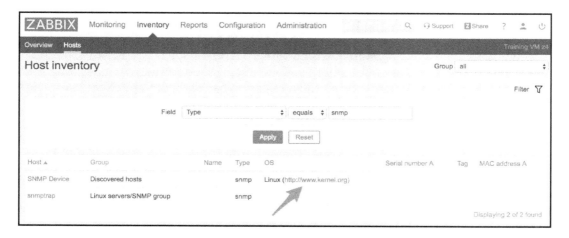

At this time, the columns displayed on this page cannot be customized.

This allows you to link to websites that provide more information or to web management interfaces for various devices. Note that, other than recognizing URLs, fields are not interpreted in any way; for example, **Location latitude** and **Location longitude** fields are just text fields.

Populating inventory data automatically

Manually populated inventory data is useful, but doing that on a large scale may not be very feasible. Zabbix can also collect some inventory values automatically for us. This is possible because any item can populate any inventory field. We will use one of our existing items and create a new one to automatically populate two inventory fields.

Let's start by adding the new item. Navigate to **Configuration** | **Hosts**, switch to **Linux servers** from the **Group** drop-down, and click on **Items** for **A test host**. Then, click on **Create item**. Fill in the following values:

- **Name**: The full OS name
- **Key**: system.uname
- **Type of information**: Text
- **Update interval**: 300
- **Host inventory field**: Software application A

When you're done, click on **Add** at the bottom. We now have an item configured to place data in the inventory field, but this alone won't do anything. We have our inventory set to manual mode. From the navigation bar preceding the item list, click on **A test host** and switch to the **Host inventory** tab. Then, choose **Automatic**. Notice how something changed—our field **Software application A** here got disabled, and a link appeared to the right of the field:

This is the field we chose during the item configuration earlier. The link shows which item is supposed to populate this field and allows convenient access to the configuration of the item. Note that the field we manually populated earlier, **Type**, did not lose the value. Actually, the automatic mode can be said to be a hybrid one. Fields that are configured to obtain their values automatically do so; other fields may be populated manually. Click on **Update**.

Values from items are placed in the inventory whenever an item gets a new value. For the full OS version item, we set the interval to a fairly low one: 300 seconds. The agent item, on the other hand, has a large interval. This means that we might have to wait for a long time before the value appears in that inventory field. To make it happen sooner, restart the agent on **A test host**.

The inventory field we chose, **Software application A**, is not very representative, but there is no way of customizing inventory fields at this time. If you have data that does not match existing inventory fields well, you'll have to choose the best fit or just use something not really related to the actual data.

With the item supposed to have the value placed in the **Inventory** field, let's return to **Inventory** | **Overview** and choose **Software application A** from the **Grouping by** drop-down. This should display only one host:

1. Click on **1** in the **Host count** column, and you should be able to see that, as expected, it is **A test host**. The column we chose is not listed in the current view, though.
2. Click on **A test host** in the **Host** column and switch to the **Details** tab.

Here, we can see system information from the `system.uname` item:

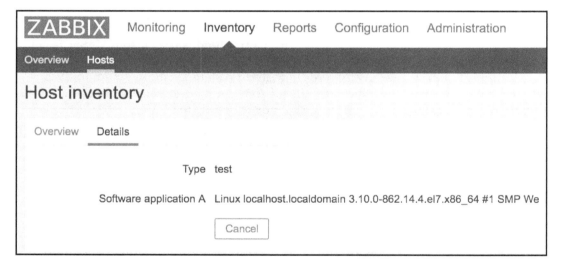

We used both the overview and host pages of the inventory section. The **Overview** page is useful to see the distribution of hosts by inventory field. The host page allows you to see individual hosts by using the filter at the top-right of the page.

When we ended up on the hosts page, the filter was preset for us to match an exact field value, but we may also search for a substring. For example, if we have systems with OS information containing CentOS 7.5 and CentOS 6.2, we may filter just by **CentOS** and obtain a list of all the CentOS systems, no matter which exact version they are running:

While being able to access inventory data in the frontend is useful sometimes, faster and easier access might be preferred. It is also possible to include inventory data in notifications. For example, an email could include system location, whom to contact when there's a problem with the system, and some serial numbers, among other things. We will discuss notifications in `Chapter 7`, *Acting upon Monitored Conditions*.

 If we go to **Administration** | **General** | **Other** (from the drop-down on the right), then we have the option to set the default host inventory mode. This option is only valid for new added hosts. It will not change the default behavior for already existing hosts.

Host maintenance

We want to know about problems as soon as possible, always. Well, not always—there are those cases when we test failover or reconfigure storage arrays. There is also maintenance—the time when things are highly likely to break and we do not want to send loads of emails, SMS messages, or other things to our accounts or to other people. Zabbix offers host group and host-level maintenance that enables us to avoid excessive messaging during such maintenance periods.

Hosts being under maintenance can result in three main consequences:

- Data is not collected for those hosts
- Problems for those hosts are hidden or not shown in the frontend
- Alerts are not processed for those hosts

These consequences can also be customized in quite some detail per host group, host, and other factors. We will explore most of those customization possibilities in this chapter, except alert processing, which we will discuss in Chapter 7, *Acting upon Monitored Conditions*.

Creating maintenance periods

We will create a couple of maintenance periods and see how they affect several views in the frontend. We will discuss the available time period options and set up two different maintenance periods:

- One that will not affect data collection
- One that stops data collection

 Before working with maintenance periods, ensure that the time zones configured for the PHP and Zabbix server hosts match. Otherwise, the time displayed in the frontend will differ from the time the actual maintenance takes place. In fact, it is also very important to have a proper ntpd or chronyd service on your hosts and server configured, otherwise weird time issues can occur when hosts lag behind the server and/or proxies.

Collecting data during maintenance

Navigate to **Configuration** | **Maintenance** and click on **Create maintenance period**. In the resulting form, fill in these values:

- **Name:** Enter Normal maintenance
- **Maintenance type: With data collection**
- **Active since**: Make sure this is set to the start of your current day or earlier
- **Active till**: Make sure this is set to a year or so in the future
- **Description**: Enter we keep data during this maintenance

What's that? Are we really creating a year-long maintenance period? Not really. Switch to the **Periods** tab:

Maintenance periods

Maintenance   Periods   Hosts and groups

* Name	Normal maintenance
Maintenance type	**With data collection** No data collection
* Active since	2018-11-01 00:00
* Active till	2019-11-02 00:00
Description	we keep data during this maintenance

Update   Clone   Delete   Cancel

Here, the Zabbix terminology is a bit confusing. The main tab has since-till fields, which allow us to set what we could call the main period. The **Periods** tab allows us to add individual periods, which we can call subperiods. Any maintenance entry in Zabbix must have at least one subperiod defined. Maintenance in Zabbix is active when the main period overlaps with subperiods. Let's repeat that:

We should not add a maintenance entry without any sub periods defined.

No sub periods are defined here yet, so let's click on **New**.

To keep things simple here, let's add a one-time period. In the **Date** field, set the date and time to the current values. We can leave the **Maintenance period** length at the default, which is 1 hour.

When you're done, click on the small **Add** link after the **Maintenance period** section—do not click on the **Add** button yet. Only after clicking on that small **Add** link should you click on the **Add** button, an error should appear:

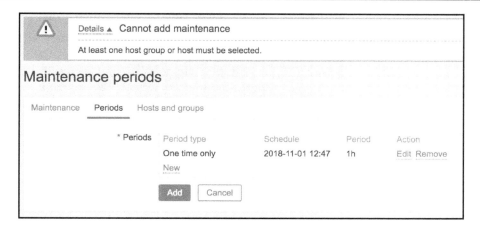

That didn't seem to work too well—apparently, a maintenance entry without any hosts or groups assigned to it cannot be created. Switch to the **Hosts and groups** tab. For our first maintenance period, select the **Linux servers** from the **Host groups** box, and choose **A test host** from the **Hosts** box. Then, click on the **Add** button, but this time not the small **Add** link, as shown in the following screenshot, as that one is used to add extra tag lines:

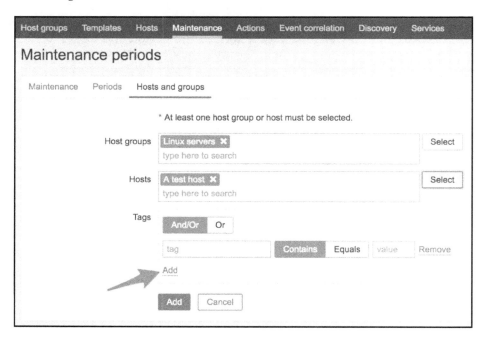

Maintenance in Zabbix is active when the main period overlaps with sub-periods. As you can see, with Zabbix 4.0, tags have been added to the maintenance periods for hosts and groups. This can be very useful if we have added tags to our triggers. Then, it is possible to only create maintenance periods for hosts who's triggers contain certain tags.

You may freely add any number of hosts and host groups, and they may overlap. Zabbix will correctly figure out which hosts should go into maintenance. The maintenance entry should appear in the list:

The reminder to click on the small **Add** link was repeated several times for a reason—it is too easy to forget to click on it and actually miss your changes in some cases. For example, if you were adding the second sub period and forgot to click on the small link, it would be silently discarded. Watch out for similar traps in other forms!

As you can also see in the preceding screenshot, when you click the filter on top of the page, it is now possible to filter the maintenance periods in a more easy way by selecting the state of the maintenance periods you would like to see.

With the maintenance entry added, let's try to see the effect this has on several sections in the frontend. In the console, run the following command:

```
$ cat /dev/urandom | md5sum
```

Navigate to **Monitoring** | **Problems.** Select **A test host** from the **Hosts** selection box and make sure you also mark the **Show suppressed problems** option:

Wait for the trigger to fire. When it shows up, look at the **Host** column—this time, there's an orange wrench indicator. This shows us that maintenance is currently active for this host. Move the mouse cursor over this indicator:

You may click on the indicator to keep the message open, as with other pop-up messages in Zabbix.

The message shows the name of the maintenance we used—normal maintenance. It also tells us that this maintenance is configured to keep collecting data, and below, that the description of the maintenance is shown. This allows us to easily inform other users why this maintenance is taking place. Still on the problem page, look at the filter. Notice how the **Show suppressed problems** checkbox was marked by us. Unmark it and click on **Apply**. All problems for **A test host** should disappear—well, from this view at least. To avoid being confused later, mark that checkbox and click on **Apply** again. Remember, most filter options are remembered between visits to a specific page, so we will not see hosts in maintenance in this view later if we leave it unmarked.

Let's check how another page looks when a host is in maintenance. Navigate to **Monitoring** | **Dashboard** and click on **Edit dashboard**. Next, click on the gear in the top-right corner of the **Problems** widget and also check the **Show suppressed problems** option here, then click **Apply**:

Note that we can choose many more options for our widget. We can even choose to only show problems for certain hosts or host groups or even only those where the trigger is tagged with a certain tag, or decide to not show problems with a certain severity level.

 You could add tags such as application or OS to your triggers or development and production, and then filter in the frontend problems related only to application or OS, or development or production.

The host that's under maintenance is denoted here in the same way. Again, moving the mouse cursor over the orange icon will reveal the maintenance name, type, and description.

The maintenance status can also be seen in other frontend sections. We will review some of them in Chapter 21, *Visualizing Data with Graphs and Maps*.

We created and checked one maintenance entry. During this maintenance, data from our host was still collected, and triggers were checking that data. The status was shown in the frontend, and we could choose to hide hosts that were in maintenance. Now let's try something different—maintenance that also stops data from being collected in Zabbix.

Not collecting data during maintenance

Follow these steps:

1. Navigate to **Configuration** | **Maintenance** and click on **Create maintenance period**. In the resulting form, fill in these values:

   - **Name**: Enter Maintenance with all data dropped
   - **Maintenance type**: Choose **No data collection**
   - **Active since**: Make sure this is set to the start of your current day or earlier
   - **Active till**: Make sure this is set to a year or so in the future
   - **Description**: Enter We don't need no data

2. Switch to the **Periods** tab and click on **New**.

3. In the **Date** field, set the date and time to the current values as shown in the following screenshot:

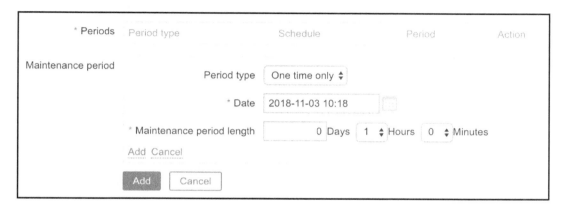

4. Click on the small **Add** link—again, that first one, not the **Add** button.

5. Now, switch to the **Hosts and groups** tab. Make sure the host selection says **Another host**.

6. Now, click on the **Add** button. There should be two maintenance entries in the list:

7. Go to **Monitoring | Latest data** and make sure **Linux servers** is selected in the **Host groups** field in the filter.

Notice how data stopped coming in for the items in **Another host**—the timestamp is not being updated anymore. That's because of the maintenance without data collection that we created. As such, triggers will not fire, and problems for such hosts will not appear in the frontend, no matter what the filter settings are.

Let's take a quick look at **Configuration** | **Hosts**. This is another location where the maintenance status can be seen. Hosts that are in maintenance will have **In maintenance** listed in the **Status** column—this replaces the normal **Enabled** text:

We discovered the way maintenance can affect data collection and the displaying of problems. Another important reason to use it is skipping or modifying notifications. We will discuss notifications in `Chapter 7`, *Acting upon Monitored Conditions*.

Maintenance period options

So far, the only type of maintenance sub-periods we've used is one-time maintenance. We decided to call those periods that were configured in a separate tab sub-periods to distinguish them from the main period, configured in the first tab, **Maintenance**. We also discovered that maintenance would be active only during the time in which the main period overlaps with sub periods. But *what's the point of defining the same thing twice? Couldn't the one-time period be the only thing to specify?* The benefit of the main period becomes more apparent when configuring recurring maintenance, so let's explore the options available for sub-periods. Navigate to **Configuration** | **Maintenance**, start creating a new maintenance, and play with the available sub periods as we explore them.

One-time only maintenance

This is the maintenance sub-period type we've already used. It starts at the specified date and time, proceeds for the amount of time specified in minutes, hours, and days, and that's it. This type of sub-period must still overlap with the main period.

Daily maintenance

For daily maintenance, we have to specify the starting time and the length of the maintenance period:

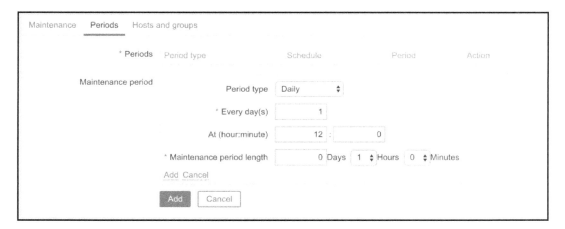

During the main period, maintenance will start every day at the specified time. It will start every day with the **Every day(s)** option set to the default, **1**. We can change this and make the maintenance only happen every second day, third day, and so on.

Weekly maintenance

For weekly maintenance, we have to specify the starting time and the length of the maintenance period, the same as for daily maintenance:

We also have to choose on which days of the week the maintenance will take place—we can choose one or more. During the main period, maintenance will start every specified day of the week at the specified time. It will start every week with the **Every week(s)** option set to the default, **1**. We can change this and make the maintenance only happen every second week, third week, and so on.

Monthly maintenance

Monthly maintenance has two modes:

- By day of month
- By day of week

For both of these, we have to specify the start time and the length of the maintenance period, the same as in daily and weekly maintenance modes. Additionally, we have to choose which months the maintenance will happen in—we may choose one month or more. In **Day of month** mode (option **Date** set to **Day of month**), we have to enter a day in the **Day of month** field. Maintenance will happen on that day only in each of the months we select.

In **Day of week** mode (option **Date** set to **Day of week**), we have to choose which days of the week the maintenance will take place on—we may choose one or more:

As this has to happen monthly, not weekly, we also have to choose whether this will happen on the **first**, **second**, **third**, **fourth**, or **last** weekday in any of the selected months:

In addition to this, we may also ask Zabbix to run this maintenance on the last such day in the selected months, for example, every **April**, **August**, and **December**, to run the maintenance on the last **Wednesday** that month.

With all these recurring maintenance modes, it is possible to create nearly any scenario—one thing that might be missing is the ability to run monthly maintenance on the last day of every month.

So, the benefit of having this sort of a double configuration, that is, this overlap between the main period and the sub-periods, is that we can have recurring maintenance that starts at some point in the future and then stops at some point later completely automatically—we don't have to remember to add and remove it on a specific date.

Ad hoc maintenance

The maintenance functionality in Zabbix is aimed at a well-planned environment where maintenance is always planned in advance. In practice, people often want to place a host in maintenance quickly and then simply remove it manually a bit later. With all the periods and other things maintenance entry requires, it's not quick enough. A slightly hackish workaround is to create a new host group (ex-maintenance) and a maintenance period that is always active (make sure to set its end date far enough in the future). Include that host group in the maintenance entry, and then adding a host to the chosen host group will add that host to maintenance. Of course, you will have to remember to remove the host from the host group afterwards. Another workaround is to use the API.

Users, user groups, and permissions

In Zabbix, hosts need to be placed in 1 or more host group(s). Users also need to be placed in 1 or more group(s). Hosts have gathered the information and, they have items linked to them, directly or from templates. Permissions in Zabbix are set on a group level.

Authentication methods

Before we look at more detailed user configuration, it might be helpful to know that Zabbix supports three authentication methods. Navigate to **Administration** | **Authentication** to take a look at authentication configuration:

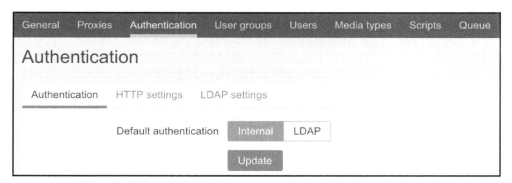

As can be seen in the preceding screenshot, these are the three authentication methods:

- **HTTP**: Users are authenticated with web server HTTP authentication mechanisms. Support for HTTP authentication basically allows the use of any of the authentication methods for Zabbix that the web server supports, and in the case of the Apache HTTPD daemon, there are many. If you like to use HTTP authentication, then click the **HTTP settings** tab and fill in the necessary information.

- **LDAP**: Users are authenticated using an LDAP server. This can be handy if all enterprise users that need access to Zabbix are already defined in an LDAP structure. Only user passwords are verified; group membership and other properties are not used. A Zabbix user account must also exist for the login to be successful. If you would like to use the **LDAP** authentication, then you will need to fill in the settings in the **LDAP** tab and select **LDAP** from the **Authentication** page instead of internal.

- **Internal**: With this method, users are authenticated using Zabbix's internal store of users and passwords. We will be using this method.

Creating a user

The initial Zabbix installation does not contain many predefined users—let's look at the user list. Navigate to **Administration** | **Users**:

That's right; only two user accounts are defined—**Admin** and **guest**. We have been logged in as Admin all the time. On the other hand, the guest user is used for unauthenticated users. Before we logged in as Admin, we were guest. The user list shows some basic information about the users, such as which groups they belong to, whether they are logged in, when their last login was, and whether their account is enabled. A guest user can be unwanted, as they could reveal certain information that should not be visible to anybody, so use with care!

 By granting access permissions to the guest user, it is possible to allow anonymous access to resources. This user will be active by default!

Let's create another user for ourselves. Click on the **Create user** button located in the upper-right corner. We'll look at all of the available options for a user account, while filling in the appropriate ones:

- **Alias**: Enter `monitoring_user`. This is essentially a username.
- **Name**: Enter `monitoring`. In this field, you would normally enter the user's real name.
- **Surname**: Enter `user`. This field normally contains the user's real surname.
- **Groups**: Just like hosts, user accounts can be grouped. A user must belong to at least one group, so let's assign our new user to a group, at least temporarily. Click on the **Select** button next to the **Groups** field, and mark the checkbox next to **Zabbix administrators**. Then, click on **Select.**

- **Password**: Choose and enter a password, and then retype it in the next field.
- **Language**: The frontend has translations in various levels of maturity, and each user can choose their own preference. We'll leave this as **English (en_GB).**

> If a language you would like to use is not listed, it might still be there—just incomplete. See `Appendix B`, *Being Part of the Community*, for more details on how to enable it and contribute to Zabbix translations.

- **Theme**: The Zabbix frontend supports theming. Currently, there are only four themes included, though. We'll leave the theme as **System default.**
- **Auto-login**: Marking this option will automatically log the user in after they have logged in at least once manually. Automatic login is performed with browser cookies. We won't be using automatic login for this user.
- **Auto-logout**: You can make a particular account automatically log out after a specific period of inactivity. The minimum time period that can be set is `90` seconds. The maximum is about `1 day`, and time suffixes are supported. There is no need to set automatic logout here.

> What's more, at the time of writing, this option does not work as expected and should not be relied on, as there are cases where a user will not be logged out. See the URL at the end of this chapter, in the *Further reading* section, for more information.

- **Refresh**: This is the time, in seconds, between page refreshes when in the **Monitoring** section. While smaller values might be nice to look at when first setting up and having items with short check intervals, they somewhat increase the load on the server, and if the page contains a lot of information, then it might not even finish loading before the next refresh kicks in. Let's set this to `60s` for this user—after all, they can always refresh manually when testing something. Note that some pages do not perform a full page refresh; instead, they just reload some elements on that page. A graph page, for example, only reloads the graph image.
- **Rows per page**: Each user can have an individual maximum rows-per-page setting. If the returned data exceeds this parameter, the interface splits the data into multiple pages. We won't change this parameter.

- **URL (after login)**: A user might wish to always see a specific page after logging in – be it the overview, trigger list, or any other page. This option allows the user to customize that. The URL that's entered is relative to the Zabbix directory, so let's make this user always see **Monitoring** | **Problems** when they log in, by entering `tr_status.php` here.

The final result should look as follows:

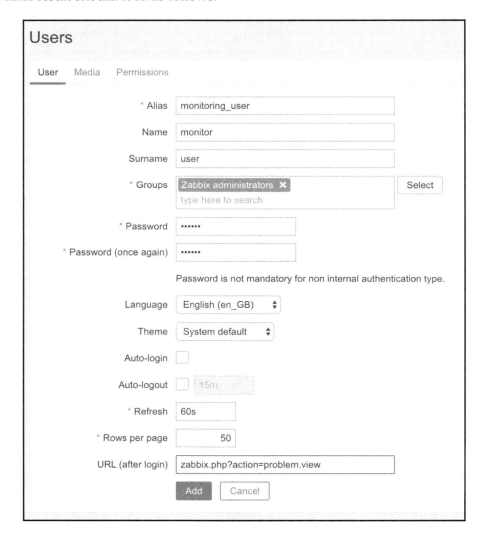

If it does, click on the **Add** button at the bottom.

Now, it would be nice to test this new user. It is suggested that you launch another browser for this test so that any changes are easy to observe. Let's call the browser where you have the administrative user logged in *Browser 1* and the other one *Browser 2*. In *Browser 2*, open the Zabbix page and log in as monitoring_user, supplying whatever password you entered before. Instead of the dashboard, the **Monitoring | Problems** page is opened.

Also, the page is notably different than before—the main menu entries **Configuration** and **Administration** are missing here. Also the **Host** and **Host groups** entries are both empty and nothing can be selected; no issues are visible. Go to **Monitoring | Overview**. The **Group** drop-down is set to all and **Type** is set to **Triggers**, but the **Details** view claims that there's **No data found**. *How come?*

By default, users don't have access to any systems. When our new user logs in, nothing is displayed in the monitoring section, because we did not grant any privileges, including read-only. We did assign this user to the **Zabbix administrators** group, but that group has no permissions set by default.

Back in *Browser 1*, click on monitoring_user in the **Alias** column. One minor thing to notice—instead of a **Password** input field, this time, a button that says **Change password** is visible. If you ever have to reset a password for a user, clicking on this button will reveal the password input fields again, allowing a password update along with any other changes that might have been made:

But there's a tab we still haven't used—**Permissions**. Let's switch to it.

There's also a **Media** tab. There, users can have various media assigned to them so that Zabbix knows how to alert them. Media types include email addresses and numbers to send SMS messages to. We will discuss notification functionality in Chapter 7, *Acting upon Monitored Conditions*.

The first thing to notice is the **User type** drop-down. It offers three user types. We'll leave it at **Zabbix User** for this user:

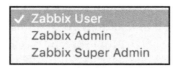

For reference, these types have the following meanings:

- **Zabbix User**: These are normal users that only have access to the **Monitoring**, **Inventory**, and **Reports** sections in the **Main** menu
- **Zabbix Admin**: These users, in addition to the previous three sections, have access to the **Configuration** section, so they are able to reconfigure parts of Zabbix
- **Zabbix Super Admin**: These users have full access to Zabbix, including the **Monitoring**, **Configuration**, and **Administration** sections

The following is a section that looks very similar to what we are looking for; there are **Host groups** and permissions:

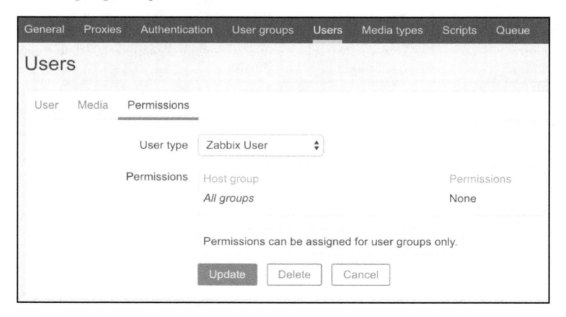

There's just one problem—there is no way to change these permissions.

A helpful message at the bottom of the page explains why. It says **Permissions can be assigned for user groups only**.

We conveniently skipped adding or configuring any groups and permissions, so now is a good time to fix that.

Creating user groups

Instead of modifying the default user groups, we will add our own. Navigate to **Administration | User groups** and take a look at the list of current user groups:

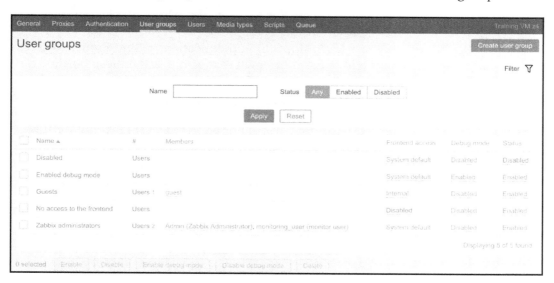

As can be seen, there are already a few predefined groups, giving you some idea of how users could be organized. That organization can be based on system categories, systems, management roles, physical locations, and so on. For example, you might have a group of administrators in headquarters and some in a branch location. Each group might not be interested in the **UPS** status in the other location, so you could group them as HQ admins and Branch admins. A user can belong to any number of groups, so you can create various schemes, as real-world conditions require.

Let's create a new group for our user. Click on **Create user group** in the upper-right corner. Let's fill in the form and find out what each control does:

- **Group name**: Enter Our users.
- **Users**: Here, we can add users to the group we are creating. Our current installation has very few users, so finding the correct username with all users displayed is easy. Select monitoring_user and click on the button or just type the name in the box and select the correct user.
- **Frontend access**: This option allows us to choose the authentication method for a specific group. It allows for a configuration where most users are authenticated against LDAP, but some users are authenticated against the internal user database. It also allows us to set no GUI access for some groups, which can then be used for users that only need to receive notifications. We'll leave this option as **System default**.

If your Zabbix installation uses LDAP for user authentication, setting **Frontend access** to **Internal** for a user group will make all users in that group authenticate against the internal Zabbix password storage. It is not a failover option—internal authentication will always be used. This is useful if you want to provide access to users that are not in the LDAP directory, or create emergency accounts that you can pull out of a safe when LDAP goes down. Such an approach will not work with HTTP authentication, as it happens before Zabbix gets to decide anything about the authentication backend:

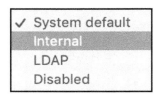

- **Enabled**: With a single option, all the users in this group can be disabled or enabled. As the predefined groups might tell you, this is a nice way to easily disable individual user accounts by simply adding them to a group that has this checkbox unmarked. We want our user to be able to log in, so this option will stay marked.
- **Debug mode**: This option gives users access to frontend debug information. It is mostly useful for Zabbix developers or Zabbix administrators. We will discuss debug mode in Appendix A, *Troubleshooting*.

With the main settings covered, let's switch to the **Permissions** tab:

Now that's more like it! We can finally see controls for various permission levels. There are three sections, labeled **Read-write**, **Read**, **Deny**, and **None**. Our user had no permissions to see anything, so we will want to add some kind of permissions. Click on **Select** left of the **Read-write** box. This opens a new window with host groups.

It also provides us with another valuable bit of information. have finally got the essential information together—in Zabbix, permissions can be set for user groups on host groups only.

Mark the checkbox next to **Linux servers/SNMP group** and click on the **Select** button.

We can now see that **SNMP devices** has been added to the **Read-write** box. Next, click on the Read box. This time, mark the checkbox next to the **Linux servers** entry, and then click on **Add**. You will see that Zabbix also adds the **Linux servers/Test group** but with permissions set to **None**. This is because, when we created our **Linux servers** host group, we had the option to select **Apply permissions and tag filters to all subgroups**, but we left that box unmarked. If we had marked that option, then all the subgroups from the **Linux servers** group would have inherited the permissions from the **Linux servers** group.

The final form should look like this:

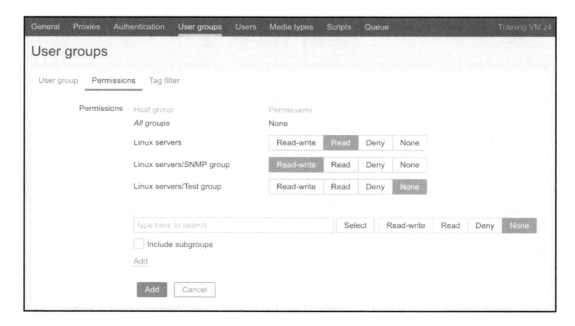

This looks about right, so click on the **Add** button at the bottom. The group will be successfully added, and we will be able to see it in the group list.

Let's get back to *Browser 2*. Navigate to **Monitoring** | **Latest data**. Click on **Select** next to the **Host groups** field. Great, both of the groups we selected when configuring the permissions are available. Mark the check-boxes next to them and click on **Select**. Then, click on **Apply**. Now, our new user can view data from all the hosts. But we also added write permissions to one group for this user, so *what's up with the* **Configuration** *menu?* Let's recall the user-creation process—*wasn't there something about user types?* Right, we were able to choose between three user types, and we chose **Zabbix User**, which, as we discussed, was not allowed to access configuration.

It is important to keep in mind that, at this time, a Zabbix User that has write access granted will not be able to configure things in the frontend, but they will get write access through the API. This could cause security issues. We will discuss the API in `Chapter 19`, *Working Closely with Data*.

To continue exploring user permissions, we'll create another, more powerful user. In *Browser 1*, go to **Administration | Users**, and click on the **Create user** button. Fill in these values:

- **Alias**: Enter `advanced_user`.
- **Name**: Enter `advanced`.
- **Surname**: Enter `user`.
- **Groups**: Click on **Select**, mark the checkbox next to **Zabbix administrators**, and click on **Select**.
- **Password**: Enter a password in both fields. You can use the same password as for `monitoring_user` to make it easier to remember.
- **Refresh**: Enter `60s`.
- **URL (after login)**: Let's have this user view a different page right after logging in. The overview page might do—enter `overview.php` here.

Now, switch to the **Permissions** tab and select **Zabbix Admin** from the **User type** drop-down. This is will make quite a big difference, as we will soon see:

When done, click on the **Add** button.

Let's use *Browser 2* now. In the upper-right corner, click the logout icon, and then log in as `advanced_user`. This user will land on the overview page, and this time, we can see the **Configuration** section. That's because we set the user type to **Zabbix Admin**. Let's check out what we have available there—open **Configuration** | **Hosts** and select **all** from the **Group** selection box:

How could there be no hosts available? We set this user as the **Zabbix Admin** type. should probably look at the user list back in *Browser 1*:

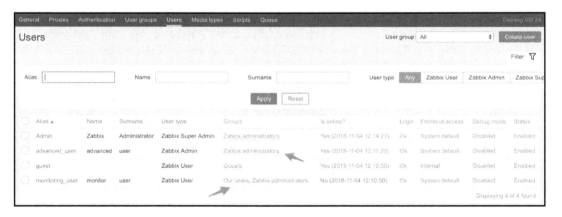

Here, we can easily spot our mistake—we added **advanced_user** to the **Zabbix administrators** group, but we set permissions for the **Our users** group. We'll fix that now, but this time, we'll use the user properties form. Click on **advanced_user** in the **Alias** column, and in the resulting form, click on **Select** next to the **Groups** field. Mark the checkbox next to **Our users**, and then click on **Select**:

When done, click on **Update**. In *Browser 2*, simply refresh the host's **Configuration** tab—it should reveal our hosts, **SNMP device**, and **snmptraps**, which **advanced_user** can configure.

Suddenly, we notice that we have granted configuration access to the snmptraps host this way, which we consider an important host that should not be messed with and that neither of our two users should have access to anyway. How can we easily restrict access to this host while still keeping it in the **SNMP devices** group?

In *Browser 1*, navigate to **Configuration** | **Host groups** and click on **Create host group**. Enter the following details:

- **Group name**: Enter Linux servers/Important SNMP hosts
- **Configuration** | **Hosts**: Go to host snmptraps and in the **Group** box, select **Linux servers/Important SNMP Hosts**

When done, click on **Update**.

Open **Administration** | **User groups**, click on **Our users** in the **Name** column, and switch to the **Permissions** tab. In the group details, click on the **Deny** box. Click select and select **Linux servers/Important SNMP Hosts**, and then click on the **Update** button:

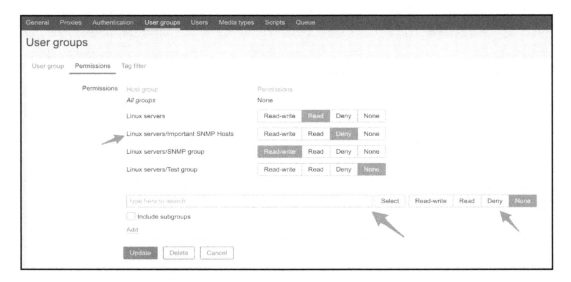

Now is the time to look at Browser 2. It should still show the host configuration with two hosts. Refresh the list and the snmptraps host will disappear. After our changes, advanced_user has configuration access only to the **SNMP device** host, and there will be no access to the monitoring of the snmptraps host at all, because we used **Deny**. For monitoring_user, nothing has changed—there was no access to the **SNMP devices** group before.

Permissions and maintenance

The maintenance configuration that we looked at in this chapter follows the rules of host group permissions in its own way. Host group permissions impact the way Zabbix administrators can configure maintenance entries:

- Zabbix admins can create new maintenance entries and include host groups and hosts they have write permissions on
- Zabbix admins can edit existing maintenance entries if they have write permissions on all the hosts and host groups included in those maintenance entries

Summary

In this chapter, we explored another aspect of host properties in Zabbix—host inventory. Host inventory may be manually populated, but the more useful aspect of it is its ability to receive values from any item in any inventory field. This still allows you to manually edit inventory fields that do not receive values from items.

Host and Host group maintenance allows us to create on-time or recurring maintenance entries on a daily, weekly, and monthly basis. Problems with hosts that are in maintenance are distinguished visually in the frontend, and in many views we can also choose not to show such problems at all.

It's important to remember the main rules about permissions in Zabbix:

- Permissions can be assigned to user groups only
- Permissions can be granted on host groups only

This means that, for fancy permission schemes, you might have to do some planning before starting to click around. We can also safely say that, to avoid mysterious problems in the future, every host should be in at least one host group, and every user should be in at least one user group. Additionally, there were two factors that combined to determine effective permissions—the permissions set for groups and the user type. We can try summarizing the interaction of these two factors:

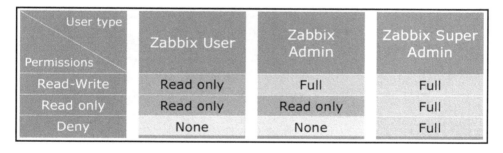

User type / Permissions	Zabbix User	Zabbix Admin	Zabbix Super Admin
Read-Write	Read only	Full	Full
Read only	Read only	Read only	Full
Deny	None	None	Full

Looking at the preceding table, we can see that the **Zabbix Super Admin** user type cannot be denied any permissions. On the other hand, **Zabbix User** cannot be given write permissions. Still, it is very important to remember that, at this time, they would gain write privileges through the Zabbix API.

With this knowledge, you should be able to group hosts, manage host inventories, and host maintenance, as well as create groups, sub-groups, and users, not to mention assign fine-grained permissions.

In the next chapter, we'll look at a way to check whether item values indicate a problem or not. While we have items collecting data, items in Zabbix are not used to configure thresholds or any other information to detect bad values. Items don't care what the values are as long as the values are arriving. To define what a problem is, a separate configuration entity, called a trigger, is used. Trigger logic, written as an expression, can range from very simple thresholds to fairly complex logical expressions.

Questions

1. Are status icons for Zabbix Active and passive?
2. How many status icons are there?
3. Can we collect data during a maintenance period?
4. Can we deny super admins access to hosts?

Further reading

Read the following articles for more information regarding what was covered in this chapter:

- **Supported macros**: https://www.zabbix.com/documentation/4.0/manual/appendix/macros/supported_by_location
- **Maintenance**: https://www.zabbix.com/documentation/4.0/manual/maintenance
- **User profile**: https://www.zabbix.com/documentation/4.0/manual/web_interface/user_profile?s[]=auto&s[]=logout#configuration

6
Detecting Problems with Triggers

We have gained quite comprehensive knowledge of what kind of information we can gather using items. However, so far, we only have a single thing we are actively monitoring, so we have only created a single trigger (we did that in Chapter 2, *Getting Your First Notification*). Triggers can do way more. Let's recap what a trigger is.

A trigger defines when a condition is considered worthy of attention. It *fires* (that is, becomes active) when item data, or a lack of it, matches a particular condition, such as too high system load or too low free disk space.

Let's explore both of these concepts in more detail now. In this chapter, we will look at the following topics:

- Getting to know more about the trigger-and-item relationship
- Discovering trigger dependencies
- Constructing trigger expressions
- Preventing trigger flapping
- Checking for missing data
- Using event tags for correlation

Triggers

Triggers are things that fire. They look at item data and raise a flag when the data does not fit whatever condition has been defined. As mentioned before, simply gathering data is nice, but awfully inadequate. If you want any historical data gathering, including notifications, there would have to be a person looking at all of the data all of the time, so we have to define thresholds at which we want the condition to be considered worth looking into. Triggers provide a way to define what those conditions are.

Earlier, we created a single trigger that was checking the system load on **A test host**. It checks whether the returned value is larger than a defined threshold. Now, let's check for some other possible problems with a server, for example, when a service is down. The SMTP service going down can be significant, so we will try to look for such a thing happening now.

Navigate to **Configuration | Hosts**, click on any of the **Triggers** links, and click on the **Create trigger** button. In the form that opens, we will fill in some values, as follows:

- **Name**: The content of this field will be used to identify the trigger in most places, so it should be human-readable. This time, enter SMTP service is down. Notice how we are describing what the problem actually is. As opposed to an item, which gathers statuses, a trigger has a specific condition to check, thus, the name reflects it. If we have a host that should never have a running SMTP service, we could create a trigger named SMTP service should not be running.

- **Expression**: This is probably the most important property of a trigger. What is being checked, and for what conditions, will be specified here. Trigger expressions can vary from very simple to complex ones. This time, we will create a simple one, and we will also use some help from the frontend for that. Click on the **Add** button next to the **Expression** field to open the expression building dialog. It has several fields to fill in as well, so let's look at what those are:
  - **Item**: Here, we can specify which item data should be checked. To do that, click on the **Select** button. Another popup will open. Select **Linux servers** from the **Group** drop-down, and then select **Another host** from the **Host** drop-down. We are interested in the SMTP service, so click on **SMTP server status** in the **Name** column. The popup will close, and the **Item** field will be populated with the name of the chosen item.

- **Function**: Here, we can choose the actual test to be performed. Perhaps we can try remembering what the SMTP server status item values were right, 1 was for the server running, and 0 was for the server being down. If we want to check when the last value was 0, the default function **Last (most recent)** seems to fit quite nicely, so we won't change it.
- **Last of (T)**: This is a function parameter if the function supports a time period. We used **180** in seconds for our first trigger to check the values during the previous 3 minutes, but when taking the last item value, a time period would make no sense.
- **Time shift**: We will discuss this functionality later in this chapter, in the *Relative thresholds or time shift* section.
- **Result**: This field allows us to set the constant used in the previous function. We want to find out whenever an SMTP server goes down (or the status is **0**). So, here, the default of **0** fits as well:

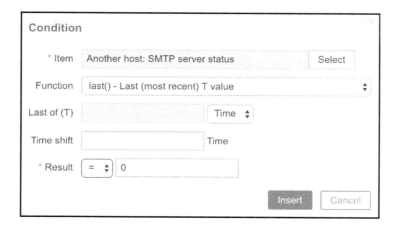

With the values set as illustrated in the previous screenshot, click on the **Insert** button. The **Expression** field will now be populated with the {Another host:net.tcp.service[smtp].last()}=0 trigger expression.

- **Severity**: There are five severity levels in Zabbix, and an additional **Not classified** severity level, as shown in the following screenshot:

We will consider this problem to be of average severity, so click on **Average**.

Before continuing, make sure that the SMTP server is running on another host, and then click on the **Add** button.

The **Allow manual close** option is useful if you like to acknowledge a problem from a log file for example. This allows you to keep the problem open and close it manually when acknowledging the problem.

Let's find out what it looks like in the overview now:

1. Go to **Monitoring** | **Overview** and make sure that the **Type** drop-down has **Triggers** selected
2. Then, expand the filter, choose **Any** in the **Acknowledge status** drop-down, and click on **Filter**:

Great, we can see that both hosts now have a trigger defined. Since the triggers differ, we also have two unused cells:

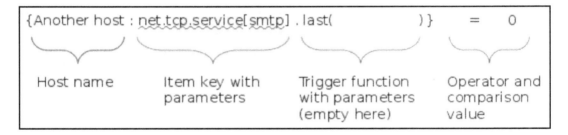

Let's look at the `trigger` expression in more detail. It starts with an opening curly brace, and the first parameter is the hostname. Separated by a colon is the item key—this is `net.tcp.service[smtp]` here. The item key must be replicated exactly as in the item configuration, including any spaces, quotes, and capitalization. After the exact item key comes a dot as a separator, which is followed by the more interesting and trigger-specific thing—the trigger function. One of the most common functions is being used here—`last()`. It always returns a single value from the item history. There are trigger functions that require at least a parameter to be passed, but for the `last()` function, this is optional, and if the first parameter is just a number, it is ignored.

Older versions of Zabbix required a parameter to be passed, even if it would have been ignored. It is still common to see syntax such as `last(0)` being used. Thus, `last(0)` and `last()` all return the latest single values for one item, so the use of the function **last(300) or last(5m)** function is incorrect.

On the other hand, if the first parameter is a number prefixed with a hash, it is not ignored. In that case, it works like an *n*th value specifier. For example, `last(#9)` would retrieve the 9th most recent value. As we can see, `last(#1)` is equal to `last(0)` or `last()`. Another overlapping function is `prev`. As the name might suggest, it returns the previous value; thus, `prev()` is the same as `last(#2)`.

Hostname, item key, trigger function, operators—they are all case-sensitive.

Continuing with the trigger expression, curly braces are closed to represent a string that retrieves a value, that is, host and item reference, followed by the trigger function. Then, we have an operator, which in this case is a simple equals sign. The comparison here is done with a constant number, `0`.

If item history is set to `0`, no values are stored and no triggers are evaluated, even if those triggers would only check the last value. This is different from previous versions of Zabbix, where only triggers referencing the last value would still work.

The trigger-and-item relationship

You might have noticed how items in Zabbix do not contain any configuration for the *quality* of the data—if the CPU load values arrive, the item does not care whether they are `0` or `500`. Any definition of a problem condition happens in a trigger, whether it's a simple threshold or something more complex.

And when we created this trigger, we could click on any of the **Triggers** links, but we paid attention to the host selected in the drop-downs when choosing the item. It actually does not matter which of those **Triggers** links we click on, as long as the proper host is selected in that popup, or we manually enter the correct host name.

A trigger does not belong to a host like an item does. A trigger is associated with any number of hosts it references items from.

If we clicked on **Triggers for host A** and then chose an item from host **B** for that trigger, the created trigger would not appear for host **A**, but would appear for host **B**.

This decoupling of problem conditions from the value collection has quite a lot of benefits. Not only is it easy to check for various different conditions on a single item, a single trigger may also span multiple items. For example, we could check the CPU load on a system in comparison with the user session count. If the CPU load is high and there are a lot of users on the system, we could consider that to be a normal situation. But if the CPU load is high while there is a small number of users on the system, it would be a problem. An example trigger is as follows:

```
{host:system.cpu.load.last()}>5 and {host:user.sessions.last()}<100
```

This would trigger if the CPU load was above 5, but only if there were fewer than 100 users on the system.

Remember that we cannot just start referencing items in trigger expressions and expect that to work. Items must exist before they can be used in trigger expressions.

A trigger could also reference items from multiple hosts. We could correlate a database statistic with the performance of an application on a different host, or free disk space on file servers with the number of users in the **Lightweight Directory Access Protocol (LDAP)**.

We will discuss and configure some slightly more advanced trigger expressions later in this chapter.

Trigger dependencies

We now have one service being watched. There are some more being monitored, so now we can try to create a trigger for an HTTP server. Let's assume that our host runs software that is a bit weird. The web service is a web email front-end, and it goes down whenever the SMTP server is unavailable. This means that the web service depends on the SMTP service.

Go to **Configuration** | **Hosts**, click on **Triggers** next to **Another host**, and then click on **Create trigger**. Fill in the following values:

- **Name:** Web service is down.

- **Expression**: Click on **Add**, and then again on **Select** next to the **Item** field. Make sure that **Linux servers** is selected in the **Group** drop-down and **Another host** in the **Host** drop-down, and then click on **Web server status** in the **Name** column. Both the function and its parameter are fine, so click on **Insert**:

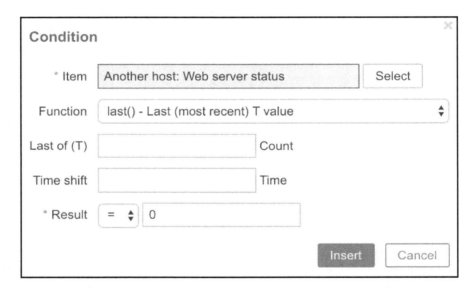

This inserts the {Another Host:net.tcp.service[http,,80].last()}=0 expression.

- **Severity**: The value of this field should be **Average**.

- **Description**: Trigger expressions can get very complex. Sometimes, the complexity can make it impossible to understand what a trigger is supposed to do without serious dissection. Comments provide a way to help somebody else, or yourself, understand the thinking behind such complex expressions later. While our trigger is still very simple, we might want to explain the reason for the dependency, so enter something such as Web service goes down if SMTP is inaccessible.

Now, switch to the **Dependencies** tab. To configure the dependency of the web frontend on the SMTP service, click on the **Add** link in the **Dependencies** section. In the resulting window, make sure that **Linux servers** is selected in the **Group** drop-down and **Another host** is selected in the **Host** drop-down, and then click on the only entry in the **Name** column, that is, **SMTP service is down**:

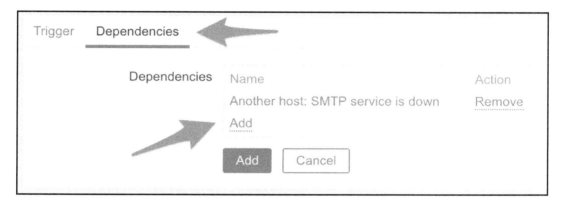

When done, click on the **Add** button at the bottom. Notice how, in the trigger list, trigger dependencies are listed in the **Name** column. This allows for a quick overview of any dependent triggers without opening the details of each trigger individually:

Both triggers in the dependency list and items in the **Expression** column act as links, allowing easy access to their details.

Item name colors in the **Expression** column match their state: green for **OK**, red for **Disabled**, and grey for **Unsupported**.

With the dependency set up, let's find out whether it changes anything in the front-end. Navigate to **Monitoring | Overview**, make sure **Type** is set to **Triggers**, expand the filter, then switch **Triggers status** to **Any**, and click on **Filter**:

The difference is visible immediately. Triggers involved in the dependency have arrows drawn over them. So, an upward arrow means something depends on this trigger—or *was it the other way around?* Luckily, you don't have to memorize that. Make sure that the web service and the SMTP service are down on another host first. Move the mouse cursor over the **SMTP service is down** trigger for **Another host**, which is the upper cell with the arrow:

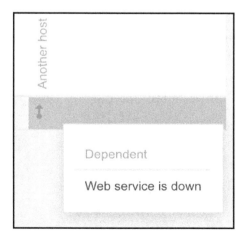

A popup appears, informing us that there are other triggers that are dependent on this one. Dependent triggers are listed in the popup. If we click on the arrow and then on **Description** from the popup menu, we will see the description we added in the trigger box before.

Let's see what happens if we turn our SMTP service on and keep our web service down. After a few seconds, when Zabbix notices that the SMTP service is up, we can see that our trigger has changed. We can now see that our web service is down and that the arrow is pointing downward, telling us that there is a dependency on this trigger:

The web server trigger has disappeared from the list and has been replaced by the SMTP server trigger. That's because Zabbix does not show dependent triggers if the dependency upstream trigger is in the **PROBLEM** state. This helps to keep the list short and concentrate on the problems that actually cause downtime.

Trigger dependencies are not limited to a single level. We will now add another trigger to the mix. Before we do that, we'll also create an item that will provide an easy way to manually change the trigger state without affecting system services. In the frontend, navigate to **Configuration | Hosts**, click on **Items** next to **Another host**, and then click on **Create item**. Fill in the following values:

- **Name**: Testfile exists
- **Key**: vfs.file.exists[/tmp/testfile]

When you are done, click on the **Add** button at the bottom. As the key might reveal, this item simply checks whether a particular file exists and returns 1 if it does, and 0 if it does not.

Using a constant filename in /tmp in real-life situations might not be desirable, as any user could create such a file. The reason we have chosen to do it in tmp is because we then don't have to care about the permissions for our file, as in real life, Zabbix would need the correct permissions.

In the bar above the **Item** list, click on **Triggers**, and then click on the **Create trigger** button. Enter these values:

- **Name**: Testfile is missing.
- **Expression**: Click on **Add** and then on **Select** next to the **Item** field. In the item list for **Another host**, click on **Testfile exists** in the **Name** column, and then click on **Insert** (again, the default function works for us). The **Expression** field is filled with the following expression:

    {Another Host:vfs.file.exists[/tmp/testfile].last()}=0

- **Severity**: The severity value should be **Warning**.

When you are done, click on the **Add** button at the bottom. Let's complicate the trigger chain a bit now. Click on the **SMTP service is down** trigger in the **Name** column, switch to the **Dependencies** tab, and click on **Add** in the **Dependencies** section. In the upcoming dialog, click on the **Testfile is missing** entry in the **Name** column. This creates a new dependency for the **SMTP service** trigger:

Click on **Update**. Now, we have created a dependency chain, consisting of three triggers—**Web service is down** depends on **SMTP service is down**, which in turn depends on **Testfile is missing**. Zabbix calculates chained dependencies, so all upstream dependencies are also taken into account when determining the state of a particular trigger—in this case, **Web service is down** depends on those two other triggers. This means that only a single trigger will be displayed in the **Monitoring** | **Overview** section. If we place the *most important* trigger at the bottom and the ones depending on it above, we would get a dependency chain like this:

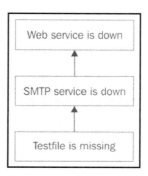

Now, we should move on to fixing the problems the monitoring system has identified. Let's start with the one at the top of the dependency chain—the missing file problem. On another host, execute the following:

```
$ touch /tmp/testfile
```

This should create an empty file and deal with the only trigger currently on the trigger list. Wait for the trigger list to update. You will see that the list gets updated and that the trigger that tells us that the **SMTP service is down** will be visible in the trigger box.

Looking at the list, we can see one big difference this time—the SMTP trigger now has two arrows, one pointing up and the other pointing down. Moving your cursor over them, you will discover that they denote the same thing as before—the triggers that this particular trigger depends on or that depend on this trigger. If a trigger is in the middle of a dependency chain, two arrows will appear, as has happened for the **SMTP service is down** trigger here.

The arrows here are shown in the same direction as in our previous schematic. We could say that the dependent trigger is *supported* by the *more important* trigger, as if we had bricks placed one on top of another. If any of the bricks disappear, the bricks above it will be in trouble.

Our `testfile` trigger worked as expected for the chained dependencies, so we can remove that dependency now:

1. Go to **Configuration | Hosts**, click on **Triggers** next to **Another host**, and click on the **SMTP service is down** trigger in the **Name** column
2. Switch to the **Dependencies** tab, click on **Remove** in the **Action** column, and click on the **Update** button

Note that you always have to save your changes in the editing form of any entity. In this case, simply removing the dependency won't be enough. If we navigate to some other section without explicitly updating the trigger, any modifications will be lost. Now, you can also restart any stopped services on another host.

Constructing trigger expressions

So far, we have used only very simple trigger expressions, comparing the last value to a constant. Fortunately, that's not all that trigger expressions can do. We will now try to create a slightly more complex trigger.

Let's say we have two servers, **A test host** and **Another host**, providing a redundant **SSH File Transfer Protocol** (SFTP) service. We would be interested in any one of the services going down. Navigate to **Configuration | Hosts**, and click on **Triggers** next to **Another host**. Then, click on the **Create trigger** button. Enter the following values:

- **Name:** `One SSH service is down.`
- **Expression:** Click on the **Add** button. In the resulting popup, click on **Select** next to the **Item** field. Make sure **Another host** is selected in the **Host** drop-down, click on the **SSH server status** item in the **Name** column, and then click on **Insert**. Now, position the cursor at the end of the inserted expression and enter `or` without quotes (that's a space, `or`, and a space). Again, click on the **Add** button. In the resulting popup, click on **Select** next to the **Item** field. Select **A test host** from the **Host** drop-down, click on the **SSH server status** item in the **Name** column, and click on **Insert**.
- **Severity:** The value of severity should be **Average** (remember, these are redundant services).

The final trigger expression should look like this:

```
{Another host:net.tcp.service[ssh].last()}=0 or {A test
host:net.tcp.service[ssh].last()}=0
```

When you are done, click on the **Add** button at the bottom.

In Zabbix versions preceding 2.4, a pipe character, |, was used instead of a lowercase `or`.

The process we followed here allowed us to create a more complex expression than simply comparing the value of a single item. Instead, two values are compared, and the trigger fires if either of them matches the comparison. That's what the `or` operator does. Another logical operator is `and`. Using the SSH server as an example trigger, we could create another trigger that would fire whenever both SSH instances go down. Getting the expression is simple, as we just have to modify that single operator, that is, change `or` to `and`, so that the expression looks like this:

```
{Another host:net.tcp.service[ssh].last()}=0 and {A test
host:net.tcp.service[ssh].last()}=0
```

Trigger expression operators are case-sensitive, so `AND` would not be a valid operator—a lowercase `and` should be used.

Trigger expressions also support other operators. In all the triggers we created, we used the most common one—the equality operator, =. We could also be using the inequality operator, <>. That would allow us to reverse the expression, like this:

```
{A test host:net.tcp.service[ssh].last()}<>1
```

Zabbix versions preceding 2.4 used the hash, #, instead of <> for the *not equal* comparison.

While not useful in this case, such a trigger is helpful when the item can have many values and we want the trigger to fire whenever the value isn't the expected one.

Trigger expressions also support the standard mathematical operators +, −, *, and /, and comparison operators <, >, <=, and >=, so complex calculations and comparisons can be used between item data and constants.

Let's create another trigger using a different function. In the frontend section **Configuration** | **Hosts**, choose **Linux servers** from the **Group** drop-down, click on **Triggers** next to **A test host**, and click on the **Create trigger** button. Then, enter the following values:

- **Name**: `Critical error from SNMP trap`
- **Expression**: `{A test host:snmptrap.fallback.str(Critical Error)}=1`
- **Severity**: The value of severity should be **High**

When you are done, click on the **Add** button at the bottom.

This time, we used another trigger function, `str()`. It searches for the specified string in the item data and returns `1` if it's found. The match is case-sensitive.

This trigger will change to the **OK** state whenever the last value for the item does not contain the string specified as the parameter. If we want to force this trigger to the **OK** state manually, we can just send a trap that does not contain the string the trigger is looking for. Sending a `success` value manually can also be useful when another system is sending SNMP traps. In the case where the problem trap is received successfully but the resolving trap is lost (because of network connectivity issues, or for any other reason), you might want to use such a fake trap to make the trigger in question go back to the **OK** state. If using the built-in trap-processing functionality, it would be enough to add trap information to the temporary file. If using the scripted solution with Zabbix trapper items, `zabbix_sender` could be used. SNMP trap management was discussed in `Chapter 4`, *Monitoring SNMP Devices*.

Preventing trigger flapping

With the service items and triggers we wrote, the triggers would fire right away, as soon as the service was detected as being down. This can be undesirable if we know that a service will be down for a moment during an upgrade because of log rotation or backup requirements. We can use a different function to achieve a delayed reaction in such cases. Replacing the `last()` function with `max()` allows us to specify a parameter, and thus react only when the item values have indicated a problem for some time. For the trigger to fire only when a service has not responded for 5 minutes, we could use an expression such as this:

```
{A test host:net.tcp.service[ssh].max(300)}=0
```

For this example to work properly, the item interval must not exceed 5 minutes. If the item interval exceeds the trigger function's checking time, only a single value will be checked, making the use of a trigger function such as `max()` useless.

Remember that, for functions that accept seconds as a parameter, we can also use the count of returned values by prefixing the number with #, like this:

```
{A test host:net.tcp.service[ssh].max(#5)}=0
```

In this case, the trigger would always check the five last returned values. Such an approach allows the trigger period to scale along if the item interval is changed, but it should not be used for items that can stop sending in data.

Using trigger functions is the easiest and most widely applied solution for potential trigger flapping. The previous service example checked that the maximum value over the last 5 minutes was 0, thus, we were sure that there are no values of 1, which would mean **service is up**.

For our CPU load trigger, we used the `avg(180)` function, checking the average value for the last 3 minutes. We could also have used `min(180)`—in this case, a single drop below the threshold would reset the 3-minute timer, even if the overall average was above the threshold. *Which one should you use?* That is entirely up to you, depending on what the functional requirements are. One way is not always better than the others.

Checking for missing data

Some items are always expected to provide values, such as the CPU load item. The problem condition for this item is usually value too large. But there are some items that are different, for example, an item with the `agent.ping` key. This item only tells us whether the agent is available to the server, and it only returns 1 when the agent is up. And yes, that's it—it does not send 0 when the agent is down; there is no value at all. We can't write a trigger with the `last()` function, as the last value is always 1. The same goes for `min()`, `max()`, and `avg()`. Luckily, there is a function we can use in this case: `nodata()`. It allows the trigger to fire if an item is missing data for some period of time. For example, if we created an `agent.ping` item on A test host, the trigger could look like this:

```
{A test host:agent.ping.nodata(300)=1}
```

Here, the `nodata()` function is checking whether this item is missing data for `300` seconds, or 5 minutes. If so, the trigger will fire. *What's the comparison with* `1`? All trigger functions in Zabbix return a number. The `nodata()` function returns `1` if the item is missing data and `0` if there's at least one value in the specified time period. Note that it might not be a good idea to try and guess what return values are available for a trigger function—if you are not sure, you'd better check the manual for details. To make it easier, I've added the link for you at the end of this chapter, in the *Further reading* section.

The `nodata()` function is said to be time-based. Normal trigger functions are evaluated when an item receives a new value. This makes a lot of sense for triggers against items such as the CPU load item we created earlier—when a value arrives, we compare it to the threshold. It wouldn't work that well with our `agent.ping` item, though. If values were coming in, everything would be good—the trigger expression would be evaluated, and this function would return `0`. If values stopped coming in, it would not get evaluated and would never fire. Then, if a new value arrived, the function would get evaluated, would see that new value, and declare that everything was perfect.

So, in this case, the trigger is not evaluated only when a new value comes in. Instead, this function is evaluated every 30 seconds. This interval is hardcoded. To be more specific, any trigger that includes at least one time-based function in the expression is recalculated every 30 seconds. With the 30-second interval, you should never use a parameter lower than 30 for the `nodata()` function. To be safe, never use a parameter lower than 60 seconds. In Zabbix version 4.0.0, the following trigger functions are time-based:

- `date()`
- `dayofmonth()`
- `dayofweek()`
- `nodata()`
- `now()`
- `time()`

Refer to the Zabbix manual if you're using a later version—there might be changes to this list.

 Starting from Zabbix 3.2, `nodata()`, `date()`, `dayofmonth()`, `dayofweek()`, `now()`, and `time()` functions are also calculated for unsupported items. The other functions require the referenced item to be in a supported state.

Triggers that time out

There are systems that send a trap upon failure, but no recovery trap. In such cases, manually resetting every single case isn't an option. Fortunately, we can construct a trigger expression that times out by using the function we just discussed—nodata(). An expression that would make the P state timeout after 10 minutes looks like this:

```
{Another host:snmptrap.fallback.str(Critical Error)}=1 and
{Another host:snmptrap.fallback.nodata(600)}=0
```

For now, we want to have more precise control over how this trigger fires, so we won't change the trigger expression to the previous example's.

Note that adding the nodata() function to a trigger will make that trigger reevaluate every 30 seconds. Doing this with a large amount of triggers can have a significant impact on the performance of the Zabbix server.

Triggers with adaptable thresholds

There are monitored metrics that have rather different threshold needs, depending on the possible range of the value, even when measuring in percentages instead of absolute values. For example, using bytes for a disk space trigger will not work that well when disks can range from a few dozen megabytes to hundreds of terabytes or even petabytes. Applying our knowledge of trigger expressions, we could vary our threshold depending on the total disk size. For this, we will have to monitor both free and total disk space:

```
(
    {host:vfs.fs.size[/,total].last()}<=100GB
        and
    {host:vfs.fs.size[/,pfree].last()}<10
) or
(
    {host:vfs.fs.size[/,total].last()}>100GB
        and
    {host:vfs.fs.size[/,pfree].last()}<5
)
```

A trigger that requires item values like this with the last function will only work when all involved items have collected at least one value. In this case, two items are referenced, each twice.

The previous expression has been split for readability. In Zabbix versions prior to 2.4, it would have to be entered on a single line, but since Zabbix 2.4, newlines and tab characters are supported in trigger expressions.

This expression will make the trigger act differently in two cases of disk configuration:

- Total disk space being less than or equal to 100 GB
- Total disk space being more than 100 GB

Depending on the amount of total disk space, a different threshold is applied to the free disk space as a percentage—10% for smaller disks and 5% for larger disks.

You might easily expand this to have different thresholds for disks between 100 MB, 10 GB, 100 GB, 10 TB, and higher.

Triggers with a limited period

We discussed hosts and host group maintenance in `Chapter 5`, *Managing Hosts, Users, and Permissions*. That allowed us to stop alerting, but when doing so, the smallest entity the maintenance could affect was a host; we could not create a maintenance for a specific trigger without the use of tags. While this is slightly different functionally, we could limit the time for which a trigger is active on the trigger level, too. To do so, we can use several of those time-based trigger functions. Taking our CPU load trigger as an example, we could completely ignore it on Mondays (perhaps there's some heavy reporting done on Mondays):

```
{A test host:system.cpu.load.avg(180)}>1 and
{A test host:system.cpu.load.dayofweek()}<>1
```

The `dayofweek()` function returns a number with Monday starting at 1, and the previous expression works unless the returned value is 1. We have to append a trigger function to an item even if it does not take item values at all, such as in this case. It is quite counter-intuitive seeing the `dayofweek()` function after the CPU load item, but it's a best practice to reuse the same item.

We could also make this trigger ignore weekend mornings:

```
{A test host:system.cpu.load.avg(180)}>1 and
{A test host:system.cpu.load.dayofweek()}>5 and
{A test host:system.cpu.load.time()}<100000
```

Here, we are checking for the day value to be above 5 (with 6 and 7 being Saturday and Sunday). Additionally, the trigger `time()` function is being used. This function returns the time in `HH:MM:SS` format, so our comparison makes sure it is not 10:00:00 yet.

Note that this method completely prevents the trigger from firing, so we won't get alerts, won't see the trigger on the frontend, and there won't be any events being generated.

We will also discuss a way to limit alerts themselves based on time in `Chapter 7`, *Acting Upon Monitored Conditions*.

Relative thresholds or time shift

Normally, trigger functions look at the latest values—`last()` gets the last value and `min()`, `max()`, and `avg()` look at the specified time period, counting back from the current time. For some functions, we may also specify an additional parameter called **time shift**. This will make the function act as if we had traveled back in time; in other aspects, it will work exactly the same. One feature this allows is creating a trigger with relative thresholds. Instead of a fixed value such as 1, 5, or 10 for a CPU load trigger, we can make it fire if the load has increased compared to a period some time ago:

```
{A test host:system.cpu.load.avg(3600)}/
{A test host:system.cpu.load.avg(3600,86400)}>3
```

In this example, we have modified the time period that we are evaluating—it has been increased to one hour. We have stopped comparing the result with a fixed threshold; instead, we are looking at the average values from some time ago—specifically, 86400 seconds, or one day, ago. Functionally, this expression checks whether the average CPU load for the last hour exceeds the average CPU load for the same hour one day ago more than 3 times.

This way, the CPU load can be 1, 5, or 500—this trigger does not care about the absolute value, just whether it has increased more than three times.

The second parameter for the avg() function we used was the time shift. To understand how it gets the values, let's assume that we have added a new item and that the time shift is set to 1 hour. It is **13:00:00** now, and a new value for the item has come in. We had previous values for 1 hour at **12:10:00**, **12:20:00**, and so on, up to **12:50:00**. The time shift of one hour would get no values at all, as it would first step 1 hour back to **12:00:00** and then look for all the values 1 hour ago—but the first value we had was at **12:10:00**:

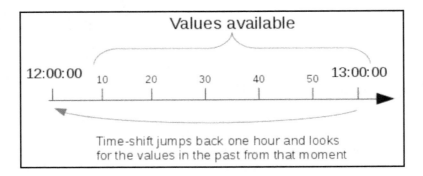

As of Zabbix version 4.0.0, the following functions support the time shift parameter:

- avg()
- band()
- count()
- delta()
- forecast()
- last()
- max()
- min()
- percentile()
- strlen()
- sum()
- timeleft()

> Triggers always operate on history data, never on trend data. If history is kept for one day, a time shift of one day should not be used, as it is likely to miss some values in the evaluation.

Verifying system time

Zabbix can verify a huge number of things, among which is the current time on monitored systems. Let's create a quick configuration to do just that. We will create an item to collect the current time and then a trigger to compare that time with the current time on the Zabbix server. Of course, for this to work properly, the clock on the Zabbix server must be correct—otherwise, we would complain that it is wrong on all the other systems.

The first thing is the item to collect—the current time. Go to **Configuration | Hosts**, click on **Items** next to **Another host**, and then click on **Create item**. Fill in the following values:

- **Name**: Local time
- **Key**: system.localtime
- **Units**: unixtime

When you are done, click on the **Add** button at the bottom. This item returns the current time as a Unix timestamp. While a unit is not required for our trigger, we entered unixtime there. This will translate the timestamp to a human-readable value in the frontend. We discussed item units in more detail in Chapter 3, *Monitoring with Zabbix Agents and Basic Protocols*.

In the bar above the item list, click on **Triggers**, then click on the **Create trigger** button. Enter these values:

- **Name**: Incorrect clock on {HOST.NAME}.
- **Expression**: Click on **Add** and then on **Select** next to the **Item** field. In the item list for **Another host**, click on **Local time** in the **Name** column and click on **Insert**. The **Expression** field is filled with this expression: {Another host:system.localtime.last()}=0. This isn't actually what we need, but we tried to avoid the function drop-down here, so we will edit the expression manually. Change it to read this: {Another host:system.localtime.fuzzytime(30)}=0. (Another option is to use the drop-down, select the fuzzytime() function from the list, and add 30 for time.)
- **Severity**: Select the **Warning** option.

When you're done, click on the **Add** button at the bottom. The `fuzzytime()` function accepts a time period as a parameter. This makes it compare the timestamp of the item with the current time on the Zabbix server. If the difference is greater than the time specified in the parameter, it returns 0, which is the problem condition we wanted to catch. Again, if you are not sure about the return value of some trigger function, you'd better check the Zabbix manual. You can change your local time by using the `timedatectl` command.

 Don't forget that an incorrect time on the Zabbix server can result in a huge number of alerts about all other systems.

Human-readable constants

Using plain numeric constants is fine while we're dealing with small values. When an item collects data that is bigger, such as disk space or network traffic, such an approach becomes very tedious. You have to calculate the desired value, and from looking at it later, it is usually not obvious how large it really is. To help here, Zabbix supports so-called **suffix multipliers** in expressions—the abbreviations **K**, **M**, **G**, **T**, and so on are supported. This results in shorter and way more easy-to-read trigger expressions. For example, checking disk space for a host called `host` looks like this at first:

```
{host:vfs.fs.size[/,free].last()}<16106127360
```

With suffix multipliers, it becomes this:

```
{host:vfs.fs.size[/,free].last()}<15G
```

This is surely easier to read and modify if the need arises.

Another type of constant is time-based. So far, we've only used time in seconds for all the trigger functions, but that tends to be a bit unreadable. For example, 6 hours would be 21,600, and it just gets worse with longer periods. The following time-based suffixes are supported:

- s: seconds
- m: minutes
- h: hours
- d: days
- w: weeks

The s suffix would simply be discarded, but all others would work as multipliers. Thus, 21,600 would become 6h, which is much more readable. The SSH service trigger example we looked at earlier would also be simpler:

```
{A test host:net.tcp.service[ssh].max(5m)}=0
```

We have now covered the basics of triggers in Zabbix. There are many more functions that allow the evaluation of various conditions that you will want to use later on. The frontend function selector does not contain all of them, so sometimes you will have to look them up and construct the expression manually. For a full and up-to-date function list, refer to the official documentation at https://www.zabbix.com/documentation/4.0/manual/appendix/triggers/functions.

Customizing how triggers are displayed

With all the details explored regarding trigger configuration, we should be able to create powerful definitions on what to consider a problem. There are also several configuration options available to customize the way triggers are displayed.

Triggering severities

Navigate to **Administration** | **General** and choose **Trigger severities** in the drop-down in the upper-right corner:

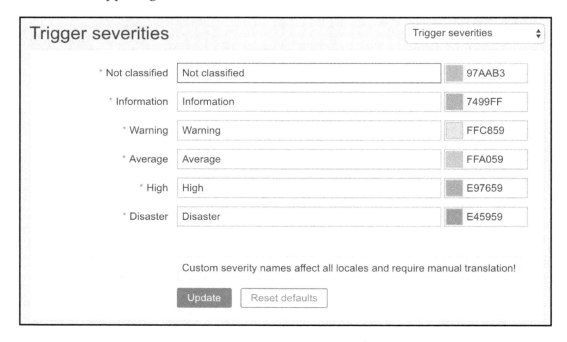

In this section, we can customize severity labels and their colors. As the information box at the bottom of this page says, changing severity labels will require updating translations that anybody might be using in this Zabbix instance.

Triggering display options

Navigate to **Administration** | **General** and choose **Trigger displaying options** in the drop-down in the upper-right corner:

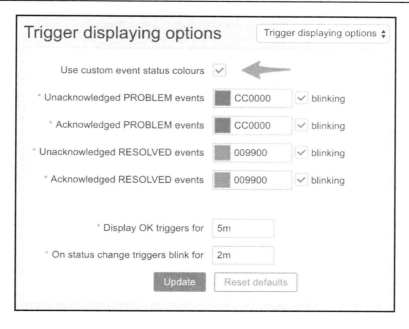

It's not just trigger severity labels that we can modify; we can even change the default red and green colors, which are used for the **PROBLEM/OK** states. Even better, the color can be different, depending on whether the problem has been acknowledged or not. We discussed trigger state blinking in **Monitoring | Overview** and other frontend sections for 30 minutes. On this page, we can selectively enable or disable blinking based on the trigger state and acknowledgement status, as well as customize the length of time for which a trigger change is considered recent enough to blink. The default can be seen here, defined in seconds: 2m. The **Use custom event status colours** option allows us to turn on the customization of colors for acknowledged/unacknowledged problems. This option was added in version 4.0.

Event details

After we have configured the triggers, they generate events, which in turn are acted upon by actions.

We looked at a high-level schema of information flow inside Zabbix, including item, trigger, and event relationships in `Chapter 2`, *Getting Your First Notification.*

But *can we see more details about them somewhere?* In the frontend, go to **Monitoring |** **Problems**, and click on date and time in the **Time** column for the latest entry with a **Problem** status.

If you see no problems listed, expand the filter, click on **Reset and** **select History from the Show option**, and make sure that the time period that's selected is long enough to include some events, for example, to last 1 day.

This opens up the **Event details** page, which allows us to determine the event flow with more confidence. It includes things such as event and trigger details and action history. The **Event list** section in the lower-right corner, which includes the **previous 20** events, acts as a control, allowing you to click on any of these events and once again see the previous 20 events from the chosen event. As this list only shows events for a single trigger, it is very handy if you need to figure out the timeline of one, isolated problem:

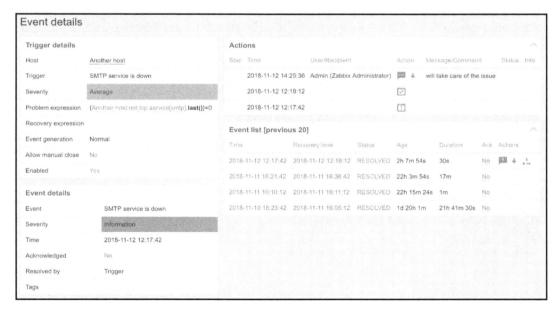

Another handy feature that's new in version 4.0 is, as you can see, the use of icons. They are visible in multiple places, such as, for example, in the problem page and the event page. They show us a quick overview of what happened with a specific item. Here is a list of icons that you might encounter and their meaning:

 - comments have been made. The number of comments is also displayed.

 - problem severity has been increased (e.g. Information → Warning)

 - problem severity has been decreased (e.g. Warning → Information)

 - problem severity has been changed, but returned to the original level (e.g. Warning → Information → Warning)

 - actions have been taken. The number of actions is also displayed.

 - actions have been taken, at least one is in progress. The number of actions is also displayed.

 - actions have been taken, at least one has failed. The number of actions is also displayed.

Event generation and recovery expression

Trigger events are generated whenever a trigger changes state. A trigger can be in one of the following states:

- **OK**: The normal state, when the trigger expression evaluates to `false`
- **PROBLEM**: A problem state, when the trigger expression evaluates to `true`
- **UNKNOWN**: A state when Zabbix cannot evaluate the trigger expression, usually when there is missing data

> Refer to `Chapter 20`, *Zabbix Maintenance*, for information on how to get notifications about triggers becoming **UNKNOWN**.

No matter whether a trigger goes from **OK** to **PROBLEM**, **UNKNOWN**, or any other state, an event is generated.

> There is also a way to customize this with the **PROBLEM events generation mode** multiple option in the trigger properties. We will discuss this option in `Chapter 10`, *Advanced Item Monitoring*.

We found out before that we can use certain trigger functions to avoid changing the trigger state after every change in data. By accepting a time period as a parameter, these functions allow us to react only if a problem has been going on for a while. But what if we would like to be notified as soon as possible, while still avoiding trigger flapping if values fluctuate near our threshold? Here, a specific Zabbix macro (or variable) helps and allows us to construct trigger expressions that have some sort of hysteresis—the remembering of state.

A common case is measuring temperatures. For example, a very simple trigger expression would read like this:

```
server:temp.last()>20
```

It would fire when the temperature was 21 and go to the **OK** state when it's 20. Sometimes, temperature fluctuates around the set threshold value, so the trigger goes on and off all the time. This is undesirable, so an improved expression in versions before 3.2 would look like this:

```
({TRIGGER.VALUE}=0 and {server:temp.last()}>20) or
({TRIGGER.VALUE}=1 and {server:temp.last()}>15)
```

As this was rather complex, this feature was replaced in Zabbix 3.2 with a new, more user-friendly **Recovery expression**. The only thing we need to do now in our trigger is select the **Recovery expression** box from the **OK event generation** option:

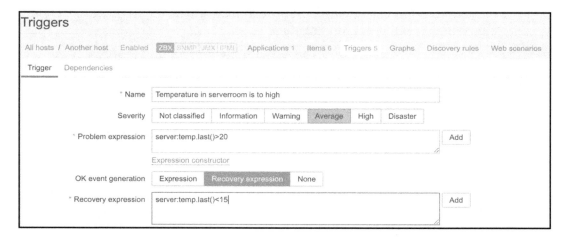

You can also think of this as the trigger having two thresholds. One for the error state and one for the OK state. We expect it to switch to the **PROBLEM** state when the values pass the upper threshold at 20 degrees but resolve only when they fall below the lower threshold at 15 degrees:

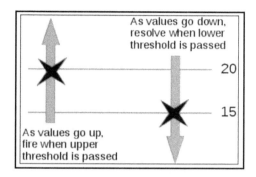

How does that change the situation when compared to the simple expression that only checked for temperatures over 20 degrees? Let's have a look:

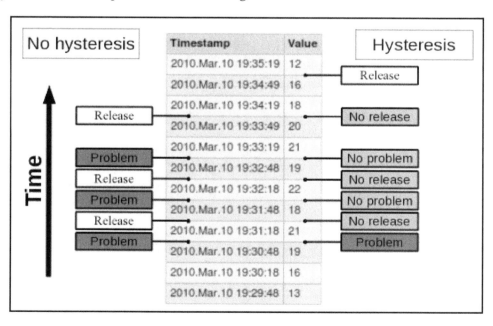

In this example case, we have avoided two unnecessary problem states, and that usually means at least two notifications as well. This is another way of preventing trigger flapping.

Using event tags for correlation

Correlation in Zabbix can be used on two different levels:

- On trigger level
- On Global level

Trigger level-based correlation: As the name suggests, this occurs on triggers and can be used to relate different problems to a solution by closing, for example, a trigger. Trigger-based event correlation, in short, allows us to correlate separate problems reported by one trigger. It's very useful for log-monitoring, SNMP traps, and so on. In Chapter 10, *Advanced Item Monitoring*, we will see how we can use trigger-based correlation in our log monitoring to close triggers based on tags.

Global-based correlation: This is a way to correlate problems to a solution based on different triggers by making use of global rules. Global event correlation allows us to do some preprocessing of problems based on the event tag information on a trigger. Here, we will create a global correlation rule and, based on this rule, problems can be closed. This allows us to focus on the root cause of the problems instead of having to look through a list of trigger problems.

Let's have a look at our event correlation screen by going to **Configuration** | **Event correlation** and clicking on **Create correlation**:

When creating a new condition, we have several options to chose from:

- **Old event tag**: Specify the old event tag for matching
- **New event tag**: Specify the new event tag for matching
- **New event host group**: Specify the new event host group for matching
- **Event tag pair**: Specify new event tag and old event tag for matching (values are used)
- **Old event tag value**: Specify the old event tag name and value for matching
- **New event tag value**: Specify the new event tag name and value for matching

Let's imagine we have a trigger on a MS SQL Server that monitors a log for this application and detects an error. Let's also imagine we have added a tag on this trigger with the name `Application` with the problem tag:

Next, we have another trigger that monitors the service state of this MS SQL Server with the `Service` tag and `stopped` value:

We now have two triggers in error state, one that warns us of the errors in the log file and another trigger that warns us that the service is stopped. What we have to do now in our global correlation rule is create a rule that closes the old event and only keeps the new event open:

In our condition, we will create a rule that says that **Old event tag Application equals Ms SQL Server** and that the new tag service should contain stopped in our **Operations** tab. We can then add that old events can be closed by Zabbix:

This will allow us to focus on only one problem by closing the old event, meaning that we are only focusing on the newly created event.

Of course, it can happen that we first see the service as stopped and then the error in the log file. For cases like this, we have to create another correlation rule.

Summary

This chapter was packed with concepts concerning reacting to events that happen in your monitored environment. We learned how to describe conditions that should be reacted to as trigger expressions. Triggers themselves have useful functionality with dependencies, and we can make them depend on each other. We also explored several ways of reducing trigger flapping right in the trigger expression, including using functions such as `min()`, `max()`, and `avg()`, as well as trigger hysteresis.

Among other trigger tricks, we looked at the following:

- Using the `nodata()` function to detect missing data
- Using the same `nodata()` function to make a trigger time out
- Creating triggers that have different used disk space threshold values based on the total disk space

- Creating triggers that only work during a specific time period
- Having a relative threshold, where recent data is compared with the situation some time ago

 Remember that if item history is set to 0, no triggers will work, even the ones that only check the very last value.

Trigger configuration has a lot of things that can both make life easier and introduce hard-to-spot problems. Hopefully, the coverage of the basics here will help you leverage the former and avoid the latter.

With the trigger knowledge available to us, we will take the time in the next chapter to see where we can go after a trigger has fired. We will explore actions that will allow us to send emails, or even run commands, in response to a trigger firing.

We have seen the different sorts of events and we have seen how we can configure global event correlation in Zabbix.

Questions

1. Can we use time notations like 5 m in our trigger functions or do we need to write it in seconds?
2. Does Zabbix have support for host dependencies?
3. How do I know if my trigger that fired has dependencies?
4. Does Zabbix have support for recovery expressions on triggers?

Further reading

Read the following articles for more information regarding what was covered in this chapter:

- **Trigger expression**: https://www.zabbix.com/documentation/4.0/manual/config/triggers/expression
- **Unit symbols**: https://www.zabbix.com/documentation/4.0/manual/appendix/suffixes

7
Acting upon Monitored Conditions

Now that we know more about triggers, let's see what we can do when they fire. Just seeing a problem on the frontend is not enough; we probably want to send notifications using email or SMS, or maybe even attempt to remedy the problem automatically.

Actions ensure something is done in connection with a trigger firing. Let's try to send notifications and automatically execute commands.

In this chapter, we will cover the following topics:

- Limiting conditions when alerts are sent
- Sending out notifications
- Escalating once a threshold is reached
- Using scripts as media
- Integrating with issue management systems
- Remote commands
- Understanding global scripts

Actions

The trigger list would be fine to look at, and would be way better than looking at individual items, but that would still be an awful lot of manual work. That's where actions come in, providing notifications and other methods to react upon in the event of a change in conditions.

The most common method is email. If you had an action set up properly when we first configured a fully working chain of item-trigger-action in Chapter 2, *Getting Your First Notification*, you will have received an email whenever we started or stopped a service, created the test file, and so on. Now, let's look at what actions can do in more detail.

Limiting conditions when alerts are sent

Our previous action, which we created in Chapter 2, *Getting Your First Notification*, matched any event, as we had not limited its scope in any way. Now, we will try matching only a specific condition:

1. Navigate to **Configuration | Actions**, select **Triggers** as the event source, and then click on **Create action**.

   The following activities rely on a correctly configured email setup (done in Chapter 2, *Getting Your First Notification*) and a user group called Our users (added in Chapter 5, *Managing Hosts, Users, and Permissions*).

2. In the **Name** field, enter SNMP action.

3. Now, look at the **Conditions**. By default, there were two conditions that were already added in earlier versions. In Zabbix 4, this is no longer the case, and **Maintenance status** has been renamed to **Problem is suppressed,** while the option **Trigger value** has made way for **Trigger severity**. A few new conditions have been added so that we can react based on our tags.

4. For now, let's add **Problem is not suppressed** and **Trigger severity is greater than or equals Not classified**:

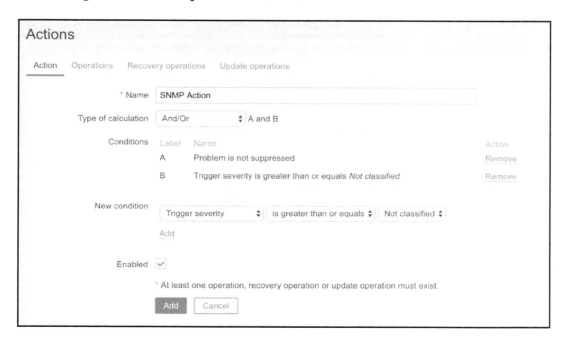

For our action right now, let's leave the default conditions in place and move to operations. Operations are the actual activities that are performed:

1. Switch to the **Operations** tab and click on the **New** link in the **Action operations** block. To start with, we will configure a very simple action—sending an email to a single user group. This form can be fairly confusing.

2. Click on **Add** in the **Send to User groups** section, and, in the window that appears, click on **Our users**. The result should look like this:

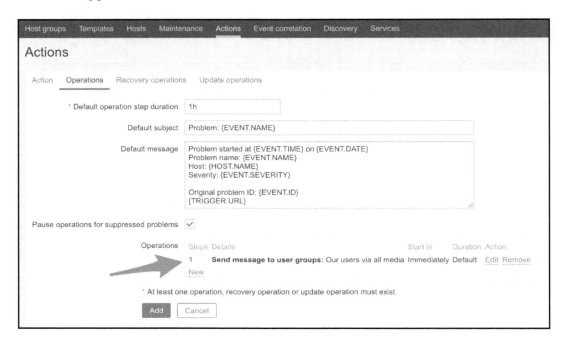

3. Continue from here and click on the main **Add** link in the **Operation details** block (just below the **Conditions** section).

4. Finally, click on the **Add** button at the bottom. As we want to properly test how emails are sent, we should now disable the action we added previously.

5. Mark the checkbox next to **SNMP Action**, click on the **Disable** button at the bottom, and then confirm disabling in the popup.

Now, we require triggers on our **SNMP trap** items.

Navigate to **Configuration | Hosts**, click on **Triggers** next to **snmptraps**, and click on **Create trigger**. Enter the following information:

- **Name**: SNMP trap has arrived on {HOST.NAME}
- **Expression**: {snmptraps:snmptraps.nodata(30)}=0
- **Severity**: **Information**

Such a trigger will fire whenever a trap arrives, and clear itself approximately 30 seconds later. We discussed the `nodata()` trigger function in `Chapter 6`, *Detecting Problems with Triggers*. When done, click on the **Add** button at the bottom.

We will also want to have a trigger fire on **Another host**:

1. Let's copy the one we just created. Mark the checkbox next to it and click on **Copy**.
2. Choose **Hosts** in the **Target type** drop-down, **Linux servers** in the **Group** drop-down, and then select **Another host**:

When done, click on **Copy**.

  To prevent our trap going in the item that has no trigger against it, go to **Configuration | Hosts**, click on **Items** next to **Another host**, and either remove the **Experimental SNMP trap** item, or change its item key.

One link is still missing—none of the two users in the `Our users` group has user media defined. To add media, navigate to **Administration | Users**, and click on **monitoring_user** in the **Alias** column. Switch to the **Media** tab and click **Add**, enter the email address in the **Send to** field, and then close the popup by clicking on **Add**. We now have to save this change as well, so click on **Update**.

Now, we have to make a trigger fire. Execute the following from **Another host**:

```
$ snmptrap -Ci -v 2c -c public <Zabbix server> "" "NET-SNMP-
MIB::netSnmpExperimental" NET-SNMP-MIB::netSnmpExperimental s
"Critical Error"
```

Refer to `Chapter 4`, *Monitoring SNMP Devices*, for information on receiving SNMP traps.

Replace `<Zabbix server>` with the IP or DNS name of the Zabbix server. This value should end up in the `snmptraps` item in `Another host` and make the associated trigger fire. You can verify that the trigger fires in the **Monitoring | Triggers** section:

To make our next trap end up in the `snmptraps` host, go to **Configuration | Hosts**, click on **Items** next to **Another host**, and either remove the `smptraps` item or change its item key.

Then, send another trap from `Another host`:

```
$ snmptrap -Ci -v 2c -c public <Zabbix server> "" "NET-SNMP-
MIB::netSnmpExperimental" NET-SNMP-MIB::netSnmpExperimental s
"Critical Error"
```

As `Another host` no longer has any `snmptraps` item, this value should go to the `snmptraps` host instead. By now, we should have received an email from our new action. Let's check out another view—the event view. Open **Monitoring | Events** and, take a look at the final few entries:

If you don't see the SNMP events, make sure that both the **Group** and **Host** drop-downs have **all** selected.

We can see that three events have been successfully registered by now; first, the SNMP trap item reporting an error on **Another host**, then resolving it, and, finally, the trigger on the **snmptraps** host has fired. But the last column, titled **ACTIONS**, is notably different. While the first **PROBLEM** event has some numbers listed, the most recent one has nothing. Here's why.

In Zabbix, only users that have at least read-only access to at least one of the systems, referenced in the trigger, receive notifications.

The `snmptraps` host was located in the important **SNMP host group**, and permissions on it for our user group were explicitly set to `deny`.

That allows us to overlap **host group** permissions with action conditions to create quite sophisticated notification scenarios.

Additional action conditions

So far, we have only used the two default action conditions. Actually, Zabbix provides quite a lot of different conditions that determine when an action is invoked. Let's look at some examples of what other conditions are available:

- **Application**: Allows us to limit actions to specific applications. For example, an action could only react when items belonging to the MySQL application are involved. This is a free-form field, so it must match the actual application name. We may also match or negate a sub-string.
- **Host**: Allows us to single out an important (or unimportant) host for action invocation.
- **Host group**: Similar to the **Host** condition, this one allows us to impose a limit based on the host group membership.
- **Problem is suppressed**: Specifies whether the problem is suppressed—yes or no.
- **Tag**: Specifies what event tag to include or exclude, or whether it should contain a specific part.
- **Tag value:** Same as tag, but relates to the value of the tag.
- **Template**: Equals, or not, a specific template.
- **Trigger**: This condition allows us to match individual, specific triggers.
- **Trigger name**: A bit more flexible than the previous one, with this condition, we can limit invocation based on the trigger name—for example, only acting upon triggers that have the `database` string in their names.
- **Trigger severity**: We can limit the action to happen just for the highest two trigger severities, or maybe just for a couple of the lowest severities.
- **Time period**: Operations may only be carried out if a problem has occurred in a specified time period, or they can be suppressed for a specified time period instead.

There are more action conditions that are useful in specific use cases—check the list in the action condition configuration so that you're able to use them later.

Complex conditions

In the action properties, in the **Conditions** tab, there was also a **Type of calculation** drop-down at the very top:

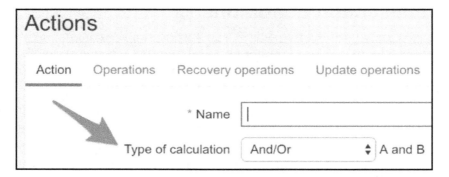

It appears when the action has two or more conditions; hence, as far as we are concerned, it was always present; the default action came with two conditions already. Now, let's find out what functionality it offers:

- **And**: All the conditions must be true for the action to match
- **Or**: It is enough for one condition to be true for the action to match
- **And/Or**: Conditions of the same type are evaluated as **Or**; conditions of different types are evaluated as **And**
- **Custom expression**: Full freedom option—you write a formula to define how the conditions should be evaluated

The first two options are clear enough. **And/Or** automatically creates the expression and the logic is based on condition types. For example, let's say we have the following conditions:

- **A**: `Application = MySQL`
- **B**: `Application = PostgreSQL`
- **C**: `Trigger severity = High`
- **D**: `Host group = Database servers`

The And/Or option would create a formula: `(A or B) and C and D`. This works in a lot of situations, but we might add another condition for a **Host group**, as follows:

- **E**: `Host group = Production servers`

Actual placeholder letters are likely to be different in the Zabbix frontend as the conditions are ordered. Adding or removing a condition can change the letters of the existing conditions—be careful when using custom expressions and when conditions are changed.

The formula would be (A or B) and C and (D or E). The new **Host group** condition, being the same type, is *or-ed* with the previous **Host group** condition. It is probably not what the user intended, though. In this case, the desired condition was *hosts that are both in the database server and production server groups*. The **And/or** option no longer helps help, so we can use a **Custom expression**. In this case, we would simply type the formula in the input field provided:

```
(A or B) and C and (D and E)
```

Grouping for D and E here is optional; we added it only for clarity.

The situation is even more complicated when negating a number of conditions. If you would like to skip an action in case a problem occurs for a host in either group A or group B, having two not host group conditions such as (A and B) wouldn't work; it would only match if a host was in both groups at the same time. Making the expression check for (A or B) would match unless a host is in both host groups again. For example, if the problem happens on a host that's in group A, Zabbix would check that the host matched the first condition. It would tell that the action shouldn't be performed, but there's the second part including *or*. The host wouldn't be part of group B, and thus the action would be performed. Unfortunately, there's no simple solution for such cases. Creating two actions, each only negating a single host group, would work.

Dependencies and actions

Another way to limit the notifications sent is trigger dependencies, which come in really handy here. If a trigger that is dependent on an already active trigger fires, we have seen the effect on the frontend—the dependent trigger did not appear in the list of active triggers. This is even better with actions; no action is performed in such a case. If you know that a website relies on a **Network File System** (**NFS**) server, and have set a corresponding dependency, the NFS server going down would not notify you about the website problem. When there's a problem to solve, not being flooded with emails is a good thing.

There's a possible race condition if the item for the dependent trigger is checked more often. In such a case, the dependent trigger might fire first, and the other one a short time later, thereby still producing two alerts. While this is not a huge problem for the trigger displaying in the frontend, this can be undesirable if it happens when actions are involved. If you see such false positives on a frequent basis, change the item intervals so that the dependent one always has a slightly longer interval.

Media limits for users

We looked at what limits an action can impose, but there are also possible limits per media. Navigate to **Administration** | **Users** and click on **Admin** in the **ALIAS** column. Switch to the **Media** tab and click on **Add**, next to the only media we have created here:

 Admin level users may change their own media. Normal users cannot change their own media.

When considering limits, we are mostly interested in two sections here—**When active** and **Use if severity**.

As the name indicates, the first of these allows us to set a period when media is used. Days are represented by the numbers 1-7, and a 24-hour clock notation of HH:MM–HH:MM is used. Several periods can be combined, separated by semi- colons. This way, it is possible to send an SMS to a technician during weekends and at night, an email during workdays, and an email to a help desk during working hours.

 In case you are wondering, the week starts on Monday.

For example, a media active period like this might be useful for an employee who has different working hours over the course of the week:

```
1-3,09:00-13:00;4-5,13:00-17:00
```

Notifications would be sent out as follows:

- Monday to Wednesday, from 09:00 until 13:00
- Thursday and Friday, from 13:00 until 17:00

 This period works together with the time period condition in actions. The action for this user will only be carried out when both periods overlap.

Use if severity is very useful as well, since that poor technician might not want to receive informative SMS messages at night—just those indicating a potential disaster.

Click on **Cancel** to close this window.

 In older versions, it was not possible to add multiple email addresses. Since the release of Zabbix 4.0, it is now possible to add multiple addresses for one user.

Sending out notifications

Since both of the users specified in the action operations have explicitly been denied access to the snmptraps host, they were not considered valid for action operations.

Let's give them access to this host now:

1. Go to **Administration | User groups** and click on Our users in the **Name** column.
2. Switch to the **Permissions** tab, then mark the read-write box in **Important SNMP hosts**, and then click on **Update**. Both users should now have access to the desired host.

Out triggers have been deactivated by now, so we can send another trap to activate the one on the `snmptraps` host.

 Notice how no messages were sent when the triggers deactivated, because of the `Trigger value = PROBLEM` condition. We will enable recovery messages later in this chapter.

Run the following commands on `Another host`:

```
$ snmptrap -Ci -v 2c -c public <Zabbix server> "" "NET-SNMP-
MIB::netSnmpExperimental" NET-SNMP-MIB::netSnmpExperimental s
"Critical Error"
```

Wait for a while so that the trigger fires again. Check your email, and you should have received a notification regarding the host that we were previously not notified about, `snmptraps`. Let's see the event list again. Open **Monitoring** | **Problems** and look at the latest entry.

 If the **Actions** column shows a number in an orange color, wait a couple more minutes. We will discuss the reason for such a delay in `Chapter 20`, *Zabbix Maintenance*.

Oh, but *what's up with the weird entry in the* **Actions** *column?* Those two differently colored numbers look quite cryptic. Let's try to find out what they could mean by opening **Reports** | **Action log** and looking at the last few entries:

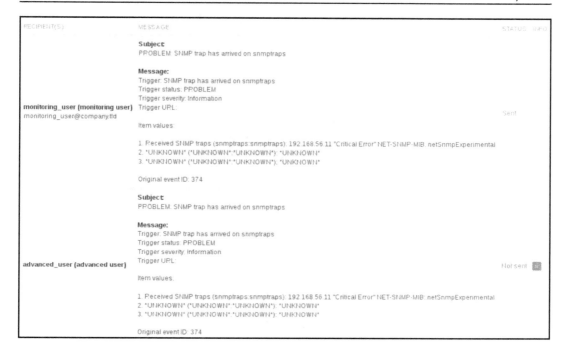

 If you don't see any entries, increase the displayed time period.

The **STATUS** column says that sending the message succeeded for the **monitoring_user**, but failed for the **advanced_user**. Thus, green numbers in the event list mean successfully sent notifications, while red numbers mean failures. To see why it failed, move the mouse cursor over the red **X** in the **INFO** column:

You can click the red **X** to make the popup stay when the mouse cursor moves away, which allows us to copy the error text.

Earlier versions would show the name of our user in the pop-up box (`advanced_user`). This is no longer the case, so we have to look in the recipient column for the exact recipient.

Excellent—that clearly explains what the error is; our `advanced_user` had no media entries defined. We can easily deduce that numbers in the event list represent notification counts—green for successful ones and red for unsuccessful ones. It also shows us that actions should not be configured to send messages for users that do not have media correctly set, as such entries pollute the action log and make it harder to review interesting entries.

While the action log provides more detail, we could have established the error in the event list as well. Return to **Monitoring | Problems** and move the mouse cursor over the red, right-most number 1 in the **Actions** column. A popup will appear. Click on the number 1 to make the popup stay and move the mouse cursor over the red **X** in the **INFO** column. The same informative popup will appear, in this case telling us that there's no media defined for this user.

Using macros

Let's take a careful look at the emails we received (if you have already deleted them, just send a couple more SNMP traps). The subject and body both mention the trigger name—SNMP trap has arrived on snmptraps. It looks like it was a good idea to include the hostname macro in the trigger name. While there's another solution we will explore right now, a general suggestion is to always include the hostname in the trigger name. Doing so will avoid cases when you receive an alert, but have no idea which host has the problem. For example, if we had omitted the hostname `macro` from our trigger, the email alerts would have said SNMP trap has arrived.

Another solution is possible in regards to the aforementioned problem; we can use the macro in the action log to help in this particular case.

To proceed, navigate to **Configuration | Actions**, click on **SNMP action,** and then the **operations** tab. In the Name column, change the default subject field contents to the following:

```
{TRIGGER.STATUS}: {TRIGGER.NAME} on {HOST.NAME}
```

The use of the word `macros` can be confusing here. Zabbix calls them `macros`, although they might be more correctly regarded as `variables`. In this book, we will follow Zabbix terminology, but feel free to read `macro` as `variable`.

The field already contained two macros—`{TRIGGER.STATUS}` and `{TRIGGER.NAME}`. The benefit of a macro is evident when we have a single action covering many cases. We don't have to create a myriad of actions to cover every possible situation; instead, we use macros to have the desired information, related to the particular event, replaced. Macro names usually provide a good idea of what a macro does. In this case, we improved the existing subject line, which already contained trigger name and status macros, by adding the hostname macro, though it is still recommended to include the hostname in trigger names.

To confirm your changes, click on **Update**. Make the trigger change state by sending SNMP traps as before, and then check your email. The subject now includes the hostname. But wait, now the hostname is included twice—*what have we done?* The subject is now as follows:

```
PROBLEM: SNMP trap has arrived on snmptraps on snmptraps
```

We used the same macro in the trigger name and in the action subject. You should decide where you would like to specify the hostname and always follow that rule.

There's also something else slightly strange in the emails. At the end of the message body, there are a number of lines with **UNKNOWN** in them:

```
Received SNMP traps (snmptraps:snmptraps): 192.168.56.11 "Critical
Error"    NET-SNMP-MIB::netSnmpExperimental
*UNKNOWN*  (*UNKNOWN*:*UNKNOWN*):  *UNKNOWN*
*UNKNOWN*  (*UNKNOWN*:*UNKNOWN*):  *UNKNOWN*
```

Let's look at the corresponding action configuration:

```
Item values:
{ITEM.NAME1}  ({HOST.NAME1}:{ITEM.KEY1}):  {ITEM.VALUE1}
{ITEM.NAME2}  ({HOST.NAME2}:{ITEM.KEY2}):  {ITEM.VALUE2}
{ITEM.NAME3}  ({HOST.NAME3}:{ITEM.KEY3}):  {ITEM.VALUE3}
```

The number that is appended in these macros, such as in {ITEM.NAME1}, is the sequential number of the item in the trigger expression. The trigger that sent the notifications for us referenced a single item only, hence the first reference works, referencing the second and third items fails, and that outputs *UNKNOWN* in the message. The default action is meant to be used as an example; in this case, demonstrating the ability to reference multiple items. If most of your triggers reference only a single item, it might be desirable to remove the second and third lines. At this time, there is no way to conditionally print the item value, if it exists.

Sometimes, the receiver of the message might benefit from additional information that is not directly obtainable from event-related macros. Here, an additional class of macros helps—the ones used in trigger expressions also work for macro contents. Imagine a person managing two servers that both rely on an NFS server, which is known to have performance problems. If the system load on one of these two servers increases enough to fire a trigger, the alert receiver would want to know the load on the second server as well, and also whether the NFS service is running correctly. That would allow them to do a quick evaluation of where the problem most likely lies. If the NFS service is down, or is having performance problems of its own, then the system load on these two servers most likely has risen because of that, and the NFS server admin will have to take care of that. For this person to receive such information, we can add lines such as these to the email body:

```
CPU load on Another host: {Another host:system.cpu.load.last()}
NFS service is: {NFS Server:nfs.service.last()}
```

 Make sure to adjust item intervals and trigger expressions to avoid race conditions for these items.

Note that there is no built-in NFS service item; you have to create proper hosts and items to be able to reference them like this.

As can be seen in the preceding example, the same syntax is used as in trigger expressions, including the functions that are supported. This also allows the receiver to be informed immediately regarding average load over a period of time by adding a macro such as this:

```
Average CPU load on Another host for last 10 minutes: {Another
host:system.cpu.load.avg(600)}
```

You can find a full list of supported macros in the official Zabbix documentation at `https://www.zabbix.com/documentation/4.0/manual/appendix/macros/supported_by_location`.

Sending recovery messages

The setup we used only sent out messages when the problem happened. That was ensured by the `Trigger value = PROBLEM` condition, which was added by default. One way to also enable the sending of messages when a trigger is resolved would be to remove that condition, but it will not be useful when escalation functionality is used. Thus, it is suggested leaving that condition in place and enabling recovery messages on the action level instead.

Let's enable recovery messages for our SNMP trap action:

1. Go to **Configuration | Actions**, click on **SNMP action** in the **Name** column, and select the **Recovery operations** tab. Now, we can customize the recovery message. Instead of sending similar messages for problems and recoveries, we can make recoveries stand out a bit more. Hey, that's a good idea. We will be sending out emails to management, so let's add some *feel good* thing here.

2. In the **Operations** box from our recovery tab, we tell Zabbix to send messages to our user group `Our users` through all media.

> Do not remove the trigger value condition when enabling recovery messages. Doing so can result in recovery messages being escalated, and thus generate a huge amount of useless messages.

3. Click on the **Update** button.

   This will make the outgoing recovery messages have a sort of a double affirmation that everything is good—the subject will start with `Resolved:` `with the name of the event:`. To test the new configuration, set the trap to generate a problem and wait for the problem to resolve. This time, two emails should be sent, and the second one should come with our custom subject.

In the email that arrives, note the line at the very end that looks similar to this:

```
Original event ID: 1313
```

The number at the end of the line is the event ID—a unique identifier of the occurrence of the problem. It is actually the so-called **original event ID**. This is the ID of the original problem, and it is the same in the problem and recovery notifications. A very useful approach is automatically matching recovery messages with the problem ones when sending this data to an issue management or ticketing system. Recovery information can be used to automatically close tickets, or provide additional information for them.

This ID was produced by a macro, {EVENT.ID}, and, as with many other macros, you can use it in your actions. If you would want to uniquely identify the recovery event, there's yet another macro for that—{EVENT.RECOVERY.ID}.

There are a lot of macros, so make sure to consult the Zabbix manual for a full list of them.

You may or may not have already noticed but, in our recovery operation, we had no option to send out the recovery option right away or with a delay, as we could with our error message. This is an option that is not yet available. Also, imagine a scenario where we send out our error message after 10 minutes, but the problem is already resolved after 5 minutes. In this case, we will get an OK email after 5 minutes but no error message, as we delayed that one by 10 minutes. This can be confusing. Zabbix has introduced another tab—**Update operations**. This works in the same way as the recovery operations tab, but will send us an update if someone clicks the **Ack** button in Zabbix for this issue. Everybody involved will then receive updates.

Escalating once a threshold is reached

We know how to perform an action if a threshold is reached, such as the temperature being too high, the available disk space being too low, or a web server not working. We can send a message, open a ticket in a tracker, run a custom script, or execute a command on a remote machine. But all of these are simple if-then sequences; if it's this problem, then do this. Quite often, the severity of the problem depends on how long the problem persists. For example, a connection loss to a branch office that lasts a couple of minutes might not be critical, but it's still worth noting down and emailing IT staff. The inability to reach a branch office for five minutes is quite important, and, at this point, we would like to open a ticket in the help desk system and send an SMS to IT staff. After 20 minutes of the problem not being fixed, we would email an IT manager. Let's look at what tools Zabbix provides to enable such gradual activities and configure a simple example.

In the frontend, perform the following operations:

1. Navigate to **Configuration** | **Actions** and click on **Disabled** next to the **Test action** in the **Status** column to enable this action
2. Then, click on **Enabled** next to the **SNMP action**
3. Now, click on **Test action** in the **Name** column

Currently, this action sends a single email to the user Admin whenever a problem occurs. Let's extend this situation:

- Our first user, Admin, will be notified five minutes after the problem happens, with a one-minute interval. After that, they would be notified every five minutes until the problem is resolved.
- advanced_user is lower-level management who would like to receive a notification if a problem is not resolved within five minutes.
- monitoring_user is a higher-level manager who should be notified in 20 minutes if the problem is still not resolved, and if it has not yet been acknowledged.

While these times would be longer in real life, in this instance, we are interested in seeing escalation in action.

Now, we are ready to configure escalations. Switch to the **Operations** tab.

Looking at the operations list, we can see that it currently contains only a single operation—sending an email message to the `Admin` user immediately and only once, which is indicated by the **Steps Details** column having only the first step listed:

The first change we would like to perform is to make sure that `Admin` receives notifications every minute for the first five minutes after the problem happens. Before we modify that, though, we should change the default operation step duration, which, by default, is `3600`, and cannot be lower than `60` seconds. Looking at our requirements, two factors affect the possible step length:

- The lowest time between two repeated alerts, in our case, 1 minute.
- The biggest common divisor for the starting time of delayed alerts. In our case, the delayed alerts were required at 5 and 20 minutes, thus, the biggest common divisor is 5 minutes.

Normally, you would set the default step duration to the biggest common divisor of both of these factors. Here, that would be `60` seconds, but we may also override step duration inside an operation. Let's see how that can help us have a simpler escalation process.

Enter `300` in the **Default operation step duration**—that's five minutes in seconds, so 5m should give the same result as `300`. Now, let's make sure that `Admin` receives a notification every minute for the first five minutes. Click on **Edit** in the **Action operations** block.

Notice how the operation details also have a **Step duration** field. This allows us to override the action level step duration for each operation. We have an action level step duration of 300 seconds, but these steps should be performed at one-minute intervals, so enter 60 in the **Step duration** field. The two **Steps** fields denote the step this operation should start and end with. Step 1 means **immediately**, thus, the first field satisfies us. On the other hand, it currently sends the message only once, but we want to pester our administrator for five minutes. In the **Steps** fields, enter 6 in the second field.

Step 6 happens 5 minutes after the problem happened, step 1 is right away, which is 0 minutes, step 2 is one minute, and so on. Sending messages for 5 minutes will result in six messages in total, as we send a message both at the beginning and the end of this period.

The final result should look like this:

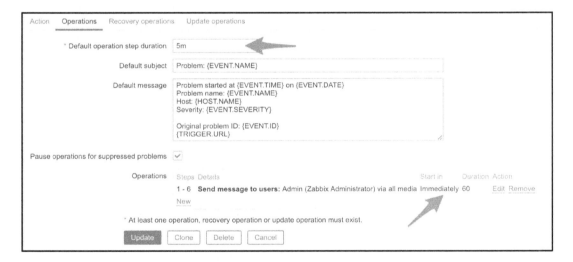

If it does, click on **Update** in the **Operations** block, not the button at the bottom yet. Now, on to the next task: Admin must receive notifications every five minutes after that, until the problem is resolved.

We have to figure out what values to incorporate in the **Steps** field. We want this operation to kick in after five minutes, but notification at five minutes is already covered by the first operation, so we are probably aiming for 10 minutes. But *which step should we use for 10 minutes?* Let's try to create a timeline. We have a single operation currently set that overrides the default period. After that, the default period starts working, and even though we currently have no operations assigned, we can calculate when further steps would be taken:

Step	Operation	Interval (seconds)	Time passed
1	Send message to user `Admin`	Operation, 60	0
2	Send message to user `Admin`	Operation, 60	1 minute
3	Send message to user `Admin`	Operation, 60	2 minutes
4	Send message to user `Admin`	Operation, 60	3 minutes
5	Send message to user `Admin`	Operation, 60	4 minutes
6	Send message to user `Admin`	Operation, 60	5 minutes
7	None	Default, 300	6 minutes
8	None	Default, 300	11 minutes

Operation step duration overrides periods for the steps included in it. If an operation spans steps 5-7, it overrides periods 5-6, 6-7, and 7-8. If an operation is at step 3 only, it overrides period 3-4.

We wanted to have 10 minutes, but it looks like this is not possible with this particular configuration—our first operation puts step 7 at 6 minutes, and reverting to the default intervals puts step 8 at 11 minutes. To override interval 6-7, we would have to define some operation at step 7, but we do not want to do that. *Is there a way to configure it in the desired manner?* This should be feasible by observing the following:

1. Click on **Edit** in the **Operations** column and change the second **Steps** field to 5, and then click on **Update** in the **Operation details** block. Do not click on the main **Update** button at the bottom.

2. Now, click on **New** in the **Operations** block. Let's configure the simple things first.

3. Click on **Add** in the **Send to Users** section in the **Operation details** block, and click on **Admin** in the resulting popup. With the first operation updated, let's model the final few steps again:

Step	Operation	Interval (seconds)	Time passed
...	...	...	...
5	Send message to user `Admin`	Operation, 60	4 minutes
6	None	Default, 300	5 minutes
7	None	Default, 300	10 minutes
8	None	Default, 300	15 minutes

With the latest modifications, it looks like we can send a message after 10 minutes have passed—that would be step 7, but we actually removed message sending at step 6, after 5 minutes. The good news is that if we now add another operation to start at step 6, that finishes the first five-minute sending cycle and then keeps on sending a message every 5 minutes. Perfect!

Enter 6 in the first **Steps** field. We want this operation to continue until the problem is resolved, so 0 goes in the second **Steps** fields. Once complete, click on the **Add** control at the bottom of the **Operation details** block.

We can see that Zabbix helpfully calculated the time when the second operation should start, which allows us to quickly spot errors in our calculations. There are no errors here; the second operation starts at 5 minutes, as desired.

With that covered, our lower-level manager, `advanced_user`, must be notified after five minutes, but only once. That means another operation, as follows:

1. Click on **New** in the **Operations** block.
2. Click on **Add** in the **Send to Users** section and, in the popup, click on `advanced_user` in the **Alias** column.
3. The single message should be simple. We know that step 6 happens after five minutes have elapsed, so let's enter 6 in both **Steps** fields, and then click on **Add** at the bottom of the **Operation details** block. Again, the **Start in** column shows that this step will be executed after five minutes, as expected.

If two escalation operations overlap steps, and one of them has a custom interval and the other uses the default, the custom interval will be used for the overlapping steps. If both operations have a custom interval defined, the smallest interval is used for the overlapping steps.

We are now left with the final task—notifying the higher-level manager after 20 minutes, and only if the problem has not been acknowledged. As before, click on **New** in the **operations** block, and then click on **Add** in the **Send to Users** section. In the popup, click on monitoring_user in the **Alias** column. Now, let's continue with our planned step table:

Step	Operation	Interval (seconds)	Time passed
...	...	...	...
7	None	Default, 300	10 minutes
8	None	Default, 300	15 minutes
9	None	Default, 300	20 minutes

Since steps just continue with the default period, this shows us that step 9 is the correct one. As we want only a single notification here, enter 9 in both of the **Steps** fields.

It is not required to fill all steps with operations. Some steps in-between can be skipped if the planned schedule so requires.

An additional requirement was to notify this user only if the problem has not been acknowledged.

To add such a restriction, execute the following:

1. Click on **New** in the **Conditions** area.
2. The **Operation condition** block is displayed, and the default setting already has **Not Ack** chosen, so click on **Add** in the **Operation condition** block. The form layout can be a bit confusing here, so make sure not to click on **Add** in the **Operation details** block instead. While we're almost done, there's one more thing we can do to make this notification less confusing for upper management.

   Currently, everybody receives the same message—some trigger information and the last values of items that are being referenced in triggers. Item values might not be that interesting to the manager, hence we can try omitting them from those messages. Untick the **Default message** checkbox and notice how we can customize the subject and message for a specific operation.

For the message, remove everything that goes below the `Trigger URL` line. For the manager, it might also be useful to know who was notified and when. Luckily, there's another helpful macro, `{ESC.HISTORY}`. Let's modify this message by adding an empty line and then this macro. Here's what the final result for this operation should look like:

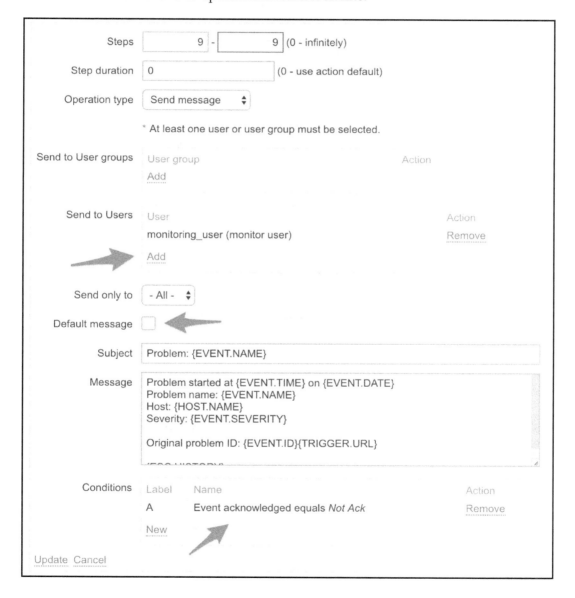

It's all fine, so click on **Add** at the bottom of the **Operation details** block. We can now review action operations and verify that each operation starts when it should.

Everything seems to match the specification. Let's switch to the **Recovery operations** tab and, similar to the **SNMP action**, change the **Recovery subject** to Resolved: {TRIGGER.NAME}. This time, we wanted to avoid **Resolved: OK:**, opting for a single mention that everything is now fine. Add the users in the recovery operation. We can finally click on **Update**. With this notification setup in place, let's break something. On Another host, execute the following command:

```
$ rm /tmp/testfile
```

It will take a short time for Zabbix to notice this problem and fire away the first email to the Admin user. This email won't be that different from the ones we received before. But now let's be patient and wait a further 20 minutes. During this time, the Admin user will receive more messages. What we are really interested in is the message content in the email to the monitoring_user. Once you receive this message, look at what it contains:

```
Trigger: Testfile is missing
Trigger status: PROBLEM
Trigger severity: Warning
Trigger URL:
Problem started: 2016.04.15 15:05:25 Age: 20m
1. 2016.04.15 15:05:27 message sent        Email admin@company.tld
"Zabbix Administrator (Admin)"
2. 2016.04.15 15:06:27 message sent        Email admin@company.tld
"Zabbix Administrator (Admin)"
3. 2016.04.15 15:07:27 message sent        Email admin@company.tld
"Zabbix Administrator (Admin)"
4. 2016.04.15 15:08:27 message sent        Email admin@company.tld
"Zabbix Administrator (Admin)"
5. 2016.04.15 15:09:27 message sent        Email admin@company.tld
"Zabbix Administrator (Admin)"
6. 2016.04.15 15:10:27 message failed       "advanced user
(advanced_user)" No media defined for user "advanced user
(advanced_user)"
6. 2016.04.15 15:10:27 message sent        Email admin@company.tld
"Zabbix Administrator (Admin)"
7. 2016.04.15 15:15:28 message sent        Email admin@company.tld
"Zabbix Administrator (Admin)"
8. 2016.04.15 15:20:28 message sent        Email admin@company.tld
"Zabbix Administrator (Admin)"
```

As in all other notifications, the time here will use the local time on the Zabbix server.

It now contains a lot more information than just what happened; the manager has also received a detailed list of who was notified of the problem. The Admin user has received many notifications, but advanced_user has not received the notification because their email address is not configured. There's some work to do in terms of either this user, or the Zabbix administrators, fixing this issue. And, in this case, the issue is escalated to the monitoring_user only if nobody has acknowledged the problem before, which means nobody has even looked into it.

The current setup would cancel escalation to the management user if the problem is acknowledged. We may create a delayed escalation by adding yet another operation that sends a message to the management user at some later step, but does so without an acknowledgement condition. If the problem is acknowledged, the first operation to the management user would be skipped, but the second one would always work. If the problem is not acknowledged at all, the management user would get two notifications.

If we look carefully at the prefixed numbers, they are not sequential numbers of entries in the history; they are actually the escalation step numbers. That gives us a quick overview of which notifications happened at the same time, without comparing timestamps. The Email string is the name of the media type that's used for this notification.

Let's fix this problem now; on Another host, execute the following command:

```
$ touch /tmp/testfile
```

In a short while, two email messages should be sent—one to the Admin user and one to monitoring_user. As these are recovery messages, they will both have our custom subject:

```
Resolved: Testfile is missing
```

Our test action had escalation thresholds that are too short for most real-life situations. If reducing these meant creating an action from scratch, that would be very inconvenient. Let's see how easily we can adapt the existing one. In the frontend, navigate to **Configuration | Actions**, click on **Test action** in the **Name** column, and then switch to the **Operations** tab. We might want to make the following changes, assuming that this is not a critical problem and does not warrant a quick response, unless it has been there for half an hour:

- Increase the interval between the additional repeated messages that the Admin user receives
- Increase the delay before the messages to the advanced_user and monitoring_user are sent
- Start sending messages to the Admin user after the problem has been there for 30 minutes

 In the next few steps, be careful not to click on the **Update** button too early as that will discard the modifications in the operation that we are currently editing.

Let's start by changing the **Default operation** step duration to 1,800 (30 minutes). Then, click on **Edit** in the **Action** column next to the first entry (currently spanning steps 1-5). In its properties, set the **Steps** fields to 2 and 6, and then click on the **Update** control in the operation details block.

For both operations that start at step 6, change that to step 7. For the operation that has 6 in both of the **Steps** fields, change both occurrences the same way as before, and again, be careful not to click on the **Update** button yet.

The final result should look like this:

If it does, click on that **Update** button.

The first change for the default operation step spaced all steps out, except the ones that were overridden in the operation properties. That mostly achieved our goals to space out notifications to the Admin user and delay notifications to the two other users. By changing the first step in the first operation from 1 to 2, we achieved two goals. The interval between steps 1 and 2 went back to the default interval for the action (as we excluded step 1 from the operation that did the overriding with 60 seconds), and no message was sent to the Admin user right away. Additionally, we moved the end step a bit further so that the total number of messages the Admin user would receive at one-minute intervals would not change. That resulted in some further operations not being so nicely aligned to the 5-minute boundary, so we moved them to step 7. Let's compare this to the previous configuration:

Before				**After**
STEPS DETAILS		START IN	DURATION (SEC)	START IN
1 - 5	Send message to users: Admin (Zabbix Administrator) via all media	Immediately	60	00:30:00
6 - 0	Send message to users: Admin (Zabbix Administrator) via all media	00:05:00	Default	00:35:00
6	Send message to users: advanced_user (advanced user) via all media	00:05:00	Default	00:35:00
9	Send message to users: monitoring_user (monitoring user) via all media	00:20:00	Default	01:35:00

This allows us to easily scale notifications and escalations up from a testing configuration to something more appropriate to the actual situation, as well as adapting quickly to changing requirements. Let's create another problem. On `Another host`, execute the following command:

```
$ rm /tmp/testfile
```

Wait for the trigger to fire and for a couple of emails to arrive for the `Admin` user, and then *solve* the problem:

```
$ touch /tmp/testfile
```

That should send a recovery email to the `Admin` user soon. Hey, wait ..., *why for that user only?* Zabbix only sends recovery notifications to users who have received problem notifications. As the problem did not get escalated for the management user to receive the notification, that user was not informed about resolving the problem either. A similar thing actually happened with `advanced_user`, who did not have media assigned. As the notification was not sent when the event was escalated (because no email address was configured), Zabbix did not even try to send a recovery message to that user. No matter how many problem messages were sent to a user, only a single recovery message will be sent per action.

So, in this case, if the `Admin` user resolved or acknowledged the issue before `monitoring_user` received an email about the problem, `monitoring_user` would receive neither the message about the problem, nor the one about resolving it.

As we can see, escalations are fairly flexible and allow you to combine many operations when responding to an event. We could imagine one fairly long and complex escalation sequence of a web server going down to proceed as follows:

1. Email the administrator
2. Send an SMS to admin
3. Open a report at the help desk system
4. Email management
5. Send an SMS to management
6. Restart Apache
7. Reboot the server
8. Power cycle the entire server room

Well, the last one might be a bit over the top, but we can indeed construct a fine-grained stepping up of reactions and notifications about problems.

Runner analogy

Did that escalation thing seem terribly complicated to you? If so, we can try an analogy that was coined near Salt Lake City.

Imagine there's a runner running through a forest, with a straight route. On this route, there are posts. The runner has a preferred speed (we might call it a **default speed**), which means that it normally takes T seconds for the runner to go from one post to the next one.

On the posts, there may be instructions. The runner starts from the very first post, and checks for instructions there. Instructions can order the runner to do various things:

- Send an SMS to somebody at this post only
- Send an SMS to somebody from this post until post N
- Change speed from this post until the next post so as to arrive sooner or later
- Change speed from this post until post N

The route is taken by the runner no matter what. If there are no instructions at the current post, the runner just continues to the next post.

If this analogy clarified how the action escalation steps are processed by the runner, it might be worth reviewing this section and possibly gaining a better understanding of the details, too.

Using scripts as media

While Zabbix supports a decent range of notification mechanisms, there always comes a time when you need something very specific and the default methods just don't cut it. For such situations, Zabbix supports custom scripts to be used as media.

Let's try to set one up:

1. Open **Administration | Media types** and click on **Create media** type. Enter the following values:

   - **Name**: Test script
   - **Type**: **Script**

- **Script name**: `testscript`
- **Script parameters**: Click on the **Add** control and enter `{ALERT.MESSAGE}` in the new field:

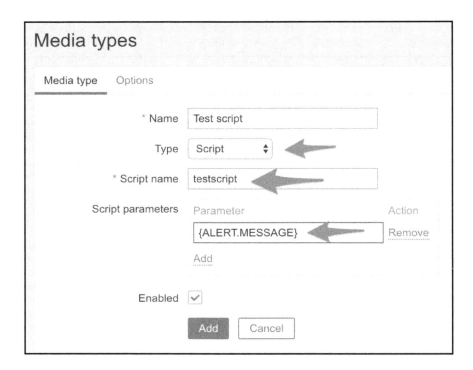

The `{ALERT.MESSAGE}` macro will be expanded to the message body from the action configuration. Currently, two additional macros are supported in the script parameters – `{ALERT.SENDTO}` and `{ALERT.SUBJECT}`. Consult the Zabbix manual to check whether any new macros are added in later versions.

2. When you are done, click on the **Add** button at the bottom.

Now, we should make sure that this media is used at some point:

1. Go to **Administration** | **Users**, click on `monitoring_user` in the **ALIAS** column, and switch to the **Media** tab.
2. Click on **Add** in the **Media** section. In the **Type** drop-down, select **Test script** and, in the **Send to** field, enter `user@domain.tld`:

The email address won't be passed to our script, but Zabbix does not allow us to save a media entry with an empty **Send to** field.

When you are done, click on **Add** and confirm these changes by clicking on **Update** in the user editing form. Before we continue with the script itself, navigate to **Configuration** | **Actions** and then click on **Disabled** next to **SNMP action** to enable this action.

We entered the script name, but *where should the script be placed?* Now is the time to return to where we haven't been for some time. Take a look at `zabbix_server.conf` and check what value the `AlertScriptsPath` option has. The default location will vary depending on the method of installation. If you installed it from the source, it will be `/usr/local/share/zabbix/alertscripts`. Distribution packages are likely to use some other directory. As with `root`, create a file called `testscript` in that directory:

```
# touch /path/to/testscript
# chmod 755 /path/to/testscript
```

Populate it with the following content:

```
#!/bin/bash
for i in "$@"; do
    echo "$i" >> /tmp/zabbix_script_received.log
done
```

As you can see, we are simply logging each passed parameter to a file for examination. Now, generate some SNMP traps so that the `snmptraps` trigger switches to the **PROBLEM** state. Wait for the email to arrive, and then check the `/tmp/zabbix_script_received.log` file. It should have content similar to this:

```
Trigger: SNMP trap has arrived on snmptraps
Trigger status: PROBLEM
Trigger severity: Information
Trigger URL:
Item values:
1. Received SNMP traps (snmptraps:snmptraps): 192.168.56.11 "Critical
Error" NET-SNMP-MIB::netSnmpExperimental
2. *UNKNOWN* (*UNKNOWN*:*UNKNOWN*): *UNKNOWN*
3. *UNKNOWN* (*UNKNOWN*:*UNKNOWN*): *UNKNOWN*
Original event ID: 397
```

We can see that the whole message body from action properties is passed here with newlines intact. If we wanted to also know the user media **Send to** value to identify the Zabbix user who received this data, we would also pass the {ALERT.SENDTO} macro to our alert script. Similarly, to get the subject from the action properties, we would use the {ALERT.SUBJECT} macro.

 If you see message content losing newlines, check the quoting in your script; all newlines are preserved by Zabbix.

From here, basically anything can be done with the data: passing it to issue management systems that do not have an email gateway, sending it through some media not supported directly by Zabbix, or displaying it somewhere.

Now, let's revisit action configuration. Open **Configuration** | **Actions** and click on **Test action** in the **Name** column. Now, we have a script being executed whenever monitoring_user receives a notification. But *what if we would like to skip the script for notification, and only use it in a specific action?* Thankfully, we don't have to create a separate user just for such a scenario:

1. Switch to the **Operations** tab and, in the **operations** block, click on **Edit** next to the last operation. This will send a message to monitoring_user.
2. Take a look at the **Send only to** drop-down. It lists all media types, and allows us to restrict a specific operation to a specific media type only. In this drop-down, choose **Email**.
3. Click on the **Update** link at the bottom of the **Operation details** block, and then the **Update** button at the bottom.

By using the **Send only to** option, it is possible to use different notification methods for different situations without creating multiple fake user accounts. For example, a user might receive an email for the first few escalation steps, and then an SMS would be sent.

Integrating with issue management systems

Sending out messages to technicians or the help desk is nice, but there are times and conditions when it is desirable to automatically open an issue in some management system. This is most easily achieved by using two main integration methods:

- Email gateways
- APIs that decent systems provide

To implement such an integration, the following steps should be taken:

1. Create a Zabbix user for the ticketing system notifications.
2. Configure media for this user (the email address that the system receives an email at, or the script to run).
3. Assign read-only access for resources tickets should be automatically created for (remember, no alerts are sent or scripts run if the user does not have access to any of the hosts involved in the event generation).
4. Create a separate action, or add this user as a recipient to an existing action operation with a custom message (by unmarking the **Default message** checkbox when editing the operation).

There's also a *step 5*—either proper message contents should be formatted so that the receiving system knows what to do with the message, or a script should be created to access the ticketing system API. This is specific to each system, but let's look at a few examples. These examples provide only basic information; for added bonus points, you can add other macros, such as final or average value ones. Note that the specific syntax might change between ticketing system versions, so check the documentation for the version you are using.

Bugzilla

Bugzilla is a famous free bug tracker, sometimes abused as a general issue management system. Still, Zabbix can monitor the status of software tests and open new tickets if, for example, compilation fails. The following would be configured as the message body:

```
@{TRIGGER.NAME}
@product = <some existing product>
@component = <some existing component>
@version = 1.8
{DATE} - {TIME}
{TRIGGER.NAME}.
```

The From address is used to determine the user account that is creating the bug report.

Computer Associates Unicenter Service Desk Manager

CA Service Desk Manager (formerly Unicenter Service Desk), from Computer Associates, is a solution that provides a ticketing system, among other features. The following would be configured as the message body:

```
"start-request"
%CUSTOMER= <some existing user account>
%DESCRIPTION= {DATE} - {TIME}
{TRIGGER.NAME}.
%SUMMARY= {TRIGGER.NAME}.
%PRIORITY= {TRIGGER.NSEVERITY}
%CATEGORY= <some existing category>
"end-request"
```

Use the `{TRIGGER.NSEVERITY}` macro here—that's numeric trigger severity, with `Not classified` being 0 and `Disaster` being 5.

Atlassian JIRA

Atlassian JIRA is a popular ticketing system or issue tracker. While it also supports an email gateway for creating issues, we could look at a more advanced way to do that—using the API that JIRA exposes. Media type and user media would have to be created and configured, similar to what we did in the *Using scripts as media* section earlier in this chapter, although it is proposed that you create a special user for running such scripts.

As for the script itself, something like this would simply create issues with an identical summary, placing the message body from the action configuration in the issue summary:

```
#!/bin/bash
json='{"fields":{"project":{"key":"PROJ"},"summary":"Issue
automatically created by
Zabbix","description":"'"$1"'","issuetype":{"name":"Bug"}}}'
curl -u username:password -X POST --data "$json" -H "Content-Type:
application/json" https://jira.company.tld/rest/api/2/issue/
```

For this to work, make sure to replace the project key, username, password, and URL to the JIRA instance, and possibly also the issue type.

 For debugging, add the curl flag −D−. That will print out the headers.

This could be extended in a variety of ways. For example, we could pass the subject from the action properties as the first parameter, and encode the trigger severity among other pipe-delimited things. Our script would then parse out the trigger severity and set the JIRA priority accordingly. That would be quite specific for each implementation, although, hopefully, this example provided a good starting point.

Remote commands

The script media type is quite powerful, and it could even be used to execute a command in response to an event. For the command to be executed on the monitored host, though, it would require some mechanism to connect, authorize, and so on, which might be somewhat too complicated. Zabbix provides another mechanism to respond to events—remote commands. Remote commands can be used in a variety of cases, some of which might be initiating a configuration backup when a configuration change is detected, or starting a service that has died. We will set up the latter scenario:

1. Navigate to **Configuration** | **Actions** and click on **Create action**. In the **Name** field, enter `Restart Apache`.
2. Go to **Conditions** and, in the **New condition** block, choose **Host** in the first drop-down. Then, select equals and, in the selection box, start typing `another`.
3. In the drop-down that appears, click on **Another host**.
4. Click on **Add** to add the condition (but do not click on the global **Add** button yet).

Let's create another condition. In the **New condition** block, in the first drop-down, choose **Trigger name**. Leave the second drop-down at the default value. In the input field next to this, enter `Web service is down`, and then click on **Add** control. The end result should look as follows:

Now, switch to the **Operations** tab. In the **operations** block, click on **New**. In the **Operation details** block that just appeared, choose **Remote command** in the **Operation type** field. Zabbix offers five different types of remote command:

- Custom script
- IPMI
- SSH
- Telnet
- Global script

We will discuss SSH and telnet items in `Chapter 10`, *Advanced Item Monitoring*. We will discuss IPMI functionality in `Chapter 14`, *Monitoring IPMI Devices*. Global scripts will be covered later in this chapter but for now, let's look at the custom script functionality.

For custom scripts, you may choose to run them either on the Zabbix agent, server, or the Zabbix proxy. Running on the agent will allow us to gather information, control services, and do other tasks on the system where problem conditions were encountered. Running on the server will allow us to probe the system from the Zabbix server's perspective, or maybe access the Zabbix API and take further decisions based on that information. Running on a proxy, the script will be executed by the Zabbix server or proxy, depending on whether the host is monitored by the Zabbix server or the Zabbix proxy.

> If you like to run remote commands, then don't forget to configure the **EnableRemoteCommands** option on your agents in the Zabbix config file.

For now, we will create an action that will try to restart the Apache web server if it is down. Normally, that has to be done on the host that had the problem. In the **Target list** section, click on the **New** link. The drop-down there will have **Current host** selected, which is exactly what we wanted, so click on the **Add** control just below it.

In the **Commands** textbox, enter the following:

```
sudo /usr/bin/systemctl restart httpd (or apache2)
```

> This will be distribution-specific, but most Linux systems today use systemd, and so does Ubuntu and CentOS. In other cases, it may be the case that you have to use init.

We are restarting Apache just in case it has stopped responding, instead of simply dying. You can also enter many remote actions to be performed, but we won't do that now, so just click on the **Add** control at the bottom of the **Operation details** block. To save our new action, click on the **Add** button at the bottom.

> When running remote commands, the Zabbix agent accepts the command and immediately returns 1—there is no way for the server to know how long the command took, or even whether it was run at all. Note that the remote commands on the agent are run without a timeout.

Our remote command is almost ready to run, except, on the agent side, there's still some work to be done, so open zabbix_agentd.conf as root and look for the EnableRemoteCommands parameter. Set it to 1 and uncomment it, save the config file, and then restart zabbix_agentd.

That's still not all. As remote commands are passed to the Zabbix agent daemon, which is running as a `zabbix` user, we also have to allow this user to actually restart Apache. As evidenced by the remote command, we will use `sudo` for this, so edit `/etc/sudoers.d/zabbix` on `Another host` as `root` and add the following line:

```
zabbix  ALL=NOPASSWD: /usr/bin/systemctl
```

For additional safety measures, use the `visudo` command. It should also check your changes for syntax validity. On some systems, `sudo` is only configured to be used interactively. You might have to comment the `requiretty` option in `/etc/sudoers`.

Again, change the script name if you need a different one. This allows the `zabbix` user to use `sudo` and restart the Apache web server. Just restart it; don't stop or do any other operations.

Make sure that the SMTP server is running on `Another host`, otherwise the web service trigger will not be triggered as we had a dependency on the SMTP trigger. Alternatively, remove that dependency.

Now, we are ready for the show. Stop the web server on `Another host`. Wait for the trigger to update its state and check the web server's status. It should start again automatically.

By default, all actions get two conditions. One of them limits the action to fire only when the trigger goes into the **PROBLEM** state, but not when it comes back to the **OK** state. For this action, it is a very helpful setting; otherwise, the web server would be restarted once when it was found to be down, and then restarted again when it was found to be up. Such a configuration mistake would not be obvious, so it might stay undetected for a while. You should also avoid enabling recovery messages for an action that restarts a service.

Note that remote commands on agents only work with passive agents; they will not work in active mode. This does not mean that you cannot use active items on such a host. You may do this, but remote commands will always be attempted in passive mode by the server connected directly to that agent. There might be a situation where all items are active and, thus, a change in configuration that prevents server-to-agent connection from working is not noticed, and then the remote command fails to work. If you have all items active and want to use remote commands, it might be worth having a single passive item to check whether that type of item still works.

While the need to restart services like this indicates a problem that would be best fixed for the service itself, sometimes it can work as an emergency solution, or in the case of an unresponsive proprietary software vendor.

Global scripts

Looking at values and graphs on the frontend is nice and useful, but there are cases when extra information might be needed right away, or there might be a need to manually invoke an action, such as starting an upgrade process, rebooting the system, or performing some other administrative task. Zabbix allows us to execute commands directly from the frontend—this feature is called **global scripts**. Let's see what is available out of the box. Navigate to **Monitoring** | **Problems** and click on the hostname in any of the entries:

The second part of this menu has convenience links to various sections in the frontend. The first part, labeled **SCRIPTS**, is what we are after. Currently, Zabbix ships with three preconfigured scripts—**Detect operating system**, **Ping**, and **Traceroute**. We will discuss them in a bit more detail later, but for now just click on **Ping**. A pop-up window will open with the output of this script:

```
Ping                                                        ×

ping -c 3 127.0.0.1; case $? in [01]) true;; *) false;; esac

PING 127.0.0.1 (127.0.0.1) 56(84) bytes of data.
64 bytes from 127.0.0.1: icmp_seq=1 ttl=64 time=0.013 ms
64 bytes from 127.0.0.1: icmp_seq=2 ttl=64 time=0.021 ms
64 bytes from 127.0.0.1: icmp_seq=3 ttl=64 time=0.023 ms

--- 127.0.0.1 ping statistics ---
3 packets transmitted, 3 received, 0% packet loss, time 1999ms
rtt min/avg/max/mdev = 0.013/0.019/0.023/0.004 ms

                                                    Cancel
```

Notice the slight delay; the target host was pinged three times, and we had to wait for that to finish to get the output.

Global scripts are available by clicking on the host in several locations in the frontend from such a context menu. These locations are as follows:

- **Monitoring** | **Dashboard** (in the **Problems** widget)
- **Monitoring** | **Overview** (when hosts are located on the left-hand side)
- **Monitoring** | **Latest data** (when showing data from more than one host)
- **Monitoring** | **Maps**
- **Inventory** | **Hosts**, where clicking on the **Host name** will open the inventory overview
- **Reports** | **Triggers top 100**

Calling those three scripts while preconfigured hinted at the fact that we can configure our own. Let's do just that.

Configuring global scripts

We will start by examining the existing scripts. Navigate to **Administration** | **Scripts**:

The same three scripts we saw in the menu can be seen here. Let's see what they do:

- **Detect operating system**: This script calls nmap and relies on sudo
- **Ping**: Uses the ping utility, and pings the host three times
- **Traceroute**: Calls the traceroute utility against the host

These three scripts are all executed on the Zabbix server, so they should work for any host, a server with a Zabbix agent, a switch, a storage device, and so on.

We will discuss other options in a moment, but for now, let's see whether all of these scripts work. Ping should work for most people. Traceroute will require the traceroute utility to be installed. As for operating system detection, it is unlikely to work for you out of the box. Let's try and make that one work.

 If Zabbix administrators are not supposed to gain root shell access to the Zabbix server, do not configure sudo, as shown here. There's a feature in nmap that allows for the execution of commands. Instead, create a wrapper script that only allows the -O parameter with a single argument.

Start by making sure that nmap is installed on the Zabbix server. As the script uses sudo, edit /etc/sudoers.d./zabbix (or use visudo) and add a line like this:

```
zabbix ALL=NOPASSWD: /usr/bin/nmap
```

In distribution packages, a Zabbix server might run as the `zabbixs` or `zabbixsrv` user instead; use that username in the `sudoers` configuration.

Adapt the `nmap` path if necessary. Similar to restarting the Apache web server, you might have to uncomment the `requiretty` option in `/etc/sudoers`. Again, all of these changes have to be executed on the Zabbix server. When finished, run the operating system detection script from the menu, using one of the locations mentioned earlier:

```
sudo /usr/bin/nmap -O 192.168.1.29


Starting Nmap 6.40 ( http://nmap.org ) at 2018-12-15 12:16 CET
Nmap scan report for 192.168.1.29
Host is up (0.00034s latency).
Not shown: 998 closed ports
PORT    STATE SERVICE
22/tcp open  ssh
80/tcp open  http
MAC Address: 08:00:27:B2:77:88 (Cadmus Computer Systems)
```

 The `SELinux` security framework may prevent global scripts from working.

Hooray, that worked! The `nmap` command took some time to run. When running global scripts on the agent, they obey the same timeout as the remote commands we discussed earlier in this chapter. This script was run on the server. In this case, there's a 60-second timeout in the frontend.

Now, on to examining other script options, and also configuring some scripts of our own. When there's a problem on a system, it might be resource starvation. We might want to find out which processes on a system are stressing the CPU the most.

Navigate back to **Administration** | **Scripts** and click on **Create script**. For our first script, fill in the following:

- **Name:** `Top CPU using processes`
- **Commands:** `top -n 1 -b | grep -A 10 "^[ ]*PID"`

In our case, we will leave the other options as is. Here is a short overview of all the options:

Column	Description
Type	Click the button to select a type script or IPMI
Execute on	• **Zabbix agent**—the script will be executed by the Zabbix agent on the host. • **Zabbix server (proxy)**—the script will be executed by the Zabbix server or proxy, depending on whether the host is monitored by a server or proxy. • **Zabbix server**—the script will be executed by the Zabbix server only. The option to execute scripts on the Zabbix agent has been available since the release of Zabbix 2.0 (providing remote commands are enabled in the Zabbix agent config file).
Commands	Enter the full path to the commands to be executed within the script. The following macros are supported in the commands—{HOST.CONN}, {HOST.IP}, {HOST.DNS}, {HOST.HOST}, and {HOST.NAME}. If a macro may resolve to a value with spaces (for example, hostname), don't forget to quote as needed. Since Zabbix 2.2, user macros are supported in script commands.
Description	Enter a description for the script.
User group	Select the user group that the script will be available to (or **All** for all user groups).
Host group	Select the host group that the script will be available for (or **All** for all host groups).
Required host permissions	Select the permission level for the host group—**Read** or **Write**. Only users with the required permission level will have access to executing the script.
Enable confirmation	Mark the checkbox to display a confirmation message before executing the script. This feature might be especially useful with potentially dangerous operations (such as a reboot script) or ones that might take a long time.
Confirmation text	Enter a custom confirmation text for the confirmation popup enabled with the preceding checkbox (for example, **Remote system will be rebooted. Are you sure?**). To see how the text will appear, click on **Test confirmation** next to the field. Since Zabbix 2.2, the confirmation text will expand hostname macros—{HOST.HOST}, and {HOST.NAME}, host connection macros—{HOST.IP}, {HOST.DNS}, and {HOST.CONN}, and user macros. The macros will not be expanded when testing the confirmation message.

When done, click on **Add**. For the top command, we told it to only print the process list and to do so once only. Then, we grabbed the header line and the next 10 lines after it – assuming the header line starts with any amount of spaces and a PID string.

We enabled remote commands on Another host earlier. If you skipped that, make sure to enable them before proceeding.

Navigate to **Monitoring | Problems**, click on **Another host** in the **Host** column, and then choose **Top CPU using processes**.

You may use any other location where this context menu is available. We listed these locations earlier:

```
Top CPU using processes                                                    ×

 top -n 1 -b | grep -A 10 "^[ ]*PID"

 PID USER      PR  NI    VIRT    RES    SHR S %CPU %MEM    TIME+ COMMAND
   1 root      20   0  128140   6720   4168 S  0.0  0.3  0:02.61 systemd
   2 root      20   0       0      0      0 S  0.0  0.0  0:00.00 kthreadd
   3 root      20   0       0      0      0 S  0.0  0.0  0:00.19 ksoftirqd/0
   5 root       0 -20       0      0      0 S  0.0  0.0  0:00.00 kworker/0:0H
   7 root      rt   0       0      0      0 S  0.0  0.0  0:00.00 migration/0
   8 root      20   0       0      0      0 S  0.0  0.0  0:00.00 rcu_bh
   9 root      20   0       0      0      0 S  0.0  0.0  0:00.72 rcu_sched
  10 root       0 -20       0      0      0 S  0.0  0.0  0:00.00 lru-add-dra+
  11 root      rt   0       0      0      0 S  0.0  0.0  0:00.04 watchdog/0
  13 root      20   0       0      0      0 S  0.0  0.0  0:00.00 kdevtmpfs


                                                               Cancel
```

In this specific case, the systemd process is using most of the CPU. The Zabbix agent, which is running on this system, is not even in the top 10 here. Well, to be fair, on this system, nothing much is happening anyway. All of the processes are reported to be using no CPU at all.

Other similar diagnostic commands might show some package details, **Media Access Control** (**MAC**) addresses, or any other information that's easily obtained from standard utilities. Note that getting a list of processes that use the most memory is not possible with top on most operating systems or distributions; the ps command will probably have to be used. The following code might provide a useful list of the top 10 memory-using processes:

```
ps auxw --sort -rss | head -n 11
```

We are grabbing the top 11 lines here because that also includes the header.

Now, let's configure another script, one that will allow us to reboot the target system. Navigate to **Administration | Scripts** and click on **Create script**. Fill in the following:

- **Name**: `Management/Reboot`.
- **Commands**: `reboot`.
- **User group**: This command is a bit riskier, so we will limit its use to administrative users only; choose **Zabbix administrators**.
- **Host group**: As this would not work on SNMP devices, it would not make sense to make it show up for hosts other than Linux systems here; choose **Selected** and start typing `Linux` in the text field. Choose **Linux servers** in the drop-down.
- **Required host permissions**: We wouldn't want users with read-only access to be able to reboot hosts, so choose **Write**.
- **Enable confirmation**: This is a potentially destructive action, so mark this checkbox.
- **Confirmation text**: With the previous checkbox marked, we may fill in this field. Type **Reboot this system?**.

 Even though the group selection field might look similar to other places where multiple groups can be selected, here, only one host group may be selected.

We may also test what this confirmation message will look like; click on **Test confirmation**:

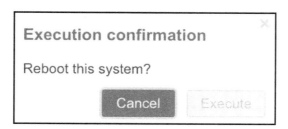

While the **Execute** button is disabled right now, we can see that this would look fairly understandable. Click on **Cancel** in the confirmation dialog. The final result should look like the following. If it does, click on the **Add** button at the bottom:

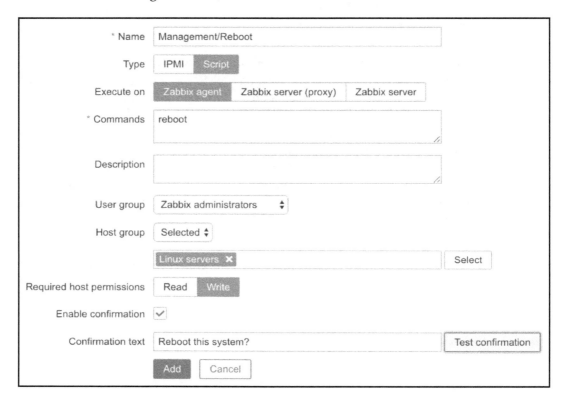

Now, let's see what this script would look like in the menu. Navigate to **Monitoring** | **Problems** and click on **Another host** in the **Host** column. In the pop-up menu, move the mouse cursor over **Management**:

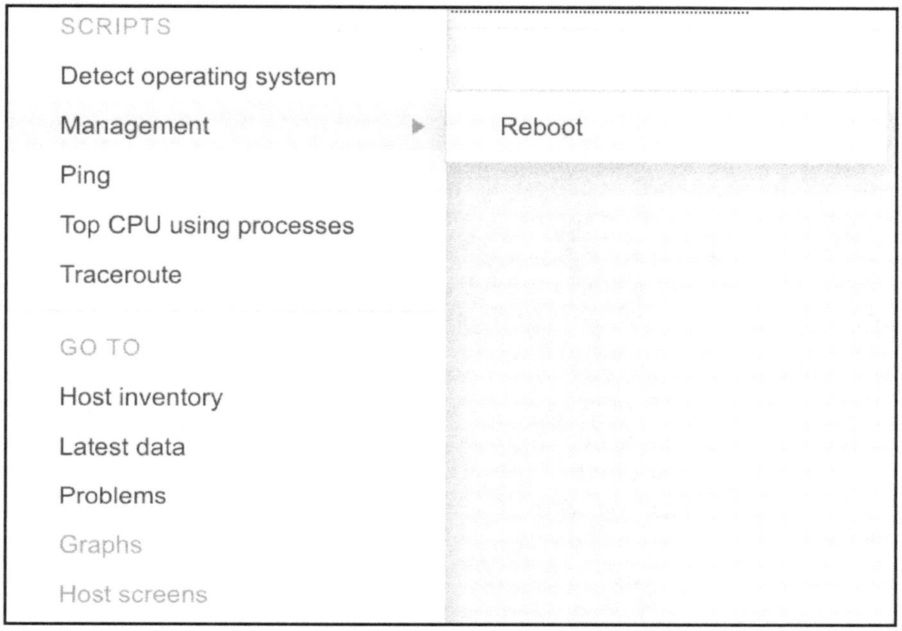

SCRIPTS

Detect operating system

Management ▶   Reboot

Ping

Top CPU using processes

Traceroute

GO TO

Host inventory

Latest data

Problems

Graphs

Host screens

Notice how the syntax we used created a submenu; the slash is used as a separator. We could group **Ping**, **Traceroute**, and **Top CPU using processes** as **Diagnostics**, add more entries in the **Management** section, and create a useful toolset. Note that we can also use `zabbix_get` on the server here and poll individual items that we might not want to monitor constantly. Entries can be nested this way as many times as needed, but beware of creating too many levels. Such mouseover menus are hard to use beyond the first few levels, as it is too easy to make a wrong move and suddenly, all the submenus are closed.

Regarding the **Reboot** entry, if it seemed a bit risky to add, fear not—it does not work anyway. First, we had to use `sudo` for it in the command. Second, we had to configure `sudoers` to actually allow the running of that command by the `zabbix` user.

Reusing global scripts in actions

Some of the global scripts, added this way only make sense when used interactively. Most of the data gathering or diagnostic ones would probably fall under this category. But our reboot entry might be reused in action operations, too. Instead of configuring such commands individually in global scripts and each action, we would have a single place to control how the rebooting happens. Maybe we want to change the reboot command to issue a pending reboot in 10 minutes. That way, a system administrator who might be working on the system has some time to cancel the reboot and investigate the problem in more detail.

We already have the global script for rebooting created. If we had a trigger that warranted rebooting the whole system, we would create an action with the appropriate conditions. In the action properties, global scripts may be reused by choosing **Remote command** in the **Operation type** drop-down when editing an operation. Then, in the **Type** drop-down, **Global script** must be selected and a specific script chosen:

As these scripts can be used both from the frontend and in actions, they're not just called frontend scripts; they are global scripts.

Summary

We started this chapter by discussing actions. Actions are the things controlling what is performed when a trigger fires, and they have a very wide range of things to configure at various levels, including conditions of various precision, message contents, and actual operations performed, starting with simple email sending and using custom scripts, and ending with the powerful remote command execution. We also learned about other things affecting actions, such as user media configuration and user permissions.

Let's refresh our memory on what alerting-related concepts are available:

Trigger is a problem definition including a severity level, with the trigger expression containing information on calculations and thresholds. Event is something happening—that is, a trigger changing state from **PROBLEM** to **OK,** and so on. Action is a configuration entity, with specific sets of conditions that determine when it is invoked and the operations to be performed. Operation is an action property that defined what to do if this action is invoked, and escalations were configured with the help of operations. Alert or notification is the actual thing sent out—an email, SMS, or any other message.

In addition to simple one-time messages, we also figured out how the built-in escalations work in Zabbix, and escalated a few problems. While escalations allow us to produce fairly complex response scenarios, it is important to pay attention when configuring them. Once enabled, they allow us to perform different operations, based on how much time has passed since the problem occurred, and other factors. We discussed common issues with notifications, including the fact that users must have permission to view a host to receive notifications about it, and recovery messages only being sent to the users who received the original problem message.

By now, we have learned of three ways to avoid trigger flapping, resulting in excessive notifications:

- By using trigger expression functions such as min(), max(), and avg() to fire a trigger only if the values have been within a specific range for a defined period of time
- By using hysteresis and only returning to the **OK** state if the current value is some comfort distance below (or above) the threshold
- By creating escalations that skip the first few steps, thus only sending out messages if a problem has not been resolved for some time

The first two methods are different from the last one. Using different trigger functions and hysteresis changes the way the trigger works, impacting how soon it fires and how soon it turns off again. With escalations, we do not affect the trigger's behavior (thus they will still show up in **Monitoring** | **Triggers** and other locations), but we introduce delayed notification whenever a trigger fires.

Finally, we figured out what global scripts are and tried manually pinging a host and obtaining a list of the top CPU-using processes on it. As for action operations, we discussed several ways to react to a problem:

- Sending an email
- Running a command (executed either on the Zabbix agent or server)
- Running an IPMI command
- Running a command over SSH or Telnet
- Reusing a global script

The last one allowed us to configure a script once and potentially reconfigure it for all systems in a single location.

When configuring triggers and actions, there are several little things that can both make life easier and introduce hard-to-spot problems. Hopefully, the coverage of the basics here will help you to leverage the former and avoid the latter.

In the next chapter, we will see how we can avoid configuring some of the things we already know, including items and triggers, on each host individually. We will use templates to manage such configurations on multiple hosts easily.

Questions

1. Can we send delayed notifications to a user and escalate problems when the issue is not resolved until it is fixed ?
2. Can we increase the severity level of a trigger when our action sends a message indicating that there is a problem ?

Further reading

Read the following articles for more information on what was covered in this chapter:

- **Conditions**: `https://www.zabbix.com/documentation/4.0/manual/config/notifications/action/conditions`
- **E-mail**: `https://www.zabbix.com/documentation/4.0/manual/config/notifications/media/email`

8
Simplifying Complex Configurations with Templates

Our current setup has two hosts with similar enough environments, so we copied items from one over to another. But *what do we do when there are a lot of hosts with similar parameters to monitor?* Copying items manually is quite tedious. It's even worse when something has to be changed for all the hosts, such as an item interval or a process name. Luckily, Zabbix provides a means to configure these things in a unified fashion with the templating system.

We will cover the following topics in this chapter:

- Identifying template candidates
- Creating a template
- Linking templates to hosts
- Using multiple templates
- Using mass update
- Nested templates
- Identifying template candidates

Templates allow a Zabbix administrator to reduce their workload and streamline the configuration. But to deploy the templates properly, we have to first identify use cases that require or benefit from them. Or, to put it simply—we have to identify what templates in Zabbix actually are.

When we created the second monitored Linux host, we manually copied items from the first host. If we wish, we can also copy over triggers. Such copying around isn't the best job ever, so instead, we can create items and triggers for a template, which are then linked to the host in question. As a result of the linkage, the host immediately gets all the items and triggers defined in the template. Later, when we want to change some item parameters for all the hosts, we only have to do it once. Changes made to the template propagate to the linked hosts. So, templates make the most sense for items and triggers that you want to have on multiple hosts, such as those Linux machines. Even if you have only a single device of a certain class, it might be worth creating a template for it in case new devices appear that could benefit from the same configuration.

For example, if we had Apache HTTPD and MySQL running on a host, we could split all items and triggers that are relevant for each of these services into separate templates:

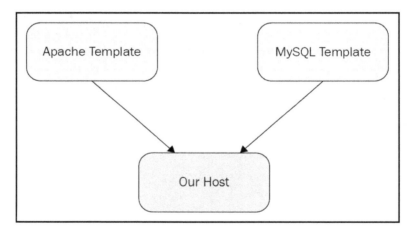

Modifying an item in the MySQL template would propagate those changes downstream in the host. Adding more hosts would be simple; we would just link them to the appropriate templates. Making a change in the template would apply that change to all the downstream hosts.

While the **snmptraps** host we created seems like a good candidate for directly-created objects, we could have a situation where SNMP agents send in traps that are properly distributed between configured hosts in Zabbix, but every now and then a device would send in a trap that wouldn't have a host or corresponding SNMP item configured. If we still wanted traps like that to get sorted in corresponding items in our generic trap host, we would again use templates to create such items for corresponding hosts and our generic host.

Templates are a valuable tool in the Zabbix configuration. That all sounds a bit dry, though, so let's set up some actual templates.

Creating a template

Open **Configuration** | **Templates**. As we can see, there are already 81 predefined templates, compared with only 38 in Zabbix 3.0. Zabbix has done a great job in providing us with a bunch of standard templates to start with. We will create our own specialized one, though; click on **Create template**. This opens a simple form that we have to fill in:

- **Template name**: C_Template_Linux
- **Groups**: Custom templates

The C_ at the front of the name stands for **custom**. We are also creating a new group to hold our templates in, and instead of going through the group configuration, we use the shortcut for group creation on this form. When you type in the name, a box will be shown with our new group name and (new) behind it. Just click on it and the new group will be created, as there is no group yet with the name Custom templates. Don't worry about (new) being in the name of the group, that's just an indication to show us that this is a new group. When you are done, click on **Add**.

We now have the template, but it has no use—there are no items or triggers in it. Go to **Configuration** | **Hosts,** where we will use a lazy and quick solution; we will copy existing items and triggers into the new template. Select **Linux servers** in the **Group** drop-down, then click on **Items** next to **Another host**. Mark all items by clicking in the checkbox in the header, next to wizard, and click on the **Copy** button at the bottom.

> Remember that to select a sequential subset of checkboxes, you can use range selection; select the first checkbox for the range, hold down *Shift*, and click on the last checkbox for the range.

On the next screen, do the following:

1. Choose **Templates** in the **Target type** drop-down, and **Custom templates** in the **Group** drop-down.
2. That leaves us with single entry, so mark the checkbox next to **C_Template_Linux** in the **Target** section.
3. Click on **Copy**. All items should be successfully copied.

In this case, the destination template did not have any items configured. As it is not possible to have two items for a single host with the same key, attempting to copy over an already-existing item would fail.

In the upper-left corner, click on the **Details** link. That expands the messages, and we can see that all of these items were added to the target template:

Now we have to do the following steps with triggers:

1. Click on **Triggers** in the navigation bar above the item list, then click the checkbox in the header next to **Severity.**

2. Uncheck the **One SSH service is down**, because this trigger spans both hosts. If we copied this trigger to the template, that would create all kinds of weird effects.

> The sequence here—copying items first, then triggers—was important. A trigger cannot be created if an item it references is missing, so attempting to copy triggers first would have failed. Copying a trigger will not attempt to copy the items the trigger is referencing.

Follow these steps:

1. Click on the **Copy** button at the bottom.

2. In the next screen, choose **Templates** in the **Target type** drop-down and **Custom templates** in the **Group** drop-down.

3. Mark the checkbox next to **C_Template_Linux** in the **Target** section, then click on **Copy**.

All triggers should be successfully copied. Of course, we don't have to create a host first; create entities on it, then copy them to a template. When creating a fresh template, you'll want to create entities on the template directly. If you have been less careful and haven't thought about templating beforehand, copying like this is a nice way to create the template more quickly.

Linking templates to hosts

Now we'd like to link this template to our very first host, **A test host**. First, let's compare item lists between the freshly-created template and that host:

1. Open **Configuration | Hosts** in one browser window or tab and **Configuration | Templates** in another.

2. In the first window, choose **Linux servers** in the **Group** drop-down, then click on **Items** next to **A test host**.

3. In the other one, select **Custom templates** in the **Group** drop-down, then click on **Items** next to **C_Template_Linux**. Place the windows next to each other and compare the listings:

NAME ▲	TRIGGERS	KEY	NAME ▲	TRIGGERS	KEY
CPU load	Triggers 1	system.cpu.load	CPU load		system.cpu.load
Full OS name		system.uname	Experimental SNMP trap		netSnmpExperimental2
ICMP ping performance		icmppingsec	ICMP ping performance		icmppingsec
incoming traffic on interface		net.if.in[io]	Incoming traffic on interface enpOs8		net.if.in[enpOs8]
incoming traffic on interface enpOs8		net.if.in[enpOs8]	Incoming traffic on interface io		net.if.in[io]
SMTP server status	Triggers 1	net.tcp.service[smtp]	Local time	Triggers 1	system.localtime
SNMP trap fallback	Triggers 1	snmptrap.fallback	SMTP server status	Triggers 1	nettcp.service[smtp]
SNMP trap tests		snmptrap[test]	SNMP trap fallback		snmptrapfallback
SSH server status	Triggers 1	net.tcp.service[ssh]	snmptraps	Triggers 1	snmptrap2
Web server status	Triggers 1	net.tcp.service[http,80]	SNMP traps tests		snmptrap[test]
Zabbix agent version		agent.version	SSH server status		nettcp.service[ssh]
			Testfile exists	Triggers 1	vfs.file.exists[smp.testfile]
			Web server status	Triggers 1	nettcp.service[http,80]
			Zabbix agent version		agentversion

We can see that the template has three more items than the host. Looking at the lists on the left side of the screenshot and the right, we can see that items available on the template (right) but not on the host (left) are both SNMP-related items that we added later, experimental SNMP trap and snmptraps, the local time item, and also the check for a file, Testfile, exists. If the template has four items that the host is missing, but in total, it only has three items more, then that means the host should have one item that the template doesn't. That's right, the full OS name exists for the host but is missing in the template. Keep that in mind, and return to **Configuration | Hosts**.

Make sure the **Group** drop-down says either **all** or **Linux servers**, and click on **A test host** in the **Name** column. We finally get to use the **Templates** tab—switch to it. Start typing C in the **Link new templates** input field. In the drop-down, our new template, **C_Template_Linux**, should be the very first one. Click on it. Even though it might seem that this template is now added, it actually isn't; if we were to update the host now, it would not be linked:

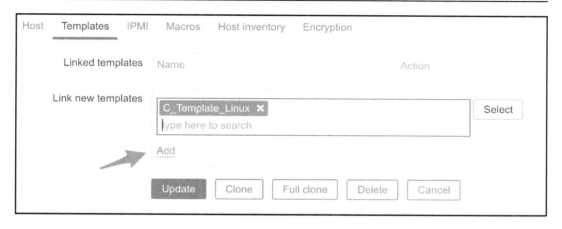

Click on the **Add** control just below the template name. This form can be highly confusing, so try to remember that you have to do that extra click here. With the template added to the list, notice that it's actually a link. Clicking it will open template properties in a new window. When looking at host properties, this offers quick access to template properties. Such convenient links are available in many places in the Zabbix frontend:

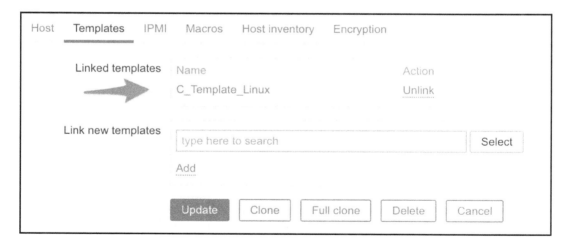

In the end, click on the **Update** button at the bottom. We are now welcomed with a message that tells us that our host is updated with the information from our template:

When a template is linked to a host, identical entities that already exist on the host are linked against the template, but no historical data is lost. Entities that exist on the template only are added to the host and linked to the template.

Do not confuse templates with host groups. They are completely different things. Groups serve a logical host grouping (and permission assigning), but templates define what is monitored on a host, what graphs it has, and so on. What's more, a single host group can contain both ordinary hosts and templates. Adding a template to a group will not affect hosts in that group in any way; only linking that template will. Think of groups as a way to organize the templates the same way as hosts are organized.

Now, we can check out how linked items appear in the configuration:

1. Open **Configuration** | **Hosts**
2. Click on **Items** next to **A test host**:

☐	• • •	Full OS Name	system.uname
☐	• • •	C_Template_Linux: ICMP ping performance	icmppingsec
☐	• • •	C_Template_Linux: Incoming traffic on interface enp0s3	net.if.in[enp0s3]

There are two observations we can make right away:

- Almost all items are prefixed with a template name (**C_Template_Linux** in this case) in grey text. Obviously, this indicates items that are linked from the template. Clicking on the template name would open an item listing for that template.
- A single item (full OS name) is not prefixed. Remember, this was the only item existing on the host, *but not on the template*. If entities exist on the host only, linking does not do anything to them; they are left intact and attached to the host directly.

Let's see what a linked item looks like. Click on **SMTP server status** in the **Name** column:

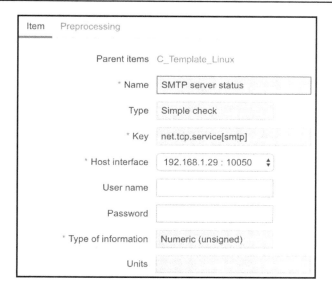

Hey, *what happened? Why are most fields greyed out and can't be edited?* Well, that's what a template is about. Most of the entity (in this case, an item) parameters are configured in the template. As we can see, some fields are still editable. This means that we still can disable or enable items per individual host, even when they are linked in from a template. The same goes for the update interval, history length, and a few other parameters.

We now want to make this particular item for this host slightly different from all other hosts that the template will be linked to, so let's change these things:

- **Update interval**: 360
- **History storage period**: 60

When you are done, click on **Update**. Now, this host will have two parameters customized for a single item, while all other hosts that will get linked against the template will receive values from the template. Let's link one more host to our template now. Navigate to **Configuration | Templates**. Here we can see a full list of templates, along with the hosts linked to them. The linkage area in this screen shows various entries and listed entities there have different colors:

- **Gray**: Templates
- **Green**: Enabled hosts
- **Red**: Disabled hosts

Go back to **Configuration** | **Hosts** and go to **Another host** to the **Template** tab. Link this host with our template **C_Template_Linux**, just as we did in previous task, with our **A test host**. Take a look at the item SMTP server status on both hosts, and you will see that our **Another host** has the interval defined from our template, while our **A test host** has the updated values.

 You used to be able to link templates to hosts from the Template section in Zabbix. However, Zabbix SIA has been cleaning up the interface to make things easier for end users and less confusing, and this functionality was lost in the process.

Handling default templates

In the template list, you can see many predefined templates. *Should you use them as is? Should you modify them? Or just use them as a reference?*

It depends. Carefully evaluate the default templates and decide whether you really want to use them as is. Maybe item intervals are too low or the history storage period is too high? If there's anything you would like to change, the suggested approach is to clone those templates and leave the defaults as-is. That will allow you to update the official templates later and always have the latest version for reference.

Regarding keeping them in sync, the easiest way is XML import, and we will discuss that in Chapter 19, *Working Closely with Data*.

And talking of community-supplied templates, this is something many of you will want to improve. The user who supplied the template might have had completely different requirements; they might have misunderstood some aspect of Zabbix configuration or handled an older device that does not expose as much data as the one you are monitoring. Always evaluate such templates very carefully and don't hesitate to improve them. I've added some URLs at the end of this chapter to get you started including the official page from Zabbix to share templates.

Changing the configuration in a template

Let's try changing an item that is attached to the template:

1. Open **Configuration** | **Templates**, select **Custom templates** from the **Group** drop-down and click on **Items** next to **C_Template_Linux**.
2. Click on **SMTP server status** in the **Name** column. As we can see, all fields are editable when we edit a directly-attached instance of an item.
3. Change the **History storage period** field to read **14d**, then click on **Update**.

When an item is updated in a template, the change is propagated to all linked hosts. This means that with a single action, both linked hosts have their history-keeping period set to **14** days now. But we changed two item properties for one downstream host before, and we just changed one of those for the upstream template. *What about downstreaming the host's other item?* Let's find out:

1. Go to **Configuration** | **Hosts**, choose **Linux servers** in the **Group** drop-down, and click on **Items** next to **A test host**.
2. In the Name column, click on **SMTP server status**:

We can see that our downstream change for **Update interval** has been preserved, but the **History storage period** value has been overwritten with the one set for the template. That's because only changed properties are set to downstream when editing template-attached items. Now click on **Cancel**.

Macro usage

We previously added triggers from **Another host** to our template, but we didn't do that for **A test host**. Let's find out whether it has some triggers we could use in the template. Click on **Triggers** in the **Navigation** bar above the **Items** list. From the directly-attached triggers in the list (the ones not prefixed with a template name), one is a trigger that takes into account items from two different hosts and we avoided copying it over before. The other directly-attached triggers are the ones that we are interested in. Mark the checkboxes next to the **CPU load too high on A test host for last 3 minutes** and **Critical error from SNMP trap** triggers in the **Name** column, then click on the **Copy** button at the bottom. In the next window, choose **Templates** in the **Target type** drop-down, **Custom templates** in the **Group** drop-down, then mark the checkbox next to the only remaining target (**C_Template_Linux**), and click on **Copy**.

The two triggers we copied are added to the template. This causes the following:

- As **A test host** is linked to the modified template and it already has such triggers; these two triggers for that host are updated to reflect the linkage.
- **Another host** does not have such triggers, so the triggers are created and linked to the template.

While we are still in the trigger list, select **Another host** in the **Host** drop-down. Look carefully at the CPU load trigger that was added to this host in the previous operation:

Wait, that's definitely incorrect. The trigger refers to **A test host**, while this is **Another host**. The trigger name was correct when we first added it, but now the same trigger is applied to multiple hosts. In turn, the reference is incorrect for all the hosts except one. Let's try to fix this:

1. Select **Custom templates** in the **Group** drop-down
2. Click on the **CPU load too high on A test host for last 3 minutes** trigger in the **Name** column
3. Change the **Name** field to `CPU load too high on {HOST.NAME} for last 3 minutes`
4. Click on the **Update** button

Yes, that's right, macros to the rescue again.

The use of the word `macros` can be confusing here—Zabbix calls them `macros`, although they might be more correctly considered `variables`. In this book, we will follow Zabbix terminology, but feel free to read `macro` as variable.

In the trigger list for the template, the trigger name has now changed to **CPU load too high on {HOST.NAME} for last 3 minutes**. That's not very descriptive, but you can expect to see such a situation in the configuration section fairly often—Zabbix does not expand most macros in configuration. To verify that it is resolving as expected, navigate to **Monitoring | Problems** and expand the filter. Set the **Show** selection box to **History**, and in **Problem** enter CPU in the **Filter by name** field, then click on the **Apply** button under the filter:

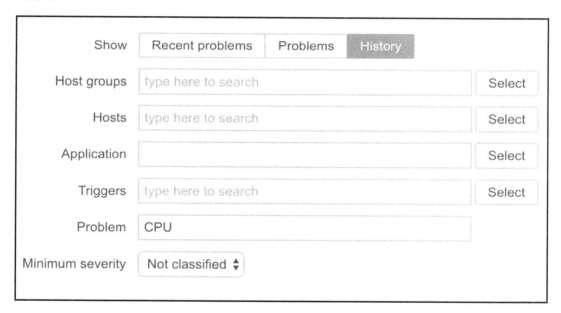

Notice how the trigger name includes the correct hostname now. In most cases, it is suggested to include a macro such as this in trigger names to easily identify the affected host.

The macro we used here, {HOST.NAME}, resolves to the host's visible name. We had no visible name specified and the hostname was used. If a host had the visible name defined, we could also choose to use the hostname with a macro {HOST.HOST}.

Zabbix made some changes in 4.0. Problem and event names used to be generated on the fly in the frontend, and on the server side, based on the respective trigger name with all the macros expanded. That lead to severe performance issues and also made it impossible to see historical information about problems if the trigger name had changed.

Now, problem and event names are stored directly in the events and problem tables when an event is generated for a problem or recovery. This change leads to a better separation of triggers and problems and improves performance, especially that of the frontend, and maintains historical problem names.

User macros

The macros we used before are built-in. Zabbix also allows users to define macros and use them later. In this case, it might be even more important to call them variables instead, so consider using that term too. Let's start with a practical application of a user macro and discuss the details a bit later.

Go to **Configuration** | **Templates** and click on **C_Template_Linux** in the **Templates** column. Switch to the **Macros** tab and add one new macro:

- **Macro**: {$CPU_LOAD_THRESHOLD}
- **Value**: 1

When done, click on **Update**. We have defined one macro on the template, but it is not used at this time. Click on **Triggers** next to **C_Template_Linux**, then click on **CPU load too high on {HOST.NAME} for last 3 minutes** in the **Name** column. Change the trigger properties:

- **Name**: CPU load too high on {HOST.NAME} for last 3 minutes (over {$CPU_LOAD_THRESHOLD})

- **Expression**:
  {C_Template_Linux:system.cpu.load.avg(180)}>{$CPU_LOAD_THR ESHOLD}

Notice how we used the same user macro name, both in the trigger name and expression, as in the template properties. When done, click on **Update**. The changes we just did had no functional impact—this trigger works exactly the same as before, except it has a more explanatory name. We replaced the trigger threshold with the macro, parametrizing it instead of having a hard-coded value. Now we can try overriding this value for a single host; navigate to **Configuration | Hosts** and click on **A test host** in the **Name** column. Switch to the **Macros** tab and switch to the **Inherited and host macros** mode:

Notice how, in this form, we can see the macro we just created on the template. There's also a {$SNMP_COMMUNITY} macro—we will discuss where that one comes from a bit later. We can also see which exact template is providing the macro that we created. Although we remember that in this case, in real-world setups, it is an extremely helpful feature when many templates are linked to a host. To customize this value on this host, click on the **Change** control next to **{$CPU_LOAD_THRESHOLD}**. The **Effective value** column input field becomes editable; change it to 0.9.

Zabbix 3.0 was the first version that allowed us to resolve macros like this. In previous versions, we would have to know the exact macro name to be able to override it. There was also no reasonable way to identify the template supplying the macro.

When done, click on **Update**. Now we finally have some use for the macro; by using the same name on the host level, we were able to override the macro value for this single host. To double-check this change, go to **Monitoring** | **Problems** and expand the filter. Set the **Show status** box to **History** and enter CPU in the **Filter problem** field, then click on **Apply**.

Create some load on both machines. Remember that we could use something such as cat /dev/urandom | md5sum to generate some CPU load. On our problem page, after some time, we would see problems:

This list confirms that **Another host** is getting the macro value of 1 from the template, but **A test host** has it changed to 0.9. We are still using the same template and the same trigger, but we changed the trigger threshold for this single host.

Remember the {$SNMP_COMMUNITY} macro we saw in the **Inherited and host macros** section from the macro tab on our host . So far, we have covered two locations where user macros may be defined—the **template** and **host level**. There's actually another location available. Click on the menu on **Administration** | **General** and select **Macros** in the drop-down in the upper-right corner. This form looks the same as the template and host macro properties, and there's one macro already defined here:

We'll talk more about this macro in a moment, but first, let's figure out how these three levels interact. As an example, we can look at a hypothetical use of the macro we just defined:

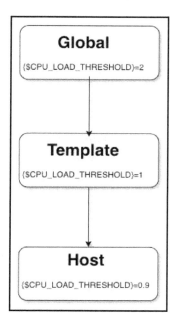

In addition to our template and host-level definitions, we could define this macro on the global level with yet another value; in this example, we used **2**. Now, all other templates and hosts that would not have this macro defined would use the global value of **2**. This change would not affect our template and host, as they have a macro with the same name already defined. In general, the macro definition that's closest to the host wins. Zabbix first looks for a macro on the host, then the template, then the global level.

> The macro's name is up to us, as long as we use the allowed symbols: uppercase letters, numbers, underscores, and a dot.

But *what happens if two templates define the same macro and are linked directly to a host?* One of the macro values will be used, and the choice will depend on Zabbix's internal IDs; do not rely on such a configuration. One way to explicitly override the macro value would be by introducing yet another template that would be linked directly to the host and would pull in the two original templates.

We used a user macro in the trigger name and expression as a threshold. *Where else can they be used?* Here are some examples:

- **Item key parameters and item name**: We might run SSH on the default port 22, but override it for some hosts. Note that user macros cannot be used in the key itself, only in parameters that are enclosed by square brackets.
- **Trigger function parameters**: We might change the trigger to {C_Template_Linux:system.cpu.load.avg({$CPU_LOAD_TIME})}>{ $CPU_LOAD_THRESHOLD} and then use {$CPU_LOAD_TIME} to change the averaging time for some hosts.
- **SNMP community**: This is where the {$SNMP_COMMUNITY} default macro we saw in the global configuration is used. If that macro had been used in SNMP item properties, we could use the same template on various SNMP devices and change the SNMP community as needed.

> If you are designing templates that use user macros, it is suggested to define such macros on the template level in addition to, or instead of, the global macro. Exporting such a template will not include global macros, only the macros that are defined on the template level.

Entities such as items and triggers are configured once in the template. When the template is applied to many hosts, macros provide a way to create personalized configurations for linked hosts.

Using multiple templates

There are two monitored hosts now. They both have some services monitored and linked to the same template. Suddenly, the situation changes: one of the hosts gets a new function and the email server is removed. Our options from the Zabbix viewpoint include simply disabling email-related items for that host, or creating a separate template for it and removing email-server-related entities from the main template, instead leaving them on the other server. There's a better approach, though: splitting email-server-related entities into a separate template.

Navigate to **Configuration** | **Templates**, then click on the **Create template** button. Enter C_Template_Email in the **Template name** field, select **Custom templates** in the **Groups** box if it's not already selected, then click on **Add**:

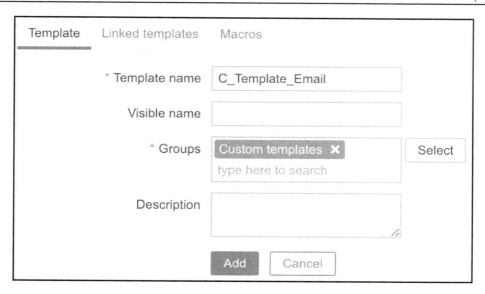

Now, let's populate this template:

1. Select **Custom templates** in the **Group** drop-down and click on **Items** next to **C_Template_Linux**
2. Mark the checkboxes next to **SMTP server status** and **Testfile** in the **Name** column, then click on the **Copy** button at the bottom
3. In the next screen, select **Templates** in the **Target type** drop-down, and **Custom templates** in the **Group** drop-down
4. Mark the checkbox next to **C_Template_Email**, then click on **Copy**

That deals with the items—now let's take care of the triggers:

1. Click on **Triggers** in the navigation bar above the **Items** list
2. Mark the checkboxes next to **SMTP service is down** and **Testfile is missing** in the **Name** column. Then click on the **Copy** button
3. In the next screen, select **Templates** in the **Target type** drop-down, **Custom templates** in the **Group** drop-down and mark the checkbox next to **C_Template_Email**, then click on **Copy**

 We also have to pull in our test file item and trigger, as the SMTP trigger depends on the test file trigger. We could not copy the SMTP trigger, as that would leave an unsatisfied dependency.

We now have a simple dedicated email server template that we can link to the hosts. It has the same item and trigger regarding the SMTP service as our custom Linux template. There's a problem though—as they both have an item with the same key, we cannot link these templates to the same host; it would fail. Attempting to do so would probably result in a message such as this:

Details ▲ Cannot update host

Item "net.tcp.service[smtp]" already exists on "Another host", inherited from another template.

We will perform some steps to change the template linkage:

- Unlink **C_Template_Linux** from **A test host** and **Another host**
- Remove SMTP related items and triggers from **C_Template_Linux**
- Link **C_Template_Email** to them both
- Link **C_Template_Linux** back to both hosts

This way, SMTP-related items and triggers will become templated from the email template, while preserving all collected data. If we deleted those items from the Linux template and then linked in the email template, we would also remove all collected values for those items.

Go to **Configuration** | **Hosts**, mark the checkboxes next to **A test host** and **Another host**, then click on **Mass update**. Switch to the **Templates** tab and mark the **Link templates** checkbox and the **Replace** checkbox. This will unlink the linked templates, but keep the previously templated entities as directly-attached ones:

We will discuss host mass update in more detail later in the chapter in the **Using mass update** section.

Click on **Update**. Now we will modify the Linux template to remove SMTP related items and triggers.

Navigate to **Configuration | Templates**, click on **Items** for **C_Template_Linux**, and mark the checkboxes next to **SMTP server status** and **Testfile exists** in the **Name** column. At the bottom, click on the **Delete** button and confirm the popup. If you expand the details, you will see that the triggers that were depending on these items got deleted, too—we did not have to delete them manually:

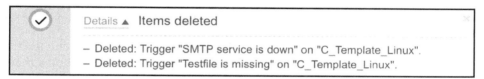

Now we are ready to link in our new email template, and link back the modified Linux template. We can even do that in one step and we will again use the mass update function to do that. Go to **Configuration | Hosts**, mark the checkboxes next to **A test host** and **Another host**, then click on **Mass update**. Switch to the **Templates** tab, mark the **Link templates** checkbox, and type C_ in the input field. Both of our templates will show up; click on one of them, then type C_ again, and click on the other template:

Click on the **Update** button. Take a look at the template-linkage list in **Configuration
| Templates** after this operation. Each of the custom templates now has two hosts
linked:

Name ▲	Applications	Items	Triggers	Graphs	Screens	Discovery	Web	Linked templates	Linked to
C_Template_Email	Applications	Items 2	Triggers 2	Graphs	Screens	Discovery	Web		Another host, A test host
C_Template_Linux	Applications	Items 11	Triggers 4	Graphs	Screens	Discovery	Web		Another host, A test host

Displaying 2 of 2 found

A single host can be linked against multiple templates. This allows for a modular
configuration where each template only provides a subset of entities, thus a server
can be configured to have any combination of basic Linux, email server, web server,
file server, and any other templates.

Of course, with a single item and trigger, this process seems too complex, but usually
the email server would have more parameters, such as mail-server process counts,
SMTP, IMAP, POP3 service status, spam and virus filter status, and queue length. At
that point, the ability to quickly make a collection of metrics monitored on a machine
with a couple of clicks is more than welcome.

> The method of unlinking, redesigning, and linking back is a
> common and suggested approach to changing template
> configurations. Just be careful not to change item keys while
> templates are unlinked, or to delete items while they are linked.

Unlinking templates from hosts

We talked about one server losing the email server duties, and linking both templates
to both hosts was not the correct operation. Let's deal with that now:

1. Open **Configuration | Hosts** and choose **Linux servers** in the **Group** drop-
   down.
2. Our first test host will not be serving SMTP any more, so click on **A test
   host** in the **Name** column and switch to the **Templates** tab:

This section properly lists two linked templates. We now want to unlink **C_Template_Email**, but there are two possible actions: **Unlink** and **Unlink and clear**. *What's the difference then?* Let's try it out and start with the one that looks safer.

3. Click on **Unlink** next to **C_Template_Email**, then click on **Update**. Expand the **Details** link to see what happened:

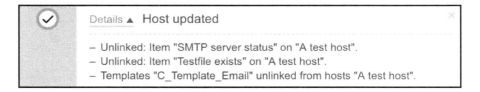

Both item and trigger got unlinked, so it seems. Was that *what we wanted?* Let's see.

4. Click on **Items** next to **A test host**:

Well, not quite—SMTP-related items are still there. So a simple unlink does unlinking only, and leaves a copy of the items on the previously-linked host. That is handy if we want to create a different item or leave an item on the host to keep data for historical reasons, but not this time. To solve the current situation, we can manually delete both triggers and items, but that wouldn't be so easy if the host additionally had a bunch of directly-attached entities. In that case, we would have to manually hunt them down and remove them, which allows for mistakes to be made. Instead, let's try a different route: relink this template, then remove it without a trace:

1. Click on **A test host** in the navigation header and switch to the **Templates** tab.
2. Start typing C_ in the **Link new templates** field, then click on **C_Template_Email**.
3. Carefully click on the small **Add** control just below it and then click on **Update**. Expanding the details will show the SMTP item and trigger getting linked to the template again. We are now back at our starting point with two templates linked—time to unlink again.
4. Click on **A test host** in the **Name** column and switch to the **Templates** tab.
5. Click on **Unlink and clear** next to **C_Template_Email** in the **Linked templates** block, then click on **Update**, and expand **Details**:

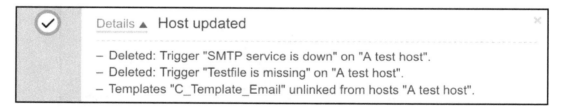

And now it's done. Both items and triggers are actually deleted. Look at the host list; notice how the **Templates** column again offers a quick overview. This comes in handy when you might want to quickly verify a template linkage for all the hosts in a particular group:

Name ▲	Applications	Items	Triggers	Graphs	Discovery	Web	Interface	Templates
Another host	Applications 1	Items 13	Triggers 7	Graphs	Discovery	Web	192.168.1.25: 10050	C_Template_Email, C_Template_Linux
A test host	Applications	Items 12	Triggers 5	Graphs	Discovery	Web	192.168.1.29: 10050	C_Template_Linux

Using mass update

Similar to items, a mass update can also be used for hosts, and we've already used it a couple of times. Let's explore in more detail what functionality mass update might offer here. Go to **Configuration | Hosts**. In the hosts list, mark the checkboxes next to **A test host** and **Another host** and click on the **Mass update** button at the bottom. Then switch to the **Templates** tab and mark the **Link templates** checkbox.

Selecting a template is done the same way as in the host properties; we can either type and search by that substring, or click on the **Select** button to choose from a list. We may specify multiple templates in that field, and there is no extra control to click like in the host properties—we had to click on **Add** there. In this form, it is enough to have the template listed in the first field. Switching between mass update and updating an individual host can be quite challenging as these forms work differently—be very, very careful.

There are also two checkboxes. Before we discuss what they do, let's figure out what happens by default. If we list a template or several and then update the configuration, that template is linked to all selected hosts in addition to the existing templates. The existing ones are not touched in any way. The checkboxes modify this behavior:

A short overview of the options we have:

- **Replace**: Existing templates are unlinked. As before, any entities coming from those templates are not touched. Items, triggers, and everything else that was controlled by that template stays on the host. If the templates we had specified in this form have items with the same keys, such items are be linked to the new templates.

- **Clear when unlinking**: Existing templates are unlinked and cleared—that is, anything coming from them is deleted. It's almost like clearing the host, except that directly-attached entities would not be touched; only templated entities are affected.

Of course, if there are any conflicts, such as the same item key being present in two templates, such a linkage would fail.

We will not modify the template linkage at this time, so click on the **Cancel** button here.

Nested templates

The one host still serving emails, **Another host,** now has two templates assigned. But *what if we separated out in individual templates all services, applications, and other similar data that can be logically grouped?* This would result in a bunch of templates that we would need to link to a single host. This is not tragic, but *what if we had two servers like that? Or three? Or 20?* At some point, even a configuration with templates can become hard to manage—each host can easily have a template count of a dozen in large and complicated environments.

This is where simplicity is coupled with powerful functionality. Behind the scenes, templates aren't that different from hosts. Actually, they are hosts, just somewhat special ones. This means that a template can be linked to another template, thus creating a nested configuration.

How does that apply to our situation? Let's create a simple configuration that would allow the easy addition of more hosts of the same setup. In **Configuration | Templates**, click on the **Create template** button. In the **Template name** field, enter C_Template_Email_Server, mark **Custom templates** in the **Groups** box.

Switch to the **Linked templates** tab. Here, we can link other templates to this one. In the **Link new templates** selection box, add the following templates by typing C_ and then selecting both **C_Template_Email** and **C_Template_Linux.** Another option is to press the **Select** button and to select them from the list of templates. Press the small **Add** button in the **Link new templates** section (not the one all the way at the bottom):

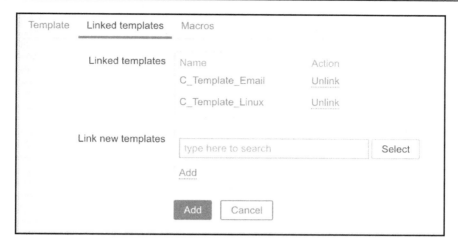

When you are done, click on the **Add** button at the bottom. We now have a template that encompasses a basic Linux system configuration with an email server installed and running, so we still have to properly link it to a host that will serve this role:

1. Open **Configuration | Hosts**, click on **Another host** in the **Name** column and switch to the **Templates** tab.
2. In the **Linked templates** section, click on both **Unlink** links.
3. In the **Link new templates input** field, type email and click on **C_Template_Email_Server**.
4. Click on the small **Add** button, then click on **Update** at the bottom of the form. The action successfully completes, so expand the **Details** link.

As we can see here, all elements were unlinked first and updated later. Essentially, the previous templates were unlinked, but the items and triggers were left in place and were then relinked to the new template. The biggest benefit from such a sequence was keeping all the historical item data.

The biggest thing we did here was create a nested template. Such a template is linked against other templates, thus it inherits all the items, triggers, and other characteristics, while usually making some modifications to the original template conditions. In this case, our nested template contains entities from two other templates, like this:

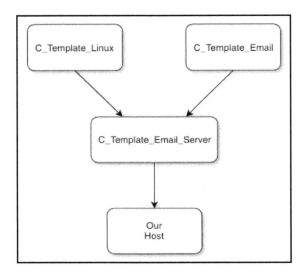

While that seems to be only a little gain from the previous situation of two templates linked to a single host, it is a very valid approach when your monitored environment is slightly larger. If there's a single host that requires a specific combination of multiple templates, it is fine to link those templates directly to the host. As soon as the count increases, it is more convenient to set up template nesting, creating a single template to link for these hosts. When you have done that, adding a new host of the same class requires linking against a single template only, which greatly simplifies configuration and minimizes the chance of mistakes.

Looking at the host list, we can see all templates that affect this host in the **Templates** column:

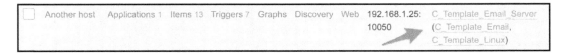

Notice how the new **C_Template_Email_Server** template is listed first, and the two other templates are listed in parentheses. Templates that are linked directly to the host are listed first, and second-level templates that are pulled in by the first level are listed in parentheses. Only the first two levels are shown her—if we had more levels of nesting, we would not see them in the host list.

Let's review a templated item now. From the host list, perform the following steps:

1. Click on **Items** next to **Another host**.
2. Click on **SMTP server status** in the **Name** column. This time we are interested in the very first row here, **Parent items**:

This is something that shows up in templated items. Higher-level items can be seen and accessed here, and for this item, there are two levels displayed. Templates that are closer to the host are listed last, and the very first template is the one the item originates from. If we had more than two levels, they would be shown as well. This line works as a quick way to get information on where a particular item originates from and what could modify it, as well as a convenience access to the upstream item. If we spot a simple mistake in some templated item, we can go to higher-level items with one click, instead of going to **Configuration | Templates**, finding the correct page and/or template, then repeating that for the item. The same parent entity convenience access line is available for triggers and other entities, too.

When using a nested template setup, the inherited macro resolution helper is even more helpful. If we had a single host and a single template, without the helper, we'd first check the macro on the host; if it's not defined there, we'd check for it on the template, and if not defined there either, on the global level. With nested templates, we would have to check all the templates individually. With the helper, we can see the outcome and which exact template is providing the value from that same macro tab in the host properties.

Template nesting is a convenient way to group templates and apply a single template to the target hosts, while still having different functionality properly split up and reused in multiple lower-level templates. Nevertheless, care should be taken not to create excessive nesting. Two levels of nesting are quite common, but one advanced Zabbix user admitted that designing a templating system with five levels of nesting was a bit excessive, and they would restrict themselves to a maximum of four levels next time.

Summary

In Zabbix, templates play a major role in simplifying the configuration and allowing large-scale changes. If you are a proficient user of word processors, you probably use styles. The same concept is used in text, CSS styles for the web, and elsewhere—separating content from the presentation helps to reduce the amount of work required when changes have to be made.

While the comparison to styles might seem far-fetched at first, it actually is similar enough. Just like styles, you can separate a host from the services you provide, and you can define these services in a centralized fashion. In the same way that a word document has a heading style that allows you to change the font size for all headings of that level with one action, templates in Zabbix allow you to change some parameter for all linked hosts, whether direct or nested.

We used several locations that allow us to modify template linkages in Zabbix:

- **Host properties**: This allows us to link, unlink, and unlink and clear multiple templates from a single host
- **Host mass update**: This allows us to link multiple templates to multiple hosts, as well as unlinking, or unlinking and clearing, all the previously linked templates (but not unlinking, or unlinking and clearing, a specific template)
- **Template properties**: This allows us to link and unlink (and clear) linked templates

In the preceding list, we could also talk about templates where we talk about hosts. That would be used when managing nested template configuration.

Macros in Zabbix are like variables—they provide a generic placeholder that is later replaced with a host-specific value. We looked at some built-in macros and also user macros that allow us to define our own variables to have customized items, triggers, and other entities on the host level.

As we saw with all the rearrangement of items and triggers in templates, it is easier to plan a sane template policy before getting to the actual configuration. It is strongly suggested that you sit down and draw at least a very basic hierarchy of monitored things before rushing into the configuration—that will make things easier in the long run.

In the next chapter, we will look at the ways data can be visualized in Zabbix. We'll start with graphs and network maps, and see how various runtime information can be displayed. We will discuss graph customization and usage in detail.

Questions

1. Can I use an item with a trigger in a template on multiple hosts and have different thresholds for the trigger?
2. If I use templates, can I still make host-level changes on my items?
3. Can I link my template to a group so that the group gets all items, triggers, and so on from the template?

Further reading

Read the following articles for more information also the Zabbix share website is the official Zabbix website to share you templates:

- **Configuring a template**: https://www.zabbix.com/documentation/4.0/manual/config/templates/template
- **User macros**: https://www.zabbix.com/documentation/4.0/manual/config/macros/usermacros
- **Zabbix share**: https://share.zabbix.com/
- **zabbix-community-repos**: https://github.com/monitoringartist/zabbix-community-repos

Visualizing Data with Screens and Slideshows

9

We will explore a few visualization options in this chapter. Compound elements (which have nothing to do with map elements) allow us to combine individual elements and other sources to provide a more informative or good-looking overview. We might want to see a map of our network together with a graph of main outbound links, and perhaps also a list of current problems.

We cover the functionality of screens and slide-shows in this chapter, but keep in mind that Zabbix SIA would like to remove this functionality in future versions. The idea is that it is deprecated and can be replaced with the revamped home screen, as it can be shared and supports widgets.

We will cover the following topics:

- Configuring and sharing dashboards
- Screens that can include other entities, including global and templated or host screens
- Slideshows that change displayed information on a periodic basis automatically
- Showing data on a big display

Configuring and sharing dashboards

The new dashboard in Zabbix has improved a lot over the years, and the idea of Zabbix SIA is that the dashboard should be a single piece of information that gathers all kind of information. It's probably inspired by the success of things such as Grafana.

Let's take a look at the dashboard more closely. Since we've already seen how to configure some of the widgets, let's take a look how we can configure our dashboard and share it with others.

Configuring the dashboard

The configuration of our dashboard can be done very easily by clicking in the top-right on the **Edit dashboard** button:

By clicking this button, we arrive at some sort of configuration mode for our dashboard, and when we move our mouse over one of the widgets, we see that a box is drawn around the widget:

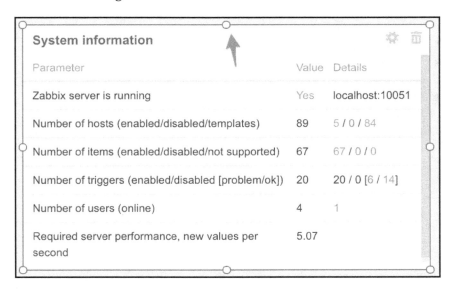

Moving our mouse over one of these lines allows us to change the size of the widget. Moving our mouse away to the middle will change our mouse cursor into four arrows, which indicates that we are now able to move our widget around.

In short, we are now able to resize our widget and change the position of our widgets. This allows us to change the look of the dashboard by resizing widgets as we need. Think of the problem widget; we can now create a widget with the exact size we need to see the number of problems.

Looking at the **Edit dashboard** button that we clicked on earlier, we now see that it has changed into four different options:

The first icon is the wheel. When we click on the wheel, we are able to configure the dashboard and change the owner and the name of our dashboard:

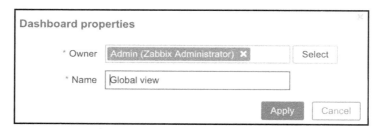

The **Add widget** button gives us the option to add new widgets to our dashboard:

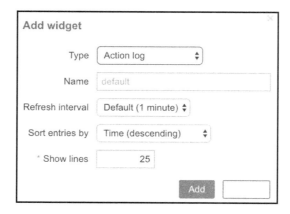

Here, we can select the type of widget we'd like to add and configure the name we'd like to give it, set the refresh interval per widget, the way we sort things, and the number of lines to show. As we can see, there is a nice long list of widgets to choose from—let's hope that this is only the start of it:

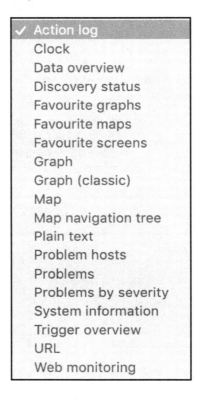

We will not go over every widget as this would take up too much time, and after all, widgets are not too difficult to configure. However, there is one widget that is very interesting. The **Graph** widget appears twice in this list, once as **Graph** and once as **Graph (classic)**.

As it turns out, Zabbix has improved not only the look and the functionalities of the dashboard, but also how graphs look in our dashboard. Graph (classic) is still the old graph style that we know from our items, and the Graph widget contains the new look, not to say the Graphana-style look:

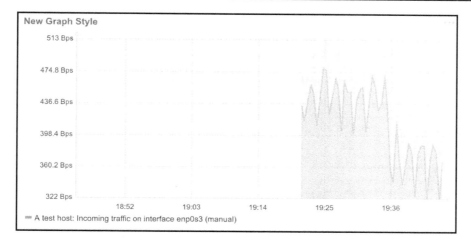

This is a much more appealing look than what we are used to. Too bad it only works in the frontend at the moment, but this was a well-thought-out decision as it would have cost resources from our Zabbix server. Once done and happy with our look, we can save the changes by clicking on the **Save changes** button.

Sharing our dashboard

Now that our dashboard looks how we want it to look, it's time to look into how we can share it with the rest of our team:

1. Click on the Actions button next to **Edit dashboard**:

2. We are presented with a new pop-up menu where we can select sharing, create new, clone, and delete. I think the last three options speak for themselves, so let's have a look at sharing:

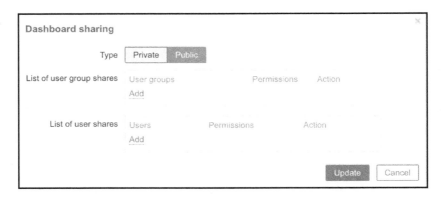

If you have experience with graphs and maps sharing, this popup should look familiar to you. The box type allows us to choose between making our dashboard available to the **public** or making it **private**.

Public speaks for itself; we share it with everybody else. When choosing **Private**, it is only visible to us. However, after the **Type** tab, we have two more options to choose from—**List of user group shares** and **List of user shares**.

If we don't want to make our dashboard publicly available, we still have the option to share it with specific users or with specific groups of users. This allows us to build dashboards and share them with other users or specific groups of users .

The third button with the two arrows pointing to both the corners of the screen is the button to go fullscreen, however there are still some parts visible from the menu, such as the name and the buttons—edit dashboard, for example. The Fullscreen button has changed a bit and now has four arrows, instead of two, pointing to all corners of our screen:

This is what we call the kiosk mode in Zabbix; it allows us to remove all unnecessary information from the screen so that we can maximize the view of our dashboard for monitors without any distraction.

Top-level navigation, user-level content, and the dashboard and all widgets in view mode (except for the map navigation tree) are now readable by a screen-reader. All interactive elements (except maps) can now be accessed by pressing the *Tab* key.

Screens

The graphs and maps we are familiar with cannot be combined into a single page on their own—for that, we may use an entity called a **screen**.

Let's create one together:

1. Navigate to **Monitoring** | **Screens**, and click on the **Create screen** button.
2. Enter Local servers in the **Name** field and 2 in the **Columns** field. We will be able to add more later, if needed:

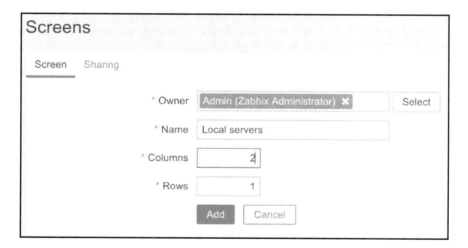

As with network maps, screens may also be created and shared by users.

3. Click on **Add**, and then click on **Constructor** next to **Local servers**. We are presented with a fairly unimpressive view:

So, it's up to us to spice it up.

4. Click on the left-hand **Change** link, and we have an editing form replacing the previous cell's contents. The default resource type is graph, and we created some graphs earlier.

5. Click on **Select** next to the **Graph** field. In the upcoming window, make sure **A test host** is selected in the **Host** drop-down, and then click on **CPU load & traffic**.

6. That's all we want to configure here for now, so click on **Add**.

7. Now, click on the right-hand **Change** link and then on **Select** next to the **Graph** field.

8. In the next window, click on **Used diskspace (pie)**. Remember *how we tuned the pie chart dimensions before?* When inserting elements for screens, we override their configured dimensions.

9. Our pie chart has to share space with the other graph, so enter 390 in the **Width** field and 290 in the **Height** field, and then click on **Add**.

10. While we can immediately see the result of our work here, let's look at it in all its glory; go to **Monitoring | Screens** and click on **Local servers** in the **Name** column:

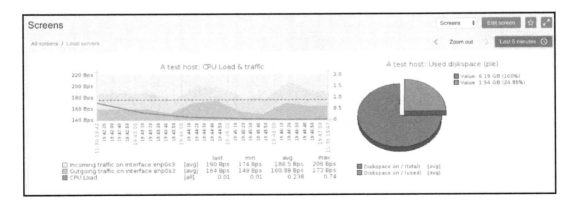

It is not required to save a screen explicitly, unlike most other configuration sections. All changes are immediately saved.

We now have both graphs displayed on a single page. But hey, take a look at the preceding screen: the controls there look very much like the ones we used for graphs. And they are—using these controls, it's possible to do the same things as with graphs, only for all the screen elements. We can make all screen elements display data for a longer period of time or see what the situation was at some point in the past.

Two graphs are nice, but earlier, we talked about having a map and a graph on the same page. Let's see how we can make that happen.

Click on **All screens** shown in the preceding screenshot, and click on **Constructor** next to **Local servers**. We want to add our map at the top of this screen, but we can see here that we created our screen with two columns and single row, so we have to add more. *Couldn't we do that in the general screen properties, using the same fields we used when we created the screen?* Of course we could, but with one limitation: increasing the column and row count that way will only add new columns and rows to the right or at the bottom, respectively. There is no way to insert rows and columns at arbitrary positions using that form. That's why we will use a different approach.

Reducing the column and row count is only possible from the right-hand side and bottom when using the generic screen properties form. Any elements that have been configured in the removed fields will also be removed.

Look at those + and - buttons around the screen. They allow you to insert or remove columns and rows at arbitrary positions. While the layout might seem confusing at first, understanding a few basic principles should allow you to use them efficiently:

- Buttons at the top and bottom operate on columns
- Buttons on the left and right operate on rows
- + buttons add a column or row before the column or row they are positioned at
- - buttons remove the column or the row where they are positioned

In this case, we want to add another row at the bottom:

1. Click on the lower-left + icon in the first column, the column that has + controls only, not the one that has a graph already. This adds a row below our graphs with two columns, both having a **Change** link, just like before.
2. Click on the first **Change** link. It's not a graph we want to add, so choose **Map** from the **Resource** drop-down.
3. Click on **Select** next to the **Map** field, and then click on **First map**. If we leave other parameters as they are, the map will appear on top of the left-hand column. Having it centered above both columns would look better. That's what the **Column** span option is—enter 2 in that field, and then click on **Add**.

As can be immediately seen, this screen element now spans two columns. This capability is not limited to maps; any element can span multiple columns or rows.

Dynamic screens

We now have a screen that contains a network map and two graphs, showing data about **A test host**. Now, we should create a screen showing data for **Another host**. We'll probably have to repeat all the steps we performed for this one as well. That would be quite bad, especially for many hosts, *wouldn't it?* That's why there is a different, much easier approach.

Click on the **Change** link after the **CPU load & traffic** graph in the screen configuration, and look at the last parameter in there:

Let's find out what a dynamic item means—mark this option and click on **Update**. While that seem to have done, edit the other graph, mark the **Dynamic item** checkbox, and click on **Update**. It's now time to check out the result—go to **Monitoring | Screens**, and click on **Local servers** in the **Name** column. Look at the available drop-downs at the top of the screen:

As soon as we marked some elements as dynamic, we were given the choice of other hosts. Let's check out how well this works. Select **Linux servers** from the **Group** drop-down and **Another host** from the **Host** drop-down:

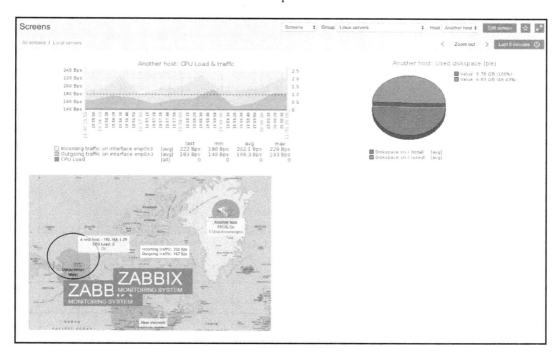

Wonderful! Elements marked as dynamic now show data from the selected host, while non-dynamic elements show the same data no matter which host is selected. The static elements could be maps, like in our screen, but they could also be graphs if the **Dynamic item** option hasn't been checked for them. That would allow us to switch a screen to show server information in some graphs, but other graphs could keep on showing general network information.

> Only graphs from hosts can be added to screens; graphs from templates cannot. For a dynamic screen item, there is a risk that the host from which the graph was initially selected gets deleted, thus breaking the screen. Old versions of Zabbix allowed us to include graphs from templates here, and that functionality might return later.

Additional screen elements

This is a nice, simple screen, but there were many more available screen elements to choose from, so let's create another screen:

1. Go to the list of screens. If a screen is shown in the monitoring view, click on **All screens**, and then click on the **Create screen** button.
2. In the resulting form, enter `Experimental screen` in the **Name** field, enter `2` for both the **Columns** and **Rows** fields, and then click on **Add**.
3. In the screen list, click on **Constructor** next to **Experimental screen**.
4. Click on the **Change** link in the upper-left cell.
5. In the **Resource** drop-down, choose **Simple graph**, and then click on **Select** next to the **Item** field.
6. Select **A test host** from the **Host** drop-down.

As we can see, all the simple graphs that are available without any manual configuration can also be added to a screen. Here, click on the **CPU Load** entry. In the **Width** field, enter `600`, and then click on **Add**. Click on the **Change** link in the upper-right cell. Choose **History of events** from the **Resource** drop-down, change **Show lines** from **25** to **10**, and then click on **Add**.

Well, suddenly our graph doesn't look that great anymore—it should be taller to fit this layout. We could place it below the events list, but that would require deleting it and reconfiguring the lower-right cell. Well, not quite. Drag the graph to the lower-right cell and release the mouse button:

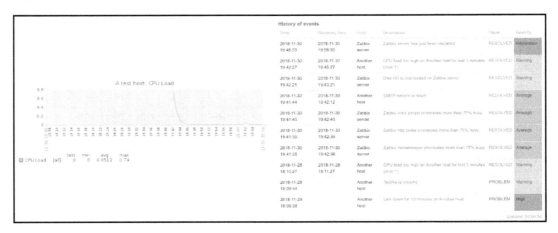

Previous Zabbix versions highlighted the target cell to inform the user that the object would be placed there. This functionality has been lost since Zabbix 3.0.0.

The element (in this case, a graph) is moved from one cell to another, requiring no reconfiguration of individual cells. The upper-left cell is now empty, so click on **Change** there. Select **Triggers info** from the **Resource** drop-down and **Linux servers** from the **Group** box, select **Vertical** in the **Style** option, and then click on **Add**.

This screen element provides us with high-level information on trigger distribution by severity. Let's populate this screen even more now:

1. Click on the **Change** link in the lower-left corner.
2. In the screen element configuration, select **Triggers overview** from the **Resource** drop-down, and start typing linux in the **Group** field.
3. Click on **Linux servers** from the drop-down. We have more triggers than hosts in this group; select **Top** for the **Hosts location** option, and click on **Add**. The elements are misaligned again, *right?*

We'll try out some alignment work now. Click on the second + button from the top in the first column (next to the overview element we just added). This inserts a row before the second row. Drag the **Triggers overview** element (the one we added last) up one row, to the first cell in the row we just added. Click on the **Change** link for the **History of events** element (upper-right cell), enter 20 in the **Show lines** field and 2 in the **Row span** field, and click on **Update**.

Our screen now looks quite nice, except that the lower-left corner is empty.

Click on **Change** in that cell, select **System info** from the **Resource** drop-down, and then click on **Add**. The screen looks fairly well-laid-out now. Let's look at it in the monitoring view by going to **Monitoring** | **Screens** and clicking on **Experimental screen** in the **Name** column:

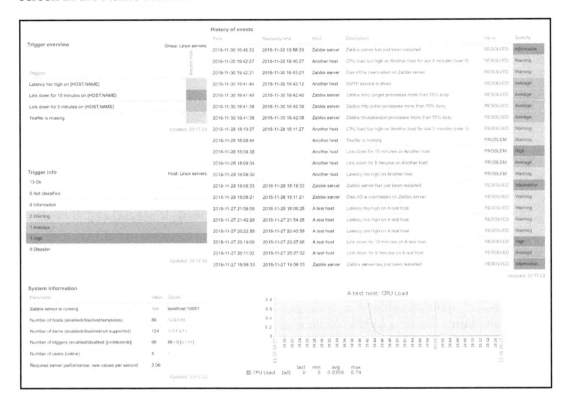

It was mentioned earlier that all graphs show the same time period in a screen. That is true if the graphs are added as normal screen elements. It is possible to add graphs that show a static period of time using the URL screen element, which allows us to include any page in a screen. In that case, the URL should point back to the Zabbix frontend instance. For example, showing a simple graph could be achieved using a URL such as `http://zabbix.frontend/zabbix/chart.php?period=3600&itemids[0]=23704&width=600`.

You can find out the item ID by opening the simple graph of that item and looking at the URL. Note that the width of the graph image should be manually adjusted to match the screen cell width and avoid scrollbars in the screen cell. This way, we could configure a screen that shows hourly, daily, weekly, monthly, and yearly graphs of the same item.

As we discovered, screens in Zabbix allow very flexible visual layouts. You can choose to have a map, followed by more detailed graphs; or you can have graphs of the most important information for a group of servers, and a trigger summary at the top; or any other combination: there are many more possible screen elements to be added. It might be a good idea to try out all of the available screen elements and see what information they provide.

 As screens can contain lots of information, they can be performance-intensive, especially if many users look at them at the same time.

Templated screens

The screens we have configured so far are global screens—they can contain lots of different elements, are available in the **Monitoring** | **Screens** section, and, if some elements are set to be dynamic, we can choose any other host in the drop-down to see its data. Zabbix also offers another way to configure and use screens: templated screens, also known as **host screens**. These are configured on a template and are then available for all the hosts that are linked to that template. Let's create a simple screen: navigate to **Configuration** | **Templates** and click on **Screens** next to **C_Template_Linux**. Then, click on the **Create screen** button. In the **Name** field, enter Templated screen, and click on **Add**. As with **global screens**, click on **Constructor** in the **Actions** column. So far, the configuration has been pretty much the same. Now, click on the **Change** link in the only cell, and expand the **Resource** drop-down. The list of available resources is much smaller than it was in the global screens. Let's compare those lists.

The global screen resources are as follows:

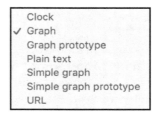

The templated screen resources are as follows:

As can be seen, global screens offer 19 different types of elements, while templated screens offer only 7.

For our screen right now, leave the **Resource** drop-down at **Graph** and click on **Select** next to the **Graph** field. Notice how the current template is selected and cannot be changed—all elements added to a templated screen must come from the same template.

In the popup, perform the following steps:

1. Click on **CPU load & traffic** in the **Name** column, and then click on **Add**.
2. Click on the + icon in the upper-right corner to add another column, and click on the **Change** link in the rightmost cell.
3. In the **Resource** drop-down, choose **Simple graph**, click on **Select** next to the **Item** field, and then click on **CPU Load** in the **Name** column.
4. Click on the **Add** button.

5. Navigate to **Configuration | Hosts** and take a look at the available columns for each host. There is no column for screens. Templated or host screens are only configured on the template level; they do not get a copy on the host whereas items, triggers, and other entities do.

Let's go to **Monitoring | Screens**. If we look at the screen list there, the screen we just configured cannot be found. Templated or host screens can only be accessed from the host pop-up menu in the following locations:

- **Monitoring | Dashboard** (in the **Problems** widget)
- **Monitoring | Problems** (if hosts are in problem state)
- **Monitoring | Overview** (if hosts are in the leftmost column)
- **Monitoring | Latest data** (if filtering by the **Host** field isn't done)
- **Monitoring | Maps**

They are also available from these two pages:

- Global search results
- The host inventory page

Let's move on to **Monitoring | Maps**: click on **Host group elements** in the **Name** column. In the map, click on either **A test host** or **Another host**. This time, the **Host screens** entry in the menu is enabled—click on that one:

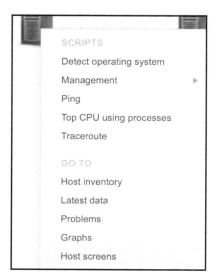

The screen we configured earlier opens, showing the data from this specific host:

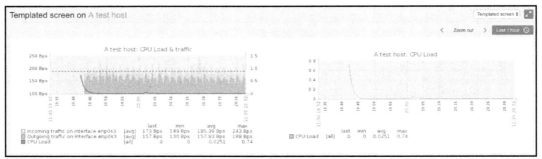

If we had multiple screens configured in this template, they would be available in the drop-down in the upper-right corner. Remember that these screens will only be available for hosts that are linked to this template.

One thing to notice on this screen is the difference in height for both graphs. When configuring the screen, we did not change the height value, and it was the same for both graphs, 100. Unfortunately, that's not the height of the whole graph, but only of the graph wall area. As a result, if you have different item counts, a trigger or a percentile line will result in a different graph height. For a screen, this means a tedious configuration to get the dimensions to match. The same also applies to width—there, having one or two Y-axis values will result in a different graph width.

 If the legend is disabled for a custom graph, the height will not vary based on item count. There is currently no way to show the legend for a custom graph when it is displayed on its own and hide it when the custom graph is included in a screen.

Should we use a templated or global screen? Several factors will affect that decision:

- The availability of the elements (global screens have many more)
- Navigation (**Monitoring** | **Screens** versus the popup menus)
- Which and how many hosts need such a screen

Slide shows

We now have a couple of screens, but to switch between them, a manual interaction is required. While that's mostly acceptable for casual use, it would be hard to do if you wanted to display them on a large display for a helpdesk. Manual switching would soon get annoying even if you simply had Zabbix open on a secondary monitor all the time.

Another functionality comes to the rescue: slideshows. Slideshows in Zabbix are simple to set up, so go to **Monitoring** | **Screens**. *Why a screen page?* Zabbix changed the slideshow operations in 3.0 to be the same way as maps and screens by moving both viewing and configuration to the monitoring section.

Slideshows didn't get their own section, though; to access them, perform the following steps:

1. Choose **Slide shows** from the drop-down in the upper-right corner.
2. Click on the **Create slide show** button. Enter `First slide show` in the **Name** field, and click on the **Add** control in the **Slides** section. Slides are essentially screens, which is what we can see in the popup.
3. Click on **Local servers**. We do not change the default value in the **Delay** field for this slide or screen. Leaving it empty will use the value of 30s from the preceding **Default delay** field.
4. Click on **Add** in the **Slides** section, and then click on **Experimental screen**. This time, enter 5s in the **Delay** field for this screen:

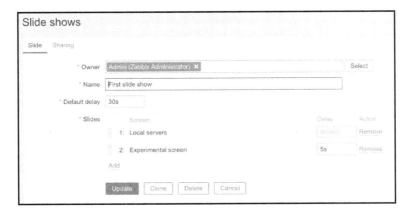

Notice the handles on the left-hand side—the same as in graphs and icon mapping; we can reorder the slides here. We won't do that now; just click on the **Add** button at the bottom.

If you want to add a single element to a slideshow, such as a map or graph, you will have to create a screen that contains only this element.

Now, click on **First slide show** in the **Name** column. It starts plain, showing a single screen, and it then switches to the other screen after 30 seconds, then back after 5 seconds, and so the cycle continues. As we have dynamic screen items included in the slideshow, we can also choose the host in the upper-right corner—this will affect the dynamic screen items only.

We could show more screens; for example, a large high-level overview for 30 seconds, and then cycle through the server group screens, showing each one for 5 seconds.

Take a look at the buttons in the upper-right corner:

The first button allows us to add this slideshow to the dashboard favorites, the same as with graphs and screens. The third button is the full-screen one again. But the middle button allows us to slow down or speed up the slideshow; click on it:

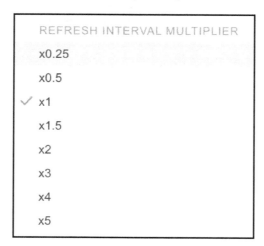

Instead of setting a specific time, we can make the slideshow faster or slower by applying a multiplier, thus maintaining the relative time for which each slide should be displayed.

There's also another reason to choose global screens over templated or host screens: only global screens can be included in slideshows.

Old versions of Zabbix had a memory leak in the slideshow functionality. There have also been several cases of memory leaks in browsers. If you see browser memory usage consistently increasing while using Zabbix slideshows, consider upgrading. If that is not possible, one of the slides could reload the page using a URL element and JavaScript, which, in most cases, should reduce memory usage. The website `http://www.phpied.com/files/location-location/location-location.ht ml` suggests 535 different ways of doing this.

Both screens and slideshows can also be created by normal users and then shared since Zabbix 3.0, the same way how we share maps in `Chapter 21`, *Visualizing Data with Graphs and Maps*. As with maps, other users will need access to all the elements and sub-elements included in such screens and slideshows to be able to access them.

Showing data on a big display

While visualization on an individual level is important, the real challenge emerges when there's a need to create views for a large display, usually placed for help desk or technical operators to quickly identify problems. This poses several challenges.

Challenges

Displaying Zabbix on a large screen for many people requires taking into account the display location, the experience level of the people who will be expected to look at it, and other factors that can shape your decisions on how to configure this aspect of information. Since Zabbix 3.2, Zabbix SIA has made more and more progress on the front dashboard to make it more dynamic and polished. It's probably best to create graphs in this dashboard and share them with other users. Another solution that is to use some third-party software, such as Grafana.

Non-interactive display

In the majority of cases, data displayed on such a screen will be non-interactive; people are expected to view it, but not click around. Such a requirement is posed because drill-down usually happens on individual workstations, leaving the main display accessible for others. Additionally, somebody could easily leave the main display in an unusable state, so no direct access is usually provided. This means that data placed on the display must not rely on the ability to view problem details. It should be enough for the level of technical support to gather the required knowledge.

Information overload

Having to place all information regarding the well-being of the infrastructure of an organization can result in a cluttered display, where too many details in a font that's way too small are crammed on the screen. This is the opposite of the previous challenge; you would have to decide which services are important and how to define each of them. This will require you to be working closely with the people responsible for those services so that correct dependency chains can be built. This is the method used most often to simplify and reduce displayed data while still keeping it useful.

 Both of these challenges can be solved with careful usage of screens and slideshows that display properly-dependent statuses. Do not rely on slide shows too much—it can become annoying to wait for that slide to come by again, because it was up for a few seconds only and there are now 10 more slides to cycle through.

Displaying a specific section automatically

There are some more requirements for a central display: it should open automatically upon boot and display the desired information, for example, a nice geographical map. While this might be achieved with some client-side scripting, there's a much easier solution, which we have already explored.

As a reminder, go to **Administration** | **Users**, click on **monitoring_user** in the **Alias** column, and look at two of the options: **Auto-login** and **URL (after login)**:

Auto-login	☐
Auto-logout	☐ 15m
* Refresh	60s
* Rows per page	50

If we marked the **Auto-login** option for a user that is used by such a display station, it would be enough to log in once, and that user would be logged in automatically upon each page access. This feature relies on browser cookies, so the browser used should support and store cookies. The **URL (after login)** option allows the user to immediately navigate to a specified page. All that's left is that the display box launches a browser upon boot and point, to the Zabbix frontend URL, which should be simple to set up. When the box starts up, it will, without any manual intervention, open the specified page (which will usually be a screen or slideshow). For example, to open a screen with an ID of 21 whenever that user accesses the Zabbix frontend, a URL like this could be used:
`http://zabbix.frontend/zabbix/screens.php?elementid=21`. To open that screen in Zabbix's fullscreen mode, a fullscreen parameter has to be appended: `http://zabbix.frontend/zabbix/screens.php?elementid=21&fullscreen=1`.

When displaying data on such large screens, explore the available options and functionality carefully; perhaps the latest data display is the most appropriate in some cases. When using trigger overviews, evaluate the host/trigger relationship and choose which should be displayed on which axis.

Summary

In this chapter, we first looked at configuring and sharing the new Zabbix dashboards and then learned to combine graphs, maps, and other data on a single page by using screens. Screens are able to hold a lot of different elements, including the statistics of currently-active triggers, and even history and any custom page, by using the URL element. The URL element also allows us to create a screen that contains graphs showing different time periods. The screens are available on both the global and template levels.

Especially useful for unattended displays, slideshows allow us to cycle through screens. We can set the default delay and override it for individual screens. To include a single map or graph in a slideshow, we still have to create a screen containing that map or graph.

In the next chapter, we will try to gather data using more advanced methods. We'll look at reusing already-collected data with calculated and aggregate items, running custom scripts with external checks, and monitoring log files. We will also try out the two most popular ways to get custom data in Zabbix—user parameters on the agent side and the great `zabbix_sender` utility.

Questions

1. How can we create slideshows?
2. If I have a slideshow that has a standard delay of five seconds, can I slow down or speed up the slideshow?
3. Should I create screens and slideshows to show in our NOC, or is there a better way?

Further reading

The following are a few links to the information in the Zabbix documentation that we have looked at in this chapter:

- **Screens**: `https://www.zabbix.com/documentation/4.0/manual/config/visualisation/screens`
- **Slide shows**: `https://www.zabbix.com/documentation/4.0/manual/config/visualisation/slides`

10
Advanced Item Monitoring

Having set up passive and active Zabbix agent items, simple checks such as ICMP ping or TCP service checks, or SNMP and IPMI checks, *can we go further?* Of course we can. Zabbix provides several more item types that are useful in different situations—let's try them out.

In this chapter, we'll explore log file monitoring; computing values on the server from the already collected data; running custom scripts on the Zabbix server or agents; sending in complete custom data using a wonderful utility, `zabbix_sender`; and running commands over SSH and Telnet. Among these methods, we should be able to implement the monitoring of any custom data source that isn't supported by Zabbix out of the box.

Let's have a short overview of the topics that we'll touch on:

- Log file monitoring
- Event tags
- Reusing data on the server
- External checks
- User parameters
- SSH and Telnet items
- Dependent items and value preprocessing

Log file monitoring

Log files can be a valuable source of information. Zabbix provides a way to monitor log files using the Zabbix agent. For that, two special keys are provided:

- `log`: Allows us to monitor a single file
- `logrt`: Allows us to monitor multiple rotated files

Both of the log monitoring item keys only work as active items. To see how this functions, let's try out the Zabbix log file monitoring by actually monitoring some files.

Monitoring a single file

Let's start with the simpler case, monitoring a single file. To do so, we could create a couple of test files. To keep things a bit organized, let's create a directory, /tmp/zabbix_logmon/, on A test host and create two files in there, logfile1 and logfile2. For both files, use the same content as this:

```
2018-08-13 13:01:03 a log entry
2018-08-13 13:02:04 second log entry
2018-08-13 13:03:05 third log entry
```

 Active items must be properly configured for log monitoring to work; we did that in Chapter 3, *Monitoring with Zabbix Agents and Basic Protocols*.

With the files in place, let's proceed to creating items:

1. Navigate to **Configuration | Hosts**, click on **Items** next to **A test host**, then click on **Create item**. Fill in the following:

   - **Name**: First logfile
   - **Type: Zabbix agent (active)**
   - **Key**: log[/tmp/zabbix_logmon/logfile1]
   - **Type of information**: **Log**
   - **Update interval**: 1s

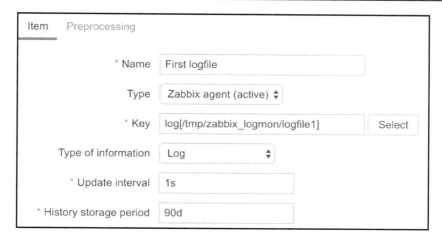

2. When done, click on the **Add** button at the bottom.

As mentioned earlier, log monitoring only works as an active item, so we used that item type. For the key, the first parameter is required; it's the full path to the file we want to monitor. We also used a special type of information here, **log**. But what about the update interval, *why did we use such a small interval of one second?* For log items, this interval isn't about making an actual connection between the agent and the server; it's only about the agent checking whether the file has changed: it does a `stat()` call, similar to what `tail -f` does on some platforms/filesystems. A connection to the server is only made when the agent has anything to send in.

> With active items, log monitoring is both quick to react, as it's checking the file locally, and avoids excessive connections. It could be implemented as a somewhat less efficient passive item, but that's not supported.

With the item in place, it shouldn't take longer than three minutes for the data to arrive—if everything works as expected, of course. Up to one minute could be required for the server to update the configuration cache, and up to two minutes could be required for the active agent to update its list of items. Let's verify this: navigate to **Monitoring** | **Latest data** and filter by host, A test host. Our First logfile item should be there, and it should have some value as well:

| | First logfile | 2018-12-01 11:09:29 | 2018-08-13 13:03:05 third ... |

Even short values are excessively trimmed here. It's hoped that this will be improved in further releases. If the item is unsupported and the configuration section complains about permissions, make sure permissions actually allow the Zabbix user to access that file. If the permissions on the file itself look correct, check the execute permission on all the upstream directories too. Here and later, keep in mind that unsupported items will take up to 10 minutes to update after the issue has been resolved.

As with other non-numeric items, Zabbix knows that it can't graph logs, hence there's a **History** link on the right-hand side; let's click on it:

Timestamp	Local time	Value
2018-12-01 11:09:29		2018-08-13 13:03:05 third log entry
2018-12-01 11:09:29		2018-08-13 13:02:04 second log entry
2018-12-01 11:09:29		2018-08-13 13:01:03 a log entry

All of the lines from our log file are here. By default, Zabbix log monitoring parses whole files from the very beginning. That's good in this case, but *what if we wanted to start monitoring some huge existing log file?* Not only would that parsing be wasteful, we would also likely send lots of useless old information to the Zabbix server. Luckily, there's a way to tell Zabbix to only parse new data since the monitoring of that log file started. We could try that out with our second file and, to keep things simple, we could also clone our first item. Let's proceed with the following steps:

1. Navigate to **Configuration | Hosts,** click on **Items** next to **A test host,** then click on **First logfile** in the **Name** column. At the bottom of the item configuration form, click on **Clone** and make the following changes:

   - **Name:** Second logfile
   - **Key:** log[/tmp/zabbix_logmon/logfile2,,,,skip]

There are four commas in the item key; this way, we're skipping some parameters and only specifying the first and fifth parameters.

2. When done, click on the **Add** button at the bottom.

The same as before, it might take up to three minutes for this item to start working. Even when it starts working, there will be nothing to see in the latest data page; we specified the `skip` parameter and hence only new lines would be considered.

 Allow at least three minutes to pass after adding the item before executing the following command. Otherwise, the agent won't have the new item definition yet.

To test this, we could add some lines to Second logfile. On A test host, execute the following:

```
$ echo "2018-12-1 10:34:05 fourth log entry" >>
/tmp/zabbix_logmon/logfile2
```

 This and further fake log entries increase the timestamp in the line itself; this isn't required, but looks a bit better. For now, Zabbix would ignore that timestamp anyway.

A moment later, this entry should appear in the latest data page:

If we check the item history, it's the only entry, as Zabbix only cares about new lines now.

 The skip parameter only affects behavior when a new log file is monitored. While monitoring a log file with and without that parameter, the Zabbix agent doesn't re-read the file, it only reads the added data.

Filtering for specific strings

Sending everything is acceptable with smaller files, but *what if a file has lots of information and we're only interested in error messages?* The Zabbix agent may also locally filter the lines and only send to the server the ones we instruct it to. For example, we could grab only lines that contain the `error` string in them. Modify the Second logfile item and change its key to the following:

```
log[/tmp/zabbix_logmon/logfile2,error,,,skip]
```

Add an error after the path to the log file. Note that now there are three commas between `error` and `skip`; we populated the second item key parameter. Click on **Update**. The same as before, it may take up to three minutes for this change to propagate to the Zabbix agent, so it's suggested to let some time pass before continuing. After making a cup of tea, execute the following on A test host:

```
$ echo "2018-12-1 10:45:05 fifth log entry" >>
/tmp/zabbix_logmon/logfile2
```

This time, nothing new will appear in the **Latest data** page; we filtered for the `error` string, but this line had no such string in it. Let's add another line:

```
$ echo "2018-12-1 10:54:05 sixth log entry - now with an error" >>
/tmp/zabbix_logmon/logfile2
```

Checking the history for the `logfile2` item, we should only see the latest entry:

Timestamp	Local time	Value
2018-12-01 11:56:27		2018-12-1 10:54:05 sixth log entry - now with an error
2018-12-01 11:42:08		2018-12-1 10:34:05 fourth log entry

How about using some more complicated conditions? Let's say we would like to filter for all `error` and `warning` string occurrences, but for warnings only if they're followed by a numeric code that starts with the numbers 60-66. Luckily, the filter parameter is actually a regular expression. Let's modify the second log monitoring item and change its key to the following:

```
log[/tmp/zabbix_logmon/logfile2,"error|warning 6[0-6]",,,skip]
```

We changed the second key parameter to `"error|warning 6[0-6]"`, including the double quotes. This regular expression should match all errors and warnings that start with the numbers 60-66. We had to double quote it, because regular expression contained square brackets, which are also used to enclose key parameters. To test this out, let's insert our log file several test lines in, but just like with the previous test, let's wait three minutes:

```
$ echo "2018-12-1 11:01:05 seventh log entry - all good" >>
/tmp/zabbix_logmon/logfile2
$ echo "2018-12-1 11:02:05 eighth log entry - just an error" >>
/tmp/zabbix_logmon/logfile2
$ echo "2018-12-1 11:03:05 ninth log entry - some warning" >>
/tmp/zabbix_logmon/logfile2
```

```
$ echo "2018-12-1 11:04:05 tenth log entry - warning 13" >>
/tmp/zabbix_logmon/logfile2
$ echo "2018-12-1 11:05:05 eleventh log entry - warning 613" >>
/tmp/zabbix_logmon/logfile2
```

We could speed up the process by reloading the Zabbix server configuration cache. This is done every 60 seconds. We still have to wait till the active agent asks for the Zabbix server for the latest update; this is done every 120 seconds. The server configuration can be reloaded on the Zabbix server by running the following command:

```
zabbix_server -R config_cache_reload
```

Based on our regular expression, the log monitoring item should do the following:

- Ignore the seventh entry, as it contains no error or warning at all
- Catch the eighth entry, as it contains an error
- Ignore the ninth entry, it has a warning but no number following it
- Ignore the tenth entry, it has a warning, but the number following it doesn't start within the 60-66 range
- Catch the eleventh entry, it has a warning, the number starts with 61, and that is in our required range, 60-66

Eventually, only the eighth and eleventh entries should be collected. Verify that, in the latest data page, only the entries that matched our regular expression were collected:

Timestamp	Local time	Value
2018-12-01 12:04:54		2018-12-1 11:05:05 eleventh log entry - warning 613
2018-12-01 12:03:57		2018-12-1 11:02:05 eighth log entry - just an error
2018-12-01 11:56:27		2018-12-1 10:54:05 sixth log entry - now with an error
2018-12-01 11:42:08		2018-12-1 10:34:05 fourth log entry

The regular expression we used wasn't very complicated. *What if we would like to exclude multiple strings or do some other, more complicated, filtering?* With the PCRE regular expressions, that could be somewhere between very complicated and impossible. There's a feature in Zabbix, called **global regular expressions**, which allows us to define regular expressions in an easier way. If we had a global regexp named Filter logs, we could reuse it in our item like this:

```
log[/tmp/zabbix_logmon/logfile2,@Filter logs,,,skip]
```

 Regular expression support in Zabbix has been switched from POSIX extended regular expressions to **Perl Compatible Regular Expressions** (**PCRE**) for enhanced regular expressions and consistency with the frontend. This was switch implemented in Zabbix 3.4.

Global regular expressions are covered in more detail in Chapter 11, *Automating Configuration*.

Monitoring rotated files

Monitoring a single file wasn't terribly hard, but there's a lot of software that uses multiple log files. For example, the Apache HTTP server is often configured to log to a new file every day, with the date included in the filename. Zabbix supports monitoring such a log rotation scheme with a separate item key, logrt. To try it out, follow these steps:

1. Navigate to **Configuration | Hosts,** click on **Items** next to **A test host,** then click on **Create item**. Fill in the following:

    - **Name:** Rotated logfiles
    - **Type: Zabbix agent (active)**
    - **Key:** logrt["/tmp/zabbix_logmon/access_[0-9]{4}-[0-9]{2}-[0-9]{2}.log"]
    - **Type of information: Log**
    - **Update interval:** 2s

2. When done, click on the **Add** button at the bottom.

But the key and its first parameter changed a bit from what we used before. The key is now `logrt`, and the first parameter is a regular expression, describing the files that should be matched. Note that the regular expression here is supported for the file part only; the path part must describe a specific directory. We also double quoted it because of the square brackets that were used in the `regexp`. The `regexp` should match filenames that start with `access_`, followed by four digits, a dash, two digits, a dash, two more digits, and ending with `.log`. For example, a filename such as `access_2018-12-31.log` would be matched. One thing we did slightly differently was the update interval was set to two seconds instead of one. The reason is that the `logrt` key is periodically re-reading directory contents, and this could be a bit more resource intensive than just checking a single file. That's also the reason why it's a separate item key, otherwise we could have used the regular expression for the file in the log item.

 The Zabbix agent doesn't re-read directory contents every two seconds if a monitored file still has lines to parse; it only looks at the directory again when the already known files have been fully parsed.

With the item in place, let's proceed by creating and populating some files that should be matched by our regular expression. On A test host, execute the following:

```
$ echo "2018-12-1 03:00:00 rotated first" >
/tmp/zabbix_logmon/access_2018-12-30.log
```

Checking the latest data page, the rotated log file item should get this value. Let's say that's it for this day and we'll now log something the next day:

```
$ echo "2018-12-1 03:00:00 rotated second" >
/tmp/zabbix_logmon/access_2015-12-31.log
```

Checking the history for our item, it should've successfully picked up the new file:

Timestamp	Local time	Value
2018-12-01 12:48:01		2018-12-1 03:00:00 rotated second
2018-12-01 12:46:03		2018-12-1 03:00:00 rotated first

As more files with a different date appear, Zabbix will finish the current file and then start on the next one.

The Zabbix agent doesn't send more than what is specified in the option `maxlines` of a log file per second. The limit prevents overloading of network and CPU resources, and overrides the default value provided by the `MaxLinesPerSecond` parameter in the agent configuration file.

Alerting on log data

With the data coming in, let's talk about alerting on it with triggers. There are a few things somewhat different than the thresholds and similar numeric comparisons that we've used in triggers so far.

If we have a log item that's collecting all lines and we want to alert on the lines containing some specific string, there are several trigger functions of potential use:

- `str()`: This checks for a substring; for example, if we're collecting all values, this function could be used to alert on errors: `str(error)`
- `regexp`: Similar to the `str()` function, this allows us to specify a regular expression to match
- `iregexp`: This is a case-insensitive version of `regexp()`

These functions only work on a single line; it's not possible to match multiline log entries.

For these three functions, a second parameter is supported as well; in that case, it's either the number of seconds or the number of values to check. For example, `str(error,600)` would fire if there's an `error` substring in any of the values over the last 10 minutes.

That seems fine, but there's an issue if we only send error lines to the server by filtering on the agent side. To see what the problem is, let's consider a *normal* trigger, like the one checking for **CPU load** exceeding some threshold. Assuming we have a threshold of 5, the trigger currently in the **OK** state, and values such as 0, 1, and 2 arriving, nothing happens; no events are generated. When the first value above 5 arrives, a **PROBLEM** event is generated and the trigger switches to the **PROBLEM** state. No other values above 5 wouldn't generate any events; nothing would happen.

And the problem would be that it would work this way for log monitoring as well. We would generate a **PROBLEM** event for the first error line, and then nothing. The trigger would stay in the **PROBLEM** state and nothing else would happen. The solution is somewhat simple: there's a selection box in the trigger properties, **Multiple**, in the **PROBLEM event generation mode** option:

Marking this checkbox would make the mentioned **CPU load** trigger generate a new **PROBLEM** event for every value above the threshold of 5. Well, that wouldn't be very useful in most cases, but it would be useful for the log monitoring trigger. It's all good if we only receive error lines; a new **PROBLEM** event would be generated for each of them.

Note that even if we send both errors and good lines, errors after good lines would be picked up, but subsequent errors would be ignored, which could be a problem as well.

With this problem solved, we arrive at another one: once a trigger fires against an item that only receives error lines, this trigger never resolves; it always stays in the **PROBLEM** state. While that's not an issue in some cases in others, it's not desirable. There's an easy way to make such triggers time out by using a trigger function we're already familiar with, `nodata()`. If the item receives both error and *normal* lines, and we want it to time out 10 minutes after the last error arrived even if no *normal* lines arrive, the trigger expression could be constructed like this:

```
{host.item.str(error)}=1 and {host.item.nodata(10m)}=0
```

Here, we're using the `nodata()` function the other way around: even if the last entry contains errors, the trigger would switch to the **OK** state if there were no other values in the last `10` minutes.

 We also discussed triggers that time out in `Chapter 6`, *Detecting Problems with Triggers*, in the *Triggers that time out* section.

If the item receives error lines only, we could use an expression like the previous one, but we could also simplify it. In this case, just having any value is a problem situation, so we would use the reversed `nodata()` function again and alert on values being present:

```
{host.item.nodata(10m)}=0
```

Here, if we have any values in the last 10 minutes, that's it; it's a **PROBLEM**. If there aren't any values, the trigger switches to **OK**. This is somewhat less resource intensive as Zabbix doesn't have to evaluate the actual item value.

Yet another trigger function that we could use here is `count()`. It would allow us to fire an alert when there's a certain number of interesting strings—such as errors—during some period of time. For example, the following will alert if there are more than 10 errors in the last 10 minutes:

```
{host.item.count(10m,error,like)}>10
```

Another solution can be to keep the problem open and, after we have checked it ourselves, close it by hand. This can be done by selecting the **Allow manual close** box in the trigger:

Yet another way could be if we receive log files with errors and OK to make use of the **OK event generation** option. We would then create a trigger that alerts us when there's, for example, an error in the log and recover when it sees the word **OK** in the log.

Let's try this with our first log file. Click on triggers on `A test host` and add the following triggers:

- **Name:** `Warning on errors in logfile1`
- **Severity: Warning**
- **Problem expression:** `{A test host:log[/tmp/zabbix_logmon/logfile1].str(error)}=1`
- **OK event generation: Recovery expression**
- **Recovery expression:** `{A test host:log[/tmp/zabbix_logmon/logfile1].str(ok)}=1`

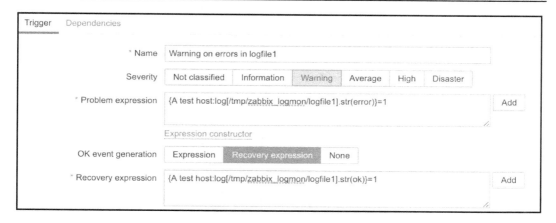

Now, let's create some errors in our log file (make sure you wait long enough, like with the other tests):

```
echo "error" >> /tmp/zabbix_logmon/logfile1
```

Let's check the dashboard to see whether we get a warning; we should be able to see a problem for our A test host.

Now, let's fix this error by sending the word ok to our log file and see what happens:

```
echo "ok" >> /tmp/zabbix_logmon/logfile1
```

We can check this in the dashboard by seeing whether our error is gone but, to get more proof, let's go to **Monitoring | Problems** and select **A test host** in the **Hosts** selection box in our filter. We can now see that there was an issue at **13:04:42** and that the issue has been resolved at **13:09:32**; in **Actions**, we can see the actions that were taken:

Event tags

Event tags are another way to get information in Zabbix and, besides the extra information, they help to close items in Zabbix in an automated way. Let's build on the previous task where we monitored and closed a log file with the recovery expression.

Another way to close our item can be by using tags. Remember, we can add tags to our triggers. By adding the log tag here and giving it the {ITEM.VALUE} value, the value will be added from the item in our tag. This will be, in our case, error or ok. Since we only want to close it when we receive the ok value, we have to filter for the word ok. This we can do with the regsub function. So, if we bring all this together in our trigger, then we need to select the following options:

- **OK event generation**: **Expression**
- **OK event closes**: **All problems if tag values match**
- **Tag for matching:** log
- **Tags**: In the first box, add, log, and in the second box, {{ITEM.VALUE}.regsub(ok)}

In this case, when the tag matches the ok value, our trigger will be closed.

What we see here is that the tag log gets populated with the latest values retrieved from our item and by making use of the regular expression function, regsub, we're able to extract the word ok from it.

Because we selected the **OK event closes** option with the `log` tag, the trigger gets closed automatically when the item receives the `ok` value in the log.

We'll see all of the tag information in our triggers in the dashboard, problem page, and so on. This can be useful as well. You could, for example, tag a program with the tag service and give the tag the name of the service, so that if the application is stopped, people know what service to restart.

Be careful not to select **OK event closes: All problems if tag values match** by not adding a tag in the **Tags** box, as this will result in the trigger being closed when the log gets populated with the next line.

Extracting part of the line

Sometimes, we only want to know that an error was logged. In those cases, grabbing the whole line is good enough. But sometimes, the log line might contain an interesting substring, maybe a number of messages in some queue. A log line might look like this:

```
2015-12-20 18:15:22 Number of messages in the queue: 445
```

Theoretically, we could write triggers against the whole line. For example, the following `regexp` should match when there are 10,000 or more messages:

```
messages in the queue: [1-9][0-9]{4}
```

But *what if we want to have a different trigger when the message count exceeds 15,000?* That trigger would have a regular expression like this:

```
messages in the queue: (1[5-9]|[2-9].)[0-9]{3}
```

And if we want to exclude values above 15,000 from our first regular expression, it would become the following:

```
messages in the queue: 1[0-4][0-9]{3}
```

That's definitely not easy to maintain. And that's with just two thresholds. But there's an easier way to do this, if all we need is that number. Zabbix log monitoring allows us to extract values by regular expressions. To try this out, let's create a file with some values to extract. Still on `A test host`, create the `/tmp/zabbix_logmon/queue_log` file with the following content:

```
echo "2018-12-1 12:01:13 Number of messages in the queue: 445" >>
/tmp/zabbix_logmon/queue_log
echo "2018-12-1 12:02:14 Number of messages in the queue: 5445" >>
/tmp/zabbix_logmon/queue_log
echo "2018-12-1 12:03:15 Number of messages in the queue: 15445" >>
/tmp/zabbix_logmon/queue_log
```

Now, on to the item, go to **Configuration | Hosts**, click on **Items** next to **A test host**, then click on **Create item**. Fill in the following:

- **Name**: Extracting log contents
- **Type: Zabbix agent (active)**
- **Key**: log[/tmp/zabbix_logmon/queue_log,"messages in the queue: ([0-9]+)",,,,\1]
- **Type of information: Log**
- **Update interval**: 1s

We quoted regular expression because it contained square brackets again. The regular expression itself extracts the text messages in the queue, followed by a colon, a space, and a number. The number is included in a capture group; this becomes important in the last parameter. To the key, we added \1 which references the capture group contents. This parameter, output, tells Zabbix not to return the whole line, but only whatever is referenced in that parameter. In this case, that's the number.

We may also add extra text in the output parameter; for example, a key such as log[/tmp/zabbix_logmon/queue_log messages in the queue, "([0-9]+)",,,,Extra \1 things], would return Extra 445 things for the first line in our log file. Multiple capture groups may be used as well, referenced in the output parameter as \2, \3, and so on.

When done, click on the **Add** button at the bottom. Some three minutes later, we could check the history for this item in the latest data page:

Timestamp	Local time	Value
2018-12-01 13:23:29		15445
2018-12-01 13:23:29		5445
2018-12-01 13:23:29		445

Hooray! Extracting the values is working as expected. Writing triggers against them should be much, much easier as well. But one thing to note: for this item, we're unable to see the graphs. The reason is the **Type of information** property in our log item; we had it set to **Log**, but that type isn't considered suitable for graphing. Let's change it now.

Go to **Configuration | Hosts**, click on **Items** next to **A test host**, and click on **Extracting log contents** in the **Name** column. Change **Type of information** to **Numeric (unsigned)**, then click on the **Update** button at the bottom.

 If the extracted numbers have the decimal part, use **Numeric (float)** for such items.

Check this item in the latest data section; it should have a **Graph** link now. But checking that reveals that it has no data. *How so?* Internally, Zabbix stores values for each type of information separately. Changing that doesn't remove the values, but Zabbix only checks the currently configured type. Make sure to set the correct type of information from the start. To verify that this works as expected, run the following on A test host:

```
$ echo "2018-12-1 18:16:13 Number of messages in the queue: 113" >>
/tmp/zabbix_logmon/queue_log
$ echo "2018-12-1 18:17:14 Number of messages in the queue: 213" >>
/tmp/zabbix_logmon/queue_log
$ echo "2018-12-1 18:18:15 Number of messages in the queue: 150" >>
/tmp/zabbix_logmon/queue_log
```

Checking out this item in the **Latest data** section, the values should be there and the graph should be available, too. Note that the date and time in our log file entries still doesn't matter; the values will get the current timestamp assigned.

Value extracting works the same with the `logrt` item key.

Another way to get data out of a log file could be by making use of the **Preprocessing** tab in our item as shown in the following screenshot. We have the option here to retrieve a whole log line and then pre-process it with, for example, the **Regular expression** option to cut out information. Only after our regular expression has run will the information be stored into the database:

Parsing timestamps

Talking about the timestamps on the lines we pushed into Zabbix, the date and time in the file didn't match the date and time displayed in Zabbix. Zabbix marked the entries with the time it collected them. This is fine in most cases when we're doing constant monitoring; content is checked every second or so, gathered, timestamped, and pushed to the server. When parsing some older data, the timestamps can be way off, though. Zabbix does offer a way to parse timestamps out of the log entries.

Let's use our very first log file monitoring item for this.

Navigate to **Configuration | Hosts**, click on **Items** next to **A test host**, and click on **First logfile** in the **Name** column. Notice the **Log time format** field; that's what we'll use now. It allows us to use special characters to extract the date and time. The supported characters are as follows:

- y: Year
- M: Month
- d: Day

- h: Hour
- m: Minute
- s: Second

In our test log files, we used the time format like this:

```
2018-12-13 13:01:03
```

The time format string to parse out date and time would look like this:

```
yyyy-MM-dd hh:mm:ss
```

Note that only the supported characters matter; the other ones are just ignored and can be anything. For example, the following would work exactly the same:

```
yyyyPMMPddPhhPmmPss
```

You can choose any characters outside of the special ones. *Which ones would be best?* Well, it's probably best to aim for readability. Enter one of the examples here in the **Log time format** field:

Log time format   yyyy-MM-dd hh:mm:ss

When specifying the log time format, all date and time components must be present; for example, it's not possible to extract the time if seconds are missing.

When done, click on the **Update** button at the bottom. Allow for a few minutes to pass, then proceed with adding entries to the monitored file. Choose the date and time during the last hour for your current time and run on A test host:

```
$ echo "2018-12-01 16:40:13 a timestamped log entry" >>
/tmp/zabbix_logmon/logfile1
```

Now, check the history for the **First logfile** item in the latest data page:

There's one difference from the previous cases. The **Local time** column is populated now, and it contains the time we specified in our log line. The **Timestamp** column still holds the time when Zabbix collected the line.

Note that only numeric data is supported for date and time extraction. The standard Syslog format uses short textual month names such as Jan, Feb, and so on; such a date/time format isn't supported for extraction at this time.

Viewing log data

With all of the log monitoring items collecting data, let's take a quick look at the displaying options. Navigate to **Monitoring | Latest data** and click on **History** for **Second logfile**. Expand the **Filter**. There are a few very simple log viewing options here:

The field in the preceding screenshot is explained as follows:

- **Items list**: We can add multiple items and view log entries from them all at the same time. The entries will be sorted by their timestamp, allowing us to determine the sequence of events from different log files or even different systems.
- **Value** and **Selected**: Based on a substring, entries can be shown, hidden, or colored.

As a quick test, enter `error` in the **Value** field and click on **Filter**. Only the entries that contain this string will remain. In the **Selected** drop-down menu, choose **Hide selected** and now only the entries that don't have this string are shown. Now, choose **Mark selected** in the **Selected** drop-down menu and notice how the entries containing the `error` string are highlighted in red. In the additional drop-down menu that appears, we can choose red, green, or blue for highlighting:

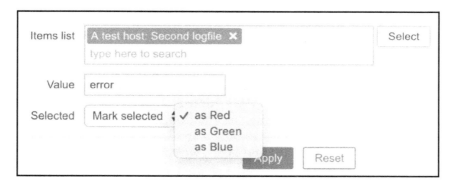

Let's add another item here; click on **Select** behind the **Items** list entry. In the popup, choose **Linux servers** in the **Group** drop-down menu and **A test host** in the **Host** drop-down menu, then click on **First logfile** in the **Name** column. Notice how the entries from both files are shown, and the coloring option is applied on top of that.

That's pretty much it regarding log viewing options in the Zabbix frontend. Note that this is very limited functionality and, for a centralized Syslog server with full log analysis options on top of that, a specialized solution should be used; there are quite a lot of free software products available.

Reusing data on the server

The items we've used so far were collecting data from some Zabbix agent or SNMP device. It's also possible to reuse this data in some calculation, store the result, and treat it as a normal item to be used for graphs, triggers, and other purposes. Zabbix offers two types of such items:

- **Calculated**: These items require writing exact formulas and referencing each individual item. They're more flexible than aggregate items, but aren't feasible over a large number of items and have to be manually adjusted if the items to be included in the calculation change.

- **Aggregate**: These items operate on items that share the same key across a host group. Minimum, maximum, sum, or average can be computed. They can't be used on multiple items on the same host, but if hosts are added to the group or removed from it, no adjustments are required for the aggregate item.

Calculated items

We'll start with calculated items that require typing in a formula. We're already monitoring total and used disk space. If we additionally wanted to monitor free disk space, we could query the agent for this information. This is where calculated items come in: if the agent or device doesn't expose a specific view of the data, or if we would like to avoid querying monitored hosts, we can do the calculation from the already retrieved values.

To create a calculated item that would compute the free disk space, do the following:

1. Navigate to **Configuration | Hosts**, click on **Items** next to **A test host**, and then click on **Create item**. Fill in the following information:

   - **Name**: `Diskspace on / (free)`
   - **Type**: **Calculated**
   - **Key**: `calc.vfs.fs.size[/,free]`
   - **Formula**: `last("vfs.fs.size[/,total]")-last("vfs.fs.size[/,used]")`
   - **Units**: `B`
   - **Update interval**: `1800s`

2. When done, click on the **Add** button at the bottom.

We chose a key that wouldn't clash with the native key in case somebody decides to use that later, but we're free to use any key for calculated items.

All of the referenced items must exist. We can't enter keys here and have them gather data by extension from the calculated item. Values to compute the calculated item are retrieved from the Zabbix server caches or the database; no connections are made to the monitored devices.

With this item added, let's go to the **Latest data** page. As the interval was set to 1,800 seconds, we might have to wait a bit longer to see the value, but eventually it should appear:

	Diskspace on / (free)	2018-12-01 18:02:43	4.65 GB
	Diskspace on / (total)	2018-12-01 18:02:20	6.19 GB
	Diskspace on / (used)	2018-12-01 18:02:24	1.54 GB

 If the item turns unsupported, check the error message and make sure the formula you typed in is correct.

The interval we used (1,800 seconds) wasn't matched to the intervals of both referenced items. Total and used disk space items were collecting data every 3,600 seconds, but calculated items aren't connected to the data collection of the referenced items in any way. A calculated item isn't evaluated when the referenced items get values; it follows its own scheduling, which is completely independent from the schedules of the referenced items and is semi-random. If the referenced items stopped collecting data, our calculated item would keep on using the latest value for the calculation, as we used the last() function. If one of them stopped collecting data, we would base our calculation on one recent and one outdated value. And if our calculated item could get very incorrect results if called at the wrong time, because one of the referenced items has significantly changed but the other hasn't received a new value yet, there's no easy solution to that, unfortunately. The custom scheduling discussed in Chapter 3, *Monitoring with Zabbix Agents and Basic Protocols*, could help here, but it could also introduce performance issues by polling values in uneven batches, and it would also be more complicated to manage. It's suggested to be used only as an exception.

The free disk space that we calculated might not match the *available* disk space reported by system tools. Many filesystems and operating systems reserve some space that doesn't count as used, but counts against the available disk space.

We might also want to compute the total of incoming and outgoing traffic on an interface, and a calculated item would work well here. The formula would be like this:

```
last(net.if.in[enp0s8])+last(net.if.out[enp0s8])
```

There's no need anymore to calculate total traffic on an interface in Zabbix 4.0 as there's now an item that can do this for us. We can make use of `net.if.total[<paramenters>]` now.

Did you spot how we quoted item keys in the first example, but not here? The reason is that calculated item formula entries follow a syntax of `function(key,function_parameter_1, function_parameter_2...)`. The item keys we referenced for the disk space item had commas in them like this: `vfs.fs.size[/,total]`. If we didn't quote the keys, Zabbix would interpret them as being `vfs.fs.size[/ with a function parameter of total]`. That wouldn't work.

Quoting in calculated items

The items we referenced had relatively simple keys: one or two parameters and no quoting. When the referenced items get more complicated, it's a common mistake to get quoting wrong. That, in turn, makes the item not work properly or at all. Let's look at the formula that we used to calculate free disk space:

```
last("vfs.fs.size[/,total]")-last("vfs.fs.size[/,used]")
```

The referenced item keys had no quoting. But what if the keys have the filesystem parameter is quoted like this:

```
vfs.fs.size["/",total]
```

We would have to escape the inner quotes with backslashes:

```
last("vfs.fs.size[\"/\",total]")-last("vfs.fs.size[\"/\",used]")
```

The more quoting the referenced items have, the more complicated the calculated item formula gets. If such a calculated item doesn't seem to work properly for you, check the escaping very, very carefully. Quite often users have even reported some behavior as a bug that turns out to be a misunderstanding about the quoting.

Referencing items from multiple hosts

The calculated items we've created so far referenced items on a single host or template. We just supplied item keys to the functions. We may also reference items from multiple hosts in a calculated item; in that case, the formula syntax changes slightly. The only thing we have to do is prefix the item key with the hostname, separated by a colon, the same as in the trigger expressions:

```
function(host:item_key)
```

Let's configure an item that would compute the average CPU load on both of our hosts:

1. Navigate to **Configuration** | **Hosts**, click on **Items** next to **A test host**, and click on **Create item**. Fill in the following:

   - **Name**: Average system load for both servers
   - **Type**: **Calculated**
   - **Key**: calc.system.cpu.load.avg
   - **Formula**: (last(A test host:system.cpu.load)+last(Another host:system.cpu.load))/2
   - **Type of information**: **Numeric (float)**

2. When done, click on the **Add** button at the bottom.

For triggers, when we referenced items, those triggers were associated with the hosts that the items came from. Calculated items also reference items, but they're always created on a single, specific host. The item we created will reside on A test host only. This means that such an item could also reside on a host that isn't included in the formula—for example, some calculations across a cluster could be done on a meta-host that holds cluster-wide items but isn't directly monitored itself.

Let's see whether this item works in **Monitoring | Latest data**. Make sure both of our hosts are shown and expand all entries. Look for three values, **CPU Load** both for **A test host** and **Another host**, as well as **Average system load for both servers**:

	Host	Name ▲	Last check	Last value	Change	
▼	Host	Name ▲	Last check	Last value	Change	
▼	A test host	**cpu** (2 Items)				
		Average system load for both servers	2018-12-01 18:13:44	0.81		Graph
		CPU Load	2018-12-01 18:13:11	1.62	+0.64	Graph
▼	Another host	**cpu** (1 Item)				
		CPU Load	2018-12-01 18:13:27	0		Graph

You can filter by `load` in the item names to see only relevant entries.

The value seems to be properly calculated. It could now be used like any normal item, maybe by including it and individual **CPU load** items from both hosts in a single graph. If we look at the values, the system loads for individual hosts are **1.62**, and **0**, and the average is calculated as **0.81**. Sometimes, it can be that this isn't an exact fit, even far away from the rounding. *Why would we get such a difference?* Data for both items that the calculated item depends on comes in at different intervals, and the calculated value is computed at a slightly different time—hence, while the value itself is correct, it might not match the exact average of values seen at any given time. Here, both **CPU Load** items had some values and the calculated average was correctly computed.

 When we make use of items in calculated items, we reference them from existing items so we need to be careful to copy the exact item over as is. That means parameters have to match with the original item—also, quotes and macros if we used them in our original item. We discuss a few additional aspects regarding calculated items in `Chapter 11`, *Automating Configuration*.

Aggregate items

The calculated items allowed us to write a specific formula, referencing exact individual items. This worked well for small-scale calculations, but the **CPU Load** item we created last would be very hard to create and maintain for dozens of hosts, and impossible for hundreds. If we want to calculate something for the same item key across many hosts, we would probably opt for *aggregate items*. They would allow us to find out the average load on a cluster or the total available disk space for a group of file servers, without naming each item individually. As with the calculated items, the result would be a normal item that could be used in triggers or graphs.

To find out what we can use in such a situation:

Go to **Configuration | Hosts**, select **Linux servers** in the **Group** drop-down menu and click on **Items** next to **A test host**, then click on **Create item**. Now, we have to figure out what item type to use. Expand the **Type** drop-down menu and look for an entry named **Zabbix aggregate**. That's the one we need, so choose it and click on **Select** next to the **Key** field. Currently, the key is listed as grpfunc, but that's just a placeholder; click on it. We have to replace it with the actual group key: one of grpsum, grpmin, grpmax, or grpavg. We'll calculate the average for several hosts, so change it to grpavg. This key, or group function, takes several parameters:

- group: As the name suggests, the host group name goes here. Enter Linux servers for this parameter.
- key: This is the key for the item to be used in calculations. Enter system.cpu.load here.
- func: This is a function used to retrieve data from individual items on hosts. While multiple functions are available, in this case we'll want to find out what the latest load is. Enter last for this field.
- param: This is a parameter for the previous function, following the same rules as normal function parameters (specifying either seconds or value count, prefixed with #). The function we used, last(), can be used without a parameter, so simply remove the last comma and the placeholder that follows it.

For individual item data, the following functions are supported:

Function	Details
avg	Average value
count	Number of values
last	Last value
max	Maximum value
min	Minimum value
sum	Sum of values

For aggregate items, two levels of functions are available. They're nested—first, the function specified as the `func` parameter gathers the required data from all hosts in the group. Then, `grpfunc` (`grpavg` in our case) calculates the final result from all the intermediate results retrieved by `func`.

All of the referenced items must exist. We can't enter keys here and have them gather data by extension from the aggregate item. Values to compute the calculated item are retrieved from the Zabbix server caches or the database; no connections are made to the monitored devices.

The final item key should be `grpavg[Linux servers,system.cpu.load,last]`.

If the referenced item key had parameters, we would have to quote it.

To finish the item configuration, fill in the following:

- **Name:** Average system load for Linux servers
- **Type of information**: **Numeric (float)**

The final item configuration should look like this:

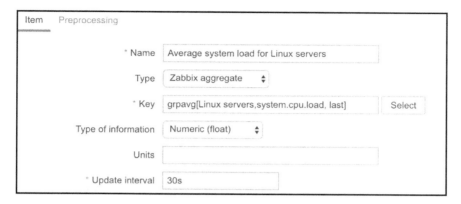

When done, click on the **Add** button at the bottom. Go to **Monitoring | Latest data**, make sure all hosts are shown, and look for the three values again—**CPU Load** both for **A test host** and **Another host**, as well as **Average system load for Linux servers**:

	Host	Name ▲	Last check	Last value	Change	
▼	Another host	- other - (1 Item)				
		CPU Load	2018-12-02 13:18:27	0.87	+0.51	Graph
▼	A test host	- other - (3 Items)				
		Average system load for both servers	2018-12-02 13:18:14	0.9	+0.49	Graph
		Average system load for Linux servers	2018-12-02 13:18:15	0.9	+0.49	Graph
		CPU Load	2018-12-02 13:18:11	1.43	+0.98	Graph

You can filter by `load` in the item names again.

The computed average across both hosts doesn't match our result if we look at the values on individual hosts, and the reason is exactly the same as we mentioned with the calculated items.

As the key parameters indicate, an aggregate item can be calculated for a host group—there's no way to pick individual hosts. Creating a new group is required if arbitrary hosts must have an aggregate item calculated for them. We discussed other benefits from careful host group planning in `Chapter 5`, *Managing Hosts, Users, and Permissions*.

We used the `grpavg` aggregate function to find out the average load for a group of servers, but there are other functions, as follows:

Function	Details
grpmax	The maximum value is reported. We can find out what the maximum SQL queries per second are across a group of database servers.
grpmin	The minimum value is reported. The minimum free space for a group of file servers could be determined.
grpsum	Values for the whole group are summed. The total number of HTTP sessions could be calculated for a group of web servers.

This way, a limited set of functions can be applied across a large number of hosts. While less flexible than calculated items, it's much more practical in case we want to do such a calculation for a group that includes hundreds of hosts. Additionally, a calculated item has to be updated whenever a host or item is to be added or removed from the calculations. An aggregate item will automatically find all of the relevant hosts and items. Note that *only enabled items on enabled hosts will be considered.*

Nothing limits the use of aggregate items by servers. They can also be used on any other class of devices, such as calculating average **CPU Load** for a group of switches, monitored over SNMP.

Aggregating across multiple groups

The basic syntax allows us to specify one host group. Although we mentioned earlier that aggregating across arbitrary hosts would require creating a new group, there's one more possibility—an aggregate item may reference several host groups. If we modified our aggregate item key to also include hosts in a `Solaris servers` group, it would look like this:

```
grpavg[[Linux servers,Solaris servers],system.cpu.load,last]
```

That is, multiple groups can be specified as comma-delimited entries in square brackets. If any host appears in several of those groups, the item from that host would be included only once in the calculation. There's no strict limit on the host group count here, although both readability and overall item key length limit—2,048 characters—should be taken into account.

Both calculated and aggregate items can reuse values from any other item, including calculated and aggregate items. They can also be used in triggers, graphs, network map labels, and anywhere else where other items can be used.

User parameters

The items we've looked at so far allowed us to query the built-in capabilities of a Zabbix agent, query SNMP devices, and reuse data on the Zabbix server. Every now and then, a need arises to monitor something that isn't supported by Zabbix out of the box. The easiest and most popular method to extend Zabbix data collection is user parameters. They're commands that are run by the Zabbix agent and the result is returned as an item value. Let's try to set up some user parameters and see what things we should pay extra attention to.

Just getting it to work

First, we'll make sure that we can get the agent to return any value at all. User parameters are configured on the agent side—the agent daemon contains the key specification, which includes references to commands. On A test host, edit zabbix_agentd.conf and look near the end of the file. An explanation of the syntax is available here:

```
UserParameter=<key>,<shell command>
```

This means that we can freely choose the key name and command to be executed. It's suggested that you keep key names to lowercase alphanumeric characters and dots. For starters, add a very simple line like this:

```
UserParameter=quick.test,echo 1
```

Just return 1, always. Save the configuration file and restart the Zabbix agent daemon. While it might be tempting to add an item like this in the frontend, it's highly recommended to test all user parameters before configuring them in the frontend. That'll provide the results faster and overall make your life simpler. The easiest way to test an item is with zabbix_get; we discussed this small utility in Chapter 3, *Monitoring with Zabbix Agents and Basic Protocols*. Run on A test host:

```
$ zabbix_get -s 127.0.0.1 -k quick.test
```

If testing user parameters on a different host, run `zabbix_get` from the Zabbix server or make sure the agent allows connections from the localhost—that's configured with the server parameter in `zabbix_agentd.conf`.

That should return just 1. If it does, great—your first user parameter is working. If not, well, there's not much that could go wrong. Make sure the correct file was being edited, the agent daemon was really restarted, and that the correct host was queried.

 This trivial user parameter actually illustrates a troubleshooting suggestion. Whenever a user parameter fails and you can't figure out why, simplify it and test every iteration with `zabbix_get`. Eventually, you'll get to the part that's responsible for the failure.

We won't actually add this item in the frontend as it won't provide much value. Instead, let's re-implement an item that is already available in the Zabbix agent, counting the number of logged-in users. Edit `zabbix_agentd.conf` again and add the following near our previous modification:

```
UserParameter=system.test,who | wc -l
```

Notice how we can chain multiple commands. In general, anything the underlying shell would accept would be good. Save the file and restart the Zabbix agent daemon. Now, quick test again by running this command from the Zabbix server (don't forget to replace `127.0.0.1` with the IP of your host) or from the host:

```
$ zabbix_get -s 127.0.0.1 -k system.test
```

That should return a number, as you are probably running `zabbix_get` from the same system; it should be at least 1. Let's create an item to receive this data in the frontend:

1. Open **Configuration** | **Hosts**, make sure **Linux servers** is selected in the **Group** drop-down menu, click on **Items** next to **A test host**, then click on **Create item**. Fill in these values:

   - **Name**: `Users logged in`
   - **Type**: **Zabbix agent (active)**
   - **Key**: `system.test`

We're using the active item type with our user parameter. User parameters are suggested to be used as active items as they can tie up server connections if they don't return very quickly. Notice how we used exactly the same key name as specified in the agent daemon configuration file.

2. When you're done, click on **Add**.
3. Now check **Monitoring | Latest data**. As this is an active item, we might have to wait for the agent to request the item list from the server, then return the data, which can take up to two minutes in addition to the server updating its cache in one minute. Sooner or later, the data will appear.

The great thing is that it's all completely transparent from the server side—the item looks and works as if it was built in.

We have gotten a basic user parameter to work, but this one replicates the existing Zabbix agent item, so it still isn't that useful. The biggest benefit provided by user parameters is the ability to monitor virtually anything, even things that aren't natively supported by the Zabbix agent, so let's try some slightly more advanced metrics.

Querying data that the Zabbix agent doesn't support

One thing we might be interested in is the number of open TCP connections. We can get this data using the `netstat` command (chances are `netstat` isn't installed on your distribution out of the box, but it should be possible to install this `util` from the `net-tools` package. If not, check out the following tip). Execute the following on the Zabbix server:

```
$ netstat -t
```

The `-t` switch tells `netstat` to list TCP connections only. As a result, we get a list of connections (trimmed here):

```
Active Internet connections (w/o servers)
Proto Recv-Q  Send-Q   Local Address            Foreign Address
State
tcp    0       0        localhost:zabbix-trapper  localhost:52932
TIME_WAIT
tcp    0       0        localhost:zabbix-agent    localhost:59779
TIME_WAIT
tcp    0       0        localhost:zabbix-agent    localhost:59792
TIME_WAIT
```

In modern distributions, the ss utility might be a better option. It'll also perform better, especially when there are many connections. An alternative command for ss, matching the aforementioned netstat command, would be ss -tstate connect.

To get the number of connections, we'll use the following command:

```
netstat -nt | grep -c ^tcp
```

Here, grep first filters out connection lines and then just counts them. We could have used many other approaches, but this one is simple enough. Additionally, the -n flag is passed to netstat, which instructs it to perform no resolving on hosts, hence giving a performance boost.

Edit zabbix_agentd.conf and add the following line near the other user parameters:

```
UserParameter=net.tcp.conn,netstat -nt | grep -c ^tcp
```

In the frontend, go to **Configuration** | **Hosts**, click on **Items** next to **A test host**, then click on **Create item** and fill in the following values:

- **Name**: Open connections
- **Type**: **Zabbix agent (active)**
- **Key**: net.tcp.conn

When you're done, click on the **Add** button at the bottom. *Did you notice that we didn't restart the agent daemon after modifying its configuration file?* Do that now. Using such an ordering of events will give us values faster, because the agent queries the active items list immediately after startup, and this way the server already has the item configured when the agent is restarted. Feel free to check **Monitoring** | **Latest values**:

	Open connections	2018-12-02 13:38:53	28	Graph

Flexible user parameters

We're now gathering data on all open connections. But looking at the `netstat` output, we can see connections in different states, such as `TIME_WAIT` and `ESTABLISHED`:

```
tcp    0    0    127.0.0.1:10050    127.0.0.1:60774        TIME_WAIT
tcp    0    0    192.168.56.10:22   192.168.56.1:51187     ESTABLISHED
```

If we want to monitor connections in different states, *would we have to create a new user parameter for each?* Fortunately, no. Zabbix supports so-called flexible user parameters, which allow us to pass parameters to the command executed.

Again, edit `zabbix_agentd.conf` and modify the user parameter line we added before to read as follows:

```
UserParameter=net.tcp.conn[*],netstat -nt | grep ^tcp | grep -c "$1"
```

> The `ss` utility again might be better in modern distributions. For example, filtering for established connections could be easily done by the established `ss -t state`.

We've made the following changes:

- First, the addition of `[*]` indicates that this user parameter itself accepts parameters
- Second, adding the second `grep` statement allows us to use such passed parameters in the command
- We also moved the `-c` flag to the last `grep` statement to do the counting

> *Was it mentioned that it might be easier with* `ss`*?*

All parameters we would use now for this key will be passed to the script—`$1` substituted for the first parameter, `$2` for the second, and so on. Note the use of double quotes around `$1`. This way, if no parameter is passed, the result would be the same as without using `grep` at all.

Restart the agent to make it pick up the modified user parameter.

Back in the frontend, follow these steps:

1. Navigate to **Configuration** | **Hosts**, click on **Items** next to **A test host**, click on **Open connections** in the **Name** column, and then click on the **Clone** button at the bottom of the editing form. Change the following fields:

   - **Name**: Open connections in $1 state
   - **Key**: net.tcp.conn[TIME_WAIT]

2. Click on the **Add** button at the bottom.
3. Now click on **Open connections in the TIME_WAIT state** in the **Name** column, click on **Clone**, and modify the **Key** field to read net.conn[ESTABLISHED]; then click on the **Add** button at the bottom.

See the man page for netstat for a full list of possible connection states.

Take a look at **Monitoring** | **Latest data**:

Open connections	2018-12-02 13:45:05	28
Open connections in ESTABLISHED state	2018-12-02 13:45:05	1
Open connections in TIME_WAIT state	2018-12-02 13:45:05	27

It's possible that the values don't match; summing open connections in all states might not give the same number as all open connections. First, remember that there are more connection states, so you'd have to add them all to get a complete picture. Second, as we saw before, all of these values aren't retrieved simultaneously, so one item grabs data, and a moment later another comes in, but the data has already changed slightly.

 We're also counting all of the connections that we create either by remotely connecting to the server, just running the Zabbix server, or by other means.

We're now receiving values for various items, but we only had to add a single user parameter. Flexible user parameters allow us to return data based on many parameters. For example, we could provide additional functionality to our user parameter if we make a simple modification like this:

```
UserParameter=net.conn[*],netstat -nt | grep ^tcp | grep "$1" | grep -c "$2"
```

We added another `grep` command on the second parameter, again using double quotes to make sure the missing parameter won't break anything. Now, we can use the IP address as a second parameter to figure out the number of connections in a specific state to a specific host. In this case, the item key might be `net.conn[TIME_WAIT,127.0.0.1]`.

Note that the item parameter ordering (passing state first and IP second) in this case is completely arbitrary. We could swap them and get the same result, as we're just filtering the output by two strings with `grep`. If we were to swap them, the description would be slightly incorrect, as we're using positional item key parameter references in it.

Level of the details monitored

There're almost unlimited combinations of what details one can monitor on some target. It's possible to monitor every single detailed parameter of a process, such as detailed memory usage, the existence of PID files, and many more things, and it's possible to simply check whether a process is running.

Sometimes, a single service can require multiple processes to be running, and it might be enough to monitor whether a certain category of processes is running as expected, trusting some other component to figure that out. One example could be Postfix, the email server. Postfix runs several different processes, including `master`, `pickup`, `anvil`, and `smtpd`. While checks could be created against every individual process, often it would be enough to check whether the `init` script thinks that everything is fine.

We would need an `init` script that has the `status` command support. As `init` scripts usually output a textual string, `Checking for service Postfix: running`, it would be better to return only a numeric value to Zabbix that would indicate the service state. Common exit codes are 0 for success and nonzero if there's a problem. That means we could do something like the following:

```
/etc/init.d/postfix status > /dev/null 2>&1 || echo 1
```

That would call the `init` script, discard all `stdin` and `stderr` output (because we only want to return a single number to Zabbix), and return 1 upon a non-successful exit code. That should work, *right?* There's only one huge problem-parameters should never return an empty string, which is what would happen with such a check if Postfix was running. If the Zabbix server were to check such an item, it would assume the parameter is unsupported and deactivate it as a consequence. We could modify this string so that it becomes the following:

```
/etc/init.d/postfix status > /dev/null 2>&1 && echo 0 || echo 1
```

This would work very nicely, as now a Boolean is returned and Zabbix always gets valid data. But there's a possibly better way. As the exit code is 0 for success and nonzero for problems, we could simply return that. While this would mean that we won't get nice Boolean values only, we could still check for nonzero values in a trigger expression like this:

```
{hostname:item.last()}>0
```

As an added benefit, we might get a more detailed return message if the `init` script returns a more detailed status with nonzero exit codes. As defined by the Linux Standard Base, the exit codes for the status commands are the following:

Code	Meaning
0	Program is running or service is OK
1	Program is dead and `/var/run` pid file exists
2	Program is dead and `/var/lock` lock file exists
3	Program isn't running
4	Program or service status is unknown

There're several reserved ranges that might contain other codes, used by a specific application or distribution—those should be looked up in the corresponding documentation.

For such a case, our user parameter command becomes even simpler, with the full string being as follows:

```
UserParameter=service.status[*],/etc/init.d/"$1" status > /dev/null
2>&1; echo $?
```

We're simply returning the exit code to Zabbix. To make the output more user friendly, we'd definitely want to use value mapping. That way, each return code would be accompanied on the frontend with an explanatory message like the preceding. Notice the use of `$1`. This way, we can create a single user parameter and use it for any service we desire. For an item like that, the appropriate key would be `service.status[postfix]` or `service.status[nfs]`. If such a check doesn't work for the non-root user, `sudo` would have to be used.

In open source land, multiple processes per single service are less common, but they're quite popular in proprietary software, in which case a trick like this greatly simplifies monitoring such services.

 Most distributions have moved to `systemd`. In that case, the user parameter line would be
`UserParameter=service.status[*],systemctl status "$1"`
`> /dev/null 2>&1; echo $?`.

Environment trap

Let's try to find out what other interesting statistics we can gather this way. A common need is to monitor some statistics about databases. We could attempt to gather some MySQL query data; for example, *how many queries per second are there*? MySQL has a built-in query per second measurement, but that isn't quite what most users would expect. That particular value is calculated for the whole uptime MySQL has, which means it's quite useful, though only for the first few minutes. Longer-running MySQL instances have this number approaching the average value and only slightly fluctuating. When graphed, the queries per second graph gets flatter and flatter as time passes.

The flexibility of Zabbix allows us to use a different metric. Let's try to create a slightly more meaningful MySQL query items. We can get some data on the **Select** statements with a query like this:

```
mysql> show global status like 'Com_select';
```

That is something we should try to get working as a user parameter now. A test command to parse out only the number we're interested in would be as follows:

```
$ mysql -N -e "show global status like 'Com_select';" | awk '{print
$2}'
```

We're using `awk` to print the second field. The `-N` flag for `mysql` tells it to omit column headers. Now, on to the agent daemon configuration—add the following near our other user parameters on our Zabbix server:

```
UserParameter=mysql.queries[*],mysql -u zabbix -N -e "show global
status like 'Com_$1';" | awk '{print $$2}'
```

It's basically the user parameter definition with the command appended, but we've made a few changes here. Notice how we used `[*]` after the key and replaced `select` in `Com_select` with `$1`—this way, we'll be able to use query type as an item key parameter. This also required adding the second dollar sign in the `awk` statement. If a literal dollar sign placeholder has to be used with a flexible user parameter, such dollar signs must be prefixed with another dollar sign. And the last thing we changed was adding `-u zabbix` to the `mysql` command. Of course, it's best not to use `root` or a similar access for database statistics, if possible—but if this command is supposed to be run by the Zabbix agent, *why specify the username again?* Mostly because of an old and weird bug where MySQL would sometimes attempt to connect with the wrong user. If you'd like to see the current status of that issue, see `https://bugs.mysql.com/bug.php?id=64522`. With the changes in place, save and close the file, then restart the agent daemon.

> You might want to create a completely separate database user that has no actual write permissions for monitoring.

Now, the same as before, let's do a quick `zabbix_get` test on our Zabbix server command line:

```
$ zabbix_get -s 127.0.0.1 -k mysql.queries[select]
```

Well, you might have seen this one coming:

```
ERROR 1045 (28000): Access denied for user 'zabbix'@'localhost' (using
password: NO)
```

Our database user did require a password, but we specified none. *How could we do that?* The mysql utility allows us to specify a password on the command line with the -p flag (for example, -p<password>, with no spaces between -p and the password), but it's best to avoid it. Placing passwords on the command line might allow other users to see this data in the process list, so it's a good idea to develop a habit: no secret information on the command line, ever.

 On some platforms, some versions of the MySQL client will mask the passed password. While that's a nice gesture from MySQL's developers, it won't work on all platforms and with all software, so such an approach should be avoided just to make it a habit. The password in such a case is likely to be written to the shell history file, making it available to attackers even after the process is no longer running.

How could we pass the password in a secure manner then? Fortunately, MySQL can read the password from a file that we could secure with permissions. A .my.cnf file is searched in several directories, and in our case the best option might be placing it in the user's home directory. On the Zabbix server, execute the following as the zabbix user:

```
$ touch ~zabbix/.my.cnf
$ chown zabbix:zabbix ~zabbix/.my.cnf
$ chmod 600 ~zabbix/.my.cnf
$ echo -e "[client]\npassword=<password>" > ~zabbix/.my.cnf
```

 If your password contains the hash mark #, enclose it in double quotes in this file.
You can change to the zabbix user with su - zabbix or use sudo.

Use the password that the Zabbix database user has. You can remind yourself what it was by taking a look at zabbix_server.conf. If running the preceding commands as root, also run chown -R zabbix.zabbix ~zabbix after creating the file. Note that we first create and secure the file, and only then place the password in it. Before we proceed with the agent side, let's test whether MySQL utilities pick up the password file. As the zabbix user, run the following:

```
$ mysqladmin -u zabbix status
```

Run the preceding code either in the same su session or as sudo -u zabbix mysqladmin -u zabbix status.

If everything went well with the file we put the password in, it should return some data:

```
Uptime: 10218  Threads: 23  Questions: 34045  Slow queries: 0  Opens:
114  Flush tables: 2  Open tables: 140  Queries per second avg: 3.331
```

If that doesn't work, double-check the password, path, and permissions to the file. We use `mysqladmin` for this test, but both `mysql` and `mysqladmin` should use the same procedure for finding the `.my.cnf` file and reading the password from it.

Now that we know it's working, let's turn to `zabbix_get` again (no agent restart is needed as we didn't modify the agent configuration file this time):

```
$ zabbix_get -s 127.0.0.1 -k mysql.queries[select]
```

But the result seems weird:

```
ERROR 1045 (28000): Access denied for user 'zabbix'@'localhost' (using
password: NO)
```

In some cases, when using `systemd`, the home directory might be set—if so, skip the next change, but keep in mind this potential pitfall.

It's failing still, and with the same error message. If we carefully read the full error, we'll see that the password is still not used. *How could that be?*

It doesn't matter which user account we run `zabbix_get` as—it connects to the running agent daemon over a TCP port. So when the user parameter command is run, information about the user running `zabbix_get` has no impact at all.

The environment isn't initialized for user parameter commands. This includes several common variables and one we're quite interested in: HOME. This variable is used by the MySQL client to determine where to look for the `.my.cnf` file. If the variable is missing, this file (and in turn, the password) can't be found. *Does that mean we're doomed?* Of course not, we wouldn't let such a minor problem stop us. We simply have to tell MySQL where to look for this file, and we can use a very simple method to do that. Edit `zabbix_agentd.conf` again and change our user parameter line to read as follows:

```
UserParameter=mysql.queries[*],HOME=/var/lib/zabbix mysql -u zabbix -N
-e "show global status like 'Com_$1';" | awk '{print $$2}'
```

If you installed from packages, use the directory that is set as the home directory for the `zabbix` user.

This sets the `HOME` variable for the `mysql` utility and that should allow the MySQL client to find the configuration file that specifies the password. Again, restart the Zabbix agent and then run the following:

```
$ zabbix_get -s 127.0.0.1 -k mysql.queries[select]
1788
```

You'll see a different value, and finally we can see the item is working. But *what's that number?* If you repeatedly run `zabbix_get`, you will see that the number is increasing. That looks a lot like another counter—and indeed, that's the number of `SELECT` queries since the database engine startup. We know how to deal with this. Back in the frontend, let's add an item to monitor the `SELECT` queries per second:

1. Navigate to **Configuration | Hosts**, click on **Items** next to **A test host**, then click on the **Create item** button. Fill in these values:

    - **Name:** `MySQL $1 queries per second`
    - **Type: Zabbix agent (active)**
    - **Key:** `mysql.queries[select]`
    - **Type of information: Numeric (float)**
    - **Units:** `qps`
    - **Preprocessing** tab: **Preprocessing steps (Change per second)**
    - **New application:** `MySQL`

The preceding details are shown in the following screenshot:

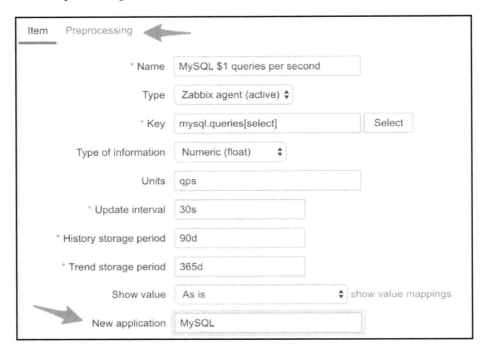

2. When you're done, click on the **Add** button at the bottom.

Notice how we used **Delta (speed per second)** together with **Numeric (float)** here. For the network traffic items, we chose **Numeric (unsigned)** instead, as there the value could overflow the float. For this query item, that's somewhere between highly unlikely and impossible, and we'll actually benefit a lot from increased precision here. The qps unit is just that—a string. It doesn't impact the displaying of data in any way besides appearing next to it.

Again, we might have to wait for a few minutes for any data to arrive. If you are impatient, feel free to restart the Zabbix agent daemon, then check the **Latest data** page:

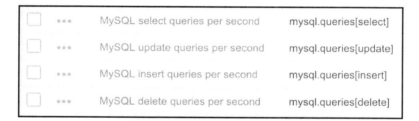

The data is coming in nicely and we can see that our test server isn't too overloaded.

Let's benefit from making that user parameter flexible now:

1. Navigate back to **Configuration | Hosts**, click on **Items** next to **A test host**, then click on **MySQL select queries per second** in the **Name** column.

2. At the bottom of the form, click on the **Clone** button and change `select` in the key to `update`, then click on the **Add** button at the bottom. Clone this item two more times, changing the key parameter to insert and delete. Eventually, there should be four items:

		MySQL select queries per second	mysql.queries[select]
	•••	MySQL update queries per second	mysql.queries[update]
	•••	MySQL insert queries per second	mysql.queries[insert]
	•••	MySQL delete queries per second	mysql.queries[delete]

The items should start gathering the data soon; let's try to see how they look all together:

1. Click on **Graphs** in the navigation header above the item list, then click on **Create graph**

2. Enter `MySQL queries` in the **Name** field and click on **Add** in the **Items** section.

3. Mark the check boxes next to the four MySQL items we created and click on **Select** at the bottom, then click on the **Add** button at the bottom

4. Let's go to **Monitoring** | **Graphs**, then select **A test host** in the **Host** drop-down menu and **MySQL queries** in the **Graph** drop-down menu. The graph, after some time, might look like this:

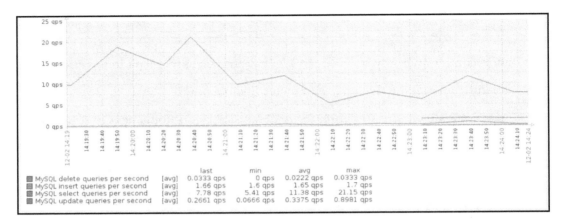

As we can see, the `select` queries are at the top here and the `delete` ones are almost non-existent. There are other query types, but this should be enough for our user parameter implementation.

Things to remember about user parameters

We saw that the flexibility of user parameters is basically unlimited. Still, there might be cases when additional measures have to be applied.

Wrapper scripts

Commands to be executed can be specified in the Zabbix agent daemon configuration file on a single line only. Pushing whole scripts there can be very messy and sometimes it can be hard to figure out the quotation. In such cases, a wrapper script has to be written. Such a script can be useful if parsing data requires more complex actions, or if parsing out multiple different values can't be easily done with flexible user parameters.

It's important to remember that using user parameters and custom scripts requires these to be distributed on all monitored hosts—that involves the scripts themselves and changes to the Zabbix agent daemon's configuration file.

This can soon become hard to manage. Various systems will require different user parameters, so you'll either end up with a messy agent configuration file containing all of them or a myriad of different combinations. There's a quite widespread feature to help with this problem: configuration file inclusion. You can specify the inclusion of individual files by adding to `zabbix_agentd.conf` entries such as these:

```
Include=/etc/zabbix/zabbix_agentd.d/zabbix_lm_sensors.conf
Include=/etc/zabbix/zabbix_agentd.d/zabbix_md_raid.conf
```

If such a file is missing, Zabbix will complain but will still start up. Inclusions can be nested—you can include one file that, in turn, includes several others, and so on.

It's also possible to include whole directories—in that case, all files placed there will be used. This method allows other packages to place, for example, user parameter configuration in a specific directory, which will then be automatically used by Zabbix:

```
Include=/etc/zabbix/zabbix_agentd.d/
```

Or, to be sure that only files ending with `conf` are included, use this:

```
Include=/etc/zabbix/zabbix_agentd.d/*.conf
```

Then, other packages would only need to place files such as `zabbix_lm_sensors.conf` or `zabbix_md_raid.conf` in the `/etc/zabbix/userparameters` directory, and they would be used without any additional changes to the agent daemon configuration file. Installing the Apache web server would add one file, installing Postfix another, and so on.

When not to use user parameters

There are also cases where user parameters are best replaced with a different solution. Usually, that will be when the following happens:

* The script takes a long time
* The script returns many values

In the first case, the script could simply time out. The default timeout on the agent side is three seconds, and it's not suggested to increase it in most cases.

In the second case, we might be interested in 100 values that a script could return in a single invocation, but Zabbix doesn't allow several values to be obtained from a single key or from a single invocation, so we would have to run the script 100 times—not very efficient.

If a script supplies values for multiple trapper items, it might be worth adding a `nodata()` trigger for some of them—that way, any issues with the script and missing data would be discovered quickly.

There're several potential solutions, with some drawbacks and benefits for each case:

- A special item (usually an external check, discussed in the following, or another user parameter) that could send the data right away using `zabbix_sender` if the data collection script is quick. If not, it could write data to temporary files or invoke another script with `nohup`.

- `crontab`: This is a classic solution that can help both when the script takes a long time and when it returns many values. It does have the drawback of having interval management outside Zabbix. Values are usually sent right away using `zabbix_sender` (discussed later in this chapter), although they could also be written to temporary files and read by other items using the `vfs.file.contents` or `vfs.file.regexp` keys.

- A special item (usually another user parameter) that adds an `atd` job. This solution is a bit more complicated, but allows us to keep interval management in Zabbix while still allowing the use of long-running scripts for data collection. See `http://zabbix.org/wiki/Escaping_timeouts_with_atd` for more details.

External checks

All of the check categories we explored before cover a very wide range of possible devices, but there's always that one that doesn't play well with standard monitoring protocols, can't have the agent installed, and is buggy in general. A real-life example would be a UPS that provides temperature information on the web interface, but doesn't provide this data over SNMP. Or, maybe we would like to collect some information remotely that Zabbix doesn't support yet—for example, monitoring how much time an SSL certificate has until it expires.

In Zabbix, such information can be collected with external checks or external scripts. While user parameters are scripts run by the Zabbix agent, external check scripts are run directly by the Zabbix server.

First, we should figure out the command to find out the remaining certificate validity period. We have at least two options here:

- Return the time when the certificate expires
- Return 0 or 1 to identify that the certificate expires in some period of time

Let's try out both options.

Finding a certificate expiry time

We could find out the certificate expiry time with an openssl command such as this:

```
$ echo | openssl s_client -connect www.google.com:443 2>/dev/null | openssl x509 -noout -enddate
```

Feel free to use any other domain for testing here and later.

We're closing stdin for the openssl command with echo and passing the retrieved certificate information to another openssl command, x509, to return the date and time when the certificate will expire:

```
notAfter=Jan 30 08:59:00 2019 GMT
```

The resulting string isn't something we could easily parse in Zabbix, though. We could convert it into a UNIX timestamp like this:

```
$ date -d "$(echo | openssl s_client -connect www.google.com:443 2>/dev/null | openssl x509 -noout -enddate | sed 's/^notAfter=//')" "+%s"
```

We're stripping the non-date part with sed and then formatting the date and time as a UNIX timestamp with the date utility:

```
1546425338
```

Looks like we have the command ready, but *where would we place it?* For external checks, a special directory is used. Open zabbix_server.conf and look for the ExternalScripts option. You might see either a specific path or a placeholder:

```
# ExternalScripts=${datadir}/zabbix/externalscripts
```

If it's a specific path, that's easy. If it's a placeholder such as the preceding, it references the compile-time data directory. Note that it's not a variable. When compiling from the sources, the `${datadir}` path defaults to `/usr/local/share/`. If you installed from packages, it's likely to be `/usr/lib/`. In any case, there should be a `zabbix/externalscripts/` subdirectory in there. This is where our external check script will have to go. Create a script, `zbx_certificate_expiry_time.sh`, there with the following contents:

```bash
#!/bin/bash
date -d "$(echo | openssl s_client -connect "$1":443 2>/dev/null |
openssl x509 -noout -enddate | sed 's/^notAfter=//')" "+%s"
```

Notice how we replaced the actual website address with a `$1` placeholder—this allows us to specify the domain to check as a parameter to this script. Make that file executable:

```
$ chmod 755 zbx_certificate_expiry_time.sh
$ chown zabbix:zabbix zbx_certificate_expiry_time.sh
```

And now, for a quick test, type the following:

```
$ ./zbx_certificate_expiry_time.sh www.google.com
1548838740
```

Great, we can pass the domain name to the script and get back the time when the certificate for that domain expires. Now, on to placing this information in Zabbix.

In the frontend, go to **Configuration | Hosts**, click on **Items** next to **A test host**, and click on **Create item**. Fill in the following:

- **Name**: `Certificate expiry time on $1`
- **Type**: **External check**
- **Key**: `zbx_certificate_expiry_time.sh[www.google.com]`
- **Units**: `unixtime`

We specified the domain to check as a key parameter, and it'll be passed to the script as the first positional parameter, which we then use in the script as $1. If more than one parameter is needed, we would comma-delimit them, the same as for any other item type. The parameters would be properly passed to the script as $1, $2, and so on. If we need no parameters, we would use empty square brackets [], or just leave them off completely. If we wanted to act upon the host information instead of hardcoding the value like we did, we could use some macro; for example, {HOST.HOST}, {HOST.IP}, and {HOST.DNS} are common values. Another useful macro here would be {HOST.CONN}, which would resolve either to the IP or DNS, depending on which one is selected in the interface properties.

When done, click on the **Add** button at the bottom. Now, check this item in the **Latest data** page:

	Certificate expiry time on www.google.com	2018-12-02 14:49:54	2019-01-30 10:59:00

The expiry time seems to be collected correctly and the unixtime unit converted the value into a human-readable version. *What about a trigger on this item?* The easiest solution might be with the fuzzytime() function again. Let's say we want to detect a certificate that will expire in seven days or less. The trigger expression would be as follows:

```
{A test
host:zbx_certificate_expiry_time.sh[www.zabbix.com].fuzzytime(604800)}
=0
```

The huge value in the trigger function parameters, 604800, is seven days in seconds. *Can we make it more readable?* Sure we can—this would be exactly the same:

```
{A test
host:zbx_certificate_expiry_time.sh[www.google.com].fuzzytime(7d)}=0
```

The trigger would alert with one week left and, from the item values, we could see exactly how much time exactly is left. We discussed triggers in more detail in Chapter 6, *Detecting Problems with Triggers*.

We're conveniently ignoring the fact that the certificate might not be valid yet. While our trigger would fire if the certificate wasn't valid for a week or more, it would ignore certificates that would only become valid in less than a week.

Determining certificate validity

A simpler approach might be passing the threshold to the OpenSSL utilities and letting them determine whether the certificate will be good after that many seconds. A command to check whether the certificate is good for seven days would be as follows:

```
$ echo | openssl s_client -connect www.google.com:443 2>/dev/null |
openssl x509 -checkend 604800
Certificate will not expire
```

That looks simple enough. If the certificate expires in the given time, the message would say `Certificate will expire`. The great thing is that the exit code also differs based on the expiry status, so we could return 1 when the certificate is still good and 0 when it expires.

This approach returns 1 upon success, similar to many built-in items. We could also follow the `openssl` command with `echo $?`, which would return 0 upon success.

```
$ echo | openssl s_client -connect www.google.com:443 2>/dev/null |
openssl x509 -checkend 604800 -noout && echo 1 || echo 0
```

In this version, values such as `7d` aren't supported, although they're accepted. Be very careful to use only values in seconds.

In the same directory as before, create a script, `zbx_certificate_expires_in.sh`, with the following contents:

```
#!/bin/bash
echo | openssl s_client -connect "$1":443 2>/dev/null | openssl x509 -
checkend "$2" -noout && echo 1 || echo 0
```

This time, in addition to the domain being replaced with `$1`, we also replaced the time period to check with a `$2` placeholder. Make that file executable:

```
$ chmod 755 zbx_certificate_expires_in.sh
```

And now, for a quick test, type the following:

```
$ ./zbx_certificate_expires_in.sh www.zabbix.com 604800
1
```

It looks good. Now, on to creating the item—in the frontend:

1. Go to **Configuration** | **Hosts**, click on **Items** next to **A test host**, and click on **Create item**. Start by clicking on **Show value mappings** next to the **Show value** drop-down menu. In the resulting popup, click on the **Create value** map. Enter `Certificate expiry status` in the **Name** field, then click on the **Add** link in the **Mappings** section. Fill in the following, as shown in the following screenshot:

   - `0: Expires soon`
   - `1: Does not expire yet`

   We're not specifying the time period here as that could be customized per item.

2. When done, click on the **Add** button at the bottom and close the popup. Refresh the item configuration form to get our new value map and fill in the following:

   - **Name:** `Certificate expiry status for $1`
   - **Type: External check**
   - **Key:** `zbx_certificate_expires_in.sh[www.google.com,60 4800]`
   - **Show value: Certificate expiry status**

When done, click on the **Add** button at the bottom. And again, check this item in the **Latest data** page.

It seems to work properly. It doesn't expire yet, so we're all good. One benefit over the previous approach could be that it's more obvious which certificates are going to expire soon when looking at a list.

It's important to remember that external checks could take quite a long time. With the default timeout being three or four seconds (we'll discuss the details in Chapter 20, *Zabbix Maintenance*), anything longer than a second or two is already too risky. Also, keep in mind that a server poller process is always busy while running the script; we can't offload external checks to an agent like we did with the user parameters being active items. It's suggested to use external checks only as a last resort when all other options to gather the information have failed. In general, external checks should be kept lightweight and fast. If a script is too slow, it'll time out and the item will become unsupported.

Sending in the data

In some cases, there might be custom data sources where none of the previously discussed methods would work sufficiently well. A script could run for a very long time, or we could have a system without the Zabbix agent but with the capability to push data. Zabbix offers a way to send data to a special item type, Zabbix trapper, using a command-line utility, **Zabbix sender**. The easiest way to explain how it works might be to set up a working item like that:

1. Navigate to **Configuration | Hosts**, click on **Items** next to **A test host**, click on **Create item**, then fill in the following:

    - **Name:** Amount of persons in the room
    - **Type:** **Zabbix trapper**
    - **Key:** room.persons

2. When you're done, click on the **Add** button at the bottom.

We now have to determine how data can be passed into this item, and this is where zabbix_sender comes in. On the Zabbix server, execute the following:

```
$ zabbix_sender --help
```

If you've installed from a distribution, then `zabbix_sender` needs to be installed first from the repository.

We won't reproduce the output here, as it's somewhat lengthy. Instead, let's see which parameters are required for the most simple operation, sending a single value from the command line:

- `-z` is to specify the Zabbix server
- `-s` is to specify the hostname, as configured in Zabbix
- `-k` is for the key name
- `-o` is for the value to send

Note that the hostname is the hostname in the Zabbix host properties—not the IP, not the DNS, and not the visible name. Let's try to send a value:

```
$ zabbix_sender -z 127.0.0.1 -s "A test host" -k room.persons -o 1
```

 As usual, the hostname is case sensitive. The same applies to the item key.

This command should succeed and show the following output:

```
info from server: "processed: 1; failed: 0; total: 1; seconds spent:
0.000046"
sent: 1; skipped: 0; total: 1
```

 If you're very quick with running this command after adding the item, the trapper item might not be in the Zabbix server configuration cache. Make sure to wait at least one minute after adding the item.

Let's send another value—again using `zabbix_sender`:

```
$ zabbix_sender -z 127.0.0.1 -s "A test host" -k room.persons -o 2
```

This one should also succeed, and now we should take a look at **Monitoring** | **Latest data** over at the frontend. We can see that the data has successfully arrived and the change is properly recorded:

Now we could try being smart. Let's pass a different data type to Zabbix:

```
$ zabbix_sender -z 127.0.0.1 -s "A test host" -k room.persons -o
nobody
```

We're now trying to pass a string to the Zabbix item even though, in the frontend, its data type is set to an integer:

```
info from server: "processed: 0; failed: 1; total: 1; seconds spent:
0.000074"
sent: 1; skipped: 0; total: 1
```

Zabbix didn't like that, though. The data we provided was rejected because of the data type mismatch, so it's clear that any process that's passing the data is responsible for the data contents and formatting.

Now, security-concerned people would probably ask—*who can send data to items of the trapper type?* zabbix_sender can be run on any host by anybody, and it's enough to know the hostname and item key.

It's possible to restrict this in a couple of ways—for one of them, see **Configuration** | **Hosts**, click on **Items** next to **A test host**, and click on **Amount of persons in the room** in the **Name** column. Look at one of the last few properties, **Allowed hosts**. We can specify an IP address or DNS name here, and any data for this item will be allowed from the specified host only:

Allowed hosts	192.168.1.23

Several addresses can be supplied by separating them with commas. In this field, user macros are supported as well. We discussed user macros in Chapter 8, *Simplifying Complex Configurations with Templates*.

Another option to restrict who can send the data to trapper items is by using the authentication feature with PSK or SSL certificates. That's discussed in `Chapter 18`, *Encrypting Zabbix Traffic*.

Using an agent daemon configuration file

So far, we specified all of the information that `zabbix_sender` needs on the command line. It's also possible to automatically retrieve some of that information from the agent daemon configuration file. Let's try this (use the correct path to your agent daemon configuration file):

```
$ zabbix_sender -c /usr/local/etc/zabbix_agentd.conf -k
room.persons -o 3
```

This succeeds, because we specified the configuration file instead of the Zabbix server address and the hostname—these were picked up from the configuration file. If you're running `zabbix_sender` on many hosts where the Zabbix agent also resides, this should be easier and safer than parsing the configuration file manually. We could also use a special configuration file for `zabbix_sender` that only contains the parameters it needs.

> If the `ServerActive` parameter contains several entries, values are sent only to the first one. The `HostnameItem` parameter isn't supported by `zabbix_sender`.

Sending values from a file

The approach we used allows us to send one value every time we run `zabbix_sender`. If we had a script that returned a large number of values, that would be highly inefficient. We can also send multiple values from a file with `zabbix_sender`. Create a file like this anywhere, for example, in `/tmp/`:

```
"A test host" room.persons 4
"A test host" room.persons 5
"A test host" room.persons 6
```

Each line contains the hostname, item key, and value. This means that any number of hosts and keys can be supplied from a single file.

> Notice how values that contain spaces are double quoted—the input file is whitespace (spaces and tabs) separated.

The flag for supplying the file is `-i`. Assuming a filename of `sender_input.txt`, we can run the following:

```
$ zabbix_sender -z 127.0.0.1 -i /tmp/sender_input.txt
```

That should send all three values successfully:

```
info from server: "processed: 3; failed: 0; total: 3; seconds spent:
0.000087"
sent: 3; skipped: 0; total: 3
```

When sending values from a file, we could still benefit from the agent daemon configuration file:

```
$ zabbix_sender -c /usr/local/etc/zabbix_agentd.conf -i
/tmp/sender_input.txt
```

In this case, the server address would be taken from the configuration file, while hostnames would still be supplied from the input file. *Can we avoid that and get the hostname from the agent daemon configuration file?* Yes, that's possible by replacing the hostname in the input file with a dash, like this:

```
-  room.persons 4
"A test host" room.persons 5
-  room.persons 6
```

In this case, the hostname would be taken from the configuration file for the first and the third entry, while still overriding that for the second entry.

> If the input file contains many entries, `zabbix_sender` sends them in batches of 250 values per connection.

When there's a need to send lots of values constantly, we might wish to avoid repeatedly running the `zabbix_sender` binary. Instead, we could have a process write new entries to a file without closing the file, and then have `zabbix_sender` read from that file. Unfortunately, by default, values would be sent to the server only when the file is closed—or with every 250 values received. Fortunately, there's also a command-line flag to affect this behavior. The `-r` flag enables a so-called **real-time mode**. In this mode, `zabbix_sender` reads new values from the file and waits for 0.2 seconds. If no new values come in, the obtained values are sent. If more values come in, it waits for 0.2 seconds more, and so on up to one second. If there's a host that's constantly streaming values to the Zabbix server, `zabbix_sender` would connect to the server once per second at most and send all of the values received in that second in one connection. Yes, in some weird cases, there could be more connections—for example, if we supplied one value every 0.3 seconds exactly.

If sending a huge number of values and using a file could became a performance issue, we could even consider a named pipe in place of the file—although that would be a quite rare occurrence.

Sending timestamped values

The data that we sent so far was considered to be received at that exact moment—the values had the timestamp assigned by the server when it got them. Every now and then, there's a need to send values in batches for a longer period of time or import a backlog of older values. This can be easily achieved with `zabbix_sender`—when sending values from a file, it supports supplying a timestamp. When doing so, the value field in the input file is shifted to the right and the timestamp is inserted as the third field. For a quick test, we could generate timestamps one, two, and three days ago:

```
$ for i in 1 2 3; do date -d "-$i day" "+%s"; done
```

Take the resulting timestamps and use them in a new input file:

```
- room.persons 1462745422 11
"A test host" room.persons 1462659022 12
- room.persons 1462572622 13
```

With a file named `sender_input_timestamps.txt`, we would additionally use the `-T` flag to tell `zabbix sender` that it should expect the timestamps in there:

```
$ zabbix_sender -c /usr/local/etc/zabbix_agentd.conf -T -i
/tmp/sender_input_timestamps.txt
```

All three values should be sent successfully.

> When sending in values for a longer period of time, make sure the history and trend retention periods for that item match your needs. Otherwise, the housekeeper process could delete the older values soon after they're sent in.

Looking at the graph or latest values for this item, it's probably slightly messed up. The timestamped values we just sent in are likely to be overlapping in time with the previous values. In most cases, sending in values normally and with timestamps for the same item isn't suggested.

> If the Zabbix trapper items have triggers configured against them, timestamped values should only be sent with increasing timestamps. If values are sent in a reversed or chaotic older-newer-older order, the generated events won't make sense.
> If data is sent in for a host that's in a no-data maintenance, the values are also discarded if the value timestamp is outside the current maintenance window. Maintenance was discussed in `Chapter 5`, *Managing Hosts, Users, and Permissions*.

SSH and Telnet items

We've looked at quite a lot of fairly custom and customizable ways to get data into Zabbix. Although external checks should allow us to grab data by any means whatsoever, in some cases, we might need to collect data from some system that's reachable over SSH or even Telnet, but there's no way to install an agent on it. In that case, a more efficient way to retrieve the values would be to use the built-in SSH or Telnet support.

SSH items

Let's look at the SSH items first. As a simple test, we could re-implement the same Zabbix agent parameter we did as our first user parameter, determining the number of the currently logged-in users by running `who | wc -l`. To try this out, we need a user account we could use to run that command, and it's probably best to create a separate account on `A test host`. Creating one could be as simple as the following:

```
# useradd -m -s /bin/bash zabbixtest
# passwd zabbixtest
```

Don't create unauthorized user accounts in production systems. For remote systems, verify that the user is allowed to log in from the Zabbix server.

With the user account in place, let's create the SSH item. In the frontend, follow these steps:

1. Go to **Configuration | Hosts**, click on **Items** next to **A test host**, and click on **Create item**. Fill in the following:

   - **Name:** Users logged in (SSH)
   - **Type: SSH agent**
   - **Key:** ssh.run[system.users]
   - **User name:** zabbixtest (or whatever was the username for your test account)
   - **Password:** Fill in the password used for that account
   - **Executed script:** who | wc -l

   The fields are shown in the following screenshot:

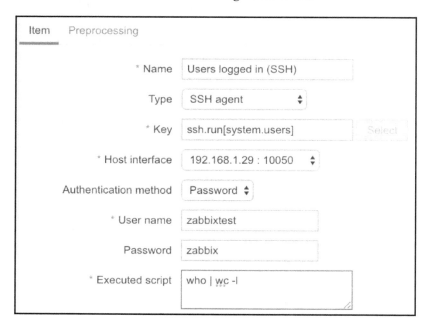

The username and password will be kept in plain text in the Zabbix database.

2. When done, click on the **Add** button at the bottom.

For the key, we could customize the IP address and port as the second and third parameters respectively. Omitting them uses the default port of 22 and the host interface address. The first parameter for the item key is just a unique identifier. For SSH items, the key itself must be ssh.run, but the first parameter works in a similar fashion to the whole key for user parameters. In the **Latest data** page, our first SSH item should be working just fine and returning values as expected. This way, we could run any command and grab the return value.

 In most cases, it's suggested to use user parameters instead of SSH checks' we should resort to direct SSH checks only when it's not possible to install the Zabbix agent on the monitored system.

The item we just created uses a directly supplied password. We could also use key-based authentication. To do so, in the item properties, choose **Public key** for the **Authentication method** drop-down menu and fill in the name of the file that holds the private key in the **Private key file** field. Although the underlying library allows skipping the public key when compiled with OpenSSL, Zabbix currently requires specifying the public key filename in the **Public key file** field. If the key is passphrase-protected, the passphrase should be supplied in the **Key passphrase** field. But *where should that file be located?* Check the Zabbix server configuration file and look for the SSHKeyLocation parameter. It isn't set by default, so set it to some directory and place the private and public key files there. Make sure the directory and all key files are only accessible by the Zabbix user.

 Encrypted or passphrase-protected keys aren't supported by default in several distributions, including Debian.
The libssh2 dependency might have to be compiled with OpenSSL to allow encrypted keys. See
https://www.zabbix.com/documentation/3.0/manual/installation/known_issues#ssh_checks for more detail.

Telnet items

In the case of a device that can neither have the Zabbix agent installed nor supports SSH, Zabbix also has a built-in method to obtain values over Telnet. With Telnet being a really old and insecure protocol, that's probably one of the least suggested methods for data gathering.

Telnet items are similar to SSH items. The simplest item key syntax is the following:

```
telnet.run[<unique_identifier>]
```

The key itself is a fixed string, while the first parameter is a unique identifier, the same as for the SSH items. Also, the second and third parameter are IP address and port, if they're different from the host interface IP and the default Telnet port, 23. The commands to run will go in the **Executed script** field, and the username and password should be supplied as well.

 The username and password are transmitted in plain text with Telnet. Avoid it if possible.

For the login prompt, Zabbix looks for a string that ends with : (colon). For Command Prompt, the following are supported:

- $
- #
- >
- %

When the command returns, the beginning of the string, up to one of these symbols is trimmed.

Custom modules

Besides all of the already covered methods, Zabbix also offers a way to write loadable modules. These modules have to be written in C and can be loaded in the Zabbix agent, server, and proxy daemons. When included in the Zabbix agent, from the server perspective, they act the same as the built-in items or user parameters. When included in the Zabbix server or proxy, they appear as simple checks.

Modules have to be explicitly loaded using the `LoadModulePath` and `LoadModule` parameters. We won't be looking at the modules in much detail here, but information about the module API and other details are available at `https://www.zabbix.com/documentation/4.0/manual/config/items/loadablemodules`.

Value preprocessing and dependent items

A new powerful tool added in Zabbix is preprocessing items and dependent items. We touched briefly on preprocessing when we had to add a network card and calculate the **Change per second**. But there's much more that we can do now out of the box without the need for knowledge of scripting. As value mapping is something we have together in an item, we'll combine it with dependent items as it makes more sense here.

Let's start by creating a new item on our `A test host`:

- **Name:** `Zabbix master item`
- **Type: Zabbix agent(active)**
- **Key:** `mysql.dependent`
- **Type of information: Text**
- **New applications: MySQL-Master**

If all goes well, when we look at the latest data, we now see text value in our history as shown in the following screenshot:

| | Zabbix master item | 2018-12-02 16:12:03 | Aborted_clients 0 Abo... | History |

When we click on **History**, it should show us all of the values from our MySQL:

Timestamp	Value	
2018-12-02 16:14:03	Aborted_clients 0	
	Aborted_connects	2
	Access_denied_errors	0
	Aria_pagecache_blocks_not_flushed	0
	Aria_pagecache_blocks_unused	15737
	Aria_pagecache_blocks_used	1
	Aria_pagecache_read_requests	80
	Aria_pagecache_reads	0
	Aria_pagecache_write_requests	24
	Aria_pagecache_writes	0
	Aria_transaction_log_syncs	0
	Binlog_commits 0	
	Binlog_group_commits	0
	Binlog_snapshot_file	
	Binlog_snapshot_position	0

Now, this looks nice but let's say we're only interested in two lines, `Innodb_deadlocks` and `Aborted_clients`, and we want to see the values from those two lines also. It turns out that with the new dependent items and preprocessing, this is going to be a piece of cake.

Let's go back to our list of items on `A test host` and click on the three dots (...) before the item, **Zabbix master item** as shown in the following screenshot:

Now, click on **Create dependent item** from the pop-up menu that appears. This will create a new item that is dependent on our **Zabbix master item**:

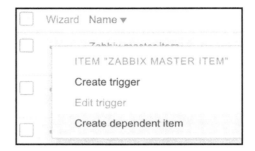

In our new item that appears, we have to add a few things. Let's start with the easy ones first:

- **Name**: Innodb_deadlocks
- **Type**: **Dependent item**
- **Key**: Innodb.deadlocks
- **Type of information**: **Character**
- **New application**: MySQL-Dependent

Notice how we now have **Master item** as an option, and how it's already making a reference to our first item our **Zabbix master item**:

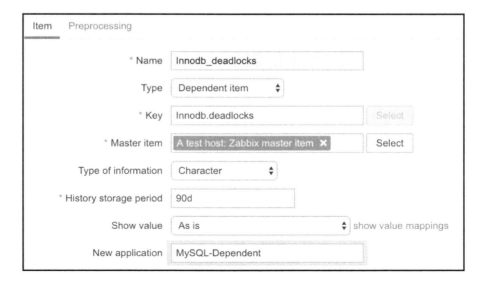

We still have things to do, as this will not work. We need to tell Zabbix now how to retrieve this information from our master item. This is where our preprocessing comes into play.

Let's go to the **Preprocessing** tab and add the following information in it:

- **Name**: **Regular expression**
- **Parameters**: In the first box, add `Innodb_deadlocks\s(\d.*)` and in the second box, `\1`:

Click on **Update** when done.

Create another dependent item for our `Aborted_clients` item. This time, use the following information in our item:

- **Name**: `Aborted_clients`
- **Type**: **Dependent item**
- **Key**: `Aborted.clients`
- **Type of information**: **Character**
- **Application**: `MySQL-Dependent`

Just like with the previous item, we need to create a reprocessing step. Use the following information:

- **Name**: **Regular expression**
- **Parameters**: In the first box, `Aborted_clients\s(\d.*)` and in the second box, `\1`

When ready click **Add**, we now should have one master item with two dependent items.

Let's check this by going to **Configuration | Hosts**, then **A test host**, and clicking on **Items**. Open the filter and select **MySQL-Master** and **MySQL-Dependent** from the subfilter. We should now see three items, one master and two dependent items, in our item list:

	Wizard	Name ▼		Triggers	Key	Interval	History	Trends	Type	Applications	Status	Info
	•••	Zabbix master item			mysql.dependent	30s	90d		Zabbix agent (active)	MySQL-Master	Enabled	
	•••	Zabbix master item: Innodb_deadlocks			Innodb.deadlocks		90d		Dependent item	MysQL-Dependent	Enabled	
	•••	Zabbix master item: Aborted_clients			Aborted.clients		90d		Dependent item	MysQL-Dependent	Enabled	

We didn't changed the **History** of the master item but if you have no need to keep it, then you could change the **History** to 0 days. The item then will only be used to create the dependent items and no data will be kept in the database.

Now, let's check whether we have some data; let's go to the latest data page and filter on **Application** by selecting the **MySQL-Dependent** items from the list:

Name ▲	Last check	Last value
MysQL-Dependent (2 Items)		
Aborted_clients	2018-12-02 16:47:06	0
Innodb_deadlocks	2018-12-02 16:47:06	0

Yippee! We have two items with values in our latest data page and we had to write 0 lines of code for this. In previous versions, we probably had to write a script to send us data for both items.

As you have probably noticed, there's much more to choose from in our preprocessing options than only **Regular expression**; some we used already when configuring our network card and others we didn't. Let's have a quick overview of what's possible:

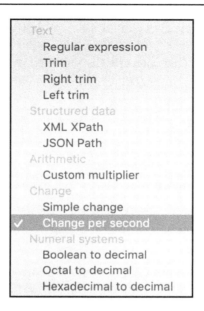

We have the following fields from the previous screenshot:

- **Regular expression**: This matches the value to the `<pattern>` regular expression and replaces the value with `<output>`. `pattern` is replaced with a regular expression and `output` with the formatting template. A `\N` (where N = 1...9) escape sequence is replaced.
- **Trim**: This removes specified characters from the beginning and end of the value.
- **Right trim**: This removes specified characters from the end of the value.
- **Left trim**: This removes specified characters from the beginning of the value.
- **XML XPath**: This extracts a value or fragment from XML data using **XPath** functionality.
- **JSON Path**: This extracts a value or fragment from JSON data using a simple subset of **JSONPath** functionality.
- **Custom multiplier**: This multiplies the value by the specified integer or floating-point value.
- **Simple change**: This calculates the difference between the current and previous value.
- **Changer per second**: This calculates the value change (the difference between the current and previous value) in speed per second.

- **Boolean to decimal**: This converts the value from Boolean format into decimal.
- **Octal to decimal**: This converts the value from octal format into decimal.
- **Hexadecimal to decimal**: This converts the value from hexadecimal format into decimal.

Summary

In this chapter, we looked at more advanced ways to gather data.

We explored log monitoring and either tracking a single file or multiple files and matching a regular expression. We filtered the results and parsed some values out of them.

Calculated items gave us a field to type any custom formula and the results were computed from the data the server already had, without querying the monitored devices again. Any trigger function could be used, providing great flexibility.

Aggregate items allowed us to calculate particular values, such as the minimum, maximum, and average for items over a host group. This method is mostly useful for cluster or cluster-like systems, where hosts in the group are working to provide a common service.

External checks and user parameters provided a way to retrieve nearly any value—at least any that can be obtained on the command line. While very similar conceptually, they also have some differences that we'll try to summarize now:

External checks	User parameters
Are executed by the Zabbix server process	Are executed by the Zabbix agent daemon
Are executed on the Zabbix server	Are executed on the monitored hosts
Can be attached to any host	Can only be attached to the host where the Zabbix agent daemon runs
Can reduce server performance	Have no notable impact on server performance if set up as active items

As can be seen from this comparison, external checks should be mostly used with remote systems where the Zabbix agent can't be installed, because they can be attached to any host in the Zabbix configuration. Given the possible negative performance impact, it's suggested to use user parameters in most situations.

Note that it's suggested for user parameters to have an active Zabbix agent type. That way, a server connection isn't tied up in case the executed command fails to return in a timely manner. We also learned that we should take note of the environment the agent daemon runs in, as it isn't initialized.

For scripts that return a large number of values or for scripts that take a long time to run, it was suggested to use the `zabbix_sender` command-line utility with a corresponding Zabbix trapper item. This not only allowed us to send in anything at our preferred rate, it also allowed us to specify the timestamp for each value.

And for those cases where we have to execute a command on a remote host to get the value, the built-in support of SSH or even Telnet items could come in handy.

Armed with this knowledge, we should be able to gather any value that traditional methods such as Zabbix agents, SNMP, IPMI, and other built-in checks can't retrieve.

Value preprocessing and dependent items provided us with a way to extract specific items from a master item and do some preprocessing of data on our items before it was put into the database.

In the next chapter, we'll cover several ways to automate configuration in Zabbix. That'll include network discovery, low-level discovery, and active agent auto-registration.

Questions

1. Does Zabbix support log rotation?
2. When using a calculated item, will it read information from the database or will it poll the data from the items?
3. I have an aggregated item for a group of servers—can I use `Zabbix-get` to retrieve the item value for that group?

4. Is it a good idea to place username and password in the Zabbix user parameters?
5. Can we use preprocessing only on dependent items?
6. I have dependent items on a master item but I don't want to keep the data from the master item as it contains too much. Is it possible to not keep it?

Further reading

Read the following articles for more information:

- **Log file monitoring**: https://www.zabbix.com/documentation/4.0/manual/config/items/itemtypes/log_items
- **Calculated items**: https://www.zabbix.com/documentation/4.0/manual/config/items/itemtypes/calculated
- **Aggregate checks**: https://www.zabbix.com/documentation/4.0/manual/config/items/itemtypes/aggregate
- **SSH checks**: https://www.zabbix.com/documentation/4.0/manual/config/items/itemtypes/ssh_checks
- **Telnet checks**: https://www.zabbix.com/documentation/4.0/manual/config/items/itemtypes/telnet_checks
- **Dependent items**: https://www.zabbix.com/documentation/4.0/manual/config/items/itemtypes/dependent_items
- **Creating an item**: https://www.zabbix.com/documentation/4.0/manual/config/items/item?s[]=hexadecimals[]=decimal#item_value_preprocessing

11
Automating Configuration

So far, we have largely executed the manual configuration of Zabbix by adding hosts, items, triggers, and other entities. With the exception of templates as discussed in Chapter 8, *Simplifying Complex Configurations with Templates*, we haven't looked at ways to accommodate larger and more dynamic environments. In this chapter, we will discover ways to automatically find out about resources such as network interfaces or filesystems on hosts by using low-level discovery, scanning a subnet using network discovery, and allowing hosts to register themselves using active agent auto-registration.

While learning about these methods, we will also explore related features, such as global regular expressions, and find out more details regarding the features we are already aware of—including context for user macros.

As Zabbix has several ways to manage automatic entity configuration and they all operate in a different manner, it is highly recommended never using the term **auto-discovery** when talking about Zabbix—nobody would know for sure which functionality is meant. Instead, it is always recommended specifying whether it's **low-level discovery** (**LLD**), network discovery, or active agent auto-registration.

We will cover the following topics in this chapter:

- LLD
- Creating custom LLD
- Global regular expressions
- Network discovery
- Active agent auto-registration

LLD

Currently, we are monitoring several parameters on our hosts, including network traffic. We configured those items by finding out the interface name and then manually specifying it for all of the relevant items. Interface names could vary from one system to another, and there could be a different number of interfaces on each system. The same could happen with filesystems, CPUs, and other entities. They could also change—a filesystem could get mounted or unmounted. Zabbix offers a way to deal with such different and potentially dynamic configurations with a feature called LLD. In the Zabbix documentation and community, it is usually known as LLD, and that is how we will refer to it in this book, too.

LLD normally enables us to discover entities on existing hosts (we will discuss more advanced functionality related to discovering hosts with LLD in Chapter 16, *Monitoring VMware*). LLD is an extremely widely used feature, and there are few Zabbix users who do not benefit from it. There are several LLD methods that are built in, and it is fairly easy to create new ones, too. The LLD methods that are available are as follows:

- Network interfaces (Zabbix agent)
- CPUs and CPU cores (Zabbix agent)
- **Simple network management protocol (SNMP) Object identifiers (OIDs)**
- **Java Management Extensions (JMX)** objects
- **Open Database Connectivity (ODBC)** queries
- Windows services
- Filesystems (Zabbix agent)
- Host interfaces
- Custom LLD

We'll discuss Windows service discovery in Chapter 22, *Monitoring Windows*. ODBC monitoring can be a bit cumbersome in the case of many databases being monitored, so we won't spend much time on it and won't be covering ODBC LLD in this book. Refer to the official documentation on it at
https://www.zabbix.com/documentation/4.0/manual/discovery/low_level_discovery#discovery_using_odbc_sql_queries.

Network interface discovery

Network interfaces on servers seem simple to monitor, but they tend to get more complicated as the environment size increases and time goes by. Back in the day, we had **eth0**, and everybody was happy. Well, not everybody—people needed more interfaces, so we had **eth1, eth2**, and so on. It would already be a challenge to manually match the existing interfaces to Zabbix items so that all interfaces are properly monitored. Then, Linux-based systems changed the interface naming scheme, and now, you could have **enp0s25** or something similar, or a totally different interface name. That would not be easy to manage on a large number of different systems. Interface names on Windows are even more fun—they could include the name of the vendor, driver, antivirus software, firewall software, and a bunch of other things. In the past, people have even written VB scripts to sort of create fake eth0 interfaces on Windows systems.

Luckily, LLD should solve all that by providing a built-in way to automatically discover all the interfaces and monitor the desired items on each interface. This is supported on the majority of the platforms that the Zabbix agent runs on, including Linux, Windows, FreeBSD, OpenBSD, NetBSD, Solaris, AIX, and HP-UX.

Let's see how we can discover all the interfaces automatically on our monitored systems. Navigate to **Configuration | Templates** and click on **Discovery** next to **C_Template_Linux**. This is the section that lists the LLD rules—currently, we have none. Before we create a rule, it might be helpful to understand what an LLD rule is and what other entities supplement it.

A **Discovery rule** is a configuration entity that tells Zabbix what it should discover. In the case of network interfaces, an LLD rule would return a list of all interfaces. Assuming our system has interfaces called **ETH0** and **ETH1**, the LLD rule would just return a list of them:

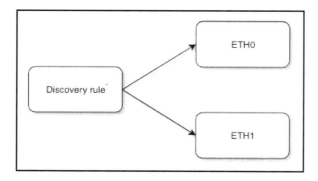

Then, the LLD rule contains prototypes. In the first place, prototypes for items would be required, although LLD allows us to add trigger and custom graph prototypes as well. *What actually are prototypes?* We discussed templates in Chapter 8, *Simplifying Complex Configurations with Templates.* You can think of LLD prototypes as mini-templates. Instead of affecting the whole host, they affect items or triggers, or custom graphs on a host. For example, an item prototype for network interface discovery could tell Zabbix to monitor incoming network traffic on all discovered interfaces the same way.

Getting back to creating an LLD rule, in the empty list of LLD rules, click on **Create discovery rule** in the upper-right corner and then fill in the following details:

- **Name**: Interface discovery
- **Key**: net.if.discovery
- **Update interval**: 120s

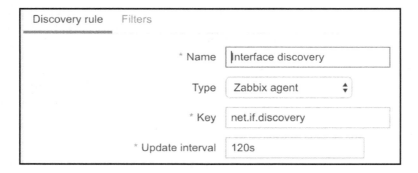

When done, click on **Add**. The discovery rule is added, although it won't do much useful work for now. The key we used, net.if.discovery, is supposed to return all the interfaces on the system. As you probably spotted, the properties of an LLD rule look quite similar to item properties—there's an update interval, and there are flexible intervals. Overall, the built-in agent LLD rules are actually items. Later, we will look at the details of how they operate.

A discovery rule returns macros. In the same way as before, it might be safer to think about them as variables, although we will again refer to them as macros here. These macros return various properties of the discovered entities. In the case of the network interface discovery by the Zabbix agent, these macros return interface names. LLD macros always use the syntax of {#NAME}, that is, the name wrapped in curly braces and prefixed with a hash mark. The macros can be later used in prototypes to create items for each discovered interface. The built-in LLD rule keys return a fixed set of such macros, and we will discuss each set whenever we look at the specific discovery method, such as network interfaces first, and the filesystem and others later. We have an LLD rule now, but it just reveals the interfaces. Nothing is done about them without the prototypes. To derive any benefit from the previous step, let's create some prototypes. Still in the LLD rule list, click on **Item prototype** in the **ITEMS** column next to **Interface discovery**. Then, click on the **Create item prototype** button, and fill in the following:

- **Name**: Incoming traffic on $1
- **Key**: net.if.in[{#IFNAME}]
- **Units**: Bps
- **Preprocessing step** (in the **Preprocessing** tab): **Change per second**

The fields can be seen in the following screenshot:

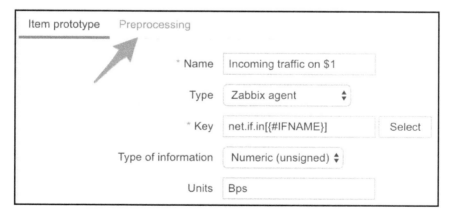

Our prototype here uses a discovery macro in the item key parameters. Actually, this is required. These macros will be replaced with different values when creating the final items, so the resulting item keys will be different. We could create item prototypes without using LLD macros in the key parameters, but the resulting discovery would fail as it would attempt to create one item per LLD macro.

When done with the configuration, click on the **Add** button at the bottom. Let's see whether this item prototype now works as intended. We set the interval in our LLD rule to a low value—120 seconds. As we cannot force items and discovery rules to run manually, this will allow us to play with various configuration changes and see the results much sooner. Wait for a few minutes and go to **Configuration | Hosts**. Then, click on **Discovery** next to **A test host**. Something's not right—in the **Info** column, there's a red error icon. Move your mouse cursor over it to see what the error message is:

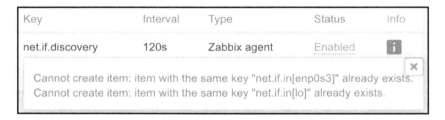

It's complaining that an item that would have to be created based on the LLD item prototype already exists. That is correct; we created an item exactly like that earlier, when we manually added items for interface monitoring.

 If an LLD rule attempts to create items that have already been created, the discovery fails and no items will be created.

As is always the case, item uniqueness is determined by the item key, including all the parameters. Unfortunately, there is no way to merge manually configured items with LLD-generated ones. There is also no easy way to keep the collected history. We could change the item key either for the existing item or for the item prototype slightly and keep the manually added item for historic purposes and then remove it later when the new, LLD-generated item has collected sufficient historical data.

In this case, we could apply a small hack to the existing item key.

Navigate to **Configuration | Templates**, and click on **Items** next to **C_Template_Linux**. Click on **Incoming traffic on interface enp0s3** in the **Name** column. In the properties, make the following changes:

- **Name**: Incoming traffic on interface $1 (manual)
- **Key**: net.if.in[enp0s3,]

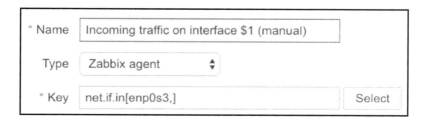

* Name	Incoming traffic on interface $1 (manual)	
Type	Zabbix agent	
* Key	net.if.in[enp0s3,]	Select

That is, add (manual) to the name and a trailing comma inside the square brackets. The first change was not strictly required, but it will allow us to identify these items. The second change does not change anything functionally—the item will still collect exactly the same information. We changed the item key, though. Even a small change like this results in the key being different, and the discovery rule should be able to create those items now. When done, click on **Update**. Now, make the same changes to the outgoing network traffic item and the loopback interface item.

This trick works because the item key accepts parameters. For item keys that accept no parameters, it is not possible to add empty square brackets to indicate no parameters.

With the item keys changed, we could also monitor outgoing traffic automatically:

1. Go to **Configuration | Templates**, click on **Discovery** next to **C_Template_Linux**, and then **Item prototype** next to **Interface discovery**.
2. Click on **Incoming traffic on {#IFNAME}** and then on the **Clone** button.
3. Change Incoming to Outgoing in the **Name** field, and change the **Key** field to read net.if.out[{#IFNAME}].
4. When done, click on the **Add** button at the bottom.
5. Allow a few minutes to pass and then head back to **Configuration | Hosts**.

6. Click on **Discovery** next to **A test host**. The error icon should be gone. If not, track down any other items mentioned here and make the same changes to them.

7. Once there are no errors listed in this section, navigate to **Configuration** | **Hosts**, click on **Items** next to **A test host**, and then click on the **Discovered** sub-filter under **DISCOVERY**. There should be several new items, and they should all be prefixed with the LLD rule name, **Interface discovery**, as shown in the following screenshot:

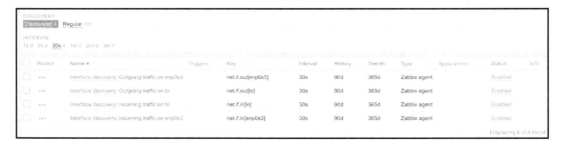

Clicking on the discovery rule name will open the list of prototypes in the LLD rule.

The number of items created depends on the number of interfaces on the system—for each interface, two items should be created.

Our first discovery rule seems to be working nicely now; all interfaces on the system have been discovered and network traffic is being monitored on them. If we wanted to monitor other parameters on each interface, we would add more prototypes, using the discovery macro in the item key parameters so that the created items have unique keys.

In our LLD item, we made use of the {#IFNAME} macro. This was not a random choice. Zabbix has a list of built-in macros for LLD rules. The list can be found for every LLD rule in the documentation. I have added the correct link at the end of this chapter.

Automatically creating calculated items

For our manually created network traffic items, we created calculated items to collect the total incoming and outgoing traffic. We did this in `Chapter 10`, *Advanced Item Monitoring*. While we could go ahead and create such calculated items manually for all LLD-created items, too, that would necessitate a huge amount of manual work.

Let's try to create a calculated item per interface according to the LLD rule instead. Go to **Configuration** | **Templates**, click on **Discovery** next to **C_Template_Linux**, and then click on **Item prototype** next to **Interface discovery**. Then, click on **Create item prototype**. Fill in the following values:

- **Name:** `Total traffic on $1`
- **Type: Calculated**
- **Key:** `calc.net.if.total[{#IFNAME}]`
- **Formula:**
  `last(net.if.in[{#IFNAME}])+last(net.if.out[{#IFNAME}])`
- **Units:** `B`

> We did not change **Type of information**, as we intentionally left it at **Numeric (unsigned)** for the network traffic items we referenced here. To remind yourself why, refer to `Chapter 3`, *Monitoring with Zabbix Agents and Basic Protocols*.

When done, click on the **Add** button at the bottom. If you check the latest data page, this item should start gathering data in a couple of minutes.

> The item key for calculated items is for our own convenience. The key does not affect the data collection in any way—that is completely determined by the formula.

But let's say we're not that interested in very detailed statistics on the total traffic, but more in a longer-term trend. We could modify the item we just created to collect the sum of average incoming and outgoing traffic over the past 10 minutes and do so every 10 minutes. Let's go back to **Configuration** | **Templates**, click on **Discovery** next to **C_Template_Linux**, and then click on **Item prototype** next to **Interface discovery**. Then, click on **Total traffic on {#IFNAME}**. Change these four fields:

- **Name:** `Total traffic on $1 over last 10 minutes`
- **Key:** `calc.net.if.total.10m[{#IFNAME}]`

- **Formula**:
  ```
  avg(net.if.in[{#IFNAME}],10m)+avg(net.if.out[{#IFNAME}],10m)
  ```
- **Update interval**: 10m

> In the formula, we could also have used 600 instead of 10m and, for **Update interval**, we could have used 600 instead of 10m or we could have used 600s.

When done, click on the **Update** button at the bottom. We now have to allow a couple of minutes for the discovery rule to run again and then up to 10 minutes for this item to get the new value.

Let's discuss the changes we made. The most important one was the **Formula** update. We changed the last() function for both item references to avg(). We can use any trigger function in calculated items. We also supplied a parameter for this function after a comma, and that was the reason we had to double-quote item keys in the disk space item. The referenced keys contained a comma. That comma would be misunderstood by Zabbix to separate the item key from the function parameters.

> Additional parameters can be specified by adding more commas. For example, in avg(net.if.in[{#IFNAME}],10m,1d), 1d would be a time shift, as that's the second parameter for the avg() trigger function. We learned more about trigger functions in Chapter 6, *Detecting Problems with Triggers*.
> If we only want to display the total on a graph, there is no need to create an item – stacked graphs allow us to do that. We discussed stacked graphs in Chapter 21, *Visualizing Data with Graphs and Maps*.

The total traffic item (or items) should be updated in the latest data to display the average total traffic over the past 10 minutes. Normally, we would probably use an even longer interval for these averages, such as one hour, but 10 minutes supplies us with the data a bit more quickly. This approach could also be used to configure a floating average for an item. For example, a formula such as this would calculate the floating average over 6 hours for the CPU load:

```
avg(system.cpu.load,6h)
```

Calculated items do not have to reference multiple items; they can also reference a single item to perform a calculation on it. Such a floating average could be used for better trend prediction or for writing relative triggers by comparing current CPU load values to the floating average.

Automatically creating triggers

Creating items for all discovered entities is useful, but even looking through them would be quite a task. Luckily, LLD allows us to create triggers automatically as well. The same as with items, this is done by creating prototypes first; actual triggers will be created by the discovery process later.

To create the prototypes, follow these steps:

1. Navigate to **Configuration | Templates**, click on **Discovery** next to **C_Template_Linux**, and then click on **Trigger prototypes**. In the upper-right corner, click on **Create trigger prototype**, and configure it as follows:

    - **Name**: Incoming traffic too high for {#IFNAME} on {HOST.NAME}.
    - **Expression**: Click on **Add** next to this field. In the popup, click on **Select prototype**, and then click on **Incoming traffic on {#IFNAME}** in the **Name** column. Click on **Insert** and modify the generated expression. Change =0 to >5K. This will alert you whenever the incoming traffic exceeds 5,000 bytes per second, as the item is collecting in bytes per second.
    - **Severity**: Select **Warning**.

    The fields can be seen in the following screenshot:

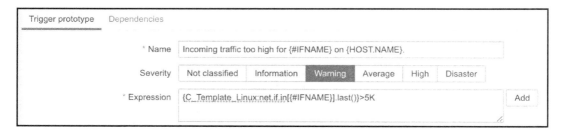

2. When done, click on the **Add** button at the bottom.

That was for incoming traffic; now, let's create a prototype for outgoing traffic. Click on the name of the prototype we just created, and then click on **Clone**. In the new form, change Incoming in the **Name** field to Outgoing and net.if.in in the **Expression** field to net.if.out, and then click on the **Add** button at the bottom.

With both prototypes in place, let's go to **Configuration** | **Hosts** and click on **Triggers** next to **A test host**. It is likely that there are several new triggers here already. For the incoming traffic, we created that prototype first, so discovery might have had a chance to process it already. Nevertheless, it should not take longer than a few minutes for all of the LLD-created triggers to show up. Make sure to refresh the page manually to see any changes—configuration pages do not get automatically refreshed like monitoring ones do:

In the same way as with items, triggers are prefixed with the LLD rule name. Notice how we got one trigger from each prototype for each interface, the same as with the items. The {#IFNAME} LLD macro was replaced by the interface name as well. Note that we did not have to worry about making the created triggers unique—we must reference an item key in a trigger, and that already includes the appropriate LLD macros in item key parameters.

The threshold we chose here is very low—it is likely to fire even on our small test systems. *What if we had various systems and we wanted to have a different threshold on each of them?* The concept we discussed earlier, user macros, would help here. Instead of a hardcoded value, we would use a user macro in the trigger expression and override it on specific hosts as required. We discussed user macros in Chapter 8, *Simplifying Complex Configurations with Templates*.

Automatically creating graphs

We have items and triggers automatically created for all interfaces, and we could also have a graph created for each interface, combining incoming and outgoing traffic.

In the same way as before, this is done with the help of prototypes:

1. Go to **Configuration** | **Templates**, click on **Discovery** next to **C_Template_Linux**, and then click on **Graph prototypes**. Click on **Create graph prototype** and enter Traffic on {#IFNAME} in the **Name** field.
2. Click on **Add prototype** in the **Items** section, and mark the checkboxes next to the incoming and outgoing network traffic items. Then, click on **Select**. Choose **Gradient line** for both items in the **Draw style** drop-down:

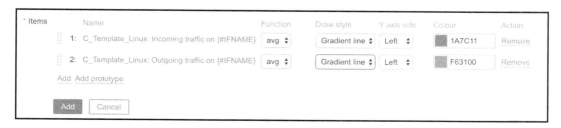

3. When done, click on the **Add** button at the bottom. Note that we had to specify the LLD macro in the graph name—otherwise, Zabbix would be unable to create graphs, as they would have had the same name.

With the prototype in place, let's go to **Configuration** | **Hosts** and click on **Graphs** next to **A test host**. If you see no graphs, wait a couple of minutes and refresh the page—the graphs should show up, one for each interface, again prefixed with the LLD rule name:

Navigating to **Monitoring** | **Graphs** and selecting **A test host** in the **Host** drop-down will show all of these graphs in the **Graph** drop-down. This way, traffic on a specific interface can be easily reviewed by selecting the appropriate graph—and without configuring those graphs manually first.

 There is no way to automatically create a graph with all the discovered items in it at this time.

Filtering discovery results

Looking at the items, triggers, and graphs that were created, besides real interfaces, the loopback interface also got discovered, and all of those entities got created for it. In some cases, it would be useful to monitor that interface as well, but for most systems, such data would not be useful.

If we look at the list of items in the configuration, the LLD-generated items had the checkbox next to them disabled. This is no longer the case, and we can now delete the discovered items. The controls in the **STATUS** column allow us to enable or disable them individually. LLD-generated items on a host cannot be edited, except for being disabled or enabled. Note that in the frontend, this can be done by selecting a list of items all at once, something that was not possible with the older 3.0 version.

Disabling an LLD-generated item on many hosts could be a massive manual task. We could think about disabling the prototype, but that would not work for two reasons:

- Firstly, we only want to disable items for the loopback interface, but the same prototype is used for items on all interfaces.
- Secondly, state changes in the prototype are not propagated to the generated items. The initial state in which these items are created – enabled or disabled – will be kept for them.

What about other changes to these items, such as changing the item key or some other property? Those would get propagated downstream, but only when the discovery itself was run by the Zabbix server, and not when we made the changes to the prototype in the frontend. In practice, this means that we would have to wait for up to the LLD rule interval to see these changes applied downstream.

Luckily, there's a way to easily avoid creating items for some of the discovered entities, such as in our case, not creating items for the loopback interface. This is possible by filtering the entities LLD returns on the LLD rule level. Let's change our existing rule to ignore interfaces with the name `lo`.

 If we wanted to keep LLD-generated items but disable or enable several of them on different hosts, in some cases, that might be worth doing through the Zabbix API—we will have a brief introduction to the API in `Chapter 19`, *Working Closely with Data*.

Navigate to **Configuration | Templates** and click on **Discovery** next to **C_Template_Linux**. Then, click on **Interface discovery** in the **Name** column. Notice how there's another tab here—**Filters**. Switch to that tab, and in the first and only **Filters** entry, fill in the following:

- **Macro**: `{#IFNAME}`, and select **matches** in the drop-down
- **Regular expression**: @**Network interfaces for discovery**

These fields can be seen in the following screenshot:

When done, click on **Update**. LLD filters work by only returning matching entries. In this case, we wanted to exclude the entry lo and keep everything else. The filter we used will exclude lo but match everything else—including eth0, enp0s3, and loop.

The regular expression here is a reference to the **Network interfaces for discovery** regular expression that is available as standard in Zabbix under the **Administration | General | Regular expression** menu:

Network interfaces for discovery	1	»	^[Ss]ystem$	[Result is FALSE]
	2	»	^[Ll]o[0-9.]*$	[Result is FALSE]
	3	»	^NULL[0-9.]*$	[Result is FALSE]
	4	»	^(In)?[Ll]oop[Bb]ack[0-9._]*$	[Result is FALSE]
	5	»	^Software Loopback Interface	[Result is FALSE]
	6	»	^Nu[0-9.]*$	[Result is FALSE]

By using the @ sign in front of the name, we make a reference to this regular expression. We could have written our own expression if we wanted in this box.

To see whether this worked, navigate to **Configuration** | **Hosts** and click on **Items** next to **A test host**. In the list, notice how both `lo` interface items have an orange icon with an exclamation mark in the **Info** column. If you move the mouse cursor over it, a message explains that this item is no longer classed as discovered and will be deleted at a later date:

In this case, the item is not discovered because it got excluded by the filter, but the reason does not matter that much; it could be an interface being removed or having its name changed as well. *But why will it be removed after that specific amount of time, a bit more than 29 days?* If we look at the properties of our LLD rule again, there's a field called **Keep lost resources period**:

$$\boxed{\text{* Keep lost resources period} \quad \boxed{30\text{d}}}$$

Here, we may specify how long items will be kept for when they are not discovered again, and the default is 30 days. The tooltip helpfully told us how much time we have left before the item will be deleted and at what precise time it will be deleted. Other entities, including triggers and custom graphs, are kept as long as the underlying items are kept.

 An LLD rule is only evaluated when it gets new data. If the rule stops getting data, items would tell you that they are supposed to be deleted, but they won't be deleted until the rule gets new data and is evaluated.

Now, navigate to **Monitoring** | **Latest data** and click on **Graph** for **Incoming traffic on lo**. Let some time pass. You will notice that items that are scheduled for deletion still continue collecting data. This might have been undesirable when we had initially been monitoring a lot of things on a device, overloaded it, and then applied filtering, hoping to remedy the situation. There is no way to directly control this, but we may temporarily set the resource—keeping to `0`, which would remove the items that are no longer discovered the next time the LLD rule runs. In the LLD rule properties, set the value of this field to `0` and click on **Update**. After a couple of minutes, check the item list for **A test host** in the configuration—both of the automatic `lo` interface items should now be gone.

What if we would like to have a different set of items for different discovered entities, for example, monitoring more things on interfaces with a specific name? That is not easily possible, unfortunately. One way would be by creating two different LLD rules with different item prototypes, and then filtering for one set of entities in one LLD rule, and another set in the other LLD rule. Still, that is more complicated than you might expect. LLD rules have the same uniqueness criteria as items—the key. With some items, we can use a little trick and have one item with a key called `key` and another with `key[]`. Specifying empty square brackets will denote empty parameters, but from a functional perspective, the item will be exactly the same. Unfortunately, the agent LLD keys do not accept parameters, so this trick won't work. One workaround would be specifying an alias on an item key—we will discuss how that can be done in `Chapter 20`, *Zabbix Maintenance*.

Filesystem discovery

We have found out that a Zabbix agent has built-in support for discovering network interfaces. It can also discover other things, one of the most popular being filesystems. Before we configure that, let's find out what we can expect from such a feature.

Introducing the LLD JSON format

The discovery does not just look a bit like an item in the frontend; it also operates in the same way underneath. The magic happens based on the content of a specific item value. All the things that are discovered are encoded in a JSON structure. The easiest way to see what's returned is to use `zabbix_get` and query a Zabbix agent. On A test host, run the following command:

```
$ zabbix_get -s 127.0.0.1 -k net.if.discovery
```

Here, `net.if.discovery` is just an item key, not different from other item keys. This will return a small string, similar to the following:

```
{data:[{{#IFNAME}:enp0s3},{{#IFNAME}:enp0s8},{{#IFNAME}:lo}]}
```

While it's mostly understandable, it would be even better with some formatting. The easiest way is to use Perl or Python tools. The Python method would be as follows:

```
$ zabbix_get -s 127.0.0.1 -k net.if.discovery | python -mjson.tool
```

The Perl method would be one of these:

```
$ zabbix_get -s 127.0.0.1 -k net.if.discovery | json_pp
$ zabbix_get -s 127.0.0.1 -k net.if.discovery | json_xs
```

The latter method should be faster, but requires the JSON::XS Perl module. For our purposes, performance should not be a concern, so choose whichever method works for you. The output will be similar to this:

```
{
    data : [
        {
            {#IFNAME} : enp0s3
        },
        {
            {#IFNAME} : enp0s8
        },
        {
            {#IFNAME} : lo
        }
    ]
}
```

The number of interfaces and their names might differ, but we can see that for each discovered interface, we are returning one macro—the interface name. The key for filesystem discovery is similar—vfs.fs.discovery. We can now run this:

```
$ zabbix_get -s 127.0.0.1 -k vfs.fs.discovery | json_pp
```

This would most likely return lots and lots of entries. Here's a snippet:

```
{
    data : [
        {
            {#FSNAME} : /dev/pts,
            {#FSTYPE} : devpts
        },
        {
            {#FSNAME} : /,
            {#FSTYPE} : xfs
        },
        {
            {#FSNAME} : /proc,
```

```
        {#FSTYPE} : proc
    },
    {
        {#FSNAME} : /sys,
        {#FSTYPE} : sysfs
...
```

Two things can be seen here:

- It definitely returns way more than we would want to monitor
- It returns two values for each filesystem—name and type

While we could filter according to filesystem name, some monitored systems could have the root filesystem only, some could have separate /home, and so on. The best way would be to filter by filesystem type. In this example, we only want to monitor filesystems of type xfs.

With this knowledge in hand, let's navigate to **Configuration** | **Templates**, click on **Discovery** next to **C_Template_Linux**, and then click on **Create discovery rule**. Fill in the following values:

- **Name**: Filesystem discovery
- **Key**: vfs.fs.discovery
- **Update interval**: 2m

The same as with network interface discovery, we set the update interval to 2m or 120s. The default in the form, 30 seconds, is very low and should not be used. Discovery can be resource intensive, and, if possible, should be run on an hourly basis or so. Now, switch to the **Filters** tab, and fill in these values:

- **Macro**: {#FSTYPE}
- **Regular expression**: matches ^xfs$

Replace the filesystem type with the one used on your system. Multiple filesystem types can be accepted, like this: ^ext4|xfs$. We can also use @File systems for discovery. This will use the regular expression that's already available in Zabbix.

When done, click on the **Add** button at the bottom. We have the discovery now, but no prototypes. Click on **Item prototypes** next to **Filesystem discovery**, and then click on **Create item prototype**. Fill in the following values:

- **Name:** Free space on {#FSNAME}
- **Key:** vfs.fs.size[{#FSNAME},free]

When done, click on the **Add** button at the bottom. We now expect the discovery to get the list of all filesystems and discard most of those, except the ones precisely with the type xfs, and then create a free disk space item for each of them. We filter by one LLD macro, {#FSTYPE}, but use another {#FSNAME} in the actual item configuration.

After a couple of minutes have passed, navigate to **Configuration** | **Hosts** and click on **Items** next to **A test host**. You can select **Discovered items** from the **Discovery** selection box in the filter if you like. For each filesystem of type xfs, there should be a free disk space item, as shown in the following screenshot:

☐	•••	Filesystem discovery: Free space on /boot	vfs.fs.size[/boot,free]	30s	90d	365d	Zabbix agent	Enabled
☐	•••	Filesystem discovery: Free space on /	vfs.fs.size[/,free]	30s	90d	365d	Zabbix agent	Enabled

With more prototypes, we could also monitor total space, inode statistics, and other data. We could have triggers as required on all of these filesystems.

As this discovery returns multiple macros, it might be desirable to filter by multiple macros at the same time. For example, we might want to exclude the /boot filesystem from monitoring. Similar to the type of calculation in action conditions, as discussed in Chapter 7, *Acting upon Monitored Conditions*, we can choose between the automatic options of **And**, **Or**, and **And/Or** and there's also the **Custom expression** option. This should allow us to create discovery logic of varying complexity.

Including discovered graphs in screens

When we configure screens with normal graphs, we just choose the graph that should be included in the screen. With LLD-generated graphs, it becomes more complicated—we never know for sure how many graphs could be there for each host. Luckily, Zabbix allows us to include LLD-generated graphs in a way that automatically figures out the number of discovered entities.

To try this feature out, execute the following steps:

1. Go to **Monitoring | Screens**, go to the list of screens, and click on **Constructor** next to **Local servers.**

2. Click on the + icon in the lower-left corner to add another row here, and then click on **Change** in the lower-left cell.

3. In the **Resource** drop-down, select **Graph prototype.**

4. Click on **Select** next to the **Graph prototype** field.

5. In the popup, choose **Linux servers** in the **Group** drop-down and **A test host** in the **Host** drop-down, and then click on **Traffic on {#IFNAME}** in the **Name** column.

6. In the **Width** field, enter 400.

7. Click on **Add.**

Notice how this cell does not seem that useful in the screen configuration—no data is displayed, and the title just says **Traffic on {#IFNAME}**. Let's check this screen in the monitoring view and see whether it's any better.

Depending on the number of network interfaces your system had, the lower-left corner of the screen will have a different number of graphs. If there's only one interface (excluding `lo`), the screen will look decent. If there are more, all of them will be displayed, but they will be stuffed in a single cell, making the screen layout less appealing:

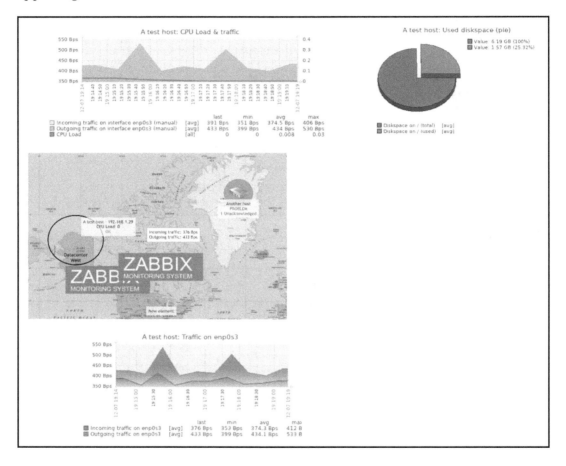

We did not set **Dynamic item** for this screen element. When the host selection is changed in the monitoring section, these graphs always show data for **A test host**. We discussed screen configuration in more detail in `Chapter 9`, *Visualizing Data with Screens and Slideshows*.

To improve this, return to the constructor of the **Local servers** screen and click on the **Change** link in the lower-left corner. Change **Column span** to 2. Our screen has two columns, so the network interface graphs will now use full screen width. Additionally, take a look at the **Max columns** field—by default, it is set to 3. If your system had three or more network interfaces discovered, the graphs would take the width of three columns, not two, breaking the screen layout again. Let's set it to 2. When done, click on **Update**, and then check the screen in the monitoring view again:

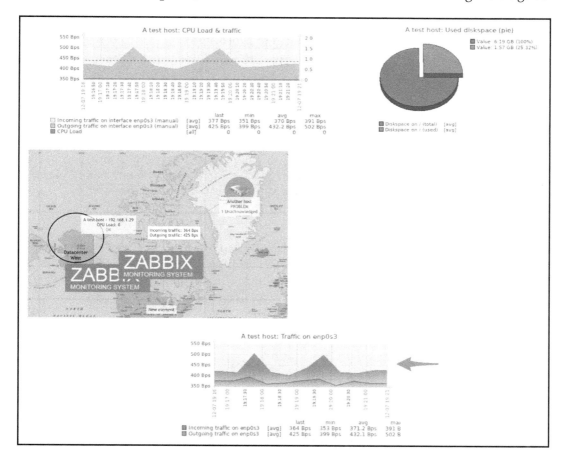

This looks better now; the network traffic graphs take full screen width, and any further traffic graphs will be placed underneath in two columns. This was a custom graph prototype that we added. Now, let's see how this works for simple graphs by following these steps:

1. Open the constructor of the **Local servers** screen again and click on the + icon in the lower-left corner.
2. Click on the **Change** link in the lower-left table cell and select **Simple graph prototype** in the **Resource** drop-down.
3. Then, click on **Select** next to the **Item prototype** field.
4. Choose **Linux servers** in the **Group** drop-down and **A test host** in the **Host** drop-down, and then click on **Free space on {#FSNAME}** in the **Name** column.
5. Set both **Max columns** and **Column span** to 2 again, and click on **Add**.
6. Check this screen in the monitoring view. All of the discovered filesystems should be shown in this screen, below the network traffic graphs.

This works the same way in templated screens (also known as host screens), except that we may only select item and graph prototypes from a single template:

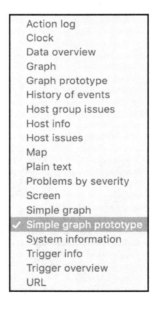

Custom thresholds with user macro context

The triggers we created from the network interface LLD prototypes always used the same threshold. We could use a user macro and customize the threshold for an individual host, but all interfaces would get the same threshold on that host. With filesystem monitoring, it could be desirable to have different thresholds on different filesystems. For example, we could use 80% warning on the root filesystem, 60% on the /boot filesystem, and 95% on the /home filesystem. This is possible, using the user macro context.

Refer to Chapter 8, *Simplifying Complex Configurations with Templates*, for further details on user macros.

The normal syntax for user macros is {$MACRO}. The context is specified inside the curly braces, separated by a colon, like so {$MACRO:context}. A trigger prototype to check for the filesystem being 80% full in our LLD rule could have an expression like this:

```
{C_Template_Linux:vfs.fs.size[{#FSNAME},free].last()}<20
```

 It might be a good idea to use trigger functions such as avg() or max() to avoid trigger flapping, as discussed in Chapter 6, *Detecting Problems with Triggers*.

This would trigger an alert on any filesystem having less than 20% free disk space or in excess of 80% utilization. We could rewrite it to use the user macro as the threshold value:

```
{C_Template_Linux:vfs.fs.size[{#FSNAME},free].last()}<{$FS_FREE_THRESH
OLD}
```

This would allow us to customize the threshold per host, but not per filesystem. Expanding on this, we would instruct the LLD rule to put the discovered filesystem as the macro context, as follows:

```
{C_Template_Linux:vfs.fs.size[{#FSNAME},free].last()}<{$FS_FREE_THRESH
OLD:{#FSNAME}}
```

As the LLD prototypes are processed, the LLD macros are replaced with the discovered values in created items. The trigger for the root filesystem that would be created on the host would look like this:

```
{A test
host:vfs.fs.size[{#FSNAME},free].last()}<{$FS_FREE_THRESHOLD:/}
```

The trigger for the /home filesystem would look like this:

```
{A test
host:vfs.fs.size[{#FSNAME},free].last()}<{$FS_FREE_THRESHOLD:/home}
```

When Zabbix evaluates this trigger, it will first look for a macro with this context value on the host. If that is not found, it will look for this macro with this context in the linked templates. If it's not found there, it will look for a global macro with such a context. If it's still not found, it will revert to the macro without the context and evaluate that as a normal user macro. This means that we don't have to define user macros with all possible context values—only the ones where we want to modify the behavior. If there's a filesystem for which a specific user macro is not available, there's always the host, template, or global macro to fall back on.

This feature is really nice, but properly explaining it seems to be complicated, so here's a schematic. Without context, user macros were evaluated as in the right-hand column—that is, the host level was checked first, then template, and then global. With context, it is the same—just that the macro name with context is looked up in all three levels first, and then we fall back to the macro name without context on all three levels. The first place where there's a match will determine the value for that macro:

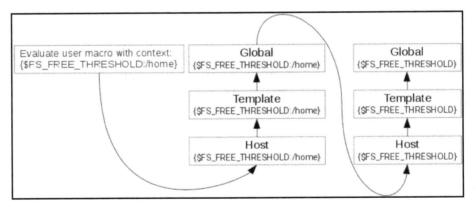

When used in triggers like this, this feature allows us to have different thresholds for different filesystems—and that can also be customized per host. We could have a user macro {$FS_FREE_THRESHOLD:/home} set to 20 on one host, 30 on another, and so on.

Of course, this is not limited to triggers—it is supported in all the locations where user macros are supported, including item-key parameters and trigger-function parameters. A trigger could check the average temperature for 5 minutes on one system and 15 minutes on another.

CPU discovery

Yet another discovery method supported by the Zabbix agent is **CPU discovery**. It returns all CPUs (or cores) present on a system. Now that we know how to get the LLD JSON, we only need to know which item key is used to return CPU information—that's `system.cpu.discovery`. Run this on `A test host`:

```
$ zabbix_get -s 127.0.0.1 -k system.cpu.discovery | json_pp
```

For a single-core system, it will return this:

```
{
    data : [
        {
            {#CPU.NUMBER} : 0,
            {#CPU.STATUS} : online
        }
    ]
}
```

The CPU discovery returns two macros for each discovered CPU:

- `{#CPU.NUMBER}` is a CPU number, as assigned by the system.
- `{#CPU.STATUS}` tells us the CPU's status, again, according to the host system.

This can be used to monitor various states on individual CPUs and cores. If our application is supposed to utilize all cores evenly, it might be useful to know when the utilization is not even. Simple CPU utilization monitoring will return the average result across all CPUs, so a runaway process that consumes 100% of a single CPU on a quad-core system would only register as having 25% utilization. We might also want to know when a CPU is not online for some reason.

SNMP discovery

The discovery methods we examined before were all Zabbix-agent based. Zabbix also supports discovering entities over SNMP. This is different from the dynamic SNMP index support we discussed in Chapter 4, *Monitoring SNMP Devices*. The dynamic SNMP index allows us to monitor a specific entity by name—for example, a network interface by its name. SNMP support in LLD allows us to discover all entities and monitor them.

Let's see how we could use it to discover all network interfaces:

1. Navigate to **Configuration | Hosts,** click on **Discovery** next to the host for which you created SNMP items previously, and click on **Create discovery rule.** Populate these fields:

  - **Name**: SNMP interface discovery
  - **Type**: **SNMPv2 agent** (or choose another, supported SNMP version)
  - **Key**: snmp.interface.discovery
  - **SNMP OID**: discovery[{#IFDESCR}, IF-MIB::ifDescr]
  - **Update interval**: 120s

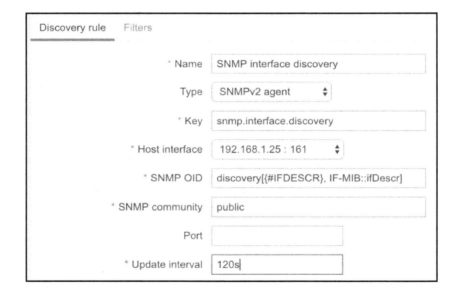

Zabbix versions before 2.4 used a different SNMP OID syntax for LLD rules. While upgrading, Zabbix would change the syntax to the current one; importing an older template would use the old syntax, which would fail in Zabbix 2.4 and later. At the present time, it is not known which Zabbix version could fix this.

2. When done, click on the **Add** button at the bottom.

The discovery itself was very similar to what we have created so far, with one exception—the SNMP OID value. For the SNMP LLD, we define the macro name and the OID table to be discovered. In this case, Zabbix would look at all the individual values in the `IF-MIB::ifDescr` table and assign them to the `{#IFDESCR}` macro, which is the name we just specified in the SNMP OID field. In addition to the macro we specified, Zabbix will also add one extra macro for each entity discovered – `#SNMPINDEX}`. That, as we will see in a moment, will be useful when creating item prototypes.

To create some prototypes, next to the new discovery rule, click on **Item prototype**, and then click on **Create item prototype**. Fill in the following:

- **Name:** `Incoming traffic on interface $1 (SNMP LLD)`
- **Type: SNMPv2 agent**
- **Key:** `lld.ifInOctets[{#IFDESCR}]`
- **SNMP OID:** `IF-MIB::ifInOctets.{#SNMPINDEX}`
- **Units:** `Bps`
- **Preprocessing: Change per second**

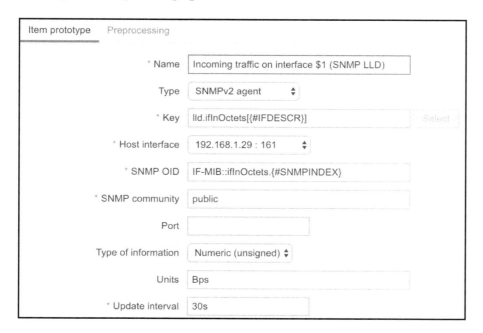

When done, click on the **Add** button at the bottom.

Notice how we prefixed `lld` to the item key. That way, there is no chance it could clash with the items we created manually earlier. As for the SNMP OID, we used the built-in `{#SNMPINDEX}` macro, which should uniquely identify values in the SNMP table. If we add such an item manually, we would find out which is the correct index for the desired interface and use that number directly. That's for the incoming traffic—to make this more complete, click on **Incoming traffic on interface {#IFDESCR} (SNMP LLD)** in the **Name** column, and then click on the **Clone** button at the bottom. In the **Name** field, change `Incoming` to `Outgoing`. In both of the **Key** and **SNMP OID** fields, change `In` to `Out` so that the **OID** has `ifOutOctets`. When done, click on the **Add** button at the bottom. Navigate to **Configuration | Hosts** and click on **Items** next to the host we just worked on. After a couple of minutes, there should be new items here, according to those two prototypes. As this is a configuration page, make sure to refresh it every now and then, otherwise the changes will not be visible.

If the items don't show up after a longer period of time, go to the discovery list for that host and check the **Info** column—there could be an error listed there.

Most likely, the loopback interface will be in the list as well. We did not apply any filtering for this LLD rule:

SNMP interface discovery: Incoming traffic on interface enp0s3 (SNMP LLD)	lld.ifInOctets[enp0s3]
SNMP interface discovery: Incoming traffic on interface lo (SNMP LLD)	lld.ifInOctets[lo]
SNMP interface discovery: Incoming traffic on interface enp0s8 (SNMP LLD)	lld.ifInOctets[enp0s8]

As before, let's create a graph prototype for these items:

1. Click on **Discovery rules** in the navigation header above the item list, click on **Graph** prototypes next to **SNMP interface discovery**, and then click on the **Create graph prototype** button. In the **Name** field, enter `Traffic on {#IFDESCR} (SNMP)`. Click on **Add prototype** in the **Items** section, mark the checkboxes next to both of the prototypes, and click on **Select**.
2. Click on the **Add** button at the bottom. If you look at the list of graphs in the configuration section for this host after a few minutes, a new graph should appear for each interface there.

The `ifDescr` OID is usually the interface name. It is quite common to use the `ifAlias` OID for a more user-friendly description. We could change our discovery to `ifAlias` instead of `ifDescr`, but not all systems will have a useful `ifAlias` value on all interfaces, and we might want to know the `ifDescr` value anyway. Zabbix can discover multiple OIDs in a single LLD rule as well. Let's go back to the discovery rule configuration for this host and click on **SNMP interface discovery** in the **Name** column. Modify the **SNMP OID** field to read the following:

```
discovery[{#IFDESCR}, IF-MIB::ifDescr, {#IFALIAS}, IF-MIB::ifAlias]
```

Further OIDs are added as extra parameters, where the macro name is always followed by the OID. We could also add more OIDs, if needed:

```
key[{#MACRO1}, MIB::OID1, {#MACRO2}, MIB::OID2, {#MACROn}, MIB::OIDn]
```

In this case, though, `ifAlias` should be enough. Click on the **Update** button at the bottom, and then click on **Graph prototypes** next to the **SNMP interface discovery** entry. Click on **Traffic on {#IFDESCR} (SNMP)** in the **Name**column, and change the name for this graph prototype:

```
Traffic on {#IFDESCR} ({#IFALIAS}) (SNMP)
```

This way, if an interface has `ifAlias` set, it will be included in the graph name. We still keep the `ifDescr` value, as that is a unique interface identifier, and some interfaces might have nothing to return for the `ifAlias` OID. Let's go to the graph configuration for this host. After a few minutes have passed, the graph names should be updated, with `ifAlias` included in the parentheses.

> If you are monitoring a Linux system that's running the Net-SNMP daemon, `ifAlias` will most likely be empty.

This approach also provides an easy way to monitor selected interfaces only. If you have a large number of network devices and only a few selected ports are to be monitored, the description for those ports could be changed on the device—for example, they could all be prefixed with `zbx`. This will show up in the `ifAlias` OID, and we would filter by the `{#IFALIAS}` macro in the LLD rule properties.

> The macro names are user configurable and could be different on a different Zabbix installation. Only the built-in `{#SNMPINDEX}` macro will always have the same name.

Creating custom LLD rules

The built-in low-level discovery support is great for discovering filesystems, network interfaces, CPUs, and other entities. But *what if we have some custom software that we would like to discover components with or perhaps are running an older Zabbix agent on some system that does not support a particular type of discovery yet?* The great thing about LLD is that it is very easy to extend with our own discovery rules. Let's take a look at two examples:

- Reimplementing CPU discovery on Linux
- Discovering MySQL databases

 An LLD rule never returns item values. It discovers entities that allow the creation of items from prototypes. Items receive values from agents, SNMP devices, using `zabbix_sender`, or any of the other data collection methods.

Reimplementing CPU discovery

First, let's try to do something that is already available in recent Zabbix agents—discovering CPUs. We do this both because it could be useful if you have a system running an old agent and because it shows how straightforward LLD can be on occasion. To do this, let's consider the following script:

```
for cpu in $(ls -d /sys/devices/system/cpu/cpu[0-9]*/); do
    cpui=${cpu#/sys/devices/system/cpu/cpu}
    [[ $(cat ${cpu}/online 2>/dev/null) ==    1 || ! -f
${cpu}/online]] &&    status=online || status=offline;
cpulist=$cpulist,'{{#CPU.NUMBER}:'${cpui%/}',
{#CPU.STATUS}:'$status'}'
done
echo '{data:['${cpulist#,}']}'
```

It relies on `/sys/devices/system/cpu/` holding a directory for each CPU, named `cpu`, followed by the CPU number. In each of those directories, we look for the online file—if that file is there, we check the contents. If the contents are `1`, the CPU is considered to be online; if something else, it is considered to be offline. In some cases, changing the online state for `CPU0` will not be allowed—this file would then be missing, and we would interpret that as the CPU being online. We then append `{#CPU.NUMBER}` and `{#CPU.STATUS}` macros with proper values and eventually print it all out, wrapped in the LLD data array. Let's use this as a user parameter.

We explored user parameters in `Chapter 10`, *Advanced Item Monitoring*.

We will concatenate it all in a single line, as we don't need a wrapper script for this command. In the Zabbix agent daemon configuration file on `A test host`, add the following:

```
UserParameter=reimplementing.cpu.discovery,for cpu in $(ls -d
/sys/devices/system/cpu/cpu[0-9]*/); do
cpui=${cpu#/sys/devices/system/cpu/cpu}; [[ $(cat ${cpu}/online
2>/dev/null) == 1 || ! -f ${cpu}/online ]] && status=online ||
status=offline;
cpulist=$cpulist,'{{#CPU.NUMBER}:'${cpui%/}',{#CPU.STATUS}:'$status'}'
; done; echo '{data:['${cpulist#,}']}'
```

For more complicated cases or production implementation, consider a proper JSON implementation, such as the `JSON::XS` Perl module.

Restart the agent daemon and, on the same system, run this:

$ zabbix_get -s 127.0.0.1 -k reimplementing.cpu.discovery

On a quad-core system, it would return something similar to this:

```
{data:[{{#CPU.NUMBER}:0,{#CPU.STATUS}:online},{{#CPU.NUMBER}:1,{#CPU.S
TATUS}:online},{{#CPU.NUMBER}:2,{#CPU.STATUS}:offline},{{#CPU.NUMBER}:
3,{#CPU.STATUS}:online}]}
```

You can reformat JSON for better readability using Perl or Python; we did that earlier in this chapter.

We can now use this item key for an LLD rule the same way as with the built-in item. The item prototypes would work exactly the same way, and we wouldn't even need to use different LLD macros.

On most Linux systems, you can test this by bringing some CPUs or cores offline—for example, the following will bring the second CPU offline:

 # echo 0 > /sys/devices/system/cpu/cpu1/online

Discovering MySQL databases

With the CPU discovery reimplemented, let's try to discover MySQL databases. Instead of user parameters, let's use a Zabbix trapper item, which we will populate with Zabbix sender.

We explored Zabbix sender in Chapter 10, *Advanced Item Monitoring*.

We will use a different item type now. This is completely normal—the item type used for LLD does not matter as long as we can get the correct JSON into the Zabbix server. Let's start by creating the LLD rule with a number of item prototypes and proceed with generating JSON after that. With this rule, we could discover all MySQL databases and monitor their sizes using a user parameter. The following assumes that your Zabbix database is on A test host. Navigate to **Configuration | Hosts**, click on **Discovery** next to **A test host**, and then click on **Create discovery rule**. Fill in the following:

- **Name**: MySQL database discovery
- **Type**: **Zabbix trapper**
- **Key**: mysql.db.discovery

When done, click on **Add**. Now, click on **Item prototypes** next to **MySQL database discovery**, and then click on **Create item prototype**. Here, fill in the following:

- **Name**: Database $1 size
- **Type**: **Zabbix agent (active)**
- **Key**: mysql.db.size[{#MYSQL.DBNAME}]
- **Units**: B
- **Update interval**: 300
- **Applications**: **MySQL**

When done, click on the **Add** button at the bottom. For this item, we used an active agent, as this is suggested for user parameters, and we also set the update interval to 5 minutes—usually, the database size won't change that quickly. We are only interested in more long-term trends. We now have the item, which will be a UserParameter variable, and that item, in turn, will be created by an LLD rule that is populated by Zabbix sender. Let's set up the UserParameter variable now. In the Zabbix agent daemon configuration file for A test host, add the following:

```
UserParameter=mysql.db.size[*],HOME=/home/zabbix mysql -Ne select
sum(data_length+index_length) from information_schema.tables where
table_schema='$1';
```

This `UserParameter` variable will query the total database size, including both actual data and all indexes. Notice how we are setting the HOME variable again. Don't forget to save the file and restart the agent daemon afterward. It's also a good idea to test it right away:

```
$ zabbix_get -s 127.0.0.1 -k mysql.db.size[zabbix]
```

This will most likely return a number:

```
147865600
```

If it fails, double-check the MySQL parameter configuration we used in Chapter 10, *Advanced Item Monitoring*.

Notice how it takes some time for this value to be returned. For large databases, it might be a better idea to use Zabbix sender for such an item as well.

With the LLD rule and item prototype in place, let's get to sending the JSON for discovery. The following should discover all databases that are accessible to the current user and generate the LLD JSON for Zabbix:

```
for db in $(mysql -u zabbix -Ne show databases;); do
    dblist=$dblist,'{{#MYSQL.DBNAME}:'$db'}'
done
echo '{data:['${dblist#,}']}'
```

We are removing the trailing comma in the JSON database list—JSON does not allow a trailing comma, and including it will make the discovery fail. Zabbix will complain that the incoming data is not a valid JSON.

The principle here is similar to the CPU discovery reimplementation from earlier—we find all the databases and list them in the JSON after the proper macro name. It should return a line similar to this:

```
{data:[{{#MYSQL.DBNAME}:information_schema},{{#MYSQL.DBNAME}:zabbix}]}
```

And now on to actually sending this to our LLD rule—we will use Zabbix sender for that.

If you tested this and thus modified the `dblist` variable, run `unset dblist` before running the following command:

```
$ zabbix_sender -z 127.0.0.1 -s A test host -k mysql.db.discovery
-o $(for db in $(mysql -u zabbix -Ne show databases;); do
dblist=$dblist,'{{#MYSQL.DBNAME}:'$db'}'; done; echo
'{data:['${dblist#,}']}')
```

This command should be run as the user the Zabbix agent daemon runs as; otherwise, it might include databases that the Zabbix user has no permission for, and such items would become unsupported.

Visiting the item list for A test host in the configuration should reveal that one item created for each database:

It might take up to 3 minutes for the first value to appear in the **Latest data** page first, up to a minute for the configuration cache to refresh, and then up to 2 minutes for the active agent to update its configuration from the server.

Also remember that the rule is only evaluated when it gets new data. If a database was removed and scheduled for deletion, it would never get deleted if the trapper item got no more data.

After some time has passed, the values should be visible in the **Monitoring** | **Latest data** page:

NAME ▲	LAST CHECK	LAST VALUE
MySQL (6 Items)		
Database information_schema size	2016-05-11 10:45:42	144 KB
Database zabbix size	2016-05-11 10:45:42	77.89 MB

LLD rules cannot be nested—for example, we cannot discover tables in the databases we discovered. If the tables had to be discovered, it would required a separate, independent LLD rule.

Global regular expressions

Now that we know about some of the automation features, let's take a look at a feature in Zabbix that allows us to define regular expressions in an easier – and sometimes more powerful – way. This feature can be used in low-level discovery, as discussed here, and in other locations.

There are quite a lot of places in Zabbix where regular expressions can be used. We already looked at icon mapping in Chapter 21, *Visualizing Data with Graphs and Maps*, and log filtering in Chapter 10, *Advanced Item Monitoring*. In all these places, we defined the regular expression directly. But sometimes, we might want to have a single expression that we could reuse, or the expression could be overly complicated when typed in directly. For example, our filtering of loopback interfaces earlier was not the most readable thing. This is where global regular expressions can help.

Let's see how we could have used this feature to simplify that filtering:

Navigate to **Administration | General**, choose **Regular expressions** from the drop-down, and click on **New regular expression**. To see what we could potentially do here, expand the Expression type drop-down:

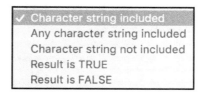

Character string included and **Character string not included** both seem pretty straightforward. This expression would match or negate the matching of a single string. **Any character string included** is a bit more complicated, according to the **Delimiter** drop-down (which appears when we choose **Any character string**). We could enter multiple values and, if any of those were found, it would be a match:

For example, leaving the **Delimiter** drop-down at the default setting, retaining the comma, and entering `ERROR, WARNING` in the **Expression** field, would match either the `ERROR` or `WARNING` string.

The two remaining options, **Result is TRUE** and **Result is FALSE**, are the powerful ones. Here, we could enter `^[0-9]` in the **Expression** field and match when the string either starts or does not start with a number. Actually, only these last two work with regular expressions; the first three are string-matching options. They do not even offer any extra functionality besides making things a bit simpler; technically, they are not regular expressions, but are supported here for convenience.

Previously, when we wanted to filter out an interface with the name `lo`, we used a filter that referenced us to the following regular expression rule—**Network interfaces for discovery**.

Creating something familiar is fairly complicated. Let's create a global regular expression that would do the same:

1. Enter **Name** as `Exclude loopback`.
2. In the **Expressions** block, fill in the following:

   - **Expression type: Result is FALSE**
   - **Expression:** `^lo$`

The fields can be seen in the following screenshot:

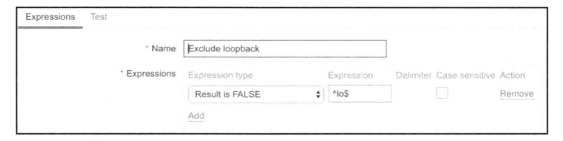

3. Click on the **Add** button at the very bottom.

Using `lo` with **Character string not included** would exclude anything containing `lo`, not just the exact string `lo`.

Now, let's reference it in our global regular expression:

1. To do so, go to **Configuration | Templates**, click on **Discovery** next to **C_Template_Linux**, and click on **Interface discovery** in the **Name** column. Switch to the **Filters** tab and replace the value in the **Regular expression** column with `@Exclude loopback`.

> Here, no quoting should be used—just the @ sign and then the global regular expression name, precisely as configured in the administration section.

2. When done, click on **Update**. The new configuration should work exactly the same. Another solution could be to just write the regular expression itself in this box.

> No check is carried out when a global regular expression gets its name changed—this way, you could break configuration elsewhere, so it should be done with great care, if at all.

Another place where global regular expressions come in handy is log monitoring. Similar to LLD rule filters, we just use an @ prefixed expression name instead of typing the regular expression directly. For example, we could define a regular expression as follows:

```
(ERROR|WARNING) 13[0-9]{3}
```

It would catch any errors and warnings with the error code in the 13,000 range—because that might be defined to be of concern to us. Assuming we named our global regexp `errors and warnings 13k`, the log monitoring key would look like this:

```
log[/path/to/the/file,@errors and warnings 13k]
```

Testing global regexps

Let's return to **Administration** | **General**, choose **Regular expressions** in the drop-down, and click on **New regular expression**. Add three expressions here, as follows:

- First expression:
  - **Expression type: Character string included**
  - **Expression**: A
  - **Case sensitive**: yes
- Second expression:
  - **Expression type: Result is TRUE**
  - **Expression**: ^[0-9]
- Third expression:
  - **Expression type: Result is FALSE**
  - **Expression**: [0-9]$

This should match a string that contains an uppercase A, starts with a number, and does not end with a number. Now, switch to the **Test** tab and enter 1A2 in the **Test string** field; then, click on **Test expressions**. In the following screenshot of the result area, it shows that a string starting with a number and containing an uppercase A corresponds, but then, the string ends with a number, which we negated. As a result, the final test fails:

Zabbix uses PCRE. In older versions, it was only the frontend using the PCRE and the backend would use the POSIX regular expressions. In Zabbix 4.0, this is no longer the case. https://regex101.com/ is a good site to test your PCRE regular expressions.

Usage in the default templates

As we created our own global regular expression, you probably noticed that there were a few already existing there.

Let's navigate to **Administration | General** and choose **Regular expressions** in the drop-down again. Besides the one we created for the loopback interface filtering, there are five existing expressions:

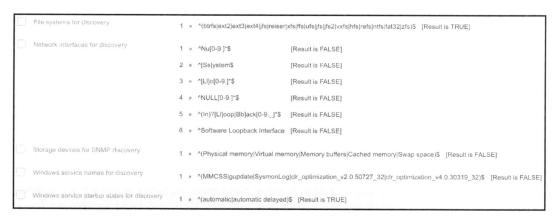

The expressions shown in the preceding screenshot can be shown as follows:

- One of them, **Network interfaces for discovery**, actually does almost the same thing as ours did, except that it also excludes interfaces whose names start with **Software Loopback Interface,** which is for MS Windows monitoring.
- **File systems for discovery** can be used to limit the types of filesystems to monitor, besides xfs, which we filtered for; it includes a whole bunch of other filesystem types.

- **Storage devices for SNMP discovery** excludes memory statistics from storage devices when monitoring over SNMP. Windows service names for discovery is used to exclude services that we don't need to know the status of in Windows and could easily get extended.
- The final one, **Windows service startup states for discovery**, will exclude services not marked as to start automatically or automatic delayed.

Network discovery

LLD is concerned with discovering entities on an individual host. Zabbix also supports a way to scan a network address range and perform some operation based on what has been discovered there—that's called **network discovery**.

Configuring a discovery rule

To see how this could work, let's have a simple discovery rule. We can discover our test systems, or we can point the discovery at another network range that is accessible to the Zabbix server.

To create a network discovery rule, execute the following:

1. Navigate to **Configuration** | **Discovery** and click on **Create discovery rule**.
2. Fill in the name and IP range as desired, and then click on **New** in the **Checks** block. Choose **ICMP ping** in the **Check type** drop-down and click on **Add** in this block. Additionally, change **Delay** to 2m so that we can more easily see the effects of any changes:

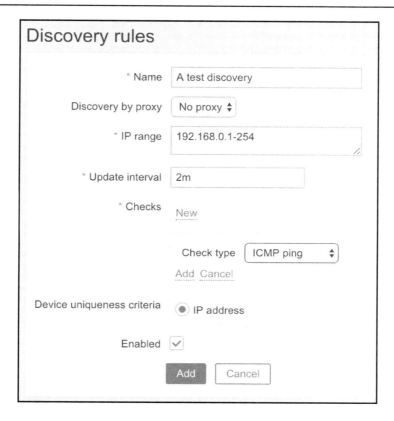

Make sure `fping` is properly configured—we did that in `Chapter 3`, *Monitoring with Zabbix Agents and Basic Protocols.*

3. When done, click on the **Add** button at the bottom.

Viewing the results

After a few minutes have passed, check the **Monitoring** I **Discovery** section:

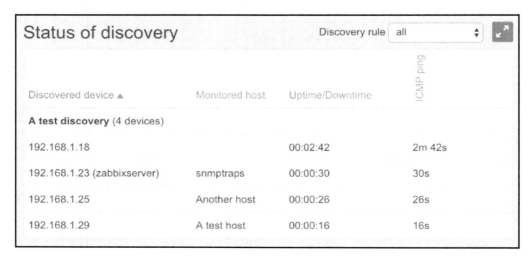

All the devices that respond to the ping in the configured range will be listed here. If a device is already monitored as a host in Zabbix, it will be listed in the **Monitored host** column. We will also see for how long the host is known to be up, and, in the **ICMP ping** column, we also see the time the service is running. In older versions, this column would just be marked green and we would have had to move the mouse over the column to see how long the status was running. It can happen that only one host is listed, as already monitored here. *How come?* Hosts are recognized here by their IP addresses, so we used 127.0.0.1. The address by which it was discovered differs, so it's not really considered to be the same host or device.

Hosts are not clickable here at this time—probably the easiest way to get to the host properties is by copying and pasting the hostname in the global search field.

Now, follow these steps:

1. Navigate back to **Configuration | Discovery** and click on **A test discovery** in the **NAME** column. Click on **New** in the **Checks** block and choose a service that is accessible and would be easy to control on these hosts – perhaps **SMTP** again. Click on **Add** in the **Checks** section, and then click on **New** there again. This time, choose a service that is not present on any host in the configured range—**FTP** might be a good choice. Then, click on **Add** in this block again:

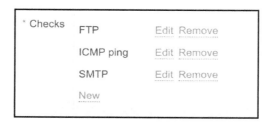

2. Finally, click on **Update**. After a couple of minutes, visit **Monitoring | Discovery**:

Discovered device ▲	Monitored host	Uptime/Downtime	ICMP ping	SMTP
A test discovery (4 devices)				
192.168.1.18		00:15:31	15m 31s	
192.168.1.23 (zabbixserver)	snmptraps	00:13:19	13m 19s	
192.168.1.25	Another host	00:13:15	13m 15s	2m 30s

SMTP has appeared, which is great. *But why is there no* **FTP** *column? Could this view be limited to two services?* It's not limited to a specific number of services, but a service that is not discovered on any of the hosts does not show up at all at this time. If a service was initially discovered on a number of systems but not on others, the column would be shown and the systems where the service was not discovered would get a gray cell.

Let's break something now—bring down the SMTP service on one of the hosts, and wait for a couple of minutes. The **SMTP** cell for that host should turn red, and the popup should start tracking downtime for that service now. If all services on a host went down, the host itself would be considered as down, and that would be reflected in the **Uptime/Downtime** column:

Discovered device ▲	Monitored host	Uptime/Downtime	ICMP ping	SMTP
A test discovery (4 devices)				
192.168.1.18		00:31:03	31m 3s	
192.168.1.23 (localhost)	snmptraps	00:28:51	28m 51s	10s
192.168.1.25	Another host	00:28:47	28m 47s	18m 2s
192.168.1.29	A test host	00:28:37	28m 37s	

Reacting to the discovery results

The discovery monitoring page is interesting at first, but not that useful in the long term. Luckily, we can make Zabbix perform operations in response, and the configuration is somewhat similar to how we reacted to triggers firing.

To see how this is configured, follow these steps:

Navigate to **Configuration | Actions** and switch to **Discovery** in the **Event source** drop-down in the upper-right corner. Then, click on **Create action**. Fill in the name of Network discovery test, switch to the **New conditions** drop-down box, and expand the first drop-down in the **New condition** section:

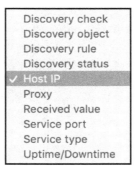

The available conditions are completely different from what was available for trigger actions. Let's review them:

- **Discovery check**: A specific check in a specific discovery rule must be chosen here.
- **Discovery object**: Either a device or service can be chosen here. In our example, the discovered host would be a device object and SMTP would be a service object.
- **Discovery rule**: A specific network discovery rule must be chosen here.
- **Discovery status**: This condition has possible values of **Up**, **Down**, **Discovered**, and **Lost**. For devices, they are considered to be discovered or up if at least one service on them can be reached. Here is what the values mean:
    - **Discovered**: This device or service is being seen for the first time or after it was detected to be down
    - **Lost**: This device or service has been seen before, but it has just disappeared
    - **Up**: The device or service has been discovered, no matter how many times it might have happened already
    - **Down**: The device or service has been discovered at some point, but right now, it is not reachable, no matter how many times that has happened already
- **Host IP**: Individual addresses or ranges may be specified here.
- **Proxy**: Action may be limited to a specific Zabbix proxy. We will discuss proxies in `Chapter 17`, *Using Proxies to Monitor Remote Locations*.
- **Received value**: If we are polling a Zabbix agent item or an SNMP OID, we may react to a specific value—for example, if undertaking discovery according to the `system.uname` item key, we could link all hosts that have `Linux` in the returned string to the Linux template.
- **Service port**: Action may be limited to a specific port or port range on which the discovery has happened.
- **Service type**: Action may be restricted to a service type. This is similar to the **Discovery check** condition, except that choosing SMTP here would match all SMTP checks from all network discovery rules, not just a specific one.
- **Uptime/Downtime**: Time in seconds may be entered here to limit the action only after the device or service has been up or down for a period of time.

Most of these are pretty self-explanatory, but let's take a closer look at two of them. The **Discovery status** condition allows us to differentiate between the initial check or being discovered after downtime and periodic checks. As an example, if we matched the **Up** status and added the host to a **Host group**, this addition would be checked and performed every time the host can be reached. If somebody removed that host from that host group, it would be readded during every discovery cycle. If we matched the **Discovered** status, it would only happen when the host is first discovered and when it goes down and then up again. Automatic readdition to the group is most likely to happen later in this case.

The **Uptime/Downtime** condition allows us to react with a delay, not immediately. For example, we might want to have an uptime of a few hours before monitoring a device, as it might be a temporary troubleshooting laptop that is attached to the network. Probably even more importantly, we might not want to delete a host with all its history if that host is down for 5 minutes. Checking for a week-long downtime might be reasonable – if nobody bothered with that host for a week, it's safe to delete.

For now, let's leave the conditions empty and switch to the **Operations** tab. Adding a new operation and expanding the **Operation type** drop-down will reveal all the available operations. We will discuss them in more detail a bit later, but for now, let's choose **Add to host groups**. In the input field, start typing linux, and choose **Linux servers** from the drop-down. Then, click on the small **Add** control in the **Operation details** block. Be very careful here, as it is easy to lose some configuration. When done, click on the **Add** button at the bottom:

After a couple of minutes, go to **Configuration** | **Hosts** to observe the results. If discovering our test systems, we should see that one new host has been added.

 Even though we did not tell the action to add the host itself, it still happened. If the operation implies that there's a host—for example, adding it to a host group or linking to a template—the host will be automatically added.

Why only one host? The other host already existed as per **Monitoring** | **Discovery** earlier. For this host, you will see either its hostname or the IP address used as the hostname in Zabbix. If the Zabbix server was able to perform a reverse lookup on the IP address, the result will be used as the hostname. If not, the IP address will be used as the hostname.

 If multiple addresses reverse-resolved to the same name, others would be added as `name_2` and so on.

Click on **New host** in the **Name** column. In the **Groups** section, this host is in the **Linux servers** group, as expected. But it is also in some other group, **Discovered hosts**. *Where did that come from?*

By default, all hosts discovered by network discovery are added to a specific group. *Which group?* That's a global setting.

Navigate to **Administration** | **General** and then choose **Other** in the drop-down. The **Group for discovered hosts** setting allows us to choose which group that is. *What if you don't want the discovered hosts to end up in that group?* In the action operations, we could add another operation, **Remove from host group**, and specify the **Discovered hosts** group.

Now let's review all available discovery operations:

- **Send message**: The same as for trigger actions, we may send a message to users and user groups. This could be used both to supplement an action that adds devices (*Hey, take a look at this new server we just started monitoring*) or as a simple notification that a new device has appeared on the network (*This new IP started responding, but I won't automatically monitor it*).
- **Remote command**: Zabbix can attempt to run a remote command on a passive Zabbix agent or Zabbix server, a command using IPMI, SSH, or Telnet, and even a global script. This would only succeed if remote commands are enabled on the Zabbix agent side. We discussed remote commands in `Chapter 7`, *Acting upon Monitored Conditions*.
- **Add host**: A host will be added and only included in the **Discovered hosts** group.
- **Remove host**: A host will be removed. This probably makes the most sense to perform when a host has not been discovered, and, to be on the safe side, only when the downtime exceeds a specified period of time.
- **Add to host group**: A host will be added to a host group. If there is no such host, one will be added first.
- **Remove from host group**: A host will be removed from a host group.
- **Link to template**: A host will be linked to a template. If there is no such host, one will be added first.
- **Unlink from template**: A host will be unlinked from a template.
- **Enable host**: A host will be enabled. If there is no such host, one will be added first.
- **Disable host**: A host will be disabled. This could be used as a safer alternative to removing hosts, or we could disable a host first and remove it later. If there is no such host, one will be added first.

When linking to a template, the host still needs all the proper interfaces, as required by the items in that template. During discovery, only successful discovery checks result in the adding of interfaces of a corresponding type. For example, if we only found SNMP on a host, only an SNMP interface would be added. If both SNMP and Zabbix agent discovery checks succeeded on a host, both interfaces would be added. If some checks succeed later, additional interfaces are created.

Uniqueness criteria

But *what about multi-homed hosts that have multiple interfaces exposed to Zabbix network discovery?*

1. Let's return to **Configuration | Discovery** and click on **A test discovery**.
2. Look at the **Device uniqueness criteria** option—the only setting there is **IP address**. In the **Checks** block, click on **New** and choose **Zabbix agent** in the **Check type** drop-down. In the **Key** field, enter system.uname, and then click on **Add** in the **Checks** block.
3. Notice how the **Device uniqueness criteria** got a new option—**Zabbix agent "system.uname"**, as shown in the following screenshot:

By default, with the uniqueness criteria set to **IP address**, Zabbix will create a new host for each discovered IP address. If there's a system with multiple addresses, a new host will be created for each address. If the uniqueness criteria is set to a Zabbix agent item, it will look at all the IP addresses it has seen before and the values it got back for that item key. If the new value matches some previous value, it will add a new interface to the existing host instead of creating a new host. It works the same way with SNMP—adding an SNMP check will add another uniqueness criteria option, and Zabbix will compare values received for that specific OID. It is common to discover SNMP devices by the SNMPv2-MIB::sysDescr.0 OID.

 Both a Zabbix agent and SNMP must be preconfigured to accept connections from the Zabbix server.

Now that we have discussed network discovery, I'll give you one short suggestion about it—don't use it. Well, maybe not that harsh, but do not cling to it too much. There are use cases for network discovery, but quite often, there's a decent list of devices that should be monitored coming either from a **configuration management database** (**CMDB**) or some other source. In that case, it is better to integrate and automatically update your Zabbix configuration based on that authoritative source. If your answer to *What's your most definitive list of hosts in your environment?* is *Zabbix*, then network discovery is for you.

Active agent auto-registration

We just explored network discovery—it scanned a network range. Zabbix also supports a feature that goes the other way around, where Zabbix agents can chime in and Zabbix server can automatically start monitoring them. This is called **active agent auto-registration**.

Whenever a Zabbix agent connects to the Zabbix server, the server compares the incoming agent hostname with the existing hosts. If a host with the same name exists, it proceeds with the normal active item monitoring sequence. This includes both enabled and disabled hosts. If the host does not exist, the auto-registration sequence kicks in, that is, an event is generated.

The fact that an event is generated every time an unknown agent connects to the Zabbix server is important. If you do not use active items or auto-registration, switch off active checks on the agent side. Otherwise, every such check results in a network connection, a log entry on the agent and server side, and an event in the Zabbix database. There have been cases where that increases the database size and results in significantly reduced performance. In some instances, there are millions of such completely useless auto-registration events, which is up to 90% of the total event count. It is recommended checking the server log for entries such as the following:

```
cannot send list of active checks to [127.0.0.1]: host [Register me]
not found
```

If found, they should all be solved. The first pair of square brackets tells us where the connection came from, and second, what host the agent claimed to be.

Similar to trigger and network discovery events, we may react to that event with an action. Let's configure an auto-registration action now:

1. Head to **Configuration** | **Actions** and switch to **Auto registration** in the **Event source** dropdown.
2. Then, click on **Create action**.
3. Enter Testing registration in the **Name** field, and then switch to the **Operations** tab.
4. Click on **New** in the **operations** block. The **Operation type** dropdown reveals a subset of operations that are available for network discovery.

In previous versions, we could not remove hosts, remove hosts from host groups, and unlink hosts from templates, but now it seems that this has been fixed. The operations are functionally the same as for network discovery, so we won't look into them much, just choose **Add host** this time, and click on the small **Add** in the **Operation details** block. Then, click on the **Add** button at the bottom. With the action in place, probably the easiest way to test this is to fake a new agent. Edit the agent daemon configuration file on A test host and change the **Hostname** parameter to Register me. Then, restart the agent daemon.

Go to **Configuration** | **Hosts**—there's a new host again. If you check the host properties, it is included in the **Discovered hosts** group; the same group is used here as in the network discovery. Let's change the **Hostname** parameter back to the previous value in the agent daemon configuration file and restart the agent.

We haven't looked at the conditions for auto-registration yet—let's return to **Configuration** | **Actions**, click on **Testing registration**, and switch to the **Conditions** tab. The drop-down next to the **New condition** section reveals the available conditions:

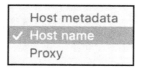

As we can see, the list of available conditions is much shorter here. We can filter by hostname. For example, if all our **Linux hosts** have linux in the name, we could detect them that way. We can also filter by proxy if we use Zabbix proxies for the auto-registration. There's also an entry called **Host metadata**. *What's that?*

Auto-registration metadata

When a Zabbix agent connects to the server, it sends its hostname. But it may additionally send some custom string to the server. What exactly it sends is controlled by a configuration parameter called **HostMetadata** in the agent daemon configuration file. This could be used to define which type the host is—database or application. Alternatively, it could list individual services running on a host. As we can match against received metadata in the auto-registration action, we could list all the running services, delimited with pipes. In the action conditions, we could look for |MySQL| and link the new host to the appropriate templates.

 Metadata is still limited to 255 characters.

Controlling the metadata parameter directly in the configuration file is possible, but it could be cumbersome. There's a way to make an agent dynamically obtain that value. Instead of HostMetadata, we would define HostMetadataItem and specify an item key. We could use one of the built-in item keys or configure a user parameter and run a script. Note that we can also use the system.run item key here and specify any command directly in the HostMetadataItem parameter, even if remote commands are not enabled—as it is not arriving from the network, it is not considered to be a remote command. For example, the following is a valid HostMetadataItem line:

```
HostMetadataItem=system.run[rpm -qa mariadb]
```

If the mariadb package is present on an RPM-based system, the agent would send that in the metadata; we could match it in the action conditions and link that host to the MariaDB/MySQL template.

There's also another use case for this parameter. You might have noticed that as long as there's an auto-registration action, somebody could maliciously or accidentally create lots and lots of hosts, potentially slowing down Zabbix significantly. There is no secret challenge mechanism to prevent that, but we can use metadata here. Action conditions could check for a specific secret string to be included in the metadata—if it's there, create the host. If not, send an email for somebody to investigate. Note that the key can't be too long, as the 255-character length limit still applies.

Summary

In this chapter, we learned about a number of features in Zabbix that allow automatic configuration, creation, and maintenance:

- Low-level discovery or LLD
- Network discovery
- Active agent auto-registration

LLD allows entities to be discovered by using Zabbix agents—it has built-in support for network interfaces, filesystems, and CPUs. We talked about customizing thresholds and other values per discovered entity with user macro context support. Zabbix can also discover SNMP tables, such as network interfaces, but it is not limited to that—any SNMP table can be discovered. We also looked at creating custom discoveries, including MySQL database discovery.

LLD offers a way to filter results by regular expressions, and we checked out how global regular expressions can make that easier here and also in other places, such as log monitoring.

After that, we explored network discovery, which is all about scanning an address range and automatically adding hosts, potentially linking them to proper templates, and then adding them to host groups.

In the other direction, there's active agent auto-registration, where active agents can chime in and the server starts monitoring them automatically. Metadata support for this feature allows quite fine-grained rules on what templates to link in or what host groups the hosts should belong to. We noted that, if not used, active checks should be disabled on agents; otherwise, an unnecessary load would be placed on the entire Zabbix infrastructure.

In the next chapter, we will explore the built-in web monitoring feature. It allows us to define scenarios that consist of steps. Steps check a page and may look for a specific HTTP response code or string in the returned page. We will also try out logging in to applications and extracting data from one page and then passing it to another.

Further reading

Read the following article for more information regarding what was covered in this chapter:

Discovery of network interfaces: https://www.zabbix.com/documentation/4.0/manual/discovery/low_level_discovery/network_interfaces

Monitoring Web Pages 12

In this chapter, we will look at the built-in capability of Zabbix to monitor web pages. We will check different sections of a web page and monitor it for failures, as well as monitoring download speed and response time. We'll also find out how Zabbix can extract a value from a page and then reuse that value. Besides more advanced scenarios and step-based solutions, we will also explore web-monitoring-related items that are available for the Zabbix agent.

In this chapter, the following topics will be covered:

- Monitoring a simple web page
- Logging into the Zabbix interface
- Authentication options
- Using agent items

Monitoring a simple web page

The internet is important in every aspect of modern life—socializing, business, entertainment, and everything else happens over the wire. With all the resources devoted to this network, many are tasked with maintaining websites—no matter whether we have an internally-hosted site or one trusted to an external hosting provider, we will want to know at least its basic health status. We could start by monitoring a few simple things on a real-life website.

Creating a web-monitoring scenario

Web monitoring in Zabbix happens through scenarios that, in turn, consist of steps. Each step consists of a URL and things to check on it. This allows both the checking of a single page and verifying that several pages work properly in succession. The web-monitoring scenarios in Zabbix are assigned to hosts, and they can also be templated.

To see how this works, we could monitor a couple of pages from the open mapping project, OpenStreetMap.

While we could attach a web-monitoring scenario to any of the existing hosts, that wouldn't correctly depict what the scenario is monitoring, so we will create a dedicated host. As there's only one OpenStreetMap website, we won't use templates for this:

1. Navigate to **Configuration** | **Hosts**, click on **Create host**, and fill in these values:

   - **Name**: OpenStreetMap
   - **Groups**: Web pages

   We don't have to change any other values here, so click on the **Add** button at the bottom.

2. We're now ready to create the scenario itself—in the list of hosts, click on **Web** next to OpenStreetMap and then click on **Create web scenario**. In the scenario properties, enter these values:

   - **Name**: Main page
   - **New application**: Webpage
   - **Update interval**: 300

Now on to the individual steps. The steps for web monitoring are the actual queries performed on the web server; each step has a URL. Switch to the **Steps** tab and click on **Add** in the **Steps** section. Fill in these values in the new popup:

- **Name**: First page.
- **URL**: http://www.openstreetmap.org/.
- **Required string**: Enter OpenStreetMap is a map of the world, created by people like you. This field will search for a particular string in the returned page, and this step will fail if such a string is not found. We can use PCRE regular expressions here, but not global regular expressions, as discussed in Chapter 11, *Automating Configuration*.
- **Required status codes**: Enter 200. Here, acceptable HTTP return codes can be specified, separated by commas. Again, if the return code doesn't match, this step will be considered a failure. A status code of 200 means **OK**.

The required string is only checked against the page source, not against the HTTP headers. The scenario only downloads the content the step URL points at; other elements of the web page are never downloaded. Since Zabbix 3.4, macros are supported in the update interval field, and time suffixes.

The form should look like this:

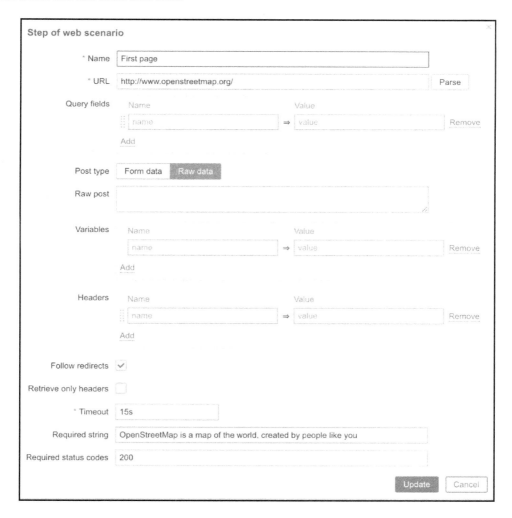

If it does, click on the **Add** button. Let's also check whether the **GPS traces** page can be accessed.

Again, click on **Add** in the **Steps** section, and enter these values:

- **Name**: Traces
- **URL**: http://www.openstreetmap.org/traces/
- **Required string**: Public GPS traces
- **Required status codes**: 200

In the **Required string** field, we entered the text that should be present on the traces page. When done, click on **Add**.

The final step of the configuration should look like this:

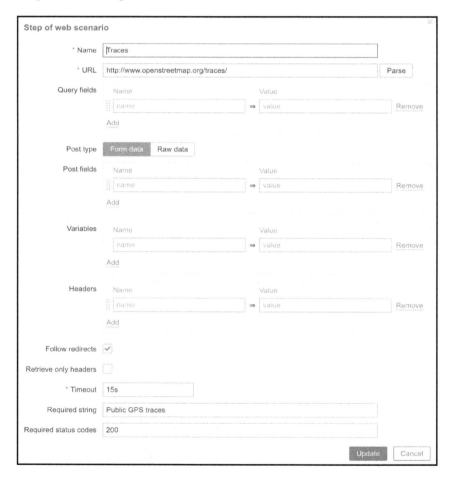

If everything looks fine, click on the **Add** button at the bottom. Let's see what web monitoring visually looks like. Open **Monitoring | Web** and click on **Main page** next to **OpenStreetMap**. It looks as if all the steps were completed successfully, so we can consider the monitored website to be operating correctly as the **Status** column happily says **OK,** or at least the parts that we are monitoring. As with plain items, we can see when the last check was performed:

We also have an overview of how many steps each scenario contains, but that's all very vague. Click on **Main page** in the **Name** column—maybe there's more information. Indeed, there is! Here, we can see statistics for each step, such as **Speed**, **Response time**, and **Response code**. And, if that's not enough, there are predefined pretty graphs for **Speed** and **Response time.** Note that these are stacked graphs, so we can identify the moments when all of the steps together take more time.

Above the graphs, we can see those familiar timescale controls, the new time selector controls, so these graphs provide the same functionality as anywhere else, including clicking and dragging to zoom in or selecting by time, months, or years:

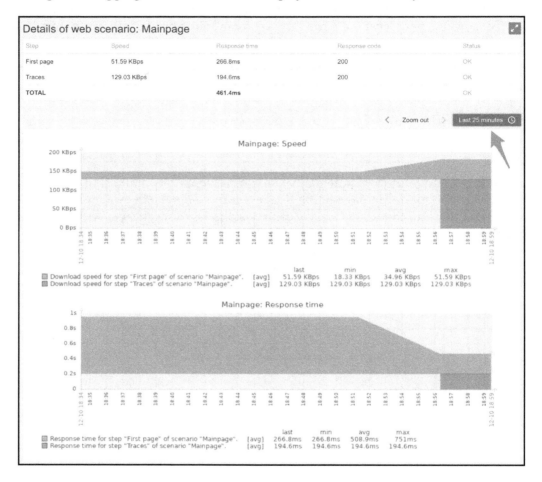

We can see the relative time each step took and how fast it was compared to the others. In this case, both operations together, on average, take slightly less than a second.

While this view is very nice, it isn't very flexible. *Can we have direct access to underlying data, perhaps?* Let's visit **Monitoring** | **Latest data** to find out. Choose **Webpages** in the **Host groups** field, and click on **Apply**. Items within the **Webpage** application will show up.

Take a look at the data, all of the collected values are accessible as individual items, including download **Speed**, **Response time**, **Response code**, and even the last error message per scenario.

We can reuse these items, creating whatever graphs we please. If we want we could create a pie chart of response times for each step or a non-stacked graph of download speeds. Of course, as with all items, we get simple graphs without any additional configuration:

	Host	Name ▲	Last check	Last value	Change	
▼	OpenStreetMap	**Webpage** (9 Items)				
		Download speed for scenario "Mainpage".	2018-12-10 19:01:22	103.01 KBps	+12.7 KBps	Graph
		Download speed for step "First page" of scenario "Mainpage".	2018-12-10 19:01:22	52.11 KBps	+532 Bps	Graph
		Download speed for step "Traces" of scenario "Mainpage".	2018-12-10 19:01:22	153.92 KBps	+24.88 KBps	Graph
		Failed step of scenario "Mainpage".	2018-12-10 19:01:22	0		Graph
		Last error message of scenario "Mainpage".				Hist...
		Response code for step "First page" of scenario "Mainpage".	2018-12-10 19:01:22	200		Graph
		Response code for step "Traces" of scenario "Mainpage".	2018-12-10 19:01:22	200		Graph
		Response time for step "First page" of scenario "Mainpage".	2018-12-10 19:01:22	264.1ms		Graph
		Response time for step "Traces" of scenario "Mainpage".	2018-12-10 19:01:22	163.6ms	- 30ms	Graph

There's also a failed step item, which returns 0 if none of the steps failed. As that value is 0 when everything is fine, we can check for it not being 0 in a trigger, and alert based on that.

 While we could use value mapping to show **Success** when the failed step is 0, we would have to add a value map entry for every step number—value mapping does not support ranges or default values yet.

Other scenarios and step properties

Before we continue with alerting, let's review the other options on the scenario level:

- **Attempts**: Web pages are funny beasts. They mostly work, but that one time when the monitoring system checks it, it fails. *Or is it just that users reload a page that fails to load once and never complain?* No matter what, this field allows us to specify how many times Zabbix tries to download a web page. For pages that experience the occasional hiccup, a value of 2 or 3 could be appropriate.

- **Agent**: When a web browser connects to a web server, it usually sends along a string identifying itself. This string includes the browser name, version, operating system, and, often, other information. This information is used for purposes such as gathering statistics, making a specific portion of a site work better in some browser, denying access, or limiting experience on the site. Zabbix web monitoring checks also send user-agent strings to web servers. By default, it identifies as `Zabbix`, but you can also choose from a list of predefined browser strings or enter a custom string by choosing the **Others** option:

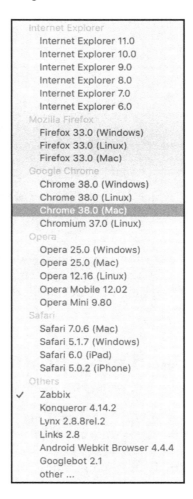

- **HTTP proxy**: If needed, an HTTP proxy can be set per scenario. A username, password, and port can be specified as well:

| HTTP proxy | http://[user[:password]@]proxy.example.com[:port] |

 The default HTTP proxy can be set with the `http_proxy` and `https_proxy` environment variables for the Zabbix server process – these variables will be picked up by `libcurl`, which is used underneath for the web monitoring. If a proxy is specified on the scenario level, it overrides such a default proxy setting. There is no way to set a proxy on the step level.

We'll discuss the remaining fields, **Variables** and **Headers**, a bit later in logging into the Zabbix interface.

 Web monitoring in Zabbix does not support JavaScript at all.

Alerting on web scenarios

Let's create a trigger that warns us when any one of the steps in the scenario fails. As discovered previously, the failed step item holds 0 when all is good. Anything else is a sequential number of the step that failed. As a web scenario stops at any failure, a failed step number of 3 means that the first two steps were executed successfully, and then the third step failed. If there were any further steps, we don't know their state—they were not processed.

To create a trigger, we always need an item key. We could try to find it in the item list. Go to **Configuration** | **Hosts** and click on **Items** next to the **OpenStreetMap** host, no items. The reason is that these items are special—they are items that are internal to Zabbix web scenarios (not to be confused with the internal monitoring items, discussed in Chapter 20, *Zabbix Maintenance*), and thus are not available for manual configuration. We should be able to select them when creating a trigger, though. Click on **Triggers** in the navigation header, and then click on **Create trigger**.

In the trigger-editing form, enter these values:

- **Name**: {HOST.NAME} website problem.
- **Expression**: Click on **Add**, then click on **Select** next to the **Item** field in the resulting popup. Select **Web pages** in the **Group** drop-down and **OpenStreetMap** in the **Host** drop-down.
- Then, click on **Failed step of scenario Main page** in the **Name** column. We have to find out when this item is not returning zero.
- In the **Function** drop-down, choose **last() - Last (most recent T value)**.
- For **Result**, choose <> and **0**.

The final trigger expression should be as follows:

```
{OpenStreetMap:web.test.fail[Main page].last()}<>0
```

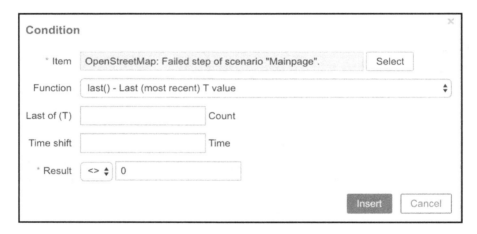

When you are done, click on the **Add** button at the bottom. We can see how the web.test.fail[Main page] item key was used, thus, web scenario items are very much like normal items. They have names and keys, even though they can't be seen in the item configuration view. This way, we can create triggers for all web scenario items, such as response time and download speed, to also spot performance issues, or for return codes so that we can spot exact at what step it has failed. The same items are available for custom graphs, too.

The trigger we created would alert upon the first failure in this web scenario. You might want to make this monitoring less sensitive, and there are at least two ways to achieve that:

- Set **Attempts** in the scenario properties to a larger value.
- Check item values over a longer period of time. We discussed such a strategy in Chapter 6, *Detecting Problems with Triggers*.

The count function could be a good candidate here as we could count the number of values over a certain period of time that are over a value, for example, count(10m,0,gt) would count the values for the last 10 minutes that are over 0.

If a web-monitoring step fails, Zabbix stops and does not proceed to the next step. If the website you are monitoring has multiple sections that can work independently of one another, you should create a separate scenario for each.

When web monitoring fails, it could be very useful to know what exactly we received from the web server. Unfortunately, Zabbix does not store retrieved content anywhere by default. We'll discuss a way to temporarily view all the retrieved web pages in the *Controlling running daemons* section of Appendix A, *Troubleshooting*.

Logging into the Zabbix interface

Our first steps in website testing were fairly simple. Let's do something a bit fancier now. We will attempt to log in to the Zabbix frontend, check whether that succeeds, and then log out. We should also verify that the logout operation was successful, by the way.

We will use the default Admin user account for these tests. Note that this will pollute the audit log with login/logout entries for this user.

We will do this with a greater number of individual steps for greater clarity:

1. Check the first page
2. Log in
3. Check login

4. Log out
5. Check logout

We will set up this scenario on **A test host**. Go to **Configuration** | **Hosts**, click on **Web** next to **A test host**, and click on **Create web scenario**. Fill in these values:

- **Name**: Zabbix frontend
- **New application**: Zabbix frontend
- **Variables**: Enter these lines:

```
{user}=Admin
{password}=zabbix
```

Remember that the host we assign the web scenario to does not matter much—actual checks are still performed from the Zabbix server.

The variables we filled in use a different syntax than other macros/variables in Zabbix. We will be able to use them in the scenario steps, and we'll see how exactly that is done in a moment. And now, on to the steps. Switch to the **Steps** tab. For each of the steps, first click on the **Add** link in the **Steps** section. Then, click on the **Add** button in the step properties, and proceed to the next step. For all the steps, adapt the URL as needed—the IP address or hostname and the actual location of the Zabbix frontend.

Step 1 – checking the first page

On the first page, fill in the following details:

- **Name**: First page
- **URL**: http://127.0.0.1/zabbix/index.php
- **Required string**: Zabbix SIA
- **Required status codes**: 200

In the URL, we also appended index.php to reduce the amount of redirects required. The **Required string** option will be checked against the page contents. That also includes all the HTML tags, so make sure to list them if your desired string has any included. We also chose a text that appears at the bottom of the page to ensure that the page has loaded completely. And the status code—the HTTP response code of 200 is OK; we require that specific code to be returned.

 Make sure you add the correct IP address of your Zabbix server in the URL field as this is the IP where your frontend is running.

Step 2 – logging in

And now, on to logging in:

- **Name**: Log in
- **URL**: http://127.0.0.1/zabbix/index.php

- **Post type**: The **Form data** option is selected with the following values:
    - **Name**: name, **Value**: {user}
    - **Name**: password, **Value**: {password}
    - **Name**: enter, **Value**: Sign in
- **Required status codes**: 200
- **Variables**: The fields of this option are filled with the following values:
    - **Name**: {sid}
    - **Value**: regex:name="csrf-token" content="([0-9a-z]{16})":

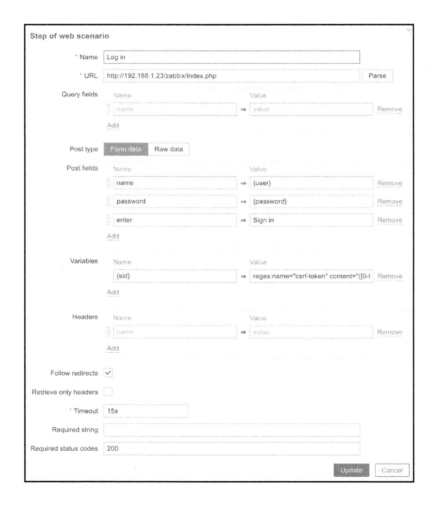

The **Post type** variables can be specified as attribute and value pairs. When using the **Form data** option, our values are URL-encoded. In raw mode, attributes and values are displayed on a single line, as in older Zabbix releases, such as 3.0, and are not URL-encoded.

In our post type, we are using the variables we specified earlier, and we pass them according to the input field names in the login form. The last variable, enter, is a hidden input in the Zabbix frontend login page, and we must pass a hardcoded value of Sign in to it. To find out these values for other pages, you can check the page source, use browser debugging features, or sniff the network traffic.

 Also take note of how we get the content of the {sid} variable (session ID) using a variable syntax with a regular expression: regex:name="csrf-token" content="([0-9a-z]{16})". This variable will be required in the *Step 4 – logging out* section. Variables can be used in later steps and override scenario-level variables or variables from previous steps.

Step 3 – checking login

We could assume that the logging in has succeeded, but it is always best to check such things. We may have missed a hidden variable, or made a mistake with the password. So, we'll use a separate step to be sure that logging in really succeeded. Note that all further steps in this scenario will act as a logged-in user until we log out. Zabbix keeps all received cookies for later steps during the whole scenario. When logged in, one distinguishing factor is the profile link, which uses the top-nav-profile class—and that will be the string we check for:

- **Name**: Check login
- **URL**: http://127.0.0.1/zabbix/index.php
- **Follow redirects**: **Yes**
- **Required string**: Administration
- **Required status codes**: 200

Step 4 – logging out

Now that we have verified that the frontend is accessible and that we can log in and retrieve logged-in content, we should also log out, otherwise the Zabbix database will become polluted with open session records. We'll discuss session maintenance in Chapter 20, *Zabbix Maintenance*.

The two important variables here are reconnect and sid. reconnect simply has to be set to 1. As for sid, we extracted that value in the *Step 2 – logging in* section, so we have all the components to log out:

- **Name**: Log out
- **URL**: http://127.0.0.1/zabbix/index.php
- **Query fields**: This option is filled with the following values:
    - **Name**: reconnect, **Value**: 1
    - **Name**: sid, **Value**: {sid}
- **Required status codes**: 200

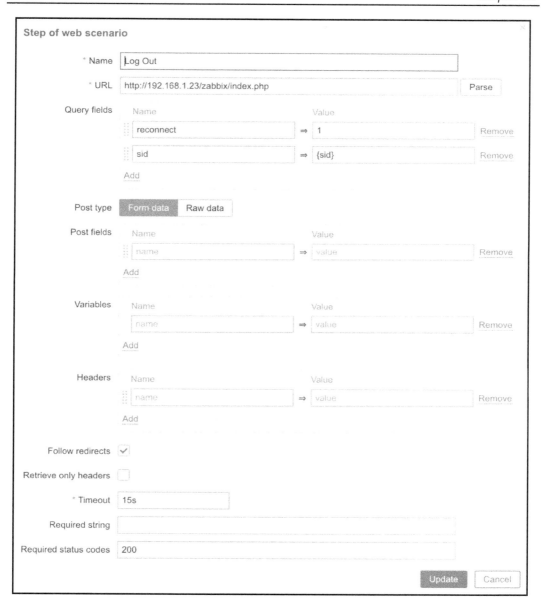

Step 5 – checking logout

We will check whether there's a string that we only expect to see on the login page. Logging out could have failed invisibly otherwise. Let's add a string to check for in our item:

- **Name:** `Check logout`
- **URL:** `http://127.0.0.1/zabbix/index.php`
- **Required string:** `Username`
- **Required status codes:** `200`

If everything looks good, click on the **Add** button at the bottom of the page to save this scenario. We could let the scenario run for a while and discuss some of the step parameters we didn't use:

- **Headers**: Custom HTTP headers that will be sent when performing a request. They are specified as attribute and value pairs. Headers on the step level will overwrite the headers specified for the scenario.
- **Follow redirects**: This specifies whether Zabbix should follow redirects. If enabled, it follows up to 10 hardcoded redirects, so there is no way to check whether there's been a specific number of redirects. If disabled, we can check for the HTTP response code being `301` or some other valid redirect code.
- **Retrieve only headers**: If the page is huge, we may opt to retrieve headers only. In this case, the **Required string** option will be disabled, as Zabbix does not yet support matching strings in headers.
- **Timeout**: This specifies the timeout for this specific step. It is applied both to connecting and performing the HTTP request, separately. Note that the default timeout is rather long, at `15` seconds, which can lead to Zabbix spending up to 30 seconds on a page.

 We could have used a user macro for part or all of the URL—that way, we would only define it once and then reference it in each step. We discussed user macros in `Chapter 8`, *Simplifying Complex Configurations with Templates*.

After the scenario has had some time to run, let's go to **Monitoring** | **Web page**. Choose **Linux servers** in the **Group** drop-down and click on **Zabbix frontend** in the **Name** column:

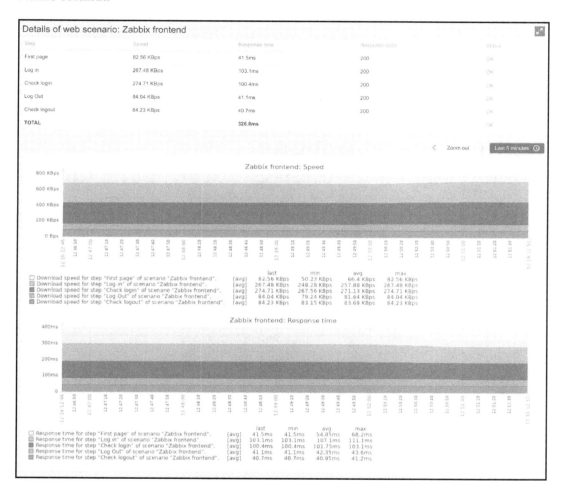

The scenario seems to be running correctly—the login and logout seem to have worked properly. Note that, if it fails for you, the failure could actually be in the previous step. For example, if it fails on *Step 3 – checking login*, the actual fault is likely to be in *Step 2 – logging in*, that is, the login failed.

The approach we took, with five steps, was not the simplest one. While it allowed us to split each action into its own steps (and provided nice graphs with five values), we could have used a much simpler approach. To check the login and logout, the simplest approach and the minimum number of steps would have been these:

- Log in and check whether it is successful
- Log out and check whether it is successful

As an extra exercise, create a new scenario that achieves the same goal in two steps.

Authentication options

In the scenario properties, there was also a tab that we didn't use: **Authentication**. Check it out here:

For **HTTP authentication**, Zabbix currently supports two options—**Basic** and **NTLM**. Digest authentication is not supported at this time, as you can see:

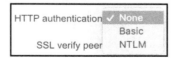

Choosing one of the **HTTP authentication** methods will provide input fields for a username and password.

All the other options are SSL/TLS-related. The checkboxes allow us to validate the server certificate—the **SSL verify peer** option checks the certificate validity, and **SSL verify host** additionally checks that the server hostname matches the **Common Name** or the **Subject Alternate Name** in the certificate. The certificate authority is validated against the system default. The location of the CA certificates can also be overridden by the SSLCALocation parameter in the server configuration file.

The last three fields enable us to set up client authentication using a certificate. Zabbix supports all possible combinations of certificate, a key, and key password, such as a single unencrypted file, a completely separate certificate, and key and key password. The client certificate files must be placed in the directory specified by the SSLCertLocation parameter in the server configuration file. Key files, if any, must be placed in the directory specified by the SSLKeyLocation parameter in the server configuration file.

Using agent items

The web-scenario-based monitoring we just set up is quite powerful, but there might be cases where a more simple approach would be enough. On the agent level, there are some interesting item keys that allow us to retrieve web pages and perform simple verification. An additional benefit is the ability to do that from any agent, so it is very easy to check web page availability from multiple geographically-distributed locations. There are three web page-related item keys:

- web.page.get
- web.page.perf
- web.page.regexp

Also keep in mind the simpler item keys, such as net.tcp.service, which was discussed in Chapter 3, *Monitoring with Zabbix Agents and Basic Protocols*.

Getting the page

The simplest web page-related agent item key, `web.page.get`, allows us to retrieve page content. As with scenario-based web monitoring, it does not retrieve any included content, such as images. Let's create a simple item with this key:

1. Navigate to **Configuration | Hosts**, and select **Linux servers** in the **Group** drop-down
2. Click on **Items** next to **A test host**, and click on **Create item**. Fill in the following values:

    - **Name**: `Zabbix main page`
    - **Key**: `web.page.get[127.0.0.1,/zabbix/index.php]`
    - **Type of information**: **Text**
    - **New application**: `ZABBIX`

We are creating an agent item for our Zabbix server, which means that this web item will be checked by the local agent.

When done, click on the **Add** button at the bottom. In this item, we specified / as the second parameter, but that is optional by default; the `root` on the web server is requested. If there is a case where your web server is not running on the standard port, `80`, we can specify this as the third parameter:

```
web.page.get[www.site.lan,/,8080]
```

Instead of checking the results of each of the items we are creating individually, let's create all three items first and then verify the results.

 HTTPS, at this time is not supported, even when you specify the correct port.

Checking page performance

Another web page-related agent item is `web.page.perf`. It returns the loading time of the page in seconds. While still in the item list, click on **Create item**, and fill in the following:

- **Name**: `Zabbix main page load time`

- **Key**: `web.page.perf[127.0.0.1,/zabbix/index.php]`
- **Type of information**: **Numeric (float)**
- **Units**: s
- **Applications**: **ZABBIX**

When you've done that click on the **Add** button at the bottom. We changed **Type of information**, as this item key returns the time it took to load the page in seconds, and that value will usually consist of a decimal part.

Extracting content from web pages

When creating the web-monitoring scenario, we extracted content from a page to be reused later. With simpler agent monitoring, it's still possible to extract some content from a page. As a test, we could try to extract the text after `remembers me for` and up to `days`. Click on **Create item** again, and fill in the following:

- **Name**: `Zabbix remembers me for`
- **Key**: `web.page.regexp[127.0.0.1,/zabbix/index.php,,"Remember me for.(\d.)",,\1]`
- **Type of information**: **Character**
- **Applications**: **ZABBIX**

When you've done that click on the **Add** button at the bottom.

 The item key works with Zabbix server page contents at the time of writing. If the web page gets redesigned, consider it an extra challenge to adapt the regular expression.

For this item, we are extracting search results from the page directly. The important parameter here is the fourth one, it is a regular expression that will be matched in the page source. In this case, we are looking for the `remember me for` string and including two digits after it. When the regular expression contains a comma, it's best to double-quote it. A comma is the **item key parameter separator**, so it could be misinterpreted. Then, in the last parameter, we request only the contents of the first capture group are included. By default, the whole matched string is returned. For more details on value extraction with this method, refer to the *Log file monitoring* section in `Chapter 10`, *Advanced Item Monitoring*. We also chose **Type of information** as **Character**, which will limit the values to 255 symbols, just in case it matches a huge string.

For this key, the fifth parameter allows us to limit the length of the returned key. If you want to extract a number and send it over SMS, limiting the length of the extracted string to 50 characters would reduce the possibility of the message being too long.

A practical application of this item would be extracting statistics from an Apache web server when using `mod_status` or similar functionality with other server software.

None of the three `web.page.*` items supports HTTPS, authentication, or redirects at this time.

With the items configured, let's check their returned values—head to **Monitoring** | **Latest data**, clear out the **Host groups** field, select **Linux servers** in the **Hosts** field, and then click on **Filter**. Look for items in the Zabbix application:

Zabbix main page	2018-12-16 14:01:08	HTTP/1.1 200 OK ...		Hist...
Zabbix remembers me for	2018-12-16 14:01:10	30		Hist...
Zabbox main page load time	2018-12-16 14:01:09	61.4ms	+10ms	Graph

Each item requests the page separately.

The items should be returning full page contents, the time it took to load the page, and the result of our regular expression. The `web.page.get` item always includes headers, too. If you see empty values appearing every now and then in the `web.page.get` and `web.page.regexp` items, this is probably happens because the request has timed out. While web scenarios had their own timeout setting, the agent items obey the agent timeout of 3 seconds by default. The `web.page.perf` item returns 0 upon a timeout.

The Zabbix `web.page.get` item currently does not work properly with chunked transfer encoding, which is widely used. Extra data is inserted in the page contents. This was expected to be fixed in Zabbix 3.0, by using `libcurl` for these agent items as well, but that development was not finished. At the time of writing, it is not known when this will be fixed.

Using these items, we could trigger when a page takes too long to load, when it doesn't work at all, or when a specific string cannot be found on the page by using `str()` and similar trigger expressions either on the whole page item or on the content extraction item.

 Web scenarios are executed on the Zabbix server, agent items on the agent. We will discuss running web scenarios on remote systems in `Chapter 17`, *Using Proxies to Monitor Remote Locations*.

The items we created all went to the same Zabbix agent. We can also create a host with multiple interfaces and assign items to each interface. This allows us to check a web page from multiple locations but keep the results in a single host. We still have to make the item keys unique—if needed, either use the trick with empty key parameters, extra commas in key parameters, or key aliasing, discussed in `Chapter 20`, *Zabbix Maintenance*. Note that templates can't be used in such a setup.

Extracting content using the HTTP agent

If we need to monitor a web page over HTTPS, there could be another solution for the items we have seen for http. The HTTP agent is new in 4.0. This item type allows us to poll data using the HTTP/HTTPS protocol. Trapping is also possible, using the Zabbix sender or Zabbix sender protocol. Let's go to our host **A test host** go to items and click **Create item**:

- **Name**: `OpenStreetMap main page`
- **Type**: HTTP agent
- **Key**: `openstreetmap.main`
- **URL**: `https://www.openstreetmap.org/`
- **Required status codes**: `200`
- **Retrieve mode**: Headers
- **Type of information**: Text
- **New application**: OSM

Give the item some time, then go to **Monitoring | Latest data**, select **A test host** from the **Host** selection box, and click on **Apply**. We should now see the headers and the confirmation that our status code, 200, is OK:

The advantage of using this type of item is that we can make use of the **Preprocessing** tab, and that it supports HTTPS. There's much more this item can do, but that discussion is outside the scope of this book. At the end of this chapter, I have added some URLs that will give you more insight into this new item type.

Summary

In this chapter, we learned to monitor web pages based on various parameters, including response time, transfer speed, HTTP return code, and text contained in the page itself. We also learned how to set up multiple scenarios, and steps as well as setting up variables to be used in those steps. As a more advanced example, we logged in to the Zabbix frontend and logged out of it. For that to work, we extracted the session ID and reused it in subsequent steps. With this knowledge, it should be possible to monitor most of the functionality web pages have.

For production systems, there will usually be way more applications, scenarios, and steps. Web monitoring can be used for many different purposes, the most popular being site availability and performance, but there are many different cases you could monitor, including things such as watching the slashdot front page for a company name and replacing the usual first web page with a simpler one to withstand the coming load-slashdotting-easier.

As a simpler alternative, we explored web page items on the agent side. They have three features:

- Retrieving full page contents
- Finding out page load times
- Extracting a string from a page using regular expressions

Web scenarios are only available on the server side, while simpler items are only available on the agent side.

Having mostly concentrated on monitoring the Linux system so far, we'll leave that here and look at monitoring Windows in the next chapter. We'll look at the native agent for Windows, performance counter and **Windows Management Instrumentation** (WMI) monitoring, and service discovery and Windows Event Log monitoring.

Questions

1. Does Zabbix web monitoring allow us to create scenarios and can they skip steps?
2. Can user macros be used in my scenarios?
3. Is HTTPS supported in scenarios?
4. When using the new HTTP agent item, is there support for trapping?

Further reading

Check out the following articles for more information:

- **HTTP agent**: https://www.zabbix.com/documentation/4.0/manual/config/items/itemtypes/http
- **Web monitoring**: https://www.zabbix.com/documentation/4.0/manual/web_monitoring

High-Level Business Service
Monitoring

13

Monitoring IT systems usually involves poking at lots of small details: CPU, disk, memory statistics, process states, and a myriad of other parameters. All of these are very important, and every detail should be available to technical people. But in the end, the goal of these systems isn't to have enough disk space; the goal is to serve a specific need. If we only look at the low-level detail, it can be very hard to figure out what impact the current problem might have on users. Zabbix offers a way to have a higher-level view, called **IT services**. Relationships between individual systems can be configured to see how they build up to deliver services, and **Service Level Agreement (SLA)** calculation can be enabled for any part of the resulting tree.

We'll cover the following topics in this chapter:

- Deciding on the service tree
- Setting up IT services
- Viewing reports
- Specifying uptime and downtime

Deciding on the service tree

Before configuring things, it's useful to think through the setup, and doubly so with IT services. A large service tree might look impressive, but it might not represent the actual functionality well and might even obscure the real system state.

Disk space being low is important, but it doesn't actually bring the system down; it doesn't affect the SLA. The best approach likely would be to only include specific checks that identify a service being available or operating in an acceptable manner; for example, the SLA might require some performance level to be maintained. Unless we want to have a large, complicated IT service tree, we should identify key factors in delivering the service and monitor those.

What are the key factors? If the service is simple enough and can be tested easily, we could have a direct test. Maybe the SLA requires that a website is available; in that case, a simple `web.page.get` item would suffice. If it's a web page-based system, we might want to check the page itself, log in, and perform some operation as a logged in user; this is possible with web scenarios.

We discussed web monitoring in more detail in Chapter 12, *Monitoring Web Pages*.

Sometimes, it might not be possible to use the interface directly—maybe it isn't possible to have a special user for monitoring purposes, or we aren't allowed to connect to the actual interface. In that case, we should use lower-level monitoring, concentrating on the main pieces of the system that must be available. We should still attempt to have the highest-level checks possible. For example, we could check whether web server software is running, whether we can connect to a TCP port, and whether we can connect to the backend database from the frontend system. Memory or disk usage on the database system and database low-level health don't matter from the high-level monitoring point of view. It should all be monitored, of course, but having the delete query rate too high usually doesn't affect the top-level service. On the other hand, if a service goes down, we might be unable to see, in the same tree, that it happened because a disk filled up—but that's an operational failure, and we can expect that the personnel responsible are using such low-level triggers with proper dependencies to resolve the issue.

Setting up IT services

The best way to learn about a feature is to use it. We don't have any business services in our environment, so we could use a similar approach as with the network map link indicator feature, where we created *fake* items and triggers to simulate network issues. We'll create items and triggers that will act as high-level service monitors.

We'll invent two companies, called **Banana** and **Pineapple**. Our company will be hosting various services for these two companies:

- A code repository system for **Banana**
- A warehouse analytics system for **Pineapple**
- A ticketing system for **Banana** and **Pineapple**

Our service tree could look like this:

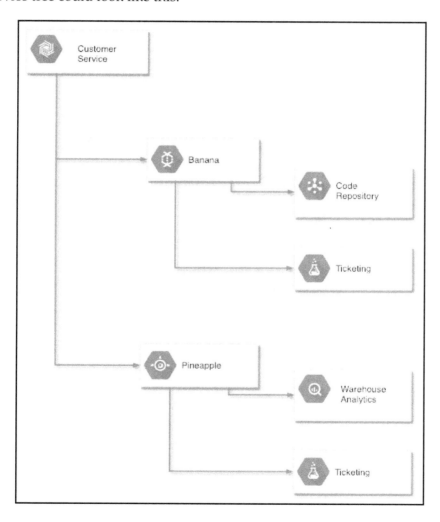

If everything is green at the top level, we know that all of our customers are happy. If not, we see which customer is having an issue with a system, and we can see which system is affected. The ticketing system going down would affect both customers. And anything below these services—well, that's operational monitoring.

Unfortunately, IT service functionality is not that easy to evaluate without collecting data for a longer period of time; SLA graphs are more interesting when we have data for a few weeks or more. Maybe we could send in data and pretend it's past data. Actually, we can do that. The small but great `zabbix_sender` tool, which we discussed in Chapter 10, *Advanced Item Monitoring*, allows us to specify a timestamp for each value. This means that we'll create Zabbix trapper items and push values to those.

Creating test items and triggers

Let's create some test items and triggers that we can use for our SLA's. Follow these steps:

1. Navigate to **Configuration | Hosts** and click on **Create host**. Normally, items such as these would reside in different hosts, but for our test setup a single host will be best. Enter IT services in the **Host name** and **Group** fields and make sure no other groups are selected in the **Groups** select box, then click on the **Add** button at the bottom.

2. Switch to **IT services** in the **Group** drop-down menu, click on **Items** next to **IT services**, then click on **Create item**. This way, we create three different items with these settings:

   - **Name:** Code repository service
   - **Type:** **Zabbix trapper**
   - **Key:** code_repo
   - **New application:** IT services

3. You can use the item cloning feature to create the remaining two items more rapidly. Use the **Applications** field instead of the **New application** field for the remaining items:

- **Name**: Warehouse analytics service
- **Type: Zabbix trapper**
- **Key**: warehouse_analytics
- **Application: IT services**

And for the last item, use the following:

- **Name**: Ticketing service
- **Type: Zabbix trapper**
- **Key**: ticketing
- **Application: IT services**

The final list of items should look like this:

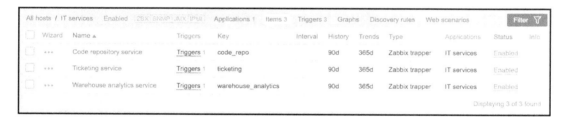

4. Now, click on **Triggers** in the navigation bar above the item list, then click on **Create trigger**. Create three triggers with their settings as follows. For the first trigger, enter the following:

- **Name**: Code repository down
- **Expression**: {IT services:code_repo.last()}=0
- **Severity: High**

For the second trigger, enter the following:

- **Name**: Warehouse analytics down
- **Expression**: {IT services:warehouse_analytics.last()}=0
- **Severity: High**

And for the third trigger, use the following:

- **Name**: `Ticketing down`
- **Expression**: `{IT services:ticketing.last()}=0`
- **Severity**: **High**

The result should look like this:

	Severity	Value	Name ▲	Expression	Status	Info	Tags
☐	High	OK	Code repository down	{IT services:code_repo.**last()**}=0	Enabled		
☐	High	OK	Ticketing down	{IT services:ticketing.**last()**}=0	Enabled		
☐	High	OK	Warehouse analytics down	{IT services:warehouse_analytics.**last()**}=0	Enabled		
						Displaying 3 of 3 found	

We didn't include the hostname in the trigger name here to keep them shorter; you'll likely want to do that for production systems.

In these triggers, the severity setting was very important. By default, triggers in Zabbix have the lowest severity, **Not classified**. SLA calculation in IT services ignores the two lowest severities, **Not classified** and **Information**. There doesn't seem to be a functional benefit from that, and the reasons are most likely historic. It's somewhat common for users to create quick testing triggers only to see that the SLA calculation doesn't work. When creating the trigger, the severity setting wasn't changed, as it is a relatively unimportant one for a quick test. Luckily, we knew about it and created triggers that will work in the SLA calculation.

Configuring IT services

We're getting closer to sending in our slightly fake data, but we must configure IT services before the data comes in. In Zabbix, SLA results cannot be calculated retroactively. IT services must be configured at the beginning of the period for which we want to collect the SLA. SLA state is stored separately from trigger and event information, and is calculated at runtime by the Zabbix server.

Let's go to **Configuration | Services**. The interface for managing **Services** is different from most other places in Zabbix. We have **root**, which is an immutable entry. All other service entries must be added as children to it. Click on **Add child** next to the root entry.

When clicking on an acceptable SLA in Zabbix, 99.9% is selected as the standard and not 100%

We'll start by grouping all customer services in an entry—we might have internal services later. In the **Name** field, enter `Customer services` and click on the **Add** button at the bottom.

We have two customers; click on **Add child** next to **Customer services**. Enter `Banana` in the **Name** field, enable the **Calculate SLA** checkbox, then click on **Add**.

Click on **Add child** next to **Customer services** again. Enter `Pineapple` in the **Name** field, enable the **Calculate SLA** checkbox, then click on **Add**. Notice how the **Customer services** entry can be expanded now. Expand it and observe the result, which should be like this:

The customers are in place; let's add their services now. Click on **Add child** next to **Banana**. Enter `Code repository` in the **Name** field and enable the **Calculate SLA** checkbox. This will be our *leaf* or lower-level service, and we'll now link it to a trigger. The trigger state will affect the SLA state for this service and for all upper-level services with SLA calculation enabled. Click on **Select** next to the **Trigger** field, then click on **Code repository down** in the **Name** column.

The final configuration for this service should look like this:

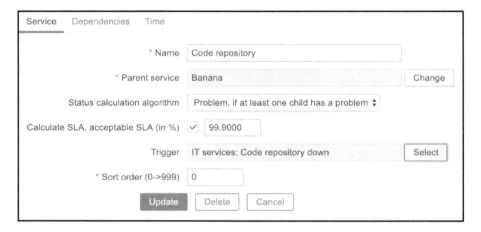

When done, click on **Add**. Then, click on **Add child** next to **Banana** again. Enter `Ticketing` in the **Name** field, enable the **Calculate SLA** checkbox, and click on **Select** next to the **Trigger** field, then click on **Ticketing down** in the **Name** column. Click on the **Add** button to add the second child service for this customer.

Our first customer is configured; now, click on **Add** child next to **Pineapple**. Enter `Warehouse analytics` in the **Name** field, enable the **Calculate SLA** checkbox, and click on **Select** next to the **Trigger** field. Click on **Warehouse analytics down** in the **NAME** column then click on the **Add** button.

We can add the ticketing service as another child service for `Pineapple`, but services here can also be defined once, then added at multiple places in the service tree. This is done by making parent services depend on additional services. Click on **Pineapple** and switch to the **Dependencies** tab. Notice how its only child service, **Warehouse analytics**, is already listed here. Click on the **Add** link and click on **Ticketing entry**. Click on the **Update** button:

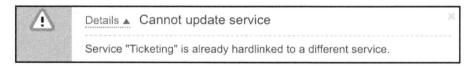

That didn't work well. If you're familiar with filesystem concepts, the error message might be a bit helpful; otherwise, it's probably a very confusing one. IT services in Zabbix have one hard link; they're attached to a parent service. To attach them to another service, we add them as a dependency, but we have to add them as a *soft link*, as only one *hard link* is allowed per service. Mark the **SOFT** checkbox next to **Ticketing** and click on **Update** again. This time, the operation should be successful and the **Ticketing entry** should now be visible for both companies.

 When deleting either a hard- or soft-linked entry, all occurrences of that service will be deleted.

If the entries are collapsed for you, expand them all and observe the final tree:

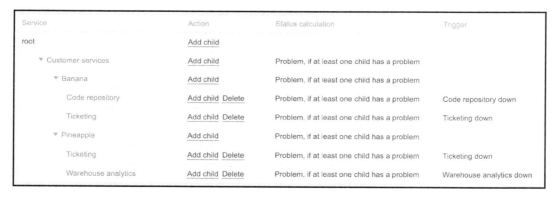

Service	Action	Status calculation	Trigger
root	Add child		
▼ Customer services	Add child	Problem, if at least one child has a problem	
▼ Banana	Add child	Problem, if at least one child has a problem	
Code repository	Add child Delete	Problem, if at least one child has a problem	Code repository down
Ticketing	Add child Delete	Problem, if at least one child has a problem	Ticketing down
▼ Pineapple	Add child	Problem, if at least one child has a problem	
Ticketing	Add child Delete	Problem, if at least one child has a problem	Ticketing down
Warehouse analytics	Add child Delete	Problem, if at least one child has a problem	Warehouse analytics down

Note that we enabled SLA calculation starting from the company level. Computing the total SLA across all customers is probably not a common need, although it could be done. In the **Status calculation** column, all of our services have **Problem, if at least one child has a problem**. In the **Service** properties, we could also choose **Problem, if all children have problems**. At this time, those are the only options for problem state propagation; setting the percentage or amount of child services isn't possible (it could be useful for a cluster solution, for example).

Sending in the data

Now is the time to send in our data, which will be a bit fake. As mentioned, IT services/SLA functionality is more interesting when we have data for a longer period of time, and we could try to send in data for a year. Of course, we won't create it manually—we'll generate it. Create a script like this on the Zabbix server:

```bash
#!/bin/bash
hostname="IT services"
time_period=$[3600*24*365] # 365 days
interval=3600 # one hour
probability=100
current_time=$(date "+%s")
for item_key in code_repo warehouse_analytics ticketing; do
        [[ -f $item_key.txt ]] && {
                echo "file $item_key.txt already exists"
                exit
        }
        for ((value_timestamp=$current_time-$time_period;
value_timestamp<$current_time;
value_timestamp=value_timestamp+$interval)); do
                echo "\"$hostname\" $item_key $value_timestamp
$([[ $(($RANDOM%$probability)) < 1 ]] && echo 0 ||
echo 1)" >> $item_key.txt
        done
done
```

This script will generate values for each of our three item keys every hour, for one year in the past, starting at the current time. For each entry, there's a small chance of getting a value of 0, which is failure. The result will be random, but it should fluctuate around our acceptable SLA level, so hopefully we'll get some services that do meet the SLA level and some that don't. As all of the values are sent in with a one-hour interval and it's quite unlikely that two failures would follow one another, no downtime should be longer than one hour. Assuming the script was saved as generate_values.sh, you just have to run it once:

$ ./generate_values.sh

Three files should be generated:

- code_repo.txt
- ticketing.txt
- warehouse_analytics.txt

The following could generate quite a lot of alert emails. If you would like to avoid that, disable the actions we added earlier.

Now run `zabbix_sender` for each of these files:

```
$ zabbix_sender -z 127.0.0.1 -T -i code_repo.txt
$ zabbix_sender -z 127.0.0.1 -T -i ticketing.txt
$ zabbix_sender -z 127.0.0.1 -T -i warehouse_analytics.txt
```

The output on each invocation should be similar to this:

```
info from server: "processed: 250; failed: 0; total: 250; seconds
spent: 0.001747"
...
info from server: "processed: 10; failed: 0; total: 10; seconds spent:
0.000063"
sent: 8760; skipped: 0; total: 8760
```

Zabbix sender processes up to `250` values per connection—refer to `Chapter 10`, *Advanced Item Monitoring*, for more details about this small, but great, utility.

If all of the preceding succeeded, great; we now have a year's worth of data.

Viewing reports

Finally, we're ready to see the results of all of the work done previously. Navigate to **Monitoring | Services** and you should see a report like this:

Service	Status	Reason	Problem time		SLA / Acceptable SLA
root					
▼ Customer services	OK				
▼ Banana	OK			1.1905	98.8095 / 99.9000
Code repository - Code repository down	OK			1.1905	98.8095 / 99.9000
Ticketing - Ticketing down	OK			0.0000	100.0000 / 99.9000
▼ Pineapple	OK			0.0000	100.0000 / 99.9000
Ticketing - Ticketing down	OK			0.0000	100.0000 / 99.9000
Warehouse analytics - Warehouse analytics down	OK			0.0000	100.0000 / 99.9000

It shows the current state of each service, the calculated SLA value, and whether it meets the projected value. In this example, out of three services, only one has met the SLA level—the **Warehouse analytics** service. You're most likely seeing a different result.

The bar doesn't actually represent **100%**—if you compare the value with how much of the bar is colored red, it doesn't seem to match. Move the mouse cursor over any of the bars to see why:

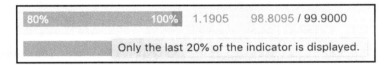

This bar only displays the last **20%**—for the SLA monitoring, we don't expect anything much below **80%** available and showing a smaller part of a full bar allows us to see the impact more.

What we are looking at right now is the report for **Last 7 days**, as can be seen in the upper-right corner. Expand the drop-down menu there and check the available options:

Play with the choices there and see how our random data either met or did not meet the expected SLA level. Unfortunately, at this time, it's not possible to generate such a report for an arbitrary period of time—if you want to see the SLA values for a specific week two months ago, you're out of luck.

There're several other reports slightly hidden on this page. Clicking on these options will give the following results:

- **Service name** will open the availability report for that service.
- **Trigger name** (if linked to the service) will open the event history for that trigger.
- The **SLA** bar will open a yearly availability graph for that service.

Let's click on **Banana** for now—this will open the availability report.

By default, it shows a weekly report for the current year. Let's switch to **Yearly** in the **Period** drop-down menu:

Service availability report: Banana					Period Yearly ⇕
Year	Ok	Problems Downtime		SLA	Acceptable SLA
2018	344d 5h 34m	7d 16h 0m		97.8213	99.9000
2017	364d 18h 0m	0d 6h 0m		99.9315	99.9000
2016	366d 0h 0m			100.0000	99.9000
2015	365d 0h 0m			100.0000	99.9000
2014	365d 0h 0m			100.0000	99.9000
2013	365d 0h 0m			100.0000	99.9000

This shows a report for the last five years, and that will almost always span six calendar years—which is why we get six entries. Here and elsewhere, Zabbix SLA calculation assumes that we'll get information about problems—if there's no information about any problem, Zabbix assumes that services were available for that period. In this page, we may also choose **Monthly**, **Weekly**, and **Daily** periods—for all of these, a year can be selected and data for all of the months, weeks, or days in that year will be displayed. When looking at the year list, we can observe that the years available are the same as in the yearly report—five years that span six calendar years:

If a trigger is linked to the service, clicking on the trigger name will show the event history for that trigger. We looked at the event view in Chapter 6, *Detecting Problems with Triggers*, so we won't spend more time on it here.

Now let's return to **Monitoring** | **Services** and click on one of the bars in the **Problem time** column. A yearly **SLA** graph is displayed:

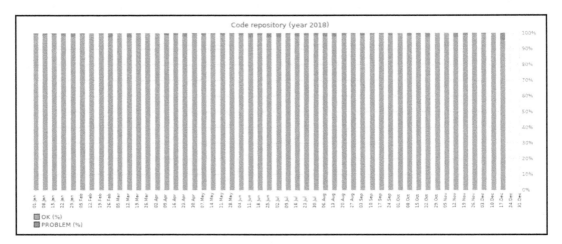

Each column represents one week. The time this service was down is displayed at the top, in red. Our service was mostly up, but we can see that there was a bit of downtime most weeks.

Both for the availability reports and the yearly graph, there's nothing to configure, and the time period can't be set to a custom time—we only have the predefined periods available here, and we can't customize SLA graph size or other parameters. For the yearly graph, we can only see the current year.

 There's no way to restrict access to IT service monitoring and reports—they're available for all users and normal permissions aren't taken into account here.

Specifying uptime and downtime

With SLA monitoring configured, we can happily proceed with making sure our systems run smoothly; we do some maintenance during a properly scheduled maintenance period, only to discover that our SLA level has dropped. *Were you sure downtime during maintenance periods wouldn't be counted against the SLA monitoring?* Wrong. Zabbix host and host group-level maintenance doesn't affect SLA monitoring. If something is down during such a maintenance, Zabbix still considers that as an unacceptable unavailability of the service.

Host and host group-level maintenance was discussed in `Chapter 5,` *Managing Hosts, Users, and Permissions*.

There's a way to avoid calculating SLA data for a specific period, though.

Let's go to **Configuration | Services** and click on **Code repository**. In the service properties, switch to the **Time** tab. Here, we can add three types of time periods:

- **Uptime**
- **Downtime**
- **One-time downtime**

Let's start with the simplest one—the **One-time downtime**. When adding a time period like that, we may enter a short description in the **Note** field, and we choose **From-Till** dates and times:

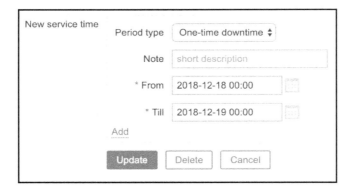

The note is not used for much, though—it's only displayed in the list of configured times, as shown in the preceding screenshot.

The **Downtime** option allows us to define times that will be excluded from the SLA calculation:

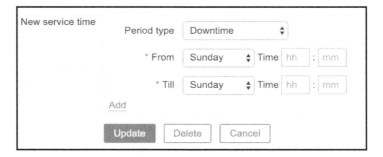

This is done on a weekly basis, where we may choose the weekday and time with minute precision. Unfortunately, here is the only place in Zabbix where a week sort of starts with **Sunday**. The biggest issue is that these periods can't cross the week border, hence it's actually impossible to add SLA calculation downtime for the weekend in one go—we would have to add one entry for **Saturday** and one for **Sunday**.

But what about the **Uptime** *option?* That one works in the reverse way. If an uptime entry is added, SLA calculation only happens during that time period; all other time is considered to be *downtime*.

Of course, when adding time periods here, we should obey the clauses from the actual agreement, not use this to hide problems from the SLA calculation, *right?*

Summary

In this chapter, we departed a bit from the low-level monitoring of CPU, disks, and memory. We discussed a higher level of monitoring, one that looked at business services, called IT services in Zabbix. We were able to configure a service tree to represent real-life dependencies and structures, link individual entries to triggers to propagate problem states to services, and configure SLA calculation for those services. We didn't have a large IT system to test against, so we sent in fake data and observed the resulting reports, including a service availability report and yearly SLA graph.

We noted two important facts about IT service functionality in Zabbix:

- Triggers with a severity of **Not classified** or **Information** are ignored when calculating the SLA.
- SLA information can't be calculated at a later time—the IT services must be configured in advance.

For those cases when a service doesn't have full-time SLA coverage, we learned about a way to specify when the SLA calculation should take place based on weekly time periods—but we also noted that host and host group-level maintenance doesn't affect the SLA calculation and the uptime/downtime configuration has to be done for the IT services themselves.

In the next chapter, we'll go back to lower-level monitoring—even lower than before. We'll cover monitoring hardware directly using the **Intelligent Platform Management Interface** (**IPMI**). Zabbix supports monitoring both normal and analog IPMI sensors, and discrete IPMI sensors. There's even a special trigger function for discrete sensors. *What is it?* See the next chapter for details.

Questions

1. Are services exportable to PDF?
2. Can I calculate my services from the beginning of the year when I configure **Services** at the end of the year?
3. Are maintenance windows taken out of service reports?

Further reading

Read the following articles for more information:

- **Service monitoring**: https://www.zabbix.com/documentation/4.0/manual/it_services
- **Services**: https://www.zabbix.com/documentation/4.0/manual/web_interface/frontend_sections/monitoring/it_services

14
Monitoring IPMI Devices

By now, we are familiar with monitoring using Zabbix agents, SNMP, and several other methods. While SNMP is very popular and available on the majority of network-attached devices, there's another protocol that is aimed at system management and monitoring: **Intelligent Platform Management Interface** (**IPMI**). IPMI is usually implemented as a separate management and monitoring module, independent of the host operating system, that can also provide information when the machine is powered down. IPMI is becoming more and more popular, and Zabbix has direct IPMI support. IPMI is especially popular on so-called **lights-out** or **out-of-band** management cards, available for most server hardware available today. As such, it might be desirable to monitor the status of hardware directly from these cards, as that does not depend on the operating system type, or even whether it's running at all.

In this chapter, we will cover the following topics:

- Getting an IPMI device
- Preparing for IPMI monitoring
- Setting up IPMI items
- Monitoring discrete sensors

Getting an IPMI device

For this section, you will need an IPMI-enabled device, usually a server with a remote management card. The examples here will use real hardware that could have vendor-specific quirks, but it should be possible to apply the general principles to any product from any vendor.

Preparing for IPMI monitoring

To gather data using IPMI, Zabbix must be configured accordingly, and the device must accept connections from Zabbix. If you installed Zabbix from packages, IPMI support should be available. If you compiled Zabbix Server from source, OpenIPMI library support should be included as well. To be sure, check the startup messages in the server log file. Make sure the line about IPMI says `YES`:

```
IPMI monitoring:            YES
```

That is not enough yet—by default, Zabbix server is configured to not start any IPMI pollers; thus, any added IPMI items won't work. To change this, open `zabbix_server.conf` and look for the following line:

```
# StartIPMIPollers=0
```

Uncomment it and set the poller count to 3, so that it reads as follows:

```
StartIPMIPollers=3
```

Save the file and restart `zabbix_server`.

On the monitored device side, add a user that Zabbix can use. The IPMI standard specifies various privilege levels, and for monitoring, the user level might be the most appropriate. The configuration of IPMI users could be done using the vendor-supplied command-line tools, the web interface, or using some other method. Consult vendor-specific documentation for details on this step.

Setting up IPMI items

Before we can add IPMI items to Zabbix, we should test the IPMI access. By default, IPMI uses UDP port 623, so make sure it is not blocked by a firewall. Check whether your Zabbix server has the `ipmitool` package installed—if not, install it, and then execute the following:

```
$ ipmitool -U zabbix -H <IP address of the IPMI host> -I lanplus -L
user sdr
Password:
```

Provide the password that you set in the IPMI configuration. We are using user-level access, as specified by the `-L user` flag, so that administrative privileges should not be required for the Zabbix IPMI user. The `-I lanplus` flag instructs `ipmitool` to use the IPMI v2.0 LAN interface, and the `sensor` command queries the host for the available sensors. If your device has IPMI running on a non-default port, you can specify the port with the `-p` flag.

 Zabbix does not use `ipmitool` to query IPMI devices; it uses the OpenIPMI library instead. This library historically has had a few bugs, and a working `ipmitool` instance does not guarantee that IPMI monitoring will work with Zabbix server. When in doubt, test with the latest version of OpenIPMI.

The output will contain a bunch of sensors, possibly including the following:

```
BB +5.0V        | 4.97 Volts    | ok
Baseboard Temp  | 23 degrees C  | ok
System Fan 2    | 3267 RPM      | ok
Power Unit Stat | 0x00          | ok
```

That looks like useful data, so let's try to monitor the fan's RPM in Zabbix. Do the following in the frontend:

1. Navigate to **Configuration | Hosts**. To keep things organized, let's create a new host for our IPMI monitoring—click on **Create host**, and then enter the following values:

    - **Name**: IPMI host.
    - **Groups**: Click on **Select** and choose **Linux servers**, or type it in the **Groups** box and select the group when it shows up.
    - **IPMI interfaces**: Click on the **Add** control and enter the IPMI address, and then click on **Remove** next to **Agent interfaces**.

 Some IPMI solutions work on the primary network interface, intercepting IPMI requests. In such cases, simply set the same IP address to be used for IPMI.

2. Switch to the **IPMI** tab, and enter the following values:

    - **IPMI username**: Enter the username used for IPMI access
    - **IPMI password**: Enter the password you set for IPMI access

If you set a long IPMI password, you will see an error that the max allowed password field is 20 characters, as shown in the following screenshot. This is normal, as the maximum password length for IPMI v2.0 is 20 characters:

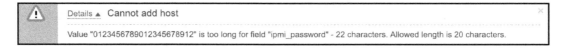

Details ▲ Cannot add host ✕

Value "0123456789012345678912" is too long for field "ipmi_password" - 22 characters. Allowed length is 20 characters.

3. If you have a different configuration for IPMI, such as a different privilege level or port, set them appropriately. When done, click on the **Add** button at the bottom.

For this host, we reused the **Linux servers** group—feel free to add it in a separate group.

Creating an IPMI item

Now that we have the host part of IPMI connectivity sorted out, it's time to create actual items. Make sure **Linux servers** is selected in the **Group** drop-down, then click on **Items** next to the **IPMI host**, and then click on **Create item**. Enter these values:

- **Name:** System Fan 2 (or, if your IPMI-capable device does not provide such a sensor, choose another useful sensor)
- **Type:** **IPMI agent**
- **Key:** System_Fan_2
- **IPMI sensor:** System Fan 2
- **Units:** !RPM

When done, click on the **Add** button at the bottom.

Even though the previous unit blacklist in Zabbix still works, it is now deprecated. So, the correct way to prevent the conversion of these units is now !ms, !rpm, !RPM, !%.

For this item type, the item key is only used as an item identifier, and we could enter any string in there. We opted to use the sensor name with spaces replaced by underscores to make it easier to identify the item in trigger expressions and other places. The IPMI sensor name will determine what data will be collected.

On some devices, the sensor name could have a trailing space. This is not obvious from the default sensor output in `ipmitool`. If the sensor name seems correct but querying it from Zabbix fails, try to retrieve data for a single sensor from the Zabbix server:

```
$ ipmitool -U zabbix -H <IP address of the IPMI host> -I lanplus -L
user sensor get "System Fan 2"
```

This will print detailed information for that sensor. If it fails, the sensor name is probably incorrect.

Let's check out the results of our work; open **Monitoring** | **Latest data** and then select **IPMI host** in the filter:

NAME ▲	LAST CHECK	LAST VALUE
- **other** - (1 Item)		
System Fan 2	2016-05-18 12:26:49	3348 RPM

Notice how the value is displayed fully and is not shortened to 3.3K. The !RPM unit is still included in a hardcoded unit blacklist, and items that use such units do not get the unit multiplier prefix added, but it's best to use the ! as this is the new way of blacklisting, plus it allows us to be more flexible. We will discuss the unit blacklist in more detail in `Chapter 20`, *Zabbix Maintenance*.

Great! The hardware state information is being gathered correctly. What's even better, this information is retrieved independently of the installed operating system or specific agents, and is retrieved even if there is no operating system running, or even installed.

 There is no built-in low-level discovery support at this time. If you would like to discover available sensors, it might be best done with an external check or Zabbix trapper item type for the low-level discovery rule itself.

Monitoring discrete sensors

The sensor list shows some sensors where the value is quite clear, such as for temperatures and fan RPMs. Some of these can be a bit trickier, though. For example, your sensor listing could have a sensor called `Power Unit Stat` or something similar. These are discrete sensors. You might think that they return 0 for an **OK** state and 1 for **Failure**, but they're usually more complicated than that. For example, the power unit sensor can actually return information about eight different states in one retrieved value.

Let's try to monitor it and see what value we can get in Zabbix for such a system:

1. Navigate to **Configuration | Hosts**, click on **Items** next to **IPMI host**, and click on **Create item**. Fill in the following:

   - **Name**: `Power Unit Stat` (or, if your IPMI-capable device does not provide such a sensor, choose another useful sensor)
   - **Type: IPMI agent**
   - **Key**: `Power_Unit_Stat`
   - **IPMI sensor**: `Power Unit Stat`

2. When done, click on the **Add** button at the bottom.

 If normal sensors work but discrete ones do not, make sure you try with the latest version of the OpenIPMI library. Discrete sensors in OpenIPMI-2.0.16, 2.0.17, and 2.0.18 often have an additional 0 (or some other digit or letter) appended at the end.

Check this item in the **Latest data** section—it will likely return 0. But *what could it return?* It's actually a decimal representation of a binary value, where each bit could identify a specific state, most often a failure. For this sensor, the possible states are listed in *Intelligent Platform Management Interface Specification Second Generation v2.0*.

 The latest version of this specification can be found at `http://www.intel.com/content/www/us/en/servers/ipmi/ipmi-ho me.html`.

According to that specification, the meanings of the individual hex values are as follows:

00h	Power off/Power down
01h	Power cycle
02h	240 VA Power down
03h	Interlock power down
04h	AC lost/power input lost (the power source for the power unit was lost)
05h	Soft power control failure (the unit did not respond to a request to turn on)
06h	Power unit failure detected
07h	Predictive failure

Looking at the description of the first bit, a binary value of 0 means that the unit is running and reports no problems. A binary value of 1 means that the unit is powered down. We could compare the returned value to 0, and that would indicate that everything is fine with the unit, but *what if we want to check some other bit, such as predictive failure?* If only that bit were set, the item would return 128. As mentioned before, discrete items return a decimal representation of the binary value. The original binary value is 10000000 (or 07h in the previous table), where the eighth bit, counting from the least significant, is set. By the way, this is also the reason why we left the **Type of information** field as **Numeric (unsigned)** and **Data type** as **Decimal** for this item—although the actual meaning is encoded in a binary representation, the value is transmitted as a decimal integer.

Thus, to check for a predictive failure, we could compare the value to 128, *couldn't we?* No, not really. If the system is down and reports a predictive value, the original binary value would be 10000001, and the decimal value would be 129. It gets even messier when we start to include other bits in there. This is also the reason it's not possible to use value mapping for such items at this time—in some cases, a value could mean all bits are set, and there would have to be a value-mapping entry for every possible bit combination. Oh, and we cannot detect a system being down just by checking for a value of 1—a value of 129 and a whole bunch of other values would also mean that.

If we can't compare the last value in a simple way, *can we reasonably check these discrete sensor values at all?* Luckily, yes; Zabbix provides a bitwise trigger function called band(), which was originally implemented specifically for discrete IPMI sensor monitoring.

Using the bitwise trigger function

The special `band()` function is somewhat similar to the simple `last()` function, but instead of just returning the last value, it applies a bitmask with a bitwise AND to the value and returns the result of this operation. If we wanted to check for the least significant bit, the one that lets us know whether the unit is powered on, we would use a bitmask of 1. Assuming some other bits have been set, we could receive a value of `170` from the monitored system. In binary, that would be `10101010`. Bitwise AND would multiply each bit down as shown in the column :

	Decimal value	Binary value
Value	170	10101010
Bitwise AND (multiplied down)		
Mask	1	00000001
Result	0	00000000

The general syntax for the `band()` trigger function is as follows:

```
band(#number|seconds,mask)
```

 It also supports a third parameter, `time shift`—we discussed time shifts in `Chapter 6`, *Detecting Problems with Triggers*.

When thinking about binary representation, we have to use decimal numbers in Zabbix. In this case, it is simple – the trigger expression would be as follows:

```
{host:item.band(#1,1)}=1
```

We are checking the last value received with `#1`, applying a decimal mask of `1`, and verifying whether the last bit is set.

As a more complicated example, let's say we wanted to check for bits (starting from the least significant) 3 and 5, and we received a value of `110` (in decimal):

	Decimal value	Binary value
Value	110	01101110
Bitwise AND (multiplied down)		
Mask	20	00010100
Result	4	00000100

A simple way to think about the operation of the mask would be that all the bits that match a 0 in the mask are set to 0, and all other bits pass through it as is. In this case, we are interested in whether both bits 3 and 5 are set, so the expression would be as follows:

```
{host:item.band(#1,20)}=20
```

In our value, only bit 3 was set, and the resulting value from the function was 4, which does not match 20—neither bits are set, so the trigger expression evaluates to FALSE. If we wanted to check for bit 3 being set and bit 5 not being set, we would compare the result to 4. And if we wanted to check for bit 3 not being set and bit 5 being set, we would compare it to 16—because in binary that's 00010000.

Now let's get back to checking for the predictive failure bit being set—it was the eighth bit, so, our mask should be 10000000, and we should compare the result to 10000000. But both of these should be in decimal format, so we should set both the mask and comparison values to 128.

Let's create a trigger in the frontend with this knowledge:

1. Go to **Configuration | Hosts**, click on **Triggers** next to **IPMI host**, and click on **Create trigger**.
2. Enter Power unit predictive failure on {HOST.NAME} in the **Name** field, and then click on **Add** next to the **Expression** field.
3. Click on **Select** next to the **Item** field, and then choose Power Unit Stat.
4. Set the **Function** drop-down to **Bitwise AND of last (most recent) T value and mask = N**, enter 128 in both the **Mask** and **N** fields, and then click on **Insert**. The resulting trigger expression should be as follows:

```
{IPMI host:Power_Unit_Stat.band(,128)}=128
```

Notice *how the first function parameter is missing?* As with the last() function, omitting this parameter is equal to setting it to #1, as in the earlier examples. This trigger expression will ignore the 7 least significant bits and check whether the result is set to 10000000 in binary, or 128 in decimal.

Bitwise comparison is possible with the count() function, too. Here, the syntax is potentially more confusing: both the pattern and mask are to be specified as the second parameter, separated by a slash. If the pattern and mask are equal, the mask can be omitted. Let's try to look at some examples to clear this up.

For example, to count how many values had the eighth bit set during the previous 10 minutes, the function part of the expression would be as follows:

```
count(10m,128,band)
```

Our pattern and mask were the same, so we could omit the mask part. The previous expression is equivalent to the following:

```
count(10m,128/128,band)
```

If we would like to count how many values had bit 5 set and bit 3 not set during the previous 10 minutes, the function part of the expression would be as follows:

```
count(10,16/20,band)
```

Here, the pattern is 16 or 10000, and the mask is 20 or 10100.

Beware of adding too many IPMI items against a single system—it is very easy to overload the IPMI controller.

With the release of Zabbix 4.0, it's now possible to use `id:` and `name:` in the IPMI sensor field:

- `name:` allows us to specify the sensor by its full name instead of its short name
- `id:` gives us the option to specify the ID of the specific sensor we would like to monitor

All of this information can easily be found in the Zabbix server log file. For this, it's best to start the Zabbix server in debug level 4.

Summary

IPMI, while not yet as widespread as SNMP, can provide software-independent hardware monitoring for some devices, usually servers. It is becoming more and more popular as an out-of-band monitoring and management solution that can help us watch over hardware states for compliant devices.

Zabbix supports monitoring normal sensors, such as voltage, RPM, or temperature, as well as discrete sensors that can pack a lot of information into a single integer. To decrypt the information hidden in that integer, Zabbix offers a special trigger function, called `band()`, which enables us to do bitwise masking and matching specific bits.

IPMI, covered in this chapter, is at a fairly low level in the system stack. In the next chapter, we will discuss ways to monitor Java applications using the JMX protocol. Zabbix supports JMX through a dedicated process called the Zabbix Java gateway, which we will set up.

Questions

1. What do I have to write in the IPMI sensor field in my item?
2. Can I make use of LLD to discover my IPMI items?

Further reading

Read the following article for more information:

- **IPMI checks:** https://zabbix.com/documentation/current/manual/config/items/itemtypes/ipmi

15
Monitoring Java Applications

Among all the other features that Zabbix can query directly is monitoring Java application servers using the **Java Management Extensions (JMX)** protocol. Actually, it's not just application servers—other server software written in Java can be monitored as well. Even standalone Java applications can be monitored, as the JMX framework does not have to be implemented by application developers—it is provided with Java. The main Zabbix daemons are written in C, but the JMX protocol is somewhat complicated, especially all the authorization and encryption methods. Thus, a separate component is used for JMX monitoring: the Zabbix Java gateway. This gateway runs as a separate process and queries JMX interfaces on behalf of the Zabbix server.

In this chapter, we'll set up the Java gateway and monitor a simple property on it. We'll cover the following topics:

- Setting up the Zabbix Java gateway
- Monitoring JMX items
- Querying JMX items manually
- JMX discovery

Setting up the Zabbix Java gateway

Let's start by getting the gateway up and running. If you installed from packages, there's likely a Java gateway package available; just install that one. If you installed from source, the Java gateway can be compiled and installed by running the following from the Zabbix source directory:

```
$ ./configure --enable-java && make install
```

If the compilation fails because it is unable to find `javac`, you might be missing Java development packages. The package name could be similar to `java-1_8_0-openjdk-devel`. Consult your distribution's documentation for the exact package name.

By default, when compiling from source, Zabbix Java gateway files are placed in the `/usr/local/sbin/zabbix_java` directory. From here on, we will use files found in that directory. If you installed from packages, consult the package configuration information to locate those files. The configuration file can probably be found at `/etc/zabbix/zabbix_java_gateway.conf`.

Let's try something simple: just starting up the gateway. Go to the Java gateway directory and run the following:

```
# ./startup.sh
```

The Zabbix Java gateway comes with a convenient startup script, which we used here. If all went well, you should see no output, and a Java process should appear in the process list. Additionally, the gateway should listen on port `10052`. While this port is not an officially-registered port for the Zabbix Java gateway, it's just one port above the Zabbix trapper port, and there does not seem to be any other application using that port. With the gateway running, we still have to tell Zabbix server where the gateway can be found. Open `zabbix_server.conf` and look for the `JavaGateway` parameter. By default, it is not set, and we have to configure the gateway IP or hostname here. As we can point the server at a remote system, we are not required to run the Java gateway on the same system as where Zabbix server is located, in some cases, we might want to place the gateway closer to the Java application server, such as by setting this parameter to the localhost IP address:

```
JavaGateway=127.0.0.1
```

Right below in our config file is a parameter called `JavaGatewayPort`. By default, it is set to `10052`, which is the same unregistered port as our running gateway already listens on—so we won't change that. The next parameter is `StartJavaPollers`. As with IPMI pollers, no Java pollers are started by default. We won't hammer our Java gateway much, so enable a single Java poller as follows:

```
StartJavaPollers=1
```

With this, Zabbix server should be sufficiently configured. Restart it to apply the Java gateway configuration changes. Great! We have the gateway running, and Zabbix server knows where it is. Now, we just need something to monitor. If you have a Java application server that you can use for testing, try monitoring it. If not, or for something simpler to start with, you could monitor the gateway itself. It is a Java application, and thus, the JMX infrastructure is available. There's one thing we should change before enabling JMX for the gateway. Java is quite picky about DNS and name resolution in general. If JMX functionality is enabled and the local system hostname does not resolve, Java applications are likely to fail to start up. For a local Java gateway, check the /etc/hosts file. If there is no entry for the current hostname, add the following line:

```
127.0.0.1 testhost
```

We're ready to enable JMX functionality for the gateway now; it is not enabled by default. To enable JMX on the Zabbix Java gateway, edit the startup.sh (or zabbix_java_gateway.conf) script we used earlier, and look for the following line:

```
# uncomment to enable remote monitoring of the standard JMX objects on
the Zabbix Java Gateway itself
```

As the first line says, uncomment the two lines following it.

A single variable is assigned across two lines in this script !

One parameter in there is worth paying extra attention to, as follows:

```
-Dcom.sun.management.jmxremote.port=12345
```

This sets the JMX port, the one that the gateway itself will query. Yes, in this case, we will start a process that will connect to itself on that port to query JMX data. The port is definitely not a standard one, as you might guess, it's just a sequence of 12345. Other Java applications will most likely use a different port, which you will have to find out by yourself.

If you installed from packages, a recent package should include the same lines in the `init` script. If not, consider reporting that to the package maintainers, and use the following parameters in addition to the `port` parameter, listed in the previous code:

```
-Dcom.sun.management.jmxremote
-Dcom.sun.management.jmxremote.authenticate=false
-Dcom.sun.management.jmxremote.ssl=false
```

The first parameter tells Java to enable JMX, and the last two parameters instruct Java not use any authentication or encryption.

> In previous versions, JMX functionality in the Zabbix gateway didn't work with Java 1.9. If this happens, the solution is to downgrade to Java 1.8. I was unable to find any reference in the Zabbix manual about this in 4.0

With this change done, run the shutdown and startup scripts:

```
# ./shutdown.sh
# ./startup.sh
```

We are finally ready to add actual hosts and JMX items.

> You should always check the log files for errors on the server side and the Java gateway side. You will quickly notice if there are communication issues. Both log files can be found under `/var/log/zabbix/`, if you installed from packages.

Monitoring JMX items

Let's create a separate host for JMX monitoring:

1. Navigate to **Configuration | Hosts** and click on **Create host**
2. Enter `Zabbix Java gateway` in the **Host name** field, clear everything in the **Groups** box, enter `Java` in the **Groups** field, and then select **Java (new)**
3. Remove the default agent interface and click on **Add** next to **JMX interfaces**

In our case, the gateway is running on the localhost, so we can leave the IP address as the default, `127.0.0.1`. *But what about the port?* We had the Java gateway listen on `10052`, but then there was also port `12345` in the `startup.sh` script. If any confusion arises, we should think about which functionality is available on each of these ports. On port `10052`, we had the gateway itself, which was the port Zabbix server connects to. We already saw this port set in the server configuration file. Normally, the gateway would then connect to some other Java application to query JMX information:

Port `12345` was in the lines we uncommented in the gateway's `startup.sh` script, and that was the JMX interface for the gateway. That was also what we wanted to monitor—our Java application. After the Zabbix server connects to the Java gateway on port `10052`, we expect the gateway to connect to itself, on port `12345`:

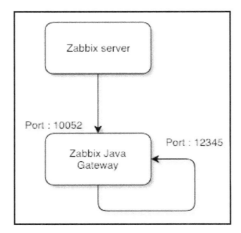

Thus, in the host interface, we would want to use port 12345 and surprise—that is also the default:

The JMX system can actually return a different IP address and port that the JMX querying client should connect to. Zabbix uses Java functionality that automatically obeys this information, but in some cases, it can be wrong. If you see error messages and the Zabbix Java gateway seems to connect to a different address or port than the one configured in the host properties, check the configuration of the target Java application, specifically the Djava.rmi.server.hostname and Dcom.sun.management.jmxremote.rmi.port parameters.

The rest of the host configuration should be sufficient for our need—click on the **Add** button at the bottom. Now, make sure **Java** is selected in the **Group** drop-down, click on **Items** next to **Zabbix Java gateway**, and click on **Create item**. Enter the following data:

- **Name:** Used heap memory
- **Type:** JMX agent
- **Key:** jmx[java.lang:type=Memory,HeapMemoryUsage.used]
- **Units:** B

When done, click on the **Add** button at the bottom. Check this item in the latest data section after a few minutes—it should be collecting values successfully.

Querying JMX items manually

Creating items on the server and then waiting for them to be updated through the gateway can be quite cumbersome if we don't know the exact parameters beforehand. We could query the gateway manually using netcat and similar tools, but that's not that easy either. There was an easier method with zabbix_get, but since 3.0.7, zabbix_get can no longer be used to query data from the Zabbix Java gateway.

There are some good community solutions, which can be found at https://www.zabbix.org/wiki/Docs/howto/zabbix_get_jmx.

Another good solution is to use tools such as JConsole. This tool comes with the standard JDK.

Let's connect to the JMX interface by just running `jconsole` and in the **Remote Process** field, add the IP and the port to connect to our machine. Keep the username and password empty, as we configured our Java gateway with the `authenticate=false` option. For other applications, you should add a password in your production environment:

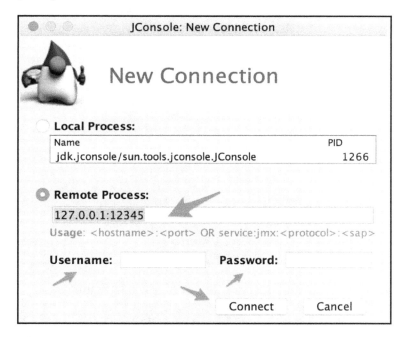

When you are finished, click on **Connect** and ignore the warning about SSL.

Let's have a look where we can find our **HeapMemoryUsage** item:

1. Click on **MBeans** | **java.lang** | **Memory** | **HeapMemoryUsage**.
2. In the right-hand pane, you can see the attribute value with
   the **HeapMemoryUsage** name and the
   `javax.management.openmbean.CompositeDataSupport` value:

This is not telling us much, so let's double-click on the value,
`javax.management.openmbean.CompositeDataSupport`. A box will
open and show us the possible names with their respective values. In the
following screenshot we will see a list of items that can be used with there
respective values. The value from that item should match with what we
monitored in our JMX item used heap memory attribute, for example we
can monitor **HeapMemoryUsage** committed, init max or used values in this
case.

What to monitor?

With a Java application server, monitoring is not initiated by the actual Java application developers often enough. Also quite often it's not clear what would be a good set of things to monitor first. In general, the same advice applies as with any other system: somebody who knows the monitored application should determine what is monitored. It's even better if the available Java developers are reasonable and actually implement additional JMX items to monitor application-specific logic. If that isn't easy to achieve, you can always start with a basic set of memory usage, thread count, garbage collector, and other generic metrics. Here are a few potentially useful parameters:

- `jmx["java.lang:type=ClassLoading","LoadedClassCount"]`: How many classes have been loaded

- `jmx["java.lang:type=Memory",NonHeapMemoryUsage.used]`: We already monitored the heap memory usage on the gateway; this will monitor the non-heap memory usage

In general, it's hard to suggest a static list of things to monitor for JMX—there are several garbage collectors, and exact keys for garbage-collection monitoring will differ depending on which one is in use. Zabbix also provides a couple of templates out of the box for generic and Tomcat-specific JMX monitoring, which could be a good start.

What if we want to use multiple Java gateways—maybe one at each data center, or even one on each Java application server so that JMX connections do not happen over the network? Zabbix server only supports a single Zabbix gateway. Attaching multiple Java gateways to a single server is actually possible using Zabbix proxies, but we will discuss that in `Chapter 17`, *Using Proxies to Monitor Remote Locations*.

> Since Zabbix 3.4, it is also possible to use custom JMX endpoints in the item. This allows us to monitor applications such as JBoss. Endpoints are set per item, so it is also possible to monitor multiple Java applications on one host with different endpoints.

JMX discovery

As we saw in the *What to monitor?* section, it's not always easy to monitor JMX items. As an example, Java has different garbage collectors and they can even change during the lifetime of the application, as it is the developer who decides what garbage collector fits best. Here, **low-level discovery** (**LLD**) comes to the rescue. Instead of creating a template with all possible combinations and seeing unsupported items all over our machines, we just discover what is on our hosts.

Let's go to our host Zabbix Java gateway and discover all garbage collectors:

1. Go to **Configuration | Hosts**
2. Select **Java** from the **Group** selection box
3. Click on **Discovery** behind the Zabbix Java gateway host
4. Click on **Create discovery rule** in the upper-right corner

Let's create our global discovery rule by adding the following:

- **Name**: `Global JMX Discovery Rule`
- **Type**: **JMX agent**
- **Key**:
  `jmx.discovery[beans,"java.lang:type=GarbageCollector,name=*"]`
- **Update interval**: `300s`

When ready, click the **Add** button:

Next, we have to create our discovery item as we only have our global discovery rule. As you can see, we added in the key to discover beans. We could have added attributes here as well.

This is the list of items we can select:

- Attributes (retrieve JMX MBean attributes, default)
- Beans (retrieve JMX MBeans)

We could also replace `java.lang:type` with `*:type,`the other garbage collectors not under `java.lang` would also be discovered. Try not to add only an `*` to do a global search but look for a specific type , such as in our case, garbage collectors, else this will cost you lots of resources.

Time to create our discovery item; let's go to **Item prototype | Create item prototype**. Add the following parameters in our item:

- **Name**: `java.gc {#JMXOBJ}-CollectionCount`
- **Type**: **JMX agent**
- **Key**: `jmx[{#JMXOBJ},CollectionCount]`
- **Type of information**: **Numeric (unsigned)**
- **New application prototype**: `{#JMXDESC}`

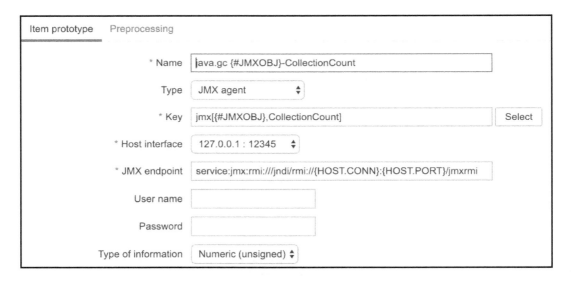

Give it some time, then go to **Monitoring | Latest data** and select **Zabbix Java gateway** in **Host**:

As you can see, we now have the latest data for the collection count for our garbage collectors configured on the machine. In our case, the **MarkSweepCompact** and **Copy** Garbage Collectors were detected.

Because we added the `{#JMXDESC}` macro in the new application prototype, we now have a new item in the latest data for every newly-detected JMX object visible like in the preceding screenshot.

Zabbix maintains a list of supported macros for JMX LLD with a perfect explanation of what every macro does. This information can be found at `https://zabbix.com/documentation/4.0/manual/discovery/low_level_discovery/jmx#supported_macros`.

> Since Zabbix 4.0.0, it's possible to work with custom MBeans that return non-primitive data types, which override the `toString()` method.

Summary

Java is sometimes called the *king of the enterprise*. It's so popular in large systems, despite often-cited drawbacks, such as memory usage, that one might wonder what makes it so attractive. One reason could be that it lowers maintenance costs—at least, that is claimed sometimes, and it would make a lot of sense in large, long-life systems. Developing a system is usually cheap compared to maintaining it over a long period of time. Given the widespread usage of Java-based systems, the built-in JMX support is very handy—except maybe the limiting endpoint support. In this chapter, we looked at setting up a separate daemon, called the Zabbix Java gateway, and performing the initial configuration to make it work with a Zabbix server. We also monitored heap memory usage on the gateway itself, and that should be a good start for JMX monitoring. For easier debugging, we looked at some scripts and the use of `jconsole`. We noticed that monitoring Java can be difficult, as many different items can exist on the same Java version, for example: garbage collectors. We saw how we can solve this problem with the use of LLD items for JMX.

Lately, we have been discussing the monitoring of somewhat niche products and protocols. The next chapter will continue that trend—we will discuss the built-in VMware monitoring that enables us to discover and monitor all virtual machines from a hypervisor or a vCenter.

Questions

1. Can I install multiple Java gateways?
2. Are JMX items processed by the Zabbix agent or the Zabbix server?
3. What ports do we need to open for JMX monitoring?

Further reading

Check out the following articles for more information:

- **JMX monitoring**: `https://zabbix.com/documentation/current/manual/config/items/itemtypes/jmx_monitoring`
- **Java gateway**: `https://zabbix.com/documentation/4.0/manual/concepts/java`
- **Docs/howto/zabbix get jmx**: `https://www.zabbix.org/wiki/Docs/howto/zabbix_get_jmx`
- **Discovery of JMX objects**: `https://zabbix.com/documentation/4.0/manual/discovery/low_level_discovery/jmx`

16
Monitoring VMware

There are a lot of virtualization solutions available today. Their target markets and popularity differ, but for enterprise shops that can afford it, VMware solutions are quite widespread. Zabbix offers built-in support for monitoring VMware. This support includes the following:

- Monitoring vSphere and/or vCenter
- Automatically discovering all hypervisors
- Automatically discovering all virtual machines

Monitoring VMware doesn't involve any custom layers; Zabbix accesses the VMware API directly, and the monitoring of such an environment is very easy to set up.

In this chapter, the following topics will be covered:

- Preparing for VMware monitoring
- Automatic discovery
- Available metrics
- The underlying operation
- VMware LLD configuration

Technical requirements

For this chapter, you'll need access to an API of a VMware instance, including a username and password. It might be a good idea to try this in a smaller or non-production environment first.

 Even though Zabbix has optimized the number of API calls, when discovering a large environment from vCenter, the vCenter API endpoint could get overloaded, as Zabbix would connect to it and request data for all of the vSphere instances and virtual machines that have been discovered. It might make sense to split the monitoring over individual vSphere instances instead.

Preparing for VMware monitoring

To try out VMware support, we'll need the following:

- The IP address or hostname on which we have access to the VMware API
- The username for an account with permissions to retrieve the information
- The password for that account

First, the server must be compiled with VMware support. If you have installed from packages, this support most likely is included. If you installed from source, check whether the Zabbix server log file lists VMware monitoring as enabled:

```
VMware monitoring: YES
```

When compiling from source, the following options are needed for VMware support:

- --with-libcurl
- --with-libxml2

As with several other features we've explored so far, the Zabbix server doesn't start any VMware-specific processes by default. Edit zabbix_server.conf and look for the StartVMwareCollectors parameter. Add a new line and tell Zabbix to start two VMware collectors:

```
StartVMwareCollectors=2
```

Restart the server. *Why two collectors?* Zabbix developers recommend the number of collectors is based on the number of monitored VMware instances. For the best performance, it's suggested to start more collectors than the monitored instance count, but less than double the monitored instance count. Or if we put that in an equation, it'll be as follows: *instances < StartVMwareCollectors < (instances * 2)*. We'll start small and monitor a single instance for now, so we'll have *1 < StartVMwareCollectors < 2*. It's also recommended to always start at least two VMware collectors, so the choice is obvious here. If we had two VMware instances to monitor, it would be three collectors: *2 < StartVMwareCollectors < 4*.

A VMware instance is a vSphere or vCenter instance, not an individual virtual machine. That is, the number of collectors depends on the endpoints Zabbix actually connects to for data collection.

We'll start by unleashing Zabbix on the VMware API and allowing it to automatically discover everything using the templates that're shipped with Zabbix. Once we see that it works as expected, we'll discover how we can customize and expand this monitoring, as well as look under the hood a bit at the mechanics of VMware monitoring.

Automatic discovery

We'll create a separate host, which will be the starting point for the discovery. This host won't do anything else for us besides monitor generic VMware parameters and discover all other entities.

Follow these steps to setup our monitoring in Zabbix:

1. Go to **Configuration | Hosts** and click on **Create host.**
2. Enter VMware in the **Host name** field, clear out existing groups in the **In groups** block, and enter VMware in the **New group** field.
3. Switch to the **Macros** tab and fill in values for these three macros:

   - {$URL}: The VMware API/SDK URL in the form https://server/sdk
   - {$USERNAME}: The VMware account username
   - {$PASSWORD}: The VMware account password

The API or SDK is available on vSphere or vCenter systems.

4. Switch to the **Templates** tab, start typing `vmware`, choose **Template VM VMware**, and click on the **Add** control in the **Link new templates** section.
5. When done, click on the **Add** button at the bottom.

What's next? Well, nothing. If everything has been done right, everything should be monitored automatically. Hypervisors should be discovered and monitored, and virtual machines discovered, placed in groups based on hypervisors, and monitored as well. It might not happen immediately, though. Like other **Low-Level Discovery (LLD)** rules in default templates, VMware discovery also has a one hour interval—wait, *LLD rules?* Yes, VMware discovery also uses LLD functionality. We discussed it in detail in `Chapter 11`, *Automating Configuration*. VMware support takes it a step further, though: besides item, trigger, and graph prototypes, it also uses host prototypes. We'll cover host prototypes a bit later. For now, we can either leave the discovery to happen, or we can go to **Configuration** | **Templates**, click on **Discovery** next to **Template VM VMware**, and reduce the update interval for all three discovery rules. Just make sure to set it back later.

After waiting for a while—or after reducing the intervals—check **Configuration** | **Host groups**. You should see several new host groups, prefixed with **Discover VMware VMs**. Depending on how large the monitored VMware instance is, the new group count could be from two up to many. There'll be a group called **Hypervisors** and a group for virtual machines per cluster. If there're clusters, there'll also be a group for hypervisors per cluster.

 If there aren't any clusters configured, the group for virtual machines will just be called `vm`.

Available metrics

With some groups and hosts automatically created, let's see what data they're collecting. Navigate to **Monitoring** | **Latest data** and select **Hypervisors** in the **Host groups** field. Then, click on **Filter**:

NAME ▲	LAST CHECK	LAST VALUE
CPU (5 Items)		
CPU cores	2015-11-02 10:49:58	4
CPU frequency	2015-11-02 10:49:56	2.53 GHz
CPU model	2015-11-02 10:49:57	Intel(R) Xeon(R) CPU
CPU threads	2015-11-02 10:49:59	8
CPU usage	2015-11-02 10:59:51	61 MHz
Datastore (2 Items)		
Average read latency of the datastore datastore1	2015-11-02 10:59:44	0
Average write latency of the datastore datastore1	2015-11-02 10:59:45	0

There'll be more items for each hypervisor. Some of them might not have data yet, but a bit of patience should reveal all of the details.

Datastore items might appear later; they're discovered by the datastore discovery LLD rule in **Template VM VMware Hypervisor** with a default interval of one hour.

Now, filter by hypervisor virtual machine group in the **Host groups** field or by a single discovered virtual machine in the **Hosts** field:

NAME ▲	LAST CHECK	LAST VALUE
CPU (2 Items)		
CPU usage	2015-11-02 11:17:14	10 MHz
Number of virtual CPUs	2015-11-02 11:17:13	1
Disks (4 Items)		
Average number of kilobytes read from the disk Hard disk 1	2015-11-02 11:16:50	0 Bps
Average number of kilobytes written to the disk Hard disk 1	2015-11-02 11:16:52	1 KBps
Average number of reads from the disk Hard disk 1	2015-11-02 11:16:51	0
Average number of writes to the disk Hard disk 1	2015-11-02 11:16:53	0
Filesystems (4 Items)		
Free disk space on /	2015-11-02 11:16:54	2.64 GB
Free disk space on / (percentage)	2015-11-02 11:16:55	68.03 %
Total disk space on /		
Used disk space on /	2015-11-02 11:16:57	1.24 GB

Again, there should be more items, and some could still be missing values. They all should eventually get populated, though.

> Disks, filesystems, and interface items might appear later; they're discovered by the **disk device discovery**, **mounted filesystem discovery**, and **network device discovery** LLD rules in the **Template VM VMware Guest** template, with a default interval of one hour.

Once all of the LLD rules on the host level have run, we'll see quite a lot of items being covered by the default templates. In many cases, these templates might even be enough. Sometimes, you might want to extend them, though. The same as with other default templates, it's strongly suggested you clone the template first and then make the modifications to the new template.

But *what other things could be supported besides the already included items?* To see the full list of supported VMware item keys, visit the item type section in the Zabbix manual. VMware items are listed after *Simple checks*, and at the time of writing this, the full URL is `https://www.zabbix.com/documentation/4.0/manual/config/items/itemtypes/simple_checks/vmware_keys`. Why below *Simple checks*? That's the item type for all VMware keys. When adding new items, the type must be set to simple check. The same as other simple checks, these items are processed by the Zabbix server directly.

Many items have been added since the first implementation of VMWare monitoring in Zabbix. If you're still using the templates that came with Zabbix 3.0, it's probably a good idea to download the latest version of the templates and check out the VMWare keys available in the previous URL. Currently, discovered VMware hosts can't have other templates linked in or other item types added. It's not possible to merge VMware monitoring and other monitoring, such as a Zabbix agent, on the same host. If both virtualization and OS-level statistics are to be monitored, separate hosts must be used for that.

The underlying operation

While automatic discovery and monitoring works great, it's useful to understand how exactly it works, both to be able to extend it and to solve problems as they arise. We'll look at two areas in more detail:

- LLD configuration in the default templates and host prototypes
- Server operation and configuration details

VMware LLD configuration

Let's dissect the default templates and how they operate. We only linked a single template, and it ended up discovering all hypervisors and virtual machines; it's time to find out how that happened. The top-level template, **Template VM VMware**, also does some direct monitoring, although not much; it has items for VMware **Event log**, **Full name**, and **Version,** as shown in the following screenshot:

	Wizard	Name ▲	Triggers	Key	Interval
☐	•••	Event log		vmware.eventlog[{$URL}]	1m
☐	•••	Full name		vmware.fullname[{$URL}]	1h
☐	•••	Version		vmware.version[{$URL}]	1h

These would be collected on the vCenter or vSphere level. It all grows more interesting and complicated when we look at the LLD rules on this template. It discovers VMware clusters, hypervisors, and individual virtual machines. Admittedly, cluster discovery isn't that complicated; it only has a single item prototype to monitor cluster status. Hypervisor discovery uses an LLD feature we haven't looked at yet: **host prototypes**.

Host prototypes

If we go to **Configuration** | **Templates** and click on **Discovery** next to **Template VM VMware**, we'll see that there's a single host prototype in the **Discover VMware hypervisors** LLD rule. Click on **Host prototypes** and then click on **{#HV.NAME}** in the **Name** column:

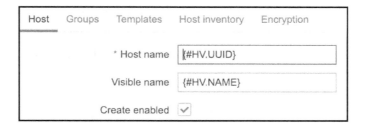

Host	Groups	Templates	Host inventory	Encryption

* Host name	{#HV.UUID}
Visible name	{#HV.NAME}
Create enabled	✓

Here, LLD macros are used again. We looked at their use in item and trigger prototypes, but here they're used for the **Host name** and **Visible name** in the host prototype. The interesting part is the use of different macros in these fields. **Host name**, the one used to identify the host, isn't the hypervisor name, but its UUID. The human-friendly name goes in the **Visible name** field. When a hypervisor is referenced, it must be done by the UUID and it'll be referenced by that UUID in the server log messages.

The **Templates** tab doesn't hold many surprises; it instructs Zabbix to link any discovered hypervisors to **Template VM VMware Hypervisor**. Let's switch to the **Groups** tab now:

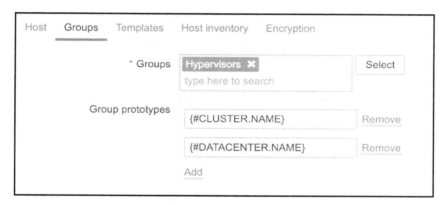

This is a bit more interesting. Host prototypes can instruct created hosts to be placed in existing host groups, listed in the **Groups** field. Additionally, they can instruct new groups to be created based on **Group prototypes** and created hosts to be included in those groups. Group prototypes are similar to other prototypes; the resulting names must be unique, and that means we should use some LLD macro in the group name.

The {#DATACENTER.NAME} macro was added in Zabbix 3.2 and adds the VMWare hypervisor data center name. If there aren't any clusters configured, there won't be any per-cluster groups created.

The **Discover VMware VMs** LLD rule in this template is similar; it holds a single host prototype to be used for all discovered virtual machines. Just as with hypervisors, the UUID is used for the hostname, and that would also be the one that appears in the server log file:

In the frontend, we may search both by the **Host name** and **Visible name**. If searching by the hostname—and this might be common, as we'll see it in log files—the visible name will be shown as usual, with the hostname displayed below it and made bold to indicate that it matched the search:

In the **Templates** tab, we can see that the created hosts will be linked to **Template VM VMware Guest**. It's worth looking at the **Groups** tab for this host prototype. Besides adding all discovered virtual machines to an existing group, **Virtual machines**, two group prototypes are used here:

As seen in the hostgroup page earlier, a group would be created per hypervisor and per cluster, holding all virtual machines on that hypervisor or in that cluster.

Summarizing default template interaction

We've looked at what the default set of VMware templates does, but it can be a bit confusing to understand how they interact and what configuration entity creates what. Let's try to summarize their interaction and purpose in a diagram. Here, hosts that receive the listed template are represented with a thick border, while various LLD rules are shown with a thin border:

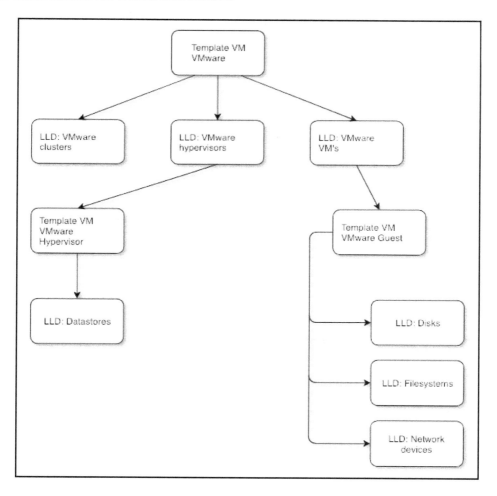

If a template has host prototypes, hence resulting in more hosts being created, it points to another thick-bordered host box, which in turn is linked to another template.

But remember that, for this tree to start working, we only had to create a single host and link it to a single template, **Template VM VMware**.

Server operation and configuration details

We know how Zabbix deals with information once that information has been received, but there's a whole process to get it. That process is interesting on its own, but there're also parameters to tune in addition to StartVMwareCollectors, which we discussed earlier. First, let's examine how the values end up in items. The following diagram shows a data flow starting with VMware and ending with the Zabbix history cache:

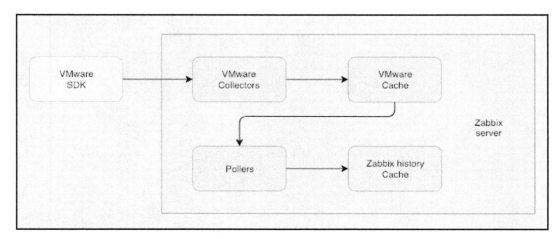

Here, the steps happening inside the Zabbix server are grouped, and arrows indicate the data flow direction; connections are actually made from the VMware collectors to the VMware SDK interface. The collectors start by grabbing data and placing it in a special cache; caches are indicated with a dashed border here. Then pollers—the same processes that are responsible for passive Zabbix agents, SNMP, and other item types—grab some values from that cache and place them in the Zabbix history cache. For now, ignore the details in the history cache; we'll discuss it more in Chapter 20, *Zabbix Maintenance*.

Why the intermediate VMware cache? When VMware items are added, there're quite a lot of them, with various intervals. If Zabbix were to make a connection to VMware for every value, it would be a performance disaster. Instead, VMware collectors grab everything from the VMware SDK interface, place that in the cache, and then the pollers pick the required values from that cache. This way, a lot of items can get their values grabbed from the VMware cache instead of having to bother VMware every single time.

Now is a good time to look at the VMware-related configuration parameters in the server configuration file. We already covered StartVMwareCollectors, the processes that connected to the VMware interface and placed information in a special VMware cache. This cache by default is set to 8 MB, and this size can be controlled with the VMwareCacheSize parameter. *How would we know when that should be changed?* The best way is to monitor the usage and adjust accordingly. We'll discuss the monitoring of internal caches in Chapter 20, *Zabbix Maintenance*.

Sometimes, connections to the VMware interface could get stuck. It could either be a single slow instance that slows down the monitoring of other instances, or it could be a single request going bad. In any case, connections to VMware instances will time out after 10 seconds by default. This time can be controlled with the VMwareTimeout parameter.

We just have two VMware-specific parameters left, VMwareFrequency and VMwarePerfFrequency. Zabbix queries some of the information using the VMware internal performance counters. At the time of writing this, the following item keys on the hypervisor level are extracted from the following performance counters:

- vmware.hv.network.in
- vmware.hv.network.out
- vmware.hv.datastore.read
- vmware.hv.datastore.write
- vmware.hv.perfcounter

On the virtual machine level, the following keys are extracted from the following performance counters:

- `vmware.vm.cpu.ready`
- `vmware.vm.net.if.in`
- `vmware.vm.net.if.out`
- `vmware.vm.perfcounter`
- `vmware.vm.vfs.dev.read`
- `vmware.vm.vfs.dev.write`

What does this actually mean? The item keys, listed previously, get new information as often as `VMwarePerfFrequency` is set to. To put it differently, it doesn't make sense to set the frequency of any items listed here lower than `VMwarePerfFrequency`. All other items, including low-level discoveries, get their information as often as `VMwareFrequency` is set to, and it doesn't make sense to set the frequency of other items and LLD rules lower than `VMwareFrequency`.

We could also say that both of these parameters should be set to match the lowest frequency for their corresponding items, but we have to be careful; setting these too low could overload VMware instances. By default, both of these parameters are set to 60 seconds. This is fine for small and average environments, but on a large VMware instance, we might want to increase them both, while potentially increasing `VMwareTimeout` as well.

 If you see weird graphs, verify whether the item update interval isn't less than `VMwarePerfFrequency`.

Summary

To monitor VMware, just a single template is all we need. Well, that's not entirely true; the other two templates for hypervisors and virtual machines must be present, too, but besides that, Zabbix can automatically discover all hypervisors and virtual machines, just like we did in the beginning of this chapter.

We looked in detail at the default templates: how they work and interact and what each provides. The main template discovered everything, and then created hosts and linked in hypervisor and virtual machine templates as needed.

In the end, we looked at lower-level details, including how data is passed through the VMware cache, how often that happens, and how we can tune all of that.

In the next chapter, we'll discuss a new Zabbix process: Zabbix proxy. Zabbix proxies are remote data collectors that are really great. Similar to agents, they can operate in passive or active mode, and they support almost everything Zabbix server supports, including monitoring Zabbix agents, SNMP devices, VMware, and much more. We'll set up both active and passive proxies, and discuss the best way to handle a proxy becoming unavailable.

Questions

1. How many templates do we need to monitor VMware?
2. How can I increase debug logging only for VMware?
3. Does Zabbix support monitoring for KVM, Xen, and Hyper-V?

Further reading

Read the following articles for more information:

- **VMware monitoring item keys**: `https://www.zabbix.com/documentation/4.0/manual/config/items/itemtypes/simple_checks/vmware_keys`
- **Virtual machine monitoring**: `https://www.zabbix.com/documentation/4.0/manual/vm_monitoring`

17
Using Proxies to Monitor Remote Locations

The Zabbix server can do monitoring using lots of different methods: it can communicate with Zabbix agents, SNMP devices, and IPMI devices; run commands; and do a whole lot of other things. A problem arises when the number of devices to be monitored increases; a single endpoint (our Zabbix server) is supposed to communicate with lots of others, and a large number of connections can cause problems both on the Zabbix server and in the network components between the Zabbix server and monitored devices.

It gets worse if we have to monitor remote environments—be it a branch office, another data center, or a customer site. *Zabbix agents?* Port 10050 must be open to all servers. *SNMP?* Port 161 must be open to all devices. It becomes unmanageable really quickly.

A solution is to use Zabbix proxies. A Zabbix proxy is a remote data-collector process that is capable of collecting data using all the methods the Zabbix server supports. In this chapter, we will set up a Zabbix proxy, use it for gathering data, and discuss the best methods to determine whether the proxy itself is available.

 Zabbix proxies are not available for Windows.

We will cover the following topics in this chapter:

- Active proxies and passive proxies
- Setting up an active proxy
- Proxy benefits
- Proxy limitations

- Proxies and availability monitoring
- Setting up a passive proxy
- Tweaking the proxy configuration

Active proxies and passive proxies

The Zabbix proxy first appeared in Zabbix version 1.6, back in 2008. Since then, it has proven to be a very good solution. When the Zabbix proxy first appeared, it supported connecting to the Zabbix server only, similarly to active agent. Zabbix version 1.8.3 introduced a capability of the server to connect to the proxy, and now, active proxies and passive proxies are available. While the Zabbix agent can communicate with the server in both ways at the same time by having active and passive items on the same host, the Zabbix proxy communicates with the server only in one way at a time; the whole proxy is designated as active or passive.

The proxy mode does not change the direction of connections to or from the monitored devices. If using active items through a proxy, the agent will still be the one making the connections, and if using passive items, the agent will be accepting connections. It's just that instead of the server, the agent will now communicate with the proxy.

In both active and passive mode, server-proxy communication requires a single TCP port, to a single address only, to be open. That is much easier to handle on the firewall level than allowing connections to and from all of the monitored devices. There are more benefits that a proxy may provide—but let's discuss those once we have a proxy running.

Setting up an active proxy

We'll start with an active proxy—one that connects to the Zabbix server.

When setting up the proxy for this exercise, it is suggested to use a separate machine. If that is not possible, you can choose to run the proxy on the Zabbix server system.

If installing the proxy from packages, we will have to choose a database. Zabbix proxy uses its own database. If compiling the proxy from the sources, use the `--enable` proxy parameter and the corresponding database parameter.

Additionally, the proxy must have support compiled in for all features it should monitor, including SNMP, IPMI, web monitoring, and VMware support. See `Chapter 1`, *Getting Started with Zabbix*, for compilation options.

If a proxy is compiled from the same source directory the server was compiled from, and the compilation fails, try running `make clean` first.

Which database should you choose for the Zabbix proxy? If the proxy will be monitoring a small environment, SQLite might be a good choice. Using SQLite for the Zabbix server backend is not supported, as it is likely to have locking and performance issues. On a Zabbix proxy, it should be much less of a problem. If setting up a large proxy, MySQL or PostgreSQL would be a better choice. During this chapter, we will use the proxy with a SQLite database, as that is very easy to set up.

If compiling from the sources, SQLite development headers will be needed. In most distributions, they will be provided in a package named `sqlite-devel` or similar. If you install from the package, then you have to install it with `yum` or `apt` and the package name will look similar to `zabbix-proxy-sqlite3`, but this is something you have to check. For other databases than SQLite, you need to replace `sqlite3` with the correct database name.

Edit `zabbix_proxy.conf`. We will change three parameters:

- `DBName`
- `Hostname`
- `Server`

Change them to read as follows:

```
DBName=/tmp/zabbix_proxy.db
Hostname=First proxy
Server=<Zabbix server IP address>
```

The parameters in the preceding code block are explained as follows:

- The first parameter, `DBName`, is the same as for the Zabbix server, except we do not just specify the database name here. For SQLite, the path to database file is specified here. While a relative path may be used, in most situations it will be much more complicated to start the proxy, thus an absolute path is highly suggested. We used a file in `/tmp` to make the setup of our first proxy simpler, no need to worry about filesystem permissions. *What about the database username and password?* As the comments in the configuration file indicate, they are both ignored when SQLite is used.

On a production system, it is suggested to place the database file in a location other than /tmp. In some distributions, /tmp might be cleared upon reboot. On the other hand, for performance reasons, we might choose to place the database in a tmpfs volume, gaining some performance, but losing the proxy database upon every system restart.

Placing the SQLite database on a tmpfs filesystem can also be useful if you run your proxy on embedded devices at one of you clients. In case things go wrong you could just ask your client to restart the device. You will lose some data, but the database will be created again once the proxy is up. With corrupt databases, you would have some more work to recover data or fix the corrupt DB.

- The second parameter, Hostname, will be used by the proxy to identify itself to the Zabbix server. The principle is the same as with the active agent: the value, specified here, must match the proxy name as configured on the server side (we will set that up in a moment), and is case-sensitive.

- The third parameter, Server, acts the same way as it did with active agents. The active proxy connects to the Zabbix server and we specify the server IP address here.

If you are running the proxy on the same machine as the Zabbix server, change the port the proxy listens on, set ListenPort=11051. The default port would conflict with the Zabbix server.

As with the Zabbix server, you must ensure that the appropriate pollers are configured to start. For example, if you want to monitor IPMI devices through a proxy, make sure to set the StartIPMIPollers parameter in the proxy configuration file to a value other than the default 0.

Start the Zabbix proxy now. Wait, we did not create the database for the proxy. *What will it do?* Let's look at the proxy log file—check /tmp/zabbix_proxy.log, or the location set in the proxy configuration file. Paying close attention, we can find some interesting log records:

```
3890:20181228:123654.746 using configuration file:
/etc/zabbix/zabbix_proxy.conf
3890:20181228:123654.746 cannot open database file
"/tmp/zabbix_proxy.db": [2] No such file or directory
3890:20181228:123654.746 creating database ...
```

It first failed to open an existing database file, then proceeded to create the database. The Zabbix proxy can automatically create the required SQLite database and populate it. Note that this is true for SQLite only—if using any other database, we would have to create the database manually and insert `schema`. This is also possible for SQLite—using the `sqlite3` utility, we would do it like this:

$ sqlite3 /tmp/zabbix_proxy.db < schema.sql

But `schema` only! Not just for SQLite—for all databases—the proxy needs `schema` only. No data and no image SQL files should be used. If the Zabbix proxy detects some extra data in the database, it exits, complaining that it cannot use the server database. Older proxy versions could crash or even corrupt the server database in such a case. A link to the documentation on where to find the DB schemas is provided at the end of this chapter.

Do not create an empty file. Either allow the proxy to create the database file, or create it yourself and populate it using the `sqlite3` utility. An empty file will be perceived as an empty database and the proxy will fail to start.
If a proxy complains that it cannot work with a server database, it will have found entries in the `users` table.

We could also verify that the Zabbix proxy is listening on the port it should be by running the following:

$ ss -ntl | grep 10051

The output should confirm that everything is correct:

LISTEN   0   128   *:10051   *:*

If installing on the same machine, check for port `11051`, or whichever other port you chose.

There are a few log entries that indicate something is not working properly:

```
cannot send heartbeat message to server at "192.168.56.10": proxy
"First proxy" not found
cannot obtain configuration data from server at "192.168.56.10": proxy
"First proxy" not found
```

Zabbix 3.0 introduced the IP address in these messages. If you struggled with figuring out which proxy is the issue in a larger environment before, it should no longer be a problem.

We only configured and started the proxy daemon, but we did not configure anything related to proxies on the server side. Let's monitor a host through our new proxy.

Monitoring a host through a proxy

Now that we have the proxy configured and running, we have to inform Zabbix about it somehow. To do this, perform the following steps:

1. Open **Administration | Proxies** in the frontend, then click on the **Create proxy** button.
2. Enter `First proxy` in the **Proxy name** field:

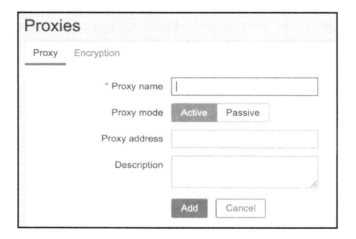

 The proxy name we enter here must match the one configured in the `zabbix_proxy.conf` file, and is case-sensitive.
Zabbix 4.0 added some extra security. If we fill in **Proxy address** with the IP of our proxy, then only requests from this comma-delimited list of IP addresses will be accepted.

3. Next, we need to select **Another host** in **Configuration | Hosts** and select `First proxy` from the **Monitored by proxy** drop-down menu:

4. When done, click on **Update**.

The next time the proxy connects to the server, the names should match and the proxy should get the information on what it is supposed to monitor. But *when will that next time be?* By default, the Zabbix proxy connects to the Zabbix server once per hour. The first connection attempt happens upon proxy startup, and at one-hour intervals from then on. If you configured the frontend part soon after the proxy was started, it could take up to an hour for the proxy to get the configuration data and start working. There are two ways to force rereading of the configuration data from the Zabbix server:

- Restart the proxy
- Force-reload its configuration cache

The first one would be acceptable on our test proxy, but it would not be that nice on a larger production proxy that is actively collecting data already. Let's see how we can force-reload the configuration cache. First, run the following:

```
# zabbix_proxy --help
```

In the output, pay attention to the runtime-control section and the first parameter in it:

```
  -R --runtime-control runtime-option     Perform administrative
functions
         Runtime control options:
           config_cache_reload           Reload configuration cache
```

When an active proxy is told to reload its configuration cache, it connects to the server, gets the new configuration data, and then updates the local cache. Let's issue that command now:

```
# zabbix_proxy --runtime-control config_cache_reload
```

 Runtime commands depend on the PID file being properly configured. When you run the previous command, it looks for the PidFile option in the default proxy configuration file, looks up the PID from the PID file, and sends the signal to that process. If multiple active proxies are running on the system, a signal can be sent to a specific proxy by specifying its configuration file with the -c option.

The reload command should be processed successfully:

```
zabbix_proxy [19293]: command sent successfully
```

Check the proxy log file now:

```
forced reloading of the configuration cache
received configuration data from server at "192.168.56.10", datalen
6545
```

First, the proxy logs that it has received an order to reload the configuration cache. Then it connects to the server and successfully retrieves the configuration data from the server.

> We will discuss reloading of the configuration cache in somewhat greater detail in Appendix A, *Troubleshooting*.

You can verify whether the proxy can successfully connect to the server by opening **Administration** | **Proxies** again. Look at the **Last seen (age)** column for the new proxy. Instead of saying never, it should show some time period. If it does not, check that both the Zabbix server and proxy are running, and that you can open a connection from the proxy host to the Zabbix server, port 10051:

Name ▲	Mode	Encryption	Compression	Last seen (age)	Host count	Item count	Required performance (vps)	Hosts
First proxy	Active	NONE	ON	2s	0	0	0	
								Displaying 1 of 1 found

But if you look at the **Hosts** column, you'll see that it is empty now. *What happened here?* We clearly added **Another host** to be monitored by this proxy—*why did it disappear?* This could be a challenging task to figure out, and a situation such as that could easily arise in a production environment. The reason for the host disappearing from the proxy configuration is active-agent auto-registration. We configured it in Chapter 11, *Automating Configuration*, and the agent has been sort of repeatedly auto-registering ever since. But *why does that affect the host assignment to proxy?* When an active agent connects and auto-registration is active, it matters where it connects to. Instead of creating a new host, the Zabbix server reassigns that host to the Zabbix server or some proxy, whichever received the agent connection. It considers that agent as having migrated from the server to some proxy or vice versa, or from one proxy to another. We assigned a host to our new proxy, the agent kept on connecting to the server, and the server reassigned that host back to be monitored directly by the server. *How could we solve it?* We have two options:

- Disable the active agent's auto-registration action and reconfigure the host manually
- Configure the agent to connect to the proxy instead

Let's try the second, fancier approach. On **Another host**, edit `zabbix_agentd.conf` and change `ServerActive` to the proxy IP address, then restart the agent.

> In the preceding screenshot, we also see a column **Compression**. All communications between the Zabbix server and proxies are now unconditionally compressed in both ways. For this the `zlib` library is required. This compression is new in Zabbix 4.0 and Zabbix SIA claims that it can save 50% of your bandwidth between proxy and server.
>
> If you installed the Zabbix proxy on the same system as the Zabbix server, make sure to specify the proxy port in this parameter, too. For example, `192.168.1.23:11051`.
>
> Do not set the proxy address in addition to the server address—in that case, the agent will try to work with both the server and proxy in parallel. See `Chapter 3`, *Monitoring with Zabbix Agents and Basic Protocols*, for more detail on pointing the agent at several servers or proxies.

Check the proxy list again. There should be **Another host** in the **Hosts** column now, and it should not disappear again. Let's check data for this host in **Monitoring | Latest data**. Unfortunately, it looks like most of the items have stopped working. While we changed the active server parameter in the agent daemon configuration file and active agent items work now, there are more item categories that could have failed:

- Passive agent items do not work because the agent does not accept connections from the proxy
- ICMP items likely do not work as `fping` is either missing or does not have proper permissions.
- While **Another host** does not have items of SNMP, IPMI, and other types, those could have started to fail because appropriate support was not compiled into the proxy, or respective pollers were not started
- If you configured the proxy on the Zabbix server system, passive items will work, as the IP address the agent gets the connections from will stay the same

Let's fix at least the passive agent items. Edit `zabbix_agentd.conf` on **Another host** and change the `Server` parameter. Either replace the IP address in there with the proxy address, or add the proxy address to it, then restart the agent. In a few minutes, most of the passive agent items should start receiving data again.

As for the ICMP items, refer to Chapter 3, *Monitoring with Zabbix Agents and Basic Protocols*, for the fping configuration. It's the same as on the server side; it's just that the changes have to be performed on the proxy system now.

In general, when a host is monitored by proxy, all connections to and from that host must and will be performed by the proxy. The agent must allow connections from the proxy for passive items and connect to the proxy for active items. Even the Zabbix sender must send data to the proxy for Zabbix trapper items, not the Zabbix server anymore.

With the host monitored by the proxy, let's check whether there is any indication of that in the frontend:

1. Open **Configuration** | **Hosts**, make sure **Linux servers** is selected in the **Group** drop-down, and take a look at the **Name** column
2. As you can see, **Another host** is now prefixed by the proxy name and reads **First proxy: Another host**:

 When having multiple proxies, it is a common practice to name them by location name—for example, proxy-London or Paris-proxy.

Before it was possible to monitor hosts by proxies from under **Administration** | **Proxies** this option was removed in Zabbix and now the only place left we can do this is on host level under **Configuration** | **Hosts**.

 If you decide to monitor **A test host** through the proxy, be very careful with its address. If the address is left at 127.0.0.1, the proxy will connect to the local agent for passive items and then report that data to the server, claiming it came from **A test host**. That would also be not that easy to spot, as the data would come in just fine; only it would be the wrong data.

Proxy benefits

With our first proxy configured, let's discuss its operation and the benefits it provides in more detail. Let's start with the main benefits:

- A proxy collects data when the server is not available
- A proxy reduces the number of connections to and from remote environments
- A proxy allows us to use incoming connections for polled items

We talked about the proxy retrieving configuration data from the server, and we talked about it having a local database. The Zabbix proxy always needs a local database, and this database holds information on the hosts the proxy is supposed to monitor. The same database also holds all the data the proxy has collected, and if the server cannot be reached, that data is not lost. *For how long?* By default, data is kept for one hour. This can be configured in the `zabbix_proxy.conf` file, in the `ProxyOfflineBuffer` parameter. It can be set up to 30 days, but beware of running out of disk space, as well as of the potential to overload the Zabbix server when connectivity is back—we will discuss that risk in more detail later:

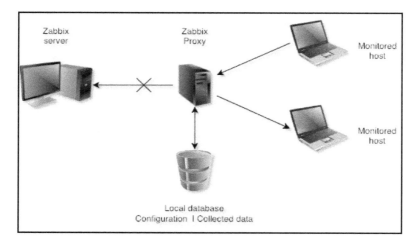

 There are more proxy-specific configuration parameters available; they are listed later in this chapter.

Fewer connections to remote environments can be very important, too. Monitoring using passive items means one connection for each value. With active items, it's a bit better; multiple values will often be sent in a single connection. But the proxy pools up to 1,000 values in a single connection. That is done even when they are of different types, such as agent, SNMP, IPMI, and SSH items. Fewer connections means healthier firewalls and other network devices, and much better performance from smaller total latency and less work for the Zabbix server to handle the incoming connections from Zabbix agents:

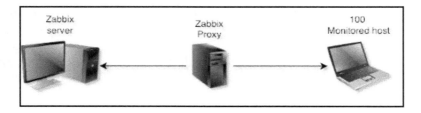

The third main benefit is the ability to receive incoming connections on the server side and still gather data by polling devices. For example, when monitoring a customer environment, the Zabbix server might have no access to the network devices. The Zabbix proxy could connect to them, collect data using SNMP, and then connect to the server to send the data. Also, keep in mind that only a single port for a single address would have to be opened in firewalls, as opposed to a lot of ports for all of the monitored devices when a proxy is not used:

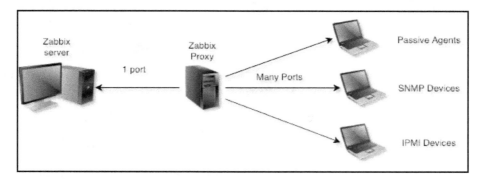

There are a few more benefits that Zabbix proxies provide:

- Single point of control for all proxies on the Zabbix server
- Ability to use multiple Java gateways

As proxies grab the configuration data from the Zabbix server, the configuration of all proxies is done on a single system. This also allows us to ship out small, preconfigured devices that are plugged into a remote environment. As long as they get network connectivity and can connect to the Zabbix server, all configuration regarding what should be monitored can be changed at will from the Zabbix server.

As for Java gateways, we discussed them in Chapter 15, *Monitoring Java Applications*. Only a single Java gateway could be configured for the Zabbix server, but a gateway may also be configured for each proxy. With proxies being simple to set up, it's fairly easy to have lots of Java gateways working on behalf of a single Zabbix server. Additionally, the Java gateway only supports connections from the server to the gateway. Using an active proxy in front of the gateway allows **Java Management Extensions (JMX)** monitoring using incoming connections to the Zabbix server:

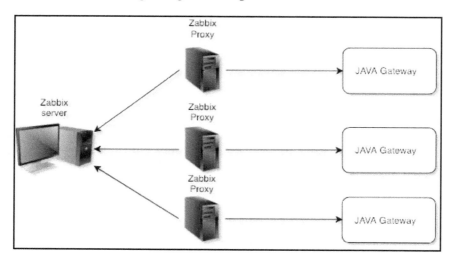

Proxy limitations

While proxies have many benefits, they do have some limitations. Well, they have pretty much one main limitation: they are only data collectors. If the server cannot be reached, the proxy cannot do independent notifications. They can't even generate events; all logic regarding triggers is processed on the server only. Remember, proxies do not process events or send out alerts. Remote commands were not supported in older versions, but are now supported since Zabbix 3.2. When we create scripts (**Administration** | **Scripts**), we now have the option to select if they need to be run from agent, server or proxy:

Remember we need to activate `EnableRemoteCommands` for this on our proxy, just like we have to do this for our host in our `zabbix_proxy.conf` file.

Proxy operation

Let's talk about how proxies operate a bit. We'll cover three things here:

- Synchronization of the configuration
- Synchronization of the collected data
- Operation during maintenance

By default, proxies synchronize the configuration once per hour, and this period can be set in the `zabbix_proxy.conf` configuration file. Look for the parameter named `ConfigFrequency`, which by default will look like this:

```
# ConfigFrequency=3600
```

This means that a Zabbix proxy can lag in configuration up to an hour, which might sound scary, but once a production installation settles, the configuration usually doesn't change that often. While testing, you might wish to decrease this period, but in a stable production setup, it is actually suggested to increase this value.

 If you must have configuration changes pushed to a proxy immediately, force the configuration to be reloaded.

The collected data is sent to the server every second by default. That can be customized in the `zabbix_proxy.conf` file with the `DataSenderFrequency` parameter.

 The active proxy won't connect to the server every second if it has no values to send—a one-second interval will be used only if it has data to send. On the other hand, if it has lots of values to send and cannot push them all in a single connection (which means 1,000 values), the next connection will be performed as soon as possible without waiting that 1 second.

Regarding host and host-group maintenance, when a host is in maintenance without data collection, data is still sent by proxy, but the server discards it. This way, changes in the maintenance status do not suffer from the default one-hour delay for a configuration sync.

Proxies and availability monitoring

With all the benefits that a proxy brings, you might be tempted to use them a lot—and a good idea that would be, too. Proxies are really great. There's still the issue of monitoring availability for hosts behind proxies. If a proxy goes down or cannot communicate with the Zabbix server, we would be missing data for all the hosts behind that proxy. If we used the `nodata()` trigger function to detect unavailable hosts (we could call such triggers **availability triggers**), that could mean thousands of hosts are declared unavailable. Not a desirable situation. There is no built-in dependency for hosts behind a proxy, but we can monitor proxy availability and set trigger dependencies for all hosts behind that proxy. But *what should we set those dependencies to?* Let's discuss the available ways to monitor proxy availability and their potential shortcomings.

Method 1 – last access item

There was the last access column in **Administration** | **Proxies**. Of course, looking at it all the time is not feasible, thus it can also be added as an internal item. To create such an item, do the following:

1. Let's go to **Configuration** | **Hosts**, click on **Items** next to the host that runs your proxy, and click on **Create item**. Fill in the following values:

   - **Name:** `$2: last access`

- **Type**: **Zabbix internal**
- **Key**: `zabbix[proxy,First proxy,lastaccess]`
- **Units**: `unixtime`

This item can be created on any host, but it is common to create it either on the Zabbix proxy host, or on the Zabbix server host.

In the key here, the second parameter is the proxy name. Thus, if your proxy was named `kermit`, the key would become `zabbix[proxy,kermit,lastaccess]`.

If items like these are created on hosts that represent the proxy system and have the same name as the proxy, a template could use the `{HOST.HOST}` macro as the second parameter in this item key. We discussed templates in `Chapter 8`, *Simplifying Complex Configurations with Templates*.

2. When done, click on the **Add** button at the bottom.

Notice how we used a special unit here: `unixtime`. Now *what would it do?* To find out, navigate to **Monitoring | Latest data**, expand the **Filter**, select the host you created the last item on, and enter `proxy` in the **Name** field, then click on the **Filter** button. Look at the way data is presented here, we can see very nicely, in a human-readable form, when the proxy last contacted the Zabbix server:

	Host	Name ▲	Last check	Last value
▼				
▼	Another host	**- other -** (1 Item)		
		First proxy: last access	2018-12-28 15:03:17	2018-12-28 15:03:16

So this item will be recording the time when the proxy last contacted the Zabbix server. That's great, but hardly enough to notice problems in an everyday routine—we already know that a trigger is needed. Here, the already-familiar `fuzzytime()` function comes to the rescue.

Navigate to **Configuration | Hosts**, click on **Triggers** next to the host you created the proxy last access item on, then click on the **Create trigger** button.

Let's say we have a fairly loaded and critical proxy—we would like to know when three minutes have passed without the proxy reporting back. In such a case, a trigger expression such as this could be used:

```
{host:zabbix[proxy,proxy name,lastaccess].fuzzytime(180)}=0
```

 One could consider using the Simple change value for the last access item, which would return 0 when the proxy is not communicating. The trigger for such an item is more obscure, thus `fuzzytime()` is the most common trigger function for this purpose.

As we might recall, the proxy connected to the server in two cases—it either synchronized the configuration, or sent the collected data. *What if, for some reason, all occurrences of both of these events are further apart than three minutes?* Luckily, the Zabbix proxy has a heartbeat process, which reports back to the server at regular intervals. Even better, this timing is configurable. Again, take a look at `zabbix_proxy.conf`, this time looking for the `HeartbeatFrequency` variable, which by default looks like this:

```
# HeartbeatFrequency=60
```

Specified in seconds, this value means that the proxy will report back to the server every minute, even if there are no new values to send. The `lastaccess` item is quite a reliable way to figure out when a proxy is most likely down or at least inaccessible, even if it would not be sending data for a longer period of time.

For our trigger, fill in the following values:

- **Name**: `Proxy "First proxy" not connected for 3 minutes`
- **Expression**: `{Another host:zabbix[proxy,First proxy,lastaccess].fuzzytime(3m)}=0`
- **Severity: High**

 Replace the proxy name with the host name on which the proxy last access item was created. If the last access item used the `{HOST.HOST}` macro, use the same macro in the trigger name and expression, too.

We could have used `180` in place of `3m`, but the time suffix version is a bit easier to read. Time suffixes were discussed in `Chapter 6`, *Detecting Problems with Triggers*. When done, click on the **Add** button at the bottom.

This combination of an item and a trigger will alert us when the proxy will be unavailable. Now we just have to set up trigger dependencies for all availability triggers behind this proxy on this proxy last access trigger.

Unfortunately, there's a common problem situation. When proxy-server communication is interrupted, the proxy last access trigger fires and masks all other triggers because of the dependency. While the proxy is unable to connect to the server for some time, it still collects the values. Once the communication is restored, the proxy sends all the values to the server, *older values first*. The moment the first value is sent, the last access item is updated and the trigger resolves. Unfortunately, at this point, the proxy is still sending values that were collected 5, 30, or 60 minutes ago. Any `nodata()` triggers that check a shorter period will fire. This makes the proxy trigger dependency work only until the proxy comes back, and results in a huge event storm when it does come back. *How can we solve it?* We could try to find out how many unsent values the proxy has, and if there are too many, ignore all the triggers behind the proxy—essentially, treating a proxy with a large value buffer the same as an unreachable proxy.

Method 2 – internal proxy buffer item

We can turn to Zabbix internal items to figure out how large the proxy buffer is—that is, how many values it has to send to the Zabbix server:

1. Let's go to **Configuration** | **Hosts**, click on **Items** next to **Another host**, and click on **Create item**. Fill in the following values:

    - **Name:** First proxy: buffer size
    - **Type: Zabbix internal**
    - **Key:** zabbix[proxy_history]

    This item must be created on a host, monitored through the proxy for which the buffer size should be monitored. If assigned to a host and monitored by the Zabbix server, this item will become unsupported.

2. When done, click on the **Add** button at the bottom.

With the default proxy configuration update interval of one hour, it might take quite some time before we can see the result of this item. To speed up the configuration update, run the following on the proxy host:

```
# zabbix_proxy --runtime-control config_cache_reload
```

The proxy will request item configurations from the server and update its own cache. After a short while, we should be able to see the result in the **Latest data** page:

	Host	Name ▲	Last check	Last value
▼				
▼	Another host	**proxy** (1 Item)		
		First proxy: buffer size	2018-12-28 15:12:18	1

What is that value, though? It's quite simply the number of values that are still in the proxy buffer and must be sent to the server. This might allow us to create a trigger against this item. Whenever the buffer is bigger than 100, 200, or 1,000 values, we consider the proxy data not up to date and make all host triggers depend on the buffer size. Except that there's still a significant problem. Values for this item are kept in the same proxy buffer it monitors and are subject to the same sequential sending, with older values being sent first. With this item, we would still suffer from the same problem as before—while the proxy was unavailable, the proxy buffer item would hold 0 or some other small value. As values start to flow in, individual host triggers would fire, and only after some time would we see that the buffer was actually really large. It would be useful for some debugging later, but would not help with masking the hosts behind the proxy. *Is there a solution then?*

Method 3 – custom proxy buffer item

A solution could be some method that would send us the proxy buffer size, bypassing the buffer itself. Zabbix does not offer such a method, thus we will have to implement it ourselves. Before we do that, let's figure out how we could obtain information on the buffer size. For that, we will delve into the proxy database.

You might have to install the SQLite 3 package to get the `sqlite3` utility.

On the proxy host, run the following:

```
$ sqlite3 /tmp/zabbix_proxy.db
```

The proxy keeps all of the collected values in a single table, `proxy_history`. Let's grab the last three collected values:

```
sqlite> select * from proxy_history order by id desc limit 3;
1659|28805|1546002875|0||0|0|0|660348055|0|0|0|0
1658|28804|1546002874|0||0|1546002874|0|658660672|0|0|0|0
1657|28799|1546002869|0||0|1|0|654297524|0|0|0|0
```

We will discuss other fields in a bit more detail in Chapter 19, *Working Closely with Data*, but for now, it is enough to know that the first field is a sequential ID. Still, *how does the proxy know which values it has sent to the server already?* Let's look at the IDs table:

```
sqlite> select * from ids where table_name='proxy_history';
proxy_history|history_lastid|1701
```

The `history_lastid` value here is the last ID that has been synchronized to the server. On a busy proxy, you might have to run these statements really quickly to see the real situation, as new values will be constantly added and sent to the server. We can get the current buffer (unsent values) size with this:

```
sqlite> select (select max(proxy_history.id) from proxy_history)-
nextid from ids where field_name='history_lastid';
```

It will calculate the difference between the biggest ID and the `history_lastid` value. On our proxy, this will likely return 0 all the time.

Try stopping the Zabbix server and see how this value increases. Don't forget to start the Zabbix server again.

Now we should put this in an item. The most important thing is to make sure this item is processed directly by the server, without involving the Zabbix proxy. We have several options:

- Passive agent item
- Active agent item
- Zabbix trapper item that is populated by `zabbix_sender`

For a passive agent, the server should query it directly. For an active agent, it should point at the Zabbix server. For the trapper item, `zabbix_sender` should be used to connect to the Zabbix server. In all three cases, the host should be assigned to be monitored by the Zabbix server. If we are using internal monitoring to collect proxy values in a dedicated host, a separate host will be needed to collect the buffer data. This way, we will avoid these values getting stuck in the proxy buffer.

For the agent items, we could use `UserParameter`, like this:

```
UserParameter=proxy.buffer,sqlite3 /tmp/zabbix_proxy.db "select
(select max(proxy_history.id) from proxy_history)-nextid from ids
where field_name='history_lastid';"
```

 You might have to use the full path to the `sqlite3` binary.

As for the Zabbix trapper approach, it could be run from `crontab` or using any other method. The command would be similar to this:

```
zabbix_sender -z zabbix_server -s target_host -k item_key -o $(sqlite3
/tmp/zabbix_proxy.db "select (select max(proxy_history.id) from
proxy_history)-nextid from ids where field_name='history_lastid';")
```

Here, we use the basic `zabbix_sender` syntax, but the value is obtained from the SQLite query. See `Chapter 10`, *Advanced Item Monitoring*, for more information on `UserParameters` and `zabbix_sender`. The Zabbix trapper item would receive the same data as the internal buffer monitoring—the buffer size. The trigger would check for this buffer exceeding some threshold.

Note that all three methods are likely to result in some missing values for the buffer item—the values would not be available while the connection between the server and proxy is down. The active agent item approach would suffer less as it has an in-memory buffer, but it there might still be missing values. If it would be valuable to know how the buffer changed during the communication breakdown. This item could be used for the trigger and an internal item, as discussed earlier, for more complete buffer statistics.

Regarding triggers and dependencies, it is suggested to make the buffer trigger depend on the last access trigger. This way, hosts behind the proxy will be silenced if the proxy disappears completely, and when the proxy comes back with a large buffer, the buffer trigger will keep those hosts silent.

Setting up a passive proxy

So far, we configured and discussed only one way a proxy can work, as an active proxy. A proxy may also be configured to accept incoming connections from the server, and similar to the agent; it is called a **passive proxy** in that case:

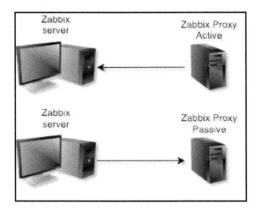

As opposed to the Zabbix agent, where this mode was set on the item level and a single agent could work in both active and passive mode, a Zabbix proxy can only work in one mode at a time.

Let's switch our active proxy to the passive mode. First, edit `zabbix_proxy.conf` and set the `ProxyMode` parameter to 1. This is all that's required to switch the proxy to the passive mode—now restart the proxy process.

> As opposed to the passive agent, the `Server` parameter is currently ignored by the passive proxy.

In the frontend, perform the following steps:

1. Navigate to **Administration | Proxies** and click on **First proxy** in the **Name** column.
2. Choose **Passive** in the **Proxy mode** drop-down, and notice how an **Interface** section appears.

3. Set the IP address and port of your proxy:

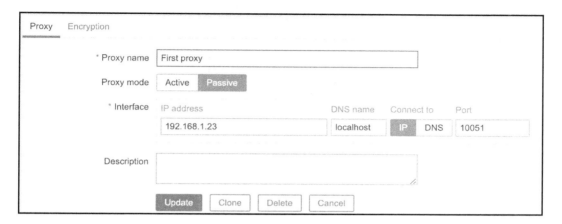

When done, click on **Update**. Now, *when will the server send configuration information to the passive proxy?* By default, the interval is one hour. Unfortunately, scheduling sending configuration data is done the same way as the polling of passive items—it's distributed in time and could happen any time from now, until one hour has passed.

 Don't forget to change the proxy port if you are not running the proxy on the standard port `10051`.

Well, let's try to force-reload the configuration cache on the proxy:

```
# zabbix_proxy --runtime-control config_cache_reload
zabbix_proxy [3587]: command sent successfully
```

That seemed promising. Let's check the proxy log file:

```
forced reloading of the configuration cache cannot be performed for a
passive proxy
```

Well, that's not good. The configuration cache-reloading command is ignored by passive proxies.

Currently, there is no way to force send that data from the server side either. Restarting the server won't help—it could make things worse, if the sending was scheduled while the server was not running. What we could do in our small installation is reduce that interval. Edit `zabbix_server.conf` and look for the `ProxyConfigFrequency` option. Set it to `180`, or some similarly small value, and restart the server. After a few minutes, check the server log file:

```
sending configuration data to proxy "First proxy" at "192.168.56.11",
datalen 6363
```

Such a line indicates the successful sending of the configuration data to the passive proxy. Note that `ProxyConfigFrequency` affects communication with all passive proxies; we cannot set this interval to a different value for different proxies.

When would one choose an active or passive proxy? In most cases, an active proxy would be preferred, as it can result in a smaller number of connections and we may force it to reload its configuration from the server. If the proxy cannot or should not connect to the server, a passive proxy could be used. A common situation when a passive proxy is used is when the Zabbix server is located in the internal network, and the proxy is monitoring a DMZ. We wouldn't want to have connections from the DMZ to the internal network, thus the choice of a passive proxy.

Tweaking the proxy configuration

While many configuration parameters for a proxy are the same as for the server (the pollers to start, port to listen on, and so on), and some are the same as for the agent daemon (hostname), there are some proxy-specific parameters. Knowing about these can be helpful when diagnosing a proxy-related problem, or when the proxy must be deployed in a specific environment. For an active proxy, the following parameters affect it:

Option	Description
ProxyLocalBuffer	Proxy will keep data in the local database for this many hours. By default, all data that is synchronized to the Zabbix server is removed. This could be useful if we would like to extract some data that is not stored permanently on the Zabbix server, such as network-discovery values.
ProxyOfflineBuffer	Proxy will keep data for this many hours if the Zabbix server is unavailable. By default, data older than one hour is discarded.

HeartbeatFrequency	By default, the Zabbix proxy sends a heartbeat message to the Zabbix server every minute. This parameter allows us to customize that.
ConfigFrequency	By default, the Zabbix proxy retrieves a new configuration from the server once per hour. You might want to increase this for large, fairly static setups, or maybe decrease it for smaller, more dynamic installations. Configuration data-retrieval can be forced by reloading the active proxy's configuration cache.
DataSenderFrequency	This parameter specifies how often the proxy pushes collected data to the Zabbix server. By default, it's one second. As all the trigger and alert processing is done by the server, it is suggested to keep this value low. If there are no values to send, an active proxy will not connect to the server except for heartbeat connections.

For a passive proxy, ProxyMode allows us to switch to the passive mode. Now the communication is controlled by parameters in the server configuration file:

Option	Description
StartProxyPollers	The number of processes that will be started and will connect to passive proxies to send configuration data and poll collected values. By default, one such process is started, and more might be needed if there are several passive proxies.
ProxyConfigFrequency	By default, Zabbix servers send configuration data to passive proxies once per hour. There is no way to force the sending of configuration data to passive proxies. This parameter affects connections to all passive proxies.
ProxyDataFrequency	This parameter specifies how often the proxy pushes collected data to the Zabbix server. By default, it's one second. The Zabbix server will connect to passive proxies even if they have no values to provide. This parameter affects connections to all passive proxies.

Summary

In this chapter, we covered a great and easily-maintainable solution for larger-scale data collection—Zabbix proxies. Zabbix proxies are also very desirable for remote environments. Similar to Zabbix agents, Zabbix proxies can operate either in active or in passive mode, reducing the hassle with configuring firewalls.

Let's recap the main benefits of Zabbix proxies:

- Connections between the Zabbix proxy and the Zabbix server are done on a single TCP port, thus allowing us to monitor devices behind a firewall or devices that are inaccessible because of network configuration.
- The Zabbix server is freed up from keeping track of checks and actually performing them, thus increasing performance.
- Local buffering on the proxy allows it to continue gathering data while the Zabbix server is unavailable, transmitting it all when connectivity problems are resolved.

Remember that active agents must point to the proxy if a host is monitored through that proxy. Passive agents must allow incoming connections from the proxy by specifying the proxy IP address in the `Server` parameter. The `zabbix_sender` utility must also send data to the proper proxy; sending data to the Zabbix server is not supported for hosts that are monitored through a proxy.

It is important to remember that proxies do not process events, do not generate trends, and do not send out alerts—they are remote data-gatherers, and alerting can happen only when the data is delivered to the Zabbix server. Additionally, proxies do not support remote commands. While scheduled for implementation in Zabbix 3.2, we will have to wait for that version to be released to know whether the development was successful.

With proxies taking over the monitoring of hosts, it is important to know that they are available, and it is also important to be silent about hosts behind a proxy if the proxy itself is not available. We discussed several ways this could be done, including proxy-buffer monitoring to avoid sending alerts when the proxy has collected a lot of data during connectivity problems, and value-sending is behind.

Zabbix proxies are easy to set up, easy to maintain, and offer many benefits, thus they are highly recommended for larger environments.

In the next chapter, we will finally discuss that **NONE** sign you might have noticed next to all hosts and proxies in the configuration section under Agent encryption. It refers to encryption configuration, which is a feature that was added in Zabbix 3.0. Zabbix supports pre-shared key and certificate-based TLS authentication and encryption. Encryption is supported for all components—server, proxy, agent, `zabbix_get`, and `zabbix_sender`. We will set up both pre-shared key and TLS-based encryption.

Zabbix has provided a template to monitor our proxies, this template is **Template App Zabbix Proxy**. This would allow us to monitor the internal health of our proxies just like we can do for our Zabbix server. In this case it's important to install a Zabbix agent on the Zabbix proxy that is being monitored by the proxy!

Questions

1. Can proxies be configured to be active/passive like Zabbix Agents?
2. When I install Zabbix proxies what do I need to change on my hosts?
3. Can I monitor JMX items from hosts behind a Zabbix proxy?

Further reading

Read the following articles for more information:

- **Database creation**: https://zabbix.com/documentation/current/manual/appendix/install/db_scripts
- **Proxies**: https://zabbix.com/documentation/current/manual/distributed_monitoring/proxies

18
Encrypting Zabbix Traffic

Communication between Zabbix components is done in plain text by default. In many environments, that isn't a significant problem, but monitoring over the internet in plain-text is likely not a good approach—transferred data could be read or manipulated by malicious parties. In previous Zabbix versions, there was no built-in solution, and various VPN, stunnel, and SSH port-forwarding solutions were used. Such solutions can still be used, but 3.0 was the first Zabbix version to provide built-in encryption.

In this chapter, we'll set up several of the components to use different types of encryption and cover the following topics:

- Overview
- Backend libraries
- Pre-shared key encryption
- Certificate-based encryption
- Being our own authority
- Setting up Zabbix with certificates

Overview

For Zabbix communication encryption, two types are supported:

- **Pre-Shared Key (PSK)**
- Certificate-based encryption

The PSK type is very easy to set up but is likely harder to scale. Certificate-based encryption can be more complicated to set up but easier to manage on a larger scale and is potentially more secure.

This encryption is supported between all Zabbix components; server, proxy, agent, and even `zabbix_sender` and `zabbix_get`.

For outgoing connections (such as server-to-agent or proxy-to-server), only one type may be used (we need to choose between no encryption or PSK or certificate-based). For incoming connections, multiple types may be accepted. This way, an agent could work with encryption by default for active or passive items from the server, and then work without encryption with `zabbix_get` for debugging.

Backend libraries

Behind the scenes, Zabbix encryption can use one of three different libraries: **OpenSSL**, **GnuTLS**, or **mbed TLS**. *Which one to choose?* If using packages, the easiest and safest is to start with whichever the packages are compiled with. If compiling from source, choose the one that's easiest to compile with. In both cases, that's likely to be the library that's endorsed by the packagers and maintained well. The Zabbix team has made a significant effort to implement support for all three libraries in as similar a way as possible from the user's perspective. There could be differences regarding support for some specific features, but those are likely to be more obscure ones: if such problems do come up later, switching from one library to another should be as easy as recompiling the daemons. While in most case, it would likely not matter much which library you're using, it's a good idea to know that; one good reason for supporting these three different libraries is also the ability to switch to a different library if the currently used one has a security vulnerability.

 These libraries are used in a generic manner, and there's no requirement to use the same library for different Zabbix components; it's totally fine to use one library on the Zabbix server, another on the Zabbix proxy, and yet another with `zabbix_sender`.

In this chapter, we'll try out encryption with the Zabbix server and `zabbix_sender` first and then move on to encrypting agent traffic using both PSK and certificate-based encryption. If you have installed from packages, your server most likely already supports encryption. Verify that by looking at the server and agent startup messages:

```
3237:20181226:100436.209 TLS support: YES
```

One way to find out which library the binary has been compiled against would be to run `ldd /usr/sbin/zabbix_server | egrep -i "ssl|tls"`—replace the binary name as needed.

If you compiled from source and TLS support isn't present, recompile the server and agent by adding one of these parameters: `--with-openssl`, `--with-gnutls`, or `--with-mbedtls`.

PSK encryption

Let's start with a simple situation, a single new host for which the Zabbix server will accept PSK-encrypted incoming connections only for the ones we'll send some values to using `zabbix_sender`. For that to work, both the Zabbix server and `zabbix_sender` must be compiled with TLS support. The PSK configuration consists of a PSK identity and key. The identity is some string that isn't considered to be secret; it isn't encrypted during the communication, so don't put sensitive information in the identity string. The key is a hexadecimal string.

Zabbix requires the key to be at least 32 characters (hexadecimal digits) long. The maximum in Zabbix is 512 characters, but it might depend on the specific version of the backend library you're using.

We could just type the key in manually, but a slightly easier method might be using the `openssl` command:

```
$ openssl rand -hex 64
```

This will generate a 512-bit key, which we'll use in a moment. Navigate to **Configuration** | **Hosts**, click on **Create host**, and fill in these values:

- **Host name**: `Encrypted host`
- **Groups**: Have only **Linux servers** in the **Groups** block

Switch to the **Encryption** tab, and in the **Connections from host** section, leave only **PSK** marked. In the **PSK identity** field, enter `secret` and paste the key we generated earlier in the **PSK** field:

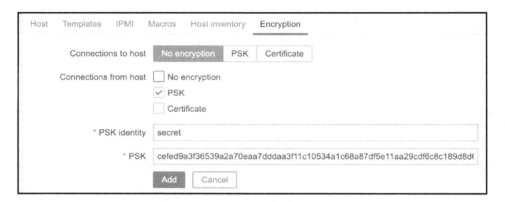

When done, click on the **Add** button at the bottom. Take a look at the **Agent encryption** column for this host:

The first block has only one field and currently says **NONE**. For connections to the agent, only one type was possible, so this column must be showing the currently selected types for outgoing connections from the server perspective. The second block has three fields. We could choose a combination of the acceptable incoming connection types, so this column must be showing what types of incoming connections from the server perspective are accepted for this host.

Now, click on **Items** next to **Encrypted host**, and click on **Create item**. Fill in these values:

- **Name**: Beers in the fridge
- **Type**: **Zabbix trapper**
- **Key**: fridge.beers

Click on the **Add** button at the bottom. Let's try to send a value now, like we did in Chapter 10, *Advanced Item Monitoring*:

```
$ zabbix_sender -z 127.0.0.1 -s "Encrypted host" -k fridge.beers -o 1
```

That should fail:

```
info from server: "processed: 0; failed: 1; total: 1; seconds spent:
0.000193"
```

Notice how the processed count is 0 and the failed count is 1. Let's check the Zabbix server log file:

```
26868:20181228:165704.100 connection of type "unencrypted" is not
allowed for host "Encrypted host"
```

Now, that's actually quite a helpful message; we didn't specify any encryption for zabbix_sender, but we did require an encrypted connection for our host.

Now is the time to get the PSK working for zabbix_sender. Run it with the --help parameter, and look at the TLS connection options section. Oh yes, there're quite a lot of those. Luckily, for PSK encryption, we only need three of them: --tls-connect, --tls-psk-identity, and --tls-psk-file. Before running the command, create a file in the current directory called zabbix_encrypted_host_psk.txt, and paste the hexadecimal key we generated earlier into it.

 It's more secure to create an empty file first, change its permissions to 400 or 600, and paste the key in the file afterward; that way, another user won't have a chance to snatch the key from the file. If a specific user is supposed to invoke zabbix_sender, make sure to set that user as the owner of the file.

Run zabbix_sender again, but with three additional encryption parameters:

```
$ zabbix_sender -z 127.0.0.1 -s "Encrypted host" -k fridge.beers -o 1
--tls-connect psk --tls-psk-identity secret --tls-psk-file
zabbix_encrypted_host_psk.txt
```

We set the connection type to psk with the --tls-connect flag and specified the PSK identity and key file now.

 Zabbix doesn't support specifying the PSK key on the command line for security reasons; it must be passed in from a file.

This time, the value should be sent successfully:

```
info from server: "processed: 1; failed: 0; total: 1; seconds spent:
0.000070"
```

To be sure, verify that this item now has data in the frontend.

Certificate-based encryption

With PSK-based encryption protecting our sensitive Zabbix trapper item, let's move to certificates. We'll generate certificates for the Zabbix server and agent and require encrypted connections on the Zabbix agent side for passive items. Certificate authorities sign certificates, and Zabbix components can trust one or more authorities. By extension, they trust the certificates signed by those authorities.

You might have a certificate infrastructure in your organization, but for our first test, we'll generate all the required certificates ourselves. We'll need a new **Certificate Authority (CA)** that will sign our certificate. Zabbix doesn't support self-signed certificates.

 It's strongly recommended to use intermediate certificate authorities to sign client and server certificates; we won't use them in the following simple example.

Being our own authority

We'll start by creating the certificates in a separate directory. For simplicity's sake, let's do this on `A test host;`, choose any directory where our certificate signing will happen.

 The following is not intended to be a good practice. It's actually doing quite a few bad and insecure things to get the certificates faster. Don't follow these steps for any production setup.

Let's create a folder with our own certificates that we can use to encrypt our traffic.

```
$ mkdir zabbix_ca
$ chmod 700 zabbix_ca
$ cd zabbix_ca
```

Generate the root CA key:

```
$ openssl genrsa -aes256 -out zabbix_ca.key 4096
```

When prompted, enter a password twice to protect the key. Generate and self-sign the root certificate:

```
$ openssl req -x509 -new -key zabbix_ca.key -sha256 -days 3560 -out
zabbix_ca.crt
```

When prompted, enter the password you used for the key before. Fill in the values as prompted; the easiest might be supplying empty values for most, except the country code and common name. The common name doesn't have to be anything too meaningful for our test, so using a simple string such as zabbix_ca will suffice.

Now, on to creating a certificate we'll use for the Zabbix server. First, let's generate a server key and **Certificate Signing Request (CSR)**:

```
$ openssl genrsa -out zabbix_server.key 2048
$ openssl req -new -key zabbix_server.key -out zabbix_server.csr
```

When prompted, enter the country code and common name strings as before. The common name doesn't have to match the server or agent name or anything else, so using a simple string such as zabbix_server will suffice. Let's sign this request now:

```
$ openssl x509 -req -in zabbix_server.csr -CA zabbix_ca.crt -CAkey
zabbix_ca.key -CAcreateserial -out zabbix_server.crt -days 1460 -
sha256
```

When prompted, enter the CA passphrase. Let's continue with the certificate we'll use for the Zabbix agent. Generate an agent key and certificate signing request:

```
$ openssl genrsa -out zabbix_agent.key 2048
$ openssl req -new -key zabbix_agent.key -out zabbix_agent.csr
```

When prompted, enter the country code and common name strings as before. The common name doesn't have to match the server or agent name or anything else, so using a simple string such as zabbix_agent will suffice. Now, let's sign this request:

```
$ openssl x509 -req -in zabbix_agent.csr -CA zabbix_ca.crt -CAkey
zabbix_ca.key -CAcreateserial -out zabbix_agent.crt -days 1460 -sha256
```

When prompted, enter the CA passphrase.

We're done with creating our test certificates. Both keys were created unencrypted; Zabbix doesn't support prompting for the key password at this time.

Setting up Zabbix with certificates

Now, on to making the passive items on A test host use the certificates we just generated. We must provide the certificates to the Zabbix agent. In the directory where the Zabbix agent configuration file is located, create a new directory called zabbix_agent_certs. Restrict access to it, like this:

```
# chown zabbix zabbix_agent_certs
# chmod 500 zabbix_agent_certs
```

From the directory where we generated the certificates, copy the relevant certificate files over to the new directory:

```
# cp zabbix_ca.crt /path/to/zabbix_agent_certs/
# cp zabbix_agent.crt /path/to/zabbix_agent_certs/
# cp zabbix_agent.key /path/to/zabbix_agent_certs/
```

Edit zabbix_agentd.conf and modify these parameters:

```
TLSAccept=cert
TLSConnect=unencrypted
TLSCAFile=/path/to/zabbix_agent_certs/zabbix_ca.crt
TLSCertFile=/path/to/zabbix_agent_certs/zabbix_agent.crt
TLSKeyFile=/path/to/zabbix_agent_certs/zabbix_agent.key
```

This will make the agent only accept connections when they're encrypted and use a certificate signed by that CA, either directly or through intermediates. We'll still use an unencrypted connection for active items. A user could supply certificates and expect all communication to be encrypted now, which would not be the case unless either of the TLSAccept or TLSConnect parameters required encryption. To prevent silently ignoring certificate files, Zabbix enforces one of TLSAccept or TLSConnect when certificates are supplied. Restart the Zabbix agent.

 If a certificate becomes compromised, the certificate authority can revoke it by listing the certificate in a **Certificate Revocation List** (**CRL**). Zabbix supports CRLs with the TLSCRLFile parameter.

Let's take a look at the host configuration list in the Zabbix frontend:

It looks like connections to `A test host` don't work anymore. Let's check the agent log file:

```
failed to accept an incoming connection: from 127.0.0.1: unencrypted
connections are not allowed
```

It looks like we broke it. We set up encryption on the agent but didn't get around to configuring the server side. *What if we would like to roll out encryption to all of the agents and deal with the server later?* In that case, it would be best to set `TLSAccept=cert,unencrypted`—then, agents would still accept unencrypted connections from our server. Once the certificates are deployed and configured on the Zabbix server, we only have to remove `unencrypted` from that parameter and restart the Zabbix agents. Let's try this out; change `zabbix_agentd.conf` again:

```
TLSAccept=cert,unencrypted
```

Restart the agent daemon and observe monitoring resuming from the Zabbix server. Now, let's make the server uses its certificate. We'll place the certificate in a place where the Zabbix server can use it. In the directory where the Zabbix server configuration file is located, create a new directory called `zabbix_server_certs`. Restrict access to it, like this:

```
# chown zabbix zabbix_server_certs
# chmod 500 zabbix_server_certs
```

> If using packages that run Zabbix server with a different username, such as `zabbixs` or `zabbixsrv`, replace the username with the proper one in the two commands.

From the directory where we generated the certificates, copy the certificates over to the new directory:

```
# cp zabbix_ca.crt /path/to/zabbix_server_certs/
# cp zabbix_server.crt /path/to/zabbix_server_certs/
# cp zabbix_server.key /path/to/zabbix_server_certs/
Edit zabbix_server.conf, and modify these parameters:
TLSCAFile=/path/to/zabbix_server_certs/zabbix_ca.crt
TLSCertFile=/path/to/zabbix_server_certs/zabbix_server.crt
TLSKeyFile=/path/to/zabbix_server_certs/zabbix_server.key
```

Now, restart the Zabbix server. Although we have specified the certificates on both agents and the server, passive items still work in unencrypted mode. Let's proceed with making them encrypted. In the Zabbix frontend, navigate to **Configuration** | **Hosts**, click on **A test host**, and switch to the **Encryption** tab. In the **Connections to host** selection, choose **Certificate**, and then click on the **Update** button. After the server configuration cache has been updated, it'll switch to using certificate-based encryption for this host.

> We're changing the configuration for A test host, not encrypted host.

Going back to our scenario where we slowly rolled out certificate-based configuration to our agents and added it to the server later, we can now disable unencrypted connections on the agent side. Change `zabbix_agentd.conf`:

```
TLSAccept=cert
```

Restart the agent. If we had followed this process from the very beginning, monitoring would have continued uninterrupted. Let's try to use `zabbix_get`:

```
$ zabbix_get -s 127.0.0.1 -k system.cpu.load
zabbix_get [5746]: Check access restrictions in Zabbix agent
configuration
```

That fails because the agent only accepts encrypted connections now. As we did for `zabbix_sender`, we can specify the certificate; but we must use the Zabbix server certificate now.

Access to the Zabbix server certificate is required for this command:

```
$ zabbix_get -s 127.0.0.1 -k system.cpu.load --tls-connect cert --tls-
ca-file /path/to/zabbix_server_certs/zabbix_ca.crt --tls-cert-file
/path/to/zabbix_server
 _certs/zabbix_server.crt --tls-key-file
/path/to/zabbix_server_certs/zabbix_server.key
0.030000
```

Certainly, this results in a more secure environment. It isn't enough to spoof the IP address to access this agent. It isn't enough to have an account on the Zabbix server to have access to all agents; access to the server certificate is needed, too. On the other hand, it makes debugging a bit more complicated, as we can't query the agent that easily, and sniffing the traffic is much harder, too.

We used PSK and certificate-based encryption with `zabbix_sender`, `zabbix_get`, and a passive agent, but the same principles apply for active agents. As an exercise, try to get the active agent items working with encryption, too.

Concerns and further reading

At this time, encryption is a very new feature in Zabbix. While it has been developed and tested extremely carefully and pedantically, it's likely to receive further improvements. Make sure to read through the official documentation on encryption for more details and in case changes are made. Right now, let's touch on basic concerns and features that're missing.

So far in this chapter, we've covered Zabbix server, agents, `zabbix_get`, and `zabbix_sender`—*what about Zabbix proxies?* Zabbix proxies fully support encryption. Configuration on the proxy side is very similar to agent configuration, and configuration on the frontend side is done in a similar way to agent encryption configuration too. Keep in mind that all involved components must be compiled with TLS support—any proxies you have might have to be recompiled. When considering encryption, think about the areas where it's needed most; maybe you have the Zabbix server and proxy communicating over the internet while all other connections are in local networks. In that case, it might make sense to set up encryption only for server-proxy communication at first. Note that encryption isn't supported when communicating with the Zabbix Java gateway, but we could easily have the gateway communicate with a Zabbix proxy on the localhost, which in turn provides encryption for the channel to the Zabbix server.

We've already figured out how upgrading and transitioning to encryption can happen seamlessly without interrupting data collection; the ability for all components to accept various connection types allows us to roll the changes out sequentially.

An important reason why we might want to implement encryption only partially is performance. Currently, Zabbix doesn't reuse connections, implement a TLS session cache, or use any other mechanism that would avoid setting up an encrypted connection from scratch every time. This can be especially devastating if you have lots of passive agent items. Make sure to understand the potential impact before reconfiguring it all.

Encryption isn't currently supported for authentication purposes. That is, we can't omit active agent hostnames and figure out which host it is based on the certificate alone. Similarly, we can't use encrypted connections for active agent auto-registration.

For certificate-based encryption, we only specified the certificates and the CA information. If the CA used is large enough, that wouldn't be very secure; any certificate signed by that CA would be accepted. Zabbix also allows verifying both the issuer and subject of the remote certificate. Unless you're using an internal CA that's used for Zabbix only, it's highly recommended to limit the issuer and subject. This can be done on the host or proxy properties in the frontend and by using the `TLSServerCertIssuer` and `TLSServerCertSubject` parameters in the agent or proxy configuration file.

Summary

In this chapter, we explored the built-in Zabbix encryption that's supported between all components; server, proxy, agent, `zabbix_sender`, and `zabbix_get`. While not supported for the Java gateway, a Zabbix proxy could easily be put in front of the gateway to provide encryption back to the Zabbix server.

Zabbix supports pre-shared key and TLS certificate-based encryption, and can use one of three different backend libraries; OpenSSL, GnuTLS, or mbed TLS. In case of security or other issues with one library, users have an option to switch to another library.

The upgrade and encryption deployment can be done in steps. All Zabbix components can accept multiple connection types at the same time. In our example, the agent would be set up to accept both encrypted and unencrypted connections, and when done with configuring all agents for encryption, we would switch to encrypted connections on the server side. Once that would be verified to work as expected, unencrypted connections could be disabled on the agents.

With the encryption being built in and easy to set up, it's worth remembering that encrypted connections will need more resources and that Zabbix doesn't support connection pooling or other methods that could decrease load. It might be worth securing the most important channels first, leaving endpoints for later. For example, encrypting the communication between the Zabbix server and proxies would likely be a priority over connections to individual agents.

In the next chapter, we'll work more closely with Zabbix data. That will include retrieving monitoring data directly from the database and modifying the database in an emergency case, such as losing all administrative passwords. We'll also discuss the XML export and import functionality and the Zabbix API.

Questions

1. What types of encryption can we use in Zabbix?
2. Is there anything at the moment that isn't encrypted?

Further reading

Read the following articles for more information:

- **Encryption**: https://zabbix.com/documentation/4.0/manual/encryption
- **Using certificates**: https://zabbix.com/documentation/4.0/manual/encryption/using_certificates
- **Using pre-shared keys**: https://zabbix.com/documentation/4.0/manual/encryption/using_pre_shared_keys

Working Closely with Data 19

Using a web frontend and built-in graphing is nice and easy, but sometimes you might want to perform some nifty graphing in an external spreadsheet application or maybe feed data into another system. Sometimes, you might want to make some configuration change that isn't possible or is too cumbersome to perform using the web interface. While that's not the first thing most Zabbix users would need, it's handy to know when the need arises. Hence, in this chapter, the following topics will be covered:

- Getting raw data
- Diving into the database
- Using XML import/export for configuration
- Starting with the Zabbix API

Getting raw data

Raw data is data as it's stored in the Zabbix database, with minor, if any, conversions performed. Retrieving such data is mostly useful for analysis in other applications.

Extracting from the frontend

In some situations, it might be a simple need to quickly graph some data together with other data that isn't monitored by Zabbix (yet you plan to add it soon, of course), in which case, a quick hack job of spreadsheet magic might be the solution. The easiest way to get data to be used outside of the frontend is actually from the frontend itself.

Let's find out how we can easily get historical data for some item:

1. Go to **Monitoring** | **Latest data** and select **A test host** from the **Hosts** filter field, and then click on **Filter**.
2. Click on **Graph** next to **CPU Load**. That gives us the standard Zabbix graph. That wasn't what we wanted, now, was it? But this interface allows us to access raw data easily using the drop-down menu in the top-right corner—choose **Values** in there, as shown in the following screenshot:

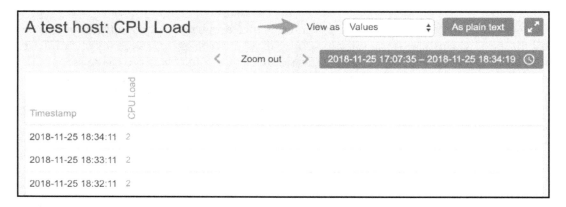

If the item has stopped collecting data some time ago and you just want to quickly look at the latest values, choose the 500 latest values instead. It'll get you the data with fewer clicks.

One thing worth paying attention to is the time period controls at the top, which are the same as the ones available for graphs, screens, and everywhere else in Zabbix. Using the new time filter, we can display data for any arbitrary period. In the previous time selector, there was a standard of one hour; in the new time selector, you'll notice that it remembers your last choice. In this case, the time selection of one hour is probably fine. For some items that're polled less frequently, we'll often want to use a much longer period:

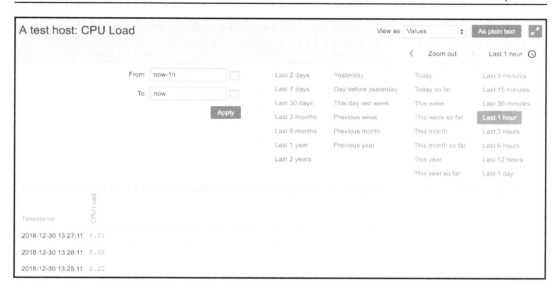

While we could copy data out of this table with a browser that supports HTML copying, then paste it into some receiving software that can parse HTML, that isn't always feasible. A quick and easy solution is in the upper-right corner—just click on the **As plain text** button.

This gives us the very same dataset, just without all of the HTML-ish surroundings, such as the Zabbix frontend parts and the table. We can easily save this representation as a file or copy data from it and reuse it in spreadsheet software or any other application. An additional benefit this data provides is that all entries have the corresponding Unix timestamps listed as well.

Technically, this page is still an HTML page. Zabbix users have asked to be provide with a proper plain-text version instead.

Querying the database

Grabbing data from the frontend is quick and simple, but this method is unsuitable for large volumes of data and is hard to automate—parsing the frontend pages can be done, but isn't the most efficient way of obtaining data. Another way to get to the data would be to directly query the database.

We'll look at the Zabbix API a bit later. It's suggested to use the API unless there are performance issues.

Let's find out how historical data is stored. Launch the MySQL command-line client (simply called `mysql`, usually available in the `path` variable) and connect to the `zabbix` database as the `zabbix` user:

```
$ mysql -u zabbix -p zabbix
```

When prompted, enter the `zabbix` user's password (which you can remind yourself of by looking at the contents of `zabbix_server.conf`) and execute the following command in the MySQL client:

```
mysql> show tables;
```

This will list all of the tables in the `zabbix` database—exactly 144 in Zabbix 4.0. That's a lot of tables to figure out, but for our current need (getting some historical data out), we'll only need a few. First are the most interesting ones—tables that contain gathered data. All historical data is stored in tables, the names of which start with `history`. As you can see, there're many of those with different suffixes—*why is that?* Zabbix stores retrieved data in different tables depending on the data type. The relationship between types in the Zabbix frontend and database is as follows:

- `history`: Numeric (float)
- `history_log`: Log
- `history_str`: Character
- `history_text`: Text
- `history_uint`: Numeric (unsigned)

To grab the data, we first have to find out the data type for that particular item. The easiest way to do that's to open item properties and observe the **Type of information** field. We can try taking a look at the contents of the history table by retrieving all fields for three records:

```
mysql> select * from history limit 3;
```

The output will show us that each record in this table contains four fields (your output will have different values):

```
+--------+------------+--------+-----------+
| itemid | clock      | value  | ns        |
+--------+------------+--------+-----------+
|  23668 | 1430700808 | 0.0000 | 644043321 |
|  23669 | 1430700809 | 0.0000 | 644477514 |
|  23668 | 1430700838 | 0.0000 | 651484815 |
+--------+------------+--------+-----------+
```

The preceding output values are explained as follows:

- The next-to-last field, `value`, is quite straightforward—it contains the gathered value
- The `clock` field contains the timestamp in Unix time—the number of seconds since the so-called Unix epoch, 00:00:00 UTC on January 1, 1970
- The `ns` column contains nanoseconds inside that particular second

An easy way to convert the Unix timestamp into a human-readable form that doesn't require an internet connection is using the GNU date command: `date -d@<timestamp>`. For example, `date -d@1234567890` will return `Sat Feb 14 01:31:30 EET 2009`.

The first field, `itemid`, is the most mysterious one. *How can we determine which ID corresponds to which item?* Again, the easiest way is to use the frontend. You should still have the item properties page open in your browser, so take a look at the address bar. Along with other variables, you'll see part of the string that reads like `itemid=23668`. Great, so we already have the `itemid` value on hand. Let's try to grab some values for this item from the database:

`mysql> select * from history where itemid=23668 limit 3;`

Use the `itemid` value that you obtained from the page URL:

```
+--------+------------+--------+-----------+
| itemid | clock      | value  | ns        |
+--------+------------+--------+-----------+
|  23668 | 1430700808 | 0.0000 | 644043321 |
|  23668 | 1430700838 | 0.0000 | 651484815 |
|  23668 | 1430700868 | 0.0000 | 657907318 |
+--------+------------+--------+-----------+
```

The resulting set contains only values from that item, as evidenced by the `itemid` field in the output.

We'll usually want to retrieve values from a specific period. Guessing Unix timestamps isn't entertaining, so we can again use the date command to figure out the opposite—a Unix timestamp from a date in human-readable form:

```
$ date -d "2016-01-13 13:13:13" "+%s"
1452683593
```

The -d flag tells the date command to show the specified time instead of the current time, and the %s format sequence instructs it to output in Unix timestamp format. This fancy little command also accepts more free-form input, such as last Sunday or next Monday.

As an exercise, figure out two recent timestamps half an hour apart, then retrieve values for this item from the database. Hint—the SQL query will look similar to this:

```
mysql> select * from history where itemid=23668 and clock >=
1250158393 and clock < 1250159593;
```

You should get back some values. To verify the period, convert the returned clock values back into a human-readable format. The obtained information can be now passed to any external applications for analyzing, graphing, or comparing.

With history* tables containing the raw data, we can get a lot of information out of them. But sometimes, we might want to get a bigger picture only, and that's when table trends can help. Let's find out what exactly this table holds. In the MySQL client, execute this:

```
mysql> select * from trends limit 2;
```

We're now selecting two records from the trends table:

itemid	clock	num	value_min	value_avg	value_max
23668	1422871200	63	0.0000	1.0192	1.4300
23668	1422874800	120	1.0000	1.0660	1.6300

Just like the history tables have history and history_uint, there are trends and trends_uint tables for **Numeric (float)** and **Numeric (unsigned)** types of information. There're no corresponding _log, _str, or _text tables as trend information can be calculated for numeric data only.

Here, we find two familiar friends, `itemid` and `clock`, whose purpose and usage we just discussed. The last three values are quite self-explanatory—`value_min`, `value_avg`, and `value_max` contain the minimal, average, and maximal values of the data. *But for what period?* The `trends` table contains information on hourly periods. So, if we would like to plot the minimal, average, or maximal values per hour for one day in some external application, instead of recalculating this information, we can grab data for this precalculated data directly from the database.

But there's one field we've missed—`num`. This field stores the number of values there were in the hour that is covered in this record. It's useful if you have hundreds of records each hour in a day that're all more or less in line but data is missing for one hour, except a single extremely high or low value. Instead of giving the same weight to the values for every hour when calculating daily, weekly, monthly, or yearly data, we can more correctly calculate the final value.

If you want to access data from the database to reuse in external applications, beware of the retention periods—data is removed from the `history*` and `trends*` tables after the number of days specified in the `History storage period` and `Trend storage period` fields for the specific items.

Using data in a remote site

We covered data retrieval on the Zabbix server. But *what if we have a remote site, a Zabbix proxy, a powerful proxy machine, and a slow link?* In situations like this, we might be tempted to extract proxy data to reuse it. However, the proxy stores data in a different way than the Zabbix server.

Just like in the previous chapter, run the following command:

```
$ sqlite3 /tmp/zabbix_proxy.db
```

This opens the specified database. We can look at which tables are present by using the `.tables` command:

```
sqlite> .tables
```

Notice how there're still all of the `history*` tables, although we already know that the proxy doesn't use them, opting for `proxy_history` instead. The database schema is the same on the server and proxy, even though the proxy doesn't use most of those tables at all. Let's look at the fields of the `proxy_history` table.

To check the table definition in SQLite, you can use the `.schema proxy_history` command.

The following table illustrates the item fields and their usage:

Field	Usage
`id`	The record ID, used to determine which records have been synchronized back to the server
`itemid`	The item ID as it appears on the Zabbix server
`clock`	The Unix time of the record, using proxy host time
`timestamp`	Relevant for time, parsed through the log file time format field, or for Windows event log monitoring—the timestamp as it appears on the monitored machine
`source`	Relevant for Windows event log monitoring only—event log source
`severity`	Relevant for Windows event log monitoring only—event log severity
`value`	The actual value of the monitored item
`logeventid`	Relevant for Windows event log monitoring only—event ID
`ns`	Nanoseconds for this entry
`state`	Whether this item is working normally or it's in the unsupported state
`lastlogsize`	The size of the log file that's been parsed already
`mtime`	The modification time of rotated log files that have been parsed already
`meta`	If set to 1, it indicates that this entry contains no actual log data, only `lastlogsize` and `mtime`

The proxy doesn't have much information on item configuration; you'll need to grab that from the Zabbix server if you're doing remote processing. For example, the proxy has item keys and intervals, but item names aren't available in the proxy database.

As can be seen, several fields will be used for log file monitoring and some others only for Windows event log monitoring.

Diving further into the database

With some knowledge of how to extract historical and trend data from tables, we might as well continue looking at other interesting, and relatively simple, things that we can find and perhaps even change directly in the database.

Managing users

We saw how managing users was an easy task using the frontend. But *what if you have forgotten the password? What if some remote installation of Zabbix is administered by local staff, and the only Zabbix super admin has left for a month-long trip without a phone and nobody else knows the password?* If you have access to the database, you can try to solve such problems. Let's find out what exactly Zabbix stores about users and how. In the MySQL console, execute this:

```
mysql> select * from users limit 2;
```

This way, we are listing all data for two users at the most:

```
+--------+--------+--------+-------------+--------------------------------+-----+
| userid | alias  | name   | surname     | passwd                         | url |
+--------+--------+--------+-------------+--------------------------------+-----+
|      1 | Admin  | Zabbix | Administrator | 5fce1b3e34b520afeffb37ce08c7cd66 |     |
|      2 | guest  |        |             | d41d8cd98f00b204e9800998ecf8427e |     |
+--------+--------+--------+-------------+--------------------------------+-----+
2 rows in set (0.00 sec)
```

The example output is trimmed on the right-hand side and fewer than half of the original columns are shown here. You can also replace the trailing semicolon in the SQL query with \G to obtain vertical output, like this:

```
select * from users limit 2 \G
```

That's a lot of fields. We'd better find out what each of them means:

Field	Usage
userid	Quite simple, it's a unique numeric ID.
alias	This is more commonly known as a username or login name.
name	This is the user's name, usually their given name.
surname	This surely can't be anything else but the surname.
passwd	The password hash is stored here. Zabbix stores MD5 hashes for authentication.
url	The after-login URL is stored in this field.
autologout	This shows whether auto-logout for this user is enabled. Non-zero values indicate timeout.
lang	This is the language for the frontend.

Field	Usage
refresh	This is the page refresh in seconds. If zero, page refresh is disabled.
type	The number is linked to the type of user—user, admin, super admin, or guest.
theme	This is the frontend theme to use.
attempt_failed	This is how many consecutive failed login attempts there have been.
attempt_ip	This is the IP of the last failed login attempt.
attempt_clock	This is the time of the last failed login attempt.
rows_per_page	This is how many rows per page are displayed in long lists.

As we can see, many of the fields are options that're accessible from the user profile or properties page, although some of these aren't directly available. We mentioned password resetting before; let's look at a simple method to do that. If passwords are stored as MD5 hashes, we must obtain those first. A common method is the command-line utility, md5sum. Passing some string to it will output the desired result, so we can try executing this:

```
$ echo "somepassword" | md5sum
531cee37d369e8db7b054040e7a943d3  -
```

The MD5 hash is printed, along with a minus sign, which denotes standard input. If we had run md5sum on a file, the filename would have been printed there instead.

 The command-line utility provides a nice way to check various sequences. For example, try to figure out what the default guest password hash, d41d8cd98f00b204e9800998ecf8427e, represents.

Now, the problem is that if we try to use this string as a password hash, it'll fail. In this case, the hash is calculated on the passed string, including the newline at the end. For the correct version, we have to pass the -n flag to echo, which suppresses the trailing newline:

```
$ echo -n "somepassword" | md5sum
9c42a1346e333a770904b2a2b37fa7d3  -
```

Notice the huge difference in the resulting string. Great, now we only have to reset the password.

The following statement changes the Zabbix administrative user password. Don't perform this on a production system, except in an emergency situation:

```
mysql> update users set passwd='9c42a1346e333a770904b2a2b37fa7d3'
where userid=1;
Query OK, 1 row affected (0.01 sec)
Rows matched: 1   Changed: 1   Warnings: 0
```

From here on, you should be able to log in to the Zabbix frontend as `Admin/somepassword`—try it out. Feel free to change the password back after that.

There's actually an easier method available. MySQL has a built-in function for calculating MD5 hashes, so all of this trickery could be replaced with a simpler approach:

```
mysql> update users set passwd=MD5('somepassword') where
alias='Admin';
```

 At this time, Zabbix doesn't use password salting. While making it simpler to reset the password, it also makes it easier to find the actual password in MD5 tables.

We also mentioned making some user a Zabbix super admin. This change is fairly simple—all we have to do is change a single number:

```
mysql> update users set type=3 where alias='wannabe_admin';
```

And that's it—the `wannabe_admin` user will become a Zabbix super admin.

Changing existing data

While once the monitoring data has been gathered, you usually won't have a need to change it, there might be some rare cases when that might be required. Back in Chapter 3, *Monitoring with Zabbix Agents and Basic Protocols*, we created items for network traffic monitoring, and we gathered data in bytes, but in network management, usually bits per second are used instead. While it would often be possible for you to simply reconfigure the items and clear the old data, *what if you need to preserve already gathered values?* Directly editing the database might be the only solution.

Before doing that, you would have to modify the item in question. If data is coming in bytes but we want bits, *what do we do?* Right, we configure the multiplier for that item and set the multiplier to 8. Additionally, change `units` to b (bits) while performing the change.

When performing the change to the item, take a quick look at a clock.

While this will deal with all future incoming values, it will leave us with inconsistent data before that moment. As we do not want to delete it, we must find some way to fix it. Our problem is twofold:

- We have incorrect data in the database.
- We have both incorrect and correct data in the database (old and new values).

This means that we can't simply convert all values, as that would break the new, correct ones.

 If you've set any triggers based on traffic amount, don't forget to change those as well.

Finding out when

Figuring out the moment when correct information started flowing in can be most easily done by looking at the frontend. Navigate to **Monitoring | Latest data**, click on **History** for that item, and then select **Values** or **500 latest values**. Look around the time you changed the item multiplier plus a minute or so, and check for a notable change in the scale. While it might be hard to pinpoint the exact interval between two checks (network traffic can easily fluctuate over eight times in value between two checks), there should be a pretty constant increase in values. Look at the times to the left of the values and choose a moment between the first good value and the last bad value.

The when in computer language

But as we now know, all time-related information in the Zabbix database is stored as Unix timestamps. For that, the GNU `date` command can help again. Execute the following on the Zabbix server, by replacing the exact time with what you deduced from the latest values:

```
$ date -d "2016-03-13 13:13:13" "+%s"
```

That'll output the Unix timestamp of that moment, which in the case of this example would be `1457867593`.

Be aware of the difference in time zones, though—values displayed in the frontend will usually have the local time zone applied. Check that the value for the timestamp you obtained matches the value in the database for that same timestamp. There's actually an easier and safer way to obtain the value timestamp. While still looking at the value history for the item in the frontend, click the **As plain text** button in the upper-right corner:

```
A test host: Incoming traffic on enp0s3
2018-12-30 14:18:39 1546172319 453
2018-12-30 14:18:09 1546172289 395
2018-12-30 14:17:39 1546172259 393
2018-12-30 14:17:09 1546172229 399
```

Notice how the third column is exactly what we wanted—the Unix timestamp. In this case, we don't have to worry about the time zone, either.

Finding out what

Now that we know the exact time that limits the change, we must also know which item we must modify for it. Wait, but we do know that already, *don't we?* Almost. What we need is the item ID to make changes to the database. The easiest way to find that out is by opening the item properties in the configuration section and copying the ID from the URL, like we did before.

Performing the change

By now, we should have two cryptic-looking values:

- The time in Unix timestamp format
- The item ID

What do we have to do now? Multiply by eight all of the values for the item ID before that timestamp. With the data we have, it's actually quite simple—in the MySQL console, we would have to execute this:

```
mysql> update history_uint set value=value*8 where itemid=<our ID>
and clock<'<our timestamp>';
```

 To be safe, you might want to perform the modifications in a transaction and check the results while the transaction is still open. If the results are satisfactory, commit the changes. If not, roll them back.

We are updating `history_uint`, because even though the data for the network traffic is a decimal number because of the **Store as item** option, we dropped the decimal part by storing the data as an integer. See `Chapter 3`, *Monitoring with Zabbix Agents and Basic Protocols*, to remind yourself why we did so. This single query should be enough to convert all of the old data into bits.

 If you have lots of historical data in total and for this item, such a query can take quite some time to complete. When running such commands on a remote system, use a tool such as `screen`.
We're only modifying the `history` table here. If the item has been collecting data for a longer period of time, we would also have to modify the corresponding `trends` or `trends_uint` tables.

Using XML import/export for configuration

The web frontend is an acceptable tool for making configuration changes to a Zabbix server, unless you have to make lots of modifications, which aren't made easier in the frontend with methods such as mass update. One simple method is exporting configuration to an XML file, making some changes, and importing it back in.

XML import/export is very often used to share templates—you can find a large number of those on `https://zabbix.org` and `http://share.zabbix.com`.

 We'll look at the Zabbix API a bit later. It's suggested to use the API to modify Zabbix configuration, as it also offers much more complete functionality than XML import/export—although the XML approach might be simpler in some cases.

Let's look at how a simple roundtrip would work.

Exporting the initial configuration

In the frontend, open **Configuration** | **Templates** and select **Custom Templates** in the **Group** drop-down menu. Mark the checkbox next to **C_Template_Email** and click on the **Export** button at the bottom. Your browser will offer to save a file called `zbx_export_templates.xml`; save it somewhere on your local machine.

Modifying the configuration

Now, with the file in hand, we can modify the configuration. This method gives us free rein over host and host-attached information, so modifications are limited only by Zabbix's functionality and our imagination. At this time, the following entities are available for XML export and import:

- Hosts
- Templates
- Host groups
- Network maps
- Map images (icons and backgrounds)
- Screens
- Value maps

Out of these, host groups and images are only exported indirectly. For hosts, all of their properties and sub-entities are exported and imported, except the web scenarios (this functionality might be available in Zabbix 3.2). Host groups are exported together with hosts or templates and, when exporting a map, the images used in it are exported in the same file. It's possible to import both a single type of entity and any number and combination of them in the same XML file.

The XML export format

Open the saved XML export in your favorite editor. In this file, you'll see all of the data that this host has, and the file will start like this:

```
<?xml version="1.0" encoding="UTF-8"?>
<zabbix_export>
    <version>4.0</version>
    <date>2018-12-30T12:22:25Z</date>
    <groups>
        <group>
            <name>Custom templates</name>
        </group>
    </groups>
    <templates>
        <template>
            <template>C_Template_Email</template>
```

In this case, each template is contained in a `<template>` block, which in turn has blocks for all of the things attached to that template. The format is simple, and most things should be obvious simply from taking a glance at the XML and maybe sometimes by comparing values in XML with values in the frontend configuration section. An exception might be the values available for each field. Those can often be gleaned from the API documentation, which we'll cover in a moment.

While we look at the exported template, we can see the same information that an exported host would have, including template linkage—that's what the second nested `<templates>` block denotes.

Scripting around the export

While manually making a single change to an exported file can be handy, it's the large changes that expose the benefit of this approach best. As the most simple approach to creating an XML file, we can use shell scripts.

For example, if we had to add a lot of similar items, we could script an XML file with them all and import them in one go. The easiest approach would be to create some items in the frontend, export that host, and write a quick script that loops over these item definitions and creates the remaining items. The same can be done for triggers and custom graphs as well. Again, it's best to create all data for a single element, export it, and examine it to find out how it should be put back together.

Unless individual entities are to be modifiable, consider using a custom **Low-Level Discovery** (**LLD**) rule, as covered in `Chapter 11`, *Automating Configuration*.

Other larger-scale problems that can be solved by an XML round-trip are the following:

- **Adding lots of devices**: If you're given a large list of switches with IP addresses, adding them all through the interface is a monstrous task. With XML, it becomes a very easy and quick one instead. To do that, simply create a single host, linked against the previously created template or several ones, and then export it to get some sort of a template. In this export, you'll basically have to change a couple of values only—notably, the connection details in the `<interfaces>` element. Then, just proceed to create a loop that creates new `<host>` entries with the corresponding IP and hostname data. Note that it's enough to only specify host information in this file—all items, triggers, graphs, and other entities will be attached based on the information that's contained in the template or templates specified in the `<templates>` block.
- **Creating many graphs with lots of arbitrary items**: Sometimes, it might be required to create not only one graph per port, but also graphs grouping items from several devices and other arbitrary collections. Export an example host and script graph items in a loop. These are located in the `<graph_elements>` block.

A graph with a huge number of items can soon become unreadable. Don't overdo items on a single graph.

Importing modified configuration

For our first XML export/import, we won't do large-scale scripting. Instead, let's make a simple modification. In the saved `zbx_export_templates.xml` file, find the item block with the `net.tcp.service[smtp]` key. An item block starts with an `<item>` tag and ends with an `</item>` tag. Copy this item block and insert it below the existing block, and then change the item name to POP3 server status and the key to `net.tcp.service[pop3]`.

Save this as a new file. Now, on to the actual import process—perform the following steps:

1. Back in the frontend, in the **Configuration** | **Templates** section, click on **Import** in the upper right-hand corner. In this form, click on **Choose file** next to the **Import file** field and choose the saved file.

2. Feel free to explore the **Rules** section, although the defaults will do for us. The only types of entities we're interested in are missing items, and the respective checkbox in the **Create new** column next to **Items** is already marked.

3. Click on **Import** to proceed. This should complete successfully, so click on **Details** in the upper-left corner. While all other records will be about updating, there should be two entries about an item being created. These will be the only ones that make any changes, as all of the updates do nothing—the data in the XML file is the same as in the database. As we're adding this item for a template, it also gets added to all other hosts and templates that're linked against this one. In previous versions, we would get detailed information about this, but in Zabbix 4.0, we only get a confirmation that the import was successful:

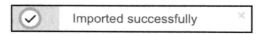

Let's verify that this item was added with the key we used in the XML file. Navigate to **Configuration** | **Hosts,** make sure **Linux servers** is selected in the **Group** drop-down menu, and click on the **Items** link next to the **Another host** entry. Our new item should be visible in the item list, showing that it's been correctly added to the linked host. Remember that we only added it to the upstream template in our import process:

| C_Template_Email: POP3 server status | net.tcp.service[pop3] |

Generating hosts

One of the possible problems that we need to solve when importing hosts in Zabbix from XML is creating a larger number of hosts. We could use a hackish script like this to generate a Zabbix host XML out of a CSV file:

```
#!/bin/bash

split="%"
agent_port=10050
useip=1

[[ -s "$1" ]] || {
        echo "Usage: pass an input CSV file as the first parameter
File should contain data in the following format:
hostname,dns,ip,hostgroup,linked_template,agent_port
agent_port is optional
For groups and templates multiple entries are separated with %
First line is ignored (assuming a header)"
        exit 1
}

echo "<?xml version=\"1.0\" encoding=\"UTF-8\"?>
<zabbix_export>
    <version>4.0</version>
    <date>$(date "+%Y-%m-%dT%H:%M:%SZ")</date>
    <hosts>"
while read line; do
        hostname=$(echo $line | cut -d, -f1)
        dns=$(echo $line | cut -d, -f2)
        ip=$(echo $line | cut -d, -f3)
        group=$(echo $line | cut -d, -f4)
        template=$(echo $line | cut -d, -f5)
        port=$(echo $line | cut -d, -f6)

        hostname1=${hostname%\"}
        dns1=${dns%\"}
        ip1=${ip%\"}
        group1=${group%\"}
        template1=${template%\"}
        port1=${port%\"}

        hostgroups=$(echo $group1 | tr "$split" "\n")
        templates=$(echo $template1 | tr "$split" "\n")

        echo "        <host>
        <host>$(echo ${hostname1#\"})</host>
```

```
                    <name>$(echo ${hostname1#\"})</name>
                    <status>0</status>
                    <description/>
                    <proxy/>
                    <ipmi_authtype>-1</ipmi_authtype>
                    <ipmi_privilege>2</ipmi_privilege>
                    <ipmi_username/>
                    <ipmi_password/>
                    <tls_connect>1</tls_connect>
                    <tls_accept>1</tls_accept>
                    <tls_issuer/>
                    <tls_subject/>
                    <tls_psk_identity/>
                    <tls_psk/>
                    <interfaces>
                        <interface>
                            <default>1</default>
                            <type>1</type>
                            <useip>$useip</useip>
                            <ip>${ip1#\"}</ip>
                            <dns>${dns1#\"}</dns>
                            <port>${port1:-$agent_port}</port>
                            <bulk>1</bulk>
                            <interface_ref>if1</interface_ref>
                        </interface>
                    </interfaces>"
        echo "              <groups>"
        while read hostgroup; do
                echo "                  <group>
                    <name>${hostgroup#\"}</name>
                </group>"
        done < <(echo "$hostgroups")
        echo "              </groups>
            <templates>"
        while read hosttemplate; do
                echo "                  <template>
                    <name>${hosttemplate#\"}</name>
                </template>"
        done < <(echo "$templates")
        echo "              </templates>"
        echo "          </host>"
done < <(tail -n +2 $1)

echo "    </hosts>
</zabbix_export>"
```

Save this script as `csv_to_zabbix_xml.sh` and make it executable:

```
$ chmod 755 csv_to_zabbix_xml.sh
```

 Some people say that the shell isn't an appropriate tool to handle XML files. The shell is a great tool for anything and perfectly fine for our simple, quick host generation.

This script takes a CSV file as the input, ignores the first line, and uses all other lines as host entries. We must specify the hostname, DNS, IP, and agent port. Additionally, for each host, we can specify multiple host groups and templates the host should be linked to by delimiting multiple entries with a percent sign. The `useip` parameter defaults to `1`; setting it to `0` will use DNS instead. Notice how we're generating all kinds of fields we aren't interested in at this time, all of the `IPMI` and `TLS` fields, setting the `bulk` parameter for the `agent` interface. Unfortunately, Zabbix XML exports are unnecessarily verbose, and it expects the same verbosity back. For a larger number of hosts, this will significantly increase the size of the XML file.

 Quoting in the CSV file allows us to use commas in host group names.

To use this file, let's create a simple CSV file called `test.csv`:

```
"Host name","Host DNS","Host IP","Host groups","Templates","port"
"test-xml-import","dns.name","1.2.3.4","Linux servers%Zabbix
servers","Template Module ICMP Ping"
```

We used a header line here, as the first line's always excluded—a single line in a file wouldn't do anything at all. Now, let's run our script:

```
$ ./csv_to_zabbix_xml.sh test.csv > zabbix_generated_hosts.xml
```

In the frontend, navigate to **Configuration** | **Hosts**, click on **Import** in the upper-right corner, choose the `zabbix_generated_hosts.xml` file in the **Import file** field, and click on **Import**. The import should be successful—verify that back in **Configuration** | **Hosts**. As this host isn't very useful right now, feel free to delete it.

Importing images

When configuring network maps, we had a chance to upload our own icons. It is highly inefficient to upload a lot of images one by one. One could script the process using a utility such as `curl`, but that requires a new connection to the frontend for every image and could break if the Zabbix interface is changed in future versions. Images are supported in XML import, though, and we can also have a file with just the images. We could write our own script for this, but there is already a script shipped with Zabbix—look for the `png_to_xml.sh` script in the `misc/images` directory. This script accepts two parameters—the directory where the images are found and the output filename. For example, if we had images in a directory called `map_icons`, we would run the script as follows:

```
./png_to_xml.sh map_icons zabbix_images.xml
```

To import the images, we would go to any page that has the **Import** button, such as **Configuration** | **Maps**, click the **Import** button, and mark the checkboxes next to the **Images** row. Only super admins can import images. Images are exported and imported in `base64` format, so there's no binary data in the XML file. An example of an exported image is this:

```
<encodedImage>iVBORw0KGgoAAAANSUhEUgAAADAAAAAwCAYAAABXAvmHAAAABmJLR0QA
/wD/AP+gvaeTAAAM70lEQVR42u2ZeXBV133HP+cub9NDSGIR
...
</encodedImage>
```

This output is significantly cut—the real `base64` value would take a few pages here.

Starting with the Zabbix API

The approaches we looked at earlier—direct database edits and XML import/export—were either risky or limited. Editing the database is risky because there's very little validation, and upgrading to a newer version of Zabbix can change the database schema, making our tools and approaches invalid. XML import/export was nice, but very limited—it didn't allow the modification of users, network discovery rules, actions, and lots of things in the Zabbix configuration.

This is where the Zabbix API could help. It's a JSON-based interface to Zabbix configuration and data. It offers way more functionality than XML import/export does, although there're still bits and pieces of configuration that can't be controlled using it.

The Zabbix API currently is frontend based—it's implemented in PHP. To use it, we connect to the web server running the frontend and issue our requests. There're a lot of ways to do this, but here, we'll try to do things in a manner that's language independent—we'll use `curl` and issue the requests from the shell.

Simple operations

The Zabbix API is request-response-based. We send a request and get a response—either the data we requested or a success/failure indicator. Let's look at some simple, practical examples of what we can do with the API. We'll use simple `curl` requests to the API. Let's try this on the Zabbix server:

```
$ curl -s -X POST -H 'Content-Type: application/json-rpc' -d ''
http://127.0.0.1/zabbix/api_jsonrpc.php
```

In this request, note the following:

- We use the `POST` method and send the JSON string with the `-d` parameter—empty for now.
- We also specify the `-s` parameter, which enables silent or quiet mode and suppresses progress and error messages.
- The URL is the Zabbix API endpoint, `api_jsonrpc.php`. This will be the same for all API requests. Additionally, we specify the content type to be `application/json-rpc`. This is required. If omitted, the Zabbix API will return an empty response, which doesn't help much. The request we issued should return a response like this:

```
{"jsonrpc":"2.0","error":{"code":-32600,"message":"Invalid
Request.","data":"The received JSON isn't a valid JSON-RPC
Request."},"id":null}
```

That didn't work, but at least there's an error message. Let's proceed with more valid requests now.

Obtaining the API version

One of the simplest ways to obtain the API version in Zabbix is probably by Zabbix itself making use of the HTTP agent item and some JSON preprocessing. For this, we'll create a new item. It doesn't really matter on what host—let's do it on A test host. Go to **Configuration | Hosts** and create a new item on our A test host host with the following parameters:

- **Name**: Check Zabbix API Version
- **Type**: HTTP agent
- **Key**: check_zabbix_api_version
- **URL**: http://<zabbix-server-ip>/zabbix/api_jsonrpc.php
- **Request type**: POST
- **Request body type**: JSON data
- **Request body**: This field is filled with the following value:

```
{
"jsonrpc": "2.0",
"method": "apiinfo.version",
"params": [],
"id": 1
}
```

- **Retrieve mode**: Body
- **Type of information**: Character

Next, we have to add some information in the **Preprocessing** tab as the result would be a JSON string looking like this:
{"jsonrpc":"2.0","result":"4.0.2","id":1}. This should look like what's shown in the following screenshot:

| Item | Preprocessing |

* Name   Check Zabbix API Version

Type   HTTP agent

* Key   check_zabbix_api_version   Select

* URL   http://192.168.1.23/zabbix/api_jsonrpc.php   Parse

Query fields   Name   Value

   name   ⇒   value   Remove

Add

Request type   POST

Timeout   3s

Request body type   Raw data   JSON data   XML data

Request body
```
{
    "jsonrpc": "2.0",
    "method": "apiinfo.version",
    "params": [],
    "id": 1
}
```

Headers   Name   Value

   name   ⇒   value   Remove

Add

Required status codes   200

Follow redirects   ☐

Retrieve mode   Body   Headers   Body and headers

Convert to JSON   ☐

HTTP proxy   http://[user[:password]@]proxy.example.com[:port]

HTTP authentication   None

SSL verify peer   ☐

SSL verify host   ☐

SSL certificate file

SSL key file

SSL key password

* Host interface   192.168.1.29 : 10050

Type of information   Character

So, in the **Preprocessing** tab, select **JSON Path** and, for the **Parameters** field, write $.result:

The end result should look similar and in the latest data, we can then read out the version from our API:

In the **Request body** field, we added some JSON information; the reason we knew what to add here was because this is well explained in the online Zabbix documentation—I added the URL as a reference at the end of this chapter.

 It's also good to know that, starting from Zabbix 2.0.4, the API version matches the Zabbix version.

Logging in

Before we can perform any useful operations through the API, we must log in. Our JSON string would be as follows:

```
$ json='{"jsonrpc":"2.0","method":"user.login","id":2,"params":{"user":"Admin","password":"zabbix"}}'
```

Now, run the curl command to get the API version. In all further API requests, we'll only change the json variable and then reuse the same curl command:

```
$ curl -s -w '\n' -X POST -H 'Content-Type: application/json-rpc' -d "$json" http://localhost/zabbix/api_jsonrpc.php
```

In this case, assuming a correct username and password, it should return the following:

```
{"jsonrpc":"2.0","result":"df83119ab78bbeb2065049412309f9b4","id":2}
```

 We use the request ID 2. That wasn't really required—we could've used 3, 5, or 1013. We could've used 1; all requests have a very obvious response, so we don't care about the ID at all. The response still did have the same ID as our request, 2.

This response also has an alphanumeric string in the `result` property, which is very important for all further work with the API. This is an authentication token or session ID that we'll have to submit with all subsequent requests. For our tests, just copy that string and use it in the `json` variable later.

Enabling and disabling hosts

Hosts may be enabled or disabled by setting a single value. Let's disable our IPMI host and re-enable it a moment later. To do this, we'll need the host ID. Usually, when using the API, we'd query the API itself for the ID. In this case, let's keep things simple and look up the ID in the host properties—as with the item before, open the host properties and copy the value for the `hostid` parameter from the URL. Also, don't forget to replace your correct authorization ID. With that number available, let's set our JSON variable:

```
$
json='{"jsonrpc":"2.0","method":"host.update","params":{"hostid":"1013
2","status":1},"auth":"df83119ab78bbeb2065049412309f9b4","id":1}'
```

 We got back to using an ID of 1. It really doesn't matter when using `curl` like this.

Run the `curl` command again; the output should look like the following:

```
{"jsonrpc":"2.0","result":{"hostids":["10132"]},"id":1}
```

This should indicate *success,* and the host should be disabled—check the host state in the frontend. Enabling it again is easy, too:

```
$
json='{"jsonrpc":"2.0","method":"host.update","params":{"hostid":"1013
2","status":0},"auth":"df83119ab78bbeb2065049412309f9b4","id":1}'
```

Run the `curl` command again to re-enable this host.

Creating a host

Now, let's move on to creating a host using the API. Let's set our JSON variable:

```
$ json='{"jsonrpc":"2.0","method":"host.create","params":{"host":"API
created
host","interfaces":[{"type":1,"main":1,"useip":1,"ip":"127.0.0.2","dns
":"","port":"10050"}],"groups":[{"groupid":"2"}],"templates":[{"templa
teid":"10186"}]},"auth": "df83119ab78bbeb2065049412309f9b4","id":1}'
```

In the default Zabbix database, the group ID of 2 should correspond to the **Linux servers** group, and the template ID of `10104` should correspond to the **Template ICMP Ping** template. If the IDs are different on your system, change them in this JSON string. Run the `curl` command now, and the host should be created successfully:

```
{"jsonrpc":"2.0","result":{"hostids":["10277"]},"id":1}
```

As part of the response, we also got the ID of the new host. Feel free to verify in the frontend that this host has been created.

Deleting a host

And the returned ID will be useful now. Let's delete the host we just created:

```
$
json='{"jsonrpc":"2.0","method":"host.delete","params":["10277"],"auth
":"df83119ab78bbeb2065049412309f9b4","id":1}'
```

 Make sure the host ID in this request is the same as what was returned in the previous request; otherwise, a different host could be deleted.

Run the `curl` command again. The host should be successfully deleted:

```
{"jsonrpc":"2.0","result":{"hostids":["10277"]},"id":1}
```

Creating a value map

Value maps couldn't be controlled via the API before Zabbix 3.0. They were needed for many templates, though, and people resorted to SQL scripts or even manually created value maps with hundreds of entries. That's dedication. Since Zabbix 3.0, things are much easier, and now, value maps are supported both in the API and XML import/export. Let's create a small value map:

```
$
json='{"jsonrpc":"2.0","method":"valuemap.create","params":{"name":"Ma
pping
things","mappings":[{"value":"this","newvalue":"that"},{"value":"foo",
"newvalue":"bar"}]},"auth":"df83119ab78bbeb2065049412309f9b4","id":1}'
```

Run the `curl` command:

```
{"jsonrpc":"2.0","result":{"valuemapids":["16"]},"id":1}
```

If you check the new value map in the frontend, it's a bit easier to read than in that JSON:

 We covered value maps in Chapter 3, *Monitoring with Zabbix Agents and Basic Protocols*.

Obtaining history and trends

The methods we've discussed so far mostly dealt with configuration. We may also query some historical data. For example, to grab item history data, we would need to know several things:

- **Item ID**
- The **Type of information** setting for that item

Both of these can be found out by opening the item properties in the configuration section—the ID will be in the URL, and the type of information will be in that drop-down menu. *Why do we have to specify the type of information?* Unfortunately, the Zabbix API doesn't look it up for us but tries to find the values only in a specific table. By default, the `history_uint` (integer values) table is queried. To get the values for the CPU load item on **A test host**, the JSON string would look like this:

```
$
json='{"jsonrpc":"2.0","method":"history.get","params":{"history":0,"i
temids":"23668","limit":3},"auth":"df83119ab78bbeb2065049412309f9b4","
id":1}'
```

 Remember to replace both `auth` and `itemid` for this query.

There're a couple extra parameters worth discussing here:

- The `history` parameter tells the API which table to query. With `0`, the `history` table is queried. With `1`, the `history_str` table is queried. With `2`, the `history_log` table is queried. With `3`, `history_int` is queried (which was the default). With `4`, the `history_text` table is queried. We must manually match this value to the setting in the item properties.
- The `limit` parameter limits the number of entries returned. This is quite useful here, as an item could have lots and lots of values. By the way, `limit` is supported for all other methods as well—we can limit the number of entries when retrieving hosts, items, and all other entities.

Now, run the `curl` command:

```
{"jsonrpc":"2.0","result":[{"itemid":"23668","clock":"1430988898","val
ue":"0.0000","ns":"215287328"},{"itemid":"23668","clock":"1430988928",
"value":"0.0000","ns":"221534597"},{"itemid":"23668","clock":"14309889
58","value":"0.0000","ns":"229668635"}],"id":1}
```

We got our three values, but the output is a bit hard to read. There're many ways to format JSON strings, but in the shell, the easiest would be using Perl or Python commands. Rerun the `curl` command and append to it `| json_pp`:

```
$ curl ... | json_pp
```

You might also have `json_xs`, which will have better performance, but performance should be no concern at all for us at this time.

This will invoke the Perl JSON tool, where `pp` stands for **pure Perl**, and the output will be a bit more readable:

```
{
  "jsonrpc" : "2.0",
  "id" : 1,
  "result" : [
    {
        "clock" : "1430988898",
        "itemid" : "23668",
        "value" : "0.0000",
        "ns" : "215287328"
    },
    {
        "ns" : "221534597",
        "value" : "0.0000",
        "itemid" : "23668",
        "clock" : "1430988928"
    },
    {
        "value" : "0.0000",
        "ns" : "229668635",
        "clock" : "1430988958",
        "itemid" : "23668"
    }
  ]
}
```

Notice how the output isn't really sorted. Ordering doesn't mean anything with JSON data, so tools don't normally sort the output.

Alternatively, use `python -mjsontool`, which will invoke Python's JSON tool module. That's a bit more typing, though.

In the output from the `history.get` method, each value is accompanied with an item ID, Unix timestamp, and nanosecond information—the same as the history tables we looked at earlier. That's not very surprising, as the API output comes from those tables. If we convert these values into human-readable format as discussed before by running `date -d@<UNIX timestamp>`, we'll see that they aren't recent—actually, they're the oldest values. We can get the most recent values by adding the `sortfield` and `sortorder` parameters:

```
$
json='{"jsonrpc":"2.0","method":"history.get","params":{"history":0,"i
temids":"23668","limit":3,"sortfield":"clock","sortorder":"DESC"},"aut
h":"df83119ab78bbeb2065049412309f9b4","id":1}'
```

These will sort the output by the clock value in descending order and then grab the three most recent values—check the returned Unix timestamps to make sure of that. If there're multiple values with the same clock value, other fields won't be used for secondary sorting.

We can also retrieve trend data—a new feature in Zabbix 3.0:

```
$
json='{"jsonrpc":"2.0","method":"trend.get","params":{"itemids":"23668
","limit":3},"auth":"df83119ab78bbeb2065049412309f9b4","id":1}'
```

The Zabbix API doesn't allow submitting historical data—all item values have to go through the Zabbix server using the `zabbix_sender` utility, which we discussed in Chapter 10, *Advanced Item Monitoring*. There're rumors that the API might be moved to the server side, which might allow merging data-submitting in the main API.

Issues with the Zabbix API

The Zabbix API is really great, but there're a few issues with it worth knowing about:

- **Audit**: Many Zabbix API operations aren't registered in the Zabbix audit log, which can be accessed by going to **Administration** | **Audit**. That can make it really complicated to find out who made a particular change and when.

- **Validation**: Unfortunately, the API validation leaves a lot to be desired. For example, using the API, one could change a host to a proxy or vice versa, or even set the `host status` value to a completely bogus value, making that host disappear from the frontend, although no new host with that name could be created. Be very, very careful with the possibility of sending incorrect data to the Zabbix API. It might complain about that data, or it might just silently accept it and make some silly changes.

- **Error messages**: Similarly, even when validating input data, the error messages aren't always that helpful. Sometimes, they'll tell you exactly what's wrong, but you may also get `incorrect parameters` for a long JSON input string.

- **Performance**: The Zabbix API's performance can be extremely bad for some operations. For example, modifying items for a template that's linked to a large number of hosts, or linking many hosts to a template, might be impossible to perform. While some of these operations could be split up, for example, linking the template to a few hundred hosts at a time, in some cases, we would have to fall back to doing direct SQL queries.

- **Missing functionality**: Although the Zabbix API allows us to control most of the Zabbix configuration, there're still some missing areas. By now, that mostly concerns things found in the **Administration** | **General** section. Once such functionality is implemented, it'll finally be possible for the Zabbix frontend to stop performing direct database queries, and the API will allow writing custom frontends without ever resorting to direct database access.

Using API libraries

While we looked at a low-level API example, you aren't likely to use shell scripts to work with the Zabbix API. The shell isn't that well suited for working with JSON data even with extra tools, so another programming or scripting language might be a better choice. For many of those languages, we wouldn't have to implement full raw JSON handling, as there're libraries available. At the time of writing this, a list of available libraries is maintained at `http://zabbix.org/wiki/Docs/api/libraries`. Alternatively, just go to `http://zabbix.org` and look for the **Zabbix API libraries** link.

All of these libraries are community supplied. There're no quality guarantees, and any bugs should be reported to the library maintainers, not to Zabbix.

For example, a Perl library called `Zabbix::Tiny` aims to be a very simple abstraction layer for the Zabbix API, solving the authentication and request ID issues, and other repetitive tasks when working with the API. It can be easily installed from the **Comprehensive Perl Archive Network (CPAN)**:

```
# cpan Zabbix::Tiny
```

To create a new user, we would save the following in a file:

```
use strict;
use warnings;
use Zabbix::Tiny;
my $zabbix = Zabbix::Tiny->new(
    server => http://localhost/zabbix/api_jsonrpc.php,
    password => 'zabbix',
    user => 'Admin',
);
$zabbix->do(
    'user.create',
    alias    => 'new_user',
    passwd => 'secure_password',
    usrgrps => [ '13' ],
    name => 'New',
    surname => 'User',
    type => 3,
);
```

This would create a new user. While most parameters are self-explanatory, the `type` parameter tells the API whether this is a user, admin, or super admin. A value of 3 denotes the super admin user type. The group ID is hardcoded to 13—that's something to customize. If the file we saved this in was called `zabbix_tiny-add_user.pl`, we would call it like this:

```
$ perl  zabbix_tiny-add_user.pl
```

While this might seem longer than our raw JSON string, it also deals with logging in, and it's easier to write than raw JSON. For more information on this particular Zabbix API library, refer to `http://zabbix.org/wiki/Docs/howto/Perl_Zabbix::Tiny_API`.

There're a lot of different Zabbix API libraries for various languages—Python alone has seven different libraries at the time of writing this. It can be a bit of a challenge to choose the best one.

If programming around a library isn't your thing, there's also a Python-based project to create command-line tools for API operations, called **Zabbix Gnomes**. It can be found at `https://github.com/q1x/zabbix-gnomes`.

Summary

In this chapter, we dove deeper into the internal data structures Zabbix uses. While that's still just a small part of a large amount of database, XML import/export, API, and other information, it should help with some of the common problems users encounter at first.

We figured out how to get raw data from the frontend, which is the easiest method for small datasets. For bigger amounts of data, we learned how to grab data from different history tables, depending on data type. We also found out how Zabbix proxies keep data in their local databases. For situations where less precision is needed, we learned about the trends table and the calculation of the hourly minimal, maximal, and average values that're stored there. We also covered resetting user passwords directly in the database and fixing item history values if the item configuration was incorrect initially.

We explored the Zabbix XML import/export functionality, which allowed us to add and partially update hosts, templates, network maps, screens, host groups, images, and value maps. We looked at the XML format in brief and created a simple script to generate hosts from a CSV file.

And in the end, we looked at the Zabbix API, which allows us to control almost all of the Zabbix configuration. We logged in, controlled the host status, added and deleted a host, created a value map and retrieved some historical item values, and formatted the output a bit with the `json_pp` tool. Although the API was really great, we also discussed various issues with it, including the lack of auditing, proper validation, and error messages. While we could only cover a small part of the Zabbix API here, we figured out how to find out further information in the Zabbix manual and step up the API usage by using a Perl library. We also discovered the list of API libraries for various languages at `http://zabbix.org/wiki/Docs/api/libraries`.

We'll continue diving into Zabbix in the next chapter. Various maintenance-related topics will be covered, including internal monitoring to find out cache usage and process busy rates, backing up our Zabbix configuration, and upgrading Zabbix when new versions come out. We'll also explore all of the parameters in the daemon configuration files.

Questions

1. Is `curl` the only option to retrieve information from the Zabbix API?
2. How can we know the version of the Zabbix API?
3. What can we use to back up our templates and hosts?

Further reading

Read the following articles for more information:

- **Information on the Zabbix API version**: `https://www.zabbix.com/documentation/4.0/manual/api/reference/apiinfo/version`
- **Zabbix API documentation**: `https://www.zabbix.com/documentation/4.0/manual/api`

20
Zabbix Maintenance

It's great when Zabbix runs smoothly; we get all of the data, nice graphs, and alerts. To keep it running like that, we should follow the health of Zabbix itself, be ready to recover from disastrous events, and upgrade to the latest version every now and then. In this chapter, we'll cover the following topics:

- **Monitoring the internals of Zabbix**: Caches, busy rates, performance items, and other data that reveals how well Zabbix is feeling
- **Making backups**: Suggestions on how to create backups and potential restore strategies
- **Upgrading Zabbix**: How to know what changes to expect from new versions and which components are compatible with others in different versions, and how to perform the upgrade itself

We'll also review generic suggestions regarding Zabbix setup to reduce performance issues and take a look at the audit log, a way to see who made changes to the Zabbix configuration and when, although this feature has some problems that we'll make sure to find out. We'll finish this chapter with a look at all of the configuration parameters in the server, proxy, and agent configuration files, concentrating on the ones we haven't discussed so far.

Internal monitoring

Zabbix can monitor a lot of things about other systems, but *what do we know about Zabbix itself?* We can see a few basic indicators in the Zabbix frontend right away. In the frontend, go to **Reports** | **System information**. Here, we can observe high-level information, such as whether the Zabbix server is running, and values such as the number of hosts, items, triggers, and users online.

This information is also visible as a widget in the dashboard. Both the widget and the report are available to super admin users only.

Let's look at the value next to **Required server performance, new values per second**. It's the main value when determining how large a Zabbix installation is:

System information

Parameter	Value	Details
Zabbix server is running	Yes	localhost:10051
Number of hosts (enabled/disabled/templates)	95	11 / 0 / 84
Number of items (enabled/disabled/not supported)	115	114 / 0 / 1
Number of triggers (enabled/disabled [problem/ok])	31	31 / 0 [9 / 22]
Number of users (online)	4	2
Required server performance, new values per second	5.86	

New values per second

Why is the new values per second setting so important? While knowing how many hosts or even items a system has is important, the underlying load could vary a lot. For example, we could have a system with 1,000 hosts, with 100 items each, but the items would be polled once every 15 minutes. In this case, the approximate expected **New Values Per Second** (**NVPS**) would be 111. Or, we could have only 10 hosts with 100 items per host, but if the interval were 10 seconds (that's a very low interval; if possible, never use such a low interval), the total expected NVPS would be 100. As we can see, host and item count have an impact, but so does the average interval. NVPS is a generic value that can be compared to other systems more easily. In our installation, the expected NVPS, based on our current host and item configuration, is likely to be somewhere between seven and nine. This means that, every second, the Zabbix server is expected to receive and process that many historical values; this also includes calculating any trigger expressions, calculating trend information for numeric items, and storing any resulting events and these historical values in the database. It's quite a lot of seemingly invisible work for each value.

We can see the value for the current configuration in the Zabbix status report, but *how can we calculate the expected NVPS for a larger system we're building, without adding all of the hosts and items?* If we had 60 items on a single host, each polled once per minute, the NVPS could be calculated like this:

```
<item count> / <item interval>
```

So, 60 items per minute would result in one NVPS. By the way, one item per minute would be `1/60` or `0.01557`. To get the total NVPS in the projected environment, we would simply multiply it all by the amount of hosts:

```
<average item count per host> / <average item interval> * <total host
count>
```

Plug in various values and see how the expected NVPS changes as one of these values is changed. The more hosts you have, the more impact the average interval and average item count per host will have.

The value that the frontend gives us is a nice way to determine the expected NVPS right now, but it isn't that easy to see how it's changed over time and how configuration changes have impacted it.

We can add an internal item that'll store this value so that we can see long-term changes and graph them:

1. Navigate to **Configuration** | **Hosts**, click on **Items** for **A test host**, and then click on the **Create item** button.
2. In this form, start by clicking on **Select** next to the **Key** field, and change the **Type** drop-down menu to **Zabbix internal** in the item helper.

   This presents us with a nice list of the available internal items. We'll set up a few of these, but won't discuss every single item in there. If you're curious about some after we're done with this topic, consult the Zabbix manual for detailed information on each internal item. *Remember how we created an item to monitor the time when the proxy last contacted the server?* That was also an internal item.

   In this list, click on `zabbix[requiredperformance]`. Fill in the following:

   - **Name**: Expected NVPS
   - **Type**: **Zabbix internal**
   - **Type of information**: **Numeric (float)**

- **Units**: NVPS
- **New application**: Zabbix performance

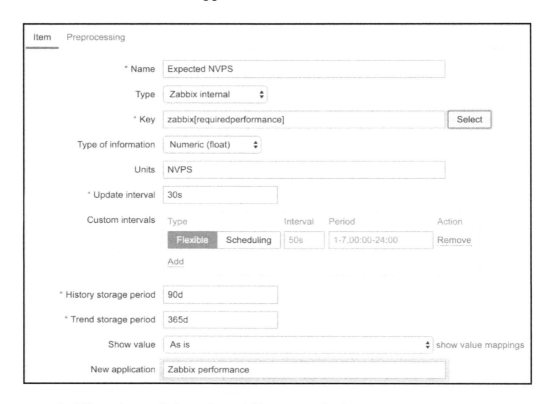

3. When done, click on the **Add** button at the bottom.

Check this item in the **Latest data** page. After a short while, it should have the value—somewhat similar to what we saw in the Zabbix status report:

▼	A test host	**Zabbix performance** (1 Item)		
☐		Expected NVPS	2018-12-31 14:29:32	5.89 NVPS

This value is likely to be different than the one we saw in the report. We just added an item to monitor the expected NVPS, which provides values of its own, so this action has affected the NVPS already.

With this item configured, let's talk about what it actually is. You might've noticed how it was stressed many times before that this is the expected NVPS. It's based on our host and item configuration and doesn't actually reflect how many values we're receiving. If we had all of the items of the active agent type and all agents were stopped, the expected NVPS wouldn't change, even though we would receive no information at all. Barring such technical issues, this number could differ from the values we normally process because of other reasons. Log monitoring items are always counted according to their interval. If we have a log item with an interval of one second, it's included as one NVPS even if the log file itself gets no values—or if it gets 10 values every second. Flexible intervals and item scheduling are ignored, and trapper items aren't included in the expected NVPS estimate at all. If we send a lot of values to trapper items, our real, processed NVPS will be higher than the expected NVPS—sometimes several times higher.

As the expected or estimated NVPS can be inaccurate, we also have a way to figure out the real NVPS value; there's another internal item for that purpose.

Let's go back to **Configuration** | **Hosts** and then **Items** for **A test host** again and click on **Create item**. Fill in the following values:

- **Name**: Real NVPS
- **Type**: **Zabbix internal**
- **Key**: zabbix[wcache,values]
- **Type of information**: **Numeric (float)**
- **Units**: NVPS
- **Preprocessing**: **Change per second**
- **Applications**: **Zabbix performance**

When done, click on the **Add** button at the bottom. In the **Key**, we used the keywords, wcache and values. The first one is supposed to stand for **write cache**, or we can think of it as a cache of the values to be written to the database. The values parameter tells it to report the number of values passing through that cache. We'll look at other possible parameters a bit later.

We could also obtain the number of processed values per type by specifying the third parameter as float, uint, str, log, or text. The third parameter defaults to all, reporting all value types.

Another thing worth noting is the **Store value;** this internal item reports a counter of all values, and this way, we're getting the number of values per second. We both obtain a value, easily comparable with the expected NVPS, and avoid a hill graph. *How would we know which internal items return a final value and which ones are counter items?* Consult the Zabbix manual as usual.

With the item in place, let's compare the expected and real values in the latest data page:

▼	A test host	**Zabbix performance** (2 Items)		
☐		Expected NVPS	2018-12-31 14:42:32	5.92 NVPS
☐		Real NVPS	2018-12-31 14:42:33	2.8 NVPS

Notice how the expected NVPS value increased again after adding another item.

In this system, parts of the monitoring infrastructure are down, so the real NVPS value is significantly lower than the expected one. You might want to mark the checkboxes next to both of these items and display an ad hoc graph to visually compare the values and see how they change over time. The expected NVPS is likely to be pretty stable, only changing when the configuration is changed. The real NVPS is likely to go up and down as the value retrieval and processing changes over time.

Zabbix server uptime

Let's try to monitor another Zabbix internal item:

1. Go to **Configuration | Hosts**, click on **Items** next to **A test host**, and then click on **Create item**. Let's monitor the uptime of the Zabbix server—not the whole system, but the Zabbix server daemon. Fill in these values:

   - **Name:** `Zabbix server uptime`
   - **Type: Zabbix internal**
   - **Key:** `zabbix[uptime]`
   - **Units:** `uptime`

2. When done, click on **Add** at the bottom and then check this item in the **Latest data** page.

   Notice how our use of the `uptime` unit resulted in the raw uptime value in seconds being converted into a human-readable format that shows how long the Zabbix server process has been running for:

	Host	Name ▲	Last check	Last value
▼	A test host	**- other -** (1 Item)		
		Zabbix server uptime	2018-12-31 14:45:34	00:27:38

We could display this item on a screen and have a trigger on it to let us know when the Zabbix server was restarted.

Cache usage

We've already discussed several caches in Zabbix and what they're used for. As these caches fill up, it can have different effects on Zabbix. Let's take a look at how we can monitor how much of some of those caches is free or used.

We could monitor the free space in the first cache we found out about, the configuration cache:

1. Let's go to **Configuration | Hosts**, then click on **Items** next to **A test host**, and click on **Create item**. Fill in the following values:

   - **Name:** `Zabbix configuration cache, % free`
   - **Type: Zabbix internal**
   - **Key:** `zabbix[rcache,buffer,pfree]`
   - **Type of information: Numeric (float)**
   - **Units:** `%`

2. When done, click on the **Add** button at the bottom.

For this item key, we used the `rcache` keyword, which stands for **read cache**. Coupled with `buffer`, it refers to the configuration cache. With `pfree`, we're requesting free space in this cache as a percentage. Notice how we're setting **Type of information** to **Numeric (float)**; we could have left it at **Numeric (unsigned)**, in which case, Zabbix would cut off the decimal part, which isn't suggested in this case. Check this item in the **Latest data** page:

A test host	**- other -** (1 Item)		
	Zabbix configuration cache, % free	2018-12-31 14:48:05	96.17 %

On our system, it's highly unlikely to see the free configuration cache size drop below 90% with the default settings.

There're other internal caches on the server we can monitor. We'll discuss what they hold in more detail, and the suggested sizes, when we look at the daemon configuration parameters a bit later, but let's have a quick list for now:

- **Configuration cache**: We're monitoring it already. It holds host, item, trigger, and other configuration information.
- **Value cache**: This holds historical values to speed up triggers, calculated items, aggregate items, and other things.
- **VMware cache**: This holds fairly raw VMware data.
- **History cache and history cache index**: These two hold historical values before they're processed for triggers and written to the database.
- **Trend cache**: This holds trend information for the current hour for all items that're receiving values.

It's a very, very good idea to monitor all of these parameters.

Note that most of the caches can be monitored for Zabbix proxies, too. This can be done by assigning the host with those items to be monitored by a specific Zabbix proxy. At that point, these internal items will return information about that proxy. Only relevant items will work; for example, monitoring the trend cache on a proxy isn't possible simply because there's no trend cache on a proxy. The same approach with having such a host assigned to a proxy works also for the items under the internal process busy rate, which we'll discuss next.

Zabbix has provided templates for this purpose; they're named **Template App Zabbix Server** and **Template App Zabbix Proxy**. Make sure when you monitor a proxy that the Zabbix agent on the proxy is being monitored by the proxy and not the Zabbix server.

Internal process busy rate

Zabbix has a bunch of processes internally, and we've already covered a few; we enabled IPMI and VMware pollers, as well as SNMP trappers. For several of these, we're also able to configure how many processes to start. *How can we know whether one process is enough or maybe we should have a hundred of them?* We'll discuss general guidelines per type a bit later, but a very important thing to know is how busy the currently running processes are. There're internal items for this purpose as well. For these items, the general syntax is as follows:

```
zabbix[process,<type>,<mode>,<state>]
```

The parameters in the preceding code are explained as follows:

- The first parameter, `process`, is a fixed keyword.
- The second parameter, `type`, is the process type, as in poller, trapper, and so on.
- The third parameter, `mode`, could be one of these:
    - `avg`: This is the average rate across all processes of the specified type.
    - `count`: This is the number of processes of the specified type.
    - `max`: This is the maximum rate across the processes of the specified type.
    - `min`: This is the minimum rate across the processes of the specified type.
    - **A number**: This is the rate for an individual process of the specified type. For example, there're five pollers running by default. With a process number specified here, we could monitor `poller 1` or `poller 3`. Note that this is the internal process number, not the system PID.

We talked about rate here; this is the amount of time a target process or processes spent in a state, specified by the fourth parameter. It could either be busy or idle.

Should we monitor the busy rate or the idle one? In most cases, the average busy time for all processes of a specific type is monitored. *Why busy?* Just by convention, as when this monitoring got implemented, the first templates monitored `busy rate`. Additionally, when debugging a specific issue, it could be helpful to monitor the busy rate for individual processes. Unfortunately, there's no way to query such values directly from the server; we would have to add an item in the frontend and then wait for it to start working. There's no built-in LLD for process types or the number of them; we would have to create such items manually or automate them using XML importing or the Zabbix API.

To see how this works, let's monitor the average busy rate for all poller processes:

1. Go to **Configuration | Hosts**, click on **Items** next to **A test host**, and then on **Create item**. Fill in these values:

   - **Name**: `Zabbix $4 process $2 rate`
   - **Type**: **Zabbix internal**
   - **Key**: `zabbix[process,poller,avg,busy]`
   - **Type of information**: **Numeric (float)**
   - **Units**: `%`
   - **New application**: `Zabbix process busy rates`

   Creating such an item on a host that's monitored through a Zabbix proxy will report data about that proxy, not the Zabbix server.

   We used positional variables in the item name again; if we wanted to monitor another process, it would be easy to clone this item and change the process name in the item key only.

2. When done, click on the **Add** button at the bottom. Check this item in the **Latest data** page:

A test host	**Zabbix process busy rates** (1 Item)		
☐	Zabbix busy process poller rate	2018-12-31 14:53:36	0.58 %

Most likely, our small Zabbix instance isn't very busy polling values. By default, there're five pollers started, and they're dealing with the current load without any issues.

As an exercise, monitor a few more process types; maybe trapper and unreachable pollers. Check the Zabbix manual section on internal items for the exact process names to be used in this item.

After adding a few more items, you'll probably observe that there're a lot of internal processes. We discussed creating such items automatically using XML importing or the API, but then there were also all of the caches we could and should monitor. Zabbix tries to help here a bit and ships with default internal monitoring templates. In the search box in the upper-right corner, enter `app zabbix` and hit the *Enter* key. Look at the **Templates** block:

Templates							
Template	Applications	Items	Triggers	Graphs	Screens	Discovery	Web
Template App Zabbix Agent	Applications 1	Items 3	Triggers 3	Graphs	Screens	Discovery	Web
Template App Zabbix Proxy	Applications 1	Items 31	Triggers 23	Graphs 4	Screens 1	Discovery	Web
Template App Zabbix Server	Applications 1	Items 42	Triggers 21	Graphs 6	Screens 1	Discovery	Web
							Displaying 3 of 3 found

While the agent template is quite simple and not of much interest at this time, the server and proxy templates cover quite a lot, with 31 and 42 items respectively. These templates will allow out-of-the-box monitoring of internal process busy rates, cache usage, queues, values processed, and a few other things. It's highly recommended to use these templates in all Zabbix installations.

These templates might still be missing a few interesting items, such as the expected NVPS item we created earlier. It's suggested to create a separate template with such missing things instead of modifying the default template. Such an approach will allow easier upgrades, as new versions could add more processes, caches, and have other improvements to the default templates. If we leave the default templates intact, we can import a new XML file, tell Zabbix to add all missing things, update existing things, and remove whatever isn't in the XML, and we'll have an up-to-date default template. If we had it modified, it could be a lot of manual work to update it.

Unsupported items and more problems

We now know quite a bit about the internal monitoring of Zabbix, but there're still more possibilities. Unsupported items are no good, so let's discuss the ways we could monitor the situation with them.

Counting unsupported items

Similar to cache usage and process busy rates, we may also monitor the count of unsupported items with an internal item.

To create such an item, follow these steps:

1. Let's go to **Configuration | Hosts**, click on **Items** next to **A test host**, and then click on **Create item**. Fill in these values:

   - **Name**: Amount of unsupported items
   - **Type**: **Zabbix internal**
   - **Key**: zabbix[items_unsupported]

2. When done, click on the **Add** button at the bottom. After a short while, check this item on the **Latest data** page:

A test host	- **other** - (1 Item)		
☐	Amount of unsupported items	2018-12-31 15:03:07	14

14? That's an extremely high value for such a small installation, although in this case it's caused by the VMware monitoring being down. At this time, a VMware timeout results in all VMware items becoming unsupported. In a perfect environment, there would be no unsupported items, so we could create a trigger to alert us whenever this item receives a value larger than 0. That wouldn't be too useful anywhere but in really small environments, though; usually, a thing becomes broken here or there, and the unsupported item count is never 0. A more useful trigger would hence be one that alerts about a larger increase in the number of unsupported items. The change() trigger function could help here:

```
{A test host:zabbix[items_unsupported].change()}>5
```

Whenever the unsupported item count increases by more than 5 in 30 seconds, which is the default item interval, this trigger will fire. The threshold should be tuned to work best for a particular environment.

Such a global alert will be useful, but in larger environments with more distributed responsibilities, we might want to alert the responsible parties only. One way to do that would be monitoring the unsupported item count per host. With this item, it probably makes most sense to create it in some base template so that it's applied to all of the hosts it's needed on.

Let's create such an item with the following steps:

1. Navigate to **Configuration** | **Templates**, click on **Items** next to **C_Template_Linux**, and then click on **Create item**. Fill in these values:

   - **Name**: Unsupported item count
   - **Type**: **Zabbix internal**
   - **Key**: zabbix[host,,items_unsupported]

2. When done, click on the **Add** button at the bottom. Check this item on the **Latest data** page:

Apparently, the test host has 0 unsupported items in this installation. We would now create a trigger on the same template, alerting us whenever a host has a non-zero count of unsupported items. Such a combination would work fairly well although, in larger installations, it could result in a large number of triggers firing if an item got misconfigured in the template or if a broken userparameter script were distributed. Unfortunately, there's no built-in item to determine the unsupported item count per host group. One workaround would be to use aggregate items, as discussed in Chapter 10, *Advanced Item Monitoring*. For example, to obtain the unsupported item count for a group called Linux servers, the aggregate item key could look like this:

```
grpsum[Linux servers,"zabbix[host,,items_unsupported]",last]
```

We should probably avoid creating a trigger for the unsupported item count on individual hosts, creating one on the aggregate item instead. While the individual items would keep collecting data, which is a bit of a load on the Zabbix server and increases database size, at least the alert count would be reasonable.

 If an item turns unsupported, all triggers that reference it stop working, even if they're looking for missing data using the nodata() function. That makes it very hard to alert somebody of such issues unless an internal item such as this is used; it's highly unlikely to become unsupported itself.

There're still more internal items. It's a good idea to look at the full list of available items for the latest version of Zabbix in the online manual.

Reviewing unsupported items

The items that tell us about the number of unsupported items either for the whole Zabbix installation or for a specific host are useful and tell us when things aren't good. But *what exactly isn't good?* There's a very easy way to review the unsupported item list in the frontend. Follow these steps:

1. Navigate to **Configuration** | **Hosts**, click on any of the **Items** links, and expand the item filter. Clear out any host, host group, or other filter option that's there, and look at the right-hand side of the filter.
2. In the **State** drop-down menu, choose **Not supported** and click on **Filter**.

This will display all of the unsupported items in this Zabbix instance. Note that we may not display all items in all states like this; the filter will require at least one condition to be set, and the state condition counts.

It's highly recommended to visit this view every now and then and try to fix as many unsupported items as possible. Unsupported items are bad. Note that by default, up to 1,000 entries will be shown. If you have more than 1,000 unsupported items, that's a pretty bad situation and should be fixed.

 If you see unsupported items in templates, it's most likely a Zabbix instance that's been upgraded from an older version. The broken item state was a bug in older versions of Zabbix. To fix this issue, the state for these items should be manually changed in the database. Look up the item ID and set the **State** value for it to 0. As usual, be very careful with direct database updates.

Internal events and unknown triggers

Alerting on unsupported items, which we covered a moment ago, is likely the best approach, as it allows us to have a small number of triggers and a relatively easy way to split up alerting about them. There's another built-in approach that allows us to alert about unsupported items and triggers in an unknown state; Zabbix has the concept of internal events.

To configure an alert based on those internal events, follow these steps:

Go to **Configuration** | **Actions**, choose **Internal** in the **Event source** drop-down menu and click on **Create action**. In the **Action** tab, enter these values:

- **Name**: A trigger changed state to `unknown`
- In the **New condition** block, select **Event type** in the first drop-down menu, and choose **Trigger in "unknown" state** in the last drop-down menu, and press **Add** (below the condition not the one at the bottom):

Switch to the **Operations** tab and enter the following values:

- **Default subject**: `{TRIGGER.STATE}: {TRIGGER.NAME}`
- Click on **New** in the **Operations** block, and then click on **Add** in the **Send to Users** section.

 We set up email for `monitoring_user` in `Chapter 2`, *Getting Your First Notification*—if another user has email properly set up in your Zabbix instance, choose that user instead.

- Click on `monitoring_user` in the popup, and then click on the small **Add** link in the **Operation details** block—the last one, just above the buttons at the very bottom. Be careful; this form is very confusing.

Switch to the **Recovery operations** tab and enter the following.

- **Recovery subject**: `{TRIGGER.STATE}: {TRIGGER.NAME}`
- Click on **New** in the **Operations** block, and then click on **Add** in the **Send to Users** section and, just like in the **Operations** tab, select the `monitoring_user`.

When done, click on the **Add** button at the bottom.

We discussed actions in more detail in `Chapter 7`, *Acting upon Monitored Conditions*.

Now, whenever a trigger becomes `unknown`, an alert will be sent.

While we can limit these actions by application, host, template, or host group, we cannot react to internal events in the same actions we use for trigger events. If we already have a lot of actions carefully splitting up notification per host groups, applications, and other conditions, we would have to replicate all of them for internal events to get the same granularity. That's highly impractical so, at this time, it might be best to have a few generic actions, such as ones that inform key responsible persons, who would investigate and pass the issue to the team assigned to that host group, application, or other unit.

If you looked carefully, then you noticed that Zabbix already provided three internal operations: one for items in a not supported state, another one for low-level discovery rules in a not supported stated, and one for triggers in an unknown state. They're all disabled and will inform the Zabbix administrators once they're enabled. My advice is to enable them and to tune them to you needs.

A list of the build in actions already provided in Zabbix:

Report not supported items	Event type equals *Item in "not supported" state*	**Send message to user groups:** Zabbix administrators via all media	Disabled
Report not supported low level discovery rules	Event type equals *Low-level discovery rule in "not supported" state*	**Send message to user groups:** Zabbix administrators via all media	Disabled
Report unknown triggers	Event type equals *Trigger in "unknown" state*	**Send message to user groups:** Zabbix administrators via all media	Disabled

Backing things up

It's a good feeling to have a backup when things go wrong. When setting up a monitoring system, it's a good idea to spend some time to figure out how backups could be made so that the good feeling isn't replaced by a bad feeling. With Zabbix, there're components and data to be considered:

- **Zabbix binaries**: Such as the binaries from Zabbix server, proxy, and agent. They're probably not worth backing up. Hopefully, they're easily available from packages or by recompiling.
- **Zabbix frontend files**: Hopefully, they're easily available as well. If any changes have been made, they're presumably stored as a patch in a version control system.
- **Zabbix configuration files**: Hopefully, these are stored in a version control system or a system configuration tool.
- **Zabbix server database**: This contains all of the monitoring-related configuration data, such as hosts and items, and it holds all of the collected values. Now that's worth backing up!

Backing up the database

Several different databases could be used for the Zabbix backend. We won't spend much time on database-specific information, besides a brief look at a simple possible way to create backups with the most widely used backend—MySQL—or one of its forks. A very simple way to back up a database with MySQL, compressing it on the way, would be this:

```
$ mysqldump zabbix --add-drop-table --add-locks --extended-insert --single-transaction --quick -u zabbix -p | bzip2 > zabbix_database_backup.db.bz2
```

Here, we're allowing the backup to drop existing tables in the target database and telling it to lock each table when restoring, which is supposed to offer better restore performance. The parameters in the preceding code are explained as follows:

- `--extended-insert`: This parameter uses one insert for many values instead of one per value—a much smaller backup and much faster restore. Performing the backup in a single transaction should ensure a consistent state across all of the tables being backed up.
- `--quick`: This parameter instructs MySQL to dump large tables partially instead of buffering all of their contents in memory.
- `bzip2`: This parameter is used to compress the data before writing it to the disk. You can choose other compression software, such as `gzip` or `xz` or change the compression level, depending on what you need more; disk space savings or a less-taxed CPU during the backup and restore. Memory usage can also be quite high with some compression utilities. The great thing is you can run this backup process without stopping the MySQL server (actually, it has to run) and even the Zabbix server.

Now, you can let your usual backup software grab this created file and store it on a disk array, tape, or some other more exotic media.

Restoring from a backup

Restoring such a backup is simple as well. We pass the saved statements to the MySQL client, uncompressing them first, if necessary:

```
$ bzcat zabbix_database_backup.db.bz2 | mysql zabbix -u zabbix -p
```

Use `zcat` or `xzcat` as appropriate if you've chosen a different compression utility.
The Zabbix server must be stopped during the restore process.

Of course, backups are useful only if it's possible to restore them. As required by any backup policy, the ability to restore from backups should be tested. This includes restoring the database dump, but it's also suggested to compare the schema of the restored database and the default schema, as well as running a copy of the Zabbix server on a test system. Make sure to disallow any outgoing network connections by the test server, though; otherwise, it might overload the network or send false alerts.

Separating configuration and data backups

While we can dump a whole database in a single file, it isn't always the best solution. There might be cases when restoring only the configuration data would be useful:

- The first is when testing a Zabbix upgrade on a less powerful system than the Zabbix server.
- When attempting to recover from a disastrous event, it would be useful to restore configuration only and resume monitoring as quickly as possible. If needed, history and trend data can be restored later in small portions to avoid overloading the database.

Usually, data tables, such as the ones holding history, trend, and event information, will be much bigger than the configuration tables. Restoring the data tables would take much longer or even be impossible on a test system. We could split all of the tables into configuration and data ones, but it's likely even more simple to back each table up separately and deal with the desired tables when restoring. An example command to do so is as follows:

```
$ for table in $(mysql -N -e "show tables;" zabbix); do mysqldump --
add-locks --extended-insert --single-transaction --quick zabbix $table
| bzip2 > zabbix_database_backup_$table.bz2; done
```

Note that, in this case, we're not performing the backup for the whole database in a single transaction, and changes to the configuration could lead to inconsistencies across the tables. It's a good idea to schedule such a backup at a time when configuration changes would be unlikely.

If the consistency of the configuration tables is a likely problem, we could instead back up the configuration tables in a single transaction and the tables that hold collected and recorded information separately:

```
$ mysqldump --add-locks --extended-insert --single-transaction zabbix
--ignore-table=zabbix.history --ignore-table=zabbix.history_uint --
ignore-table=zabbix.history_text --ignore-table=zabbix.history_str --
ignore-table=zabbix.history_log --ignore-table=zabbix.trends --ignore-
table=zabbix.trends_uint --ignore-table=zabbix.events --ignore-
table=zabbix.alerts --ignore-table=zabbix.auditlog --ignore-
table=zabbix.auditlog_details --ignore-table=zabbix.acknowledges |
bzip2 > zabbix_database_backup_config_tables.bz2
$ mysqldump --add-locks --extended-insert --single-transaction zabbix
history history_uint history_text history_str history_log trends
trends_uint events alerts auditlog auditlog_details acknowledges |
bzip2 > zabbix_database_backup_data_tables.bz2
```

Note that the configuration and data table distinction is a bit fuzzy in Zabbix, and several configuration tables still hold runtime information.

Upgrading Zabbix

Even though Zabbix is a mature product with more than 15 years behind it, it's still very actively developed. Bugs are fixed and new features are added. At some point, accumulated improvements make it worth upgrading. In this section, we'll look at the following:

- **General version policy**: Which versions are stable and which ones are supported for longer periods of time
- **The upgrade process**: What can be upgraded to what and how it should be done
- **Compatibility between Zabbix components**: Which versions of the server can be used with which versions of the agent and so on

General version policy

The Zabbix versioning scheme has changed a few times over the years. In general, the first two numbers have denoted a major version, such as 2.4, 3.0 and 4.0, while the third number has denoted a minor version number. Previously, an even second number denoted a stable branch, while an odd second number denoted a development branch. Hence, 2.3 was a development branch for 2.4, while 2.4 was the resulting stable branch. This has slightly changed since 3.0. The development releases have moved away from the odd numbering, that is, the 3.5 number. They're now called **4.0.0alpha1**, **4.0.0beta2**, and so on. This is deemed to be more user friendly, although the internal numbering is still based on 3.5 in several places—the database version, for example, which we'll explore in more detail a bit later.

The new version numbering since Zabbix 3.0 could be summed up as follows:

- A version number with just digits (and dots) in it denotes a stable release
- A version number with the `alpha`, `beta`, or `rc` (release candidate) keywords added isn't a stable release

Long-term support and short-term support

For stable branches, there're even more differences. The release and support policy has changed as well, and the current policy states that there're two types of stable branches:

- **Long-term support (LTS) branches**: These branches are supported for three years for general bug fixes and two more years for only critical and security fixes
- **Short-term support branches**: These are supported for roughly one month after the first release in the next stable branch, LTS or non-LTS

At the moment of writing, 4.0 is the current LTS branch, with 4.2 and 4.4 planned as short-term support branches, 5.0 following as the next LTS branch, and all further LTS branches aligning to `N.0` versioning. *Will this hold?* That's very hard to predict, so you might want to check the current policy at `http://www.zabbix.com/life_cycle_and_release_policy.php`.

 This support mostly references commercial services, although it strongly affects all users. We'll discuss support options in `Appendix B`, *Being Part of the Community*.

How to decide which branch to use? Consider the available features and how quickly you would be able to upgrade. *Does the latest LTS version satisfy you and you don't plan to upgrade for years?* Stick with it. Really desire a feature in a non-LTS branch and plan to upgrade when the next stable branch comes out. Go with the non-LTS branch. Anything in between, and you'll have to make a decision based on the support policy that's in effect at that time. Here's a quick lookup table to help you decide:

Use a non-LTS branch when...	Use an LTS branch when...
You need a new feature in the non-LTS branch	The LTS-branch features satisfy you
You plan to upgrade to every new version quickly	You prefer to stay with one version as long as possible
You can tolerate slight instability	You prefer a more stable version

Note that the *slight instability* mentioned in the table doesn't mean that there're serious issues with the non-LTS versions. In some cases, *more stable* might mean this bug is pretty stable, but hasn't been fixed for a long time.

The upgrade process

Read the upgrade notes from the new Zabbix version you want to install.

What was that? Yes, before performing any upgrades, take a little time, go to the Zabbix manual, and read the upgrade notes. If you're jumping over a few major versions, do read all of the upgrade notes in between. Even if you've followed Zabbix development a bit, you might've missed some change that could cause problems; removed or added configuration parameters, memory requirement changes, or API changes; the upgrade notes should list all significant changes.

It's also highly suggested to read the pages on new features and improvements, called **What's new**. While it's much less risky to miss some of those changes, knowing about them could help you use Zabbix in a more efficient way.

Let's talk about the upgrade process itself now. This process and compatibility will differ depending on the version change you're performing:

- A minor version upgrade inside the same major version is simple and easy to undo
- A major version upgrade is more complicated, and hard or impossible to undo

Minor version upgrade

This is the simplest case. For example, upgrading from 4.0.0 to 4.0.1 or from 4.0.1 to 4.0.5 would be considered a minor version upgrade.

 Zabbix uses the third number to denote a minor version.

When performing a minor version upgrade, we may upgrade any combination of components: server, agents, proxies, Java gateway, and so on. While it's suggested to keep the main components of the same version to reduce confusion, a 4.0.0 server will happily work with a 4.0.1 frontend, 4.0.2 proxies, and 4.0.3 agents. Inside one major version, all components are compatible with each other.

It's also perfectly fine to skip minor versions when upgrading; as mentioned, going from 4.0.1 directly to 4.0.5 is perfectly fine.

While minor versions won't have upgrade notes often, do make sure to check for them. And read those **What's new** pages.

Upgrading binaries

Zabbix server, agents, and potentially proxy binaries have to be updated. The exact process will depend on how you installed them in the first place. *Compiled from the source?* Perform the same steps as during the installation. *Installed from packages?* Use the distribution package management tools to perform the upgrade. This process should be fairly simple, and we discussed the details back in Chapter 1, *Getting Started with Zabbix*.

After starting the upgraded Zabbix server, in some rare cases you might see a log entry like this:

```
10852:20151231:094918.820 starting automatic database upgrade
```

For a minor version upgrade, that could be a change to the database indexes to improve performance, but we'll discuss that in more detail when we get to the major version upgrades.

Upgrading the frontend

Upgrading the Zabbix frontend from one minor to another minor version should be simple as well. If installed from the sources, copy over the new frontend files. Instead of overwriting the frontend, it might be a good idea to copy the frontend to a separate directory first, verify that it works as intended, and then move your users over.

For example, if your original installation had the Zabbix frontend in the relative path, `zabbix/`, place the new frontend files in `zabbix-<new_version>/`, rename the `zabbix/` directory to `zabbix-<old_version>/`, and create a symlink called `zabbix` that points at the new version so that you don't have to use a different URL whenever you upgrade. To skip the configuration wizard, copy over the configuration file:

```
# cp zabbix-<old_version>/conf/zabbix.conf.php zabbix/conf/
```

That should be enough. Now, you can refresh the Zabbix frontend in the browser and check the page footer; the new version number should be visible there.

This approach with keeping the old frontend versions is useful if a new version turns out to have a problem and you would like to test whether the old version also had the same problem; just load up a URL in your browser that points to the old frontend directory. If the problem indeed turns out to be a regression, simply change the symlink to point to the old directory and revert to the old version.

 If you modified the `defines.inc.php` file, make sure to perform the same modifications in the new version of the file.

You may keep and use multiple versions of the Zabbix frontend in parallel, as long as they all are of the same major version. While normally not needed, it can be very helpful when some debugging or comparison has to be performed.

Major-level upgrades

A major-level upgrade is slightly different from a minor version upgrade. As a quick reminder, definitely go and read the upgrade notes; major versions will always have some. Remember about the **What's new** pages, too.

Back to the major version upgrade itself, the most significant differences from a minor version upgrade are as follows:

- Database schema changes
- Compatibility
- Reading the upgrade notes

 When performing major-level upgrades from source, it's suggested to avoid copying the new frontend files over the old files. Leftover files from the old version might cause problems.

Let's talk about database schema changes right now, let's discuss compatibility in detail a bit later, and let's always remember to read our upgrade notes.

While the Zabbix team works hard to keep minor version upgrades without database changes, for major releases, it's open season. Changes to the database schema and its contents are made to accommodate new features, improve performance, and increase flexibility. Users wouldn't appreciate it if they couldn't keep gathered data and created configuration in the name of new greatness so, with each new version, a database upgrade patch is provided. This may include adding new tables and columns, removing tables and columns, and changing the data layout.

Given that a major version upgrade changes the database, make sure you have a recent backup. While upgrades are extensively tested, it isn't possible for the developers to test all scenarios. What has worked for a thousand people might break in some obscure way for you. Additionally, interrupting the upgrade process because of a hardware or electricity failure is likely to leave your database in a broken state. You've been warned, so get that backup ready.

You're strongly encouraged to test the upgrade on a test installation, preferably using a production dataset (maybe with trimmed history and trend data, if the available hardware doesn't permit testing with a full copy).

With a fresh backup created, we're ready to engage the major version upgrade. The database upgrade process significantly changed for Zabbix version 2.2. In older versions, we had to apply the database patch manually. If you happen to have an old Zabbix installation—old being pre-2.0—you'll have to patch it up to the 2.0 database schema manually. For your reference, the database patches are located in the `upgrades/dbpatches` directory in the source tree, but if you really want to follow that path, make sure to consult with the Zabbix community via the channels discussed in Appendix B, *Being Part of the Community*.

For upgrading to Zabbix from version 2.2 or more recent, no manual patching is required. Starting up the new server will automatically upgrade the database schema. Note that this database upgrading happens without a confirmation. Be careful not to start a more recent server binary against an older database version if you don't intend to change the database.

One last note regarding the upgrade notes: promise. While the latest Zabbix upgrades are really quick even in large installations, older versions sometimes upgraded historical data tables, and that took a long time—like, really a long time. In some reported cases, it was days. If such a change is required in any of the future versions, it'll be mentioned in the upgrade notes, and you'll be glad you read them.

Database versioning

With all of this talk about the database version and schema changes, let's take a closer look at how version information is stored and how we can check the upgrade status. Examine the dbversion table in your Zabbix database:

```
mysql> select * from dbversion;
+-----------+----------+
| mandatory | optional |
+-----------+----------+
|   4000000 |  4000003 |
+-----------+----------+
1 row in set (0.00 sec)
```

This table is the way Zabbix components determine which version of the database schema they're dealing with. There're two numbers in there: the mandatory and optional versions. The following rules are important regarding version numbers:

- Inside one major version, the mandatory version number is always the same
- If a more recent server is started, it upgrades the database to the latest mandatory and optional version
- The server and frontend can work with a database as long as its mandatory version matches their mandatory version exactly; the optional version doesn't affect compatibility

The mandatory version encodes things such as table changes, column changes, and otherwise significant changes that break compatibility. The optional version would usually denote an index change—something that's helpful but doesn't prohibit older versions from working with a more recent database.

The Zabbix server can upgrade to the latest database schema version on all versions from 2.0 onward. To upgrade the database from version 2.0 to 4.0, it isn't required to use server versions in succession; it's enough to start server version 4.0.

When a new major version of `Zabbix Server` is started, it's possible to observe the current status and database upgrade progress in the server log file:

```
10852:20151209:094918.686 Starting Zabbix Server. Zabbix 4.0.0
(revision {ZABBIX_REVISION}).
10852:20151209:094918.729 ****** Enabled features ******
...
10852:20151209:094918.730 TLS support:                NO
10852:20151209:094918.730 ******************************
10852:20151209:094918.730 using configuration file:
/usr/local/etc/zabbix_server.conf
10852:20151209:094918.820 current database version
(mandatory/optional): 4000000/ 4000000
10852:20151209:094918.820 required mandatory version:  4000000
10852:20151209:094918.820 starting automatic database upgrade
...
10852:20151209:094918.866 completed 20% of database upgrade
...
10852:20151209:094918.937 completed 100% of database upgrade
10852:20151209:094918.937 database upgrade fully completed
```

Notice how it prints out the current mandatory and optional database versions we just examined in the database, and the required mandatory version. If the mandatory or optional database version numbers are lower than the required version, the server will upgrade the database. If the database mandatory version is higher than the server version, the server will refuse to start up. During the database schema upgrade, no monitoring happens. Monitoring restarts once the database upgrade is complete.

What happens if you upgrade the fronted before upgrading and starting the server to take care of the database upgrade? You're likely to see a message that warns you that the frontend doesn't matches the current Zabbix database version.

If you see such a message when upgrading, start the new server and ensure the database upgrade is successful. If that doesn't help, make sure you're not starting some older Zabbix server binary or pointing the Zabbix server at a different database. If you see a message like that when not upgrading Zabbix, you likely have a quite significant misconfiguration.

Such a situation should never happen during the normal operation of Zabbix or minor version upgrades. Note that the Zabbix frontend stores the major version it's compatible with in the `defines.inc.php` file in the `ZABBIX_DB_VERSION` constant.

Gathering data during the upgrade

The database upgrade process can be very quick but, in some cases, it can also take quite some time. It might be required to keep gathering data even during the Zabbix upgrade, but *how can we achieve that if the monitoring doesn't resume until the upgrade is finished?*

Remember the additional Zabbix process, *the proxy?* It's able to gather data and buffer it for sending to the Zabbix server, so no data was lost even if the server was down for some time, which sounds pretty much like our situation. If all of your actual monitoring is already done by Zabbix proxies, you're already on the right track.

If you have items that're polled directly by server, you might want to set up a temporary proxy installation, maybe even on the same server, that would be running during the Zabbix server upgrade and removed later. To do this easily, use the mass update functionality in the **Configuration | Hosts** section in the frontend and set the **Monitored by Proxy** option. Make sure the proxy can actually gather data by testing it first with a single host.

 Setting up a temporary proxy installation will be notably harder if you're using active items. It would be required to reconfigure all Zabbix agents as they connect to the address specified in the `ServerActive` parameter. On the other hand, active agents do buffer data for a short while themselves, so a quick server upgrade might not miss that data anyway.

The proxy method sounds great, but it's a bit more complicated than just upgrading the server. Officially, only the same major version is supported for server-proxy compatibility. This means that we should not use proxies of the previous version with our upgraded server. Proxies, if used with a MySQL or PostgreSQL backend, can upgrade their database as well. The suggested path for using proxies to continue data collection through the major version upgrade would be like this:

1. Block all proxy-server communication (possibly using a local firewall such as `iptables`)
2. Stop the old Zabbix server, upgrade it, and start the new server

3. Stop one of the old Zabbix proxies, upgrade it, and start the new version to upgrade the local database
4. Restore the communication between the proxy and the new server
5. Proceed the same way with all the remaining proxies

This should ensure minimum data loss through the upgrade, especially if the steps for an individual proxy upgrade are scripted and happen with no delays.

 Proxy database upgrading isn't supported if using SQLite. In that case, the previous method wouldn't work, and the proxy database file should simply be removed when upgrading.

The frontend configuration file

While the database upgrade is the most important step when moving from one major version to another, it's worth paying a moment of attention to the Zabbix frontend configuration file. It's suggested to compare the old configuration file with the new one and see whether there're any new parameters or significant changes to the existing parameters. The easiest way might be comparing with the `zabbix.conf.php.example` file in the `conf/` subdirectory. This configuration file is pretty small, so spotting the differences should be easy.

 When installing from packages, the frontend configuration file could also be placed in `/etc/zabbix/`, `/etc/zabbix/web/` or `/etc/zabbix/frontend/`.

Compatibility

We've discussed upgrading the Zabbix server. But there're quite a lot of components, and the compatibility between each of them differs slightly. Actually, the official compatibility rule list is very short:

- All older versions of Zabbix agents are supported but, starting from Zabbix 4.0, agents older then 1.4 aren't supported anymore.
- Zabbix server, proxies, and Java gateways must be of the same major version.

Regarding the agents, it really is as great as it sounds. All of the old agent versions will work with the latest version of the Zabbix server or proxy, even down to 1.4—with versions older than 4.0, even back to version 1.0 from 2001. If you upgrade Zabbix server, you can keep your agents as is; although you wouldn't benefit from new features, performance, or even security improvements.

Technically, combinations outside of the support rules might work. For example, a more recent agent might work with an older server in some cases, and the Zabbix Java gateway protocol hasn't changed much, so it's likely to work with different major versions of Zabbix server, too. Such combinations aren't tested by Zabbix developers, aren't supported, and should be avoided in general.

Performance considerations

Zabbix tends to perform nicely for small installations, but as the monitored environment grows, we might run into performance problems. A full Zabbix performance discussion is out of scope here, but let's discuss the starting points to having a healthy configuration and the directions for further research:

- Monitor only what you really need, as rarely as possible, and keep the data only for as long as really needed. It's common for new users of Zabbix to use default templates as is, add a lot of new items with low intervals, and never look at the data. It's suggested to clone the default templates, eliminate all that isn't needed, and increase the intervals as much as possible. This involves trimming item lists, increasing intervals, and reducing history and trend-retention periods. There're also events, alerts, and other data—we'll discuss their storage settings a bit later.

- When using Zabbix agents, use active items. Active items will result in a smaller number of network connections and reduce the load on the Zabbix server. There're some features not supported with active items, so sometimes you'll have to use passive items. We discussed what can and cannot be done with active items in Chapter 3, *Monitoring with Zabbix Agents and Basic Protocols*.

- Use Zabbix proxies. They'll provide bulk data to Zabbix server, reducing the work the server has to do even further. We discussed proxies in Chapter 17, *Using Proxies to Monitor Remote Locations*.

We already know about the history and trend-retention periods for items, *but for how long does Zabbix store events, alerts, acknowledgment messages, and other data?* This is configurable by going to **Administration** | **General** and choosing **Housekeeping** in the drop-down menu in the upper-right corner:

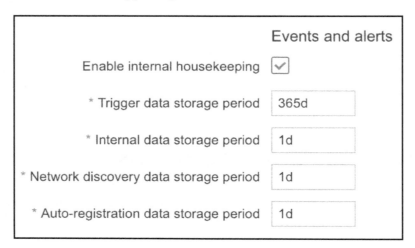

 This page is excessively long, so the preceding screenshot only shows a small section from the top.

Here, we may configure for how long to keep the following data:

- **Events and alerts**: We may choose separate storage periods for trigger, internal, network discovery, and active agent auto-registration events. Note that removing an event will also remove all associated alerts and acknowledgment messages.
- **Services**: The IT service up and down state is recorded separately from trigger events, and its retention period can be configured separately as well.
- **Audit data**: This specifies how long to store the audit data for. We'll discuss what that actually is in a moment.
- **User sessions**: User sessions that have been closed will be removed more frequently, but active user sessions will be removed after one year by default. This means that we can't be logged in longer than a year.

These values should be kept reasonably low. Keeping data for a long period of time will increase the database size, and that can impact the performance a lot.

What about the history and trend settings in here? While they're configurable per item normally, we may override those here. Also, for each of the entries, internal housekeeping may be disabled. These options are aimed at users who have to manage large Zabbix installations. When the database grows really large, its performance significantly degrades and can be improved by partitioning the biggest tables—splitting them up by some criteria. With Zabbix, it's common to partition the history and trends tables, sometimes adding events and alerts tables. If partitioning is used, parts of tables (partitions) are removed, and the internal housekeeping for those tables should be disabled. A lot of people in the Zabbix community will eagerly suggest partitioning at the first opportunity. Unless you plan to have a really large installation or know database partitioning really well, it might be better to hold off. There's no officially supported or built-in partitioning scheme yet, and one might appear in the future. If it does and your partition scheme is different, it'll be up to you to synchronize it with the official one.

Who did that?

Now who did that? This is a question occasionally heard in many places, IT workplaces included. Weird configuration changes and unsolicited reboots; accountability and a trace of actions help a lot to determine whether the questioner was the one who made the change and then forgot about it. For Zabbix configuration changes, an internal audit log is available. Just like most functionality, it's conveniently accessible from the web frontend. During our configuration quest, we made quite a lot of changes; let's see what footprints we left. Navigate to **Reports** | **Audit** and set the filter time to a period that approximately matches the initial installation of this Zabbix instance. We're presented with a list of the things we did, although you can also only see logging in and out on the first page of the audit records:

Time	User	IP	Resource	Action	ID	Description	Details
2018-10-13 11:36:03	Admin	192.168.1.18	User	Login	0		
2018-10-13 11:36:02	guest	192.168.1.18	User	Login	0		
2018-10-13 11:35:57	guest	192.168.1.18	User	Logout	0		
2018-10-13 11:34:25	guest	192.168.1.18	User	Login	0		

And *what if you set up Zabbix frontend monitoring, like we did in* Chapter 12, *Monitoring Web Pages?* You're likely to see only such records as our web scenario logs in and out every minute. But notice the filter; we may also filter by user, action, and resource:

Expand the **Action** and **Resource** drop-down menus; notice that they're quite fine-grained, especially the **Resource** drop-down menu.

In the Zabbix 1.8 version of this book, it said:

> *"In the first Zabbix 1.8 releases some actions aren't registered in the audit log. Such issues are expected to be fixed in the near future."*

Oh well. Unfortunately, it didn't get fixed in further 1.8 releases: 2.0, 2.2, 2.4 ,3.0, and—to the best of my knowledge—neither in 4.0. The Zabbix audit log is still missing lots of operations performed, especially when the API is used. While the audit log can be extremely useful, it can easily miss the specific operation you're interested in. Perform a test with the version you're interested in to be sure; the list of operations that aren't logged can easily change in a minor version.

Moving forward from the sad fact of the broken audit log, as an exercise, try to find out at what time you added the **Restart Apache** action.

While looking at this section, let's remind ourselves of another logging area; the action log that we briefly looked at before. Go to **Reports** | **Action log**. Here, all actions performed by the Zabbix server are recorded. This includes sending emails, executing remote commands, sending SMS messages, and executing custom scripts. This view provides information on what content was sent to whom, whether it was successful, and error messages, if any. It's useful for verifying whether Zabbix has sent a particular message, as well as figuring out whether the configured actions are working as expected.

Together, the action and log audit sections provide a good overview of internal Zabbix configuration changes, as well as debugging help to determine what action operations have been performed.

Exploring configuration file parameters

Let's conclude this chapter by digging into the configuration files of the Zabbix agent and server, and examining each parameter in them. We'll start with the agent configuration file and discuss the ways in which common parameters apply to other daemons. We'll skip the proxy configuration file, as the common parameters will be discussed by then, and the proxy-specific parameters were discussed in Chapter 17, *Using Proxies to Monitor Remote Locations*. We'll also skip all the parameters that start with TLS, as those are related to Zabbix daemon traffic encryption, and we discussed that in Chapter 18, *Encrypting Zabbix Traffic*.

We'll look at the parameters in the order in which they appear in the default example configuration files; no other meaning should be derived from the ordering here.

While reading the following descriptions, it's suggested to have the corresponding configuration file open. It'll allow you to verify that the parameters are the same in your version of Zabbix. Make sure to read the comments next to each parameter; they might show that some parameters have changed since the time of writing this. In general, when in doubt, read the comments in the configuration files. The Zabbix team tries really hard to make them both short and maximally relevant and helpful.

Zabbix agent daemon and common parameters

Let's start with the agent daemon parameters. For the parameters that're also available for other daemons, we'll discuss their relevance to all of the daemons here:

- PidFile: This is common to all daemons. They write the PID of the main process in this file. The default configuration files use /tmp for simplicity's sake. In production systems, this should be set to the distribution recommended location.

- LogType: This is common to all daemons and can be a file, syslog, or console. The default is file and, in that case, the LogFile parameter determines where the logs are written. The syslog value directs the daemon to log to syslog, and the console parameter tells it to log the messages to stdout.

- LogFile: This is common to all daemons. Log data is written to this file when LogType is set to file. The default configuration files use /tmp for simplicity's sake. In production systems, this should be set to the distribution-recommended location.

- LogFileSize: This is common to all daemons. When logging to a file, if the file size exceeds this number of megabytes, move it to file.0 (for example, zabbix_agentd.log.0) and log to a new file. Only one such move is performed (that is, there's never zabbix_agentd.log.1).

- DebugLevel: This is common to all daemons and specifies how much logging information to provide, starting with 0 (nearly nothing) and ending with 5 (a lot). It's probably best to run at DebugLevel 3 normally, and use something higher for debugging. For example, starting with DebugLevel 4, all server and proxy database queries are logged. At DebugLevel 5, two extra things are currently logged:

  - Received pages for web monitoring
  - Received raw data for VMware monitoring

We'll look at changing the log level for a running daemon in Appendix A, *Troubleshooting*.

- SourceIP: This is common to all daemons. If the system has multiple interfaces, outgoing connections will use the specified address. Note that not all connections will obey this parameter; for example, the backend database connections on the server or proxy won't.

- EnableRemoteCommands: This determines whether the system.run item should allow running commands. It's disabled by default.

- LogRemoteCommands: If EnableRemoteCommands is enabled, this parameter allows us to log all of the received commands. Unless system.run is used to retrieve data, it's probably a good idea to enable logging of the remote commands.

- Server: This is also available for the Zabbix proxy, but not for the Zabbix server. It's a comma-delimited list of IP addresses or host names the agent should accept connections from. It's only relevant for passive items, zabbix_get, and other incoming connections.

- ListenPort: This is common to all daemons and specifies the port to listen on.

- ListenIP: This is common to all daemons and specifies the IP address to listen on—it could also be a comma-delimited list of addresses.

- StartAgents: This is the number of processes to start that are responsible for incoming connection handling. If it's a very resource-starved system, it might be a good idea to reduce this. If this agent is expected to get lots of queries for passive items, increase this number. Note that it has nothing to do with the collector or active check processes; their numbers can't be directly changed. If set to 0, the agent will stop listening to incoming connections. This could be better security-wise, but could also make debugging much harder.

- ServerActive: This is the list of servers and ports to connect to for active checks. It follows the syntax of server:port, with multiple entries delimited by commas. If not set, no active checks are processed. We discussed this functionality in Chapter 3, *Monitoring with Zabbix Agents and Basic Protocols*.

- Hostname: This is also available for the Zabbix proxy, but not for the Zabbix server. If specified, the exact string will be sent to the Zabbix server as the host name for this system.

- HostnameItem: If Hostname isn't specified but HostnameItem is, the value in this parameter will be interpreted as an item key and the result of the evaluation will be sent to the server as the host name for this system.

- HostMetadata: This is an exact string to be sent to the server; used in active agent auto-registration.

- HostMetadataItem: If HostMetadata isn't specified but HostMetadataItem is, the value in this parameter will be interpreted as an item key and the result of the evaluation will be sent to the server as the host metadata to be used in active agent auto-registration.

- RefreshActiveChecks: This specifies how often the agent should connect to the server and ask for active items. It's set to two minutes by default. If active checks aren't used at all, it means a useless connection every two minutes from each agent; it's best not to set ServerActive at all in such a case.

- BufferSend: Active agents will send values every BufferSend seconds—by default, every five seconds. This allows us to reduce the number of network connections if multiple values are collected within a five-second window.

- BufferSize: This is a buffer to hold the values for active items. By default, it's set to 100 values. This is an in-memory buffer; don't set it too large if memory usage is a concern. The buffer is actually split in half if there's at least one log-monitoring item-one half is used for *normal* values, the other for log entries. If the buffer is full, new *normal* values will result in the dropping of older *normal* values, but it won't affect log entries. If the log entry part of the buffer is full, log file processing stops, but no entries are dropped there. If there're log items only and no *normal* items, half of the buffer is still reserved for *normal* entries. If there're only *normal* items, the whole buffer is used for them until at least one log item is added.

- MaxLinesPerSecond: This is the default maximum number of lines of log items that should be sent to the server. We discussed this in Chapter 10, *Advanced Item Monitoring*.

- Alias: This is a way to set an alias for an item key. While usable on all platforms, we discussed it in Chapter 22, *Monitoring Windows*. This parameter can also be used to create two LLD rules with the same key, even if the key itself doesn't accept parameters. One rule could use the original key, another the key that's aliased.

- Timeout: This is common to all daemons. It specifies the timeout for running commands, making connections, and so on. Since Zabbix 3.0, it has a default of three on agents and four on the server and proxy. This could affect userparameters, for example; a script that takes more than a few seconds would time out. It's highly suggested not to increase the timeout on the server side; if we have to handle many values every second, it's not good to have a server process wait on a single script that long. If you have such a script that takes a long time to return the value, consider using zabbix_sender instead, as discussed in Chapter 10, *Advanced Item Monitoring*.

- AllowRoot: By default, Zabbix daemons, if started as root, try to drop the privileges to a user specified in the User parameter (refer to the next point). If the User parameter isn't specified, the outcome depends on this parameter. If it's set to 0, startup fails. If it's set to 1, the daemon starts as the root user.

- `User`: This is common to all daemons. If daemons are started as the `root` user and `AllowRoot` is set to 0, try to change to the user specified in this parameter. This is set to `zabbix` by default.

- `Include`: This is common to all daemons. It allows you to include individual or multiple configuration files. We discussed this feature in `Chapter 10`, *Advanced Item Monitoring*. Note that files are included sequentially as if literally *included* in the location where the `Include` directive appeared. Also keep in mind that, if specified more than once, most parameters will override all previous occurrences; that is, the last option with the same name wins.

- `UnsafeUserParameters`: By default, a subset of characters is disallowed to be passed as parameters to `userparameter` keys. If enabled, this option will allow anything to be passed and is essentially equivalent to `EnableRemoteCommands`—the originally prohibited symbols make it simple to gain shell access. See the default configuration file for a full list of symbols this parameter would allow.

- `UserParameter`: This allows us to extend agents by adding custom item keys to it. We discussed this in quite a lot of detail and configured some user parameters in `Chapter 10`, *Advanced Item Monitoring*. This parameter may be specified multiple times as long the item key is unique; that's a way to add multiple user parameters.

- `LoadModulePath`: This is common to all daemons. It specifies a path to load modules, written in the C language. This is an advanced way to extend Zabbix daemons that's a bit out of scope for this book. Refer to the Zabbix manual for more details.

- `LoadModule`: This is common to all daemons. Multiple entries of this parameter may be specified for individual `.so` files to load inside the `LoadModulePath` directory.

Zabbix server daemon parameters

We'll now skip the common parameters we already discussed when looking at the agent daemon configuration file. The remaining ones are as follows:

- `DBHost`: This is useful if the backend database is on a different system. Using an IP address is highly recommended here.

- `DBName`: This is the database name; we set it in `Chapter 1`, *Getting Started with Zabbix*. As the comment explains, it should be set to the database file path when the SQLite backend is used for a proxy.

- DBSchema: This is the database schema, only useful with PostgreSQL and IBM DB2.
- DBUser and DBPassword: These are database access credentials. As the comment explains, they're ignored when the SQLite backend is used for a proxy.
- DBSocket: This is the path to the database socket, if needed. Unless the Zabbix server or proxy is compiled against a different database library than the one available at runtime, you'll likely never need this parameter.
- DBPort: If connecting to a local or remote database on a nonstandard port, specify it here.
- HistoryStorageURL: This is the URL to the Elasticsearch storage; remember there's still no official support for Elasticsearch.
- HistoryStorageTypes: This is a list of what to store in the Elasticsearch DB.
- HistoryStorageDateIndex: This enables preprocessing of history values in history storage to store values in different indices based on date.
- ExportDir: This is a directory for real-time export of events, history, and trends in newline-delimited JSON format. If set, it enables real-time export.
- ExportFileSize: This is the maximum size per export file in bytes.
- StartPollers: Pollers are internal processes that collect data in various ways. By default, five pollers are started, and this is plenty for tiny installations such as our test setup. In larger installations, it's common to have hundreds of pollers. Notice that there're no separate SNMP pollers; the same processes are responsible for passive agent and SNMP device polling. *How to know whether you have enough?* Using the internal monitoring, find out the average busy rate. If it's above 70%, just add more pollers. Pollers are responsible for the following:
  - Connecting to passive agents
  - Connecting to SNMP devices
  - Performing simple checks, such as service/port checks
  - Retrieving internal monitoring data
  - Retrieving VMware data from the VMware cache
  - Running external check scripts
- StartIPMIPollers: This specifies how many processes should be started that poll IPMI devices. We configured this parameter in Chapter 14, *Monitoring IPMI devices*.

- `StartPreprocessors`: This is the number of pre-forked instances of preprocessing workers needed for our preprocessing, such as JSON, XML, and PCRE.

- `StartPollersUnreachable`: If a host isn't reachable, it isn't polled by normal pollers anymore; special types called **unreachable pollers** now deal with that host, including IPMI items. This is done to avoid a situation where a few hosts that time out take up most of the poller time. If there aren't enough unreachable pollers, the worst thing that happens is that hosts that are declared unreachable aren't noticed as being back up as quickly. By default, only one unreachable poller is started. To know whether that's enough, observe their busy rate, especially when there're systems down in the monitored environment.

- `StartTrappers`: By default, there're five trappers. As with pollers, monitor their busy rate and add more as needed. Trappers are responsible for receiving incoming connections from the following:
    - Active agents
    - Active proxies
    - `zabbix_sender`
    - The Zabbix frontend, including server availability check, global scripts, and queue data

- `StartPingers`: These processes create temporary files and then call `fping` against those files to perform ICMP ping checks. If there're lots of ICMP ping items, make sure to check the busy rate of these processes and add more as needed.

- `StartDiscoverers`: Discoverers perform network discovery. Discovery happens sequentially for each rule. Even if there're lots of available discoverers, only one at a time works on a single discovery rule. Note that discoverers split up the rules they'll serve; for example, if there're two discovery rules and two discoverers, one discoverer will always work with a particular rule. We discussed network discovery in `Chapter 11`, *Automating Configuration*.

- `StartHTTPPollers`: These processes are responsible for processing web scenarios. Like discoverers, HTTP pollers split up the web scenarios they will serve. We discussed web monitoring in `Chapter 12`, *Monitoring Web Pages*.

- `StartTimers`: Timer processes can be quite resource intensive, especially if lots of triggers use time-based functions such as `now()`. We discussed time-based trigger functions in `Chapter 6`, *Detecting Problems with Triggers*. These processes are responsible for the following:
  - Placing hosts in and out of maintenance at second 0 of every minute; this is only done by the first timer process if more than one is started
  - Evaluating all triggers that include at least one time-based trigger function at second 0 and second 30 of every minute

- `StartEscalators`: These processes move escalations forward in steps, as discussed in `Chapter 7`, *Acting upon Monitored Conditions*. They also run remote commands, if instructed so by action operations.

- `JavaGateway`, `JavaGatewayPort`, and `StartJavaPollers`: These parameters point at the Java gateway and its port, and tell the server or proxy how many processes should connect to that gateway. Note that they all connect to the same gateway, so the gateway should be able to handle the load if the number of Java pollers is increased. We discussed Java monitoring in `Chapter 15`, *Monitoring Java Applications*.

- `StartVMwareCollectors`, `VMwareFrequency`, `VMwarePerfFrequency`, `VMwareCacheSize`, and `VMwareTimeout`: These control the way VMware monitoring works. We discussed these parameters in detail in `Chapter 16`, *Monitoring VMware*.

- `SNMPTrapperFile` and `StartSNMPTrapper`: When receiving SNMP traps, we must specify the temporary trap file and whether the SNMP trapper should be started. Note that only one SNMP trapper process may be started. We configured these parameters in `Chapter 4`, *Monitoring SNMP Devices*.

- `HousekeepingFrequency`: This specifies how often the internal housekeeper process runs or, to be more specific, how long after the previous run finished the next run should start. It's not suggested to change the default interval of one hour; the housekeeper may be disabled as needed for specific data in **Administration** | **General**, as discussed earlier in this chapter. The first run of the housekeeper happens 30 minutes after the server or proxy starts. The housekeeper may be manually invoked using the runtime control option.

- `MaxHousekeeperDelete`: For deleted items, this specifies how many values per item should be deleted in a single run, with the default being 5,000. For example, if we'd deleted 10 items with 10,000 values each, it would take two housekeeper runs to get rid of all of the values for all items. If an item had a huge number of values, deleting them all in one go could cause database performance issues. Note that this parameter doesn't affect value cleanup for existing items.

- `CacheSize`: This is the size of the main configuration cache that holds hosts, items, triggers, and lots of other information. Use of this cache depends on the size of the configuration data, which is influenced by the number of hosts, items, and other entities. Be very proactive with this parameter; if cache usage significantly increases or you plan to add monitoring for lots of new hosts, increase the configuration cache. If the configuration cache is full, the Zabbix server stops.

- `CacheUpdateFrequency`: This specifies how often the configuration cache is updated. The default of one minute is fine for most installations, although in large environments it might be a good idea to increase this parameter, as a configuration cache update itself can increase database load.

- `StartDBSyncers`: This specifies how many database or history syncers should be started (both names are used interchangeably in various places in Zabbix). These processes are responsible for calculating triggers that reference items, receiving new values, and storing the resulting events and those history values in the database—probably the most database-taxing processes in Zabbix. The default of four database or history syncers should be enough for most environments, although it could be useful to increase for big installations. Be careful with increasing this number; having too many of these can have a negative effect on performance, although you might see that, if their average busy rate decreases, the number of values processed could decrease.

- `HistoryCacheSize`: When values are collected, they're first stored in a history cache. History or database syncers take values from this cache, process triggers, and store the values in the database. The history cache getting full usually indicates performance issues; increasing the cache size is unlikely to help. If this cache is full, no new values are inserted into it, but the Zabbix server keeps running.

- `HistoryIndexCacheSize`: This cache holds information about the most recent and oldest value for all items in the history cache. It's used to avoid scanning the history cache, which could get rather large. Use of this cache depends on the number of items that collect data. As with the main configuration and trend cache, make sure to have enough room in this cache; if it's full, the Zabbix server will shut down.

- `TrendCacheSize`: This cache holds trend information for the current hour for each item—not the current hour per the clock, but the current hour based on the incoming values. That is, the last value that came in for an item determines the current hour value. For example, if values are sent in using `zabbix_sender` for the hour 09:00-10:00 yesterday, that's the current hour and its trend data is in the trend cache. As soon as the first value for the hour 10:00-11:00 arrives, the trend cache information for that item is written to the database and 10:00-11:00 becomes the new current hour. Use of this cache depends on the amount of items that collect data. As with the main configuration cache, make sure to have enough room in this cache; if it's full, the Zabbix server will shut down.

- `ValueCacheSize`: This parameter controls the size of the cache that holds historical values; but as opposed to the history cache, it holds values that're expected to be useful in the future. The values in here aren't meant to be written out to the database, but quite the opposite: values are often read into this cache from the database. The value cache is used when item values are needed for trigger calculation (for example, computing the average value for last 10 minutes), for calculated or aggregate items, for including in notifications, and other purposes. Value cache population can take a while when the server first starts up. If the value cache is full, the Zabbix server will keep running, but its performance will likely degrade. Monitor this cache and increase the size as needed.

- `Timeout`: This specifies how long Zabbix waits for the agent, SNMP device, or external check (in seconds).

- `TrapperTimeout`: This parameter controls how long trappers spend on communicating with active agents and proxies, as well as `zabbix_sender`. Being set to the maximum value of five minutes by default, this timeout is highly unlikely to be reached.

- UnreachablePeriod, UnavailableDelay, and UnreachableDelay: These parameters work together to determine how value retrieval failures should be handled. If value retrieval fails with a network error, the host is considered to be unreachable and is checked every UnreachableDelay seconds (by default, 15). This goes on for UnreachablePeriod seconds (45 by default), and if all checks fail (with the default settings, we end up with four checks), the host is marked unavailable and is checked every UnavailableDelay seconds. Note that, since Zabbix 3.0, if an item fails twice in a row but another item of the same type on the same host succeeds, the failing item is marked unsupported instead. It's probably best to leave these values at the defaults, as changing them could lead to fairly confusing results.

- AlertScriptsPath: Custom scripts to be called from actions must be placed in the directory specified by this parameter. We configured such a script in Chapter 7, *Acting upon Monitored Conditions*.

- ExternalScripts: Scripts that are to be used in external check items must be placed in the directory specified by this parameter. We configured such an item in Chapter 10, *Advanced Item Monitoring*.

- FpingLocation and Fping6Location: These parameters should point at the fping binaries for IPv4 and IPv6, if different. The fping utility is required for ICMP checks, which we configured in Chapter 3, *Monitoring with Zabbix Agents and Basic Protocols*.

- SSHKeyLocation: If using SSH items with keys, the keys must be placed in the directory specified by this parameter. We configured SSH items in Chapter 10, *Advanced Item Monitoring*.

- LogSlowQueries: Normally, SQL queries aren't logged up to DebugLevel 4. This parameter allows us to log all queries that take longer than the number of milliseconds, specified here, at DebugLevel 3. By default, since Zabbix 3.0, any query that takes longer than three seconds is logged. They appear in the log file like this:

    ```
    13890:20151223:152504.421 slow query: 3.005859 sec,
    "commit;"
    ```

- TmpDir: This is a temporary directory for any files the Zabbix server or proxy need to store. Currently, it is only used for files that're passed to fping.

- SSLCertLocation, SSLKeyLocation, and SSLCALocation: These parameters specify where certificates, keys, and certificate authority files will be looked up when the SSL functionality is used with web monitoring.

Again, all of the parameters starting with TLS are relevant for daemon traffic encryption and won't be discussed here.

The available parameters might be slightly different if you have a more recent version of Zabbix. To list the supported parameters in the configuration file you have, the following command could help:

```
$ grep "### Option" zabbix_agentd.conf
```

Now, if you get confused about some parameter, *what's the first place you should check?* If you said or thought: *comments in the configuration files themselves,* of course, great. If not, go take a look at those comments and remember that the Zabbix team really, really tries hard to make those comments useful and wants you to read them. You will save your own time that way.

Summary

After Zabbix is installed and configured, a moment comes when maintenance tasks become important. In this last chapter, we looked at three important tasks:

- **Monitoring Zabbix itself**: We covered internal items that allow figuring out how much data the Zabbix server or proxy is receiving, monitoring cache usage, and verifying how busy the internal processes are, how many unsupported items we have, and a few other things.
- **Making backups**: We discussed the suggested and popular approaches to making backups (and restoring from them, too) of the most important thing in Zabbix—its database.
- **Upgrading Zabbix**: We found out the differences between minor and major version upgrades, and how the database is automatically patched by the Zabbix server. We also learned about LTS versions, which are supported for three years and for two extra years for critical and security fixes, while the other versions are supported for about one month from when the next version is released.

While talking about upgrades, we also figured out how the compatibility between different Zabbix components works. With minor-level upgrades, it was very easy; all components, including the server, proxy, and agent, are compatible with each other. Let's try to visualize the major upgrade level compatibility matrix:

Older / Newer	Agent	Proxy	Server
Agent		Y	Y
Proxy	N		N
Server	N	N	

As a reminder, from the support perspective, the server and proxy should be of the same major version, and they support all older agent versions. Regarding the Zabbix Java gateway, it should be from the same major version as the server or proxy; although the protocol hasn't changed, there're no official tests done and no support provided for different major versions.

Before performing a major Zabbix version upgrade, make sure to take a database backup.

After dealing with these three major topics, we discussed general suggestions to keep Zabbix performance acceptable, paying extra attention to housekeeper configuration.

We also found out a way to see the changes made to the Zabbix configuration: the audit log. It allows us to see who made what changes to hosts, items, and other entities. We're a bit disappointed to find out this log doesn't actually record all operations, especially those performed through the API.

We concluded with quite a detailed look at the parameters in the server, proxy, and agent configuration files. Is it maybe worth reminding you to pay close attention to the comments in the configuration files themselves?

We'll conclude this book with two appendices, where we'll discuss the steps and methods for Zabbix troubleshooting, as well as ways to interact with and join the Zabbix community.

Questions

1. Can we use older agents with newer Zabbix servers?
2. Can I use a Zabbix 4.0.1 server with a Zabbix 4.0.0 frontend and some 3.0.3 agents?
3. When upgrading from Zabbix 3.4 to 4.0, can I keep my proxies on 3.4 after I've upgraded my Zabbix server to 4.0?

Further reading

Read the following articles for more information:

- **Zabbix server**: https://zabbix.com/documentation/4.0/manual/appendix/config/zabbix_server
- **Zabbix agent (Unix)**: https://zabbix.com/documentation/4.0/manual/appendix/config/zabbix_agentd
- **Appendixes**: https://zabbix.com/documentation/4.0/manual/appendix

Troubleshooting

Installing and configuring Zabbix can happen without a hiccup for one user and with a constant stream of problems for another. The reasons for the problems can differ from user to user—buggy libraries, bad distribution packaging, unintuitive configurations in Zabbix, or maybe even an occasional bug in Zabbix itself. Here, we will look at common problems new users experience when performing various tasks:

- Setting up the initial Zabbix installation
- Working with the web frontend
- Monitoring different devices
- Configuring thresholds and alerting

If you face a case that is more complicated than that, we will continue with more detailed debugging instructions, including:

- The Zabbix log file format
- Reloading the server and the proxy configuration cache
- Controlling running daemons
- Observing the work performed by individual daemon processes

Introduction

This chapter caused me a bit of mental agony. Having worked with Zabbix since 2001, there were a lot of potential problem cases to describe. I'd wake up in the middle of the night with an idea of a brilliant problem (and solution) to include, only to have forgotten it by the time morning came. But this could have been a never-ending chapter. A compromise was needed, and reluctantly accepted. This chapter does not aim to help you with every single problem you will ever encounter in your life, or with Zabbix. It tries to help with more common issues, and give you some hints and starting points for further debugging.

Common issues

In this section, we'll look at a few issues you might face.

Installation

There are several common stumbling blocks in the installation process, some caused by well-hidden factors.

Compilation

1. **Q**: I am trying to compile Zabbix on a 64-bit system. I have the corresponding development packages installed, but Zabbix claims they are not present.

   A: Double-check that the 64-bit development packages are installed, not just the 32-bit ones.

2. **Q**: I am trying to compile Zabbix from an SVN checkout, but the configuration script fails with this error:

   ```
   syntax error near unexpected token 'IKSEMEL,iksemel,'
   ```

   A: Install the `pkg-config` package and rerun the commands to generate the configuration script.

3. **Q**: I am trying to compile Zabbix, but it fails.

   A: It is useful to reduce the number of possible causes. Verify that you are not compiling with `--enable-static`, which is known to cause compilation problems. If compilation fails without that flag, check the `config.log` file contents in the `source` directory. It often contains exact error details.

Frontend

1. **Q**: I have installed the Zabbix frontend. What's the default username and password?

   A: The username is `Admin`, and the password is `zabbix`.

2. **Q**: I'm setting up Zabbix from an SVN checkout. When I switch languages in the frontend, nothing happens.

   A: In the `frontend` directory, in the `locale` subdirectory, there's a `make_mo.sh` script. It compiles the needed `.mo` files out of the translation source `.po` files—run it. Note that it will need Gettext tools, and the web server might have to be restarted afterward.

Backend

1. **Q**: Zabbix is working correctly, but some/all graphs are not displayed.

   A: Refer to the Apache error log for more details. Usually, this is caused by the PHP script memory limit being too low—if that is the case, increase it by setting the `memory_limit` parameter to a higher value and restarting the web server. Another possible cause is a broken `conf/zabbix.conf.php` file—verify that it does not have any weird characters, especially at the end of the file.

2. **Q**: Complex views, such as screens with many elements, sometimes fail to load. What could be causing this?

   A: Like the previous problem, check that the PHP memory limit has not been exceeded. Additionally, check the PHP script timeout (`max_execution_time parameter`) and increase it if necessary.

3. **Q**: My graphs have gaps.

   A: It's not only graphs—data is missing in the database as well. This problem should be resolved by finding out what causes the data loss. Common reasons for this are:

   - **Network problems**: If the network is unreliable, data will be missing.
   - **An overloaded monitored device**: For example, if you have added a switch with many ports and are monitoring several items on each port very often, try increasing the intervals and disabling unneeded items.
   - **An overloaded Zabbix server**: It's usually the database. Check the system load on the Zabbix database server, especially `iowait`.

4. **Q**: I had Zabbix installed and running, but it is suddenly showing me the installation screen again.

   A: Check the accessibility of the `conf/zabbix.conf.php` file.

5. **Q**: The `conf/zabbix.conf.php` file is there, but I still see the installation screen.

   A: In some distribution packages, the frontend might expect the frontend configuration file to be in `/etc/zabbix/web` or a similar location. Check the package documentation.

6. **Q**: I am trying to open a large page with many elements, but refresh kicks in before the page even finishes loading. How can I solve this?

   A: Increase the refresh period in your user profile. While the page-loading speed won't be improved by that, at least the page will get a chance to load completely.

7. **Q**: The clock on my server is correct, but the frontend shows incorrect times.

   A: Check that the time zone is set correctly in the PHP configuration.

8. **Q**: Zabbix server is running, but the frontend claims it is not.

   A: This could be caused by multiple factors:

   - Check the `conf/zabbix.conf.php` file—the frontend uses the server address and port specified there to query the Zabbix server process.
   - Make sure no firewall is blocking connections from the frontend to the Zabbix server.
   - Make sure SELinux is not blocking connections from the frontend to the Zabbix server.
   - Make sure you have at least one trapper process enabled—they accept frontend connections. It is also possible that there are not enough trappers to service all requests. This is especially likely if the message about the server being unavailable appears only every now and then. Monitor the busy rate of the trapper processes like we did in Chapter 20, *Zabbix Maintenance*.

9. **Q**: I am having a problem with a frontend that is not listed here.

   A: Check the Apache error log and PHP log—these often offer an insight into the cause. Also, go to **Administration | Users** or **User groups** and add your user to the **Enabled** debug mode group. Afterward, all frontend pages will have a small **Debug** control in the lower-right corner. Clicking on it will show a lot of detail about that specific page, including the exact API and SQL queries that were performed. Debug mode can use more resources—if some frontend pages stop working after enabling debug mode, try disabling it.

10. **Q**: I am sure that my Zabbix server is properly configured, but it still won't start .

    A: It could be that SELinux is active. Another issue can also be that coredumps are activated. The Zabbix agent and Zabbix server will not start if encryption is compiled in, as it can cause security issues with sensitive data being written in the coredump.

Locked out of the frontend

A common mistake, performed by both new and seasoned users, is locking oneself out of the frontend. This can happen in several ways, but we're more interested here in how to get back in:

1. **Q**: I forgot my password and tried to log in until the Zabbix frontend stopped responding.

   A: By default, Zabbix denies access for 30 seconds after 5 failed login attempts, so just wait for 30 seconds. You can customize these values in `includes/defines.inc.php`:

   - `ZBX_LOGIN_ATTEMPTS`: The number of unsuccessful attempts after which Zabbix denies access
   - `ZBX_LOGIN_BLOCK`: How long to deny access for, in seconds

2. **Q**: I have forgotten my Admin user password, or I have been tasked with managing a Zabbix installation where the Admin user's password is not known.

   A: You can easily reset the Admin user password by directly modifying the database:

   ```
   mysql> update zabbix.users set passwd=MD5('somepassword')
   where alias='Admin';
   ```

   Of course, replace `somepassword` with some other string. Keep in mind that, by default, MySQL saves console commands in the `~/.mysql_history` file, so you might want to set the password to some temporary version and update it in the frontend later.

3. **Q**: I changed the authentication method, but it didn't work as planned and now I can't log in anymore.

   A: You can restore Zabbix's internal authentication method by editing the database:

   ```
   mysql> update zabbix.config set authentication_type='0' where
   configid='1';
   ```

Authentication type `0` is the internal one. For the record, other types are `1` (LDAP) and `2` (HTTP). Zabbix expects only one config table entry with a `configid` value of `1`.

Monitoring

Sometimes, monitoring something proceeds without a hitch, and sometimes it just won't work.

General monitoring

1. **Q**: I added a host or item, but I don't see it in **Monitoring** | **Latest data**.

   A: Check that the filter there includes the host or its group. Make sure that the **Show items without data** checkbox is marked and that other filter options do not exclude the item you are looking for.

2. **Q**: I can see my host in latest data, and new values are coming in—but it is missing in **Monitoring | Overview**.

   A: **Overview** is probably set to display triggers—verify that the host has triggers configured. Hosts without triggers are not displayed in trigger mode.

Monitoring with the Zabbix agent

1. **Q**: I am trying to monitor a host using passive Zabbix agent checks, but it doesn't work.

   A: Common reasons why Zabbix agent items won't work include the following:

   - The Zabbix agent daemon is not running. Simple, *right?* Still, start by checking that it is actually running.
   - The Zabbix daemon is not listening on the correct port or interface. You can check which port and interface the Zabbix agent daemon is listening on by running `netstat -ntpl` on the monitored host. The default agent daemon port is `10050`.
   - The server IP address in the agent daemon configuration file is incorrect. Check the configuration file and make sure the server directive specifies the IP that the Zabbix server will be connecting from.
   - Network problems prevent the server from connecting to the agent daemon properly. This includes things such as local and network firewalls blocking connections, but also some network devices and setups actually changing the source IP address of the Zabbix server's outgoing connections. Test the connectivity by executing `telnet <monitored host IP> 10050` from the Zabbix server. If you have customized the agent listen port, use that port in this command. If the connection is not opened, debug it as a network problem. If the connection is immediately closed, the Zabbix agent daemon does not see the connection as coming from the IP address set in the configuration file. Note that, in some cases, you might actually have to use the IPv6 address, as the Zabbix agent is receiving that as one of the incoming connections.

2. **Q**: I am trying to monitor a host using active Zabbix agent checks, but it does not work.

   A: Active items are a bit trickier. Here are some things to verify:

   - Check network connectivity as with normal items—from the monitored machine, execute `telnet <Zabbix server IP> 10051`
   - If you have customized the agent listen port, use that port in this command

    The Zabbix proxy IP address and port should be used in almost all commands if the host is monitored by a proxy.

   - Make sure to wait for the Zabbix server to refresh its configuration cache, and that the time specified in the `RefreshActiveChecks` option in the agent daemon configuration file has passed, before expecting results from the active items. If you want to force the agent to reload the list of items from the server, restart the agent.
   - Check whether the host name specified in the agent daemon configuration file in the `Hostname` option matches the one configured for the host in the frontend. Note that this is not the IP address or DNS name; only the host name will work—it is also not the visible name, but the so-called technical host name. Like nearly everything else in Zabbix, it is case-sensitive.
   - Make sure that the Zabbix server you want to send active checks to (or retrieve them from) is listed in the `ServerActive` option in the agent daemon configuration file.

3. **Q**: I am verifying that I can get the value on the monitored host, but the Zabbix agent says it is not supported or gives me the wrong data.

   A: There are several possible cases:

   - You are checking things such as the process count or using the `zabbix_agentd -t` syntax as root, but various permission limitations, including grsecurity and SELinux, can prevent access for the Zabbix agent. This includes the Zabbix agent showing the number of unique running processes as 0 even when with root access you can see the actual number.
   - Another case when the local process count differs from what the Zabbix agent returns: various interpreted processes, such as Python or Perl ones, can appear to the agent as interpreter processes, only with user processes as a parameter. Processes known to display this problem include `amavisd` and `xend`. In those situations, you can use a different approach; for example, with the `proc.num[python,,,xend]` item key. This will look for Python processes with the `xend` string in their parameters.
   - The monitored instance is missing. For example, if you are asking for a metric with the `net.if.in[eth0,bytes]` key and the Zabbix agent claims it is not supported, verify that the `eth0` interface actually exists.
   - Another server has an active Zabbix agent configured with the same host name and is also sending in data for this host.

4. **Q**: I modified a parameter in the agent daemon configuration file, but it ignores my changes.

   A: Check several things:

   - Verify that the modified line is not commented out.
   - Make sure you are editing the file on the correct system.
   - Check that the Zabbix agent daemon uses the modified configuration file. All Zabbix daemons log the configuration file they are using when starting up.

- Check for `Include` directives. Pay extra attention to ones that include all files in a directory, and nested includes.
- Make sure you properly restarted the daemon. Note that simply running `zabbix_daemon` or the `zabbix_daemon restart` will not restart the daemon.

 Some distribution packages may provide a configuration file and a convenient symlink to that file. If you use `sed -i` on a symlink, it does not edit the target file—it replaces the symlink with a regular file instead. Some versions of `sed` may provide an option called `--follow-symlinks` to edit the target file.

5. **Q**: I see the configuration file specifying one value for a parameter, but the Zabbix agent uses a different value.

   A: Refer to the answer to the previous question, especially the part about making sure it's the correct file on the correct system, and that Include directives do not override the first instance of the parameter.

6. **Q**: I'm trying to use active items or autoregistration on a Windows system, but the automatically acquired hostname is all uppercase and cut at 15 characters.

   A: Set `HostnameItem=system.hostname[host]` in the agent daemon configuration file. We discussed this in `Chapter 22`, *Monitoring Windows*.

7. **Q**: I verified that an item works as expected when running `zabbix_agentd -t` or `-p`, but it does not work when I check the values in the frontend.

   A: When manually running `zabbix_agentd`, the user and environment are likely different from a running daemon, so permissions and environment values will differ. Check the detailed operations that the item is expected to perform and what could prevent it from succeeding with the Zabbix agent daemon permissions. Do not test `zabbix_agentd` directly as root. The best approach is testing against a running agent daemon with `zabbix_get`.

8. **Q**: I can get item values in the Zabbix server or with `zabbix_get`, but when I test with `zabbix_agentd -t` or `-p`, I get an error: `[m|ZBX_NOTSUPPORTED] [Collector is not started.]`.

A: Some items, including `system.cpu.util` and `proc.cpu.util`, have their values calculated by a running agent, as they need multiple samples before providing a useful value. Such items only work when an agent daemon is queried by the Zabbix server or `zabbix_get`.

User parameters

The following list details queries related to user parameters:

1. **Q**: My user parameter does not work.

   A: Here are some common causes that break user parameters:

   - A missing environment is one of the biggest stumbling blocks when setting up user parameters. The Zabbix agent does not explicitly initialize environment details, such as the `HOME` variable or other information. This can lead to an inability to read the required configuration files and other issues. Make sure to set the environment as required either by setting variables in the user parameter directly or in a wrapper script.
   - Again, restricted permissions for the Zabbix user will be confusing to debug if you run commands for testing as root, so always test user parameters as the Zabbix user. If you need root access for a check, configure access via `sudo`.
   - Returning unclean data can also easily break data retrieval. When retrieving data with user parameters, make sure it does not contain characters that make it unsuitable for storage (such as returning 26.6 C for a float datatype item) or has other weird characters (such as having a CR/LF newline at the end of the data string).
   - By default, agent items will timeout after three seconds. It is not suggested to increase this timeout in most cases, although it might be reasonably safe to do so if the `userparameter` variable is used as an active item. Remember that active items are not parallel—only one agent process works on them, one item at a time. Consider using `zabbix_sender` for such items instead.

SNMP devices

1. **Q**: My SNMP items do not work.

    A: Double-check that the SNMP version and community string are set correctly. Specifying an incorrect SNMP version will often cause timeouts, making it harder to debug. Of course, check general connectivity and permissions by using the `snmpwalk` and `snmpget` commands from the Zabbix server.

     Additionally, make sure you are not overloading the monitored device by querying lots of values too frequently.

2. **Q**: My SNMP items either do not work at all, or fails frequently.

    A: Perhaps your device does not properly support SNMP GETBULK, try disabling bulk get support in the host properties for the SNMP interface.

3. **Q**: I imported a template, but the LLD fails with an invalid SNMP OID: `pairs of macro and OID are expected`.

    A: The Zabbix SNMP LLD key syntax changed in Zabbix 2.4. Unfortunately, the XML import process was not updated accordingly, and the imported LLD rule uses the old syntax. Refer to `Chapter 11`, *Automating Configuration*, for details on the key syntax.

4. **Q**: I added MIB files, and they work with the command-line tools, but the Zabbix server seems to be ignoring the MIB files.

    A: Make sure to restart the server daemon—MIB definitions are loaded only upon startup.

5. **Q**: My SNMP items work, but some OIDs on a specific device do not, even though data appears in the `snmpwalk` output.

    A: Try `snmpget` with those OIDs. Some UPSes are known to have buggy firmware that prevents these metrics from working with GET requests, but they do work with the GETNEXT requests that `snmpwalk` uses. If this is the case, upgrade the firmware on the device.

6. **Q**: I listed all SNMP MIBs I want to use in `/etc/snmp/snmp.conf`, but `Net-SNMP` utilities do not use them all properly.

   A: Some `Net-SNMP` versions silently trim lines in this file to 1,024 symbols, including the newline character. Try splitting options on multiple lines so that a single line does not exceed 1,023 printable characters.

7. **Q**: I'm monitoring network traffic, but it returns incorrect data.

   A: If it's a high-speed interface; make sure to use 64-bit counter OIDs, such as `ifHCInOctets` and `ifHCOutOctets`.

8. **Q**: I'm adding SNMP devices to Zabbix, but adding new devices stops the monitoring of the previous devices. If I query each device with `snmpget`, they still respond as expected.

   A: If it's SNMPv3, make sure all devices have a unique `snmpEngineID` variable.

IPMI monitoring

1. **Q**: I can't get the IPMI item to work.

   A: There are several things to verify when IPMI items do not work:

   - Make sure that the Zabbix server is configured with IPMI support. Simple, but easy to miss.
   - Check whether the `StartIPMIPollers` option in the server's configuration file is set to the default value, `0`. If it is, set it to `1` and restart the Zabbix server.
   - Make sure that the sensor names are correct. You can get the sensor names with `IPMItool`, and you have to use the name as it appears in the `IPMItool` output, with spaces and without quoting it.
   - Check using the latest `OpenIPMI` version. Older `OpenIPMI` versions are known to have various issues.

ICMP checks

1. **Q**: All of my ICMP checks are failing.

   A: Here are a few possible reasons:

   - Check that `fping` has the correct permissions so that it can run as root. For this we need to set the `setuid` bit on the Zabbix server.
   - Make sure SELinux does not prevent Zabbix from running `fping`. The `grep fping /var/log/audit/audit.log` command might reveal more information.

Problems with simple checks

1. **Q**: My service works, but the `net.tcp.service` or `net.udp.service` item says it does not.

   A: Besides verifying that the correct server is queried, check whether the service responds as Zabbix expects—simple checks are documented in detail at `https://www.zabbix.com/documentation/3.0/manual/appendix/items/service_check_details`.

Problems with zabbix_sender and trapper items

1. **Q**: I send in values with a timestamp, but a different timestamp is entered in the server database.

   A: The `zabbix_sender` includes the current time on the host in a clock property for the whole request, and Zabbix server adjusts the timestamp for all values accordingly. It is not possible to tell the server not to do so, or the sender not to send it. Either fix the time on the sending system, or implement the basic protocol without sending the request timestamp.

General issues

1. **Q**: I am monitoring network traffic, but the numbers are unrealistically huge.

   A: As the data is likely provided as a counter, make sure the result is stored as delta (speed per second) on Zabbix.

2. **Q**: I'm monitoring a 10 G interface speed in bytes per second, and when the interface is loaded, I lose values.

   A: Make sure **Type of information** is set to **Numeric (unsigned)**. This way, you'll lose the precision of a fraction of a bit, but keep all the values.

3. **Q**: Zabbix does not like the formula for my calculated item.

   A: Make sure to use proper quoting, especially if the referenced item keys have quotes. For example, if the referenced item key is `key["parameter",param]` in the calculated item formula, it can be used as `last("key[\"parameter\",param]")`. Notice the escaping of the inner double quotes with backslashes.

4. **Q**: I'm trying to use an item key, such as `proc.num['apache']`, but it does not work.

   A: Zabbix supports only double quotes; do not use single quotes for quoting.

5. **Q**: I'm trying to use a trigger expression, such as `{host:item.LAST()=13}`, but it does not work.

   A: The problem could be case sensitivity, almost everything is case-sensitive in Zabbix: item keys, their parameters, host names, trigger functions, and so on. If you come from Windows, keep reminding yourself that case matters.

Triggers

1. **Q**: My trigger doesn't work, or Zabbix refuses to add my trigger.

   A: Check the trigger's syntax, paying close attention to parentheses—is the correct type used? Are they all properly closed? The same goes for quotes, and don't forget about case-sensitivity. Try splitting up complex expressions to pinpoint the error.

Actions

1. **Q**: My actions do not work.

   A: If the notifications do not appear in **Reports | Action log**, make sure the user you want to send notifications to has read permission to at least one of the hosts that participated in generating the event. Also, check the action conditions, host maintenance settings, and action operations. Make sure your actions are not disabled—Zabbix can silently and automatically disable actions if the resources referenced in action conditions or operations are deleted. Also check the user media settings, such as severity and time filter, and whether the configured media type is enabled. If the messages do appear in the action log and there are error messages, hopefully the error is helpful. If the messages appear in the action log as successfully sent, check the logs on your MTA or other receiving system.

2. **Q**: My email notifications are not sent, and I can see that error messages, such as `[127.0.0.1]`, did not issue `MAIL/EXPN/VRFY/ETRN` during the connection to MTA in e-mail server log files.

   A: These messages are most likely caused by Zabbix monitoring the SMTP service, not by notification attempts. Check the permissions, as mentioned in the previous question, and check the action log in **Reports | Action log** to find out why notifications are failing.

3. **Q**: Something happened, and my Zabbix server is sending out loads of messages. Can I quickly stop that?

A: There exists a harsh method to stop runaway or excessive escalations—you can delete all the currently-active escalations. Note that even when deleting the active escalations, Zabbix will create new ones—a good way to solve that is to have the action operation condition only send out messages when the trigger is not acknowledged, and acknowledge the problematic triggers. Beware: this will also remove correct escalations. In the correct database, execute this:

```
mysql> delete from escalations;
```

Discoveries and autoregistration

1. **Q**: I remove a host from some host group, but it gets mysteriously re-added later.

   A: Check network discovery and active agent autoregistration actions—most likely, they re-add the host.

2. **Q**: I move a host to be monitored by a specific proxy or Zabbix server instance, but it changes back to another proxy or Zabbix server instance later.

   A: Check active agent autoregistration actions and the `ServerActive` parameter on the agent. The created host will be assigned to the proxy or server that last received the autoregistration request.

3. **Q**: I disable an LLD prototype, but the downstream items or triggers are not disabled.

   A: Unfortunately, that's by design and cannot be changed. You can disable individual items and triggers in the configuration list. For changing the state of many downstream items or triggers, try using the Zabbix API.

Troubleshooting Zabbix

All of the previous Q&As cover some of the most common issues new users might encounter. There are a lot of other issues you might run into, and with new versions of Zabbix, new issues will appear. While it's good to have quick solutions to common problems, let's look at some details that could be helpful when debugging Zabbix problems.

The Zabbix log file format

One of the first places we should check when there's an unexplained issue is log files. This is not just a Zabbix-specific thing; log files are great. Sometimes. Other times, they do not help, but we will discuss some other options for when log files do not provide the answer. To be able to find the answer, though, it is helpful to know some basics about the log file format. The Zabbix log format is as follows:

```
PPPPPP:YYYYMMDD:HHMMSS.mmm
```

Here, `PPPPPP` is process ID, space-padded to six characters, `YYYYMMDD` is the current date, `HHMMSS` is the current time, and `mmm` is milliseconds for the timestamp. Colons and the dot are literal symbols. This prefix is followed by a space and then by the actual log message. Here's an example log entry:

```
10372:20151223:134406.865 database is down: reconnecting in 10 seconds
```

If there's a line in the log file without this prefix, it is most likely coming from an external source, such as a script, or maybe from some library, such as `Net-SNMP`.

During startup, output similar to the following will be logged:

```
3737:20181208:111546.489 Starting Zabbix Server. Zabbix 4.0.2
(revision 87228).
 3737:20181208:111546.489 ****** Enabled features ******
 3737:20181208:111546.489 SNMP monitoring: YES
 3737:20181208:111546.489 IPMI monitoring: YES
 3737:20181208:111546.489 Web monitoring: YES
 3737:20181208:111546.489 VMware monitoring: YES
 3737:20181208:111546.489 SMTP authentication: YES
 3737:20181208:111546.489 Jabber notifications: YES
 3737:20181208:111546.489 Ez Texting notifications: YES
 3737:20181208:111546.489 ODBC: YES
 3737:20181208:111546.489 SSH2 support: YES
 3737:20181208:111546.489 IPv6 support: YES
 3737:20181208:111546.489 TLS support: YES
```

```
3737:20181208:111546.489 ****************************
3737:20181208:111546.489 using configuration file:
/etc/zabbix/zabbix_server.conf
3737:20181208:111546.500 current database version
(mandatory/optional): 04000000/04000003
3737:20181208:111546.500 required mandatory version: 04000000
```

The first line prints out the daemon type and version. Depending on how it was compiled, it might also include the current SVN revision number. A list of the compiled-in features follows. This is very useful to know whether you should expect SNMP, IPMI, or VMware monitoring to work at all. Then, the path to the currently-used configuration file is shown—helpful when we want to figure out whether the file we changed was the correct one. In the server and proxy log files, both the current and the required database versions are present—we discussed those in Chapter 20, *Zabbix Maintenance*.

After the database versions, the internal process startup messages can be found:

```
3737:20181208:111546.507 server #0 started [main process]
3747:20181208:111546.517 server #6 started [timer #1]
3748:20181208:111546.518 server #7 started [http poller #1]
3743:20181208:111546.518 server #2 started [alerter #1]
3744:20181208:111546.518 server #3 started [alerter #2]
3745:20181208:111546.518 server #4 started [alerter #3]
3749:20181208:111546.519 server #8 started [discoverer #1]
3750:20181208:111546.529 server #9 started [history syncer #1]
3746:20181208:111546.529 server #5 started [housekeeper #1]
3742:20181208:111546.529 server #1 started [configuration syncer #1]
3769:20181208:111546.529 server #28 started [trapper #5]
3771:20181208:111546.531 server #30 started [alert manager #1]
3754:20181208:111546.532 server #13 started [escalator #1]
3756:20181208:111546.533 server #15 started [proxy poller #1]
3757:20181208:111546.535 server #16 started [self-monitoring #1]
3758:20181208:111546.535 server #17 started [task manager #1]
3761:20181208:111546.535 server #20 started [poller #3]
3764:20181208:111546.546 server #23 started [unreachable poller #1]
3765:20181208:111546.556 server #24 started [trapper #1]
3755:20181208:111546.558 server #14 started [snmp trapper #1]
3763:20181208:111546.558 server #22 started [poller #5]
3772:20181208:111546.570 server #31 started [preprocessing manager
#1]
3766:20181208:111546.570 server #25 started [trapper #2]
3751:20181208:111546.572 server #10 started [history syncer #2]
3753:20181208:111546.572 server #12 started [history syncer #4]
3759:20181208:111546.572 server #18 started [poller #1]
3762:20181208:111546.584 server #21 started [poller #4]
3767:20181208:111546.594 server #26 started [trapper #3]
```

```
3768:20181208:111546.596 server #27 started [trapper #4]
3770:20181208:111546.598 server #29 started [icmp pinger #1]
3752:20181208:111546.599 server #11 started [history syncer #3]
3760:20181208:111546.599 server #19 started [poller #2]
3774:20181208:111547.136 server #33 started [preprocessing worker
#2]
3773:20181208:111547.162 server #32 started [preprocessing worker
#1]
3775:20181208:111547.162 server #34 started [preprocessing worker
#3]
```

There will be many more lines like these; the output here is trimmed. This might help verify that the expected number of processes of some type has been started. When looking at log file contents, it is not always obvious which process logged a specific line, and this is where the startup messages can help. If we see a line such as the following, we can find out which process logged it:

```
21974:20151231:184520.117 Zabbix agent item "vfs.fs.size[/,free]" on
host "A test host" failed: another network error, wait for 15 seconds
```

We can do that by looking for the startup message with the same PID:

```
# grep 21974 zabbix_server.log | grep started
21974:20151231:184352.921 server #8 started [unreachable poller #1]
```

 If more than one line is returned, apply common sense to find out the startup message.

This demonstrates that hosts are deferred to the unreachable poller after the first network failure.

But what if the log file has been rotated and the original startup messages are lost? Besides more advanced detective work, there's a simple method, provided that the daemon is still running. We will look at that method a bit later in the chapter runtime process status.

Reloading the configuration cache

We met the configuration cache in Chapter 2, *Getting Your First Notification,* and we discussed ways to monitor it in Chapter 20, *Zabbix Maintenance.* While it helps a lot performance-wise, it can be a bit of a problem if we are trying to quickly test something. It is possible to force the Zabbix server to reload the configuration cache.

Run the following to display the Zabbix server options:

```
# zabbix_server --help
```

 We briefly discussed Zabbix proxy configuration cache-reloading in Chapter 17, *Using Proxies to Monitor Remote Locations*.

In the output, look for the runtime control options section:

```
-R --runtime-control runtime-option   Perform administrative functions
Runtime control options:
config_cache_reload   Reload configuration cache
```

Thus, reloading the server configuration cache can be initiated by the following:

```
# zabbix_server --runtime-control config_cache_reload
zabbix_server [2682]: command sent successfully
```

Examining the server log file will reveal that it has received the signal:

```
forced reloading of the configuration cache
```

In the background, the sending of the signal happens like this:

- The server binary looks up the default configuration file
- It then looks for the file specified in the PidFile option
- It sends the signal to the process with that ID

As discussed in Chapter 17, *Using Proxies to Monitor Remote Locations*, the great thing about this feature is that it's also supported for active Zabbix proxies. Even better, when an active proxy is instructed to reload its configuration cache, it connects to the Zabbix server, gets all the latest configuration, and then reloads the local configuration cache. If such a signal is sent to a passive proxy, it ignores the signal.

What if you have several proxies running on the same system—how can you tell the binary which exact instance should reload the configuration cache? Looking back at the steps that were taken to deliver the signal to the process, all that is needed is to specify the correct configuration file. If running several proxies on the same system, each must have its own configuration file already, specifying different PID files, log files, listening ports, and so on. Instructing a proxy that used a specific configuration file to reload the configuration cache would be this simple:

```
# zabbix_proxy -c /path/to/zabbix_proxy.conf --runtime-control
config_cache_reload
```

The full or absolute path must be provided for the configuration file; a relative path is not supported. The same principle applies for servers and proxies, but it is even less common to run several Zabbix servers on the same system.

Manually reloading the configuration cache is useful if we have a large Zabbix server instance and have significantly increased the `CacheUpdateFrequency` parameter.

Controlling running daemons

A configuration-cache reload was only one of the things available in the runtime section. Let's look at the remaining options in there:

```
housekeeper_execute          Execute the housekeeper
log_level_increase=target    Increase log level, affects all processes
if target is not specified
log_level_decrease=target    Decrease log level, affects all processes
if target is not specified
Log level control targets: pid
Process identifier process-type All processes of specified type (for
example, poller)
process-type,N               Process type and number (e.g., poller,3)
```

As discussed in Chapter 20, *Zabbix Maintenance*, the internal housekeeper is first run 30 minutes after the server or proxy startup. The `housekeeper_execute runtime` option allows us to run it at will:

```
# zabbix_server --runtime-control housekeeper_execute
```

Even more interesting is the ability to change the log level for a running process. This feature first appeared in Zabbix 2.4, and it made debugging much, much easier. Zabbix daemons are usually started and just work—until we have to change something. While we cannot tell any of the daemons to reread their configuration file, there are a few more options that allow us to control some aspects of a running daemon. As briefly mentioned in Chapter 20, *Zabbix Maintenance*, the `DebugLevel` parameter allows us to set the log level when the daemon starts, with the default being 3. Log level 4 adds all the SQL queries, and log level 5 also adds the received content from web monitoring and VMware monitoring.

For the uninitiated, anything above level 3 can be very surprising and intimidating. Even a very small Zabbix server can easily log dozens of megabytes in a few minutes at log level 4. As some problems might not appear immediately, you might have to run it for hours or days at log level 4 or 5. Imagine dealing with gigabytes of logs you are not familiar with. The ability to set the log level for a running process allows us to increase the log level during a problem situation and lower it later, without requiring a daemon restart.

Even better, when using the runtime log level feature, we can select which exact components should have their log level changed. Individual processes can be identified by either their system PID or by the process number inside Zabbix. Specifying processes by the system PID could be done like this:

```
# zabbix_server --runtime-control log_level_increase=1313
```

Specifying an individual Zabbix process is done by choosing the process type and then passing the process number:

```
# zabbix_server --runtime-control log_level_increase=trapper,3
```

A fairly useful and common approach is changing the log level for all processes of a certain type—for example, we don't know which trapper will receive the connection that causes the problem, so we could easily increase the log level for all trappers by omitting the process number:

```
# zabbix_server --runtime-control log_level_increase=trapper
```

And if no parameter is passed to this runtime option, it will affect all Zabbix processes:

```
# zabbix_server --runtime-control log_level_increase
```

When processes are told to change their log level, they log an entry about it and then change the log level:

```
21975:20151231:190556.881 log level has been increased to 4 (debug)
```

Note that there is no way to query the current log level or set a specific level. If you are not sure about the current log level of all the processes, there are two ways to sort it out:

Restart the daemon

Decrease or increase the log level 5 times so that it's guaranteed to be at 0 or 5, then set the desired level. As a simple test of the options we just explored, increase the log level for all pollers:

```
# zabbix_server --runtime-control log_level_increase=poller
```

Open a tail on the Zabbix server logfile:

```
# tail -f /tmp/zabbix_server.log
```

Notice the amount of data that just 5 poller processes on a tiny Zabbix server can generate. Then decrease the log level:

```
# zabbix_server --runtime-control log_level_decrease=poller
```

Runtime process status

Zabbix has another small trick to help with debugging. Run `top` and see which mode gives you a more stable and longer list of Zabbix processes—one of sorting by processor usage (hitting *Shift + P*) or memory usage (hitting *Shift + M*) might.

 Alternatively, hit *o* and type `COMMAND=zabbix_server`.

Press *C* and notice how the Zabbix processes have updated their command line to show which exact internal process it is and what is it doing as we can see here:

```
zabbix_server: poller #1 [got 0 values in 0.000005 sec, idle 1 sec]
zabbix_server: poller #4 [got 1 values in 0.000089 sec, idle 1 sec]
zabbix_server: poller #5 [got 0 values in 0.000004 sec, idle 1 sec]
```

Follow their status and see how the task and the time it takes change for some of the processes. We could also have output that could be redirected or filtered through other commands:

```
# top -c -b | grep zabbix_server
```

The -c option tells it to show the command line, the same thing we achieved by hitting *C* before. The -b option tells top to run in batch mode without accepting input and just outputting the results. We could also specify -n 1 to run it only once or specify any other number as needed.

It might be more convenient to use ps:

```
# ps -f -C zabbix_server
```

The -f flag enables full output, which includes the command line. The -C flag filters by the executable name:

```
zabbix    21969 21962  0 18:43 ?          00:00:00 zabbix_server: poller
#1 [got 0 values in 0.000006 sec, idle 1 sec]
zabbix    21970 21962  0 18:43 ?          00:00:00 zabbix_server: poller
#2 [got 0 values in 0.000008 sec, idle 1 sec]
zabbix    21971 21962  0 18:43 ?          00:00:00 zabbix_server: poller
#3 [got 0 values in 0.000004 sec, idle 1 sec]
```

The full format prints out some extra columns—if all we needed was the PID and the command line, we could limit columns in the output with the -o flag, like this:

```
# ps -o pid=,command= -C zabbix_server
21975 zabbix_server: trapper #1 [processed data in 0.000150 sec,
waiting for connection]
21976 zabbix_server: trapper #2 [processed data in 0.001312 sec,
waiting for connection]
```

 The equals sign after pid and command tells ps not to use any header for these columns.

And to see a dynamic list that shows the current status, we can use the watch command:

```
# watch -n 1 'ps -o pid=,command= -C zabbix_server'
```

This list will be updated every second. Note that the interval parameter, -n, also accepts decimals, so to update twice every second, we could use -n 0.5.

This is also the method to find out which PID corresponds to which process type if startup messages are not available in the log file—we can see the process type and PID in the output of top or ps.

Further debugging

There are a lot of things that could go wrong, and a lot of tools to help us find out why it has. If you're familiar with the toolbox, including tools such as `tcpdump`, `strace`, `ltrace`, and `pmap`, you should be able to resolve most Zabbix problems.

 Some people claim that everything is a DNS problem. Often, they are right—if nothing else helps, check the DNS. Just in case. Remember that it's probably a good idea to use IP addresses instead of DNS names for hosts in Zabbix.

As it would be quite out of scope, we won't discuss general Linux or Unix debugging here. Of course, there's still a lot of Zabbix-specific things that could go wrong. You might want to check out the Zabbix troubleshooting page on the wiki: `http://zabbix.org/wiki/Troubleshooting`. If that doesn't help, make sure to check the community and commercial support options from your local Zabbix partner or Zabbix SIA. We will discuss options, such as the Zabbix IRC channel, in `Appendix B`, *Being Part of the Community*.

Being Part of the Community

An important aspect of Zabbix is its open source nature. Zabbix is a true open source solution—it's not *open core*, and it doesn't have an Enterprise version or some proprietary plugins. Such approaches could be labeled as *fake open source*. All components of Zabbix are completely open source; there are no closed or hidden components.

Besides being open source, a lot of Zabbix development happens out in the open, too. That makes it easy to closely follow the development and to get community support. But each open source project is different in how it is run and what guidelines it has, so let's look at what you can expect to find from this aspect of Zabbix:

- Community support can be a great way to solve a problem, by chatting on the IRC channel, looking at the Wiki, discussing it on the official forum, or using the open bug tracker.
- Following the development more closely by getting the latest source code can enable you to try out fixes for problems as soon as possible, provide early feedback, and get more familiar with the internals of Zabbix.
- For product development, support contracts, or other services, commercial support might be handy.

The development of Zabbix happens out in the open, but external contributions are usually not accepted, except in one area—translations. Contributors to all the translations Zabbix has are welcome, and we will also find out how to get involved in that area.

Community and support

There's a vibrant community of Zabbix users who communicate and share through different means. You are free to choose the communication and information-exchange method you prefer, but it is good to know how things are organized.

You are welcome to ask questions and help others by answering theirs, but it is suggested to observe some basic rules, which will help you to get your answers:

- Be polite; remember that nobody is obliged to respond to you in IRC, on the forum, or elsewhere.
- If you get no response, perhaps nobody knows the answer right now—be patient. Remember that people live in different time zones, so what is the middle of the working day for you might be the middle of the night for somebody else.
- Use English, unless communicating in a dedicated native-language section. Avoid the use of single-letter substitutions for words. Keep in mind that for many participants, English is a second or third language, so pointing out mistakes should be polite. Perception of language also varies a lot—what is considered offensive in one region might be completely fine in another.
- Make sure to try to resolve the problem yourself first, by consulting the official documentation, Wiki, and other sources. It's not polite to ask community members to do your work for you. On the other hand, if you would prefer somebody to work on your Zabbix instance, a commercial support service, mentioned at the end of this chapter, might be more suitable for you.
- When asking for help, provide as much relevant information as possible. This usually includes your Zabbix version and a detailed problem description, depending on the problem you are having. That could be the database used, the operating system or distribution, and information about other dependencies. It is very helpful to note what steps you have already taken when trying to resolve the problem. Don't make others guess at the details—if they have to ask for more information, it will delay the solution.

These and other guidelines are listed at `http://zabbix.org/wiki/Getting_help` and make sure to read through those as well.

Chatting on IRC

IRC, or **Internet Relay Chat**, is a fairly old communication method and is especially popular within open source project communities. Zabbix users also like to gather for Zabbix-related discussions on a dedicated channel. Located on the Freenode network at `freenode.net`, the `#zabbix` channel is where you can expect to get help from, and communicate with, fellow Zabbix users.

The most advanced and knowledgeable community members can be found here. You may use one of the many web-IRC gateways, such as `http://webchat.freenode.net/`, or connect to any Freenode IRC server with a dedicated program called an **IRC client**. There are many different options available for different operating systems, and you are free to choose any one—it won't impact your ability to communicate with people using a different one. In addition to general communication guidelines, there are some IRC-specific ones as well:

- To reiterate the basic suggestion: be patient. Too often, people come in, ask their question, and leave a few minutes later. Other members of the channel might be sleeping, eating, or otherwise away from their computer. So ask your question and stay around for a while. If it happens to be a weekend, a while might even be several days.

- Don't ask whether you can ask you question. If it's about Zabbix, and is well thought out, just go ahead and ask. Starting with, *Hey, can I ask a question about Zabbix?* will require somebody to confirm with, *Yes, you can*, then you typing the question, and only then can the helping process start, which will take much longer.

- Don't repeat your question too often; it will only annoy others. While it might be tempting to ask again and again when new people join, they are unlikely to be the experts you are waiting for, so again, be patient. On the other hand, it usually is fine to repeat the question if no answer has appeared for a longer time—a day, for example.

- Don't type the names of people present, hoping it will get you help. That will needlessly distract them. Wait for somebody to respond instead.

Regarding politeness, remember that all communication is logged and publicly available. If you reveal yourself to be a person who is hard to communicate with, it will not only stay in people's memories, but also in the logs.

The Zabbix IRC channel also has a couple of automated helpers, called **bots**. All new bug reports and feature requests are announced in the channel by them, and they have other features as well. At this time, current bot features are described at `http://zabbix.org/wiki/Getting_help#IRC_bots`.

Not only the most knowledgeable users are available on the Zabbix IRC channel. This channel is quite popular. At the time of writing, the average number of participants is about 300. It's actually the most popular IRC channel about monitoring. The demo Zabbix instance, at `http://zabbix.org/zabbix/`, monitors the number of users on the channel, and a graph from 2006 until mid-2016 looks like this:(at time of writing the demo site was down so it was not possible to update the graph with newer statistics)

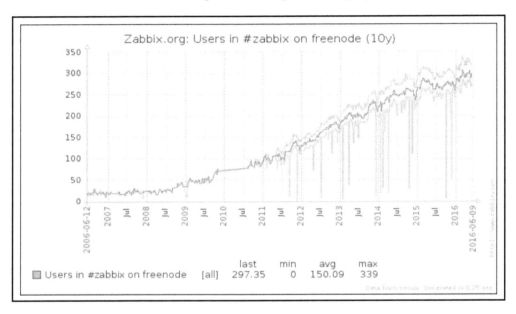

The number of participants on the channel has grown significantly since 2006. You can access the current version by going to `http://zabbix.org/zabbix/` and looking up the simple graph **Users in #zabbix on freenode** on the **Zabbix.org** host.

Using the Zabbix Wiki

The system that hosts the demo instance we discovered a moment ago also serves as a community platform. Primarily, it's a MediaWiki instance that has a large amount of useful information, and we have referred to it a few times already. Here are a few of its interesting features:

- Zabbix templates
- Zabbix technical documentation, including the Zabbix protocol documentation

- Various Zabbix guidelines, including bug-reporting guidelines and IRC etiquette
- A list of Zabbix API libraries
- Various how-tos, including instructions on high-availability setups and the installation process

The content is flexible, and it is suggested you investigate what is available on `http://zabbix.org/wiki/Main_Page` every now and then.

 This book was also supposed to cover how great it is to have new feature specifications available on the Zabbix website, but unfortunately, the Zabbix team has decided to withdraw them. You can still find old specifications at `http://zabbix.org/wiki/Category:Specifications`.

It being a Wiki, everybody is welcome to participate. See a mistake or *something missing?* Just go ahead and improve it. *Want to write instructions for some process you found non-trivial to perform?* Go ahead and create a new page. And if you are not sure about it, just ask on IRC, and somebody will surely help.

 There is also a Zabbix-related resource directory at `http://share.zabbix.com`. It does not host most of the content; instead, it usually links to templates or scripts on GitHub or a Zabbix website page. We won't look into it in any detail at this time, as the functionality is a bit limited, but it is suggested to visit it every now and then to check whether it has improved.

Using the Zabbix forum

The Zabbix forum is located at `http://www.zabbix.com/forum`. You can read it without registering, but for posting, you will need authenticated access, so register for a user account. The forum offers both a large collection of already-solved problems and a chance that you will receive assistance with new problems.

While we've looked at the general suggestions for efficient and satisfactory communication, there are some forum-specific suggestions as well:

- Choose the appropriate forum for your question. If your problem is with the development version of Zabbix, it should not be raised in the forum concerning the Zabbix website.

- Choose wisely between when to create a new thread and when to comment on an existing one. It is highly discouraged to ask different questions on an existing thread. On the other hand, it's better to search the forum before creating a duplicate thread about an existing problem.
- Enable new message notifications so that you can respond in a timely fashion if additional information is requested. That will help resolve the problem sooner.

Filing issues on the tracker

What if you have discovered a bug or have a bright idea on how to improve Zabbix? Zabbix uses an issue tracker to record such things and track the resolution process. To access the Zabbix issue tracker, navigate to `https://support.zabbix.com`. Here, you can register and log in to search existing reports as well as enter new ones.

When reporting a new issue, choose the correct project—project ZBX is used for bug reporting, and project ZBXNEXT for new feature requests. It is strongly suggested you search the tracker before filing a new report—perhaps the problem has already been reported and there is no need to create duplicate reports.

What if you have resolved the issue yourself and have a patch for fixing a bug or implementing a feature? Just attach it to the corresponding report. You should discuss your approach with Zabbix developers before coding for all but the simplest cases—perhaps they are already working on it, or perhaps your approach will conflict with some other feature in development. Make sure to get familiar with the coding guidelines, too—they are available at `http://zabbix.org/wiki/Main_Page`.

 There is also a patch repository, at `https://github.com/zabbix/zabbix-patches`, but it remains to be seen whether it becomes popular.

Meeting in person

All the discussed channels are great for communicating with other Zabbix users, getting help, and helping others. But there are also various ways to meet in person. A very popular and nice yearly event is the **official Zabbix conference**, but there are also various less formal events organized by local communities.

The Zabbix summit

The official Zabbix conference is a great event. It was first organized in 2011, and it used to happen in September, but the latest conference was renamed to *summit* and was held in October. It is a chance to find out about the latest things going on at Zabbix, learn from a lot of very inventive Zabbix users, and have a bit of fun. It happens in the birthplace and hometown of Zabbix—Riga, Latvia. There are two days packed with interesting talks, and the Zabbix team tries hard to make everybody feel welcome. If you have a chance, do try to join this event. Besides the Zabbix summit, there are also more local summits being organized in Japan, Brazil, China, and the BeNeLux. All events can be found at `https://www.zabbix.com/events`.

Local communities

Your local community might also be arranging get-togethers. Check out the listing of various communication channels at `http://zabbix.org/wiki/Usergroups`. Join the user group, follow the news, and maybe even help to organize events. Don't hesitate to add a new country to the list, too.

Following the development

So you have seen an interesting new feature mentioned on IRC and you want to try it out? Perhaps you want to see how exactly a particular change was implemented or comment on the way it was designed. Or perhaps you would like to produce a patch that depends on some changes being made in the development version. A lot of Zabbix development happens out in the open; here are the main phases you could be interested in:

- A specification being created
- A development starting in a separate feature branch
- A feature being merged into the main branches

 Specifications were public at `http://zabbix.org/wiki/Main_Page` before, but they are no longer available.

Providing feedback early is likely to be helpful and has a higher chance of impacting the design. If you are interested in a specific feature, you could previously have followed the specification on `http://zabbix.org/wiki/Main_Page`, but that phase is closed now. Zabbix uses SVN for code versioning. The feature branches in SVN provide very early access to the code, and that is a great time to try out and test the features.

We talked about testing things out; let's find out how to get code that has not been released as a version yet.

Getting the source

When looking for the Zabbix development version, there are two ways to get it, each with its strengths and weaknesses.

Daily snapshots

On the Zabbix development download page (`http://www.zabbix.com/developers.php`), there are daily snapshots of development versions provided. These usually have the same setup procedures as the released versions. The benefits of using daily snapshots include the following:

- Getting them is a simple download
- The source archive is already generated for you

The drawbacks include the following:

- There is no way to update only those parts of the development version that have actually changed
- There is no way to easily see what actually has changed
- You have no access to the feature branches
- There is no way to get an arbitrary older version

It is suggested to use daily snapshots if you want a simple, one-time peek at how the Zabbix development is progressing.

Accessing the version-control system

If you plan to follow Zabbix development for a longer period of time, or if you want to see how exactly a particular change was implemented, daily snapshots will quickly become cumbersome to use. There are no snapshots of the feature branches, so we have to use SVN if the feature has not been merged into the main branches yet.

 You can also browse the official SVN repository using a WebSVN instance: https://www.zabbix.org/websvn/wsvn/zabbix.com. It won't allow you to do a local checkout, but for a quick check on a few files, it can be more convenient.

To access SVN repositories, specific software—a client—is needed. There are many different SVN clients for various platforms, and you can choose whichever seems most convenient to you. Here, we will use the official command-line client. As this client is available on almost all Linux distributions, we may want to use it on our Zabbix test server. But before we start playing with it, we must know that the Zabbix source code repository resides at https://svn.zabbix.com/. In SVN, development is usually split into a trunk and branches. While the trunk represents the most recent development work, branches are usually used for stable version maintenance. Zabbix uses the same schema, and there are branches for stable version maintenance, such as 3.0; the development for the next stable version happens in the development section, the trunk. The changes do not happen in the version branches or trunk right away, though—they are first implemented in the development branches, which are usually located at svn://svn.zabbix.com/branches/dev/ZBX-1, with the correct ZBX or ZBXNEXT issue number at the end.

Let's say we are interested in the latest features and want to retrieve the trunk. To do this, run the following:

```
$ svn checkout svn://svn.zabbix.com/trunk zabbix-trunk
```

This will proceed to retrieve all the files in the trunk and place them in a directory called zabbix-trunk. As of writing this, the Zabbix trunk checkout uses approximately 118 MB on disk, but the amount transferred over the network will be less than that. Once the process completes, you might be tempted to proceed with compilation, but that won't be easy to do as there is no configuration script. There's a convenient script to generate the configuration:

```
$ ./bootstrap.sh
```

After this completes, we should have the configuration script. Now, we can compile this development version of Zabbix, *right?* Not quite yet. Development repositories hold only a generic database schema and content description, so we will not be able to create the database. We will have to generate the actual schema and data files ourselves. For the Zabbix frontend, specific CSS files have to be generated, too. It is also suggested you create a package, one just like those downloadable from the Zabbix site, so let's do that. But before we can generate the database schema and package, we have to use the configuration script. We can make it slightly faster and require fewer dependencies by omitting any features that are not required. This also enables the creation of a Zabbix package on another machine that does not have all the dependencies for the required functionality installed, such as SNMP or IPMI monitoring. In the simplest case, run the following:

```
$ ./configure
```

This will produce the files required for the database schema and package generation. Now, we can proceed with the schema and CSS-generation:

```
$ make dbschema
$ make css
```

 We discussed the packages required for compilation in Chapter 1, *Getting Started with Zabbix*. For the make css step, you will also need the Sass Ruby gem.

With the database schema and CSS files generated, we are ready to create a package:

```
$ make dist
```

After this command completes, the source directory should have a new archive, named zabbix-<version>.tar.gz. Here, the version will be whatever name the development part has received. From now on, we are back on the known path, as this package is pretty much the same as the one you can download from the released version area or from the daily snapshots area.

But that was a lot of work to get the same thing we could have downloaded right away—*why do it at all?* Indeed, if you only want to grab the development version once, daily snapshots should be your choice. But an SVN checkout presents other benefits. Let's understand what those are.

When writing this book, Zabbix SIA announced to its partners that it was looking in moving to Git so it can be that things have changed and that the source code is now available in Git instead on SVN.

Looking at the changesets

A collection of changes to a repository is called a **changeset**. A changeset that has been placed in a repository is said to be committed. We can list changesets that have been committed. For example, if we would like to know what the last changeset that was committed to this part of the repository is, we would issue the following command:

```
$ svn log -r PREV:HEAD
```

The `-r` subversion switch allows us to specify revisions—numeric representations of each change. `PREV` and `HEAD` are special references, being the previous version and latest version, respectively. Sometimes, we might be instructed to test or use a specific version, called a revision. In that case, it is possible to retrieve it by issuing this command:

```
$ svn up -r 1234
```

Replace `1234` with the revision number you are told to use. This will update the whole checkout to that revision, and you should now rerun the commands discussed previously, repeating the same process used after just having checked out.

But sometimes, we might need to update only one or a few files to a specific revision—that can be done by specifying the path, like this:

```
$ svn up -r 1234 frontends/php/history.php
```

You can specify both of the directories and files, and get different revisions to test behavior changes or find the specific change that introduced a problem for you.

So you have tried out a development version—maybe several revisions. Some time later, you decide to find out what changes have been made to the trunk. First, you need to determine the current revision. While in the checkout directory, run the following command:

```
$ svn info
```

Look for the line that looks like this:

```
Revision: 60013
```

With that number in hand, it's now time to update the local copy to the latest and greatest. From the local copy directory, run the following:

```
$ svn up
```

This will proceed to update everything that has changed, compared to whatever copy you have. As only changes are pulled, this will result in much less data being downloaded, compared to downloading daily snapshots over and over again. Now, you can proceed with building Zabbix as discussed before, or you can choose to view the exact changes developers have committed:

```
$ svn log -r 60000:HEAD
```

This command will display the exact changes pushed to the code repository, along with any comments that the developers decided to add. This can be used to determine what exactly was changed. But all this was about the forward-looking development version, that is, the trunk—*what if you want to see a particular bug fix for some problem in the stable version applied to that particular branch?* Just as we grabbed the trunk from the code repository, we can also grab the branch:

```
$ svn checkout svn://svn.zabbix.com/branches/3.0
```

Instead of the trunk, we are now specifying the subsection branches. After that comes the specific branch, which can be any valid branch. *What branches are there?* We can list them:

```
svn ls svn://svn.zabbix.com/branches
```

While installing a branch version is pretty much the same as installing the trunk, there's one more use case with branches. If a particular bug is fixed in the branch and you want to benefit from that before the next stable version is out, it is possible to apply this single change to the installed copy. To do that, though, the change has to be first extracted in a format that is easy to reuse. Here, another command comes to the rescue. Remember `svn log`, *which we used to look at changesets before?* It showed the revision number for each changeset. If we now have this number, we can take a look at what files a particular commit modified:

```
$ svn log -v -c 60013
```

Here, we use the –c switch to specify a single changeset, and –v to increase the verbosity level. In the changed paths section, one or more files will be listed, for example:

```
M /trunk/ChangeLog
M /trunk/src/zabbix_server/escalator/escalator.c
```

When creating a patch, we might want to omit files that don't affect actual software behavior—the changelog in this case. Creating a patch would be done as follows:

```
$ svn diff –c 60013 src/zabbix_server/escalator/
escalator.c > /tmp/zabbix.patch
```

Notice how we used subversion's diff subcommand, specified a single file, and redirected the output to a file. Now, the patch should be applied to our Zabbix installation. To do this, change to the Zabbix source installation directory, and execute the following:

```
$ patch –p 0 –i /tmp/zabbix.patch
```

 Be careful with extracting patches in this way. They will often work if the change was made soon after the release you are patching. If a lot of development has happened between the used version and the patch, the patch might depend on some other changes and not work properly.

The patch utility is instructed to use the zabbix.patch input file, and use the full path information as specified to apply the changes. After patching, we should evaluate areas the patch applies to—if it's the server, we should recompile and reinstall our server binary, the same with the agent daemon. If changes were performed on the frontend only, we'll usually want to apply the patch to the installed frontend directly, by changing to the frontend directory and applying it as root with the following command:

```
# patch –p 2 –i /tmp/zabbix.patch
```

Note that in this case, we are instructing the patch utility to strip the first two directories from the path inside the patch. When we are patching the frontend, no recompilation is necessary, and all changes will be visible immediately. *What if we applied a patch but it only made things worse?* Thankfully, that is easy to undo by applying the same patch in reverse:

```
# patch –R –p 2 –i /tmp/zabbix.patch
```

If using this command for the frontend, again, no further action is required. If it affects binaries, we have to recompile them.

 Refer to the SVN documentation for more detailed instructions, or ask on the Zabbix IRC channel for Zabbix-specific subversion repository questions.

Translating Zabbix

The Zabbix frontend is available in various languages, and that is a great achievement of the community—the Zabbix company does not do most of the translations. This is also a great opportunity to get involved and make Zabbix available in your language. Zabbix uses the online tool Pootle, which is a very easy way to get started. For more advanced contributors, po files can be downloaded and used with standalone tools. If you have decided to improve or create Zabbix support for your language, here are a few general suggestions:

- It can be a lot of work; be ready for that.
- Before starting, discuss the current state with existing translators for your language, if there are any.
- Think carefully about how the terms could be translated—*how would you translate host, item, trigger, action, operation, and other entities?*
- Don't try to translate the Zabbix manual right away—once the frontend has been fully translated and maintained for a while, manual translation can be considered. Translating and maintaining the Zabbix manual is a huge amount of work, and there is no language that has yet had a successful long-term translation of the manual.

 If a language you want to work on is available to translate but does not appear in the frontend language selection, it might be hidden. You can enable a language by editing the `include/locales.inc.php` file and changing the display property from false to true.

The exact steps and procedure for participating in the translation work may change, so I won't reproduce them here. Instead, go to `http://zabbix.org/wiki/Translating_Zabbix` and follow the steps there. It will likely include registering on the `http://zabbix.org/wiki/Main_Page` Wiki, adding yourself to the translator table, subscribing to the translator mailing list, and asking for permissions on Pootle. The latter is probably best done on the Zabbix IRC channel, and that is also the best place to ask any questions about getting involved in the translation process.

Commercial support options

Community support is great. It is often speedy, accurate, and friendly. However, even if it is always like that, there might be cases when you might need a more formal approach. Common cases where a formal agreement is pursued include the following:

- A company policy requires a support agreement for all systems put in production
- You want qualified help when implementing Zabbix
- The Zabbix installation will be managed by people who are not deeply involved and don't have much experience with it
- You need a feature developed or improved

Approaching a commercial support provider is often the best solution in such cases, and it is possible to obtain such support from the company behind the Zabbix software. Visit the Zabbix website at `http://www.zabbix.com/support.php` to obtain more information. If you are ready to discuss commercial support in more detail, it's as easy as sending an email to `sales@zabbix.com`. At the time of writing this, the sales team is very knowledgeable, helpful, and friendly, and usually lightning fast at responding, too. There's no conflict of interest or personal gain for me; this is a completely sincere and honest endorsement.

I would also advise you to have a look for a local partner. Local partners live in your timezone, speak your language, and are probably more closely situated to your company. Another advantage is that they can probably help you with more than just Zabbix, and you can still buy local support and ask them to include official Zabbix support in your contract. You can find the full list of partners and the reseller list at `http://www.zabbix.com/partners.php`. This should help you find one that is geographically convenient.

Assessment

Chapter 1: Getting Started with Zabbix

1. The three main components that we need to set up a Zabbix server are as follows:
    - Zabbix server
    - Zabbix frontend
    - Zabbix database
2. The C language
3. PHP language
4. Databases other than MySQL are supported are as follows:
    - PostgreSQL
    - MySQL forks such as MariaDB and Percona DB
    - IBM DB2
    - Oracle DB

Chapter 2: Getting Your First Notification

1. The 5 severity levels in Zabbix are as follows:
    - Disaster
    - High
    - Average
    - Warning
    - Information
    - Not classified
2. Yes, Zabbix can send messages to users or groups, or both and configuration is done under the tab configuration—**Actions**
3. Yes, for every item, there is a preprocessing tab that allows us to make some changes before Zabbix stores the data in the database.

Chapter 3: Monitoring with Zabbix Agents and Basic Protocols

1. This is from the perspective of the agent. We talk about active or passive agents but, in fact, there is only one agent that we configure to be active or passive or both. Items can then be configured for active or passive.
2. No, remember it only works for passive items and there is also the configuration cache that needs to be updated first.
3. This is a possible solution and it was needed before but, since Zabbix 4.0, we now have an item, `net.if.total`, that calculates the total throughput of our data over the interface.

Chapter 4: Monitoring SNMP Devices

1. Yes, by making use of the bulk request
2. OIDs can change from device to device. Also, with firmware updates, it can change to streamline our templates. We can also make use of dynamic indexes
3. When configuring `snmptraps` in Zabbix, the following options are there:
   - Using the Zabbix Perl script
   - Using custom scripts

Chapter 5: Managing Hosts, Users, and Permissions

1. Only a passive status is shown
2. There are 4 status icons: Zabbix Agent, SNMP, JMX, and IPMI
3. Yes we have the option to either gather or not gather data during maintenance
4. No, super admins always have full access

Chapter 6: Detecting Problems with Triggers

1. This is possible—we can use s, m, h, d, and w
2. No, but Zabbix has support for trigger dependencies (it is a feature on the development list for 4.2 for dependencies on proxies)
3. There are visible icons on triggers in the problem page
4. Yes, in the trigger, we can choose to have a recovery expression or not

Chapter 7: Acting upon Monitored Conditions

1. Yes, in our actions, we have to configure the proper operations
2. It's not built-in in Zabbix, but you could do it by creating a script that can talk to the API

Chapter 8: Simplifying Complex Configurations with Templates

1. Yes. If we use macros, we can define them on a global, template, and host level.
2. Yes. Some items are changeable on the host level even if we have used a template for it.
3. No. We can only link templates to hosts and other templates. Linking a template to a group is not possible.

Chapter 9: Visualizing Data with Screens and Slideshows

1. Slideshows are based on graphs, and we need two or more graphs to create a slideshow.
2. Yes, by making use of the refresh interval multiplier.

3. Screens are probably deprecated and it's best to not put too much effort into them. The new dashboard has the same functionality, and graphs look much nicer and have more options.

Chapter 10: Advanced Item Monitoring

1. Yes, it does, but we need to use a special item for this.
2. Calculated items will read the existing data from the database and then create a new item with it.
3. No, aggregated items are calculated just like calculated items by Zabbix serve, but they do it for a group of servers. The `zabbix-get` tool can only retrieve information from Zabbix agents.
4. No, it's not a good idea. It's best to look for another solution to do this, as we've seen for our MySQL database.
5. No, it works on all items.
6. Yes, place the history at 0 days. Zabbix will create dependent items but won't keep the data from the master item.

Chapter 12: Monitoring Web Pages

1. Yes, scenarios are supported and No, steps in scenarios cannot be skipped there are no **if-else** scenarios

2. Yes, user macros are supported for variables—we can even use regex on them.

3. Yes, scenarios support HTTP and HTTPS—only `web.page.xxx` items do not support HTTPS

4. Yes, this can be done by using the Zabbix sender or the sender protocol

Chapter 13: High-Level Business Service Monitoring

1. No. At this time, we can only show them on screen; there's no way to export them, not even on a weekly basis.
2. No, services aren't calculated retrospectively in time.

3. No. We need to configure this in our services by specifying uptime/downtime.

Chapter 14: Monitoring IPMI Devices

1. You have to use the short sensor name, and with Zabbix 4.0, you can also use an ID and long sensor name if you specify that with `name:` and `id:`
2. Not out of the box with the Zabbix built-in IPMP solution, but you could do this with scripting and the Zabbix sender.

Chapter 15: Monitoring Java Applications

1. Yes, but you need to install proxies; only one Java gateway can be installed per Zabbix server or per proxy.
2. The Java gateway will retrieve items from the JAVA application and the Zabbix server will pull the data from the gateway and process the data. We don't use Zabbix agents.
3. Ports we need to open for JMX monitoring are:
   - For communication between Zabbix server/proxy and the gateway, we need port `10052` (not IANA registered).
   - For communication between the Java gateway and an application, we need to open another port (standard in Zabbix `12345`).

Chapter 16: Monitoring VMware

1. Only one; linking Template Virt VMware with the ESX or vCenter and adding the correct macros should be enough.
2. Debug logging only for VMware can be done as follows:
   - We can increase logging global by changing the log level in the zabbix server configuration.
   - We can do it more smart and only increase VMware logs by running:

        ```
        zabbix_server -R log_level_increase="vmware
        collector"
        ```

3. Not out of the box; however, with LLD, it's probably possible to create your own implementation.

Chapter 17: Using Proxies to Monitor Remote Locations

1. No, we have to chose between active or passive.
2. Depending if the hosts is active or passive, or both, we need to point the agent to the correct proxy by changing the IP of the Zabbix server in the proxy configuration, and we need to tell Zabbix in the frontend that our host is monitored by a proxy.
3. Yes, but we need to install a Zabbix Java gateway on our proxy.

Chapter 18: Encrypting Zabbix Traffic

1. The types of encryption can we use in Zabbix are as follows:
   - Encryption by PSK file
   - Encryption by certificate
2. Sadly, yes, there's no encryption between the Zabbix server and the database, and there's no encryption between the Zabbix server/proxy and the Java gateway.

Chapter 19: Working Closely with Data

1. No, other libraries such as Perl, PHP, and Python are available but they're all community supported at the moment.
2. There's a method that doesn't need user authentication to retrieve the API version; we can call it with `curl`, or even better, use the new Zabbix HTTP item to retrieve that information.
3. We can use XML import/export to back up our hosts and templates.

Chapter 20: Zabbix Maintenance

1. Yes, we can still use 1.0 agents but, since Zabbix 4.0, the oldest agent we can use is 1.4.

2. Yes, in a major version, we can mix server and frontend even if they have minor upgrades. Agents are backward compatible till 1.4; however, we'll lose some functionality so it's best to upgrade agents when you can.

3. Proxies will still work and send data to the Zabbix server; however, they can't receive updates from the Zabbix server. Proxies need to have the same version as the Zabbix server so you need to upgrade them as soon as possible.

Other Books You May Enjoy

If you enjoyed this book, you may be interested in these other books by Packt:

Network Scanning Cookbook
Sairam Jetty

ISBN: 978-1-78934-648-0

- Install and configure Nmap and Nessus in your network infrastructure
- Perform host discovery to identify network devices
- Explore best practices for vulnerability scanning and risk assessment
- Understand network enumeration with Nessus and Nmap
- Carry out configuration audit using Nessus for various platforms
- Write custom Nessus and Nmap scripts on your own

Practical Network Automation - Second Edition

Abhishek Ratan

ISBN: 978-1-78995-565-1

- Get started with the fundamental concepts of network automation
- Perform intelligent data mining and remediation based on triggers
- Understand how AIOps works in operations
- Trigger automation through data factors
- Improve your data center's robustness and security through data digging
- Get access infrastructure through API Framework for chatbot and voice interactive troubleshootings
- Set up communication with SSH-based devices using Netmiko

Leave a review - let other readers know what you think

Please share your thoughts on this book with others by leaving a review on the site that you bought it from. If you purchased the book from Amazon, please leave us an honest review on this book's Amazon page. This is vital so that other potential readers can see and use your unbiased opinion to make purchasing decisions, we can understand what our customers think about our products, and our authors can see your feedback on the title that they have worked with Packt to create. It will only take a few minutes of your time, but is valuable to other potential customers, our authors, and Packt. Thank you!

Index

suffix multipliers 254

T

TCP connectivity 87
Telnet items
  about 436, 439
  syntax 439
Template App Zabbix Proxy 678
Template App Zabbix Server 678
template interaction
  summarizing 587
templates
  configuration, modifying in 331
  creating 323, 324, 325
  linking, to hosts 325, 326, 328, 329
  nested templates 346, 347, 349, 350
  unlinking, from hosts 342, 344
test hosts 74
test system
  load, creating 71, 74, 75
threshold
  escalating 285, 286, 288, 290, 294
  runner analogy 297
time shift 251
timestamps
  parsing 394, 395, 396
traps 162
trigger dependencies 275
trigger functions
  iregexp 386
  regexp 386
  str() 386
Trigger value 268
Triggers
  about 232, 233, 235
  customizing 255
  dependencies 237, 241, 243
  display options 256
  expressions, constructing 244, 246
  flapping, prevention 246, 247
  human-readable constants 254
  relative thresholds 251
  severities 256
  system time, verifying 253
  time out 249
  time shift 251
  trigger-and-item relationship 236
  with adaptable thresholds 249
  with limited period 250, 251
tunnel 160

U

Ubuntu/Debian
  Zabbix, installing 19
units
  about 132
  custom intervals 133
  items, copying 136, 138
unreachable pollers 709
uptime
  specifying 546, 548
User Datagram Protocol (UDP) 144
user groups
  about 215
  creating 221, 222, 223, 225, 227
user macros 334, 335, 336, 337
user parameters
  about 407
  avoiding 423
  benefits 424
  drawbacks 424
  flexible user parameters 411, 413
  level of details, monitoring 413, 414, 415
  setting up 407, 408, 409
  statistics, monitoring 415, 416, 417, 418,
    419, 420, 422
  unsupported data, querying 409, 410
  wrapper scripts 422, 423
user
  creating 216, 219, 221
users 215

V

value mapping 129, 131, 132
value preprocessing 440, 441, 443, 444, 445
VMware monitoring
  preparing for 578, 579
VMwareCollectors 579